1980-81
EDITION

ARTHUR FROMMER'S
DOLLARWI$E
GUIDE TO
Germany

By STANLEY HAGGART
and DARWIN PORTER

Sponsored by **Lufthansa**  **DB** GERMAN RAIL
German
National
Tourist Office

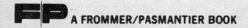 A FROMMER/PASMANTIER BOOK

Published by the Frommer/Pasmantier Publishing Corporation
A Simon and Schuster Division of
Gulf + Western Corporation
380 Madison Avenue
New York, NY 10017

ISBN 0-671-25487-1
Library of Congress Catalog Card Number: 79-57401

Manufactured in the United States of America

Cover photo by German National Tourist Office

*Lufthansa German Airlines, Germanrail, and the
German National Tourist Office shall not be responsible
for any errors, faulty information, and/or printing errors
of any sort.*

*Although every effort was made to ensure the accuracy
of price information appearing in this book,
it should be kept in mind that prices
can and do fluctuate in the course of time.*

CONTENTS

MAPS

The writers of this book gratefully acknowledge the generous contributions of Margaret Foresman and Mr. and Mrs. Pierre Français.

Inflation Alert!

The authors of this book have spent laborious hours attempting to ensure the accuracy of the information and prices appearing in this book. As we go to press, we believe we have obtained the most reliable data possible. Nonetheless, in the lifetime of this edition—particularly in its second year (1981)—the wise traveler will add at least 10% to 15% to the prices quoted in these pages.

A DOLLARWISE GUIDE TO GERMANY

The Reason Why

A NEW, WEALTHY, industrial—yet beautiful—Germany awaits you. Although many of its medieval treasures were lost during the war, much remains and much has been rebuilt in the old style. Natural scenery—particularly such places as the Black Forest, the Mosel Valley, and the Bavarian Alps—was and is a potent lure for any prospective traveler to Germany.

The people themselves are complex, the descendants of widely varied cultural backgrounds. Distinguishing differences can be noted among the Westphalians, the Lower Saxonians, the Bavarians, and the Rhinelanders. Don't expect to find a nation of happy, laughing beer drinkers running around in lederhosen with feather-topped hunting caps resting jauntily on their heads. However enough of these tradition-minded souls exist to reinforce the stereotype.

In capsule fashion, here's a running impression of Germany.

Bavarian baroque . . . cow bells . . . white-capped Alps . . . crystal-blue lakes . . . golden old cities on the banks of the Danube . . . green hills and castles along the majestic Rhine . . . the fragrance of a new harvest in the wine towns . . . the dark pines of the Black Forest . . . sailors and strippers after dark in the port of Hamburg . . . the canaries of the Harz Mountains . . . half-timbered buildings in medieval villages . . . bold, courageous modern architecture rising in industrial cities . . . operas, theaters, fairs, and festivals . . . soaring Gothic cathedrals . . . wine drinking and dancing . . . the good regional cuisine in a typical ratskeller . . . the finger-sized sausages of Nürnberg . . . the health spas with their kur baths and roulette wheels.

All in all, a land that knows how to harmonize contrasts.

THE BEST OF GERMANY: We have set for ourselves the formidable task of seeking out Germany at its best and condensing that between the covers of this book. The best includes not only descriptions of important cities, towns, villages, and sightseeing attractions, but recommendations of hotels, restaurants, bars, cafes, and nightspots as well.

This book is based on the premise that the best need not be the most expensive. Hence, our ultimate aim—beyond that of familiarizing you with the offerings of Germany—is to stretch your dollar power, to reveal that you need not always pay scalper's prices for charm, top-grade comfort, and first-rate food.

We'll devote a great deal of attention to the tourist meccas: Munich, Frankfurt, Hamburg, and Berlin, focusing on both obvious and hidden treasures. But important as they are, they do not reflect completely the widely diverse and complicated country that is Germany.

To seek out the wonders of this often perplexing land, you must also go to the Bavarian Alps, Lake Constance, the Rhine and Mosel Valleys, and the coast of the North Sea, to name only a few areas.

It may be presumptuous to give you reasons why to go to Germany. Dozens may have already occurred to you. We'll merely add a few, beginning with . . .

(1) To live in a castle and feel like a king

If this has been a long-suppressed desire, Germany offers an opportunity to fulfill it. More chances, in fact, to spend the night in a real castle than you'll find in any other country of Europe. Picture yourself perched high in the clouds (1800 feet altitude), the window of your bedchamber opening onto a wall of fortress-like houses. At night, under a full moon, the Middle Ages come alive.

(2) To take "the cure" at a spa

Regardless of your ailment—hypochondriacal or otherwise—a German spa claims a cure. No country in Europe has more health resorts. Ever since the Romans came this way 2000 years ago, "taking the waters" has been a long-established rejuvenation process throughout the land. Once the spa was the exclusive domain of royalty and the aristocracy, but today it has become a firmly entrenched middle-class institution. Of course, Germans like to take the cure in style, even or especially if nothing is wrong with them. Therefore, the spa dining table is the best in the country. The major resorts have gambling casinos, with dancing and entertainment in the evening. It's no surprise then that some spa devotees come just to have fun, spending their daytime hours golfing and horseback riding. Others take the treatment more seriously, immersing themselves in thermal pools, even taking sand baths. The curative spring is the therapeutic beverage to many Germans, as the eternal search for the fountain of youth goes on.

(3) To get the biggest hangover of the year at Munich's annual Oktoberfest

Even if you don't like to drink, you can get bombed just walking through Munich's Oktoberfest meadow when it's in full swing, filled to the brim with beer-drinking revelers. Lasting for 16 days, the festival begins late in September. Barn-like beer halls are assembled on the Theresienwiese. Beer wagons, drawn by horses, bring in kegs of the golden brew that eternally delights the Bavarians, who seem to hold all sorts of world records for beer consumption. All the famous breweries are represented, including Löwenbräu and Pschorrbräu. You'll think you're reliving the days of the Roman Empire when you see oxen roasting, beer being guzzled, screaming girls being hoisted into the air and twirled around, and throngs of merrymakers in corny hats, making the festival an eternal New Year's Eve party. Enough pork sausage is consumed "to girdle Munich," as the saying goes. However, for those who have imbibed too heavily, tents are set up which dispense coffee. Gone is the "oompah" band in these rehabilitation centers for the boozed out. Rather, the quiet, melodious sound of the zither is heard. Many of the "patients" are often successfully rejuvenated enough by the music to try their luck once again!

(4) To see if the Reeperbahn of Hamburg lives up to its reputation

If you grew up in the Bible Belt and were tantalized by sermons on the evils of Sodom and Gomorrah and have been searching for those cities ever since, you may find their spirit on the streets of Hamburg's Reeperbahn. Straight from the reels of *Mondo Cane,* this so-called sin strip is a genuine Teutonic sex circus. Mere striptease is never enough. It's a voyeuristic delight as dozens of girlie joints vie for the marks of the visiting sailor or the local businessman looking for some divertissement. The parade, or rather the posture, of erotic adventuring continues throughout the evening and into the early hours. A bit of comedy, a touch of perversity—all in all, a bold adventure!

DOLLARWISE—WHAT IT MEANS: In brief, this is a guidebook giving specific, practical details (including prices) about Germany's hotels, restaurants, sightseeing attractions, and nightlife. Establishments in all price ranges have been documented and described, from the extravagant chambers of the Vier Jahreszeiten (Four Seasons) in Hamburg to a low-budget, 12th-century knight's castle commanding a spectacular view of the Harz Mountains.

In all cases, establishments have been judged by the strict yardstick of value. If they measured up, they were included in this book—regardless of price classification. The uniqueness of this book, we think, lies in the fact that it could be used by a matron ("We always stay at the Bayerischer Hof in Munich"), or by a mark-mindful collegian ("There's this great little restaurant in Berlin that serves you a complete dinner for 12 DM").

But the major focus of the book is centered neither on the impecunious nor on the affluent. Rather, our chief concern is the average, middle-income-bracket voyager who'd like to patronize the almost wholly undocumented establishments of Germany that offer maximum value.

SOME "VORSPEISEN" OF BARGAINS: Borrowing the word in this heading from the array of tempting beginnings to the German meal, we'll preview some of the most delectable establishments awaiting you. In our journeys through every province of Germany, through its large cities and small villages, we have discovered surprising luxury offered for little cost, or establishments where the homemade or creative touch of their proprietors lifted them far above the ordinary. For a truer understanding of what dollarwise means, we'll now recall only a few as examples, though you'll find dozens more in the pages ahead—and perhaps discover others on your own when you actually go to Germany.

In the Mosel Valley at **Traben-Trarbach,** you can stay at Clauss-Feist, a heavily Germanic structure right on the banks of the river. It was created in an ornamental style around 1900, with elaborate timberwork, a domed tower, a highly pitched roof, gables, and dormers. Warmly decorated double rooms without bath cost from 40 DM ($22.94) to 52 DM ($29.83).

Or, on Germany's famed Romantic Road, in the Medieval town of **Dinkelsbühl,** still surrounded by ancient walls, you can stay in the Deutsches Haus, an inn whose fascinating carved and painted facade dates from 1440. In the individually furnished bedrooms, you're likely to find a ceramic stove in one room, a Biedermeier desk in another. For this you'll pay 45 DM ($25.81) in a bathless double.

What about restaurants? In the Bavarian capital is the Weinstadt, reportedly the oldest house in **Munich,** tracing its history back to 1468. But it's no museum, although your first glance would lead you to think so. Waitresses in regional dress hurry across the natural brick floor, serving up hearty Bavarian fare at scrubbed wooden tables lit by candles. Typical main dishes include pork chops with vegetables and a salad at 9.50 DM ($5.45). A quarter liter of an open wine begins at 2.30 DM ($1.32).

In the large Black Forest city of **Freiburg,** you can dine in the Oberkirch's Weinstuben, where you can saturate yourself with the food and flavor of the old town. The restaurant's situation is picture-postcardy—on a little square, with step-gabled roof houses. An old wrought-iron sign hangs over the restaurant's entrance, and red and white tables are set out front for wine sampling or meals. A memorable lunch in the dark-paneled weinstube costs as little as 15 DM ($8.60).

THE DEUTSCHES MARK AND THE DOLLAR: The unit of German currency is the Deutsches Mark (DM), which is subdivided into pfennigs. What the Deutsches Mark is worth in terms of U.S. money is a tricky question, the answer to which you determine the same way you determine what your stock holdings are worth: by consulting the daily market quotations from day to day, in this case the money market.

The best advice is to consult a broker immediately before you leave or upon arrival to determine the most up-to-the-minute rate of exchange.

Still, some idea of what you'll be spending will be useful as you read these pages, so we've prepared a DM-to-dollar chart to be used only as a gauge. It is based on an exchange rate of approximately 1.75 DM to one U.S. dollar.

DM	U.S. $	DM	U.S. $
0.25 (25 pfennigs)	.14	20	11.47
0.50 (50 pfennigs)	.29	25	14.34
1	.57	50	28.68
2	1.15	75	43.02
5	2.87	100	57.36
7.50	4.30	125	71.70
10	5.74	150	86.04
15	8.60	200	114.72

SOME DISCLAIMERS: No restaurant, inn, hotel, gasthaus, or nightclub paid to be mentioned in this book. What you read are entirely personal recommendations—in many cases, proprietors never knew their establishments were being visited or investigated for inclusion in a travel guide.

A word of warning: Unfortunately, costs change—and they rarely go down. All prices quoted in this book are subject to change.

Always, when checking into a hotel, inquire about the price. This policy can save much embarrassment and disappointment when the time comes to settle your bill. You cannot insist on being charged the precise prices quoted in this book, although much effort has been made to secure accurate tariffs as they were foreseeable.

An additional note: The price quoted for double or twin hotel rooms is the rate for two persons, unless otherwise indicated.

AN INVITATION TO READERS: Like all the Dollarwise books, *Dollarwise Guide to Germany* hopes to maintain a continuing dialogue between its authors and its readers. All of us share a common aim—to travel as widely and as well as possible, at the best value for our money—and in achieving that aim, your comments and suggestions can be of aid to other tourists. Therefore, if you come across an appealing hotel, restaurant, nightclub, even sightseeing attraction, please don't keep it to yourself. We'll send free copies of the next edition of this book to readers whose suggestions are printed in it. And the letters need not only apply to new establishments, but to hotels and restaurants already recommended in this guide. The fact that a listing appears in this edition doesn't give it squatter's rights in future publications. If its services have deteriorated, its chef grown stale, its prices risen unfairly, whatever, these failings need to be known. Even if you enjoyed every place and found every description accurate, a letter letting us know that, too, can cheer many a gray day. Send your comments to Stanley Haggart and Darwin Porter, c/o The Frommer/Pasmantier Publishing Corporation, 380 Madison Avenue, New York, NY 10017.

THE $15-A-DAY TRAVEL CLUB: In this book we'll be looking at how to get your money's worth in Germany, but there is a "device" for saving money and determining value on *all* your trips. It's the popular, international $15-a-Day Travel Club, now in its 16th successful year of operation. The Club was formed at the urging of numerous readers of the $$$-a-Day and Dollarwise Guides, who felt that such an organization could provide continuing travel information and a sense of community to value-minded travelers in all parts of the world. And so it does!

In keeping with the budget concept, the membership fee is low and is immediately exceeded by the value of your benefits. Upon receipt of $10 (U.S. residents), $12 (Canadian and Mexican residents), or $14 (other foreign residents) in U.S. currency to cover one year's membership, we will send all new members, by return mail (book rate), the following items:

(1) The latest edition of *any two* of the following books (please designate in your letter which two you wish to receive):

Europe on $15 a Day
Australia on $20 a Day
England and Scotland on $20 a Day
Greece and Yugoslavia on $15 & $20 a Day
Hawaii on $25 a Day
Ireland on $15 a Day
Israel on $15 & $20 a Day
Mexico and Guatemala on $10 & $15 a Day
New Zealand on $15 & $20 a Day
Scandinavia on $20 a Day
South America on $15 a Day
Spain and Morocco (plus the Canary Is.) on $10 & $15 a Day
Turkey on $10 & $15 a Day
Washington, D.C. on $25 a Day

Dollarwise Guide to Caribbean (including Bermuda and the Bahamas)
Dollarwise Guide to Canada
Dollarwise Guide to Egypt

Dollarwise Guide to England and Scotland
Dollarwise Guide to France
Dollarwise Guide to Germany
Dollarwise Guide to Italy
Dollarwise Guide to Portugal (plus Madeira and the Azores)
Dollarwise Guide to California and Las Vegas
Dollarwise Guide to New England
Dollarwise Guide to the Southeast and New Orleans
(Dollarwise Guides discuss accommodations and facilities in all price ranges, with emphasis on the medium-priced.)

The Caribbean Bargain Book
(A one-of-a-kind guide to the "off-season" Caribbean mid-April to mid-December—and the fabulous resorts that slash their rates from 20% to 60%; includes almost every island group in the Caribbean, and the Bahamas too.)

Where to Stay USA
(By the Council on International Educational Exchange, this extraordinary guide is the first to list accommodations in all 50 states that cost anywhere from $3 to $20 per night.)

(2) A copy of **Arthur Frommer's Guide to New York,** a newly revised pocket-size guide to hotels, restaurants, night spots, and sightseeing attractions in all price ranges throughout the New York area.
(3) A one-year subscription to the quarterly Club newsletter—**The Wonderful World of Budget Travel** (about which more below)—which keeps members up-to-date on fast-breaking developments in low-cost travel to all areas of the world.
(4) A voucher entitling you to a $5 discount on any Arthur Frommer International, Inc. tour booked by you through travel agents in the United States and Canada.
(5) Your personal membership card, which, once received, entitles you to purchase through the Club all Arthur Frommer Publications for a third to a half off their regular retail prices during the term of your membership.

Those are the immediate and definite benefits which we can assure to members of the Club at this time. Further benefits, which it has been our continuing aim to achieve for members, are announced to members in *The Wonderful World of Budget Travel (WWBT).* An eight-page, full-size newspaper, *WWBT* carries such continuing features as "The Traveler's Directory" (a list of members all over the world who are willing to provide hospitality to other members as they pass through their home cities) and "Share-a-Trip" (offers and requests from members for travel companions who can share costs); worldwide travel news and feature stories by our acclaimed expert travel writers; plus tips and articles on specific plans and methods for travel savings.
If you would like to join this hardy band of international budgeteers and participate in its exchange of travel information and hospitality, simply send your name and address, together with your membership fee of $10 (U.S. residents), $12 (Canadian and Mexican residents), or $14 (other foreign residents) in U.S. currency to: $15-a-Day Travel Club, Inc., 380 Madison Avenue, New York, NY 10017. Remember to specify which *two* of the books in section (1) above you wish to receive in your initial package of members' benefits. Or,

if you prefer, use the last page of this book, simply checking off the two books you want and enclosing $10, $12, or $14 in U.S currency.

Chapter I

GETTING THERE

1. Traveling to Germany
2. Traveling within Germany

YOU COULDN'T CHOOSE a more central place than Germany to start your European experience. Germany most certainly is in the heartland of Europe. Not only is it jam-packed with atmosphere, nightlife, and sightseeing interests, but it's a perfect gateway to the rest of Europe. The Eastern European countries beckon with increasing accessibility, while to the south are storybook Austria and Switzerland, as well as glamorous Italy. Directly to the west is France, to the north the Scandinavian countries. You can use Germany as your starting point to explore any of these countries with comparative ease.

Moreover, in planning a trip to Germany, there are several available methods of cutting your air transportation costs. We'll first discuss the basic structure of airfares to Western Europe, and then deal with methods of traveling within Germany once you arrive.

1. Traveling to Germany

PLANE ECONOMICS: In the reorganization of the International Air Transport Association (IATA), and the withdrawal of almost all U.S. air carriers from the organization, tariff coordination has been left, more or less, in the hands of government policies. This holds true for the North Atlantic. Each member country works out a fare agreement between the home country and the United States, specifically the Civil Aeronautics Board (CAB).

For flights between Germany and the United States, Lufthansa has introduced a fare package which will suit a wide margin of travelers, whether they go in tourist, business, or first class.

For convenience, we will list fares to Germany, as well as to most other European countries, in each category with basic conditions mentioned. When you know your exact travel plans, it is best to check with your travel agent or with Lufthansa. There you'll learn if unavoidable fuel surcharges have been added to the fares quoted.

As of December 1, 1979, the following fares are applicable on Lufthansa. The figures represent round-trip fares from New York, first class, on jet aircraft, quoted in U.S. dollars.

Athens	$2130	Nice	$2124
Belgrade	1950	Oslo	1788

Bucharest	2422	Prague	1512
Budapest	1986	Rome	2012
Copenhagen	1788	Sofia	1928
Frankfurt (A)	1856	Stockholm	1886
Helsinki	1706	Tel Aviv	2558
Istanbul	2572	Vienna	1832
Milan	1910	Warsaw	1752
Moscow	2174	Zagreb	1870
Munich (B)	1866	Zurich	1740

First-class fares apply all year and allow unlimited stopovers.

(A) Same fare applies to Bremen, Cologne, Düsseldorf, Hamburg, Hannover, Stuttgart, Saarbrücken, and Münster.

(B) Same fare applies to Berlin and Nürnberg.

The figures below represent round-trip fares from New York City, economy class (business class between U.S.A./Germany) on a jet aircraft quoted in U.S. dollars.

Note: Passengers traveling in business class will be seated in a separate section of the aircraft. They will have separate check-in facilities, as well as complimentary alcoholic beverages and headsets. They are also allowed the same baggage allowance as holders of first-class tickets.

Basic season is eastbound September 15, 1979, to May 14, 1980, and westbound from October 15, 1979, to June 14, 1980.

Peak season is eastbound May 15, 1980, to September 14, 1980, and westbound June 15, 1980, to October 14, 1980.

	Basic Season	Peak Season		Basic Season	Peak Season
Athens	$ 978	$1132	Nice	$ 764	$ 916
Belgrade	1046	1232	Oslo	694	878
Bucharest	1178	1366	Prague	734	910
Budapest	858	1010	Rome	916	1068
Copenhagen	694	878	Sofia	966	1114
Frankfurt (A)	834	1044	Stockholm	748	932
Helsinki	836	1036	Tel Aviv	1630	1630
Istanbul	1222	1428	Vienna	848	1062
Milan	764	916	Warsaw	948	1156
Moscow	974	1166	Zagreb	966	1182
Munich (B)	848	1062	Zurich	694	878

(A) The same fare applies to Bremen, Cologne, Düsseldorf, Hamburg, Hannover, Stuttgart, Saarbrücken, and Münster.

(B) Same fare applies to Berlin and Nürnberg.

Excursion Fares

One way to cut the cost of your air transportation to Europe is by using the "Excursion Fare" plan, for which you simply must comply with the minimum/maximum length of stay. For example, if the validity is 14 to 60 days, this means that your trip must be a minimum of 14 days, and the return can be no later than midnight of the 60th day following the date you commence your trip. Minimum/maximum stay will vary, depending on each country. With this type of fare you can realize a savings that can be a substantial reduction from normal round-trip fares.

Set below are excursion fares in both the basic and peak seasons, as well as the minimum/maximum stay periods.

Basic season is eastbound September 15, 1979, to May 14, 1980, and westbound October 15, 1979, to June 14, 1980.

Peak season is eastbound from May 15, 1980, to September 14, 1980, and westbound from June 15, 1980, to October 14, 1980.

Note: The applicable period for fares to cities other than those in Germany might be different. Make sure that you get in touch with your travel agent or Lufthansa for the latest information and applicable weekend surcharge.

	Basic Season	Peak Season	Validity
Athens	$ 949	$1082	14–60 days
Belgrade	570	699	14–60 days
Budapest	712	865	14–60 days
Copenhagen (A)	724	852	14–45 days
Frankfurt (B)	704	795	14–60 days
Helsinki	764	921	14–90 days
Istanbul	822	946	14–60 days
Milan	543	692	14–90 days
Moscow	828	966	14–60 days
Munich (C)	725	817	14–60 days
Nice	783	893	14–60 days
Oslo (A)	724	852	14–45 days
Prague	672	819	13–60 days
Rome	580	740	14–90 days
Sofia (A)	688	836	22–45 days
Stockholm (A)	790	918	14–45 days
Tel Aviv	1001	1089	6–120 days
Vienna	718	817	14–60 days
Warsaw	689	832	14–90 days
Zagreb	540	660	14–60 days
Zurich	684	778	14–60 days

(A) Weekend surcharge applicable, $15 each way.
(B) Same fare applies to Bremen, Cologne, Düsseldorf, Hamburg, Hannover, Stuttgart, Saarbrücken, and Münster.
(C) Same fare applies to Berlin and Nürnberg.

Apex (Advance Purchase)

You can save even more on your Apex fare by purchasing your ticket at least 30 days in advance of departure. The advance purchase requirement varies according to the country, as indicated in the table below. Please take into consideration that there is a cancellation penalty of $50 if you cancel your reservation within the purchase requirement period or thereafter.

If you are able to make firm plans far enough in advance, you'll find the following fares much to your advantage.

Basic season is eastbound September 15, 1979 to May 14, 1980 and westbound October 15, 1979 to June 14, 1980.

Peak season is eastbound May 15, 1980 to September 14, 1980 and westbound June 15, 1980 to October 14, 1980.

Note: The applicable period for fares to cities other than those in Germany might be different. Make sure you get in touch with your travel agent or Lufthansa for the latest information.

	Basic Season	Peak Season	Validity	Advance Purchase Requirement
Athens	$630	$760	7–60 days	21 days
Belgrade	545	677	14–45 days	21 days
Bucharest	611	711	14–60 days	21 days

Budapest	498	625	14–90 days	30 days
Copenhagen (A)	500	634	14–45 days	30 days
Frankfurt (B)	485	585	14–60 days	30 days
Helsinki	480	672	7–90 days	30 days
Istanbul	618	744	14–60 days	30 days
Milan	531	613	7–60 days	21 days
Moscow	557	706	14–60 days	21 days
Munich (C)	505	611	14–60 days	30 days
Nice	520	524	7–60 days	21 days
Oslo (A)	500	634	14–45 days	30 days
Prague	481	607	13–45 days	30 days
Rome	567	655	7–60 days	21 days
Sofia (A)	533	676	14–45 days	30 days
Stockholm (A)	531	667	14–45 days	30 days
Vienna	524	653	14–60 days	30 days
Warsaw	564	703	14–90 days	21 days
Zagreb	530	650	14–45 days	21 days
Zurich	(460*) 417	(591*) 534	14–60 days	30 days

* Applicable on weekends.

(A) Weekend surcharge applicable, $15 each way.

(B) Same fare applies to Bremen, Cologne, Düsseldorf, Hamburg, Hannover, Stuttgart, Saarbrücken, and Münster.

(C) Same fare applies to Berlin and Nürnberg.

Holiday Fare/Special Apex

Even more economical are Lufthansa's holiday fares to Germany and special Apex fares to many countries in Europe. Here, again, advance purchase requirements, minimum/maximum stay, and penalty for cancellation must be complied with. The round-trip fares in U.S. dollars are as follows:

	Basic Season	Peak Season	Validity	Advance Purchase
Frankfurt (D)	$425	491	14–60 days	30 days
Munich	451	526	14–60 days	30 days
Vienna	463	569	14–60 days	30 days
Warsaw	540	657	14–90 days	21 days

(D) Same fares applicable to Cologne and Hamburg.

A Warning

All fares, rules, and regulations are effective only through March 31, 1980, and they are subject to change.

THE CHOICE OF AIRLINE: To get a head start on your German travel adventure, it seems only appropriate to fly the German airline, **Lufthansa.** It makes good sense from a practical standpoint, too. True to Germanic tradition, the Red Baron's airline emphasizes punctual, efficient, yet warm and friendly service. The worldwide Lufthansa system, with one of the most modern fleets in commercial aviation, offers more flights to Germany than any other airline.

For the convenience of travelers from the U.S. and Canada, Lufthansa now serves 11 gateway cities: New York, Chicago, Boston, Philadelphia, Los Angeles, Anchorage, Toronto, Montréal, Nassau in the Bahamas, and since May 1979, Miami and San Francisco. Plans for further expansion in May 1980, include the addition of Atlanta and Dallas/Fort Worth services. From each gateway, frequent Lufthansa flights will speed you nonstop or direct to such major German cities as Frankfurt, Munich, Hamburg, and Cologne.

On most Lufthansa flights from North America to Germany, you'll fly in the spacious comfort of wide-body aircraft, while on shorter routes within Europe, you'll travel aboard dependable 737s, 727s, and the newer, wide-body Airbus A300s.

Whatever class of service you choose, you'll notice the same devotion to detail. If you fly Lufthansa's first-class Senator Service, you can expect to be coddled from check-in to arrival, regaled with a variety of German beers, all the hors d'oeuvres you can eat (heaps of caviar), and an endless array of German specialties.

If you travel at the full economy-class fare, you'll be treated to Lufthansa's popular business-class service. Designed to provide extra amenities for business travelers, Business Class Service can add a lot to the convenience and pleasure of leisure travel as well. It's available on all Lufthansa flights from the U.S. and Canada to Germany (with the exception of flights from Anchorage, Alaska, and a few New York flights which originate in South America). The benefits include seating in a separate section of the plane, where most unoccupied seats usually are located, priority meal service, free bar service, the full first-class free baggage allowance, and on wide-body flights, free movies and audio entertainment.

Budget-minded travelers who take advantage of any of Lufthansa's money-saving excursion fares will still enjoy the normal standard economy-class service. (With Lufthansa, by the way, the normal standard is very high indeed.) It may also pay you to consult your travel agent about the many special package deals that Lufthansa offers.

2. Traveling Within Germany

GERMAN FEDERAL RAILROAD: Whether you travel first or second class, Germanrail's trains deserve their good reputation for comfort, cleanliness, and punctuality. They are modern and fast, running smoothly over welded tracks. Both first- and second-class trains carry smoker and nonsmoker compartments. A snackbar or a dining car serving German dishes and international cuisine, as well as good wines and beers, will usually be on your train (unless you're taking a "local"), and you can enjoy the landscape through picture windows.

Actually, Germanrail's customer service begins long before you board the train. Special features of major rail stations include information desks and ticket offices, pictorial directional signs (eliminating language problems), and posted timetables listing departures and arrivals of trains chronologically. In addition, each car carries signs, inside and out, describing its routing, point of origin, destination, and important stops en route. Restaurants, snackbars, post and money exchange offices, newsstands and bookstores, flower shops, beauty parlors, pharmacies, and often a cinema are just some of the facilities major railroad stations offer. And they're usually located right in the center of the city.

For city sightseeing, you can leave your baggage in a locker, or check it at the station's baggage counter. In many cities Germanrail provides door-to-door baggage service, allowing passengers to have their luggage picked up at or delivered to their hotels. Accompanying baggage can be checked for an economical fee. Suitcases, plus baby carriages, skis, bicycles, or a steamer trunk, are permitted as baggage. Insurance policies of various kinds, even a

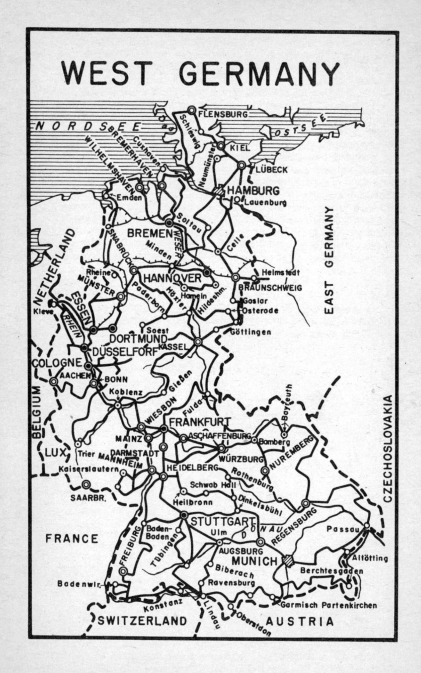

travel medical plan, may be obtained in addition to your ticket (inside Europe only).

About 20,000 passenger trains per day include the network of first-class Intercity (IC) trains offering express service every hour among 48 major German cities. IC trains carry first as well as coach class. These trains, as well as the Trans Europe Express (TEE) trains, require a surcharge (but not from holders of the Eurailpass and the first-class Germanrail Tourist Card). Seat reservations on TEEs are obligatory when crossing international borders, but should be made regardless. The luxurious interiors of IC trains match the quality of the TEE. Cushioned, adjustable seats and individual reading lights are just samples of the features you can expect. Business travelers appreciate the telephone and secretarial services offered on most of these trains. Bars, lounges, and dining rooms are available, too.

Sound sleep is almost guaranteed on Germanrail's smoothly running trains. You can make selections from different types of accommodations. Many prefer a private compartment (some even contain showers); others share bunk-type couchette compartments with five other passengers, at a price of only $7.50 per person. Advance reservations for sleeping accommodations are necessary. Travelers wanting to avoid the fatigue of long-distance driving can reach their destination on special car-sleeper trains (Auto Trains). Some daytime automobile trains are also operated.

Children below the age of 4, provided they do not require a separate seat, travel free; those between the ages of 4 and 12 pay half fare.

In several countries outside Europe, Eurailtariff tickets may be purchased either at a Germanrail office or at authorized travel agencies. Eurail tickets are valid for six months and allow unlimited stopovers en route. With a Eurail ticket, you just board the train, avoiding lines at ticket counters and currency problems.

These tickets are interchangeable for travel on many bus lines in Germany. You may, for example, take the Europabus along the Romantic Road from Frankfurt am Main via Würburg to Füssen and Munich, or along the Castle Road from Heidelberg to Rothenburg to Nürnberg. If your ticket is valid for the railroad portions—Mainz-Cologne and Koblenz-Trier—the payment of a small supplement entitles you to the corresponding boat passage on the Rhine and Mosel steamers operated by Köln-Düsseldorfer Deutsche Rheinschiffahrt AG.

For group travel the Eurailtariff allows substantial reductions. Groups of 10 to 24 members pay 25% to 30% less than the normal fare; groups of 25 or more members pay almost 50% less. Free transportation is offered to one member of a group consisting of 15 to 50 paying passengers. For youth groups of at least ten members (age below 21), the price reductions amount to 50%. Reservations for groups have to be made at least six weeks in advance.

The Eurailpass and the Eurail Youthpass are well-known travel bargains. These passes are valid in 15 Western European countries, excluding Great Britain and Yugoslavia.

But before we go into specifics about these passes, we should certainly mention that Germanrail runs trains directly from the Düsseldorf and Frankfurt Airports to the Düsseldorf and Frankfurt am Main Hauptbahnhof (railroad station), Wiesbaden, and Mainz. Travel time is all of 30 minutes, and the usual hassle of getting yourself from airport to town is considerably lessened.

GERMANRAIL TOURIST CARD: This unlimited-mileage card is available for periods of 9 or 16 days of first- or coach-class train travel in West Germany.

First-class tickets cost $145 and $200, respectively, while coach class is priced at $105 and $145. Children from 4 to 11 pay half these fares. The many bonuses include a reduced-fare round-trip rail ticket to Berlin, which also provides a free city sightseeing tour. Also included are free bus transportation on specified routes and reduced-rate steamer excursions on the Rhine between Cologne nd Mainz or on the Mosel River between Koblenz and Trier.

The Germanrail Tourist Card is also part of two packaged rail tours. A do-it-yourself **Romantic Hotel Rail Tour** allows the traveler to select his or her own itinerary from among 50 different locations in Germany. The **Historic Cities Rail Tours** are packaged for a southern circuit (five historic cities, nine days), a northern circuit (six historic cities, nine days), or a complete journey to all ten historic cities (16 days).

INSIDE GERMANY ONLY: In addition to these travel plans, Germanrail offers various other programs which can be purchased at railroad ticket offices and authorized travel agencies—but within Germany only.

Physical fitness enthusiasts, overworked managers, and nature lovers have long heeded Germanrail's advice to take the train to the countryside and enjoy the landscape "bike-back." More than 300 railroad stations in scenic areas participate in the "Bicycle at the Station" plan. Together with your bike ticket, you receive an area map with tour suggestions, telling you where to stop and visit a baroque church, a historical site, or some other attraction. You do not have to return the bicycle to the starting station—you can leave it at another station (after having made certain that its baggage counter is still open).

Other travel plans include programs for senior citizens as well as "junior citizens," city-to-city weekend tours, and district tickets. In addition, Germanrail offers reduced fares for mini-groups, holiday tickets (Vorzugskarte), conference compartments in IC trains, or even conference cars.

Before leaving for Germany, you can get complete details about the GFR and the many plans it offers at the following offices:

German Federal Railroad
630 Fifth Avenue
New York, NY 10020

German Federal Railroad
625 Statler Office Building
Boston, MA 02116

German Federal Railroad
1121 Walker St.
Houston, TX 77002

German Federal Railroad
10100 Santa Monica Boulevard
Los Angeles, CA 90067

German Federal Railroad
45 Richmond St. West
Toronto, ON M5H 1Z2
Canada

German National Tourist Office
104 South Michigan Avenue
Chicago, IL 60603

German National Tourist Office
700 South Flower Street
Los Angeles, CA 90017

German National Tourist Office
47 Fundy, P.O. Box 417
Place Bonaventure
Montréal, PQ H3A 1R3
Canada

EURAILPASS: This pass is obtainable for periods of 15 days, 21 days, and one, two, or three months at the price of $210, $260, $320, $430, and $530, respectively. The holder is entitled to unlimited first-class rail transportation and many bonuses—either free or with substantial reductions. Traveling on this pass has to be begun within six months of the day it was issued, and the first day of validity has to be stamped in at the railroad station where travel is commenced. For children, the already-mentioned rate reductions apply.

EURAIL YOUTHPASS: This is a single, convenient ticket for young people under 26 years of age. For $290, unlimited second-class rail mileage for a two-month period is offered. This pass offers the same privileges as the Eurailpass. However, seat reservations and supplements for express trains in some countries must be paid in addition.

Before leaving for Germany, you can get complete details on the German-rail Tourist Card, the Eurailpass, and the Eurail Youthpass from travel agents. You can also write to German Federal Railroad, 630 Fifth Avenue, New York, NY 10020.

WEEKEND EXCURSIONS: Many German cities and towns offer weekend packages with reductions on hotel accommodations, car rentals, restaurants, and admission to nightclubs and museums. The list of such excursions is extensive, and we have, unfortunately, not the space to review them all. The "Munich Weekend Key," however, is a particularly exciting example. It's run by the Munich Tourist Office and is offered in three price ranges, from economy to deluxe, for one, two, or three days. Included in the prices are hotel room and breakfast, a sightseeing tour of Munich or a tour of Upper Bavaria, a free ride to the top of Olympia tower, free admission to all museums and galleries in Munich, and a host of further reductions (on car rentals and admission to the Krone Circus, to name but two).

The best way to find out about the full range of the weekend excursions is to consult the **German National Tourist Office** at 630 Fifth Ave., New York, NY 10020 (tel. 212/757-8570), before you leave home, or to ask at the various local tourist offices as you travel around Germany.

CAR RENTALS: Traveling by car becomes economical if more than one person goes along for the ride. When four share expenses, it makes for a particularly dollarwise bargain. Two American car-rental organizations provide rental services, but it might make more sense to get your car from the biggest German company.

That means **Inter-Rent,** which has been in existence for more than half a century. All that experience is well reflected in its handling of overseas tourists. The company rents cars out of more than 330 stations. Their fleet ranges from the famous "Beetle" up to the Mercedes 280 SE. Inter-Rent operates airport offices at all German airports, and at such strategic locations as Frankfurt, Munich, and Berlin's Tegel. As a convenience for overseas visitors, you can pick up a car at one station and leave it at another at no extra cost.

If you don't plan to do much motoring, you might prefer the regular rental rate—that is, so much per day (week, or month) and so much per kilometer. In this classification, daily tariffs range from 37 DM ($21.22) to 88 DM ($50.48) per day, plus about 13¢ (U.S.) to 32¢ (U.S.) per kilometer.

Much more serviceable for the visitor going long distances would be the unlimited-mileage rates. In this category, daily rentals range from 55 DM ($31.55) all the way up to 138 DM ($80.16) for the more luxurious models. Regardless of the tariff you sign for at the beginning of your trip, Inter-Rent will quote you at the end whichever arrangement is cheaper. An 11% government tax is added to all rental charges and extra costs. And all major credit cards are honored by Inter-Rent, which rents cars to licensed drivers 21 years of age or older.

Inter-Rent operates a European system, with more than 1500 stations. This simplifies excursions to the surrounding countries such as France, Switzerland, and Austria.

In Germany, the telephone number of the reservation center is 520-18; the telex number is (02) 1743-46. To make reservations in the United States for Europe, you can call a toll-free number—800/421-6878. In California, call 800/262-1520.

FRANKFURT AM MAIN AND ENVIRONS

YOUR FIRST GLIMPSE of Germany will very likely be this thriving industrial metropolis. Although it's only the country's seventh-largest city, Frankfurt is Germany's most important transportation center. Its huge *flughafen* welcomes every major international airline. More than 1200 trains run in and out of its massive 19th-century station, the largest in Germany, and some of these trains run from the station right to the airport to transport arriving passengers back to town.

As the home of the Bundesbank (Federal Bank), Frankfurt is also the financial center of the Federal Republic. Since the Rothschilds opened their first bank here in their hometown in 1798, it has been a major banking city, currently containing more than 220 banks and the third-largest stock exchange in the country. It is also a heavily industrial city, with more than 2450 factories operating around the ford *(furt)* on the Main where the Frankish tribes once settled.

Frankfurt has also been the home of Germany's most important trade fairs since way back around 1200 A.D. But in spite of its commerce and industry, it is also a tourist city, offering numerous attractions to its many visitors. One out of 11 persons in Frankfurt on any given day is actually a stranger to the city.

For shoppers, Frankfurt has everything—the specialty shops are so much like those back in the States that most visitors from America will feel right at home. The Zeil is the major shopping district, with its huge department stores lining both sides of the street, offering everything from raincoats to rock records in a wide range of prices.

GETTING AROUND: Frankfurt's urban transportation system is new and rapid. The fares, paid before you board, are the same for both underground and surface transport. At tram and subway stops you'll find ticket-vending machines labeled "Fahrscheine." These machines will change up to 5 DM ($2.87).

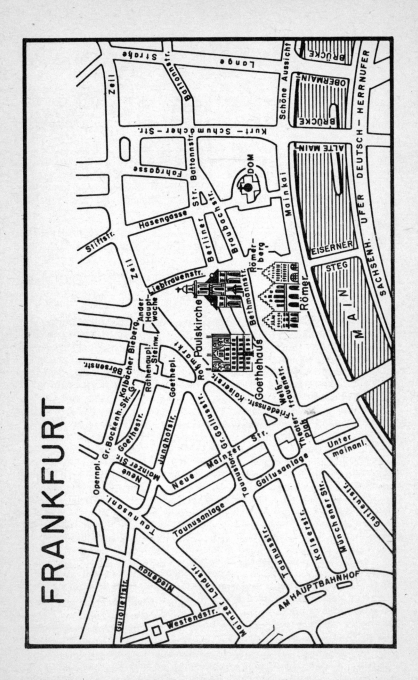

Fares vary, depending on the time of the day. During rush hours, the usual fare—1.20 DM (69¢)—goes up to 1.40 DM (80¢). This hike in price is to discourage shoppers and the "coffee-and-pastry" set from taking the lines at the same time as the workaday business people. If you are caught traveling without the proper ticket, you are subject to a fine of about 40 DM ($22.94) to 500 DM ($286.80).

1. Hotels

If you arrive during a busy trade fair, you may find many of the better hotels full. Rooms in Frankfurt are rather expensive. The cheapest living is found in private homes. You can't reserve these in advance, but you can always find a room on the spot by going to the tourist office in the railway station, near Track 24. During a particularly busy season, you may have to take a room as far as two or three miles from the city's center. The average cost for staying in a private home is 20 DM ($11.47), with an additional 4 DM ($2.29) charged for breakfast.

THE TOP CHOICES: Hotel Frankfurter Hof, Kaiserplatz (tel. 2-02-51), run by the Steigenberger chain, is the grand hotel of Frankfurt. This massively restored structure is the number one choice of traditionalists. Its position in the center of the city is ideal for tourists and business people alike, being just a few short blocks from the main railway station and near the sights of the Altstadt (Old Town).

Behind a 100-year-old, neobaroque facade, the Frankfurter Hof has successfully combined the traditional and the modern. In spite of its size—you and your friends could stay here for a month without running into one another—this comfortably furnished hotel offers a homelike atmosphere. The rooms are well maintained, furnished in restrained and dignified modern. The cost varies with size and location of your room: a single ranges from 99 DM ($56.79) to 155 DM ($88.91); doubles, from 150 DM ($86.04) to 190 DM ($108.98). All rooms have well-equipped baths. The 15% service charge, the 11% value-added tax, and the continental breakfast are included in all room prices.

In keeping with the management's belief that a fine hotel is "more than just a place to sleep," the Frankfurter Hof boasts several fine attractions: the French Restaurant, decorated in Empire style; the Grill Restaurant, with its huge lobster tank; the Lipizzaner Bar, where thirsty friends meet amid the memorabilia of the hunt—saddles, hunting horns, and etchings and paintings of horses and equestrians. The favorite spot in the hotel is the Frankfurt Stubb, recommended in the upcoming restaurant section.

Hotel Frankfurt Intercontinental, 43 Wilhelm-Leuschner (tel. 23-05-61), is West Germany's largest hotel. It has everything: you may find no reason whatsoever to leave its precincts. Right on the Main River, the south wing (21 stories) and the north wing (18 stories) offer 814 bedrooms of quiet comfort and dignity. Singles in price from 140 DM ($80.30) to a peak of 196 DM ($112.43); doubles are anywhere from 142 DM ($81.45) to 237 DM ($135.94).

The public rooms are mammoth, including a ballroom that can stuff in nearly 1000 Frankfurters. The general tone of the decor is quiet, but you get a feeling of warmth from the rich basic colors. For dining, the choice is awesome. The more formally attired guests are attracted to the downstairs Dell'Arte Restaurant, with its opera red and velvet upholstery and Austrian draperies. A fixed buffet luncheon is served from noon to 3 p.m. At the Silhouette rooftop supper club which houses the Three Coins Bar, you can not only dine, but dance to a combo every night except Monday. The Brasserie coffeeshop and the Treffpunkt restaurant are for more casual dining. The Weinstube is a cozy restaurant offering German specialties and local wines. In the Prolog Bar, you might meet the person you've been looking for all your life.

The hotel also has a swimming pool, sauna, message facilities, and a solarium.

Park Hotel, 36 Wiesenhüttenplatz (tel. 23-05-71), is considered by many discriminating guests the finest hotel in Frankfurt. In spite of its incredible size, it provides not only warmth but personal attention as well for each of its guests. Near the station, it opens onto a quiet square, offering parking (the underground garage has additional space for 150 cars). The hotel has been built in two sections—an ornately decorated 19th-century building right alongside a sleek 1970s wing. The decor is rich in autumnal tones, making for a soft, mellow atmosphere throughout. A single room with either shower or complete private bath ranges in price from 108 DM ($61.95) to 128 DM ($73.42); a double with bath is anywhere from 156 DM ($89.48) to 176 DM ($100.95). The hotel's grillroom dishes out some of the best hors d'oeuvres in Frankfurt, followed by meats from the open fire. The Parkstuben's one-plate meals are perfect for the visitor in a hurry. There's also the garden restaurant, where guests dine under a grape trellis.

Hessischer Hof, 40 Friedrich-Ebert-Anlage (tel. 74-02-51), looks like a substantial modern hotel with a severe facade. But its interior is so warm and inviting that it comes as a surprise, and does justice to its prestigious owners, the princes of Hessen. The furnishings give the hotel character: gilt-framed oil paintings, a museum-level collection of Sèvres porcelain in the dining room, antiques, and fine reproductions. The bedrooms are traditionally furnished, often with frilly decorator touches.

All 108 rooms have private bathrooms. Singles range in price from 85 DM ($48.76) to 140 DM ($80.30); twin-bedded rooms, 175 DM ($100.38) and up. Rates include breakfast; the garage cost is 10 DM ($5.74) extra.

Hotel Gravenbruch Frankfurt (tel. 06102/55-71), a property of Kempinski AG, in the suburbs, a 20-minute haul from the center of Frankfurt, is highly recommended for guests wanting to escape the bustle of the commercial city. The hotel is set back from Hwy. 459. Although the core of the hotel is in a historical building dating from 1568, the present complex has been turned into a superior deluxe hotel overlooking its private lake in a secluded park. Scheduled for completion by the autumn of 1980, the hotel will have 315 spacious and comfortably appointed rooms, each with private bath or shower, toilet, self-dial phone, radio, color TV, and full air conditioning. Singles with bath range from 110 DM ($63.10) to 160 DM ($91.78), and doubles with bath go for 165 DM ($94.64) to 260 DM ($149.14).

Many in-the-know Frankfurters drive down just to sample the savory viands of the cozy, rustic style dining room, Forsthaus Restaurant, with its tree-shaded terrace. Main dishes average around 24 DM ($13.77) to 28 DM ($16.06). You can also dine at the Forsthaus Grill, offering a French cuisine, or at the Forsthaus Schanke, converted from a 15th-century hunting lodge. After dinner, the hotel's bar presents an international band playing for dancing nightly. You can also patronize the disco and nightclub, Der Pferdfstall, in a 15th-century horse stable. Other facilities include heated indoor and outdoor swimming pools, a fitness center, a sauna, a solarium, and tennis courts, plus a beauty parlor and barbershop.

THE MODERATE RANGE: Mozart, 17 Parkstrasse (tel. 55-08-31), is a honey, perhaps the best of the small hotels in Frankfurt. It stands on the periphery of the Botanical Gardens, overlooking the U.S. Army building where Eisenhower headquartered himself in Frankfurt. Right off the busy Fürstenbergerstrasse, you'll recognize this hotel by its cold marble facade, softened by blue panels and the filmy curtains at the windows. Everything inside—walls, furniture, bed coverings—is gleaming white, with the small exception of the rosebuds at the breakfast table. The breakfast room, incidentally, could easily pass for a salon with its crystal chandeliers and Louis XV–style chairs. The cheaper rooms are those with shower and toilet; the more expensive offer a bidet, separate toilet, and tub with shower. A double with full bath is 119 DM ($68.26). Singles with shower go for 79 DM ($45.31), increasing to 93 DM ($53.34) with full bath. Members of the staff, in white-and-blue aprons, are polite and helpful.

Monopol, 11-13 Mannheimer Strasse (tel. 23-01-91), is across from the railway station. The decor: tapestries, Oriental rugs, and patterned armchairs. The bedrooms are sizable, with space often provided for a sitting area. Try to get accommodations in the rear; they're not only quieter, but less expensive. Top price for a bathless single is 46 DM ($26.39); a single with bath goes for 65 DM ($37.28) to 80 DM ($45.89). Bathless doubles are 80 DM ($45.89); doubles with bath, 100 DM ($57.36) to 120 DM ($68.83). Prices include a continental breakfast. The hotel bar is good for a tête-à-tête. The staff here is attentive and helpful.

Diana, 83-85 Westendstrasse (tel. 74-70-07), is spotless and homey. A leader in its price class, it is a copy of a private villa, with a gracious drawing room and an intimate breakfast salon. In the West End, it is set on a pleasant residential street and maintains a tone of quiet dignity. Although the Diana is postwar built, the surrounding neighborhood contains many 19th-century houses at least partially spared from bombings. The rooms at the Diana are quite comfortable. Singles with private bath or shower range in price from 40 DM ($22.94) to 52 DM ($29.83), the latter equipped with toilet as well. Doubles with complete bath are 70 DM ($40.15). Breakfast is an additional 5 DM ($2.87).

Hotel Continental, 56 Baselerstrasse (tel. 23-03-41), is the most modern hotel in the railroad station district. Around the corner are lively bars, but serenity prevails inside this continental hotel. The housekeeper has glistening standards, and there is maximum comfort in the bedrooms, especially those with the new private baths. Singles pay 52 DM ($29.83) with toilet only, 72 DM ($41.30) with full bath. A double is 88 DM ($50.48) with a partial bath, 99 DM ($56.79) with full bath. The Continental is fresh, airy, contemporary—often the preferred choice of business people who usually fill the small, but attractive lobby.

Pension Uebe, 3 Grüneburgweg (tel. 59-12-09), is a mother-daughter venture—and a successful one at that. Both the mother, Hilde Beck, and her daughter, Helga, speak English and are artistic and color conscious, having named and decorated each room after a European city, such as Munich or Vienna. Prints and decorative objects carry out the motif of the particular city. Reached by elevator, the pension occupies three floors over a grocery store and is entered through a covered passageway with window displays from an adjoining clothing store. The rooms in back are quieter; those up front face a busy intersection. There's a public bath for every four rooms. Singles are 38.50 DM ($22.08) without shower, 44.50 DM ($25.53) with shower; doubles, 67 DM ($32.50) without shower, 73 DM ($41.87) with shower. In the country-style breakfast room you order from a hand-painted breakfast menu in English. The pension is strictly for those seeking a gentle, warm, homelike atmosphere.

Hotel am Zoo, 6 Alfred-Brehm-Platz (tel. 49-07-71), is a modern little hotel just across from the entrance to the zoo gardens. The rooms are extremely clean, furnished in simple but comfortable modern pieces. Singles with showers and toilets rent for 50 DM ($28.68); doubles with bath, 80 DM ($45.89). The breakfast room on the street level is the hotel's most charming feature, with its linen-covered tables and attractive stained-glass windows. Parking facilities are available behind the hotel. The tram stops just across the street for convenient shopping and sightseeing trips.

Schwille, 50 Grosse Bockehheimer Strasse (tel. 28-30-54), is a small establishment with a charming cafe that is very popular at night, and overflows onto the sidewalk in fair weather. Guests sit at tables adorned with bright colors, admiring the original art for sale on the walls. An elevator takes guests up to the rooms, furnished in modern, with wide windows fronting either a busy street or trees out back where there is a parking lot holding only six cars. Single accommodations without bath are 48 DM ($27.53), increasing to 65 DM ($37.28) with bath. A bathless twin-bedded room is 72 DM ($41.30), increasing to 85 DM ($48.76) to 125 DM ($71.70) with private bath. Guests are offered a self-service breakfast buffet. This good breakfast is included in the rates. A ten-minute ride from the center of the city, the hotel is next to the university.

Hotel Niedenau, 5 Niedenau (tel. 72-25-36), is a family-style little hotel of only ten rooms. But it's a find. The atmosphere is intimate, and the well-furnished rooms are individualized to make them more inviting. The establishment is immaculately kept, with scrubbing and polishing going on daily. Singles without bath go for 40 DM ($22.94), rising to 52 DM ($29.83) with bath. Bathless doubles cost 75 DM ($43.02), peaking at 85 DM ($48.76) with private bath; a continental breakfast is included in the tariffs. In the vicinity of the railway station, the Niedenau is near two other suitable hotels, the Württemberger Hof and the Haus Hübner.

Hotel Rhein Main, 15 Mainlustrasse (tel. 23-23-15), is a modern hotel, offering good rooms close to the railway station. Units come with shower or bath, plus a self-dial phone. Accommodations are reached by elevator, and there are parking facilities. Tourists and business people both enjoy the hospitality of the manager, M. Erassas, who has employed a most solicitous staff. Units are small and furnished in a simple style. Everything, however, is immaculately kept. The charge is 57 DM ($32.70) for a single with shower and breakfast. Doubles cost from 125 DM ($71.70).

THE BUDGET HOTELS: Hotel-Pension Palmengarten, 8 Palmengarten-strasse (tel. 75-20-11), is a quiet little hotel within an apartment building just opposite the entrance to the famous Palmengarten. Run by Frau Hoffman, it's ideal particularly for American women traveling alone. The rooms are fairly large, always fresh and clean, and have sitting room areas with chairs or sofas. Everything is comfortable and homey. Most rooms are on the second floor, and there is an elevator. The hotel has no public lounges other than the cozy breakfast room. Singles without bath rent for an inclusive 28 DM ($16.06) to 44 DM ($25.24); with shower, 44 DM ($25.24); with private bath, from 55 DM ($31.55). Bathless doubles go for 60 DM ($34.42), increasing to 78 DM ($44.74) with shower, and peaking at 90 DM ($51.62) with private bath. Breakfast is included. An added attraction—on Sundays in summer you can hear the music of the concerts in the Palmengarten without leaving your room.

Hotel am Kurfürstenplatz, 38 Kurfürstenplatz (tel. 77-78-16). Frau Lauber, the English-speaking owner, has decorated the hotel in a mixture of styles, perking up each room with bright, cheerful colors, filmy curtains, and boxes of plants at the windows. The combination breakfast room and lounge sparkles with sunny, bright colors. The front rooms face a park complete with fountain, church spire, and lots of baby carriages. The hotel provides one bath and toilet for every three rooms. Singles rent for 28 DM ($16.06), doubles for 47 DM ($26.96), and triples for 65 DM ($37.28). There's an additional charge of 3 DM ($1.72) for use of the bath. There are some rooms with showers, and for these a single pays 40 DM ($22.94); a double, 60 DM ($34.42). Rates include breakfast, tax, and service. From October through April, 2 DM ($1.15) is added to your bill for heat.

Hotel Pension West, 81 Gräfstrasse (tel. 77-33-30), occupies part of an old house just off a busy street opposite the university. The atmosphere is like that of a private home. Managers Herr and Frau Operhalski speak no English, but you'll find that no obstacle. Everything is clean and orderly here. Single rooms without bath rent for 32 DM ($18.36); with shower, the cost is 34 DM ($19.50). Doubles without bath range from 52 DM ($29.83), going up to 64 DM ($36.71) with private bath. Breakfast, included in the rates, is served in a room on the ground floor. There are no parking facilities, but metered parking is usually available on the nearby streets.

Haus Hübner, 23 Westendstrasse (tel. 74-60-44), looks like a private mansion on a quiet street a quarter of a mile from the main station. Its elderly host has created a homelike atmosphere, giving each room subtle, but personal, differences, avoiding the institutional aura. Bathless singles cost 33 DM ($18.93), increasing to 45 DM ($25.81) with shower. Bathless doubles cost 66 DM ($37.86), but 80 DM ($45.89) with private bath, breakfast included.

The **Hotel Atlas,** 1 Zimmerweg Strasse (tel. 72-39-46), has a dozen nicely furnished rooms, lying in the vicinity of the railway station, at the corner of Maizerlandstrasse. You're welcomed by Pietro Bonetti, who speaks English among other languages, and exudes kindness and courtliness. He likes to keep a personal atmosphere, and has extended many courtesies to his American guests in the past. A single rents for 35 DM ($20.08), a double for 55 DM ($31.55), breakfast included.

Württemberger Hof, 14 Karlstrasse (tel. 23-31-06), has the family style of a Germanic gasthof, even though it's on a busy commercial street, close to the main station. The bedrooms, 67 in all, are functional and modern. The ones overlooking the street are equipped with special soundproof windows. Tariffs, including a continental breakfast, are as follows: 35 DM ($20.08) in a bathless single, 60 DM ($34.42) to 62 DM ($35.56) in a bathless double, 68 DM ($39) to 75 DM ($43.02) for a double with full bath. This is a good, standard overnight stop.

A LEFT BANK CHOICE: Hotel Maingau, 38 Schifferstrasse (tel. 61-70-01), is just right for those who want to live among the Frankfurters rather than with their fellow tourists on the right bank. The hotel opens onto a small park in the colorful apple wine district, just across the Main from the Old Town. Plenty of blond wood and plastic make up the Nordic furnishings in both the recently renovated old building and the annex. Bathless singles rent for 31.50 DM ($18.07), increasing to 41 DM ($23.52) with private shower or bath. Bathless doubles cost 49 DM ($28.11), although one with private bath will run a high of 61 DM ($34.99). The Maingau is a good point from which to launch a nighttime pub crawl of the apple wine district, beginning at the friendly restaurant and bierstube next door.

A YOUTH HOSTEL ACROSS THE MAIN: Haus der Jugend, 12 Deutsch-hherrnufer (tel. 61-90-58), is a large government building, combined with a modern annex, right on the Main. This is wholesale international living—all nationalities, both sexes. In spite of the name (*jugend* means youth), age is not a prerequisite for staying here. One woman seen checking in couldn't have been a day under 70. The mammoth-size rooms sleep from four to eight persons and rent for 6.30 DM ($3.61) to those under 20; 9 DM ($5.16) to those over 20, breakfast included. Without a youth hostel card, the cost is 1.50 DM (86¢) more. The bunkbeds are clean and comfortable, and you pay 1.80 DM ($1.03) for sheets. The hostel has a terrace cafe serving meals for only 3.50 DM ($2.01) to 8 DM ($4.59).

READERS' HOTEL SELECTIONS: "We selected a hotel between the railway station and the airport, **Hotel Stadion** (tel. 67-15-32), when we arrived late in Frankfurt by train and were to leave by plane for Canada the next morning. We paid 60 DM ($34.42), which included shower and breakfast, for a double room. The hotel has a restaurant and a large lobby. The bedrooms are well equipped and comfortable, and the service is courteous" (Agnes and Jim Nevfeld, Lethbridge, Altoona, Canada). . . . "I would like to recommend a pension in Frankfurt, **Pension Backer**, 92 Mendelssohnstrasse, near the Palmengarten (tel. 74-79-92). Singles cost from 25 DM ($14.34) and up. The price includes a breakfast of orange juice, German rolls with butter and jam, and a two-cup pitcher of strong coffee" (Lucy Jane King, Richmond Va.). . . . "**Hotel Goldner Stern,** 8 Karlsruhestrasse (tel. 23-33-09), is a spotlessly clean hotel just three minutes' walk from the railway station. It is operated by obliging people. Each room has hot and cold running water. The price of a single is from 22 DM ($12.62), which includes a continental breakfast with which cheese is served" (D. Hannay, Sanderstead, Surrey, England).

2. Restaurants

At the crossroads of European travel, Frankfurt's restaurants reflect a sophisticated international flavor. You can find everything here from haute cuisine to the city's sausage namesake. The best wines are also readily available, although many Frankfurters still prefer to wash their food down with beer and apfelwein.

THE TOP RESTAURANTS: Brückenkeller, 6 Schützenstrasse (tel. 28-42-38), is the leading restaurant in Frankfurt and the favorite watering spot of American visitors to that city. In the heart of the Old Town, you dine under medieval-looking arches at candlelit tables. Strolling musicians encourage singing and gaiety. Franconian carvings adorn the alcoves, and huge wooden barrels are decorated with scenes from Geothe's *Faust* and from the life of Martin Luther. The food is well prepared, a happy mix of German and French cuisine. A typical meal might begin with French onion soup at 5 DM ($2.87), or a more substantial platter of hors d'oeuvres at 11.50 DM ($6.60), and follow with the veal steak Cordon Bleu for 21 DM ($12.05). For the perfect finish, you might order crêpes suzette, 19 DM ($10.90) for two persons. Homemade sourdough bread is served with the meal. The wine cellar includes an excellent collection of German wines, including the best from the Rhineland. The Brückenkeller is invariably crowded, so reservations are imperative. Personal attention and efficient service are hallmarks here. It's open for dinner only.

Frankfurter Stubb, Kaiserplatz (tel. 21-56-79), in the Hotel Frankfurter Hof, takes a giant step backward to the simple German cooking of the past century. The food here is straightforward and honest. The ambience is that of an elegant cellar, with cozy dining nooks. Red and raspberry-colored fabrics soften the wood and stucco look. The attentive English-speaking waitresses are most helpful in translating the difficult German menu. For openers, try the excellent lentil soup with frankfurters, at 3.50 DM ($2.01). One of the house specialties is gekochtes ochsenfleisch mit Frankfurter grüne sosse, bouillonkartoffeln, at 14 DM ($8.03). It's delicious, but you'll have to ask the head waiter to explain it. The featured dessert is quarkpfannkuchen mit nüssen and rosinen (cottage cheese pancakes and nuts and raisins), 4 DM ($2.29)—well worth a 15-minute wait. The regular menu is served until 10 p.m., and then a smaller menu is offered until midnight for the theater crowd. The Stubb is a favorite with Americans.

Frankfurter Back Stubb, 2 Junghofstrasse (tel. 28-13-61), is an annex of the nearby Konditorei right on the corner. The ambience is a richly satisfying blend of rustic elements with some elegant overtones. Each dining room is slightly different, providing small boxes for an intimate meal. The decoration is real Stubb style, with wooden tables and chairs, as well as amusing cretonne-covered hanging lamps. The cuisine here is good but simple, offering a typical soup at 3 DM ($1.72), plus an assortment of German dishes in the 8-DM ($4.59) to 13-DM ($7.46) range.

Henninger-Turm, 60 Hainer Weg (tel. 61-04-71), is a revolving restaurant spectacle in a silo, housing barely enough for 200 million glasses of beer. The pride of the Henninger Brewery, the two restaurants, the **Panorama** and the **Frankfurter Drehscheibe** (Turntable), rotate in different directions in the largest brewery silo in the world. To go up on the elevator, adults pay 1.50 DM (86¢); children, 1 DM (57¢). On the upper part is a lookout platform with a panoramic sweep of the city from a position across the Main in Sachsenhausen. Hesse cooking is featured in the Drehscheibe, 357 feet above ground, which charges 17.50 DM ($10.04) for either a rumpsteak or a veal schnitzel with mushrooms. The soup of the day usually goes for 4 DM ($2.29). The lentil, if featured, is especially nice. Copper and tile sound the rustic keynote.

Revolving at 337 feet above the ground, the more expensive Panorama offers such dishes as lobster cream soup at 6 DM ($3.44); breast of chicken Florentine, 16 DM ($9.18); and a local specialty in season—medallions of hare with a juniper cream sauce, 17 DM ($9.75). Desserts, such as fresh strawberries in season, are in the 5-DM ($2.87) to 18-DM ($10.32) range.

Incidentally, the **Tower Bar** in the roof garden features international bands (usually Latin) on weekends, as well as Sunday afternoons. A tavern in the old-world style, called the **Turmschänke** (Tower Tavern), is at the foot of the silo, but who came all this way to stay on the ground floor?

Mövenpick am Opernplatz, 77 Neue Mainzerstrasse (tel. 28-78-57), is the spot where the Swiss have invaded Frankfurt and have given Hesse cuisine a real challenge in the doing. Having long enjoyed an outstanding reputation for cooking in their own country, the Mövenpick interests have created dramatic dining in this German city, especially in the main restaurant, **Baron de la Mouette** (a second Mövenpick at Wiesbaden is too remote for the casual tourist). In this restaurant, the roast rib of Angus beef with horseradish cream, Warwick mustard sauce, beef pan gravy, and baked potato is the daily specialty, costing 24.50 DM ($14.05). More seductive dishes of the French and international cuisine include scampi in a tarragon sauce at 24 DM ($13.77) and entrecôte Bordelaise at 24.75 DM ($14.20).

Preferred by many is the Mövenpick's pub, **Rob Roy,** named after the Scottish rebel. It's open from 11:30 a.m. to 3 p.m. and from 5 p.m. to 1 a.m., and serves apéritifs, liquors, steaks, warm snacks, seafood, and salads. Specialties include a crayfish cocktail, 13 DM ($7.46), and Angus entrecôte at 25 DM ($14.34). Scotch, the national drink of Scotland, goes for 8 DM ($4.59) to 12 DM ($6.88). Waiters in tartan vests and waitresses place the savory dishes before you.

Börsenkeller, 11 Schillerstrasse (tel. 28-11-15), is an oasis in the austere metropolis, concealing its old-world atmosphere behind a deceptively modern exterior. Dining is on the lower level, where you'll find arched cellar rooms and lots of nooks and recessed areas. During the evening, accordion music is played. The restaurant begins serving its savory viands around noon, with soups going for 3.50 DM ($2.01) and main dishes ranging from 14 DM ($8.03) to 30 DM ($17.21). Specialties include rumpsteak Rothschild with croquettes at 23.50 DM ($13.48) and pork chops in the Swiss style, 15.50 DM ($8.89). Desserts range in price from 3.75 DM ($2.15) to 10 DM ($5.74), the latter tab for a raspberry flambé. Set lunches are priced anywhere from 7.75 DM ($4.45) to 19.75 DM ($11.33). If you've just arrived in Germany, a memorable meal at the Börsenkeller will whet your appetite for exploring the countryside.

MEDIUM-PRICED DINING: Rheinpfalz-Weinstuben, 1 Gutleutstrasse, is the favorite weinstube of Frankfurt, directly across the street from the new theater. During the summer, lunch is served in the canopy-covered wine garden. It's a typical wine tavern atmosphere, with good food in hearty portions and excellent wines. Dinners are served only on weekends, when hearty German meals are available until midnight. Main dishes include rumpsteak with roast onions at 17 DM ($9.75); Pfalzer topf, a choice of three pieces of meat with mushrooms, 15.75 DM ($9.03); or schweinhaxe, 13.55 DM ($7.77). Desserts are in the 3.80-DM ($2.18) to 6.50-DM ($3.73) range. Every month you may select a new wine, a quarter liter costing from 2.40 DM ($1.38) to 4.50 DM ($2.58).

Schwarzer Stern (Black Star), 8 Kalbacher Gasse, still has its original beams and oversize wine press. A provincial country-house theme prevails throughout the three floors, with wooden churns used as hanging lamps, goat yokes and grain scoops decorating the walls. The street-floor nookery is for drinks. The upstairs restaurants are intimate, carpeted, designed more for charm than victuals. The cuisine is good, however. Set lunches are priced anywhere from 8.80 DM ($5.05) to 18 DM ($10.32). Specialties include rumpsteak Schwarzer Stern served with potato croquettes at 22.80 DM ($13.08). For a first course, try the Hungarian goulash soup, 3 DM ($1.72). The restaurant also offers what must be the largest diner in all of Frankfurt—for gargantuan appetites only. Costing 42.80 DM ($24.55), it is the large grill platter of the house, with filets of venison, ham, veal kidney, beef, veal, and more. If you need anything else after that, make it a cup of sherbet at 5 DM ($2.87). If you want to wash down your meal the German way, try one of the five kinds of beer on tap.

Zur Stadt Wien, 13-15 Weckmarkt, behind the cathedral, is a bit of Old Vienna in Old Frankfurt. The innkeeper, Mr. Jerepp, is a wine expert who shares his interest with his patrons. More than 80 wines from 12 different countries are stored in the wine cellar. The best and most traditional wine, the Grinzig, costs 35 DM ($20.08) a bottle. The restaurant is softly lit, with a rather schmaltzy but fun decor. A zither, accordion, or violin is usually playing Viennese melodies. The food is good, concentrating on German-Austrian specialties such as wienerschnitzel, 20 DM ($11.47). Tasty wiener goulaschsuppe at 5.50 DM ($3.15) is a most filling appetizer, and the Salzburger nockerl "made with nine egg whites and seven egg yolks" is a knockout at 16 DM ($9.18).

Churrasco, 6 Domplatz, is where Frankfurters go for succulent Argentine beef steaks. The black sign with the steer outside marks the spot of this dimly lit tavern, just next door to the cathedral. The Argentine beef filet comes in two sizes: 180 grams costing 19 DM ($10.90), or 300 grams going for 27.50 DM ($15.77). Cheaper orders of rumpsteak cost 13 DM ($7.46) and 19 DM ($10.90), depending on the size. All cuts are charcoal-grilled to your specifications. Rounding out the menu are a typical Argentine gazpacho at 3.50 DM ($2.01) and a limited list of desserts, ranging from 2.90 DM ($1.66) to 4 DM ($2.29). A steak and salad luncheon goes for 9.80 DM ($5.62).

BUDGET DINING: König Quelle, 19 Grosse Bockenheimer Strasse, still retains some of its old country pub-inn quality, although it has been slightly modernized. Rough plaster walls, hand-hewn beams, and stained-glass windows capture the Germany of years gone by. A curving wooden staircase leads to the mezzanine tables. The cost of a main dish is 7.50 DM ($4.30), and each day a different specialty is featured. Otherwise, you can order a main dish, complete with soup and dessert, for 18.50 DM ($10.61). The special feature of the place is its famous Nürnberg sausages, costing 8.50 DM ($4.88). Try also the pork cutlets in the Nürnberg style, 10.50 DM ($6.02), or else a mixed grill of pork and veal, with vegetables, for 16.50 DM ($9.46).

Zur Hauptwacht, an der Hauptwache, is historic, although the present building is a reconstruction. Now a restaurant-snackbar on three levels, it offers both partial and full-course meals throughout the day and evening. On a warm evening, the street level—attracting coffee drinkers and pastry eaters—is a delight. The atmosphere is casual, and many a lonely traveler has found a companion for the evening. Don't fail to ask for the special beer, Römer Pilsner. A typical German snack is likely to run 9 DM ($5.16), but expect to pay from 16.50 DM ($9.30) to 25 DM ($14.34) for a more elaborate meal.

A RUSTIC INN ON THE OUTSKIRTS: Gutsschänke Neuhof, between Neu Isenburg and Götzenhain, 20 minutes south of Frankfurt (tel. 32-14), is a dining adventure. Surrounded by woods, meadows, and fields of flowers, the inn itself is part of a huge farm estate (Hofgut Neuhof) dating from 1499. In summer, tables are set out on the wide terrace overlooking the pond. Inside, the former manor farmhouse is a maze of connecting rooms for dining. It's a totally rustic atmosphere, with pewter candlesticks and fresh-cut field flowers on the tables. On the walls hang antlers, maps, swords, rifles, and old prints. You'll sit in hefty captain's chairs while English-speaking waiters in red waist-coats proffer excellent service. The food is exceptional, beginning with the vorspeise Neuhof, an assortment of hors d'oeuvres including such delicacies as fresh crayfish with dill. Served at your table from a cart, the array of appetizers is priced by size. If you prefer a different appetizer, try the herring salad at 5 DM ($2.87) or the Hungarian goulash soup at 4 DM ($2.29). Venison is a popular main course in season, and two house specialties are gespickte rehkeule Hubertus (leg of venison) for 21 DM ($12.05), and hirschrücken steak, 26 DM ($14.91).

Vegetarians will enjoy the pichelsteiner gemüseeintopf, a delicious vegetable stew made from produce grown on the estate. Dr. Egon Schumacher, the owner of Neuhof, supplements the excellent wine cellar with wines from his own local vineyards. Gutsschänke Neuhof is open every day, serving lunch from noon to 3 p.m., and dinner from 6 p.m. to 9:45 p.m. Live music is played in the evening from Thursday through Sunday.

While you're visiting Nuehof, stop in and browse in the gift shop on the premises, which sells pottery and linens as well as homemade sausages, candy, applecakes, and delicious breads.

READER'S PENSION SELECTION IN RÜDESHEIM: "Rüdesheim, in a quaint, wine-making section along the Rhine River, is a one-hour train ride from Frankfurt. Besides walking along narrow, winding cobbled streets, you'll find many excellent restaurants and a winery to visit. The **Pension Stella,** 8 Frauensteinstrasse (tel. 55-40-26), is near the center of the city, convenient to public transportation routes, and is run by Herr and Frau Veith, two charming people who speak reasonably good English. Room rates are negotiable and range from 32 DM ($18.36) to 48 DM ($27.53). Breakfast is an additional 7 DM ($4.02), and consists of an egg, rolls or toast, assorted jams, cheese, sometimes salami, and coffee or tea. Some rooms have private showers and large balconies. Others share bath and shower. All rooms, however, have sinks and are large, clean, and attractively decorated" (Shirley Kappa, APO, New York).

3. Sights

When the bombs rained on Frankfurt in 1944, nearly all the oldest historical buildings were leveled to mere piles of rubble. Visitors to the city today wouldn't sense this, however, except in the lack of some of the old-timbered buildings in the Old Town. For in what must have been a record reconstruction, the Frankfurters have not only built up their city into a fine melange of modern and traditional architecture, but they have faithfully restored some of their most prized old buildings as well.

The **Goethe House,** 23 Grosser Hirschgraben, is among them. It's been a shrine for Goethe enthusiasts since it was opened to the public in 1863. Originally built about 1590, the red sandstone and masonry structure was faithfully restored after it was destroyed in 1944. Today, the house appears much as it did when Goethe lived here, until he joined the Weimar court in 1775. One critic wrote that the restoration has been carried out "with loving care and damn-the-expense craftsmanship."

Reflecting the fashion trends of the 18th century, the house illustrates three successive periods of style. The dining room and most of the ground floor is in baroque, but the second floor, at the top of the elaborate wrought-iron balustraded staircase, is a rococo world. The second and third floors are more classical, and contain the library where Goethe's father worked and often watched the street for the return of his son. A portrait of the severe-looking gentleman hangs behind the door.

On the second floor is an unusual astronomical clock built in 1749 and repaired in 1949 to run again for another 200 years. One room also contains a picture gallery with paintings collected by Goethe's father. Most of them painted by contemporary Frankfurt artists, these works influenced Goethe's artistic views for a great part of his life. The poet's rooms contain a puppet theater which was one of Goethe's most important childhood possessions and which played a significant role in his "Wilhelm Meister."

Annexed to the house is the **Goethe Museum,** built since the war on the site of its predecessor. The museum contains a library of 120,000 volumes and a collection of 25,000 manuscripts, as well as 15,000 graphic artworks and 400 paintings associated in some way with Goethe and his works. The house and museum are open from April to September on weekdays from 9 a.m. to 5:30 p.m. (otherwise, from 9 a.m. to 4 p.m.); Sundays, from 10 a.m. to 1 p.m. Admission is 2 DM ($1.15).

The **Altstadt (Old Town)** centers around three reconstructed 15th-century Gothic buildings with stepped gables, known collectively as the **Römer.** For more than 500 years Frankfurters had their own "Bridge of Sighs" to cross the Main to pay their taxes at the town hall in these burghers' houses. The second floor of the center house is the **Imperial Hall,** lined with the rather romanticized portraits of 52 emperors who celebrated their coronation banquets here. You can visit this hall any weekday from 9 a.m. to 1 p.m. and from 1:30 to 5 p.m.; Sundays, 10 a.m. to 4 p.m. Tickets can be purchased at the entrance to the Römer Building. The cost is 1 DM (57¢).

The elaborate facade of the Römer, with its ornate balcony and statues of four emperors, overlooks the **Römerberg Square.** On festive occasions in days gone by, the square was the scene of roasting oxen and flowing wine. Today, unfortunately, the Justitia fountain only pours forth water, but oxen are still roasted on special occasions.

Towering over the opposite side of the square is the belfry of St. Nicholas, but the dominating feature of the Old Town is the 15th-century red-sandstone tower of the **cathedral,** in whose chapel German emperors were elected and crowned for nearly 300 years.

The architecture of many buildings in the Old Town has changed over the centuries, through enlargement or reconstruction, and since the war many buildings have been rebuilt along more modern lines. The oldest structure left unscathed by the bombings of 1944 was the 12th-century chapel of the Saalhof, constructed as a palace for Frederick Barbarossa. The Goethe House, described above, also in the Altstadt, has been carefully reproduced, although the Carmelite Convent and 13th-century St. Leonard's Church have a few modifications in their restorations.

At the northern edge of the Old Town is the **Hauptwache,** an old guard house, which is the heart of modern Frankfurt. Under it is the main subway station with a modern shopping promenade, but the Hauptwache remains serene in spite of the traffic whirling around and underneath.

Städel Museum, 63 Schaumainkai, on the south bank of the Main, opposite the Old Town, is Frankfurt's most important art gallery, containing a fine representative collection of most European schools and periods of paintings. The French Impressionists are represented on the first floor by Renoir and Monet, mixed in with the best German painters of the 19th and 20th centuries. One of the best of these is Ernst Ludwig Kirchner (1880–1938). See in particular his *Nude Woman with Hat.* Also on the first floor is Johann Heinrich Wilhelm Tischbein's portrait of Goethe in the Campagna in Italy. If you're short on time, however, go directly to the second floor to view the outstanding collection of Dutch Primitives, Dutch Paintings from the 17th century, and German Masters of the 16th century. Works by Dürer, Hans Memling, Hans Holbein, Mantegna, and many others have been brought together here. One of the most impressive paintings is Jan Van Eyck's *Madonna* (1433). Lucas Cranach is represented in several works, including a large winged altarpiece, and his rather impish nude *Venus.* The museum also includes a display of works from the Italian school, including a *Madonna* by Bellini. There is also a department of prints and drawings containing 25,000 drawings and 65,000 prints of European schools. The museum is open (except Mondays) from 10 a.m. to 5 p.m.; Wednesdays, until 8 p.m. Admission is 2 DM ($1.15), Sundays free.

Liebieghaus, 71 Schaumainkai, operated in conjunction with the neighboring Städel Museum, contains the city's largest collection of sculpture, spanning thousands of years, from ancient Egyptian to baroque. One of the most impressive works is a bas relief by Andrea della Robbia. The museum is open daily, except Monday, from 10 a.m. to 5 p.m.; Wednesday, from 10 a.m. to 8 p.m. Admission is free.

The Frankfurt **Zoo** is a multifaceted institution, intent more on education than entertainment, and because of this, it is unique and interesting for both young and old. Most of the animals wander about in exhibits enough like their native habitats to make them feel completely at home. One of the best examples of this is the African Veldt Enclosure, landscaped with ills and bushes so that the animals living there can avoid encounters with other breeds. In this single exhibit, gazelles, antelopes, and ostriches roam freely. In the Exotarium, fish and various reptiles live under special climatic conditions. In an artificially cooled polar landscape, King and gentoo penguins swim and dive. Half-hour radio guided tours are available throughout the day at the Exotarium. In keeping with its educational policy, the zoo has, in addition to many typical animal exhibits, a nursery where young apes are cared for by zookeepers (this is done only when the mother cannot care for the baby properly), and a breeding aviary, where you can watch birds preparing unusual nests. A new building for small mammals with a nocturnal section opened in 1978. It is one of the largest and most diversified of its kind in the world and also contains many educational facilities. The zoo is open from 8 a.m. to 5 p.m. in winter and from 8 a.m. to 7 p.m. in summer. The Exotarium is open until 10 p.m. Admission to the zoo and Exotarium is 5 DM ($2.87); for the Exotarium alone (after closing hours of the zoo), 2 DM ($1.15). A special permit costing .50 DM (29¢) per day is required to take photographs.

The **Palmengarten** is more than just botanical gardens; it is a pleasure ground throughout the year for relaxation and music. All year the gardens flourish with flowers of all kinds of annuals and perennials, such as tulips, daffodils, iris, day lilies, and bed plants of the seasons, rose gardens, alpine gardens, and various species of trees. Flower shows and exhibitions of flowering pod plants are held from the end of February until Christmas in the gallery around the old palm house, which is connected to the Gesellschaftshaus, a restaurant with ballrooms. Conservatories with 14 greenhouses contain a huge collection of orchids, bromeliads, cacti and other succulents, tropical water lilies, insectivorous plants, and palm trees. In summer, daily concerts are given in the bandshell. Once a week in the evening there's open-air dancing and jazz. The fountains are lit at night. Admission is 2.50 DM ($1.43).

ORGANIZED TOURS: In addition to seeing the sights of Frankfurt on foot or by tram, you can enjoy many attractions from a comfortable coach seat on one of the two daily tours sponsored by the tourist office. The 2½-hour tours depart in season from the tourist office in front of the **main railway station** at 10 a.m. and 2 p.m. The English-speaking guide provides a running commentary as you drive through old and new Frankfurt. You'll get brief glimpses of the Old Town, some of the more interesting modern buildings, and a stop at Goethe's House and the Palmengarten. If you prefer a longer or more detailed look at any of the major sights, you will have to visit them on your own, however. But the tour provides a good general look at Frankfurt for 18 DM ($10.32).

If you would like a night tour of Frankfurt, you can be picked up at one of several locations in the early evening, including the Lufthansa office and the Tourist Information Office. First, you visit the Henninger Turm for a drink and an overall view of Frankfurt from the top of the revolving tower. Then you'll be whisked off to Sachsenhausen for food and fun in the apple wine quarter. For coffee and cognac, you return to the center of town to a Viennese coffeehouse. Then you're off to a nightclub to view a sex show. The cost of the entire evening, including drinks and dinner, is 90 DM ($51.62) per person. Tours can be arranged any evening except Sunday through the tourist office or by calling **Autodienst Main-Eck** at 61-20-06.

4. Frankfurt After Dark

For robust Teutonic antics after dark, business visitors and GIs head for a 16-square-block area in front of the railway station, the Hauptbahnhof. This is the main rail station of the city, bisected by Kaiserstrasse and Münchner Strasse.

Here you'll find a rowdy, even dangerous, district which the Germans call *erotische Spiele.* Doormen will practically pull you inside to view porno movies, sex shows, sex shops, even discos teeming with prostitutes.

However, if you've got only one night for Frankfurt (a typical tourist average), and aren't out for erotic thrills, you'll do better to head across the Main to a district known for its apple wine taverns or apfelweinstuben.

These taverns—there are seemingly dozens of them—are in the **Alt-Sachsenhausen** section of the left bank. Here you drink local apple wine which some Frankfurters enjoy and some foreigners consider a cousin to vinegar. Our verdict: an acquired taste. Tradition says that you won't like the apple wine until you've had three big steins. After that, what does taste matter? A glass of the apple wine at one of these taverns costs as little as 2.50 DM ($1.43). It can be your cheapest night out in Germany.

You can also go on a tavern crawl, stopping off at the much-frequented **Zum Grauen Bock,** 30 Grosse Rittergasse. A hearty gemütlich atmosphere prevails in this smoke-filled tavern. Sometimes the communal singing is so robust it's necessary to slide back the roof on a summer night. A six-foot-six accordionist stumbles over pretzel vendors as he goes from table to table, involving everyone in his song. Contact is made, instant friendships formed, if only for the evening, whether you know the words or not. Featured on the menu is something known as handkäs mit musik (cheese with vinegar, oil, and onions). You may want to let the locals enjoy the subtle pleasures of this dish while selecting instead a true Germanic specialty known as schweinehaxen, a huge pork shank with sauerkraut and boiled potatoes, 17 DM ($9.75). A good beginning is the Frankfurter bohnensuppe (bean soup), 3.20 DM ($1.84).

A more romantic setting is found at **St. John's Inn,** 20 Grosser Hirschgraben, across from Goethe's House, a short walk from an der Hauptwache. Its cozy, old-world ambience is created in part by its large brick and timbered fireplace with its raised hearth, Windsor chairs, and candle lit tables. It's possible to drop in just for drinks, although you may order food as well. The house specialty is a pot of Irish stew at 11 DM ($6.31). The peppersteak is a good buy at 17 DM ($9.75), while the gourmet might prefer the sirloin at 19 DM ($10.90). Sometimes live music is played, but chances are you'll hear records. Often it's so crowded you can't get in. Open every night at 8 (but never on Sunday).

Jimmy's Bar, in the cellar of the Hessischer Hof, 40 Friedrich-Ebert-Anlage, is popular with a crowd in their 20s and 30s. Sometimes there is live music; otherwise, it's disco dancing to records. No minimum, no cover—just the standard drink prices. Whiskey is around 8 DM ($4.59). It's a good place to take a date or find one. Although the bar opens at 7 p.m., the action doesn't begin till much later. Parking is free, and the bar is closed on Sundays.

The **Silhouette,** on the 21st floor of the Intercontinental, 43 Wilhelm-Leuschner-Strasse, provides your most elegant evening out in Frankfurt. It's a rooftop evening restaurant, with music for dancing provided by a lively combo, often Latin, every night except Mondays. The fare is in the German supper club tradition, the view is spectacular—far better than that from the Henninger Turm. Drinks average around 12 DM ($6.88) to 15 DM ($8.60). For a quick glass of draft beer (three choices), a visit to the cozy **Bierstube** in the modern wing of the hotel can be inexpensive fun. Also, snacks are available.

A real Teutonic nightlife choice is the **Paradieshof,** on Paradiesgasse, a Henninger Bräu house in the apple wine district. Upstairs, it's a beer hall, with singing and dancing. Downstairs, Frankfurt teenagers flock to the **Nachteule** (Night Owl)—entrance fee, 4 DM ($2.29). The price of the local brew is the same in the beer hall upstairs or the disco below, 4 DM ($2.29). You can have a cheap evening here with lots of fun.

5. Exploring the Environs

Unless you're rushed beyond reason, you should allow an extra day or two in Frankfurt to take a look at some of the attractions of the surrounding countryside. Here you'll stumble over little medieval towns, or you'll be awed by the sophisticated spas of the Taunus. We'll highlight some of the best attractions below.

THE TAUNUS: These wooded hills north of Frankfurt include the highest peaks of the ancient mountain range cut by the Rhine and its tributaries. The geological formations have created a number of mineral springs along the periphery of the range. Entrepreneurs have developed these springs into spas. Two of the most active Taunus spas, Bad Homburg and Bad Nauheim, are described separtely in Chapter IV. From the Taunus's highest peak, the **Grosser Feldberg,** the towers of Frankfurt, 15 miles away, become part of the panoramic view. Because of its altitude, this peak is an important telecommunications post for the German post office. A few miles south of the Grosser Feldberg is one of the Taunus's most popular landmarks.

Schloss Hotel Kronberg

The **Schloss Hotel Kronberg** (tel. 06173-7011) comes as close as one can get to living in a royal castle. Actually, a royal prince does live in a more modest place on the grounds. Architecturally, the hotel is Wagnerian in scope, with towers, turrets, and stone terraces overlooking the vast forest (where there is an 18-hole golf course, used by Eisenhower when he was a general). The Schloss attracts everyone from presidents and kings to international bankers and industrialists, including on one occasion, Nixon and Constantine of Greece.

The former castle of Queen Victoria's eldest daughter, the German Empress Frederika, was turned into a hotel in 1954, after serving as a casino for U.S. officers during and after World War II. The manager, Herr Fisher, is one of the finest men in his profession. Throughout the salons, drawing rooms, and dining halls, there are abundant antiques and a number of valuable tapestries. Guests enjoy the English library and the petite salon. Everywhere you turn, even in the intimate drinking lounge, you'll see paintings worthy of a museum. The hotel boasts the only bar in the world with originals by Turner, Sir Thomas Lawrence, and Sir Joshua Reynolds.

The hotel's 54 rooms, five of which are suites, all contain private baths. In 1967 the castle was swept by a devastating fire and during the restoration, 20 rooms and some modern furnishings were added. Some rooms still have real antiques, however. The price of a single room, including breakfast and taxes, ranges from 125 DM ($71.70) to 135 DM ($77.44). Doubles go for a whopping 185 DM ($106.12) to 220 DM ($126.19). Rates include a continental breakfast, the service charge, and government tax. The hotel is open all year.

The hotel's dining room serves good food; the service is superb, almost courtly. Since space is limited, it is imperative to telephone in advance for reservations. The menu is à la carte.

In all, the Schloss Hotel Kronberg provides pampered care in a country estate.

A Quiet Hotel on the Southern Slopes

Sonnenhof Königstein, 7 Falkensteinerstrasse, Königstein im Taunus (tel. 30-51), surrounded by fields of wildflowers and wooded hills, is ideal for nature visitors seeking a peaceful interlude. If you're just passing through Königstein on a tour of the Taunus, you may want to stop here for dinner after viewing the feudal ruins of the Königstein fortress overlooking the town. The hotel's menu is an international one, with dishes from India, Austria, Russia, Scandinavia, and Switzerland, as well as Germany. For appetizers, try the cream of oxtail soup at 6 DM ($3.44) or six snails in a shell, 8 DM ($4.59). Although roast dishes are a specialty, for example, a haunch of stag in cream, 25 DM ($14.34), there are a number of unusual seafood items on the menu, including salmon with shrimp and asparagus at 25 DM also.

If you do plan to stay over, the hotel offers 80 comfortable rooms, all overlooking the Main Valley and Taunus hills. Full-pension terms are quoted for a minimum of three days. Otherwise, a bathless single goes for 46 DM ($26.39), increasing to from 60 DM ($34.42) to 79 DM ($45.31) with bath. Bathless doubles are in the 78-DM ($44.74) bracket, although you'll pay from 100 DM ($57.36) to 140 DM ($80.30) with a complete bath, breakfast included. But whether you're staying for dinner or for the night, you'll find the whole staff attentive and the atmosphere one of relaxed elegance. A swimming pool is an additional attraction.

THE ODENWALD: Odin, chief of the Nordic gods, could probably still identify his forest today. Many of the landmarks in this farm country south of Frankfurt date back to legendary beginnings. For instance, the well in the forest where Siegfried met his death at the hand of Hagen stands today in a tiny village on the Siegfriedstrasse, one of the best roads for exploring the Odenwald.

The climate here is among the warmest in Germany, owing to the shelter of the surrounding mountains. Blossoms appear early on trees and vines, and abundant harvests are celebrated in the otherwise quiet little German towns. To reach the Odenwald, drive south from Frankfurt to Darmstadt, then take the Bergstrasse (Rte. 3) running toward Heidelberg. This scenic route leads along the western slopes of the mountains to the old town of . . .

Bensheim

Just 30 miles south of Frankfurt, Bensheim could be an inspired place for a short flying visit from Frankfurt if you're between planes and want to sample or preview a typical German town. Here, the old timbered and plastered buildings, clustered about the tiny squares and fountains, look as if they've been removed from a Christmas card. The vineyards around the town indicate that this, like the Rhine Valley, is wine country. Each September, Bensheim is the scene of the most exuberant wine festival in the Odenwald, the Bergstrasse Wine Festival.

Just west of Bensheim is its major sightseeing attraction, the ruins of **the great abbey at Lorch,** at the edge of the Rhineland Palatinate. The monastery was built in Carolingian style in the 8th century, with a massive Königshalle (King's Hall), adorned with huge columns and walls covered with mosaics.

Returning to Bensheim, you may want to sample the hospitality at the following inn: **Hotel-Restaurant Stadtmühle,** 2 Platanenallee (tel. 31-48), beside a canal, offering a trio of dining rooms, each decorated in variations of a country theme. You may be enticed to prolong your stay, enjoying one of the inn's comfortable bedrooms at a cost of 24 DM ($13.77) to 27 DM ($15.49) in a single without bath, 45 DM ($25.81) to 50 DM ($28.68) in a double without bath, including breakfast. Beginning in the early morning, hefty women who enjoy their own cooking can be seen in the kitchen preparing the meals. The Stadtmühle, the most popular dining recommendation in Bensheim, has set meals starting at a low of 9.75 DM ($5.59) and ranging upward to 21.50 DM ($12.23). Extra added attraction: In the adjoining courtyard, seek out the comic robed figure with lantern and cat. Closed in June.

After a satisfying meal at the Stadtmühle, a drive eastward from the town through the Odenwald leads to . . .

Erbach

This town's "reason for being" seems to be the magnificent baroque palace of the ruling Erbach-Erbach family. The present structure, dating from 1736, was built on the site of an earlier 14th-century castle, of which only an ancient round watch tower has survived. The palace is a museum in itself, with its huge knight's hall, endless corridors, and Gothic painted windows. But even more remarkable are the collections exhibited within the castle halls: art treasures of the Erbach-Erbach family, including medieval sculpture and ivory displays.

Concerts are given in the Erbacher Festhalle, the modern town hall. The castle and its museums are open daily from 8 a.m. to noon and from 1 to 5 p.m.

Just three miles north of Erbach, and 30 miles east of Bensheim, is yet another medieval town . . .

Michelstadt

In a valley of the Odenwald, Michelstadt reflects a more prosperous and commercial medieval town than most of the neighboring communities. Around the marketplace are old houses and the 15th-century town hall, a half-timbered structure with oriel windows and a pointed roof supported by wooden pillars.

Just outside the town is the ancient fortified **Fürstenau Castle,** built in the 14th century for the archbishopric of Mainz. In the 16th century, it was expanded into a Renaissance palace with an unusual archway connecting it to the courtyard. The castle sits in a huge English-style park which dates from 1756. The courtyard can be visited by the public.

For meals or lodgings in Michelstadt, the inn described below is the most logical choice.

Drei Hasen, 5 Braunstrasse (tel. 23-74), is a glamorized tavern, established in 1830. Glittering with copper, it is rich in the old Germanic tradition. From his post at the cash register, the innkeeper makes frequent appearances at the tables to wish his guests "bon appétit." Here you get a good accommodation in rooms that are furnished in a Directoire style. Singles without bath cost 30 DM ($17.21), rising to 38 DM ($21.80) with bath. A double without bath is 50 DM ($28.68) nightly, increasing to 56 DM ($32.12) with bath, including breakfast. The best rooms have a view of the market square. In the true inn fashion, the meals are more of a source of revenue than the beds. Be sure to sample the specialty, original Nürnberger rostbratwürste 4 DM ($2.29) each. Other recommended and featured items include schweinhaxe, which begins at 12.50 DM ($7.17), depending on the size, and Holsteiner schnitzel, 28 DM ($16.06) for two persons.

THE SPESSART: Separated from the Odenwald by the snakelike Main River, the Spessart Mountains are much more rugged than the rolling hills to the west. The oak-covered mountains are broken here and there to make room for an old village or castle, and then the trees seem to join together again to cover the land. Most of the towns in the Spessart lie along the Main, their link to the outside world. At the confluence of the Main and Tauber stands . . .

Wertheim

Towering over this medieval town are the ruins of the ancient castle of the feudal counts of Wertheim. The town itself is much better preserved than the castle, with a marketplace dating from the 16th century and narrow brick streets sheltered by overhanging timbered houses. Beside the Tauber stands the ancient city gate of Wertheim, the Kittstein Tower, a reminder of the days when Wertheim was an important 14th-century city and not the sleepy community of today.

The **Hotel Schwan,** 23 Main Platz (tel. 12-78), is an enchanting little inn, part of it incorporating the already-mentioned medieval stone tower. The inn itself is colorful and well decorated, a friendly oasis. Only a roadway separates it from the river, and in true inn fashion less attention is paid to lounges than to dining rooms. The upstairs accommodations are comfortable, doubles with bath renting from 60 DM ($34.42) to 70 DM ($40.15). Singles with bath range in price from 35 DM ($20.08) to 48 DM ($27.53). Included in these tariffs is breakfast. The innkeeper, Rolf Wiessler, has considerably upgraded the Schwan, in more contemporary taste. Although the plumbing is updated, the welcome's still as warm as ever.

Set lunches start at 10.50 DM ($6.02), going up to 18 DM ($10.32). Specialties on the à la carte menu range from veal escalope in caper sauce with mushrooms and parsley potatoes for 20 DM ($11.47) to broiled eel in sage with potato salad and a remoulade sauce for 21 DM ($12.05). Try also the jambalaya, which is a mixture of chicken, ham, and bacon cooked with rice and shrimp, for 19 DM ($10.90). The Schwan is easy to spot, with its ornate wrought-iron sign projecting over the front dining terrace.

Set farther back from the Main, among the thick forests of the mountains, is the tiny village of . . .

Mespelbrunn

Just three miles from the Weibersbrunn exit of the Frankfurt-Würzburg autobahn, the little village of Mespelbrunn seems far removed from the reality of 20th-century living. The chief attraction of the town is the well-preserved Renaissance castle of the Counts von Ingelheim. It's a lake palace, more common in France than Germany, completely surrounded by water, and still the property of nobility today. The rooms are open to the public daily from 9 a.m. to 6 p.m., March to November. The prices: 2.50 DM ($1.43) for adults, 1.50 DM (86¢) for children. Included is a museum devoted to the history of the ruling family, and those for whom beauty is not food enough can visit a nearby restaurant.

Chapter III

MUNICH

1. **Hotels**
2. **Restaurants**
3. **Sights**
4. **Munich After Dark**
5. **Some Notes on Shopping**

TO MÜNCHNERS, BEER has been the core of existence for centuries. Songs were written in praise of the brew; festivals were organized in its honor, and beer halls were the scenes of all major events.

The people of Munich don't need much of a reason for celebrating. If you arrive here in late September, you'll find them in the middle of a festival in honor of Ludwig I's engagement to Princess Theresa—and that took place in 1810! The **Oktoberfest** starts on a Saturday, lasts 16 days, and ends the first Sunday in October. Although this great Oktoberfest, where beer flows as freely as water, is the most famous of Munich's festivals, the city is actually less inhibited and more individualistic in the pre-Lenten Carnival (**Fasching**). Even the most reserved Germans are caught up in this whirl of colorful parades, masked balls, and revelry.

Between these two festival seasons, Munich remains lively all year—fairs and holidays seem to follow one on top of the other. But no "oom-pah-pah" town this. You'll find the most sophisticated clubs, the best theaters, and the finest concert halls as well. Don't go to Munich to rest—it's a city in which you can really let yourself go.

TRANSPORTATION IN THE CITY: The city has a rapid transit system. Preferred to streetcars and certainly high-priced taxis is the subway. The underground network is of recent construction, containing many convenient electronic devices, and the rides are relatively soundless. The same ticket entitles you to ride the "U" railways and the "S" railways streetcars and buses. The U-Bahn or Untergrundbahn is the line you will use most frequently, as the S-Bahn or Stadtbahn services suburban locations.

At the Marienplatz, 135 services of the U-Bahn and S-Bahn crisscross each other. It's possible to use your Eurailpass or S-Bahn journeys, as it is a state-owned railway. Otherwise, you must purchase a single-trip ticket or a strip ticket for several journeys at one of the blue vending machines positioned at the entryways to the underground stations. These tickets entitle you to ride both the "S" and "U" railway lines, and are also good for rides on streetcars and buses as well. For the network area, there are 24-hour tickets valid for any number of trips during that time.

Incidentally, the U-Bahn runs across Munich from Harras going via Schwabing to the Nürnberg autobahn and Olympia Park, and the S-Bahn lines (six from the west and five from the east) run under the city in a two-track tunnel between the main station and the east station to combine the region with the city.

And now, before we take on the town, a place to stay.

1. Hotels

Finding a room is comparatively easy. The choice of hotels is vast, ranging from simple prewar pensions to sleek, streamlined modern. Many older candidates were face-lifted for the '72 games. In general, the tabs tend to be high. Bargains are few and hard to find, although they do exist.

If you are stranded in Munich, go to the **Information Office** in front of the railway station. There a patient Bavarian woman with some 20,000 listings in her file will come to your rescue. Tell her what you can afford, pay a fee, and get a receipt, as well as a map with instructions on how to reach the accommodation in which she books you. You pay only a 2-DM ($1.15) fee per room. Keep your receipt. If you dislike the room to which you've been sent, return to the same desk and the woman will try to find another room at no extra charge. The emergency room booking office is open daily from 8 a.m. to 11 p.m., and in the Airport Arrivals Hall, Monday through Saturday, from 9 a.m. to 10 p.m.; Sunday, from 11 a.m. to 7 p.m.

DELUXE HOTELS: Bayerischer Hof and Palais Montgelas, 2-6 Promenadeplatz (tel. 22-88-71), are considered by many travelers a Bavarian version of the Waldorf Astoria. The location is swank, across from American Express, opening onto a little tree-filled square. The tastefully decorated central lounge, with English and French reproductions and Oriental rugs, is practically the living room of Munich. "Meet you in the lounge of the Bayerischer Hof" is heard often. The Palais Montgelas, sumptuously decorated, was integrated into the hotel with deluxe suites and double rooms and a number of conference and banqueting rooms.

The major dining room evokes the grandeur of a small palace, with ornate ceiling, crystal chandeliers, and French provincial chairs. Generous drinks and charcoal specialties from the rôtisserie are served in the clublike bar, where the tables are lit by candlelight and the reflected glow from the octagonally paned stained-glass windows.

Some of the best-looking women in Bavaria are found lounging on the bricked sun terrace alongside the rooftop swimming pool and garden. Other facilities include the Kleine Komödie Theatre, a sauna, massage rooms, a Trader Vic's, and the best nightclub in Munich.

Bedrooms are priced according to size, bath facilities, and view. A single goes for 96 DM ($55.07) with shower, 141.50 DM ($81.16) with complete bath. Doubles with complete bath cost from 143 DM ($82.02) to 223 DM ($127.91), including breakfast.

Grand Hotel Continental, 5 Max-Joseph-Strasse (tel. 55-79-71), is exceptional, perhaps the nicest in Munich if you appreciate a stylish, antique-filled hotel run in a personal manner (its owner is Max Billig). Just five minutes from the railway station, it is a delight for one or 100 nights. The formal lounge, with an overscale tapestry, sets the tone. The grill room is furnished as a country

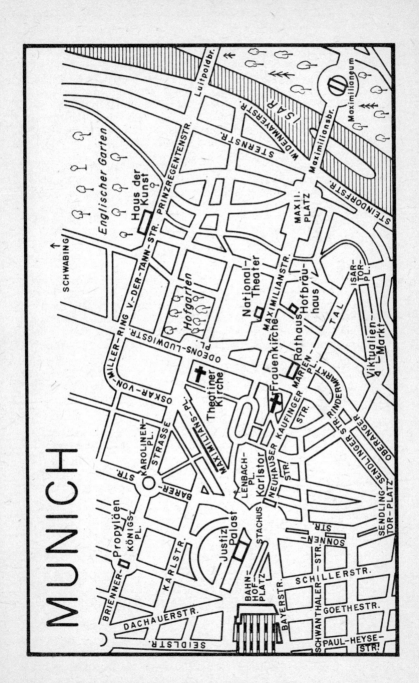

inn, with pine walls, crude tables, shelves of pewter plates, and antler horns. The more formal dining room is also provincial, with a wooden beamed ceiling, an open chateau fireplace, and high antique cupboards. That the Continental deserves its "Grand" appellation is reflected everywhere: in the French provincial coffee and card room; in the formal sitting salon, with ornate Louis XVI–style furniture, brocaded walls, and baroque doors; in the garden room, with its arbor, vines, and planters of red geraniums. In fair weather, guests seek the inner garden for dining. Breakfast is served at tables near the fish pond, splashing fountain, and ivory-covered wall. Each of the bedrooms, no matter what you pay, has style. A single with shower costs 85 DM ($48.76) to 149 DM ($85.47) with a complete bath. A double with shower goes for 163 DM ($93.50), peaking at 223 DM ($127.91) with complete bath.

Vier Jahreszeiten, 17 Maximilianstrasse (tel. 22-88-21). Whenever you see this name Four Seasons—in Germany—you're almost assured of a good hotel. In addition to the famed hotel in Munich, one of the best hotels in the north of Germany—the prestigious Vier Jahreszeiten in Hamburg—also uses this name. A substantial, quiet dignity prevails at Munich's front-ranking hotel. The tone is set as your taxi drives up to the covered entryway, where a liveried doorman greets you warmly.

Inside, you may feel as if you've arrived at an exclusive country club. One writer found that its rooms "radiated the atmosphere of the Wittelsbach era." The bedrooms are what you'd expect: immaculate comfort in spacious, well-appointed surroundings. The prices are from 117 DM ($67.11) to 162 DM ($92.92) for single rooms with bath. Doubles with bath rent for anywhere from 194 DM ($111.28) to 274 DM ($157.17). These tariffs include service, tax, and a continental breakfast. Unquestionably, the Vier Jahreszeiten offers the finest hotel dining in the Bavarian capital. In fact, it has won its fame for its gastronomic excellence. The cuisine generates from the Walterspiel Restaurant.

München Hilton, 8000 München 2, am Tucherpark (tel. 34-00-51), is a modern, 15-story hotel between the Isar River and the English Garden. Built in 1972 in the center of the former Tivoli park, it is about a ten-minute ride from the downtown shopping areas. The hotel's 491 bedrooms contain floor-to-ceiling picture windows, plus a balcony affording distant views of the Alps. Chambers are contemporary, yet elegant, with dark Macassar wood furniture, a perfect foil for the autumnal colors used throughout. Each accommodation is equipped with color TV and a self-service refrigerator bar, plus air conditioning, and direct-dial phones. Depending on the floor and location, singles range from 98 DM ($56.21) to 165 DM ($94.64); doubles, from 140 DM ($80.30) to 210 DM ($120.46).

A special feature is Poseidon's Grotto, a heated indoor swimming pool on the ground floor facing the English Garden. Overlooking the pool is an adjacent coffeeshop for drinks and snacks in the sun. Another open-air sunbathing area faces the Eisbach, a canal leading to the Isar. International specialties are featured in the grill on the ground floor. U.S. prime beef is also a specialty. Before dinner you can have a "mass" of good beer in the bar, with its wood and copper paneling. Facing the restaurant is the Atrium patio, which boasts Italian bronze sculpture and a mosaic wall. Crowning the hotel is the Marco Polo Bar/Restaurant, Asiatic in decor. Large windows with sliding thin woven wood panels open onto a panoramic view. At night, music is played for dancing (see our nightlife section).

Arabella, 5 Arabellastrasse (tel. 9-23-21), is excellent, but distantly located. The free-wheeling design of Arabella is contemporary, with many dramatic public rooms. Best of all is the skytop swimming pool. The bedrooms are modern, with private balconies, tiled baths, direct-dial telephones, and refrigerators (in some rooms). The accommodations seem more like chic living rooms than bedrooms. For example, lime-green walls, with overscale chalk-white sofas, chairs, and tables, are style pacesetters. Prices are sensible, considering what you get. Singles cost 95 DM ($48.76) to 98 DM ($56.21); twin-bedded rooms, 110 DM ($63.10) to 130 DM ($75.57). Breakfast and garage are included. Especially popular is the Safari Room, suitably adorned with leopard skins, tropical planting, cactus garden, and Toledo red chairs. However, the bars and Restaurant Capriccio have their own special flair. Guests can relax in sauna and massage rooms. Three miles from the airport, this city within a city lies off the autobahn to Nürnberg.

UPPER-BRACKET HOTELS: **Eden-Wolff-Hotel,** 4-8 Arnulfstrasse (tel. 55-82-81), opposite the railway station, misleads with its sedate exterior. The interior is not only more attractive, but warmly styled, making the Eden-Wolff one of Munich's better hotels. Each of its main-floor lounges is richly traditional, perhaps the most intimate and sophisticated being the old-world wood-paneled bar. A Bavarian theme permeates the main dining room—natural pine ceiling, gleaming brass lantern sconces, tavern chairs, and thick stone arches. Another dining room is like a richly paneled men's club, with oil paintings and brass chandeliers. Yet another contains murals depicting pastoral scenes. Quite consistently, the bedrooms borrow heavily from Bavarian styling. Most of them are substantial and lustrous, with polished woods, TV sets, and radios. Single rooms cost from 96 DM ($55.07) to 110 DM ($63.10), and twin-bedded units go from 145 DM ($83.17) to 180 DM ($103.25). All prices include breakfast. An underground garage is on the premises.

Excelsior, 11 Schützengasse (tel. 55-79-06), is one of Munich's leading hotels, owned by the same proprietors as the Königshof. Halfway between the railway station and the Stachus, it was built primarily for business people. For that reason, it is used less on weekends and grants rate reductions from Friday evening through Monday morning. The hotel has a contemporary look with a stamp of elegance in its public rooms. Especially attractive is the multitiered St. Hubertus restaurant, with its bas-relief of hunting scenes, open charcoal grill, wood paneling, and excellent cuisine, featuring Bavarian game specialties. Adjoining is an intimate bar. The bedrooms are modern. Singles go from 62 DM ($35.56) to 92 DM ($52.77); doubles or twins, from 114 DM ($65.39) to 144 DM ($82.60), according to size and placement. The hotel also offers several suites on the roof, at prices ranging from 167 DM ($95.79) to 182 DM ($104.40).

Splendid, 54 Maximilianstrasse (tel. 29-66-06), is one of the most attractive old-world hotels in Munich. Every room reflects the owner's ability to combine antiques with good reproductions, achieving harmony and style. The small living rooms, as well as the bedrooms, evoke the aura of a country home. Room prices are scaled according to size, furnishings, and bath. A bathless single is 50 DM ($28.68); a double, also without bath, 80 DM ($45.89). A single with private bath costs 75 DM ($43.02); a double with bath, from 110 DM ($63.10) to 130 DM ($75.57). A tasty breakfast is included. On sunny mornings, many guests prefer to have their morning meal on the paved patio, with its trellis and bubbling fountain.

Der Königshof, 25 Karlsplatz (tel. 55-84-12), in the heart of Munich, overlooks the famous Stachus (Karlsplatz) and the old part of the city, wherein interesting walking and shopping areas. Completely face-lifted for the 1972 Olympics, the hotel offers traditional comfort with up-to-date facilities. It is not only a commercial hotel, but attracts many tourists. All of its sleekly styled rooms have private baths, are air-conditioned and soundproofed, and feature TV sets and picture windows. Doubles or twins go for anywhere from 124 DM ($71.13) to 154 DM ($88.33). Singles are in the 72-DM ($41.30) to 102-DM ($58.51) range. On the second floor is a well-known terrace restaurant, serving a French and international cuisine. The lobby houses an intimate club bar, the King's Corner. An underground garage shelters 200 cars.

Deutscher Kaiser, 2 Arnulfstrasse (tel. 55-83-21) is a mini-skyscraper opposite the railway station. Its 15th-floor dining room provides both a panoramic view of the city and a relaxed opportunity to get your geographic bearings. In addition, the fourth-floor terrace contains a restaurant and cozy wood-paneled bar. The bedrooms feature built-in contemporary designs and room-wide picture windows. The accommodations are generously sized, combining sitting and sleeping areas. Singles with toilet and hot and cold running water rent for 52 DM ($29.83), increasing to 76 DM ($43.59) with full bath. Doubles with sink and toilet cost 98 DM ($56.21), 126 DM ($72.27) with full bath. Supplementary beds are an additional 28 DM ($16.06); use of a corridor bath is another 8 DM ($4.59). Breakfast is included.

Ambassador Hotel, 4 Mozartstrasse (tel. 53-08-40), can become your pied-à-terre in Munich, where you can have your own homelike setup—perfect for entertaining friends. For a reasonable outlay of marks, you get a studio apartment decorated in functional Nordic style, including a complete sitting room, with sofa, coffee table, reading lamp, armchairs, desk, TV, and three-channel radio. Silk draperies draw across a bed recess, with night light and telephone. In a corridor leading to an all-tile bathroom is your own little bar and refrigerator (stocked with basic materials). Singles are from 67 DM ($38.43) to 95 DM ($54.49); doubles, from 120 DM ($68.83) to 150 DM ($86.04). In addition to all this, there's an intimate lounge-bar on the lower level, plus a dignified wood-paneled dining room. Another asset: The Ambassador lies in a comparatively quiet spot, a few blocks south of the railway station. Garage space is available.

MIDDLE-BRACKET HOTELS: Schweizerhof, 26 Goethestrasse (tel. 53-96-31), is perfect for the on-the-go traveler who wants a compact, up-to-date accommodation close to the railway station. The bedrooms here are not large, but they are colorful and modern, each with a private bath or shower and telephone. A single with shower ranges in price from 50 DM ($28.68) to 80 DM ($45.89); a double or twin with bath or shower is 75 DM ($43.02) to 140 DM ($80.30). Included in these prices is an old-fashioned breakfast, featuring orange juice, eggs, honey, cheese, or ham. Parking at 7 DM ($4.02) is available 150 feet from the hotel. Diners choose between a main room in red, white, and blue, offering Swiss dishes and an open grill.

Hotel an der Oper, 10 Falkenturmstrasse (tel. 22-87-11), is a newly built hotel standing just off the Maximilianstrasse, in the vicinity of Marienplatz. It's superb either for sightseeing or shopping in the traffic-free malls. In spite of its basic, clean-cut modernity, there is a touch of elegance. The little reception area has a salon look with glistening crystal chandeliers and trim leather chairs. The luxurious cellar bar, the Opern-Taverne, is richly decorated with wood paneling and lots of crystal. Adjoining is one of the most prestigious restaurants of Munich, the Bouillabaisse. The bedrooms aren't super-chic, but they do offer first-class amenities, each with a private bath, phone, refrigerator, and small sitting areas with armchairs and tables for breakfast. Traditional elements have been combined with a severe modern. Including breakfast, a single rents for 80 DM ($45.89) nightly, a double for 110 DM ($63.10).

Adria, 8a Liebigstrasse (tel. 29-30-81), is a completely revamped hotel, offering many special appointments to remove it from the ordinary. With red-shaded lamps, global map behind the reception desk, wood panels, planter of greenery, and Oriental rugs, the lobby sets the stylish contemporary look. Some of the 54 rooms have a TV as well as a refrigerator filled with cold drinks. Armchairs or sofas and small desks add to the comfort. Singles without bath range in price from 39 DM ($22.37) to 45 DM ($25.81), increasing to 44 DM ($25.24) and 65 DM ($37.28) with bath. Bathless twin-bedded rooms go from 60 DM ($34.42); with private bath, from 78 DM ($44.74) to 110 DM ($63.10). Breakfast, included in the room rate, is the only meal served in the garden room—brightly decorated in red and white, with wrought-iron furniture.

The **München Penta Hotel,** 3 Hochstrasse (tel. 44-85-555), is 800 meters from the heart of the city. But the S-Bahn railway, which stops within the hotel complex, whisks visitors to the center in three minutes. Operated by the Forum division of Inter-Continental, the hotel is a mammoth, modern affair, with 583 rooms and three restaurants, plus an indoor pool and sauna. The Motorama shopping center is in the same building. The guest rooms are furnished in a contemporary idiom and offer air conditioning, color TV, and self-service bars. A single room with bath ranges in price from 75 DM ($43.02) to 105 DM ($60.23), and a double with bath from 105 DM ($60.23) to 140 DM ($80.30), including bell-captain room breakfast, service, and VAT.

Drei Löwen (Three Lions), 8 Schillerstrasse (tel. 59-55-21), is a trim, attractive, and tasteful 145-bedroom hotel adjacent to the railway station. It attracts clients who don't want to pay too much, yet like a quality setting where they can entertain a bit. Its dignified lounge is more like a library. Other little sitting rooms have the same sedate character—even the dining room, with its wood-paneled dado and scenic murals. The bedrooms are half traditional, half modern, all nicely styled, some with complete mini-bars. A bathless single is 48 DM ($27.53), 83 DM ($47.61) with bath. Doubles cost 115 DM ($65.96) bathless to 136 DM ($78.01) with bath. A supplementary bed can be added for 22 DM ($12.62). Use of the corridor bath is free.

Germania, 28 Schwanthalerstrasse (tel. 59-77-03), is conservative and sedate on the outside, but has many winning touches of design inside. Special features include automatic air conditioning, soundproofing, a separate private entrance, a box for shoes in the vestibule, and bathrooms lined either with pearl gray, black, or blue tiles or Venetian glass mosaic. Usually there is a sitting room adjoining the bedroom, with original paintings, etchings, Oriental rugs, and fruitwood furnishings. Large windows let in plenty of light. A bathless single ranges in price from 38 DM ($21.80) to 48 DM ($27.53), increasing to anywhere from 58 DM ($33.27) to 98 DM ($56.21) with private bath. A bathless double begins at 64 DM ($36.71), rising to 82 DM ($47.04). With bath, the double rate goes from 85 DM ($48.76) to 150 DM ($86.04)—these rates including breakfast, service charge, and taxes.

Hotel Mark, 12 Senfelderstrasse (tel. 59-28-01). This 141-bed hotel, near the south exit of the railway station, should be considered for its comfort and modest prices. Rebuilt in 1956, it offers either a shower or tub bath, plus toilet, in most rooms. The beds are good, the furnishings sleekly modern, and everything is undeniably serviceable. Included in the rates are taxes, service, and breakfast. A single with basin and toilet costs 38 DM ($21.80), increasing to 56 DM ($32.12) with bath. Doubles with shower rent for 69 DM ($39.58); with bath, from 76 DM ($43.59) to 82 DM ($47.04). Many rooms have TV. You can park your car in an underground garage for 7 DM ($4.02) nightly, or in the court for 6 DM ($3.44). The charming, tavern-style dining room has good food.

Hotel Habis, 2a Maria-Theresia-Strasse (tel. 47-27-17), wins our respect as a special small hotel of character. The location is across from Isarpark overlooking the river. Across the bridge are some of the leading museums of Munich. The hotel itself is built on a corner, with five floors of individualized bedrooms. The top floor has the old Munich architectural styling, and in general is well conceived. On the premises in a wine restaurant which combines old-style furnishings set in nooks and also has a mezzanine of rough white plaster and arches. Also on the premises is the unusual Komödientheater where shows are presented nightly except Mondays. The general decor of the hotel, especially the entrance with its gracious, curving staircase, is a moderate art noveau style. The bedrooms have strong earth colors, with painted built-in pieces, trim beds, casual wicker armchairs, and balloon lights. Most rooms have private baths, although a few have hot and cold running water with free use of the corridor baths and toilets. Singles range in price from 45 DM ($25.81) to 55 DM ($31.55); doubles, from 70 DM ($40.15) to 80 DM ($45.89).

THE BEST FOR VALUE: Bundesbahn-Hotel, im Hauptbahnhof (tel. 55-85-71), may well be the best hotel value in Munich! Although it's part of the railway station complex (right inside it), it shuts out that dreary world as soon as you enter its doors. A dignified, traditional lounge, with contemporary flair, greets you. In the snug little leather-coated bar, you can drown your troubles, or enjoy good Germanic cooking in one of several dining rooms, each tastefully and individually designed. More important, however, are the fresh bedrooms. Most of the accommodations ingeniously combine excellent French and art noveau designs; romanticists will gravitate to the top-floor rooms, with their dormer windows and built-in Tyrolean furniture (curved posts as headboards, painted armoires). Each room seems to have its own personality. The prices differ, depending on bath arrangement and size. Bathless singles cost 44 DM ($25.24); with shower, 52 DM ($29.83); with bath and toilet, from 64 DM ($36.71). A bathless twin-bedded room costs 77 DM ($44.17); with shower, 83 DM ($47.61); with complete bath, 96 DM ($55.07). A continental breakfast is included.

Europäischer Hof, 31 Bayerstrasse (tel. 55-46-21), is a nine-floor hotel opposite the railway station, which was originally built by a group of Catholic sisters. There's even a chapel on the premises. Nowadays, the operation is under the management of Siegfried and Josephine Büchl, and it's one of the best buys in Munich. Many of the accommodations overlook an inner courtyard, with a subterranean parking area, charging 6 DM ($3.44) nightly. Singles cost 34 DM ($19.50) to 38 DM ($21.80) bathless, 48 DM ($27.53) with shower, 58 DM ($33.27) with full bath. Twin-bedded rooms go for 64 DM ($36.71) bathless, 96 DM ($55.07) with full bath. These rates include breakfast, served either in the morning room or in your bedroom. Use of the corridor bath is 6 DM ($3.44). Despite its dreary station location, the hotel couldn't be more immaculate: the constantly dusting, polishing, buffing, and waxing maids make spring cleaning a year-round activity here. Most of the rooms are fair-sized, with built-in headboards, three-channel radios, a desk table, sofa, a pair of armchairs, coffee table, luggage racks, and an entry hall wardrobe.

Hotel-Pension Am Markt, 6 Heiliggeiststrasse (tel. 22-50-14), is a Bavarian-style hotel with a regional gingerbread trim that stands in the heart of the Old Town. It's not that easy to get in here, but it's worth a try. The hotel is not luxurious, but it has many decorative trappings reflecting the glory of another era. The owner, Harald Herrier, has wisely maintained an interesting, nostalgic decor in the dining room and entrance lobby. Behind his reception desk is a wall of photographs of friends or former guests of the hotel, including the late Viennese chanteuse, Greta Keller. As Mr. Herrier points out, when you have breakfast here, you are likely to find yourself surrounded by opera and concert artists who like to stay here because they are close to the houses in which they perform. The bedrooms are basic modern, quite small, but trim and neat. A few rooms have private baths, although most of the units have hot and cold running water, with free use of the corridor baths and toilets. The cost in a single is 31 DM ($17.78). In a bathless double, the rate is 52 DM ($29.83), rising to 62 DM ($35.56) with shower. Breakfast is included in the tariffs quoted.

Kraft Hotel, 49 Schillerstrasse (tel. 59-48-23), is a neat, little modern hotel that is especially attractive. Set back from a busy street, about five minutes from the railway station, it has just enough space in front to park a single car. The reception lounge is inviting, but you guessed it—absolutely tiny. An adjoining breakfast room is decorated in stark black and white, with large blow-ups of Old Munich all around. The emphasis, however, is mostly on the streamlined bedrooms, which are well kept and up to date, with many built-in units. Depending on the bath facilities you get, singles range in price from 38 DM ($21.20) to 59 DM ($33.84); doubles, from 66 DM ($37.86) to 89 DM ($51.05). Included in these tariffs are taxes, service, and breakfast. Luncheons and dinners are also available at moderate prices.

Salzburg, 1 Senfelderstrasse (tel. 59-56-27), is a modest hotel, a few minutes from the railway station, offering nicely furnished bedrooms. Each room has a good amount of space and is immaculately kept. There's an all-purpose second-floor room with a sitting area and a pleasant place for having morning coffee. Single rooms are 34 DM ($19.50). Bathless doubles are 56 DM ($32.12), 65 DM ($37.28) with shower, 67 DM ($38.43) with full bath. Rates include breakfast, tax, and service.

Modern, 16 Schillerstrasse (tel. 59-47-71), only two minutes from the station, is a great little bargain. The room furnishings are nicely coordinated, compactly designed, with built-in recessed beds, gilt-framed mirrors, and chandeliers. Doubles with perky tiled baths cost 60 DM ($34.42) to 95 DM ($54.49). Singles with shower go for 35 DM ($20.08) to 55 DM ($31.55), breakfast included. The gathering place for fellow guests is the intimate drinking lounge, which features wood paneling, red tiles, and patent leather chairs.

Haberstock, 4 Schillerstrasse (tel. 55-78-55), and its nearby sister hotel, the **Daheim,** 20 Schillerstrasse (tel. 55-01-39), are two hotels which were reconstructed in 1952. They are close to the railway station and priced reasonably. At the Haberstock, singles without bath rent for 28 DM ($16.06) to 34 DM ($19.50), from 58 DM ($33.27) to 55 DM ($31.55) with shower bath. Bathless doubles are 48 DM ($27.53) to 54 DM ($30.97); with bath or shower, from 62 DM ($35.56) to 82 DM ($47.04). These prices include breakfast. The dining room is old-fashioned, the bedrooms a mixture of traditional and modern; everything is clean and serviceable. The Daheim charges 30 DM ($17.21) in a single without bath, 54 DM ($30.97) in a double without bath, increasing to 75 DM ($43.02) in a double with bath.

Hotel Adler, 8 Ledererstrasse (tel. 22-39-91), in the center of town, is run by an ingratiating couple, Hans and Christl Faschinger, who once managed a pension, and were so successful with it that they decided to open this 60-bed hotel near Marienplatz. Culture lovers will find the Opernhaus, theaters, and the Kongressaal of the Deutsches Museum nearby. Around the corner there is the Hofbräuhaus, which you have to see if you visit Munich. The hotel is pleasantly furnished in the modern mode. In a room with a shower, one person pays from 45 DM ($25.81) to 65 DM ($37.28), that rate going up to 65 DM

($37.28) to 80 DM ($45.89) for two guests. With complete bath, the double rate is 90 DM ($51.62). The prices include breakfast, service, and tax. For 6 DM ($3.44) per day, you can garage your car. On the ground floor, the Restaurant Adler offers a wide range of German specialties.

THE PICK OF THE PENSIONS: **Pension Tirol,** 51 Goethestrasse (tel. 53-46-90), is on the second floor of an attractive prewar building, on a tree-shaded street, just an eight-minute walk from the railway station. It's owned by the kindly, English-speaking Frau Maria Schmitzberger, who makes it her business to offer genuine hospitality to her overseas guests. Her rooms are clean and comfortably furnished in a charming European way. In high season she charges from 42 DM ($24.09) to 45 DM ($25.81) for a double and 60 DM ($34.42) for a triple, including breakfast and service. Singles are tabbed at 28 DM ($16.06). A shower is included. Every room has hot and cold running water, plus central heating. There is no elevator.

Pension Schubert, 1 Schubertstrasse (tel. 53-50-87), is quite a special, small, personally run establishment with a taste of Old Germany. It's on the lower floor of an attractive villa on a quiet, tree-lined street, about five blocks from the railway station. Except for a tiny sign, you'd never know it was a pension. It's owned by English-speaking Frau Käthe Fürholzner. A few of her bedrooms have private baths (with showers), although most of her clients use a large tiled public bath. Doubles with bath rent for 50 DM ($28.68), only 40 DM ($22.94) if bathless. Bathless singles cost 30 DM ($17.21), including a special breakfast. To get to the Schubert from the station, walk along Goethes-trasse to Beethovenplatz, turn right along Beethovenstrasse to Kaiser-Ludwig-Platz, then walk along Schubertstrasse.

Hotel Uhland Garni, 1 Uhlandstrasse (tel. 53-92-77), is a stately, dignified town mansion, standing in its own small garden, just three blocks from the Bahnhof. It offers good accommodations at fair prices. The owners, Herr and Frau Hanzen-Berger, enjoy American visitors. They have a sliding price scale, based on the location and size of your room. A bathless double costs from 45 DM ($25.81) to 60 DM ($34.42), going up to the neighborhood of 70 DM ($40.15) to 90 DM ($51.62) with complete bath. Depending on the plumbing, singles range in price from 38 DM ($21.80) to 55 DM ($31.55). There are some three-bedded rooms on the top floor going for 60 DM ($34.42) to 75 DM ($43.02) if bathless, increasing to 90 DM ($51.62) to 110 DM ($63.10) with bath. The family specials, bathless four-bedded rooms cost from 80 DM ($45.80) to 90 DM ($51.62).

Pension Beck, 36 Thierschstrasse (tel. 22-07-08), is a 100-bed pension, next to the Hofbräuhaus and Deutsches Museum, with singles ranging from 15 DM ($8.60) to 24 DM ($13.77); doubles, from 30 DM ($17.21) to 42 DM ($24.09). Prices include use of the bath and shower as well as the kitchen (one on every floor), complete with refrigerator. With a private shower and toilet, the cost of a double room ranges from 64 DM ($36.71) to 78 DM ($44.74). The pension may be reached by taking tram Nos. 1, 4, or 21 to the Max II Monument stop or the S-train (use your Eurailpass) in the direction of Ostbahnhof, getting out at the third stop, Isartorplatz.

Pension Coburg, 38 Franz-Josef-Strasse (tel. 33-10-61), offers solid, mid-dle-class home comfort in Schwabing. Doubles with private showers cost 50 DM ($28.68) per night, 39 DM ($22.37) to 48 DM ($27.53) without showers. Singles go for 25 DM ($14.34) to 31 DM ($17.78). Use of the corridor bath is an extra 4 DM ($2.29). All prices include breakfast and local taxes.

Pension Westfalia, 23 Mozartstrasse (tel. 53-03-77), stands only two blocks from the meadow where the annual Oktoberfest takes place. This four-story town house is near Goethe Platz, and is reached by taking tram no. 17; it's one of the best pensions in Munich. The rooms themselves are immaculately maintained. Bathless doubles cost 36 DM ($20.65) to 40 DM ($22.94); bathless singles, 28 DM ($16.06). With a shower, a single costs 35 DM ($20.08), increasing to anywhere from 55 DM ($31.55) to 60 DM ($34.42) in a double with complete bath. Rates include breakfast, service, and tax. The owner, Herr Bertram Hoos, speaks English and was trained at the Hilton in Berlin.

Hotel Pension Terminus, 44 Bavaria Ring (tel. 77-65-85), is in a prewar building facing the meadow that's the site of the annual Oktoberfest. You have to climb three rather deceptively long flights, but upon arrival the welcome's warm and the rooms are nicely furnished in a homelike manner. Singles range from 24 DM ($13.77) to 28 DM ($16.06); doubles, 40 DM ($22.94) to 44 DM ($25.24). Bargain note: One of the three-bedded accommodations goes for 52 DM ($29.83). Breakfast is included in these tariffs. Every room has running water, and there are hall baths. The management works hard to make the atmosphere comfortable. Tram no. 19 from Karlsplatz.

Pension Dollman, 49 Thierschstrasse (tel. 22-31-91), occupies all four floors of a large stone building in an attractive, quiet residential area. It's a real find, with an elevator, a reception hall, and breakfast room on the ground floor. Large, pleasantly furnished rooms are rented, all with telephone and many with showers or private bathrooms. The owners are friendly and helpful. A bath and shower are on each floor. Singles cost 25 DM ($14.34); doubles, 35 DM ($20.08) to 38 DM ($21.80); three-bedded rooms, 53 DM ($30.40), breakfast included. There are some units with private bath, costing from 38 to 42 DM ($21.80 to $24.09) in a single, from 70 DM ($40.15) to 75 DM ($43.02) in a double, including breakfast, service, and tax. Take tram no. 20 from Karlsplatz, getting off at Liebigstrasse.

Mariandl, 51 Goethestrasse (tel. 53-41-08), is one of the better pensions of Munich, lying about a seven-minute walk from the railway station. Downstairs you'll find an old Bavarian restaurant, managed by the owner of the pension, Hans Brugger. Upstairs he rents modestly furnished rooms that are well kept, including a large breakfast of cold cuts, cheese, bread, butter, and jelly, as well as coffee. The charge in a double is 44 DM ($25.24), going up to 60 DM ($34.42) in a triple-bedded room, a peak 78 DM ($44.74) in a unit with four beds. English is spoken.

Pension Excelsior, 40 Kaulbachstrasse (tel. 34-82-13), lies one short block from the Gieselastrasse subway stop in the center of Schwabing. It is a small, pleasant pension, with good service, large and clean rooms, and some of the atmosphere of Alt München. It's housed in a turn-of-the-century building, but the conveniences are modern. All accommodations have hot and cold running water. Showers are free. The tariffs in a single range from 25 DM ($14.34) to 32 DM ($18.36). For a double, the charge rises from 57 DM ($32.70) to 59 DM ($33.84). All prices include breakfast with an egg. English is spoken.

Am St. Anna Platz Pension, 8 St. Anna Platz (tel. 22-28-60), sits on a quiet square facing St. Anna Church in the Lehel district. You're welcomed into a clean ground-floor pension where the rooms are small but nicely furnished in "modest modern." A bath and shower are on each floor. Singles go for 28 DM ($16.06); doubles, 45 DM ($25.81) to 50 DM ($28.68); three-bedded rooms, 65 DM ($37.28), breakfast included. Take tram no. 20 from Karlsplatz to Liebigstrasse.

Karl-Friedrich, 13 Mozartstrasse (tel. 53-40-78), is a family pension that, in the words of its owner, is a "good place in these days when money is scarce and not everybody is a millionaire." The host, Eugen Kranovitz-Kőváry, adds, "It's suitable for those who would like to live in a small decent house where the owner speaks English." He also speaks French and Spanish. The rooms are comfortably and pleasantly furnished. The price is 45 DM ($25.81) in a double, 26 DM ($14.91) in a single, with a good breakfast included. The bathrooms are shared. The location is fairly central—three minutes by subway to the heart of Munich.

Pension Frisch, 39 Liebigstrasse (tel. 22-67-60), is old with a 19th-century look. As it's not maintained as well as it should be, it's recommended for emergencies only. The ambience is peculiar, with a lot of furniture giving an Ali Baba aura—or at least a flea market atmosphere. A kind of do-it-yourself pension. Singles cost 28 DM ($16.06); doubles, 38 DM ($21.80); and a few triples, 53 DM ($30.40) to 65 DM ($37.28). Breakfast is included. Expect only the barest of plumbing, however. To get there, use bus no. 55 from the Main Station from Karlsplatz.

Hotel Pension Utzelmann, 6 Pettenkoferstrasse (tel. 59-48-89), is an impersonal building, but the atmosphere inside is family-like. Its owner, Mrs. Hermann Ernst, has freshened everything with furniture, carpeting, and modern toilets. The large accommodations are well kept, airy, and bright. Singles range in price from 25 DM ($14.34); doubles, 42 DM ($24.09) to 46 DM ($26.39). A bathroom is conveniently placed on each floor.

HOTELS IN SCHWABING: **Residence,** 4 Artur-Kutscher-Platz (tel. 39-90-41), provides a breath of fresh modernity in Schwabing. A corner honeycomb structure, it contains eight floors of rooms, most of which have balconies. The lounge is most attractive, its vibrant colors intermixed with chalk white and wood paneling. There's even a sauna-style swimming pool, with a wall and ceiling of natural pine, subtropical plants, and lounge chairs. Color and style are also notable features of the spacious bedrooms. Prices are set according to the floor you're assigned—those nearer the ground being cheaper. All rooms have private baths, balconies, refrigerators, and radios. Singles cost 111 DM ($63.67), going up to 134 DM ($76.86) in a double. Breakfast is extra. An underground garage is available. You can dine here at the elegant Le Pavillon restaurant, wherein glass globe lighting, bentwood chairs, and filmy white curtains; patronize the cozy, post-coach-like bar-restaurant, Die Kutsche (air-conditioned), or meet for drinks in the wood-paneled bar.

Holiday Inn, 200 Leopoldstrasse (tel. 34-09-71), acquainted Munich with this American motel chain. And this one's quite a glamorous introduction. Already the Holiday Inn has become a leading Munich hotel. Created originally to lure business for the year of the Olympics, it has offered a lot in modern living from the beginning. Every one of its rooms—it contains a total of 700 beds—is air-conditioned, with private bath and shower, queen-size bed (two in doubles), TV set, as well as direct-dial telephones. The decor is streamlined, with upholstered furniture, natural woods, and picture windows. Singles are 110 DM ($63.10); doubles, 150 DM ($86.04). A copious buffet breakfast costs another 13 DM ($7.46). A distinctive plus is the no-cost policy for children under 12 who occupy the same rooms as their parents. Guests are invited to use the marble-edged inside swimming pool, the Old Munich cocktail bar, the restaurants Schwabing-Klause and Almstuben-Grill, or the Yellow Submarine disco, an "underwater" nightclub surrounded by sharks and thousands of other deep-sea animals. The inn is in Schwabing, near the Olympic area, right at the Autobahn Nürnberg/Berlin and Frankfurt.

Leopold, 119 Leopoldstrasse (tel. 36-70-61), is a unique hotel in Schwabing, run by the Kiefer family. A 1924 villa, it offers a modern annex behind its garden, connected by a glassed-in passageway. Passing the hotel is the exit road of the superhighway. Nürnberg-Würzburg-Berlin. Think of the Leopold as a kind of motel, with plentiful parking. Two subway stations are 250 yards from the hotel; a bus and tram stop in front of the door, taking you into the center in about ten minutes. Finally, the famous English Garden is only a few minutes away by foot. Most of the public rooms are furnished in a Bavarian style, with wooden wing chairs and pine dado. The bedrooms are nicely designed, many with built-in beds, end tables, and all with armchairs or sofas. Bathless doubles are 80 DM ($45.89), 105 DM ($60.23) with private baths. Bathless singles go for 48 DM ($27.53), rising to 65 DM ($37.28) with shower, and peaking at 75 DM ($41.30) with bath, breakfast included. Whether in the old or new wing (which has an elevator), you'll have a telephone and double-soundproofed doors.

Paris, 130 Leopoldstrasse (tel. 36-20-80), is a miniature contemporary hotel in Schwabing, just past the traffic congestion of central Munich, yet easily reachable by bus and subway. It is suitable if you want a modestly priced modern accommodation. The public rooms are not important, but the bedrooms are quite good. Newly constructed, it offers streamlined rooms with uncluttered wood-grained furniture, and large windows letting in sunlight. Singles cost from 32 DM ($18.36) to 46 DM ($26.39); doubles, 59 DM ($33.84) to 75 DM ($43.02), including breakfast. You can call to have your morning meal served in your room at no extra cost, or join other guests in the sun-drenched breakfast room.

Hotel Gebhardt, 38 Goethestrasse (tel. 53-94-46), lies only three minutes from the main rail station, right in the center of town. Frau Gebhardt, the warm, friendly owner, is extremely helpful to her guests. Her rooms are pleasantly and attractively furnished, usually in autumnal colors. In a bathless single the rate is 29 DM ($16.63) to 32 DM ($18.36), rising to 38 DM ($21.80) to 48 DM ($27.53) with shower. Bathless doubles cost 55 DM ($31.55), but 58 DM ($33.27) to 75 DM ($43.02) with shower. The best bargains are the triple rooms, costing from 65 DM ($37.28) to 80 DM ($45.89), and the accommodations for four persons, from 75 DM ($43.02) to 85 DM ($48.76).

Hotel Nokolai, am Nikolaiplatz (tel. 39-70-56), is a moderately priced, small hotel in the Schwabing district, adjacent to the English Garden. It lies only a block or so from the restaurant and boutique district of Schwabing. A chocolate-brown and cream stucco building, it overlooks a tiny tree-filled plaza, and is convenient to public transportation which will take you to the center of Munich. Rising five stories high, it is in a severe modern design, with fine and attractively decorated bedrooms, all of which have private baths. There is no lobby to speak of, and your room price includes a tasty German-style breakfast. Singles go for 58 DM ($33.27); doubles, for 90 DM ($51.62).

A FORMER HUNTING LODGE ON THE OUTSKIRTS: Schloss-Hotel Grünwald, 1 Seillerstrasse (tel. 64-1935), is a hunting lodge belonging to the former rural palace of the Bavarian dukes. Deep in a forest in the Isar Valley, it has been converted into a 20-bed innlike hotel. It's on the outskirts of Munich (a distance of eight miles), yet is reachable by streetcar no. 25. The bedrooms are chock-full of museum caliber antiques: decoratively painted beds, chests, alpine chairs, ecclesiastical wooden figures, oil paintings of the early aristocracy, rare Oriental rugs, and crystal lights. Singles range in price from 43 DM ($24.66) to 70 DM ($40.15), depending on the plumbing. Likewise, doubles cost from 68 DM ($39) to 99 DM ($56.79), and some apartments are available for 128 DM ($73.42). Even if you're not overnighting, try a lunch or dinner in the modernized dining room, with its spacious wide windows. In fair weather, however, diners prefer lunches on the stone terrace, where they can enjoy a view of the nearby wooded hills and river.

A BAVARIAN INN ON THE OUTSKIRTS: Brauereigasthof Hotel Aying, 80-11 Aying bei München (tel. 08-09-5/221), is a country inn owned by the famous Aying Brewery. It's all hearts and flowers Alpine. Everything is traditional, except for the excellent bathrooms and 20th-century comfort. The beds are as large as Ping-Pong tables, and the colors are coordinated. Large double accommodations rent for a price of 110 DM ($63.10), including breakfast. Some smaller doubles are offered for 72 DM ($41.30). One person can rent one of the larger double rooms for 70 DM ($40.15), although he or she is likely to get lost in the bed alone.

The dining room pleases both the palate and the eye. On chilly days a fire burns in the fireplace, and soft candles light the meals. A well-cooked dinner might cost 30 DM ($17.21), including a simple but pure consommé, grilled veal steak with potatoes, a seasonal green salad with fresh lemon dressing, and a goodly amount of beer, followed by apple pie.

Directions: Take the autobahn toward Salzburg, leaving it at the second exit. Aying is about 18 miles from the center of Munich.

READERS' PENSION SELECTIONS: "The **Hotel am Karlstor,** 34 Neuhauserstrasse, just off Karlsplatz (tel. 59-36-96), provides a small bathless single with attractive decor and excellent separate bath and toilet facilities, elevator, and continental breakfast for 31 DM ($17.78) to 35 DM ($20.08). A single with shower goes for 45 DM ($25.81). Doubles range in price from 56 DM ($32.12) if bathless, 70 DM ($40.15) with bath. Three-bedded rooms are tabbed at 78 DM ($44.74) to 90 DM ($51.62)" (Mrs. George J. Flynn, Washington, D.C.). . . . "**Pension Marion,** 25 Luisenstrasse (tel. 59-25-54), is a short, five-minute walk from the railway station. It's a bargain at 45 DM ($25.81) for a bathless double, 48 DM ($27.53) to 60 DM ($34.42) with bath or shower, including breakfast. The pension is under the capable leadership of Franz Mosthav who proved to be very interesting as well as a gracious gentleman. Mr. Mosthav is a noted actor-director-producer for stage and screen in Europe. One evening he was kind enough to treat us to a glass of wine, an interesting conversation concerning his career, and mementos from films that he was involved in" (Mr. and Mrs. W. Brooks, St. Louis, Mo.). . . . "The **Pension Rottmüller,** 36 Gollierstrasse (tel. 50-63-09) (cross streets are Ligsalzstrasse and Ganghoferstrasse), can be reached by taking either tram 2 or 20 to Ganghofstrasse (five stops), then walking down Ganghofstrasse, away from the direction the tram takes, to Gollierstrasse. The pension is on your right, above the hobby shop on the first floor. For 38 DM ($21.80), we had a bathless double which consisted of a large bedroom and a good-sized sitting room, and breakfast of coffee, tea, rolls, butter, jam, and a boiled egg. My prime reason for writing, however, is the kindness and help extended to my wife and me by the wonderful woman who owns the pension. We do not speak each other's languages, but this did not cause any communcations problem" (Charles E. Buettner, Lindsay, Calif.).

"I stayed at the **Kreuzbräu,** 3 Brunnstrasse (tel. 24-24-66). I got a double there for 45 DM ($25.81) a night, including use of the shower. Breakfast was extra. It's within walking distance (a fairly long walk) to both the train station and the Hofbräuhaus. Who could ask for more?" (Larry Thompson, Clymer, N.Y.). . . . "**Hotel-Pension Theresia,** 51 Luisenstrasse (tel. 52-12-50), is a five-minute ride from the Hauptbahnhof (trams 12 and 7) to the Theresienstrasse stop. Walk one block east, turn right another half block. Spacious and comfortable rooms are offered for 25 DM ($14.34) single, 38 DM ($21.80) to 42 DM ($24.09) double, including breakfast, service, and tax. There is an Italian restaurant next door, and Vietnamese and Chinese restaurants are nearby. A bath or shower is 4 DM ($2.29). The proprietor, Annemarie Mosslacher, speaks fluent English, Italian, and a little French" (Rahul Sangal, New Delhi, India). . . . "**Mr. Michael Betz** of Alt Förstenried (within the city line), 8 München 71, 12 Katzbachstrasse (tel. 755-58-

02), has a large house with single rooms at 24 DM ($13.77) without breakfast and 34 DM ($19.50) with. Doubles are approximately 50% more. However, the 10 DM ($5.74) difference is Mr. Betz's special attraction. He offers a hearty Bavarian breakfast of unlimited eggs, meat, cereal, bread, butter, coffee, tea, etc., that he personally guarantees to be sufficient until the next morning. Also Mr. Betz offers constantly hot meals at any time of the day for nominal prices, as well as an assortment of drinks (both soft and alcoholic) at prices well below licensed houses. Above all, the overwhelming Bavarian hospitality of the Betzes will make anyone's visit to Munich most enjoyable. Just take the tram from the main railway station to Alt Förstenried and telephone Mr. Betz who'll come directly in his rather old Mercedes to pick you up" (Peter S. Stewart, Ossining, N.Y.).

   "We found an excellent pension, the **Pension Bosna,** on the fourth floor at 33 Dachauerstrasse. It's run by a very lovely woman, and the charge is 40 DM ($22.94) to 50 DM ($28.68) for two persons, including a breakfast with egg. We had a free shower as well. Our room was nice and clean, and we had a balcony. All in all, a real find" (Graham and Rhonda Kelly, Sydney, Australia). . . . "We found a hotel in Munich which is particularly convenient for those who, like us, are driving but prefer not to drive during their stay in a city. This was the **Hotel zur Laube,** 2 Notburgastrasse, right across the bridge from Schloss Nymphenburg and only five minutes or so from the autobahn exit. For 60 DM ($34.42) we had our only room with bath during our three-week trip. The place was, even by German standards, exceptionally clean, there was an elevator, and there was also an underground garage. The trolley stop was right outside the door, and we found this very convenient for getting into the city proper. Breakfast was included. Although the owner did not speak English, the son and daughter of the household did" (Joan and Gene Schneider, Canandaigua, N.Y.). . . . "For the longer term visitor to Munich, we recommend the **Pension Welti** (tel. 791-15-42). Herr Keis, an American, rents efficiency apartments with a living room/bedroom, bathroom, and fully equipped kitchen for 55 DM ($31.55) per night for two persons. Included in the price are a television, private phone, all linens, and daily maid service. Breakfast and underground parking are optional and extra. The pension is in a quiet residential neighborhood in Solln, convenient to public transportation and shopping areas. Take the U-Bahn to Harras and then bus 63 or 64 to Bastian-Schmidt-Platz. Walk south to Uhdestrasse 45. Call first since he is often full" (James A. Pope, Jacksonville, Fla.).

2. Restaurants

   It is said that the good people of Munich consume more beer and food than the people in any other city of Germany. If the cuisine isn't exactly delicate, it is certainly plentiful, and if you haven't already noticed, every housewife here seems destined to give her husband a bulging waistline before he's 30. So if you like food, and plenty of it, you've come to the right city.

   In many restaurants, especially the beer halls, you'll find the gemütlich atmosphere prevails until the early hours of the morning. Stamina is needed if you're going to live life as the natives do. Bernd Boehle once wrote: "If a man really belongs to Munich he drinks beer at all times of the day, at breakfast, at midday, at teatime; and in the evening, of course, he just never stops."

   Some of the local fare may frighten the timid: minced liver, dumplings, "spleen" wurst, calf's feet, pig's trotters, and pork and liver "cheese." But if your palate requires careful attention, you needn't fear. Many of the restaurants of Munich—admittedly the upper-bracket ones—feature an international cuisine, with emphasis on French dishes. A number of specialty restaurants exist, including Trader Vic's. The most classic dish of Munich, however, is "weiss-würste." These are herb-flavored white veal sausages that have been blanched in water. Traditionally, they are consumed early in the morning.

   But our main interest is lunch and dinner—and here are the spots where you'll find the best meals for the best value in Munich:

THE TOP RESTAURANTS: Tantris, 7 Johann-Fichte-Strasse (tel. 36-20-61), in Schwabing, serves some of the best food in Munich—and it's French.

In an unlikely setting, near the Holiday Inn, the restaurant stands near an Esso gasoline station. But, once you've gone down the street and inside the restaurant's doors, you're transported into an ultramodern atmosphere with fine service.

Incidentally, don't arrive without reservations, as many of the leading members of Munich's business colony like to entertain here, not only their families and friends, but foreign associates as well.

The food, as presented, is a treat to the eye as well as the palate. The soups are especially interesting, and priced in the 8.50-DM ($4.88) to 14.50-DM ($8.32) range. Among the main courses, we'd recommend the roast lamb with herbs, 74 DM ($42.25) for two persons. For 72.50 DM ($41.59) for two persons, you might enjoy suprême de turbot Marguery or a salmon soufflé. For dessert, prices begin at 10 DM ($5.74), going up to 15 DM ($8.60). One way to dine here is to order a six-course menu costing 92 DM ($52.77). It might include a mousseline de crab aux avocats, salmis de chevreuil aux girolles, and purée de persil, as well as sole à la sauce estragon, climaxed by sorbet de Johannisberg.

The choice of dishes is wisely limited, and everything is served and prepared with the utmost care. The cooking is both subtle and original, the beautiful interior adding to one's enjoyment.

Although closed Sundays, Tantris is otherwise open from noon to 3 p.m. and from 6:30 p.m. to midnight daily, except Saturdays when it only serves dinner.

Walterspiel, 17 Maximilianstrasse, in the Hotel Vier Jahreszeiten (tel. 22-88-21), is named after two brothers who entertained and catered to the tastes of kings. The atmosphere is dignified and refined, the service extremely competent, and the food prepared along classic lines, although with many imaginatively original variations.

The cuisine is rich and filling, as you'll quickly realize merely by reading a list of the appetizers offered, including some of the following suggestions: mousse of duck liver with marinated grapes at 29.50 DM ($16.92); a lobster salad with peaches and tarragon, 45 DM ($25.81); spinach salad with quail eggs and Roquefort, 13 DM ($7.46); and pigeon pâté with raisins and nuts in a Kiwi sauce, 15 DM ($8.60). Or as an alternative opening to a fine repast, you might try the clear tomato soup with Camembert dumplings at 6 DM ($3.44) or perhaps the essence of morels in champagne, 7.50 DM ($4.30).

For a main course, we'd suggest, if featured, artichoke bottoms with snails, mushrooms, and tomatoes at 23 DM ($13.19); breast of duck with peppercorns and oranges, 36.50 DM ($20.94); sauteed calf liver on a watercress puree, 23.50 DM ($13.48); scallops on leek strips with saffron, 29.50 DM ($16.92); and quenelles of pike in a lobster cream sauce, 26 DM ($14.91).

Desserts include such delectable offerings as a mocha ice soufflé at 9 DM ($5.16); raspberries Walterspiel style, 13 DM ($7.46); and a white chocolate mousse at 9 DM ($5.16).

Aubergine, 5 Maximilianplatz (tel. 59-81-71), is discreet and distinguished, a citadel of fine taste, good food, impeccable service, and lethal tariffs. It's chic, elegant, and fashionable. The owner-chef, Eckart Witzigmann, has studied with the famous Paul Bocuse of Lyon, France. His cuisine is a mixture of classic dishes along with some nouvelle cuisine offerings. At lunch you can order a set menu for 79 DM ($45.31), although the cost of the table d'hôte dinner rises to 110 DM ($63.10).

The set menu is almost invariably good, and it contains an array of widely varying specialties, including a sorbet served in between to clear your palate. Menus change every day, and can't be written until the owner returns from the market after having decided what was fresh and good that day. Fresh ingredients and top-quality produce are keys to the success of the Aubergine (eggplant).

You can also order à la carte, selecting such tempting treats as sole filet in a champagne sauce at 37 DM ($21.22) or crab salad with broccoli in vinaigrette, 44 DM ($25.24). Many specialties are for two persons, ranging in price from 69 DM ($39.58) to 74 DM ($42.45).

Maximilianstuben, 27 Maximilianstrasse (tel. 22-90-44), serves elegant dishes in a traditional setting, as befits its location near the Vier Jahreszeiten Hotel. Behind filmy curtains, while seated at candlelit tables, you must make the difficult decision of what to order. The many offerings are all just so tantalizing, running the gamut of favorite international dishes with a decided French influence. A good beginning might be artichokes hollandaise at 12.50 DM ($7.17), although many patrons prefer the spaghetti in a seafood sauce at 17 DM ($9.75), before going on to a fish or meat entree. Fresh Norwegian salmon in a tantalizing sauce is the chef's specialty, costing 37.50 DM ($21.51), as is his sirloin steak Bordelaise (a red wine sauce), costing 34.50 DM ($19.79). A rumtopf parfait with home-preserved fruit in rum is one of the best desserts, costing 12.50 DM ($7.17) per person. The restaurant is closed on most Sundays. In the evenings, a zither player entertains dinner guests.

Käfer-Schänke, 1 Schumannstrasse (tel. 47-60-11), is famous for its cookery. You have to reserve if you want a seat here. It's crowded and popular, with good reason. On the main floor is a deluxe gourmet shop, the Fauchon of Munich. The decor suggests the home of a wealthy countryman, with a few farm-style antiques placed here and there. You select your own hors d'oeuvres —the most handsome and dazzling display in Munich—and are billed according to how many pâtés or croûtes you made off with. The main dishes are waiter served, however. Often Käfer-Schänke features a week devoted to a particular country's cuisine. On our latest rounds, it was France. Main courses begin at 14 DM ($8.03), going up to 68 DM ($39) for two persons for the classic loup with fennel presented on the French Riviera. Other dishes include bouillabaisse at 7.80 DM ($4.47) and salade St. Topez (made with crab and ham) at 15.50 DM ($8.89).

Schwarzwälders Naturweinhaus, 8 Hartmannstrasse (tel. 22-72-16), is an Old Munich wine restaurant, the second-best dining choice in the Bavarian capital. Its more loyal habitués, however, put it at the top. Certainly you can easily be intoxicated into thinking so after sampling one of the superb meals here accompanied by fine German wines. From the moment you enter, the atmosphere evokes a warm and hospitable charm that sets the mood for a fine meal. You can select almost any wine you might desire from the extensive wine list. The menu is international, reflected in such main dishes as peppersteak with cognac at 28 DM ($16.06), but in season game is the specialty, and it's prepared with flair by the chef. House specialties also include pikant hirschgoulash with noodles with berries, 18.50 DM ($10.61). For dessert you might prefer the ice bombé moka and kirsch at 7.50 DM ($4.30). The restaurant is only a short walk from the Bayerischer Hof and the American Express, both of which open onto the Promenadeplatz.

Restaurant-Weinhaus zur Kanne, 36 Maximilianstrasse (tel. 22-12-36), offers intimate rooms, candlelight, and an outstanding theater collection dating back to 1794. It's popular after-theater rendezvous for opera-goers and attracts an interesting clientele of singers, politicians, and actors. The menu's more varied than in previous years, with offerings of both international and traditional Bavarian dishes. The wine list has also been expanded, with 24 "open" wines, plus nearly 140 bottled varieties as well as 40 or so in stock for guests who want something special. The owner, Claus Offermann, who is from San Francisco, runs the restaurant with his German wife. You might begin your meal here with the French onion soup au gratin at 6.50 DM ($3.73). Scrumptious entrees include a rolled filet of sole in white wine sauce, with scampi, mushrooms, green salad, and rice, at 32 DM ($18.36), and saddle of venison à la Kanne at 30 DM ($17.21). Another good selection is stuffed pork filet in tarragon sauce, with buttered noodles and a mixed salad, at 17.50 DM ($10.04). Desserts include an iced fruit salad with kirschwasser at 8.50 DM ($4.88) and crêpes Kanne at 9 DM ($5.16). Open wines range from 3.50 DM ($2.01) to 8.50 DM ($4.88). The restaurant is open from noon to 3 p.m. and from 6 p.m. till 1 a.m. Although closed Saturday, zur Kanne is open Sunday only in the evening. Reservations are recommended in the evenings.

Bouillabaisse, 10 Falkenturmstrasse, in the Hotel An der Oper (tel. 29-79-09), is highly rated in local gourmet circles. The restaurant does beautiful food in a lovely setting near the Hofbräuhaus and across from Harry's Bar. The peppersteak is served Madagaskar style here, costing 29.50 DM ($16.92), although the chef's specialty is bouillabaisse, honoring the name of the restaurant. You can order a small plate as an appetizer, costing 12 DM ($6.88), or else a large order at 22.50 DM ($12.91). An unusual hors d'oeuvre for Munich is the specially prepared squid, served here for 14 DM ($8.03). The menu generally remains the same from day to day, and somehow the kitchen manages to secure some of the finest sole in Munich. The chef prepares the fish in several ways, costing from 27.50 DM ($15.78). Scampi is another specialty prepared in several different ways too, according to your choice, at a cost of 30.50 DM ($17.50). A more classic offering is the veal schnitzel Cordon Bleu at 25 DM ($14.34). For dessert, we'd suggest the peach Melba at 7 DM ($4.02). The restaurant is closed from August 4 to September 4 and on Sundays.

A. Boettner, 8 Theatinerstrasse, off the Marienplatz (tel. 22-12-10), is one of the choicest specialty restaurants in Munich. It's tiny and totally intimate, and at times everybody seems to know everybody else. Here you're assured of some of the most savory viands in Munich. You'll do well sticking to such international fare as saddle of venison at 38 DM ($21.80) and fried goose liver on green beans, 42 DM ($24.09). For dessert, the chocolate mousse makes a particularly soothing choice at 9 DM ($5.16). The wine cellar is excellent, the relatively unadorned surroundings pleasant, and the service polite and skilled. For the discriminating gourmet only! Reservations are imperative.

BEST ALL-AROUND RESTAURANTS: Mövenpick Restaurant, im Künstlerhaus, 8 Lenbachplatz, (tel. 55-78-65). All the Swiss gastronomic know-how has been poured into this cluster of five different spots to dine in under one roof, making Mövenpick a success with Munich residents, whatever their budgets. The Mövenpick chain chose a historic building for its restaurants, in what used to be called "the house of the artists," where the literary elite would gather for coffee. Posted at the door is a menu bulletin for each of the restaurants, allowing you to select in advance.

The **Rob Roy** bar on the downstairs floor is dimly lit, with hanging mugs and plaid carpeting. The waiters, in Edwardian dress, serve authentic British ale in mugs. You can also get your favorite drink along with a Pickburger at 7.20 DM ($4.13), a toast Armstrong at 10.50 DM ($6.02), or a wienerschnitzel at 15.50 DM ($8.89).

Möpi Square is a nice outdoor section overlooking busy Lenbachplatz, where you can order a light lunch or a snack at any time. Try Salisbury steak at 9 DM ($5.16).

The palazzo-style **Venezia** is more suitable for quick lunches, with already-prepared main dishes, such as spaghetti Mexicaine, 8.95 DM ($5.13), or pork Waikiki, 14.50 DM ($8.32).

At **Pastorale** on the second floor, excellent Swiss and international dishes are served. The salad buffet is self-service—as much as you like on your plate from 8.90 DM ($5.11) to 12.50 DM ($7.17). A special dish, depending on seasonal marketing, is featured each week. The outstanding Züricher geschnetzeltes is a good choice here at 20.50 DM ($6.58), as is the entrecôte Züricher Art, 24.50 DM ($14.05).

Finally, the **Long Horn Corner** features Angus steaks, in a western ranch setting, replete with saddles, horns, stirrups, and cowhides. Dining is by candlelight. Specialties include fresh homemade goose liver at 18 DM ($10.32); a tender rib roast, 28 DM ($16.06); lammrücken Bretagne, 23 DM ($13.19); and scampi Montagnani, 28 DM ($16.06).

THE FOREIGN COLONY: Trader Vic's, Bayerischer Hof, 6 Promenadeplatz (tel. 22-88-71), just had to happen to Munich! And the invasion of South Seas magic is in full force. The Trader Vic chain has never pretended to serve an authentic South Seas cuisine—rather it prefers to offer entrees that appeal to one's fantasy of what life must be like lounging under a palm tree in the Pacific. But the cuisine is inspired by the South Seas with a dash of China, and lots of imagination. The restaurant—on the ground floor of one of the most luxurious hotels in Germany—is much as you'd expect: native drums, masks, cork floats, colored nets, spears, coconuts, and bamboo. Many of the drinks are now familiar to the globe-trotting traveler: the navy grog at 14.50 DM ($8.32), the Samoan fogcutter, also 14.50 DM, and Molokai Mike at 11 DM ($6.31). The Calcutta curry is priced anywhere from 18 DM ($10.32) to 28 DM ($16.06); the deviled crab, 24.50 DM ($14.06); the lobster mousse, 24.50 DM ($14.05). When you're tired of sauerkraut and wurst, Trader Vic's provides a viable alternative.

Chesa Ruegg, 18 Würzerstrasse (tel. 29-71-14), beside the Vier Jahreszeiten, has rough white plaster walls, a crude beamed ceiling, and a collection of large cow bells. Red-shaded kerosene lamps on the tables, plus vases of red roses and an overscale peppermill, further enhance the alpine-tavern theme. The star of this intimate dining theater is the Swiss chef. From start to finish, your meal is carefully planned and served. A meal here might consist of a rich-tasting soup at 5 DM ($2.87), followed by crab with lobster sauce at 32.50 DM ($18.64) or perhaps a venison steak at 35.80 DM ($20.53). Closed Sundays and holidays.

Goldene Stadt, 44 Oberanger (tel. 24-24-37). Come here for the finest Bohemian specialties in Bavaria! The setting is sedate, much like the ground floor of a town house. You're given a choice of three dining rooms (the central one is the most often reserved). Against a background of scenic etchings and a mural depicting scenes of Czechoslovakia, the savory cuisine from Germany's neighboring country is served. Beer is usually drunk with the meals, and the more you eat of the delicious rock salt rolls, the more you'll want to drink. A friendly and gracious English-speaking host takes your order. Borscht is the classic beginning at 4.50 DM ($2.58), but not the type you're served in New York. Most Bohemian specialties such as roast goose and duckling are in the 12.50-DM ($7.17) to 22.50-DM ($12.91) range. Desserts go for anywhere from 4.50 DM ($2.58) to 6.50 DM ($3.73). After dinner, it's customary to order apricot brandy at 7.50 DM ($4.30)—served in a glass that looks like a bud vase.

At the **Csarda Piroschka,** 1 Prinzregentenstrasse (tel. 29-54-25), the Hungarian cuisine is absolutely first rate. The location is decidedly offbeat: occupying the ground floor of the Haus der Kunst art museum, a long taxi haul from the center. The service is as smooth as the food is delicious, while violin music and candlelight create a romantic ambience. The menu is placed before you by one of the most gracious proprietors in Munich who is the epitome of Hungarian Charm. The house specialty—served to two persons only—is called Husarenspiess flambiert, costing 39 DM ($22.37). Another good dish is the Hungarian farmer's steak at 30 DM ($17.21). A good beginning is the bohnensuppe (bean soup) jókai at 5 DM ($2.87). A bottle of the Hungarian wine, Tokaji, costs 28 DM ($16.06). A 2-DM ($1.15) cover charge is levied. Closed Sundays. Go in the evening, and be sure to reserve a table in advance.

BUDGET BAVARIAN RESTAURANTS: Nürnberger Bratwurstglöckl am **Dom,** 9 Frauenplatz, is the coziest and warmest of Munich's local restaurants. You sit in carved chairs that look as if they came from some little carver's shop in the Black Forest. Country-like tablecloths add to the regional atmosphere, and the collection of memorabilia is wide ranging, including, among other things, pictures, prints, pewter, and beer steins. Upstairs—reached through a hidden stairway—is a dining room devoted to Dürer. Open from 9 a.m. to midnight, the restaurant has a strict policy of shared tables. The homesick Nürnberger comes here for just one dish: Nürnberger stadtwurst mit kraut, the delectable little sausages, costing 4.70 DM ($2.70) for four pieces. Other main dishes include steak tartare at 12.50 DM ($7.17) and a pork cutlet salad at 9.50 DM ($5.45). The service is on tin plates. A short walk from the Marienplatz, the restaurant faces the cathedral of Munich.

Weinstadt, 5 Burgstrasse (tel. 22-10-47), has been a wine house since 1850. Luckily, it survived World War II, and it is now reportedly the oldest house in Munich, tracing its history back to 1468. But it's no museum, although first appearances would lead you to think so. Real old-world charm is to be found here: vaulted ceilings, coats of arms, a trompe l'oeil facade, and wrought-iron sconces. Dining is on three levels. Waitresses in regional dress hurry across the natural brick floor, serving up hearty Bavarian food at candlelit wooden tables. Soups are priced at from 3 DM ($1.72) to 3.40 DM ($1.95); especially delectable is the bean soup with ham. A typical main dish is pork cutlet with vegetable and salad, at 9.50 DM ($5.45). Many excellent bottles of wine are priced at anywhere from 13 DM ($7.46) to 45 DM ($25.81). A quarter liter of an open wine ranges in price from 2.30 DM ($1.32) to 6 DM ($3.44).

Haxhbauer, Munzstrasse-Sparkassenstrasse (tel. 22-19-22), could get by on atmosphere alone! One of the most colorful and typical of all Bavarian restaurants in Munich, it offers the patron a choice of dining rooms. Over 100 years in the same family, it has a devoted following—and isn't as well known among foreign visitors as it deserves to be. Soups are priced from 3 DM ($1.72) to 5 DM ($2.87). Radi mit hausgeraucherterm schinken at 9 DM ($5.16)— razor-thin slices of ham, with white radishes and chive bread—makes for an excellent appetizer. The specialty of the house is either schweinshaxn or kalbshaxn (pork or veal shank), priced according to weight. Both are spit roasted, the skin cooked a crusty brown. The meat is guaranteed fresh, as the restaurant has its own butcher. For desert, the chef's specialty is apfelkücherl flambé at 8 DM ($4.59).

Spatenhaus, 12 Residenzstrasse, is the best beer house restaurant in Munich. Its wide windows overlook the Opera House on Max-Jospeh-Platz. Of course, to be loyal, you'll accompany your meal with the restaurant's own beer, called Spaten-Franziskaner Bräu, one-half liter costing 2.40 DM ($1.38). The decor is a no-nonsense one of hardwood floors and chintz draperies. Try for one of the little semiprivate dining nooks on the ground floor. The Spatenhaus is an old-fashioned, family dining room, offering Germanic main courses in the 9-DM ($5.16) to 21-DM ($12.05) range. The best bargains are at lunch; set meals cost anywhere from 9 DM ($5.16) to 14 DM ($8.03). The portions are generous, a factor to take into consideration when you order.

Donisl, 1 Weinstrasse (tel. 22-01-84). All you need to be told is that the hefty waitresses here serve dumplings as big as baseballs—and you know what kind of place Donisl is. An enterprise operated by the Pschorr beer interests, Donisl is recommended for those seeking a Bavarian ambience. The nicest place to sit is in the enclosed two-tiered courtyard; a huge antler chandelier is suspended from the ceiling, and the room is festooned with greenery, to which blue and white ribbons are attached. Portraits of roly-poly Bavarians—not unlike some of the present clientele—adorn the walls. The servings are far more than you and the people at the next table will be able to eat. Set lunches are in the 8-DM ($4.59) to 10.50-DM ($6.02) range. A different soup is offered every day for 2 DM ($1.15). Typically Bavarian dishes are in the 5.50-DM ($3.15) to 14.50-DM ($8.32) range. The restaurant opens at 7 a.m., when night-reveling Munich denizens often show up to sample rostbratwürste, delectable little sausages, five of which cost 6.50 DM ($3.73).

Vinzen Murr, 8 Rosenstrasse, near the City Hall, is good for a light snack if you're in the area, or a full meal. A short walk from the Marienplatz, this food shop offers such dishes as half roast chicken for 3.60 DM ($2.07) or different versions of pork with various sauces in the 2.50-DM ($1.43) to 7.50-DM ($4.30) range. An order of weisswürste goes for 2.50 DM ($1.43), and it's always accompanied by a glass of Pilsener Urquell at 1.50 DM (86¢).

Badische Weinstuben, 3 Lammerstrasse, in back of the Württemberger Hof Hotel, two blocks from the railroad station, is nicely decorated with old-style prints on crude white walls. Small wooden tables with chairs and benches covered with green fabric give a warm ambience. The fare is country Bavarian—blood sausages, dumpling soup, and the like. A main dish averages anywhere from 6.60 DM ($3.79) to 17 DM ($9.75). A quarter liter of wine ranges from 2.80 DM ($1.61) to 4.20 DM ($2.41).

Gasthaus zum Bögner, 72 im Tal, is in an old house, with typically Bavarian decorations and food. Lunches range from 6.50 DM ($3.73) to 14.50 DM ($8.32). Soups start at 2.30 DM ($1.32). You may have a quick snack here for as little as 2.50 DM ($1.43).

St. Georg Weinhaus, Prinzregentenplatz (tel. 47-83-18). Here you dine under the massive beams of a 500-year-old farmhouse, in one of five vaulted cellar rooms in the Upper Bavarian style. As you enter, a bar (where you can dance) is on the left. To the right are candlelit tables with colorful napkins. The restaurant is owned by a former wine merchant, Herr Hummert, who stocks the finest Rhine, Franconia, and Mosel bottles. One-quarter liter is from 2.40 DM ($1.38). This family-run winehouse has been going for more than a quarter of a century, and is noted for its simple, yet delicious, dishes. Try the lentil soup with bacon. Set dinners range in price from 9.80 DM ($5.62) to 26 DM ($14.91), with à la carte main dishes going for anywhere from 7.50 DM ($4.30) to 32 DM ($18.36). It's open nightly from 7:30.

Ratskeller, im Rathaus, Marienplatz (entrance on Dienerstrasse). Many visitors discover the tradition of the German "ratskeller" in Munich. Throughout Germany you'll find these customary cellar restaurants in the basements of town halls, serving inexpensive good food and wine. Although not as celebrated as some of its sisters (the one at Bremen, for example), the Munich

Ratskeller holds its own. The decor is much what you'd expect, with lots of dark wood and carved chairs. The most interesting tables—and the ones staked out first by the in-the-know locals—are at the rear, resting under vaulted, painted ceilings. One mural depicts a Bavarian choking a dragon to make the monster swallow poison. The ideal table is a cozy, semiprivate dining nook in the rear. A large wine vat suggests that Bavarians don't drink only beer.

The menu is a showcase of regional fare, but it also includes some international dishes. The soup of the day goes for 3 DM ($1.72). Ragoût of venison in red wine, served with juniper berries and noodles, is 18.50 DM ($10.61), and pork livers in a sauce with potato puree is 14.50 DM ($8.32). A good dessert is a fruit tart at 3 DM ($1.72). The chef has prepared an English menu made up especially for American guests and offering typical German dishes. The waiters are very helpful, and most of them speak English. Ice water is served right at the beginning of your meal, just as in the States.

Weinhaus Neuner, 8 Herzogspitalstrasse (tel. 260-39-54), is an "Altestes Weinhaus Münchens," where the food is good and the setting mellow. Between the Karlsplatz (Stachus) and Marienplatz, the wine house has been such since 1852, but originally it was the site of a Jesuit monastery. Two large dining rooms, paneled in wood, suggest an old Tyrolean atmosphere. The wine list is quite good, although many diners tenaciously stick to their favorite beer. A traditional beginning for a meal is the goulaschsuppe at 4 DM ($2.29). The chef specializes in steaks, juicy and tender, at prices ranging from 14.50 DM ($8.32) to 22.50 DM ($12.91). Each day a different specialty is offered, including Irish stew on our most recent visit, costing only 8 DM ($4.59).

A FAMOUS DELI: Alois Dallmayr, 14 Dienerstrasse, is the Fauchon's of Munich. Near the City Hall, it is perhaps the most famous delicatessen in Germany and actually is one of the most renowned in the world. After walking through it, looking at its tempting array of delicacies from all around the globe, you'll think you're lost in a millionaire's supermarket. Here you'll find the most elegant consumers in all of Munich, looking for that "tinned treasure," perhaps Scottish salmon, foie gras, English biscuits, wines and spirits, as well as fashionably out-of-season fresh produce.

Unknown to many, it's possible to dine upstairs, and the prices aren't as high as you might expect. For example, sandwiches range from 5.50 DM ($3.15) to 9 DM ($5.16), and most of them are delectable. Soups (we'd suggest the Danish crab soup) are in the 3.80-DM ($2.18) to 6.50-DM ($3.73) range. Even an American salad is featured, the Waldorf—at 5 DM ($2.87). Main dishes begin at 10 DM ($5.74), going upward to 30 DM ($17.21). If you're dining alone, you might prefer to anchor at the counter instead of a table. The bustling restaurant is usually crowded at lunchtime. Hours, Monday to Friday, are from 9 a.m. to midnight (Saturdays, 9 a.m. to 3 p.m.; closed Sundays).

FRENCH FOOD IN SCHWABING: Occam-Bistrot, 23 Occamstrasse, is a bustling student brasserie, deep in the heart of Schwabing, that does a really interesting French cuisine. In some French restaurants in Germany, the cuisine is strictly Provençale, clogging your nostrils with thyme, basil, and garlic. But at Occam-Bistrot, more restraint is the order of the day. You might begin with an appetizer in the 8.50-DM ($4.88) to 14-DM ($8.03) category that might include escargots, bisque de homard, and, of course, gratinée (that is, onion soup). Main courses, likely to average around 22 DM ($12.62), feature entrecôte Provençale and côte de boeuf Villette, the latter honoring a famous bistro in the slaughterhouse district of Paris. Finally, you might wish to conclude with a selection of "les fromages de France," and if not, then perhaps baba au rhum glacé at 6.75 DM ($3.87) or else Irish coffee at 8 DM ($4.59). Good French red or white wine comes by the carafe.

SWISS SPECIALTIES IN SCHWABING: Walliser Stuben, 33 Leopold-strasse (tel. 34-80-00), is like a Hollywood version of a Swiss tavern. Because of its skill with the Helvetian cuisine, it attracts many visitors to Schwabing. It not only serves the best food in the area, but is one of the leading Swiss-style restaurants in Germany. The atmosphere is an inviting one, with an open fireplace, lots of copper pans about, and carved wooden chairs. But the master chef, Adi Holzmuller, doesn't just rely on these old-world touches. Rather, he enchants his patrons with such classic dishes as fondue bourguignonne at 52 DM ($29.83) for two persons. The average price of his other Swiss specialties is 18.50 DM ($10.61) to 23 DM ($13.19). Very popular, and very good, are the flambé desserts. Delicious soups are priced anywhere from 3.50 DM ($2.01) to 6.50 DM ($3.73). The Swiss House in Schwabing is closed Sundays, but open otherwise from 5 p.m. to 1 a.m.

THE CORNER DRUGSTORE: Drugstore, corner of Feilitzschstrasse and Siegesstrasse, is in the heart of Schwabing. It's in a class by itself, comparable to the famous Les Drug Stores of Paris. Part of a pace-setting international craze, it combines a nightclub with boutiques and a restaurant. At the brass horseshoe bar, under the soft yellow glow of globe lamps, you listen to piped-in music (usually American) and order a mug of beer for only 2 DM ($1.15). Irish coffee, at 5.80 DM ($3.33), is the house specialty. Here you can order an American sandwich at 4.50 DM ($2.58) to 7.60 DM ($4.36) or perhaps spaghetti with a choice of sauces in the 4.70-DM ($2.70) to 6.40-DM ($3.67) range.

AT OLYMPIC CITY: The Olympia Tower offers a choice of dining experiences. You can either take your pie in the sky or else ground your chicken at one of the Wienerwald chains at the base. The television tower itself is 950 feet in height, and it costs 3 DM ($1.72) for adults, 1.50 DM (86¢) for children, to take the speediest elevator on the continent to its summit. Parking is 2 DM ($1.15).

The most expensive dining spot in the tower is the Tower Restaurant, featuring a selection of international dishes, with main courses going from 16 DM ($9.18) to 32 DM ($18.36). Soups average around 3.80 DM ($2.18) to 7.50 DM ($4.30); desserts, 6.50 DM ($3.73) to 9 DM ($5.16). Food is served from 9:30 a.m. to 10:30 p.m. While you're sampling your entrecôte, why not think about this important statistic: you're in the "tallest reinforced concrete structure in Western Europe." Before or after dinner, you'll want to take in the view, including the alpine mountain chain itself. Four observation platforms look out over the Olympic grounds. The Tower Restaurant revolves around its axis at the rate of 36, 53, or 70 minutes, giving the guest who lingers longer a changing vista of the entire Olympic grounds.

At the base of the tower is the Am Olympiasee, serving genuine Bavarian specialties. Favored items include half a roast chicken at 7 DM ($4.02). Soups are in the 3.50-DM ($2.10) to 3.80-DM ($2.18) range; desserts, 3.80 DM ($2.18). The decor is in a warm Bavarian motif.

On the observation deck is a cafeteria, serving low-cost snacks and würst (sausage) costing from 3.50 DM ($2.01) to 3.80 ($2.18); beer, 2.10 DM ($1.20).

FOOD ON THE RUN: Cornelius Schuler Buffeteria, 13 Bayerstrasse, is a large coffeeshop where you can eat sausages or sandwiches standing around small round tables, or you can sit in a dining room after passing through the self-service line with your tray. Prices are about the same as low-budget restaurants—it's faster, that's all. Set lunches begin at 4.50 DM ($2.58), going up to 8.50 DM ($4.88). Bratwurst with potato salad costs 3.50 DM ($2.01); goulash with rice, 6.50 DM ($3.73).

THE WIENERWALDS: This is Germany's most popular chain. Adopting the romantic name of the Vienna Woods, there are stylized rustic restaurants, where a gemütlich atmosphere prevails. Even though they are busy and bustling, there are still many quiet corners for relaxed dining. Service is by dirndl-clad waitresses. Prices are standard in all the restaurants. Soups are in the 1.60-DM (92¢) to 3.25-DM ($1.86) range. The house specialty, half a chicken, costs 6.50 DM ($3.73), and other main courses begin at 4.25 DM ($2.44), going up to 17 DM ($9.75). Desserts go from 2 DM ($1.15) to 4 DM ($2.29). A mug of beer is 2 DM ($1.15). Popular Wienerwalds are at 44 Leopoldstrasse in Schwabing; 12 Karlsplatz, 6 Odeonsplatz, and 23 Amalienstrasse.

HAMBURGERS: McDonald's, 26 Martin-Luther-Strasse. Actually it seems quite authentic. It even looks like this popular chain back in the States. A hamburger with tomato and cucumber costs 1.60 DM (92¢), rising to 1.80 DM ($1.03) for a cheeseburger. Apple pie is 1.45 DM (80¢).

COFFEE BREAK: Tchibo or **Frielo** coffee stores are found throughout Munich. You can only drink coffee at 1.50 DM (86¢) a cup and eat pastries at .70 DM (40¢) at most of them, but there is one restaurant, **Tchibo-Höflinger,** 85 Schleissheimerstrasse, that offers a good bargain. Ordering from the daily menu, you can eat here for a total cost of 6.50 DM ($3.73) to 10.20 DM ($5.85). Featured are soup, a main dish of either meat or fish, with vegetables, a salad, and dessert. The decoration is rather deluxe, with large tables and leather benches. A lamp hanging over each table provides bright light.

DEPARTMENT STORE DINING: In most department stores in German cities, you have two choices for eating—top-floor restaurants with scenic views or stand-up counters in the basement. The prices are widely varied. The two leading candidates in Munich are **Herties Department Store,** across from the railroad station, and **Kaufhof Department Store,** at Karlsplatz. At Herties, soups begin at 1.90 DM ($1.09), bratwurst at 4.50 DM ($2.58). Meals are generally in the 7.50-DM ($4.30) to 11.50-DM ($6.60) range. At Kaufhof, soups go from 2 DM ($1.15), and main courses include a pork cutlet at 8.95 DM ($5.13) or half a chicken at 7.75 DM ($4.45). During the day, most meals are in the 5-DM ($2.87) to 11.75-DM ($6.74) range. The fruit salad at 3.50 DM ($2.01) makes a nice finish.

FOR STUDENTS: Mensa Restaurant 15 Leopoldstrasse, is the best bargain in Munich. Technically, you should be a bona fide student, but if you look the part you usually get served. Prices run from 2 DM ($1.15) to 3.40 DM ($1.95) for a two-course lunch. To eat here, you have to insert coins in a slot machine which dispenses coupons to exchange for food. Go early as it closes at 6:30 p.m.

ROCK BOTTOM IN SCHWABING: Weinbauer, 5 Fendstrasse, off Leopoldstrasse, is a favorite in Schwabing. It's a rather small gaststätte full of smoke and students. No bright accessories are found here, just wood tables and passable food. Set lunches range from 4.50 DM ($2.58) to 11 DM ($6.31), and about ten main dishes costing less than 7 DM ($4.02) are featured daily.

Wirtsauf Seerose, 32 Feilitzstrasse, is a renovated old patrician house with a clean yellow face. It's a good bet in Schwabing for budget dining. Set lunches, attracting both young and old diners, are offered, ranging in price from 8.20 DM ($4.70) to 16.50 DM ($9.46). Soups go for 2.50 DM ($1.43) to 6 DM ($3.44), and desserts begin at 2.50 DM ($1.43). The restaurant room is known as the Grill Parzer.

READERS' EATING SELECTIONS: "You should tell your readers of the important word **'Imbiss'** in Germany. Usually you can get a great meal of meat and potatoes and kraut or salad for 8 DM ($4.59). Standing up can be tolerated for that price. There are several central ones in Munich—one on the Tal and another in the alley just down from the Hofbräuhaus. They close at 6 p.m. weekdays and 1 p.m. Saturdays, but sure help out your pocketbook and stomach. You can even point if your German is bad" (Rosemary Hensby, Kansas City, Mo.). . . . "I discovered **Gaststätte Wilhelm Tell**, 15 Schonfeldstrasse, quite by accident but was very pleased with both prices and food. They offer two menu-of-the-day choices: 5.50 DM ($3.15) and 7 DM ($4.02). I chose the 7-DM meal which included soup, fish, boiled or fried potatoes, and salad. It is off Ludwigstrasse very near the English Gardens" (George P. De Kay, London, Ontario, Canada). . . . "We found a restaurant in Munich which was a welcome change from the usual German fare when my stomach finally rebelled against sausages, Hungarian goulaschsuppe, and wienerschnitzel. It's **Ochs'n Willi**, 54 Sendingerstrasse. Steaks and baked potatoes are featured, served with German flair and garnish. The typical salads, soups, and desserts are also available. Entrees range from 9.50 DM ($5.45) to 18 DM ($10.32). The darkened beam ceiling and small tables set close together retain the German atmosphere" (Verna Richert, Morgan Hill, Calif.).

3. Sights

Munich is stocked with so many treasures and sights, the visitor who plans to do the city in one or two days makes a mistake. Not only will a person miss many of the highlights, but will also fail to grasp the spirit of Munich and to absorb fully its special flavor, unique among the cities of the world. But faced with an enormous list of important attractions and a time clock running out, the tourist may have to limit sightseeing to a few of the more vital attractions—especially in the area of museums and galleries, with which Munich is endowed. After a quick trip through the Old Town with its numerous sights, we'll survey the most important of Munich's museums and churches, and then add a few interesting excursions from the city.

THE OLD TOWN: Try to arrive at the **Marienplatz** before 11 a.m. This square, dedicated to the patron of the city, whose statue stands on a huge column in the center, is the heart of the Old Town. On its north side is the New Town Hall, built in 19th-century Gothic. At 11 a.m. each day, the **glockenspiel** on the facade performs a miniature tournament, with little enameled copper figures moving in and out of the archways.

Since you're already at the Town Hall, you may wish to climb the 55 steps to the top of its tower (an elevator is available if you are conserving your energy) for a good overall view of the Old Town. To the south of the square you can see the oldest church in Munich, St. Peter's. To the north lies **Odeonsplatz**, Munich's most beautiful square, surrounded by the Royal Palace (Residenz) and the Theatinerkirche. Adjoining the Residenz is the restored National Theater, home of the acclaimed Bavarian State Opera.

Running westward from the Odeonsplatz is the wide shopping avenue, Briennerstrasse, leading to the **Königsplatz** (King's Square). Flanking this large Grecian square are three classical buildings constructed by Ludwig I—the Propyläen, the Glyptothek, and the Antikensammlungen. Returning to the Odeonsplatz, take the busy Ludwigstrasse north to the section of Munich known as **Schwabing.** This is the Greenwich Village, Latin Quarter, or Chelsea of Munich, proud of its artist and writer element, numbering among its own such literati as Ibsen and Rilke. Painters from all over Germany found their way here. In fact, the "Blue Rider" group which so influenced abstract art in the early 20th century was originated here by Kandinsky, along with Marc and Klee. Today it still retains a frankly offbeat flavor, with racks of handmade jewelry for sale along the streets and sidewalk tables filled with young people from all over the world.

Bordering Schwabing on the east and extending almost to the Isar River is Munich's city park, the 18th-century **English Garden,** laid out by Sir Benjamin Thompson. Here you can wander for hours along the walks and among trees and flowers, even stopping for tea on the plaza near the Chinese pagoda.

MUSEUMS AND GALLERIES: Thus far, seeing Munich has been a walking experience, looking mainly at the outsides of buildings and admiring parks and squares which have been around for centuries. Now, to see some of its biggest attractions, we will have to go indoors to the museums and galleries where the city has preserved some of the finest and most varied collections of art found anywhere. If you have time to visit only one of these during your stay, it definitely should be:

Alte Pinakothek

Art lovers come to Munich just to gaze on the hundreds of famous works exhibited in this huge Renaissance building at 27 Barerstrasse (tram no. 15 or 25 or bus no. 53). The more than 900 paintings on display (many thousands more are gathering dust in the basement) represent the greatest European artists of the 14th through the 18th centuries. Begun as a small court collection of the royal Wittelsbach family in the early 1500s, the gallery is now the largest and most important in Germany. Although there are only two floors with exhibits, the museum is immense, and we do not recommend that you try to cover all the galleries in one day. If you have only a few hours to spend here, however, some works definitely merit your time.

The landscape painter par excellence of the Danube school, Albrecht Altdorfer, is represented by no less than six monumental works.

The works of Albrecht Dürer include his greatest—and final—self-portrait (1500). Here the artist has portrayed himself with almost Christ-like solemnity. Also displayed is the last great painting of the artist—his two-paneled work, *The Four Apostles* (1526).

Several of the galleries in the main branch are given over to the works of the Dutch and Flemish masters. The *St. Columba Altarpiece* (1460–62), by Roger van der Weyden, is one of the greatest of these—in size as well as importance. Measuring nearly ten feet across, this triptych is a triumph of van der Weyden's subtle linear style, and one of his last works (he died in 1464).

Several galleries display a number of works by three of the Dutch and Flemish masters, Rembrandt, Rubens, and van Dyck. Included are a series of religious panels painted by Rembrandt for Prince Frederick Hendrick of the Netherlands. A variety of French, Spanish, and Italian artists are displayed in both the larger galleries and the small rooms lining the outer wall. The Italian masters are well represented by Fra Filippo Lippi, Giotto, Botticelli, Raphael (his *Holy Family*), and Titian.

You'll also find a *Madonna* by Da Vinci, a famous self-portrait of the young Rembrandt (1629), and a number of works by Lucas Cranach, one of Germany's Renaissance painters. Cranach's famous *Venus,* is also displayed. Pieter Bruegel's *Land of Cockaigne,* where nothing has to be done and where food simply falls into one's mouth, is on view, too. Bruegel has taken the popular subject of European folk literature and satirized it in this painting. Note the little egg on legs running up to be eaten, and the plucked and cooked chicken laying its neck on a plate. In the background you'll see a knight lying under a roof with his mouth open, waiting for the pies to slip off the eaves over his head.

Important works are always on display, but exhibits are changed in two rooms on the first floor. To save yourself a fruitless search for one work, you'd be wise to buy the 1-DM (57¢) map of the gallery which will guide you through the dozens of rooms. The museum is open daily from 9 a.m. to 4:30 p.m., with additional hours on Tuesday and Thursday evenings from 7 to 9 p.m. Closed Monday. Admission is 3 DM ($1.72); free on Sundays.

Deutsches Museum (German Museum)

On an island in the Isar River, the Deutsches Museum is a world unto itself, with seven floors of exhibits, including the Zeiss Planetarium in the dome above the entrance hall. The exhibits consist of original pieces of historical apparatus and machinery, as well as scale working models and even complete reconstructions of factories, workshops, and mines.

The basement level of the museum is devoted to mineral resources and mining. Here you can see everything from a replica of an old Bavarian coal mine to exhibits of drilling equipment from 1844 to the present. On the floor above, working models show how the ore from metal and coal mines is converted into usable material.

One of the most popular exhibits is in the department of aeronautics, in the upper story of the central hall. Models of airships designed by Zeppelin and an 1895 glider help the visitor understand more about the development of aircraft. Equally popular, but more complicated to the casual observer, is the department of nuclear physics and technology (on the same level). Among the exhibits is a model of a nuclear reactor with adjustable movable parts.

Besides the purely scientific departments, you can also visit rooms devoted to musical instruments, printing and writing, and an exhibit of old automobiles. Each exhibit is designed to be understood and appreciated by every visitor— whether he or she is a scientist, a student, or simply a casual sightseer. The museum is open every day from 9 a.m. to 5 p.m. Admission is 3 DM ($1.72), 1 DM (57¢) for students and children. Guided tours are available if ordered in advance. A restaurant is on the premises.

The Residenz

When a member of the royal Bavarian family said he was going to the castle, he could have meant any number of places—especially if he was Ludwig II. But if he said he was going home, it could only be the Residenz to which he referred. This enormous palace, with a history almost as long as that of the

Wittelsbach family, was the official residence of the rulers of Bavaria from 1384 to 1918. Added to and rebuilt over the centuries, this complex of buildings is a conglomerate of various styles of art and architecture. Depending on the direction from which you approach the Residenz, your impression can be one of a German Renaissance hall (the western facade), a Palladian palace (on the north), or a Florentine Renaissance palace (on the south facing Max-Joseph-Platz).

The Residenz has been completely restored since its almost total destruction in World War II and now houses the Residenz Museum, a concert hall, the famous Cuvilliés Theatre, and the Residenz Treasury.

The **Residenz Museum** takes up the whole southwestern section of the palace, some 100 rooms of art and furnishings collected by centuries of Wittelsbachs. To see the entire collection, you'll have to take two tours, one in the morning and the other in the afternoon. You may also visit the rooms on your own.

The Ancestors' Gallery is designed almost like a hall of mirrors with one important difference: where the mirrors would normally be, there are portraits of the members of the royal family, set into gilded, carved paneling. The largest room in the museum section of the palace is the Hall of Antiquities, possibly the finest example of interior Renaissance styling in Germany (outside of churches, that is). Frescoes seemingly adorn every inch of space on the walls and ceilings alike, painted by dozens of 16th- and 17th-century artists. The room is broken into sections by wall pillars and niches, each with its own bust of a Roman emperor or a Greek hero. The hall contains pieces of furniture dating from the 16th century as well, but the center of attraction is the two-story chimney-piece of red stucco-marble. Completed in 1600, it is adorned with Tuscan pillars and a large coat of arms of the dukes of Bavaria.

On the second floor of the palace, directly over the Hall of Antiquities, the museum has gathered its enormous collection of Far Eastern porcelain. Note also the fine assemblage of Oriental rugs in the long narrow Porcelain Gallery.

Although many of the rooms have been organized as exhibit salons with glass cases and pedestals, some have been furnished as they were when the palace was actually a residence. The best example is the Elector's bedroom on the second floor. Several tapestries adorn the walls, and the room is lit by carved and gilded sconces as well as by the massive cut-glass chandelier. The focal point is the ornate bed (1750) enclosed by a balustrade.

Entrance to the museum, open from 10 a.m. to 12:30 p.m. and from 1:30 to 4:30 p.m., Tuesdays through Saturdays (Sundays, from 10 a.m. to 1 p.m.), costs 1.50 DM (86¢). You'll have to pay another 1.50 DM to visit the **Schatzkammer** (Treasure House) of the Residenz, open the same hours. If you've time to see only one item here, it should be the Renaissance statue of *St. George Slaying the Dragon* (16th century). The equestrian statue is made of gold, but you can barely see the precious metal for the thousands of diamonds, rubies, emeralds, sapphires, and semiprecious stones imbedded in it.

Room 4 is devoted to sacred objects, including several icons and numerous crucifixes, carved in ivory, ebony, or hammered in gold. The Wittelsbach equivalent to the Crown Jewels is in Room 5, with sceptres and royal orbs. The crown of the realm is also on display.

Both the Residenz Museum and the Treasury are entered from Max-Joseph-Platz on the south side of the palace. From the museum, for another 1 DM (57¢), you can visit the **Cuvilliés Theatre,** whose rococo tiers of boxes are supported by nymphs and angels. Directly over the huge center box, where the royal family sat, is a crest in white and gold topped by a jewel-bedecked crown of Bavaria held in place by a group of cherubs in flight. In summer this theater is the scene of frequent Mozart concerts.

Bavarian National Museum

King Maximilian II in 1855 began an ever-growing institution that today presents the largest and richest display of the artistic and historical riches of Bavaria. So rapidly has its collection grown in the past 100 years that the museum has had to move into larger quarters several times. Its current building, at 3 Prinzregentenstrasse, near the Haus der Kunst, contains three vast floors of sculpture, painting, folk art, ceramics, furniture, and textiles, as well as clocks and scientific instruments.

Entering the museum, turn to the right and go into the first large gallery (called the Wessobrunn Room). Devoted to early church art, from the 5th through the 13th centuries, this room contains some of the oldest and most valuable works. The desk case contains ancient and medieval ivories, including the so-called Munich ivory, from about 400 A.D. The carving shows the women weeping at the tomb of Christ while the resurrected Lord is gingerly stepping up the clouds and into heaven. The adjoining room is named for the stone figure of the *Virgin with the Rose Bush,* from Straubing (c. 1300). This is one of the few old Bavarian pieces of church art to be influenced by the spirit of mysticism.

The Riemenschneider Room (no. 16) is devoted almost entirely to a Gothic contemporary of Dürer. Characteristic of the sculptor's works is the natural, unpainted look of his carvings and statuary. Note especially the 12 apostles from the Marienkapelle in Würzburg (1510), St. Mary Magdalene, central group of the high altar in the parish church of Münnerstadt (1490–92) and the figure of St. Sebastian (1490). Also on display, in Rooms 18 and 19, are famous collections of arms and armories from the 16th to the 18th centuries.

Other salons on the main floor are devoted to various periods of German and northern Italian art (which is closely tied to the cultural evolution of Bavaria). One gallery (no. 47) is occupied by scale models of important Bavarian towns as they looked in the 16th century.

The second floor contains a fine collection of stained and painted glass—an art in which medieval Germany excelled. Also worth a visit are the two rooms of rococo costumes and textiles (nos. 67 and 68), an extravagant period in fashion and design. Other rooms on this floor include historic glassware, Meissen porcelain, and ceramics. One of the newest additions to the museum is the collection of antique clocks (Rooms 58 and 59), dating from as early as the 16th century.

In the east wing of the basement level is an extensive array of Christmas Cribs, not only from Germany, but from Austria, Italy, Moravia, and Sicily as well. The variety of materials competes with the styles themselves—wood, amber, gold, terracotta, and even wax were used in making these nativity scenes. Also on this level is a display of Bavarian folk art, including many examples of wood carving.

From April 1 to September 30 the Bavarian National Museum is open daily, except Monday, from 9:30 a.m. to 4:30 p.m. (from 10 a.m. on Sundays). Admission is 2 DM ($1.15). Reductions are granted for children and students. Free on Sundays. From October 1 to March 31, hours are Tuesday to Friday from 9 a.m. to 4 p.m. (Saturday and Sunday from 10 a.m. to 4 p.m.).

Munich Antikensammlungen

After 100 years of floating from one museum to another, the Museum of Antiquities finally found a home in the 19th-century neoclassical hall on the south side of the Königsplatz. The collection grew up around the vase collection of Ludwig I and the Royal Antiquarium, both of which were incorporated after World War I into a loosely defined group called the Museum Antiker Kleinkunst (Museum of Small Works of Ancient Art). Many of the pieces may be small in size, but never in value or artistic significance.

Entering the museum, you find yourself in the large central hall. On your left near the stairs you'll see a marble bust of King Ludwig I, who was responsible for the three classic buildings around the Grecian-style square. The five halls of the main floor house more than 650 Greek vases, collected from all parts of the Mediterranean. The pottery has been restored to a near-perfect condition, although most of it dates as far back as 500 B.C. The oldest piece is "the goddess from Aegina," dating from 3000 B.C. Although technically not pottery, this pre-Mycenaean figure, carved from a mussel shell, is on display along with the Mycenaean pottery exhibits in Room I. The upper level of the Central Hall is devoted to large Greek vases discovered in Sicily and to the art of the Etruscans.

Returning to the Central Hall, take the stairs down to the lower level to see the collection of Greek, Roman, and Etruscan jewelry. Note the similarities of today's fashions in design. Included on this level as well are rooms devoted to ancient colored glass, Etruscan bronzes, and Greek terracottas.

The **Glyptothek** is the ideal neighbor for the Museum of Antiquities. It supplements the pottery and smaller pieces of the main museum with an excellent collection of ancient Greek and Roman sculpture, e.g., the Archaic Kouroi. Included are the famous pediments from the temple of Aegina. Both the Glyptothek and the Antikensammlungen are open Tuesday through Sunday from 10 a.m. to 4:30 p.m. On Wednesdays the Antikensammlungen and on Thursdays the Glyptothek are open from noon to 8 p.m. A 2.50-DM ($1.43) ticket admits you to both. Students are admitted free, and everybody gets in free on Sundays.

Haus der Kunst

At 1 Prinzregentenstrasse, the Haus der Kunst (House of Art) is a complex of two galleries and a wing devoted to changing exhibitions. The west wing of the building houses the **Neue Pinakothek** and the **Neue Staatsgalerie** (New State Gallery), charging 2 DM ($1.14) for admission.

The works housed in the west wing are by the finest artists of the 18th, 19th, and 20th centuries. The best of the non-German collections are the 19th-century French paintings, including several Cézannes, Corots, Gauguins, Manets, and Renoirs. Vincent van Gogh is also represented by an impressive list of works, including his famous *Sunflowers*. Among the most popular German artists represented are Wilhelm Leibl and Max Beckmann. Placed throughout the gallery are sculptures, mainly in bronze, by German artists, with a Degas and Rodin here and there. Occasionally, special exhibitions such as Henry Moore sculpture are also held here.

The east wing of the Haus der Kunst, entered separately—the 4-DM ($2.29) to 5-DM ($2.87) tickets are purchased separately—is devoted to changing exhibits. You never know what to expect, from displays of Nazi and Communist posters to American patriotic banners, or even covers from *Harper's* magazine. The works of aspiring artists are often exhibited as well, and many of them can be purchased at reasonable prices.

The galleries of the Haus der Kunst are open daily from 9:30 a.m. to 4:30 p.m. From the center of town, you can take bus no. 55 from the main station—it stops right in front.

Münchner Stadtmuseum (Municipal Museum)

Munich's Municipal Museum is to the city what the Bavarian National Museum is to the whole of the province. In what was once the armory building on St. Jakobsplatz, its collections give you an insight into the history and daily lives of the people of this unique community. A wooden model shows how Munich looked in 1572.

The extensive collection of furnishings includes armoires, painted furniture, and replicas of a 1750 dining room and a salon from 1820. Toys, dolls, and hobby horses dating from centuries past are also an attraction.

The museum's main exhibit is its *Moorish Dancers* (Moriskentänzer) on the ground floor. These ten figures, each two feet high, carved in wood and painted in bright colors by Erasmus Grasser in 1480, are among the best examples of secular Gothic art in medieval Germany.

A mural of Al Jolson's *The Jazz Singer* invites you to the photo and film museum on the second floor. This department traces the early history of the camera technique, going back to 1733! Cabinet after cabinet of early cameras, many from about 1915, line the walls. Murals document scenes from early movies including the likes of Garbo and Ramon Novarro in *Mata Hari* (1931). You see photos of the sex goddesses—Dietrich, Mae West, and Jean Harlow—appreciated as much in Munich as in the U.S.

On the third floor is an array of puppets from around the world—China, Nigeria, India, and Indonesia, to name a few. The comical and grotesque figures include marionettes and hand puppets. Like a Lilliputian version of the world of the stage, the collection also includes detailed puppet theaters, miniature scenery, and one stage where visitors can practice puppeteering themselves.

One salon is devoted to the replica of an old brewery, with effective models, vats, and other equipment. The adjacent room contrasts the modern technique of bottling, depicting with large photo murals and other exhibits, right down to the beer cans.

Some readers have found the collection on the fourth floor even more impressive. The display of musical instruments is one of the greatest of its kind in the world. For example, this historical collection shows examples of the harp and violin from earliest times. In addition, an ethnological collection displays instruments in use in Africa, Oceania, the Americas, the Orient, the Middle East, Byzantium, and Europe.

Enter the Municipal Museum through the main courtyard. It is open daily, except Monday, from 9 a.m. to 4:30 p.m. Admission is 1.80 DM ($1.03).

Städtische Galerie

The ancient villa of Franz von Lenbach, this gallery exhibits works by that 19th-century artist (1836–1904). Entering the gold-colored mansion through the gardens, you'll be greeted with a large collection of early works by Paul Klee (1879–1940)—mainly those predating World War I. There's also an outstanding representation of works by Kandinsky, leader of the "Blue Rider" movement in early 20th-century art. One of his best paintings on display is the portrait of his wide-eyed mistress, Gabriele Münter (1905). There are many other 19th-century paintings throughout the villa, along with a few works from the 15th through the 18th centuries. The enclosed patio is pleasant for a coffee break. The gallery is open daily, except Monday, from 9 a.m. to 4:30 p.m. Admission is 1.50 DM (86¢). On Tuesdays, it remains open until 8 p.m.

CHURCHES OF MUNICH: As Germany's largest Catholic city, Munich naturally contains a number of outstanding churches. For those interested in ecclesiastical art and architecture, we offer a trio of the finest.

Frauenkirche (Cathedral of Our Lady)

When the smoke cleared from the bombings of 1945, only a fragile shell remained of Munich's largest church. Workmen and architects who restored the 15th-century Gothic cathedral used whatever remains they could find in the rubble, supplementing it with several modern innovations. The overall effect of the rebuilt Frauenkirche is strikingly simple, yet dignified.

The twin towers (which remained intact), with their strangely un-Gothic onion-shaped domes, have been the city's landmark since 1525. However, the red-brick exterior of the cathedral proper has retained its Gothic appearance. Instead of the typical flying buttresses, the edifice is supported by huge props on the inside which separate the side chapels. The Gothic vaulting over the nave and chancel is borne by 22 simple octagonal pillars.

Entering the main doors at the west end of the cathedral, you first notice that there are no windows (they are actually hidden, except for the tall chancel window, by the enormous pillars). According to legend, the devil thought so, too, and you can still see the strange footlike mark called "the devil's step" in the entrance hall where he stamped in glee at the stupidity of the architect. As you enter the left aisle of the three-aisled nave, you'll see photographs showing the cathedral as it looked after it was destroyed in the air raids of World War II. Many of the works of art formerly housed in the church were safely put away at that time, and are displayed in the chapels along the nave and behind the chancel.

In the chapel directly behind the high altar is the most interesting painting in the cathedral: *The Protecting Cloak,* a 1510 work by Jan Polack, showing the Virgin holding out her majestic robes symbolically to shelter all of mankind. The collection of tiny figures beneath the cloak includes everyone from pope to peasants. At the entrance to the vestry, just to the left of the choir, is a huge painting of *The Ascension of the Virgin Mary* by Peter Candid. In the south chapel adjoining the Chapel of the Holy Sacrament is one of the modern works, *The Immaculate Virgin,* a graceful bronze statue (1959) hung over a simple altar.

The Baptistry, to the right of the choir, contains the cathedral's oldest work, a stone sculpture of the suffering Christ, dating from 1380.

Returning to the entrance via the south nave, you'll pass the mausoleum of Emperor Ludwig IV, built in 1622. The elaborately carved tomb is guarded at each corner by armored soldiers with banners of the realm. In the front stands a sculpted likeness of the emperor, sword in hand.

After a tour of the church, climb the 82 steps to the elevator, and take the worthwhile trip to the top of the 300-foot south tower. From the lookout, all the landmarks of the city are identified by photographs on the walls. In fair weather, you can even see as far as the Alps. Admission to the tower is 1.50 DM (86¢).

St. Peter's Church

Munich's oldest church (1180) has turned over a new leaf—and it's a gold one at that! The white and gray interior has been decorated with painted medallions of puce and lots of gilded baroque. In contains a series of murals by Johann Baptist Zimmermann, but nothing tops the attraction of the bizarre relic in the second chapel on the left: a gilt-covered and gem-studded skeleton staring at you with two false eyes in its head, which rests on a cushion. Jewels cover the mouth of rotten teeth, quite a contrast to the fresh roses usually kept in front of the black and silver coffin.

Near the Town Hall, St. Peter's—known locally as Old Peter—also has a high steeple, although you may be discouraged from going up it by the lack of an elevator. The colored circles on the lower platform will tell you whether the climb is worthwhile, however. If the circle is white, you can be assured of a spectacular view as far as the Alps.

Theatinerkirche

Named for a small group of Roman Catholic clergy (the Theatines) and not for the Residenz Theatre just across the Odeonsplatz, this church is the finest example of Italian baroque in Munich. Dedicated to the scholar-saint Cajetan, it was begun in the mid-17th century by two Italian architects, Barelli and Zucalli. It was completed in 1768 by the son of the dwarf court jester-cum-architect, Francois Cuvilliés. The facade and the interior are both studded with cherubs. Some of them are quite mischievous, especially the "Angel of Silence," which points the way to the interior with one hand while he holds the other to his lips to form an obvious "shh."

The arched ceiling of the nave is supported by fluted columns lining the center aisle. Above the transept dividing the nave from the choir, the ceiling breaks into an open dome with an ornate gallery decorated with large but graceful statues. Nothing seems to detract from the whiteness of the interior, except the dark wooden pews and the canopied pulpit.

ON THE OUTSKIRTS—SCHLOSS NYMPHENBURG: When the call of spring made city life unbearable, the Wittelsbachs would pack up their bags and head for their country house. But they were hardly getting away from it all. The summer residence at Nymphenburg was, if anything, a more complete, more sophisticated palace than the Residenz in Munich. Begun in the style of an Italian villa in 1664 by Elector Ferdinand Maria, Nymphenburg took more than 150 years and several architectural changes before it was completed in 1823. The final plan of the palace was due mainly to Elector Max Emanuel, who in 1702 decided to enlarge the villa by adding four large pavilions connected by arcaded passageways. Gradually, the French style took over, and today the facade is a subdued baroque.

The interior of the palace is less subtle, however. Upon entering the main building, you're in the Great Hall, decorated in rococo colors and stuccos. The frescoes by Zimmermann (1756) depict incidents from mythology, especially those dealing with Flora, goddess of the nymphs, for whom the palace was named. This hall was used for both banquet and concerts during the reign of Max Joseph III, elector during the mid-18th century. Concerts are still presented here in summer. The smaller rooms are devoted to tapestries, paintings, and period furniture.

From the main building, turn left and head for the arcaded gallery connecting the northern pavilions. The first room in the arcade is the Great Gallery of Beauties, painted for Elector Max Emanuel in 1710, containing portraits of five of the loveliest ladies in the Court of Louis XIV. More provocative, however, is King Ludwig I's Gallery of Beauties in the south pavilion (the apartments of Queen Caroline). Ludwig commissioned no fewer than 36 portraits of the most beautiful women of his day. The paintings by J. Stieler (painted from 1827 to 1850) include the *Schöne Münchnerin* (lovely Munich girl), and the dancer Lola Montez, whose "friendship" with Ludwig I caused such a scandal that she was considered a factor in the Revolution of 1848, which resulted in the abdication of the king.

To the south of the palace buildings, in the rectangular block of low structures which once housed the court stables, is the **Marstallmuseum,** containing carriages, coaches, sleighs, and riding accessories from the 18th and 19th centuries. As soon as you enter the first hall, look for the Coronation Coach of Elector Karl Albrecht. Built in Paris in 1740, this so-called glass coach is ornamented with everything from acanthus leaves to dolphins. The few flat panels on the side of the coach are filled with oil paintings of Justitia, Bellona, and Ecclesia. From the same period is the hunting sleigh of Electress Amalia, with the statue of Diana, goddess of the hunt. Even the runners of the sleigh are decorated with shellwork and hunting trophies.

The coaches and sleighs of Ludwig II are displayed in the third hall. In keeping with his constant longing for the grandeur of the past, his State Coach was ornately designed for his marriage to Duchess Sophie of Bavaria—a royal wedding which never came off. The fairytale coach wasn't wasted, however, since Ludwig often rode off to one of his many castles in it, creating quite a picture through the countryside. The coach is completely gilded, inside and out. Rococo carvings cover every inch of space except for the panels, faced with paintings on copper of the French Louis XV period. In winter, the king would use his State Sleigh, nearly as elaborate as the Cinderella Coach!

Returning outdoors, you find Nymphenburg's greatest attraction—the park. Stretching for 500 acres in front of the palace, it is divided into two sections by the canal which runs from the pool at the foot of the staircase to the cascade at the far end of the gardens. From the palace steps, you can see the formal design of the gardens, laid out in an English style, with lakes, greenery, and beds of flowers.

Within the park are several pavilions. On the guided tour, you begin with **Amalienburg,** whose plain exterior belies the rococo decoration inside. Built as a hunting lodge for Electress Amalia (1734), the pavilion carries the hunting theme through the first few rooms and then bursts into salons of flamboyant colors, rich carvings, and wall paintings. The most impressive room is the "Hall of Mirrors," a symphony of silver ornaments on a faintly blue ground.

The **Badenburg Pavilion** sits at the edge of the large lake of the same name. As its name implies, it was built as a bathing pavilion, although it's difficult to visualize little Ludwig dashing in from the water with swimming suit dripping on those elegant floors. A trip to the basement, however, will help you appreciate the pavilion's practical side. Here you'll see the unique bath, surrounded by blue and white Dutch tiles. The ceiling is painted with several frescoes of bathing scenes from mythology.

The **Pagodenburg,** on the smaller lake on the opposite side of the canal, although octagonal, looks little like a Chinese pagoda from the outside. The interior, however, is decorated with pseudo-Chinese motifs, often using Dutch tiles in place of the Oriental ones.

The **Magdalenenklause** may look like a ruin, but it was intended that way when it was built in 1725. Also called the Hermitage, it was planned as a retreat for prayer and solitude. The four main rooms of the one-story structure are all paneled with uncarved, stained oak. All the furnishings are simple and the few paintings religious. It's really a drastic change from the frequent gaudiness of the other buildings.

You can park your car beside the main building and walk through the palace and gardens. Those arriving by tram (no. 17 or 21) can get off at Auffahrtsallee and go along the small canal to the palace. If you have the better part of a day, buy the 2.50-DM ($1.43) ticket to the palace, carriage museum, and the pavilions in the park. Otherwise, you'll have to pay 1 DM (57¢) for each attraction. Hours are generally the same for all sights except the Marstall-museum. The palace and pavilions are open daily except Monday from 9 a.m. to 12:15 p.m. and from 1 to 5 p.m. in summer; in winter, from 10 a.m. to 12:15 p.m. and 1 to 4 p.m. The Carriage Museum is open the same hours as those above in summer. The museum is closed on Mondays.

EXCURSION TO DACHAU: In 1933, what had once been a quiet little artists' community just ten miles from Munich became a tragic symbol of the Nazi era. Himmler and the SS set up the first German concentration camp in March of that year, on the grounds of a former ammunition factory. Dachau saw countless prisoners arrive between 1933 and 1945. Although the files show a registry of more than 206,000, the exact number of people imprisoned here is unknown.

Entering the camp today, you are faced by three memorial chapels—Catholic, Protestant, and Jewish—built in the early 1960s. Immediately behind the Catholic chapel is the "Lagerstrasse," the main camp road lined with poplar trees, once flanked by the 30 barracks, each housing 208 prisoners who had to share two washrooms and lavatories. Two of these barracks have been rebuilt to give visitors an insight into the horrible conditions endured by the prisoners.

The museum is housed in the large building which once contained the kitchen, laundry, and shower baths where prisoners were often brought for torture by the SS. Photographs and documents show the rise of the Nazi regime, the super-power of the SS, as well as exhibits depicting the persecution of Jews and other prisoners. Every effort has been made to present the facts truthfully.

The tour of Dachau is not enjoyable, but it is a moving experience. You can get to the camp by taking the frequent trains from Munich to the Dachau station for 4.60 DM ($2.64), and then the Dachau Ost bus from the station to the camp, .70 DM (40¢). The camp is open every day from 9 a.m. to 5 p.m.

OLYMPIC CITY: The center of the Olympiads—site of the 1972 World Olympics—is a 740-acre plot of land at the northern edge of the city. More than 15,000 workers from 18 countries transformed the site into a park-like setting of nearly 5000 trees, 27 miles of roads, 32 bridges, and a lake.

Olympic City has its own railway station, subway line, mayor, post office, churches, even an elementary school. It broke the skyline of Munich by the addition of a 960-foot television tower in the center of the park.

The showpiece of the city is a huge stadium, capable of seating 80,000 spectators, and topped by the largest roof in the world—nearly 90,000 square yards of tinted acryl glass. The supports for the stadium are anchored by two huge blocks, each capable of resisting 4000 tons under stress. The roof serves the additional purpose of collecting rainwater and draining it into the nearby Olympic lake.

Nearly 5000 apartments and cottages were built on the grounds to house members of the Olympic staffs and teams. After the games were over, these were turned into modern housing projects for some 10,000 residents.

Smaller halls throughout the park are used for exhibitions and such competitive events as wrestling, judo, fencing, and weight lifting. The covered swimming stadium, with four large pools, is now a municipal enterprise open to the public.

READERS' SIGHTSEEING TIPS: "A fun and inexpensive day in Munich begins by taking tram no. 7 to Peterdring, the northern end of the line. Spend the morning exploring the **Olympic Village;** then at about noon, go to the **BMW factory,** sign up for the free tour (which is given in German, English, French, or Italian as needed), and visit the museum until the tour begins. The BMW factory has the best and most thorough industrial tour we've ever seen and should not be missed by anyone who is even the least bit interested in cars, motorcycles, and/or industrial tours in general" (Larry and Trudy Phelps, Jacksonville, Fla.). . . . A second recommendation for this attraction follows: "At the **Bavarian Motor Works,** a futuristic museum houses numerous examples of BMW technology, both past and present. Included are seven decades of technically sophisticated automobiles, both street and racing, the famous shaft-drive BMW motorcycles, early aircraft engines (including the famous Fokker Dvii WW1), the first production jet engine in the world, and other exhibits of interest to young and old. Admission is free. A very good tour of the factory is also offered, and one should not miss the lavish parts display area, where one can purchase posters and other memorabilia. All in all, a great example of Bavarian technical achievement set in wonderfully clean and efficient work areas" (Paul F. Lee, Hagerstown, Md.). . . . "If you understand just a little German, you can enjoy the **Karl Valentine Turmstuberl,** the 'museum of blooming nonsense,' dedicated to the early 20th-century German comedian. It's in the tower gate of Isator, the first stop east of Marienplatz on the S-Bahn. Admission is 1.50 DM (86¢)" (Robert C. Probasco, Moscow, Idaho).

4. Munich After Dark

Munich is a city with a lively—and quite inexpensive—nightlife. It won't take you long to realize that most of it centers around . . .

THE BEER HALLS: Hofbräuhaus, 9 Platzl, is a legend among beer halls, the most famous in Bavaria. Visitors with only one night in Munich usually target the haus as their number one nighttime destination. There are several rooms spread over three floors, including one on the top floor for dancing on certain nights of the week. But with its brass band (which starts playing in the afternoon), the ground-floor Zur Schwemme is most typical of what you always expected of a beer hall—here, it's the eternal Oktoberfest! At the second-floor restaurant, strolling musicians, including an accordion player and a violinist, entertain you. Waitresses in dirndls place mugs of beer at your table between sing-alongs. For a full liter, expect to pay 3.90 DM ($2.24) to 4.80 DM ($2.75); meals are in the 7.50-DM ($4.30) to 18-DM ($10.32) range.

Augustiner, 16 Neuhauserstrasse, stands on the principal pedestrian-only street of Munich, and is handy for many, as it offers generous helpings of food, really good beer, and an attractively mellow atmosphere. Dark-wood panels and ceilings in carved plaster make the place look even older than it is. It's been around for less than a century, but beer was first brewed on this spot in 1328, or so the printed literature about the establishment claims. Waitresses in dirndls will hand you the menus, which change daily. You'll find soups in the 1.80-DM ($1.03)—usually consommé with egg—to 6-DM ($3.44) bracket. Main dishes are priced anywhere from 6.80 DM ($3.90) to 14 DM ($8.03). The menu is long, and the cuisine itself is not for dieters, as it's hearty, heavy, and definitely starchy, but that's what the customers want.

Platzl, Am Platzl, 2 Münzstrasse (tel. 29-31-01), faces its more famous competitor, the Hofbräuhaus. Actually, it's not really a competitor, as it offers an entirely different brand of fare, presenting a Bavarian folk program nightly in the large beer hall area.

The women dancers wear the dirndl (a skirt and blouse popular with many Bavarian girls); the men dress in lederhosen (leather shorts), worn with a Loden jacket and a felt hat with a badger's tail. Together they perform the schuhplattler, the thigh-slapping folk dance of the Bavarian Alps. The entrance charge is 7 DM ($4.02). The inn offers fine Bavarian food and sausages, and Platzl draft beer in a keg is placed at the table.

Mathäser Bierstadt, 5 Bayerstrasse, is a beer city, filled both afternoons and evenings with happy imbibers. To reach the Bierhalle, walk through to the back, then go upstairs. Featured is a brass band oompahing away. The largest of all Bavarian taverns, the Bierstadt contains tables and tables of drinkers joining in the songs. Even at midafternoon, the place is often packed, making you wonder if anybody is working in the entire city. In addition to the main hall, there is a downstairs tavern. Here Löwenbräu kegs spill out onto the sidewalk for stand-up sausage and kraut nibblers. Specialties of the house include knuckles of veal and pork. Be sure to try leberkäs, a kind of liver cheese. The most favored dish is the half a roast chicken at 4.80 DM ($2.75). Soups cost from 1.50 DM (86¢) to 2.50 DM ($1.43); desserts, 2.25 DM ($1.29) to 4.10 ($2.35). One-half liter of beer costs 2 DM ($1.15).

"During the spring 'Strong Beer Season,' two weeks after the end of Fasching, and during Oktoberfest, the beer house holds a special typical Bavarian program with a big brass band and yodeling," writes reader A. L. Witmer of South Haven, Michigan. "The Mathäser is also famous for its Bavarian breakfasts with weisswürste and beer."

Pschorr Bierhallen, 11 Neuhauserstrasse, is the showcase of the Pschorrbräu interests. It's a good place for both food and entertainment. Live music is played in the new wine cellar, St. Michael, from 7 p.m. until 1 a.m. The wine list provides 60 different varieties, and hot food is served until midnight. Actually, the Pschorrbräu offers a more toned-down introduction to a Bavarian beer restaurant than does, say, the Hofbräuhaus. The atmosphere is in a typical Bavarian motif, and the food is better than usually found in such places—and it's not expensively priced. For example, set lunches range from 12 DM ($6.88) to 18 DM ($10.32). The à la carte menu features soups from 2 DM ($1.15), a very luxurious steak, peppersteak flambé, costing 22 DM ($12.62).

Löwenbräu-Stuben, 2 Nymphenburgerstrasse. This beer hall should be better known. Admittedly, it's somewhat removed from the center of town yet it offers one of the best gemütlich evenings in Munich. It's especially festive when dances are held on Saturdays in the Festsaal. Main dishes begin as low as 3.70 DM ($2.12), going up to 21 DM ($12.05). On the à la carte menu, a typical main dish would be sauerbraten with dumplings and red cabbage, costing only 9.50 DM ($5.45). In summer, such Bavarian specialties are served in the open-air beer garden.

THE TOP NIGHTCLUB: The **Bayerischer Hof,** 6 Promenadeplatz. The ground-floor cellar nightclub of this deluxe hotel offers the most gilt-edged entertainment in Munich. The orchestras are the smoothest in town—and so is the clientele. Dancing goes on in front of the bandstand (the combo wisely varies the pace from fast to slow); some of the tables are placed above the dance floors, others are right in the center of the action. Large drinks are served, with most whiskeys averaging around 10.50 DM ($6.03) to 12 DM ($6.88) a drink.

The club opens at 8 p.m., then the action builds until it probably rocks the rice in the adjoining Trader Vic's.

Der Marco Polo Night Club, München Hilton, 7 am Tucherpark (tel. 34-00-51), offers revue and nightclub entertainment where you can order either dinner or drinks as well. It's one of the most prestigious show spots in Germany, featuring international performers. Usually entertainers are imported from such places as France, Italy, Spain, or Brazil. Guests pay a cover charge of 5 DM ($2.87) per person. You can see the show from the bar, although most guests ask for a table. The same selective menu of the Hilton's grill room is also available to Der Marco Polo guests. If no group is performing and only music is played for dancing, the cover charge is waived.

FAVORITE BARS: St. James Club, 10 Briennerstrasse, is dark and cozy, slightly British in atmosphere, as befits its name. The choice of drinks is wide—and so are the prices. Most libations are in the 10-DM ($5.74) to 12-DM ($6.88) range. A small combo plays every night except Sunday. You'll meet a really nice crowd of professional people here.

Less sophisticated than the former, the **Bongo Bar,** 33 Färbergraben, is in a cellar, with revolving dance floors. A floor show is often featured with striptease. More clients drink beer here than hard liquor at a minimum cost of 6 DM ($3.44).

Harry's New York Bar, 9 Falkenturmstrasse (tel. 222-700), lies in the heart of Munich, near the Hofbräuhaus. All the members of the "International Bar Flies" of the world pay an obligatory visit here when in Munich. It takes its name from the first American bar in Paris on "Sank Roo Doe Noo." The German bar continues the tradition of mixing very fortifying drinks which feature concoctions based on the original recipes. They include the Sidecar cocktail, created in 1931, costing 9.80 DM ($5.64), and the Monkey's Gland, created in 1930, also costing 9.80 DM. Attentive waiters will bring you simple food items as well, including chili con carne at 6 DM ($3.44); tomato cream soup with vodka, 4.50 DM ($2.58); and a "BLT" (bacon, lettuce, and tomato sandwich), 5.50 DM ($3.15). The roast beef sandwich at 12 DM ($6.88) is another popular item. Beer is also available on tap at 3.90 DM ($2.19). The bar shuts down on Sundays, but opens otherwise at 4 p.m.

JAZZ: Domicile, 19 Leopoldstrasse, in the Schwabing district, is the main spot for jazz in Munich—in fact, it is one of perhaps three clubs in Europe that has jazz all year long. The best artists seem to perform there from late April through early October. Everything or everyone from big bands to solo performers can be seen until 4 a.m. Students and artists—lots of stags—are drawn to the place, a typical jazz cellar, its walls decorated with enlarged transparencies of many performing jazz artists, the work of Josef Werkmeister, a rich German who photographs for pleasure. On one recent night we enjoyed Slide Hampton, Bert Thomson, Billy Brooks, Carmel Jones, and Vince Benedetti. Whiskeys go for around 5 DM ($2.87) to 7.50 DM ($4.30), or open wine for the same price.

CABARETS: In Munich when you "come to the cabaret," you may end up at the ultramodern Drugstore at the corner of Feilitzschstrasse and Siegesstrasse, in the heart of Schwabing. There its upstairs club, **Scala,** offers a varied evening's entertainment that is likely to include folk, rock, country and blues, a cabaret show, jazz, even occasional drag acts. Shows are nightly (except Mondays) at 8, and advance tickets can be purchased at the kiosk for either

12 DM ($6.88) or 16 DM ($9.18), plus a 10% surcharge. If you don't want to buy the tickets in advance, you can take your chance at the door where you'll avoid the 10% surcharge. Once inside, you'll find drinks priced at 2 DM ($1.15) each.

Nearby, **Schwabinger Podium,** 1 Wagnerstrasse, offers different entertainment nightly. A lot of "rockers" appear here. Some nights are devoted to jazz, although on other occasions we've been entertained by Dixieland as well as rock. Hours are from 8 p.m. to 1 a.m., and beer is priced at 3.30 DM ($1.92), whiskey at 6 DM ($3.44).

DISCO: **East Side,** 30 Rosenheimerstrasse, is the most popular disco in Munich and one of the best. Near the München Penta Hotel, the disco has some of the finest and most effective lights and sounds in Germany. The club caters to a select clientele, and on most nights the patrons are fairly well dressed. There's a policy, for example, against wearing jeans to the club. Your first drink is expensively priced at 12 DM ($6.88), and there are no reductions for your second or third libation. The setting is modern in the extreme.

OLD MUNICH: **Walter Novak,** 11 Occamstrasse (tel. 34-72-89), deep in the heart of Schwabing, is the closest approximation Munich has of suggesting a club that might have existed in Berlin in the heady days of the 1920s. Lotte Lenya isn't around the premises, but fine singers perform nightly. Occasionally, German folk songs are sung, and the atmosphere is vibrant and lively. The entrance is free, and you may want to order Novak's famous onion soup at 5.20 DM ($2.98), even though after eating it you may never know the secret of why it's famous. Beer begins at 3.75 DM ($2.15), a standard scotch whiskey at 4.50 DM ($2.58). Go after 10 p.m.

Alter Simpl, 57 Türkenstrasse (tel. 28-72-42), was once a literary cafe, taking its name from a satirical revue in 1903. There is no one around anymore who remembers that revue, but Alter/Simpl remained on the scene and was made famous by its mistress, Kathi Kobus. She went on to become a legend, but even she is no longer with it. Today, Toni Netzle runs the show, which is staged daily, except Sunday, from 8 p.m. to 3 a.m. Once Lale Andersen, who made "Lili Marlene" famous in World War II, frequented the cafe whenever she was in Munich. Whiskey ranges in price from 7 DM ($4.02) to 10 DM ($5.74), although gin is only 6 DM ($3.44). You can dine here as well, perhaps selecting a bowl of soup at 4 DM ($2.29), followed by a main meat dish at 12 DM ($6.88).

THE CASINO BLITZ: Although it may seem contradictory after recommending so much nightlife, you can spend your best evening in Bavaria just by taking the Casino Blitz bus to the fashionable alpine resort of Garmisch-Partenkirchen. (For a detailed description of the attractions of this southern Bavarian town, see Chapter IX.)

The Blitz Bus leaves from a side of the railway station (facing the station, it'll be on your right). The bus stop is more or less opposite the Hotel Deutscher Kaiser. It departs Monday through Friday at 5:15 p.m., returning to Munich at 11 p.m. On weekends and holidays, the departure time is 2 p.m. and the return time is the same. The round-trip fare is 10 DM ($5.74).

The bus takes you to the Casino at Garmisch-Partenkirchen, although you're under no obligation to play the roulette tables. Rather, you can explore the town, have dinner, and do some shopping. But at some point in your trip, you must make an apperance at the Casino to have your ticket validated. The Casino, incidentally, opens at 4 p.m. You must be 21 years old to enter, and able to prove it with a passport.

THEATERS, OPERA, AND CONCERTS: Perhaps nowhere else in Europe, other than London and Paris, will you find so many orchestras and artists performing. And the good news is the low cost of the seats—so count on indulging yourself and going to concerts several times. Seats often start at 7 DM ($4.02) for the higher balcony perches. You'll get good tickets if you're willing to pay anywhere from 12 DM ($6.88) to 20 DM ($11.47). Finally, you may want to consider standing room, around 4 DM ($2.29).

Practically any night of the year, you'll find a performance at the **National Theater,** on Max-Joseph-Platz (tel. 21-85-1), the home of the Bavarian State Opera. The Germans give their hearts, perhaps, their souls, to opera. Productions are beautifully mounted and presented. Tickets may be purchased weekdays from 10 a.m. to 1 p.m., 4 to 6 p.m., and one hour before each performance (during the weekend, only on Saturdays from 10 a.m. to 1 p.m.). For ticket information, telephone 22-13-16.

The regular season of the **Deutsches Theatre,** 13 Schwanthalerstrasse (tel. 59-29-11), lasts between March and June and July to December. Although closed at the moment, it is slated to reopen in time for Carnival in January 1981. Musicals are popular, but operettas and classical plays are performed as well. It is the only theater in Germany which is both a theater and a ballroom. During the "Carnival Season" in January and February, the seats are removed and stored away, replaced by tables and chairs for more than 2000 guest. Handmade decorations by artists combined with lighting effects create an enchanting ambience. Waiters serve wine, champagne, and food. There are costume balls and official black tie festivals, famous throughout Europe.

Staatstheater am Gärtnerplatz, 3 Gärtnerplatz (tel. 2-60-32-32), is yet another theater where the presentations are varied and entertaining. The program includes anything from ballet, to opera, operettas, and musicals. The ticket office is open during the same hours as those of the National Theater.

Altes Residenztheater (Cuvilliés Theater), in the Residenz (entrance at 1 Residenzstrasse; tel. 29-68-36), is a sightseeing attraction in its own right. The Bavarian State Opera and the Bayerisches Staatsschauspiel perform smaller works here in keeping with the more intimate character of the unique baroque architecture of the tiny theater. Ticket hours are the same as those for the National Theater. Nearby, the **Residenz Theater,** 1 Max-Joseph-Platz (tel. 22-57-54), features plays, comedies, and dramas in its Bayerisches Staatsschauspiel. The price of seats ranges from 8 DM ($4.59) to 34 DM ($19.50). The **Münchner Theater in der Briennerstrasse,** 50 Briennerstrasse (tel. 52-19-07), is yet another theater, presenting light musical productions.

If you speak German, you'll find at least 20 theaters offering plays of every description: classic dramas, comedies, experimental, contemporary—take your pick. The best way to find what current productions might interest you is to go to a theater ticket agency. The most convenient one is at the railway station, opposite Track 21. You'll see theater, concert, and opera posters on the wall, and can save time and energy by purchasing your tickets here.

Special mention should be made of a few unusual theaters: **Intimes Theater im Künstlerhaus,** 8 Lenbachplatz (tel. 55-34-80), where you are likely to see a production by Jean-Paul Sartre; **FTM-Freies Theater München,** 9 Wörthstrasse (tel. 45-58-13), which might show a production by Peter Handke one day, one by Bertolt Brecht the next; and the **Münchner Marionetten**

Theater, 29a Blumenstrasse (tel. 26-57-12), where you can attend puppet shows and the théâtre de marionnettes. Adults as well as children are delighted with these productions.

Finally, not to be ignored is the **Circus Krone,** 43 Marstrasse (tel. 55-81-66). It might be compared to London's Albert Hall, its productions are so varied. One night, a jazz festival; the next night, a hard rock concert; yet another night, gospel singers; and December 25 to March 31, a circus-show every night.

5. Some Notes on Shopping

The most interesting shops are concentrated on Munich's pedestrians-only street, lying between Karlsplatz and Marienplatz at the Rathaus. In general, Munich is the most varied shopping city in Germany, with merchandise-loaded shops lining many intriguing streets.

Rosenthal, 8 Theatinerstrasse, near the City Hall, attracts everybody from the pope to Queen Juliana of the Netherlands. Several factories in Bavaria combine to produce this high-quality china. In this Munich outlet, china, crystal, and cutlery are for sale, along with such prestigious names as Arabia from Finland. You might expect the merchandise to be high after all those legendary stories of Arab oil magnates purchasing dinner sets. However, you'll save about 50% of what you would at home by shopping at this fashionable Munich store. Traditional dinner sets begin at $75 and can go up into the thousands. Many gifts are also available.

In optical goods, Germany has been known since the birth of that industry. For contact lenses and other eye aids, we'd suggest you patronize **Söhnges,** 7 Briennerstrasse.

Germany's cameras are magnificent, and Leica is perhaps the most famous name. The shop of **Kohlroser,** 14 Maffeistrasse, carries a good assortment of cameras and equipment. The location is within an easy walk of the Hotel Bayerischer Hof and American Express. Look also for the Minox cameras (sometimes referred to humorously as "spy cameras"). The staff is extremely friendly. They're so democratic they even carry Japanese cameras as well.

Dirndl Ecke, 4 Platzl, across from the famous Hofbräuhaus, gets our unreserved recommendation as a stylish shop specializing in high-grade dirndls, feathered Alpine hats, and all clothing associated with the Alpine regions. Everything sold here is of fine quality—there is no tourist junk. The chic Salzburg dirndls sell for around 500 DM ($286.80); blouses with regional designs, around 90 DM ($51.62). Wide-brimmed felt hats begin at 125 DM ($71.70), and for plumage you'll pay another 85 DM ($48.76). Other merchandise includes needlework hats, beaded belts, and pleated shirts for men. You may also be attracted to the stylish capes. The shop is open weekdays from 9 a.m. to 6 p.m. (Saturdays, 9 to 1).

Galerie Weber, 11 Maximilianstrasse (tel. 29-29-88), is an elegant little shop selling original antique paintings as well as antiques. But as a side line, Frau Weber has imported silk dresses from Italy and France which she sells at low prices. All these dresses are by name designers, and the display attracts many a well-dressed, taste-conscious Munich woman.

For folk art and handicrafts, **Wallach,** 3 Residenzstrasse (tel. 22-08-71), is preferred. In fact, we consider it the finest place in Germany to obtain handicrafts, both newly made and antique. It can save much time in your search for a memorable object which will remind you of your trip to Germany. You'll find such items as antique churns, old kitchen ware, brass hunting horns, rag rug lengths sold by the yard, paintings on glass, charmingly hand-painted wooden boxes and trays, milking stools, painted porcelain clocks, wooden wall clocks, doilies, napkins, and towels.

Kunsthandlung Timberg, 15 Maximilianstrasse (tel. 29-52-35), in the central shopping mall, has the best collection of new and antique Meissen and Dresden porcelain. It's almost a miniature museum. Look for both an old or new Meissener coffee set with the blue-and-white onion design. The shop has outlets to Dresden porcelain denied to other retail stores. Important: Any purchase here can be packed and shipped safely. They've had a lot of experience in doing just that.

Ludwig Back am Rathauseck, am Marienplatz (tel. 22-82-64), is a two-level shopping bazaar selling handmade crafts from all over Germany, both old and new. You'll find it a feast of tasteful, colorful items to purchase. Items offered for sale include decorative pottery and dishes, beer steins and vases of etched glass, painted wall plaques depicting rural scenes, or decorative flower arrangements. There is much unusual kitchenware, colored flatware, calico hot pads and towels, plus a stunning collection of leather-trimmed canvas purses that are chicly casual.

READER'S SHOPPING SUGGESTION: "Your readers can find superb small wooden gifts to bring home, very reasonable, of light weight, if they ever go to Germany during the Christmas holidays and when they can shop in the tents of city squares called **'Kristkindermarkt'** at Munich" (William J. O'Dwyer, Fairfield, Conn.).

Chapter IV

THE SPA COUNTRY

1. **Bad Pyrmont**
2. **Bad Wildungen**
3. **Wiesbaden**
4. **Bad Nauheim**
5. **Bad Homburg**
6. **Bad Wiessee**
7. **Bad Reichenhall**
8. **Bad Neuenahr**
9. **Bad Oeynhausen**
10. **Bad Kissingen**

EVEN IF YOU WANDER into the most out-of-the-way places in Germany, you'll never get away from the greatest of all Teutonic institutions—the spa. With dozens of them spread throughout the country, these resorts have been as much a part of German life as beer and sausages. Some of the spas have been known since Roman times, while others are of much more recent vintage, but they all have one thing in common—"healing" waters.

These waters vary much more than just hot or cold. From seawater to thermal or radioactive springs, the Germans have learned to make the best use of all types of water for all types of ailments. The famous Kneipp treatment, commonly called hydrotherapy, was formulated by a Bavarian pastor, and through this man-made water treatment, natural mineral springs are no longer a prerequisite for the establishment of a spa. Thus, spas exist in every imaginable location, from seaside resorts to mountaintops in the Bavarian Alps.

But Germans vacation in the spas for more than just taking the waters. Between mud baths and hydrotherapy, they have a wide range of activities and facilities from which to choose. From the casinos in Baden-Baden, Bad Homburg, and Westerland, to golf courses and horse racing, there's never a dull moment during the busy summer spa season. Some of the larger spas are active all year.

In this chapter we will sample some of the variety to be found among the spas—it really would take a massive volume devoted solely to spas to cover the whole subject. In addition to the ten spas detailed in this chapter, you will find other important German resorts, such as Baden-Baden, Bad Godesberg, and Westerland, in separate chapters of this book.

1. Bad Pyrmont

This attractive spa has enjoyed a notable reputation for more than 2000 years! Its springs are of different kinds, from the brine variety in the fields to the medicinal iron waters on the southern side of the valley of the Weser Hills. In the center of town, you can drink a medicinal cocktail from the fountain at the Hyllige Born spring. Another popular pastime is taking mud baths. But Bad Pyrmont is a good place to vacation even if you don't come just to take the waters. Horseback riding in the hills, hiking, tennis, and swimming, as well as concerts and live shows, make the resort a lively place, a sort of German Tunbridge Wells.

The spa gardens are among the most beautiful in Germany, with little temples, flowering trees, and even a palm garden—an unusual touch in the temperate climate. The concert house in the Kurpark produces live shows during the busy summer. At night, the central promenade is glamorously lit, giving the spa a festive air, while guests sit out at sidewalk tables drinking beer.

ACCOMMODATIONS AND FOOD: Several fine possibilities exist in Bad Pyrmont, some with real historic atmosphere.

Hotel Fürstenhof, 328 Brunnenplatz (tel. 50-94), is virtually a museum of rare and beautiful antiques. It's been an exclusive hotel for 200 years, and in the same family for the past century. The ornate exterior, featuring long wrought-iron, double-level verandas, is as captivating as the interior, crowded with a remarkable collection of antiques, mostly Biedermeier and Chippendale. Rare Oriental carpets and rich tapestries add to the luxury of the salon and dining room.

The hotel is open from March to October, and offers first-class rooms and service (there's an English-speaking hostess) at reasonable prices. Bathless singles range from 40 DM ($22.94) to 50 DM ($28.68); bathless doubles, from 60 DM ($34.42) to 80 DM ($45.89). Singles with bath go for 60 DM ($34.42) to 70 DM ($40.15); doubles range from 90 DM ($51.62) to 100 DM ($57.36). For a real treat, ask for Queen Luise's room (she stayed here three times), in white and gold, with her portrait over the bed. Better yet, ask for Room 25 where Napoleon once slept. For 14.50 DM ($8.32) to 17.50 DM ($10.04), you can order a complete lunch, perhaps a cream soup Du Barry, followed by a pork filet Fürstenhof with vegetables and sauteed potatoes, then red currants with cream. Dinner is only 18 DM ($10.32).

Park-Hotel Rasmussen, 8 Hauptallee (tel. 44-85), is a completely renovated villa right in the heart of Bad Pyrmont, on the traffic-free promenade mall. The spacious rooms are well furnished. The beds are comfortable, and many rooms have balconies overlooking the promenade. Prices are 95 DM ($54.49) for a double with bath, 60 DM ($34.42) for a single with bath. The staff of the hotel is pleasant, although a wee bit formal for some tastes.

The hotel's restaurant, by the way, serves the best food in town. Set lunches in the quiet dining room overlooking the mall range from 18 DM ($10.32) to 28 DM ($16.06). In the evening, diners are offered a more expensive array of dishes, including trout au bleu at 20.50 DM ($11.76) and wild game for two at 42 DM ($24.09). The bar adjoining the dining room has a clublike atmosphere.

Next to Rasmussen is the **Cafe Park Hotel Konditorei,** at Hauptallee, which is a social gathering point in town. It has attractive outside tables on the mall and offers set lunches for 13.90 DM ($7.97) to 18.50 DM ($10.61). The cookery is very traditionally German.

2. Bad Wildungen

The healing mineral springs of Bad Wildungen have long attracted northern Europeans to the rolling hills and deep forests of the Waldeck region southwest of Kassel. Thousands of visitors flock here annually, seeking treatment for kidney and gall bladder disorders, or simply for the rest and relaxation combined with the spa's numerous cultural activities.

The spa gardens are well planned, augmenting the natural wooded surroundings with carefully planted flowers from all parts of the world, and several attractive buildings, including two bandshells where frequent outdoor concerts are given. The modern horseshoe-shaped arcade houses the Georg-Viktor spring, as well as several exclusive shops and a small auditorium. Lawn chairs are placed throughout the grounds for the convenience and comfort of the strollers. Admission to the Kurpark is 2 DM ($1.15).

Bad Wildungen itself is more than 700 years old. Rising above the Old Town (Altstadt) is the massive tower of the 14th-century church (Stadtkirche), the most impressive structure—and the oldest—in the town. The highlight of the church is not its interesting hallenkirche architecture, however, as much as its remarkable **Niederwildungen Altarpiece,** one of the best examples of early German painting. The wing-paneled altarpiece, painted in 1403 by Master Konrad von Soest, contains a large dramatic scene of the Crucifixion, flanked by six smaller scenes, depicting the birth, passion, and resurrection of Christ. The work shows an obvious French influence in the use of delicate colors and figures, made even more dramatic by the use of actual gold. The colors seem even more striking in contrast to the simple drab interior of the church.

THE TOP HOTEL: Staatliches Badehotel, in the Kurpark (tel. 40-61), has the most enviable position for a spa hotel—right at the entrance to the gardens, in the center of the clinical and cultural activities.

Evoking the grandeur of another era, the Badehotel is large and rambling, branching out in two great wings from the circular domed entrance. Aside from the standard conveniences of a fine hotel, it has its own private clinic and sanitorium, providing every imaginable diagnostic and therapeutic device, including carbon dioxide baths, massages, and complete medical attention by a fine professional staff.

The hotel's 74 rooms (43 more in the sanitorium) are large, sunlit, and airy, all with views of the Waldeck woodlands and spa gardens. The furnishings are sleek, comfortable, modern, and kept spotless by an efficient staff. Prices of rooms vary according to size and location. Bathless singles are 43 DM ($24.66); with bath, 85 DM ($48.76). Bathless doubles cost 82 DM ($47.04), rising to 150 DM ($86.04) with complete bath. Room rates include breakfast, service, tax, and use of the large indoor heated pool. Garage facilities are available.

The hotel's restaurant is just what the doctor ordered—that is, if you're not worried about calories. Special diets are available, but the menu offers with a tempting array that nearly everyone cheats at least once. Veal dishes are the specialty, and the kalbsschnitzel (veal scallops) cooked with herbs is a tasty choice for 22 DM ($12.62). Other dishes include trout au bleu at 18 DM ($10.32); filet of sole, 24 DM ($13.77); and nasi-goreng, at 24 DM also. A carafe of Mosel Valley wine costs 5 DM ($2.87).

3. Wiesbaden

This famous health resort has been firmly entrenched in a sheltered valley between the Rhine and the Taunus Mountains since it was first settled in Roman times. Part of its success as a spa is due, of course, to the 27 hot springs whose temperature ranges from 117° to 150°F, but its proximity to Germany's largest cities and transportation centers, such as Frankfurt, is what has made Wiesbaden the most international of spas.

Today, Wiesbaden competes with Baden-Baden as Germany's most fashionable resort. It is also one of the most important cultural centers in the country. Every May, it plays host to the **International Festival of Music, Ballet, and Drama,** when the best foreign companies perform operatic and dramatic works in German, French, and English.

There is still much of the turn-of-the-century splendor that goes with a fashionable resort city. In the Bath Quarter of Wiesbaden, around the Kurhaus and Brunnenkolonnade, most of the cultural activities of the theater and concert season take place. The **Brunnenkolonnade** is a magnificent pillared structure housing fountains fed by two of the spa's most famous springs, the Kochbrunnen and Faulbrunnen. Concert and exhibition halls are also enclosed within its walls.

The major concert halls are in the **Kurhaus,** a big, lively structure centering around an impressive cupola-crowned hall which opens into rooms in all directions. One of the smaller halls houses the **Casino,** offering the gambler an alternative to concerts from 3 on every afternoon. Roulette and baccarat are the main games played here all year.

If you prefer the outdoors, Wiesbaden offers horseback riding, excellent golf courses, swimming, tennis, and hiking. The streets of the city are enjoyable if you like to ramble about. The spa park is attractive, with old shade trees surrounding a lake. It is especially beautiful at night when the lights of the spa and the huge fountain in the lake are reflected in the water.

THE TOP HOTELS: Schwarzer Bock (Black Goat), 12 Kranzplatz (tel. 38-21), is a tradition in the area, tracing its history back to 1486. Most of its public rooms are a treasure house of Teutonic architecture and filled with antiques—Empire, Biedermeier, and Louis XVI. It's a world of wood paneling, gilt, and crystal. If you like cozy nooks, then this is your hotel. For example, the oak-paneled drinking salon lies under an ornate wood ceiling. Then there's the Chinese tea room, with screens, lanterns, vases, and a teak dragon table. The rustic tavern with an open grill is a preferred dining spot, although Le Capricorne is more elegant.

Two hundred of the bedrooms have private baths; many rooms contain television sets, radios, and air conditioning. The most sought-after accommodations are those opening onto views of the sunpocket patio. On the whole, the bedroom furnishings are traditionally Germanic and comfortable. Singles with bath go for 125 DM ($71.70); doubles with complete bath, 190 DM ($108.98). These rates include breakfast. Behind the scenes is a thermal bathhouse, with a Japanese swimming pool. In addition, there's an indoor pool, plus the usual spa facilities, including an exercise room, massage parlor, and thermal tub baths. To wind down after all this strenuous activity, guests retreat to the roof-garden terrace.

Nassauer Hof, 3–4 Kaiser-Friedrich-Platz (tel. 3-96-81), is an old favorite with modern conveniences. Recent renovations have maintained the baroque facade, but the interior has been completely modernized. With the recent addition of two new restaurants, this hotel now ranks with the most appealing in Germany. Die Pfanne features local German specialties in a rustic atmosphere at moderate prices, while Die Ente vom Lehel boasts some of the finest deluxe fare on the continent. The cozy Kamin Bar features an open fireplace and piano entertainment. The staff provides cordial service in understandable English, and the spacious rooms feature bath, TV, and stocked mini-bar. Singles range between 125 DM ($71.70) and 185 DM ($106.12); twins, between 165 DM ($94.64) and 225 DM ($129.06)—including service and tax. The hotel stands in the city center, within walking distance of Kurhaus gambling casino, State Opera and Theatre, spa, and the shopping area. There is hourly bus service to and from the nearby Frankfurt airport.

MEDIUM-PRICED HOTELS: The **Hotel Bären**, 3 Bärenstrasse (tel. 30-10-21), is standard modern, lying only a three-minute walk from the Schloss and the Marktkirche (Market Church), as well as the Kurhaus. The bedrooms are clean, efficiently appointed, and comfortable. A bathless single costs 45 DM ($25.81); with private bath or shower, 58 DM ($33.27). Two persons pay 78 DM ($44.74) in a bathless double; 98 DM ($56.21) in a double with private bath, these tariffs including breakfast, service, and the use of the thermal swimming pool. A sun-simulator and other fitness equipment are at your disposal. The cocktail bar and the restaurant, König im Bären, take care of your material well-being.

Klee, 4 Parkstrasse (tel. 30-50-61), is the best choice for the voyager on a moderate budget. A square modern hotel, it is set in a tranquil position at the edge of a park and is surrounded by its own informal gardens. All of its bedrooms have French doors opening onto little balconies. Most of the accommodations have sitting areas—large enough for entertaining. The baths are colorfully tiled, many containing double sinks. A bathless single ranges in price from 45 DM ($25.81). A single with shower is from 55 DM ($31.55); with bath, 60 DM ($34.42) to 80 DM ($45.89). Doubles with a private bath range in price from 92 DM ($51.62) to 125 DM ($71.70). These prices include service and taxes. You can have a buffet breakfast (the only meal served) on the garden terrace or in the dignified salon. The cost is 11 DM ($6.31). Guests will find a pleasantly furnished cafe and restaurant, where French-style food is served. A comfortable bar in the English style offers a fine ambience for an evening drink. The Klee is highly recommended for those who find the older, superluxurious hotels a bit too monumental.

Aukamm-Hotel, 31 Aukamm-Allee (tel. 5-68-41), built in 1970, is a well-situated and well-run hotel in this spa district, offering 160 comfortably furnished hotel rooms and apartments, each with a private bath, balcony, phone, radio, and upon request, a TV set. The rate for a twin-bedded room, including breakfast, is 162 DM ($92.93). In a single, expect to pay 105 DM ($60.23), also including breakfast, service charge, and taxes. The hotel lies only 30 minutes by car from the Frankfort airport and 15 minutes from the Rhine steamer pier.

BUDGET HOTELS: **Goldenes Ross,** 7–9 Goldgasse (tel. 30-30-67), is a pleasant, old-fashioned hotel in the center of Wiesbaden. An open courtyard for breakfast or tea, the splendidly furnished hotel-bar, Esquire Club, and a typical weinstube, add to the comfort of this small, informal, and somewhat haphazardly furnished town inn. Forget about private baths. However, in the basement is a bath house with hot springs suitable for showers or bathing. A single room ranges in price from 28 DM ($16.06) to 35 DM ($20.08), with doubles going for anywhere from 60 DM ($34.42) to 68 DM ($39). The rates vary according to the size and situation of the accommodations and include a good buffet breakfast and service.

Stadmitte, 9 Neugasse (tel. 30-08-00), is where you are welcomed by innkeepers Awe and Schneider. Guests are accommodated in their small, modest hotel at low rates. The simply furnished rooms are mainly without private baths or showers. Rates for the night, including breakfast, are 32 DM ($18.36) in a bathless single, 60 DM ($34.42) in a bathless double. In a single with shower the tariff is 45 DM ($25.81), going up to 75 DM ($43.02) in a double with shower. The hotel's nice, modern restaurant, Mauerblümchen, serves meals beginning at 10 DM ($5.74).

Hotel Oranien (VCH), 2 Platterstrassee (tel. 3-98-91), is a 110-bed hotel belonging to a nationwide hospiz organization. Right in the center of the spa, close to the park, it offers rooms that are immaculate and rather plainly furnished with modern pieces. Singles with shower bath, toilet, and telephone cost 56 DM ($32.12); doubles, 86 DM ($49.33)—breakfast and taxes included.

READERS' PENSION SELECTION: "The **Pension Kranig,** 146 Rheingaustrasse (tel. 6-16-57), 6202 Wiesbaden-Biebrich, is the least expensive around—but it is extremely clean and hospitable. A breakfast with meat, egg, and bread is included. At the Wiesbaden Station, take bus 4 to Biebrich-Rhine River Boat Terminal. This point is the boat terminus for Rhine River steamers, and is extremely useful for Eurailpass holders, who can travel 'free' on the Europabus between Munich and Wiesbaden along the 'Romantic Road,' and wish to connect with a Rhine River steamer for the Wiesbaden-Cologne trip, which is also 'free' on Eurail. Singles range in price from 25 DM ($14.34) to 30 DM ($17.21); doubles, from 46 DM ($26.39) to 52 DM ($29.83). The house has five bathrooms. Lunch and dinner are available for all guests" (Phil and Sherry Guarino, Rockford, Ill.).

READERS' HOTEL SELECTION: "We found the **Hotel Meuser,** 13 Stettinerstrasse (tel. 2-15-48), where we had a delightful double room for only 34 DM ($19.50). Singles cost 25 DM ($14.34). It is close to the dock (about 1½ blocks) and is reached by walking across the street, after debarking from a Rhine River steamer, up Wilhelm Koppstrasse, taking a diagonal right at the first intersection onto Stettinerstrasse. The proprietor, Willy Meuser, speaks a little English, but his daughter is fluent" (Jon and Karol Shafer, Enfield, Conn.).

THE TOP RESTAURANT: **Kesseler's Mutter Engel** ("Mother Angel"), 5 Bärenstrasse (tel. 30-10-44), offers the best food at the spa. It's an intimate and elegant restaurant with high cuisine standards and top-rate atmosphere and service. The aura is definitely sophisticated, with a liberal use of antiques and the pleasant touch of flowers placed on every table. Lobster, priced according to weight (even a tiny one is very expensive), is the specialty of the chef. He also does many moderately priced dishes exceedingly well. Three specialties include veal steak Cordon Bleu at 28 DM ($16.06); sole Colbert at 34 DM ($19.50); and oxtail in Madeira, 23 DM ($13.19). The wine list is quite reasonable. Mutter Engel is especially popular with visiting Yankees.

BUDGET DINING: The **Ratskeller,** 7 Markstrasse (tel. 30-13-13), is like a vaulted temple cellar, with tables set in recesses. You dine in high-backed chairs or on wooden settles. The cellar is informal, serving good basic food that makes it the outstanding choice for those on a limited budget. The restaurant is popular with families, shoppers, and business people. Although the service is somewhat helter-skelter, you're served soup practically before you sit down at lunch—even if you never eat soup! A large choice of dishes is offered, international in scope, although there are no set meals. Veal piccata costs 15.60 DM

($8.95). A more economical dish is bauern bratwursten with sauerkraut at 7.80 DM ($4.47). Chopped steak starts at a low 6 DM ($3.44), and beer at 2.40 DM ($1.38) accompanies most dishes. Desserts range from 2.50 DM ($1.43) to 8 DM ($4.59).

4. Bad Nauheim

Like many similar spas throughout Germany, Bad Nauheim grew popular in the early part of this century when the railroad became a convenient and inexpensive means of transportation. Still going strong today, the resort at the northern edge of the Taunus Mountains is a center for golf, tennis, and water sports, as well as the beginning point for energetic hikers to scale the 773-foot Johannisberg, towering over the town.

The warm carbonic acid springs of the spa are said to be particularly beneficial in the treatment of heart and circulatory disorders. The Kurpark is attractive, well-maintained, and filled with promenaders all summer long.

In accommodations, Bad Nauheim offers a number of hotels that sprouted up in an era gone by to cater to the turn-of-the-century crowds who flocked to take the waters.

THE TOP HOTEL: Hilberts Parkhotel, 2–4 Kurstrasse (tel. 31-945), a Wilhelmian hotel under a mammoth mansard roof, is the leading hotel in Bad Nauheim and one of the best known spa hotels in Germany. Right in the center of town, it shares a parklike setting with an old church. One side fronts a commercial street, but otherwise the rooms open onto stately views of park and trees.

The interior of the hotel has been completely modernized in a style contrasting to the architecture. Everyone meets in the L-shaped garden room for armchair breakfasts. There's even an indoor-outdoor dance floor.

The rooms, many with terraces, are furnished with comfortable, modern pieces. Bathless singles range from 42 DM ($24.09) to 52 DM ($29.83); bathless doubles, from 68 DM ($39) to 80 DM ($45.89). Singles with private bath are 72 DM ($41.30) to 78 DM ($44.74); doubles, 96 DM ($55.07) to 145 DM ($83.17). The prices include breakfast as well as service and tax, but you may take all your meals in the hotel's fine restaurant.

A MEDIUM-PRICED HOTEL: Blume's Hotel am Kurhaus, 3 Auguste-Viktoria-Strasse (tel. 20-72), is a huge classic-style villa, especially recommended for its tranquil setting in a residential district at the edge of the spa gardens. The furnishings are a mixture of modern and traditional. Many of the rooms have terraces, but those with the best views go quickly and are usually reserved in advance. The inclusive prices are quite reasonable, ranging from 35 DM ($20.08) to 50 DM ($28.68) per person, depending on the type of bath and location. Full pension rates range from 55 DM ($31.55) to 70 DM ($40.15) per person per day. Interesting food is served in the dining room, which has a baronial fireplace straight out of a castle.

THE BUDGET HOTELS: Rosenau, 1 Steinfurtherstrasse (tel. 8-11-55), is more of a family-style pension than a hotel. It is kept tidy, with rooms that are adequate, but sparsely furnished. Singles cost as little as 21 DM ($12.05), although you'll pay 34 DM ($19.50) with a bath or shower. Doubles with toilets go for 40 DM ($22.94), rising to 70 DM ($40.15) with bath or shower, breakfast included. Closed from mid-December to January 10.

Hotel-Restaurant Gaudes, 6 Hauptstrasse (tel. 25-08), is known mainly for its restaurant, but it offers eight rooms (no baths) at a cost of 29 DM ($16.63) in a single, from 54 DM ($30.97) in a double, breakfast included. Even if you don't stay here, you might want to patronize the dining room. The rumpsteak (entrecôte) goes for 19 DM ($10.90) per person. The mixed grill is 44 DM ($25.24) for two persons.

Christliches Hospiz "Bethel," 10–12 Lindenstrasse (tel. 45-82), is by far the best bargain at Bad Nauheim. This converted old mansion is not only comfortable, but gives a special welcome to foreign visitors. Everything is kept in good shape and is immaculately clean. A single ranges in price from 26 DM ($14.91) to 34 DM ($19.50). A double with bath goes from 52 DM ($29.83) to 70 DM ($40.15). No rooms have private baths.

WHERE TO DINE: Staatliches Kurhaus, 12 Terrassenstrasse, right in the spa gardens, is the best place to dine outside the Hilberts Parkhotel. It's a modern restaurant/cafe/weinstube combined, with outdoor tables overlooking the gardens and and bandshell. No doubt you'll want to enjoy your four o'clock tea while the band plays Mozart. Set lunches range in price from 16 DM ($9.18) to 35 DM ($20.08). À la carte dishes include soups, in the 3.70-DM ($2.12) to 6.50-DM ($3.73) range, and veal steaks at 21 DM ($12.05). The Kurhaus has a classic interior, with dining on two levels, and a good Rhine wine cellar.

READER'S RESTAURANT SELECTION: "Paprikschell-Imbiss, 11 Karlstrasse, diagonally across the street from the Hotel Gaudes, is very economical. Available are hamburgers, french fries, as well as typical German wurst dishes. The wurst dishes begin at 2 DM ($1.15), and you can order brochettes at 6 DM ($3.44), even half a chicken at 4.50 DM ($2.58)" (Luther W. Hampton, Columbia, S.C.).

5. Bad Homburg

Just ten miles north of Frankfurt lies one of Germany's most attractive spas, still basking in the dreamy grandeur of turn-of-the-century Europe. Actually, Bad Homburg has been a popular watering spot since Roman times. Royalty from all over the world has visited the spa and left their mark. King Chulalongkorn, immortalized in *The King and I,* was so impressed by it that he built an exotic Siamese temple in the Kurpark. Czar Nicholas erected an onion-domed Russian chapel nearby. The name of the town itself was popularized by Edward VII of England, when, as Prince of Wales, he visited the spa and introduced a new hat style which he called the homburg.

The spa park is an oasis in the middle of a large, rather commercial town. The spa's saline springs are used in the treatment of various disorders, especially heart and circulatory diseases. The Kurpark extends into the foothills of the Taunus Mountains, stretching in front of the modern Kurhaus (resort center). The gardens are filled with brooks, ponds, and arbors.

The town became the gaming capital of Europe when the famous Blanc brothers opened the **Casino** in the Kurpark in 1841. Predating its offspring by 25 years, the "Mother of Monte Carlo" is especially popular in summer with white-suited Frankfurt industrialists. From 3 p.m., roulette and baccarat are the games people play here. Entrance fee is 5 DM ($2.87).

The **Bad Homburg Palace,** just a few short blocks from the spa gardens, was the residence of the landgraves of Hesse-Homburg from its construction in 1680 until the mid-19th century. Its builder, Prince Friedrich II von Homburg, preserved the still-standing White Tower of the medieval castle which had stood on that site, and incorporated it into the structure of the magnificent baroque palace. In the late 19th century, the palace became a summer residence for Prussian princes and kings.

The interior of the palace contains furniture and paintings of the 18th century, including a bust of Prince Friedrich II by Andreas Schluter, Germany's greatest baroque sculptor. The former "telephone room of the empress" includes a *Cleopatra* by Pellegrini. The palace and formal gardens are open daily from 10 a.m. to 6 p.m. in season, with guided tours every 40 minutes. Admission is 2 DM ($1.15).

Within the castle enclosure, next to the White Tower, is the **Landgrafen Restaurant,** with a weinstube on the floor below. The cafe-restaurant serves four or five daily specials, mostly typical German dishes such as bratwurst, fresh salmon poached in wine, or vension stew, from 9 DM ($5.16) to 18.50 DM ($10.61). Set meals include soup, although dessert is an extra 2.70 DM ($1.55) to 6 DM ($3.44). If you wish to have a low-cost meal, try the Landgrafen platter, a mixed grill, a real bargain at 11.50 DM ($6.60). You can stop off in the afternoon for drinks, wine beginning at 3.70 DM ($2.12), beer at 3 DM ($1.72). In summer you can dine on the wide terrace with a fine view of the castle grounds.

A MEDIUM-PRICED HOTEL: Hardtwald Hotel, Philosophenweg (tel. 2-94-70), is like a modern chalet set in a forest. Run by the Scheller family since 1868, the hotel is an ideal retreat near the spa gardens. The modestly furnished rooms were built to overlook the forest. Prices are reasonable, ranging from as low as 30 DM ($17.21) for a bathless single, to 96 DM ($55.07) for a double room with private bath and toilet. Full pension is available for 20 DM ($11.47) per person per day extra. And that may be the best bargain, as the hotel is especially noted for its fine food. The dining room, heavily planted with flowers, seems to do as much business as the hotel. In summer tables are set outdoors on the large patio.

A LOW-COST PENSION: Haus Fisher am Park, 12 Landgrafenstrasse (tel. 2-49-27), is a quiet and clean town house, with only 11 rooms for paying guests. For the spa, it's a real bargain. Bathless singles rent for 23 DM ($13.19) to 27 DM ($15.49). In a double with shower, the overnight rate ranges from 49 DM ($28.11) to 57 DM ($32.70); with shower and toilet, 62 DM ($35.56)—breakfast included. The location is quiet, facing Jubiläumspark.

A BUDGET RESTAURANT: Römerbrunnen, in the Kurpark, is traditional, with tables set outside on sunny days. The food is typically German and good. A two-course menu is offered for anywhere from 7.50 DM ($4.30) to 12 DM ($6.88). A quarter of a liter of beer costs 1.80 DM ($1.03).

READER'S RESTAURANT SELECTION: "Hotel zum Johannisberg, 5 Thomasstrasse. We had a very good dinner here, enjoying an inexpensive Cordon Bleu cuisine, a dinner costing 14 DM ($8.03) to 21 DM ($12.05). A quarter of a liter of beer costs 1.80 DM ($1.03)" (Nancy Gilbert, Alexandria, Va.).

6. Bad Wiessee

If you've always believed that the best medicine is the worst tasting, you should feel right at home in Bad Wiessee—the mineral springs of this popular spa on the Tegernsee are saturated with iodine and sulfur. But the other attractions of this small town more than make up for this small discomfort. Just 30 miles south of Munich, this spa—with a huge lake at its feet and towering Alps rising behind it—is an ideal year-round resort. In summer, swimming and boating are popular pastimes; in winter, you can ski on the slopes or skate on the lake.

The springs are used for the treatment of many diseases, including rheumatism and heart and respiratory conditions. Even though the town is small (population 4000), it is sophisticated in its medicinal facilities as well as in accommodations and restaurants. There's even a small gambling casino.

WHERE TO DINE: For an elegant dining adventure in this most fashionable Bavarian spa, call on the **Restaurant See Casino,** right at the Casino, 10 Bodenschneidstrasse (tel. 86-09). Actually, you may never look at the food on your plate, so intriguing is the view. The menu is in the international tradition, with occasional German specialties such as deer in season, a steak costing 22 DM ($12.62). Other fare includes such items as scampi Provençal, 20 DM ($11.47). Soups cost about 4.50 DM ($2.58), and desserts are in the 7.50-DM ($4.30) bracket. After dinner, you may want to pay an additional 6 DM ($3.44) to enter the Casino itself.

But if the Casino isn't for you, you can try a typically Bavarian experience by going to the **Hotel Resi von der Post,** 14 Zilcherstrasse (tel. 814-44). Inside, the atmosphere is bustling, especially at mealtimes with hungry diners who know they can get delicious fish from the lake for an average of 14.50 DM ($8.32). Other main courses are in the 10.50-DM ($6.02) to 18.50-DM ($10.61) range, with soups around 2 DM ($1.15). Desserts cost from 2.75 DM ($1.58) to 14 DM ($8.03), or you may want to sample a special cheese from the Tegernsee district, Miesbacher. Many of the guests show up in Bavarian costumes.

7. Bad Reichenhall

Only the most excellent German spas can call themselves Staatsbad, denoting supreme state approval. Bad Reichenhall bears that title with pride. This old salt town is the most important curative spa in the Bavarian Alps. Mountain chains surround it, protecting it from the winds; the town's brine springs, with a salt content of as much as 24%, are the most powerful saline springs in Europe. The combination of the waters and the pure air have made Bad Reichenhall a recognized spa for centuries, although it has been a source of salt for much longer—more than 2400 years.

In 1848, King Maximilian of Bavaria stayed here, doing much to popularize Bad Reichenhall as a fashionable resort. Today, visitors come from all over the world to take the waters of the salt springs, which are supposedly effective in the treatment of asthma and other respiratory ailments. Treatment sessions are almost exclusively in the mornings at the seven resort institutes, the therapy ranging from simply drinking the water to pneumato-therapy, and even electronic lungs for the most serious cases. But although Bad Reichenhall takes the medical side of the cure seriously, spa authorities encourage visitors to enjoy the many attractions in and around the town as well.

There's a wide choice of activities: from symphony concerts to folklore presentations. The State Gaming Rooms are popular, and the ideal climate permits a complete whirl of outdoor events, from hikes into the mountains to tennis tournaments. Incidentally, the spa gardens are unusual in that the sheltered location of the town amid the lofty Alps permits the growth of several varieties of tropical plants, giving the gardens a lush, exotic appearance.

WHAT TO SEE: The **Alte Saline** (Old Salt Works), just a short walk from the Kurgarten, is the home of the ancient industry responsible for the growth and prosperity of Bad Reichenhall from Celtic times to the present. Parts of the old plant still stand today, but most of it was reconstructed in the mid-19th century in the troubadour style by Ludwig I of Bavaria. The large pumps and huge marble caverns are impressive. Tours are provided daily from April 1 to October 31. Hours are from 10 to 11:30 a.m. and from 2 to 4 p.m. Admission is 4 DM ($2.29) for adults, 2 DM ($1.15) for children.

The great fire of 1834 destroyed much of the town of Bad Reichenhall, but many of the impressive churches of the town survived. One outstanding memorial is **St. Zeno**, a 12th-century Gothic church showing a later baroque influence. Its most remarkable feature is the painted interior, centering on the carved altarpiece of the *Coronation of the Virgin*.

THE TOP HOTELS: **Steigenberger Hotel Axelmannstein**, 2–4 Salzburger-strasse (tel. 40-01), occupies an excellent position in its own eight-acre garden, complete with swimming pools, in- and outdoor. An older hotel attracting a mature clientele, it offers many rooms with views of the encircling Bavarian Alps. Nearly all of the 156 well-furnished accommodations contain private baths. A single room without bath ranges in price from 41 DM ($23.52) to 55 DM ($31.55), increasing to anywhere from 71 DM ($40.73) to 97 DM ($55.64) with private bath. Double rooms with bath cost from 102 DM ($58.51) to 150 DM ($86.04). Prices include breakfast. In July, August, and September, a supplementary charge of 10% is added to all prices.

The dining room, opening onto a garden, attracts many nonresidents. The public rooms are traditionally furnished with antiques and reproductions, including some Gobelin tapestries. The most popular gathering point is the cozy wood-paneled drinking lounge. The Hotel Axelmannstein has a cure department, sauna, fitness center, tennis courts, mini-golf, cosmetic shop, and boccia.

Luisenbad, 33 Ludwigstrasse (tel. 50-81), is a world unto itself. It's an older hotel with a newer bedroom wing placed in a garden setting. Its most outstanding feature is its indoor swimming pool, with a glass wall bringing the outdoors inside. The lounges and atmosphere are invitingly homelike; nothing is austere here, as the emphasis is placed on informality and comfort. The new bedrooms are quite handsome, with bold colors and tasteful furnishings; most contain showers and baths. A bathless single ranges in price from 44 DM ($25.24) to 52 DM ($29.83), increasing to anywhere from 66 DM ($37.86) to 98 DM ($56.21) with bath. Bathless doubles are in the 78 DM ($44.74) to 98 DM ($56.21) category; with complete bath, 106 DM ($60.80) to 180 DM ($103.25). Pension terms are available, costing an extra 36 DM ($20.65) for full board. There are facilities for thermal baths, inhalations, massages, and mud baths, plus a Finnish sauna.

The food is among the best at the resort; a set luncheon runs to 24 DM ($13.77). Among the à la carte listings are such tempting items as hamburger crab soup with cognac at 4.80 DM ($2.75); chicken paprika, 19 DM ($10.90); and game specialties, 24 DM ($13.77) to 60 DM ($34.42) for two. A pianist plays from 7:30 p.m. daily.

A MEDIUM-PRICED HOTEL: Salzburger Hof, 7 Mozartstrasse (tel. 20-62), is the best buy if you're shopping for a moderately priced hotel. Although recently built and architecturally contemporary, most of the public rooms have been given an overlay of old Bavarian charm. Public lounges are sacrificed to make room for unique dining rooms and nooks. Best of all are the compact and refreshingly furnished bedrooms, most of which contain streamlined sofas, window desks, beds with built-in headboards, and armchairs placed around a breakfast table. All of the accommodations open onto tiny balconies, and all have baths. Single rooms with breakfast range in price from 54 DM ($30.97) to 74 DM ($42.45); doubles, from 88 DM ($50.48) to 108 DM ($61.95). Your hosts, the Helmun Herkommer family, speak English.

THE BUDGET RANGE: The ornate facade at **Brauerei Bürgerbräu**, Rathausplatz (tel. 24-11), features groups of dancers. Inside, much use is made of wood and stone, and the vaulted dining rooms have an ambience typical of the popular breweries of Bavaria. The food is good, copious, and inexpensive. A large range of dishes, costing from 6.75 DM ($3.87) to 19.50 DM ($11.19), is offered. An elevator whisks you to immaculately modern and functional bedrooms, with up-to-date plumbing. Offering perhaps the best bargain at the resort, the hotel charges 29 DM ($16.63) in a single without bath, increasing that to 40.50 DM ($23.23) with shower and toilet. Depending on the plumbing, doubles range from 58 DM ($33.27) to 78.50 DM ($45.03), including breakfast. The reception is on the second floor.

8. Bad Neuenahr

Lying in the foothills of the Eifel Mountains, near the confluence of the Ahr and Rhine Rivers, this modern spa has a mild climate and wide range of facilities suitable to the international clientele who gather here. Just 20 miles south of Bonn, Bad Neuenahr attracts a diplomatic crowd from the capital to its fashionable gambling casino, the largest in Germany. Roulette, baccarat, and blackjack are played here daily from 2 p.m. till 2 a.m.

Besides the modern spa installations, including facilities for the Kneipp hydrotherapy, Bad Neuenahr is a popular gathering spot for relaxation and sport. Business people often hold conferences here, combining decisions with golf, entertainment, fine food, and wines. The spa is also a good starting point for day trips and hiking expeditions into the Ahr Valley, one of the Rhine's most attractive tributaries. The river is lined with old wine villages, crumbling chateaus, and wooded hills.

THE TOP HOTEL: Steigenberger Kurhotel, 1 Kurgartenstrasse (tel. 22-91), is an old Wilhelmian hotel with a modern extension. When the newer wing was added, an interior decorator was given a free hand to create a completely contemporary look. This is especially reflected in the spacious bedrooms, containing adequate living space, plus sitting areas. A single room with toilet ranges in price from 49 DM ($28.11) to 57 DM ($32.70), increasing from 77 DM ($44.17) to 99 DM ($56.79) with a complete bath. Doubles with bath go for anywhere from 110 DM ($63.10) to 150 DM ($86.04). The chain hotel is right in the heart of the spa, 550 yards from the main station.

Guests are given a choice of dining places, including the Kupferkessel (Copper Kettle). The Pfeffermühle (Peppermill) is also popular, as are the Kurhaus Restaurant and the gambling casino. (The chef specializes in diets for diabetics, by the way.) Elaborate meals are offered, a four-course lunch going for 25 DM ($14.34), a four-course dinner for 30 DM ($17.21).

The spa facilities here are exceptional, including therapeutic installations, plus an indoor swimming pool with thermal water. Either in the lounge with a fireplace, or in the spacious awning-shaded sun terrace, the living at the Steigenberger is easy.

A BUDGET HOTEL: Giffels' Goldener Anker, 14 Mittelstrasse (tel. 23-86), is the second-largest hotel at the spa, lying on a quiet street only 100 yards from the Kurpark. Founded in 1869, it's still managed by the same family, and the present operators, the fourth generation, carry on with the same friendly and personalized manner that has always been a hallmark of the hotel. On one recent occasion, one of their "repeaters" admitted to having patronized the establishment for 45 years. The bedrooms are nicely furnished, with some of the rear accommodations featuring little private balconies. For overnight stays, bathless singles range in price from 30 DM ($17.21) to 35 DM ($20.08), increasing to anywhere from 47.50 DM ($27.25) to 55 DM ($31.55) with some sort of plumbing. Bathless doubles are tabbed at 55 DM ($31.55), rising to anywhere from 75 DM ($43.02) to 89.50 DM ($51.34) with plumbing, the higher price for a complete bath. Full-pension terms are reasonable as well. For example, a single person pays from 49.50 ($28.39) per day, depending on his or her room assignment.

DINING AT THE CASINO: The **Kurhaus Restaurant,** 1 Felix-Rütten-Strasse (tel. 22-91), provides not only the most scenically interesting dining in the spa, but serves the best food as well. In spite of the luxurious trappings, a meal need not be expensive. Beyond the formal entrance, with its fountains and doorman, guests are offered first-rate food. Under the appellation of "medallion red and black," you'll discover a mixed grill "americaine" at 22 DM ($12.62). Standard fare includes soups at 8 DM ($4.59), rumpsteak "maître d'hotel" at 24 DM ($13.77), desserts at 9 DM ($5.16). The service is elegant, the atmosphere formal. At night, music is played for dancing. It's closed Mondays.

9. Bad Oeynhausen

The Jordan spring at Bad Oeynhausen is considered the world's greatest carbonic acid thermal salt spring, said to be beneficial for heart and vascular diseases, as well as rheumatism and certain female ailments. Lying between the Wiehen and Weser Mountains at the northern edge of the Teutoburger Wald, the resort contains attractive spa gardens, although much of the town itself is industrial and commercial.

A MEDIUM-PRICED HOTEL: Kur-und-Badehotel "Wittekind," 10 am Kurpark (tel. 2-10-96), stands like a sunny Italian villa overlooking the spa gardens. The emphasis is more on comfort than on stylized decor, and the rooms—some of them quite large—are furnished in a mixture of traditional or contemporary styles. It's all quite homey. Prices vary according to size and location of the rooms. All rooms have private toilet and bath or shower. With continental breakfast, taxes, and service included, a room will cost from 45 DM ($25.81) to 55 DM ($31.55) per person. Full pension is from 75 DM ($43.02) to 90 DM ($51.62) per person. The hotel's restaurant, the Wittekindstuben, serves the best food in town.

10. Bad Kissingen

Of the many spas in the Franconian basin north of Bavaria, Bad Kissingen stands out as the most attractive and most popular. Aside from its modern cure installations for the treatment of liver and stomach disorders, the town itself is a major attraction. It's a quiet village, nestled in the valley of the Saale River. The sleepy little marketplace is flanked by old shops and the medieval Rathaus. Parks and gardens surround the town, including the attractive Kurgarten with its palms, extensive walks, and the Rosengarten.

The huge Kurhaus is one of the most impressive buildings in the town, with arcades stretching to the mineral springs and the huge promenade hall. In summer there is always plenty to do besides taking the cure—tennis, golf, chess. This is probably the only place where chess is as much a test of the body as the mind—the board is nearly 35 feet square, with huge pieces which must be picked up and carried to the next square! For the less energetic, spectator games include horse racing at the modern track. At night, the track receives heavy competition from the gambling casino and the magnificent paneled concert hall.

THE TOP HOTEL: Steigenberger Kurhaushotel, 1 Kurhausstrasse (tel. 30-31), is the leading hotel at the spa, with direct access to the baths. Built in 1850, it was once a meeting place for some of the VIPs of Europe, including Bismarck, Leo Tolstoy, the czar of Russia, and the empress of Austria. The public rooms are serene, offering maximum comfort to well-seasoned spa habitués who gather in comfortably upholstered chairs to exchange notes on cures. The bedrooms are pleasant, usually color coordinated, with homey touches such as chintz draperies. Most of the accommodations are spacious enough to have sitting areas. A single with bath goes from 69 DM ($39.58) to 103 DM ($59.08), increasing to anywhere from 98 DM ($56.21) to 146 DM ($83.75) in a double, prices based on the size and situation of a room.

In the intimate bar, guests gather to drink and relax; breakfast is served in a private enclosed garden at the rear of the hotel. Afterward, guests take a morning stroll by the pond with its musical fountain. A meal at the hotel is elegant, enhanced by an elevated garden in the center of the two dining rooms. The cuisine is international, and the chef is quite used to some of the most esoteric dietary requests. Master Chef Herr Erich Möller, who works only during the season, has been with the hotel since 1930. His specialty is duck with sour cherries. Meals are also served on the balconies, which overlook the park and are bordered with flowers. A main dish, such as peppersteak, goes for 24.50 DM ($14.05), followed by a dessert in the 5.50-DM ($3.15) to 7.50-DM ($4.30) range. Diet menus range in price from 6.75 DM ($3.87) to 14.50 DM ($8.32).

A MEDIUM-PRICED HOTEL: Das Ballinghaus, 3 Martin-Luther-Strasse (tel. 12-34), is favored by many over the larger and more expensive Kurhaushotel. A neoclassic building, it is prim and proper, lying only a few minutes from the Kurhaus Gardens and across the street from a row of boutiques. Actually, spa devotees who come here for liver and stomach cures need never leave the grounds, as Das Ballinghaus has its own gardens and indoor swimming pool with medical baths. Behind the sedate town-house look lies a classic interior. Semimodern furnishings enhance the air of quiet dignity. The rooms are comfortable and immaculately kept. In a bathless single with toilet, the rate ranges from 56 DM ($32.12) to 60 DM ($34.42). With a private bath, the price goes from 60 DM ($34.42) to 64 DM ($36.71). In a bathless double with toilet, you pay 55 DM ($31.55) to 58 DM ($33.27) per person, 57 DM ($32.70) to 62 DM ($35.56) per person in a room with private bath. The rates include taxes, service charge, and continental breakfast.

BUDGET DINING: The **Ratskeller,** 1 Rathausplatz (tel. 25-50), is one of the most enchanting in Germany, containing several dining rooms on two levels. Decorations include a liberal mixture of pewter and antlers. Semiprivate areas are separated by ornately carved dark-wood partitions. You certainly discover Old Germany here while enjoying some of the most savory (and least expensive) dishes in the spa. The townspeople, with good reason, are proud of their Ratskeller and its specialties. Among the à la carte selections are soups in the 2.75-DM ($1.58) to 3.50-DM ($2.01) range. Eels cooked in Riesling wine are 15 DM ($8.60).

After a well-deserved rest at a spa, we're ready to face the Lorelei.

Chapter V

THE RHINELAND

FEW RIVERS OF THE WORLD claim—or deserve—as important a role in the growth of a nation as does the Rhine. It is the greatest single contributor to the history, legend, wealth—even the art of Germany, parading along its banks a capsule version of the past, present, and future of Western Europe.

Although the Rhine begins in Switzerland (as a trickling mountain stream), and eventually passes through the Netherlands in its search for the sea, most of its 850 miles snake and stretch through the mountains and plains of West Germany. For more than 2000 years it has been the chief route of trade within the continent, its deep waters enabling even the most modern of sea vessels to travel upstream from the North Sea as far as Cologne.

Trade was not the only commodity carried along the waters of the Rhine. From the earliest times, it was also the route and magnet for the intellectual, artistic, and religious minds of Europe. It has been called "a triumphal avenue of the muses," and a trip along its banks even today reveals historic and artistic treasures. Cathedrals and castles, huge modern cities, and sleepy little wine towns dot the landscape. Legends and history seem to wait around every bend of the river, or on each little mound or ruin along the banks.

From Mainz to Koblenz stretches the most scenic section of the Rhine Valley, taking in the winding portion of the river, which cuts through steep vine-covered hillsides dotted with towns whose names are synonymous with fine German wines. In this section is the most symbolic formation in the Rhineland, the legendary Lorelei, written and sung about for centuries as the rock from which the siren lured men to their doom.

The sage of the Nibelungen is, however, the most famous of the Rhine legends, associated with much of the topography along the Rhine, from the Seven Mountains near Bonn where Siegfried slew the dragon, to the city of Worms where Brünhilde plotted against the dragon-slayer.

The Rhine is also the home of many of Germany's largest and most modern cities. Cologne and Düsseldorf vie for the prestige of trade and tourism; Bonn continues as the provisional capital of West Germany.

The best way to get a really intimate look at the Rhine Valley is by taking a **boat along the Rhine River.** A wide range of cruises is offered by several shipping lines, from a 500-mile tour of the river in the luxury of a liner complete with cabins, restaurant, deck, and swimming pool, to one-day cruises between selected scenic points via smaller tour boats. The **KD German Rhine Line** runs its liners all year (less frequently in winter, of course) between Rotterdam at the North Sea and Basle, Switzerland, with all the elegance of a tropical island cruise. These tours usually last five days (one way) and vary in price according to the ship and season.

For the visitor to Germany, however, the popular tours are the one-day cruises between Mainz and Cologne, also operated by the KD German Rhine Lines. This short trip takes in the most scenic portion of the Rhine, including the Lorelei, the best of the Rhine castles, and the most interesting of the wine villages. Cruise tours are also available between almost any two major points along the full length of the Rhine. Special tickets are sold enabling you to leave or join a cruise at any of these points.

The best alternative for sightseeing on the Rhine is by car. The advantage of automobile travel is that you are free from the tour guides herding you in and out of castles, museums, and cathedrals. You will not be pressured to leave behind some sight unseen or some village unexplored. If your schedule can possibly accommodate the time, allow at least a week. Know then that you will have only scratched the surface, and promise yourself a return whenever possible.

If you wish, you can settle yourself in one of the big towns, such as Düsseldorf or Cologne, with its wide range of accommodations. But you may infinitely prefer to seek out a central, yet seemingly isolated, village with an old inn where the pace is less frenetic, the food worthy of the finest tables in Germany.

READER'S SIGHTSEEING SUGGESTION: "There are alternatives to the KD Rhine boats. Alongside the pier are smaller boats which also run cruises. Although the KD boats are larger, serve food, and sometimes have a band on board, the best seats near the windows tend to be reserved for tour groups. If one prefers a more peaceful trip to view the castles, one should consider one of these smaller boats which charge about half the price, depending on the distance traveled" (Dr. Henry Chang, New York, N.Y.).

1. Bonn

Unitl 1949, Bonn was a sleepy little university town, basking in its glorious 2000 years of history. Suddenly, it was shaken out of this quiet life and made the provisional capital of the Federal Republic of Germany. Although the city has adjusted to its important new position in the country's affairs, many of the older citizens still long for the relaxed and unhurried days before the war.

Within sight of the Seven Mountains, the home of the Nibelungen legends, Bonn has been a strategic city since Roman times. In the 13th century, it was the capital of the electors of Cologne. More than any other heritage, however, the city is proud of its intellectual and musical history. Beethoven was born here; Schumann lived here; Karl Marx and Heinrich Heine studied in Bonn's university.

Today, the capital is a bustling city of civil servants, lobbyists, secretaries, diplomats, newspaper reporters, university students, and politicians. The population and physical size of Bonn have more than doubled since the war.

In addition to political goings-on, visitors are attracted to Bonn from all over the world for the Beethoven Festival, held every two years in Beethovenhalle, a magnificent modern concert hall renowned for its excellent acoustics.

THE SIGHTS: The best way to become oriented to what Bonn has to offer is to take a guided sightseeing tour, leaving daily from 1 Mülheimer Platz (April 15 to September 30) at 10 a.m. and noon. The cost of the tour is 9 DM ($5.16) for adults, 4.50 DM ($2.58) for children. For those who prefer to explore on their own, the city has a number of fine attractions.

The **Beethoven House,** Bonn's pride and joy, is in the old section of town, just north of the marketplace, 20 Bonngasse. Beethoven was born in 1770 in the small house in back, which opens onto a little garden. On the second floor, there is a simple marble bust of the composer, the only decoration in the room where he was born. Within the house are many personal possessions of Beethoven, including manuscripts and musical instruments. In the Vienna Room, in the front of the house, overlooking the street, is Beethoven's last piano. The instrument was custom-made, with a special sounding board meant to amplify the sound enough so that the composer might possibly hear it in spite of his deafness. The house is open daily from 9 a.m. to 1 p.m. and from 3 p.m. to 6 p.m. (Sundays, from 9 a.m. to 1 p.m. only). Admission is 1.50 DM (86¢).

The **Government Quarter,** along the west bank of the Rhine, is a complex of modern white buildings, rather nondescript when compared to the architecture of the Old Town. The two most impressive structures, both along Koblenzerstrasse, are the President's Residence and the Chancellery of the prime minister. These white villas are more reminiscent of Old Bonn, long before it became an international center of diplomatic activity. Running north along the Rhine from the government buildings is a popular promenade, lined with trees and flowers as far as the **Alter Zoll,** an ancient fortress whose ruins make an excellent viewing point from which visitors can see across the Rhine to the Seven Mountains and the old village of Beuel.

The **Rhineland Museum,** 14 Colmantstrasse, contains a fine collection of art and artifacts from the Rhine Valley, including the skull of the famous Neanderthal man, found in 1856 a few miles east of Düsseldorf. The most interesting collection, however, is in the department devoted to the Roman period, with altars, stones, glass, and artifacts found in the Roman settlements in the Rhineland. The most fascinating exhibit is the altar to the Aufanic Matrons, a group of deities worshipped by the landowners of the Rhine. Open Tuesdays through Fridays from 9 a.m. to 5 p.m. (Wednesdays to 9 p.m.); Saturdays and Sundays from 10 a.m. to 6 p.m. Admission is 1 DM (57¢).

THE TOP HOTELS: Steigenberger, am Bundeskanzlerplatz/124 Reuterstrasse (tel. 201-91), is in a modern business complex on the outskirts of Bonn, opposite the government building and the Palais Schaumburg, the residence of the Federal chancellor. It's in the heart of an area that is, in fact, a city within a city. Downtown Bonn couldn't possibly handle this type of hotel, with its high-rise accommodations. Everything has a sophisticated and somewhat lavish touch, perfect for visiting diplomats. (You might spot foreign ministers, or even presidents, around the lounge fireplace.) The bedrooms are on the five upper floors; each has a private bath, TV, radio, and self-dial phone. Rates include a continental breakfast. Singles are 97 DM ($55.64) to 135 DM ($77.44); twin-bedded doubles go for 130 DM ($75.57) to 190 DM ($108.98). Expert designers and decorators have been called in to make the 160 bedrooms stylish and to provide super-comfort. Beautifully grained woods are combined with strong, pure colors, and sofas convert into beds at night, for studio-style living.

The 18th-floor dining room, adjoined by an intimate armchair lounge, opens onto a panoramic view. But the pièce de résistance is the top-floor swimming pool and sauna, with its wall of glass providing views of the Rhine. In a highly stylized Swiss chalet atmosphere, the Juliette offers disco dancing. A sun terrace on the front plaza provides outside tables. Free underground parking is available.

Königshof, 9 Adenauerallee (tel. 63-18-31), is a modern building, with wide terraces, occupying spacious grounds across the boulevard from the park. It is often filled with government officials from other nations. Neither extravagant nor elegant, the Königshof is a sound and reliable haven. A twin-bedded room with private bath overlooking the Rhine costs 110 DM ($63.10). Singles with bath go from 70 DM ($40.15) to 90 DM ($51.62).

MEDIUM-PRICED HOTELS: Sternhotel, 8 Markt (tel. 65-44-55), is the best of Bonn's hotels in the moderately priced category. It's right in the heart of town, next door to Bonn's most colorful building, the baroque town hall. The Stern has been in the hands of the Haupt family for 75 years, and they offer an informal, homey place for guests. A reception lounge has been combined with a bierstube, the furnishings harmoniously blending traditional with modern. Equally homelike are the bedrooms, the larger of which have sitting areas. A single with shower and toilet costs from 64 DM ($36.71) to 68 DM ($39), rising to anywhere from 70 DM ($40.15) to 81 DM ($46.46) with complete bath. A twin-bedded room with shower goes from 91 DM ($52.20) to 95 DM ($54.49), increasing to 100 DM ($57.26) to 120 DM ($68.83) with complete bath. Meals are graciously served in the dining room.

Astoria, 105–113 Hausdorffstrasse (tel. 23-95-07), is a new, 50-room hotel, frequented by traveling business people, members of Parliament, and diplomats. The hotel lies in the heart of "Greater Bonn," about a ten-minute walk from Parliament Center. Each unit is well furnished, containing private showers, tub baths, and toilets. Singles with shower cost 60 DM ($34.42) nightly, going up to 65 DM ($37.28) with complete bath. Doubles with shower go for 95 DM ($54.49), rising to 110 DM ($63.10) with complete bath. Breakfast, a continental one, is included in the tariffs quoted. In the evening some hot meals are served.

Schwan, 24 Mozartstrasse (tel. 63-41-08), is a bourgeois-style house on a quiet street about six minutes by foot from the railway station. Although not exactly an exciting choice, it is clean, sternly furnished in a modern idiom. Singles with private shower range from 45 DM ($25.81) to 55 DM ($31.55). A twin-bedded room with shower costs 70 DM ($40.15), going up to 80 DM ($45.89) to 85 DM ($48.76) with private bath—these tariffs including a continental breakfast.

BUDGET HOTELS: In the precincts of the Hofgarten and within walking distance of the Rhine is a harmonious group of little hotels, each offering modest accommodation at moderately low prices.

Haus Hofgarten, 7 Fritz-Tillmann-Strasse (tel. 22-34-82), is the most interesting of the three. A friendly couple presides over this unique establishment, furnished with antiques. Although the look is slightly cluttered in places, it's ideal if you appreciate the charm of another era. A good-sized breakfast room makes it a bit like living in a private home. A wide dark mahogany staircase leads to the 15 bedrooms. Large doubles with bath go for 78 DM ($44.74); if bathless, 62 DM ($35.56). Singles with bath are 52 DM ($29.83), 29 DM ($16.63) if bathless.

Benz, 17a Maarflach (tel. 22-50-51), is a second choice. Here are three floors of modern and spacious walk-up rooms, some with private baths and showers. Bathless singles cost 32 DM ($18.36) nightly, rising to 41 DM ($23.52) with shower, 49 DM ($28.11) with private bath. Doubles with shower are tabbed at 62 DM ($35.56), rising to 80 DM ($45.89) with bath, breakfast included. The Benz is frequented mainly by traveling business people. Breakfast is the only meal served. The Benz (named after its owner-manager, Henni Benz) is hidden in a narrow elbow lane, off the park. It's quiet, yet handy to the center of Bonn.

Eden, 6 am Hofgarten (tel. 63-80-71), right on the Hofgarten, is a modest place with a pleasant family management. A good breakfast is provided in the combination sitting room, lounge, and office. The decor is a bit fussy and cluttered, but clean and homey. In a bathless single, the rate ranges from 40 DM ($22.94) to 44 DM ($25.24), increasing to 54 DM ($30.97) with shower, and peaking at 60 DM ($34.42) with bath. Bathless doubles cost 67 DM ($38.43), from 84 DM ($48.18) to 94 DM ($53.92) with private bath, breakfast included.

If no accommodations are available, then two more scattered choices include the following. **Römerhof,** 20 Römerstrasse (tel. 63-47-96), is not known to many travelers, but it's a suitable accommodation on a busy street close to the northern exit of the autobahn to Cologne. In reality, it's a gasthof-type inn, where the friendly owner puts up overnight guests. The modern rooms are kept in good shape. Prices, including a continental breakfast, are 38 DM ($21.80) in a single with shower, rising to 70 DM ($40.15) in a double with shower. At the Römerhof's restaurant, you can order hearty meals in the 11-DM ($6.31) to 30-DM ($17.21) range. It's closed in July.

Hotel Weiland, 98a Breite Strasse (tel. 65-24-24), is great for a tight budget—a guest house not far from the Kölnstrasse. It's as clean as fresh violets, and the welcome is also warm. The decor is uninspired, but the rates, including breakfast, are compensatingly low: singles from 24 DM ($13.77) to 32 DM ($18.36); doubles, as little as 50 DM ($28.68) to 56 DM ($32.12) if bathless, increasing to 62 DM ($35.56) to 66 DM ($37.86) with a private shower. The receptionist on the first floor speaks English.

READER'S ACCOMMODATION SELECTION: "In Bonn, we stayed with a woman who spoke practically no English but who went out of her way more than once to be of assistance. This was at the **Hotel Gereons-Hof,** 45 Kölnstrasse. The charge is 52 DM ($29.83), plus 4 DM ($2.29) each for a bath. Singles cost 34 DM ($19.50)" (Mrs. D. A. Mifflin, Stratford, Ontario, Canada).

ON THE OUTSKIRTS: Düsseldorfer Hof, Rheinhallee, Königswinter, near Bonn (tel. 02223/22011), stands on the Rhine promenade, offering beautiful scenery from its well-furnished rooms plus a good restaurant serving reasonably priced fare. A single with a private shower bath rents for 50 DM ($28.68), increasing to 80 DM ($45.89) in a double. Both these tariffs include a continental breakfast.

MEALS WITH ATMOSPHERE: Em Höttche, 4 Markt (tel. 65-85-96), has a long and colorful history, tracing its origin back to the year 1389. Situated next to the baroque town hall, it has been restored, with carved wood paneling and columns, natural brick, old beamed ceilings, decoratively painted plaster, grandfather clocks, nooks for handholding by candlelight, and curlicue chandeliers. Favored as a dining spot are the tables set inside the walk-in fireplace, with its heavy wooden supporting posts. The front room is mostly for drinks. Set lunches range in price from 9.50 DM ($5.45) to 20 DM ($11.47). On the à la carte list, you'll find filet goulasch Stroganoff at 21 DM ($12.05) and specialties for two persons, including entrecôte, at 44 DM ($25.24). Fresh salmon is available at 26 DM ($14.91). You can complement your meal with a carafe of local wine—the best buy of the house. Closed Sundays.

Im Stiefel, 30 Bonngasse (tel. 63-48-06), is a holdout to the past, representing antiquity, although in a completely modern setting. A few doors down the street from Beethoven's House, this atmospheric restaurant is popular with students. Dining is at bare bleached tables in one of several rooms. The decor is rich in butterscotch and brown shades, with wood paneling, pewter plates, and stained glass. There's even a standup bar for mugs of beer. Recommendable is oxtail soup at 3.75 DM ($2.15). Typical German specialties are featured, including hirschragoût at 13 DM ($7.46) and eisbein (pig's knuckles) with sauerkraut at 12.50 DM ($7.17). It's closed on Sundays.

MEALS WITH A FOREIGN TOUCH: Grand Italia, 1 Bischofsplatz (tel. 63-83-62), right off the old market square, is rightly considered one of the best Italian restaurants along the Rhine. It's an excellent change of pace, and the service is good. Fish soup, a savory offering, is 17.50 DM ($10.04). Spaghetti ranges in price from 7.25 DM ($4.16) to 10.50 DM ($6.02), depending on the way it's made. Tagliatelle verde goes for 8.50 DM ($4.88). Many pizzas are in the 6-DM ($3.44) to 13-DM ($7.46) range. For dessert, you may want to sample the classic Italian dessert, zabaglione, 7 DM ($4.02).

2. Bad Godesberg

Bonn's diplomatic suburb four miles to the south is a smart, modern town built around one of the Rhine's oldest resorts. Just opposite the Siebengebirge (Seven Mountains), it has a view of the crag, Drachenfels (Dragon's Rock), where Siegfried slew the dragon. The dragons are gone from the Rhine today, but you can still see some ancient castle ruins on the hills. The most interesting is the Godesberg castle, built in the 13th century by the electors of Cologne. Its ruins have been incorporated into a modern hotel (see recommendations below). From the promenade along the Rhine, you can watch a constant flow of boats and barges wending their way up and down the river.

Most of the spa's activity centers around the Redoute Palace, a small but elegant 18th-century castle. Beethoven Hall, the main ballroom, was the scene of the meeting between the young Beethoven and Haydn. Although the town itself is mainly a residential center for the representatives of many nations in Bonn, there is seemingly no end to the entertainment and cultural facilities here. Theaters, concerts, and social functions offer a constant whirl of events.

THE TOP HOTELS: **Zum Adler,** 60 Koblenzerstrasse (tel. 36-40-71), provides a 19th-century, cultural atmosphere. This oldtime prestige hotel is modest for the caliber of guests who have either stayed or dined here, but proud nevertheless.

The Zum Adler was once a private villa, built right on the street, with a small rear garden. It is furnished with good antiques—many inlaid desks and carved mirrors—although it contains a minimum of salons. Rates include a continental breakfast. The plumbing has been completely renewed and improved, although a few bathless singles still remain, for 50 DM ($28.68). With shower or bath, the single tariff rises to 68 DM ($39). Doubles with shower go for anywhere from 72 DM ($41.30) to 85 DM ($48.76). With complete bath, the double tariff is from 100 DM ($57.36) to 145 DM ($83.17).

Rheinhotel Dreesen, 1–3 Rheinaustrasse (tel. 36-40-01), enjoys a superior position, next to the Diplomatic Corps, directly on the Rhine, with its own gardens and terraces. Sliding glass roofs and infrared heating provide a sense of being outdoors, whatever the weather. Although a sentimental favorite of oldtimers, it is frequented by travel groups and business people, as well as vacationing German families who make it a holiday resort center. Practically every dining table offers a panoramic view of the river boats. The furnishings of the bedrooms are elegant, the size generous, and the prices based on plumbing and view. The renovated accommodations have the following rates: bathless singles, from 31 DM ($17.78) to 43 DM ($24.66); with shower, 55 DM ($31.55); with private bath, from 83 DM ($47.61). Bathless doubles are in the 60-DM ($34.42) to 80-DM ($45.89) bracket; with shower or private bath, from 106 DM ($60.80) to 116 DM ($66.54). Breakfast is included.

Godesberg Castlehotel, 1 aug dem Berg (tel. 36-30-08), is a comfortable place to stay. A winding road leads up to this hilltop castle ruin, now converted into a hotel. It's distinctive and highly recommended. Its tall tower and many of its rugged stone walls were erected in 1210 by the archbishop of Cologne and are still intact. A lounge was ingeniously built against one of the stone walls, providing a sunny lounge and a view of the spa and the river. There's also a roof terrace, with tables for drinks. The bedrooms themselves have been designed with zigzag picture windows, allowing for views. Various kinds of woods have been used in the bedrooms, each of which has a shower and bath. Singles range in price from 75 DM ($43.02) to 89 DM ($51.05), the difference based on your view or lack of it. Doubles with shower or complete bath go for anywhere from 89 DM ($51.05) to 110 DM ($63.10), breakfast included. The food is especially good here (see our restaurant recommendations).

WHERE TO DINE: **Weinhaus Maternus,** 3 Poststrasse (tel. 37-91-70), attracts a diplomatic crowd to its plush tavern atmosphere. The cuisine and service are excellent. There are some excellent à la carte suggestions: onion soup at 5 DM ($2.87); deer steak (in season) at 21 DM ($17.78); piccata Milanaise at 20 DM ($11.47). For your dessert, a splashy crêpes Suzette for two, 22 DM ($12.62), will be pleasing. The wine house is easy to find—opposite the railway station, with sidewalk canopy tables in warmer weather. Unquestionably, Weinhaus Maternus offers the best food in the spa.

Godesberg Castlehotel Restaurant, 1 Auf dem Berg (tel. 36-30-08), offers excellent meals in a romantic situation. It's a part of the previously recommended 13th-century castle which was turned into a hotel. You dine in elegant style in a modern room nestled into the castle ruins. The former knight's hall has been converted into a spacious dining room with picture-window views— the true eagle's-nest style. Preferred, however, is the adjoining Weinstube, warmer in tone, with its inner wall paneled in grainy wood. Set lunches range in price from 20 DM ($11.47) to 38 DM ($21.80). The international menu appeals to the widest possible tastes. Even American fried chicken is featured.

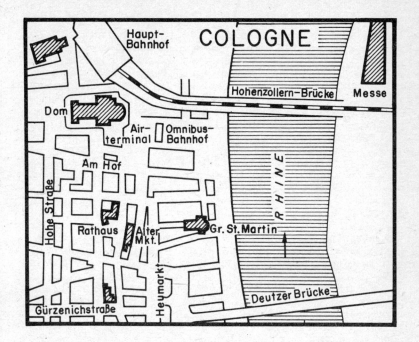

3. Cologne

The largest city in the Rhineland is so rich in antiquity that every time a new foundation is dug for a modern office building or the new subway system, the excavators come up with another relic from its past. Tragic though the World War II devastation of Cologne was—nearly all the buildings of the Old Town were damaged—it helped to reveal a period of Cologne's history that had been steeped in mystery for centuries. When the rubble was cleared away after the bombings, evidence was found proving that Cologne was as important and powerful a city during the early Christian era as it was during Roman times and the Middle Ages.

Cologne traces its beginning back to 38 B.C., when Roman legions set up camp here. As early as 5 B.C., it was given municipal rights as a capital of a Roman province. It still retains part of its original name today, an eternal tie to its strong Roman heritage as a colony of that vast empire.

Historical findings since the war have proved what an important town Cologne also was during the early Christian era. It became a city of martyrs and saints, including the patron of the city, St. Ursula, murdered by the Huns. During the prosperous Middle Ages, churches were built with the gold of the zealous merchants, as Cologne became a center for international trade. Visitors come from all over the world just to visit the medieval churches of Cologne, and rightly so, but there is much to see from every period of the city's 2000-year history—from the old Roman towers to the ultramodern Opera House.

The very word, Cologne, has become a part of the common language, since the introduction to the world many years ago of the scented water called eau de cologne. Cologne water is still produced in the city.

THE SIGHTS: The major sightseeing attractions of this ancient city lie within the Old Town, the section along the Rhine in the shape of a semicircle. The streets enclosing the Old Town are called rings, since they follow the route of the original medieval city wall, remnants of which remain in three gates, today housing museums and museum depots. Cutting through the center of the town is **Hohestrasse,** a straight street connecting the north and south Roman Gates. This main shopping street of Cologne is so narrow that vehicles are prohibited, enabling shoppers to move freely from one luxury shop or department store to the next. If you walk northward on the Hohestrasse, you'll soon reach Cologne's major attraction.

The **Cologne Cathedral** is the spiritual and geographical heart of the city, the most overwhelming edifice in the Rhine Valley. Built on the site of a pagan temple and earlier Christian churches, the majestic structure is the largest Gothic cathedral in Germany. Construction was begun in 1248 to house the relics of the Magi brought to Cologne by Archbishop Reinald von Dassel, chancellor of Frederick Barbarossa in 1164, but after the completion of the chancel, south tower, and north side aisles (about 1500), work was halted and not resumed until 1842. In 1880 the great 632-year enterprise was completed, and unlike many time-consuming constructions which change styles in midstream, the final result was as true to the Gothic style as the original plans had been.

For the best overall view of the cathedral, stand back from the south transept, where you can get an idea of the actual size and splendor of the edifice. Note that there are no important horizontal lines—everything is vertical. The west side (front) is dominated by two towering spires, perfectly proportioned and joined by the narrow facade of the nave. The first two stories of the towers are square, gradually merging into the octagonal form of the top three stories and tapering off at the top with huge finials. There is no great rose window between the spires, so characteristic of Gothic architecture, as the designers insisted that nothing was to detract from the lofty vertical lines.

Entering through the west doors (main entrance), one is immediately caught up in the grandeur of the cathedral. Although this portion of the church is somewhat bare, the clerestory and vaulting give an idea of the size of the edifice. The towering windows on the north and south aisles include the Bavarian Windows, donated by King Ludwig I of Bavaria, in 1848. Typical of most of the windows in the nave, they are colored in portrait-like pigments, which have been burned on rather than stained.

When you reach the transept, you become aware of the actual size of the cathedral. Here are the organ and choir loft, just south of the Treasury, with its liturgical gold and silver pieces. In the center of the transept—and the cathedral—is an elegant bronze and marble altar, which can be seen from all parts of the cathedral. This was to have been the site of the Shrine of the Three Kings, but the reliquary actually stands behind the high altar in the chancel.

The *Shrine of the Three Magi* is the most important and most valuable object in the cathedral. Designed in gold and silver in the form of a triple-naved basilica, it is decorated with relief figures depicting the life of Christ, the Apostles, and various Old Testament prophets. Across the front of the chancel are two rows of choir stalls divided into richly carved partitions. The unpainted oak choir dates from 1310 and is the largest still extant in Germany.

Surrounding the chancel are nine chapels, each containing important works of religious art. The Chapel of the Cross, beneath the organ loft, shelters the painted, carved oak cross of Archbishop Gero (969–976), the oldest full-size cross in the Occident. Behind the altar in Our Lady's Chapel, directly across the chancel from the Chapel of the Cross, is the famous triptych masterpiece painted by Stephan Lochner (1400–1451). When closed, the Dombild, as it is called, shows the Annunciation and when opened, it shows the Adoration of the Magi in the center, flanked by the patron saints of Cologne, St. Ursula, and St. Gereon.

The cathedral welcomes visitors at any time till 7:30 p.m., except during religious services. Daily tours take place at 10 a.m., 11, 2:30 p.m., 3:30, and 4:30. Visitors are welcome to visit the Treasury and Cathedral Tower daily from 9 a.m. to 5 p.m. Admission to each is 2 DM ($1.15).

The **Dionysos-Mosaik,** dating from the third century, was discovered in 1941 when workmen were digging an air raid shelter. Near the cathedral, this mosaic once was the decorative floor of the oecus (main room) of a large Roman villa. It was named "Dionysos" because most of the octagons and squares within the elaborately decorated and colored work are pictures dealing with the Roman god Bacchus, god of wine and dispeller of care. The mosaic is housed in the new **Roman-Germanic Museum.** On the second floor is an unusual collection of Roman antiquities found in the Rhine Valley, including Roman glass from the third and fourth centuries, as well as coins, marble busts, and jewelry. The museum and mosaic are open daily from 10 a.m. to 8 p.m. Admission is 1 DM (57¢).

The **Wallraf-Richartz Museum/Museum Ludwig,** just a short walk from the Domplatz, is Cologne's oldest museum, begun in the 19th century with a collection of Gothic works by Cologne artists. The group of works is still one of the main attractions, although today the Wallraf-Richartz shows art from 1300 to 1900, and the Ludwig, art from 1900 until today. Representative of the Gothic style in Germany is Stephan Lochner, best shown in his *Madonna in the Rose Garden,* painted in 1445. Several cathedral works are exhibited here, including the triptych of the *Madonna with the Vetch Flower* (1410). The museum is especially proud of its collection of German artists, spanning more than 500 years. It houses Germany's largest collection of works by Wilhelm Leibl, as well as paintings by Max Ernst, Paul Klee, and Ernst Ludwig Kirchner. There is also a representative collection of nearly every period and school of painting, from the Dutch and Flemish Masters to the French Impressionists to American art of the sixties and seventies (the famous Ludwig Donation). Open daily from 10 a.m. to 5 p.m.; Tuesday and Thursday, from 10 a.m. to 8 p.m.

The **Schnütgen Museum** is a curator's dream: beautiful works of art displayed in their original surroundings. Cologne's best collection of religious art and sculpture is housed in the Church of St. Cecilia, a fine example of Rhenish Romanic architecture. The works displayed here include several medieval tapestries, especially one showing rosy-checked Magi bringing gifts to the Christ child (1470). There is naturally an abundance of Madonnas, of all sizes and descriptions, carved in stone, wood, and metal. The museum is open daily from 10 a.m. to 5 p.m. (Thursdays to 8 p.m.). Admission is 1 DM (57¢) for adults, .50 DM (29¢) for children.

ORGANIZED TOURS: The only way to get a really comprehensive look at Cologne's many attractions is to take one of the tours departing from the Tourist Office opposite the cathedral. Two-hour tours are offered daily at 10 a.m. and 2 p.m. (the morning tour is only offered from May 1 through October 15), and cover the major sights of the Old Town, including a large number of Gothic and Romanesque churches, a Roman tower, the medieval city gates, the Gothic (15th-century) town hall, Roman Praetorium, and the modern opera house. The tour also includes a stop at one of the major museums. The cost for either tour is 12 DM ($6.88).

A guided walking tour leaves daily in summer at 3 p.m. from the Tourist Office. It is much more individualized than a coach trip, costing approximately $3 per person, which includes a drink and a chat in good company.

READERS' SIGHTSEEIING SELECTIONS: "At the end of the line for streetcar no. 9 (Königsforst) is a pleasant woods with many paths for exploring or just getting out of the city and enjoying the German woods. Nearby is also a **Waldsportpfad,** otherwise known as a 'Trim dich Pfad,' which is a short course track through the woods with exercise stations (with equipment of a durable type) placed approximately 100 yards apart. For example, there are poles to leapfrog over or bars to hang by. Believe it or not, Germans spend almost as much time walking and exercising as they do drinking beer in pubs! For exact directions, ask at the ticket stand at the end of the line—only 100–150 yards from there" (Margaret Manatt, La Canada, Calif.). . . . "I spent a wonderful Sunday afternoon in mid-May before catching the steamer to Mainz the next morning. Between the Hohenzollernbrücke and Zoobrücke (bridges) on the east bank of the Rhine is the exquisitely manicured **Rhine Park,** only surpassed in beauty by Holland's Keukenhof. Admission is 5 DM ($2.87). I entered just before noon and stumbled upon a seven-man jazz group playing some of the laziest 'down-home' Dixieland I'd ever heard! A wide variety of performers appear throughout the summer on the Dance Fountain stage. There are also a classic miniature railroad and two aerial tram rides, one through the park and one crossing the Rhine at Zoobrücke" (Charles H. Perlo, Somerville, Mass.).

THE TOP HOTELS: Excelsior Hotel Ernst, 1–5 Trankgasse (tel. 27-01), is, from several points of view, Cologne's most prestigious hotel. Its position alone, facing the cathedral square, should be sufficiently commanding. But its tasteful, authentic, and traditional ambience is also first rate. Add to this an outstanding Hanse Stuben restaurant on the premises, and you emerge with a winning combination. The bedrooms are spacious, with many facilities for comfort, including built-in wardrobes, bedside reading lamps, and traditional furnishings intermixed with reproductions, telephone, and radio. Doubles are priced according to size and position: 205 DM ($117.59) to 230 DM ($131.93) overlooking the cathedral. Singles range from 95 DM ($54.49) to 164 DM ($94.07). All rooms have private baths. Tariffs include service, taxes, and breakfast. The half pension is an extra 35 DM ($20.08) per person.

Dom-Hotel Köln, 2a Domkloster (tel. 23-37-51), is opposite the cathedral, standing in a world-famous area tucked away from the bustle of traffic. It is ten minutes by car from the Cologne-Bonn Airport, and the railway station is close by. One of Europe's finest, the hotel has a pleasant, comfortable atmosphere. Modern uncluttered decor lends an air of spacious restfulness. There's an excellent French restaurant, inviting bar, and an open-air terrace. The lobby recently was completely renovated. A public underground garage provides direct admittance to the hotel. There are 133 bedrooms, 90% with private baths. A single room with private bath runs from 125 DM ($71.70) to 145 DM ($83.17); a double with bath, from 175 DM ($100.38) to 240 DM ($137.66)—including a breakfast buffet, service, and tax.

Eden, 18 am Hof (tel. 23-61-23), is a recently created hotel opposite the Dom, bringing a light, airy note to the old section of the city, with its sun-mad colors and advanced architectural design. More than half of its bedrooms overlook the cathedral itself; each has its own bath, telephone, radio, mini-bar, and TV (on request). The accommodations are well conceived, with twin couches which convert to beds at night. Rates here include breakfast, taxes, and service. The largest doubles, with sitting and sleeping room, go for 185 DM ($106.12); other doubles cost 150 DM ($86.04). When you first walk in, you think you are in a tasteful and dramatic living room in a private home. Room and breakfast only are provided, although there is a Herren Bar for drinks. The restaurant next door provides set meals in the 16-DM ($9.18) to 25-DM ($14.34) range.

Europa am Dom Hotel, 38–46 am Hof (tel. 23-32-66), may not be as swank as some of its neighboring competitors, but this new hotel shares the same spectacular view of the cathedral. While its exterior is unbecomingly severe, much attention was given to bringing warmth and style to the interior. You'll find rich paneling and provincial antique reproductions in its foyer-lounge. Its terrace dining room has a festive red canopy. There's even a Treppchen-Keller in the basement, a recreation of a 12th-century wine cellar. Rustic booths, rugged stone walls, and pewter plates are just the right background to go with the good food and music. The bedrooms are completely modern in every sense, both in comfort and styling; each has a phone and radio. More than half open onto the Dom. Bathless singles are 50 DM ($28.68) to 70 DM ($40.15); with bath, 88 DM ($50.48) to 95 DM ($54.49). The average double with full bath is 180 DM ($103.25), dropping to 130 DM ($75.57) with shower. All prices include breakfast.

MEDIUM-PRICED HOTELS: Atlantic, 55 Alter Markt (tel. 23-32-69), is a modern, 70-room hotel, tucked away on a side street about a two-minute walk from the cathedral. It's recommended mostly for its straightforward, no-non-sense approach, as excessive frills do not exist. There are no public rooms to speak of, although attention has been paid to the utilitarian bedrooms. They have all you need for a refreshing overnight stay. The two price ranges depend on the type of bath arrangement you request. A bathless single costs from 32 DM ($18.36) to 50 DM ($28.68); a single with bath ranges from 45 DM ($25.81) to 78 DM ($44.74). Doubles range from 52 DM ($29.83) to 85 DM ($48.76) for a bathless room to 69 DM ($39.58) to 98 DM ($56.21) with bath. Breakfast is included. For children under 6 there is no charge if they stay in a room with their parents. A public garage is about a block away.

Hotel Baseler Hof, 2 Breslauer Platz (tel. 12-40-91), lies directly opposite the main station and the famous Dom, offering 108 pleasantly furnished rooms, all with private baths, phones, radios, and televisions. Including a breakfast buffet, the single tariff is 55 DM ($31.55), rising to 85 DM ($48.76) in a double. On the premises are a Swiss-style restaurant and a beer bar.

Hotel Turin, 9 Turinerstrasse (tel. 12-30-25), lies only 300 meters from the previously recommended Baseler Hof, and is under the same management. The hotel has no restaurant, although it does offer a breakfast room. It's a small place, but one that is well run, offering guests 39 double rooms, all with private baths, phones, and radios. Including breakfast a double room rents for 80 DM ($45.89) nightly.

Altstadt Hotel, Salzgasse (tel. 23-41-87), is a retreat hotel in the old section, just two minutes from the Rhine boat landing dock. Guests of this 42-bed hotel have passed the word along to their friends, making it a big success. Herr Olbrich learned about catering to international guests while a steward on the German-America Line, and he has furnished his little hotel most beguilingly. Each of his rooms is immaculate, individually decorated—a restful haven. Each room has a telephone and a refrigerator, with radio and television available on request. Rates are 35 DM ($20.08) for bathless singles, 53 DM ($30.40) with shower. Doubles without bath are 50 DM ($28.68); with shower, 70 DM ($40.15); with complete bath, 80 DM ($45.89). All rates include breakfast, service charge, and tax. Space is not easy to obtain, and reservations are recommended.

LOW-BUDGET INNS: **Hotel City,** 26 Ursulagartenstrasse (tel. 13-36-46), lies on a narrow, quiet street behind St. Ursula Church, away from the center of town. The hotel offers quite a lot, mainly the hearty welcome of its owner, Mr. Taeschner, who knows well what a tired traveler yearns for: comfort and a friendly atmosphere at a reasonable price. His rooms are rather small, but sufficient. The ambience is not unlike that of the home of a friend. Some accommodations have their own showers, but in others you'll have to rely on the corridor facilities. Furnishings are standard. Doubles with shower go for 57 DM ($32.70), rates including breakfast served in an intimate lounge.

Flandrischer Hof, 5 Flandrischerstrasse (tel. 23-46-95), on the outskirts of the city and connected to the Hohenzollern Ring, is a small, 26-room hotel away from the river. The accommodations are quite decent, of medium size and furnished informally. The atmosphere may be impersonal, but the quietness makes up for it. Bathless singles are 32 DM ($18.36); bathless doubles, 54 DM ($30.97). With bath, singles go for 45 DM ($25.81); doubles with bath, 70 DM ($40.15). Breakfast is included, although the room in which it's served does overlook a rather dark backyard.

Breslauer Hof, 56 Johannisstrasse (tel. 12-30-09), is a minimal little 20-room hotel directly across from the Dom and the railway station. The furnishings are in the eternal oak functional type, the floors of plastic tile. However, all is kep immaculate in true Germanic tradition. Singles cost 45 DM ($25.81); doubles, 65 DM ($37.28). All rooms contain showers. Included in the tariff is breakfast served in a cafe-style room with small tables opening directly onto the street. An elevator serves all floors, and the receptionist who sits at a corridor desk speaks a little English. The welcome's good in spite of some uprofessional aspects of the establishment.

Hotel Ludwig, 24 Brandenburgerstrasse (tel. 12-30-31), is for those seeking good, middle-class comfort, in a central location, directly by the north entrance of the main station and only 100 yards from the cathedral. Innkeeper Erich Ahles welcomes you at rates of 37 DM ($21.22) in a single room or 26 DM ($14.91) per person in a double. The bargain special would be an accommodation suitable for three, with the extra person paying an additional 22 DM ($12.62) nightly, these tariffs including a continental breakfast, tax, service charge, and free use of the showers downstairs.

Central, 3 an den Dominikanern (tel. 13-50-88), provides old-fashioned homelike comfort in a good location, directly across from the Hanse-Stube, the leading restaurant of Cologne. It's an easy walk to the Dom. An elevator whisks you to one of the upper-floor bedrooms—fairly well furnished, often with English oak. The somber effect is brightened by the use of curtains and bedcovers in flowery cretonne. A single with running water costs 32 DM ($18.36); a similar double, 67 DM ($38.43). Singles with shower go for 46 DM ($26.39), increasing to 78 DM ($44.74) for doubles with a complete bath. Included is breakfast, served in a large ground-floor lounge at small tables.

Brandenburger Hof, 2 Brandenburgerstrasse (tel. 12-28-89), is a modest, family-style hotel where you can get cheaper rates in accommodations sheltering three or four persons. A room for three goes for 56 DM ($32.12). A regular single costs 30 DM ($17.21), and doubles (depending on the size) are yours for

38 DM ($21.80) to 42 DM ($24.09). Breakfast, included in the price, is served in a homey room with a big central table around which all the guests sit. The hotel is in back of the railway station, about three blocks from the river and within walking distance of the cathedral. The furnishings are in the style of neoclassic dark wood. All the rooms are small, warm, and equipped with running water; there's a bath on each floor.

Hotel Lenz, 9 Ursulaplatz (tel. 21-00-55), is like a Black Forest guest house, and it stands incongruously in the middle of Cologne. It is convenient to the railway station, cathedral, and other major points of interest. Rooms are simply although adequately furnished. The Lenz is a real bargain, especially in its double rooms with hot and cold running water which rent for a low of 55 DM ($31.55) to 73 DM ($41.87), breakfast included. Doubles with more elaborate plumbing are in the 76-DM ($43.59) to 90-DM ($51.62) range.

READERS' HOTEL SELECTIONS: "I had a very pleasant room at **Hotel Heinzelmännchen,** 5–7 Hohe Pforte (tel. 21-12-17), at 32 DM ($18.36) for a single with breakfast. Hohe Pforte is an extension of the pedestrian street, Hohe Strasse, and the hotel can also be reached by taking buses 32 or 33 from the station. Then turn left and stop at Hohe Pforte, only a few blocks from the hotel" (Lynn Peterson, Hollywood, Calif.). . . . "We found a really nice hotel with big rooms and the best showers we had on our trip, and only one block behind the railroad station. It is the **Hotel Thielen,** 1 Brandenburgerstrasse (tel. 12-33-33). The price was about 42 DM ($24.09) for a double" (Keith A. Brintzenhoff, Macungie, Penna.). . . . **"Hotel Friedrich,** 23 Domstrasse (tel. 12-33-03), is three minutes' walk from the station. A bathless single, with hot and cold running water, costs 35 DM ($20.08). Breakfast, included in the tariff, included egg, sausage, and cheese, as well as honey and jam" (D. Hannay, Sanderstead, Surrey, England).

THE TOP RESTAURANTS: Hanse-Stube, Bahnhofstrasse (tel. 27-01), on the ground floor of the Excelsior Hotel Ernst, is rightly considered the best restaurant in Cologne. The cuisine and service are top-drawer. The setting is that of a tavern, which you can enter through the hotel itself. In case you check into your hotel at a late hour, the restaurant provides a warm kitchen until midnight. Lunches start at 31 DM ($17.78) and 39 DM ($22.37). The à la carte selections are international. To begin, try the bouillabaisse at 28 DM ($16.06), although you may not want much more, it's so satisfying. Main-dish specialties include a mixed grill of seafood at 28 DM ($16.06) and a filet Singapore at 28 DM also. The star dessert is the Salzburger nockerl at 18 DM ($10.32).

Die Bastei, 82 Konrad-Adenauer-Ufer (tel. 12-28-25), is the favored spot for your watch on the Rhine. The trick here is to aim for a window table. The split-level dining room's located on the second floor of this circular tower-type building jutting out into the river. The view from here is dramatic. The restaurant is as high class as its prices, no meals under 25 DM ($14.34), some reaching heavenward to 65 DM ($37.28). In addition to German specialties, many dishes are presented from neighboring Switzerland, Austria, and France. Dinner and dance music is played on Saturday evenings.

DINING IN THE OLD TOWN: Weinhaus in Walfisch, 13 Salzgasse (tel. 21-95-75), is a step-gabled inn in the Old Town dating back to 1626. Behind its black-and-white timbered facade, you'll find the leading atmospheric choice for dining. More important, it serves some of the best food in the city. Not too easy to find, it's on a narrow street set back from the Rhine. For starters try the Hamburger krebssuppe at 11.50 DM ($6.60). There are many main dishes for from 21 DM ($12.05) to 39 DM ($22.37), including a wide variety of fluffy omelets. Chef's specials include sole meunière at 28.50 DM ($16.35) and venison for two at 65 DM ($37.28).

Im Stapelhäuschen, 1–3 Fischmarkt (tel. 21-30-43), is one of the finest wine taverns in Cologne. Just a few minutes from the cathedral, it's housed in an office building, opening onto the old fish market platz and the Rhine. The two-story-high dining room and service bar are antique in style, and provincial cabinets hold a superb wine collection behind the service bar. A carved Madonna attached to the wall, brass objects hanging against paneled wainscoting, a copper coffee urn—everything here is rustic. A wide, wooden, cantilevered staircase leads to mezzanine tables. While wine is the main reason for coming here (it's that special), the cuisine is excellent. Proof of that is how quickly the dining room becomes crowded. Soups cost around 3 DM ($1.72) to 4.50 DM ($2.58), and dishes such as medallions of veal are priced at 21 DM ($12.05). Rumpsteak in the Balkan style (stuffed with cheese and ham) costs 18.50 DM ($10.61). Desserts are offered from 3 DM ($1.72) to 7.25 DM ($4.16).

THE BEER TAVERNS: Früh, 12 am Hof (tel. 21-26-21), is a local beer tavern-restaurant within the cathedral precincts. It's the best all-around choice for economy and hearty portions. The denizens of Cologne congregate here for well-cooked meals served on scrubbed wooden tables. A different German specialty is offered every day of the week, ranging in price from 7 DM ($4.02) to 14 DM ($8.03). To make things easier, the menu is in English. You'll find the following dishes: soup of the day, only 1.50 DM (86¢); bockwurst with sauerkraut and mashed potatoes, 7 DM ($4.02); Hungarian goulash, with boiled potatoes and a salad, 10 DM ($5.74). Desserts are in the 1.70-DM (98¢) to 2.10-DM ($1.20) range. Hot meals are served until 10 p.m.

Alt Köln am Dom, Domplatz, next door to the Excelsior Hotel Ernst, has the showpiece of Cologne, even rivaling the cathedral in tourist attention. It's the mechanical clock on its facade; when it chimes the hour, a parade of figures emerges and disappears—a festive reminder of Old Germany. Alt Köln itself is a recreation of a group of old taverns. You can either drop in for a beer or a good hot meal. Some of the upper-floor tables provide box-seat views of the Dom. For starters, try the onion soup at 4 DM ($2.29) or the goulash soup at 4.25 DM ($2.44). A chef's specialty is his Alt Köln dish (scampi, chicken, mushrooms, and pineapple) at 11.50 DM ($6.60), although you may prefer merely a hamburger at 10 DM ($5.74) or rumpsteak at 21 DM ($12.05). Main dishes are in the 12-DM ($6.88) to 24—DM ($13.77) range, and desserts are priced from 3.50 DM ($2.01) to 6 DM ($3.44).

4. Aachen

Just 40 miles west of Cologne, where the frontiers of Germany, Belgium, and Holland meet, is the ancient Imperial City of Aachen (Aix-la-Chapelle). It is inseparably associated with Charlemagne, who selected this natural spa as the center of his vast Frankish empire.

THE SIGHTS: About 800, the emperor built the octagon, the core of the **Imperial Cathedral.** Within the cathedral stands the marble "Königsstuhl," Charlemagne's throne, considered one of the most venerable monuments in Germany. For 600 years, the kings of Germany were crowned here, until Frankfurt became the country's coronation city in the mid-16th century.

The cathedral stands today an unusual mixture of Carolingian (the well-preserved dome), Gothic (the choir, completed in 1414), and baroque (the roof), all united into a magnificent upward sweep of architecture. The **Treasury,** in the adjoining treasure house, is the most valuable and celebrated ecclesiastical treasure store north of the Alps. But the cathedral holds its own share of wealth. The elaborate gold shrine in the chancel contains the relics of the Emperor Charlemagne. The pulpit of Henry II is copper studded with precious gems. Visitors to the cathedral can view the throne of Charlemagne only with a guide (request one at the Treasury). The Cathedral Treasury may be visited daily from 9 a.m. to 1 p.m. and from 2 p.m. to 5 p.m. (Sundays, 10:30 a.m.). Admission: 2 DM ($1.15).

The 14th-century **Rathaus** (Town Hall) was built on the original site of Charlemagne's palace. Part of the old structure can still be seen in the so-called Granus Tower at the east side of the hall. The richly decorated facade of the Town Hall facing the marketplace is adorned with the statues of 50 German rulers crowned in Aachen. In the center are the two most important men in the Holy Roman Empire, Charlemagne and Pope Leo III, the Majestas Domini, standing in relief above the main entrance.

On the second floor of the Rathus is the double-naved and crossbeamed **Imperial Hall,** dating from 1330, the scene of German coronation meals from 1349 to 1531, built as the successor to the Carolingian Royal Hall. This hall today contains exact replicas of the Imperial Crown Jewels, true in size and material to the originals, presently in the Vienna Secular Treasury. On the walls are the Charlemagne frescoes, painted in the 19th century by Alfred Rethel, illustrating the victory of the Christian Franks over the Germanic heathens. The hall is open weekdays from 9 a.m. to 1 p.m. and from 2 p.m. to 5 p.m. Admission is 1 DM (57¢).

As a spa, Aachen has an even longer history than it does as an Imperial City. Roman legionnaires established a military bath here in the first century A.D. At the end of the 17th century, it became known as the Spa of Kings, attracting royalty from all over Europe. In 1742, Frederick the Great took the cure here, and in 1818 the "Congress of Monarchs" brought Czar Alexander from Russia. After World War II, which badly damaged the whole town, the spa was rebuilt and today enjoys a mild reputation as a remedial center.

Its springs are among the hottest in Europe. The treatment includes baths and the *trinkkur* (drinking of water). The spa gardens are the center of the resort activity, with attractive ponds, fountains, and shade trees.

STAYING OVER: Most travelers visit Aachen on a day trip from Cologne, via the Cologne-Aachen autobahn, usually having dinner at the Ratskeller before returning to the larger city on the Rhine. However, those interested in the spa facilities can stay at one of the hotels described below.

The Top Spa Hotel

Parkhotel Quellenhof, 52 Monheimsallee (tel. 4-81-61), is a palacelike structure in a tranquil setting. Architecturally neoclassic, it is furnished with a combination of antique reproductions and modern pieces. True to spa tradition, it is stately and dignified, with an impressive indoor swimming pool. Picture windows allow a view of the garden while guests swim in thermal water. In addition there is a sauna, plus treatment rooms for chronic rheumatic diseases, gout, and skin diseases. Rates here include breakfast. Singles with full bath cost from 98 DM ($56.21) to 127 DM ($72.85). Twin-bedded rooms with bath range from 138 DM ($79.16) to 202 DM ($115.87). Most of the accommodations are large scale. The food is good as well, with a set three-course luncheon going for 23 DM ($13.19) to 27 DM ($15.49).

Economy Hotels

Am Marschiertor (Hospiz), 1–7 Wallstrasse (tel. 3-19-41), stands in the center of Aachen, not far from the main station and next to the medieval town gate, Marschiertor, a beautiful and historical part of town. It has 46 newly furnished rooms in a cozy atmosphere. Parking facilities are available and, in addition, buses stop in front of the hotel. Singles without shower cost 36 DM ($20.65), going up to 48 DM ($27.53) with shower. Doubles with shower cost 55 DM ($31.55), rising to 88 DM ($50.48) with complete bath. All these tariffs include a continental breakfast.

3 Türme, 25 Ludwigsalle (tel. 3-52-19), is right at the opposite end of the Hotel am Marschiertor on the north boulevard. Close to the gardens of Velt-manplatz, this hotel is in an old building, offering a spacious breakfast and dining room, but no reception. There are only a few rooms, some of them suffering from the noise of the busy boulevard. The style is that of an old-fashioned pension, but sufficient. Prices run from 24 DM ($13.77) to 29 DM ($16.63) in a single, from 42 DM ($24.09) to 50 DM ($28.68) in a double. Breakfast is included in the tariffs, and a bath's on each floor. The restaurant offers an interesting set of lunches, beginning with an egg salad at 7.25 DM ($4.16). For 14.50 DM ($8.32), you can order a peppersteak, although you may prefer rumpsteak à la Meyer, with roasted onions and fried potatoes, at an additional cost of 16.50 DM ($9.46). Another good main dish is a wienerschnitzel at 11 DM ($6.31).

WHERE TO DINE: Ratskeller, am Markt (tel. 3-50-01), is a charming place to dine, with its rustic atmosphere of brick and stone, oak benches and tables, hammered metal lanterns, decorative bronze and wood sculpture, and oil paintings. There are two major dining rooms. Most intimate and attractive is an extension, containing a pub where men gather to drink and play cards. Little drinking nooks upstairs are for other games. Soups begin at 4 DM ($2.29) for a Viennese consommé with little bits of chopped meat, to 5.50 DM ($3.15) for a pepper soup Madagascar with pineapple and cream. Main dishes include such chef's specialties as pork filet chasseur, with mushrooms, potatoes, and a fresh salad, costing 14 DM ($8.03); veal fricassee, 21.50 DM ($12.33); or a beef filet with a béarnaise sauce, mushrooms, grilled tomatoes, and fried potatoes, 29 DM ($16.63). A dessert specialty—quite elaborate—is a cream of hot sour cherries flambé with kirsch, 7.50 DM ($4.30).

READERS' HOTEL AND DINING SELECTIONS: "The **Hotel Frankfurter Hof,** 30–32 Bahnhofstrasse (tel. 3-48-62), offers 28 neat and clean rooms at 40 DM ($22.94) for bathless singles, peaking at 55 DM ($31.55) for singles with bath. Bathless doubles go for 65 DM ($37.28), rising to 90 DM ($51.62) with private baths. The hotel features include an elevator, a garage, telephones in rooms, central heating, and continental breakfast; it's an easy walk from the railroad station. The proprietor, Anni Piper, is friendly and accommodating. I suggest **Zum Wagenpost,** at the corner of the Rathaus, for midday dining. A paprika goulash with potatoes, butter, and a salad goes for 10.50 DM ($6.02)" (Mrs. George J. Flynn, Washington, D.C.). . . . "The **Katakomben,** 76 Ponstrasse (tel. 2-06-68), is almost a rarity, e.g., with its decent and filling zigeunerschnitzel and fried potatoes for only 7 DM ($4.02) and Hungarian chicken for 5 DM ($2.87). It is a hangout for university students, hence the presence of recreational facilities. The place is strategically on your way as you wander about the neighborhood of the cathedral" (Sabino Vengco, San Jose, Philippines).

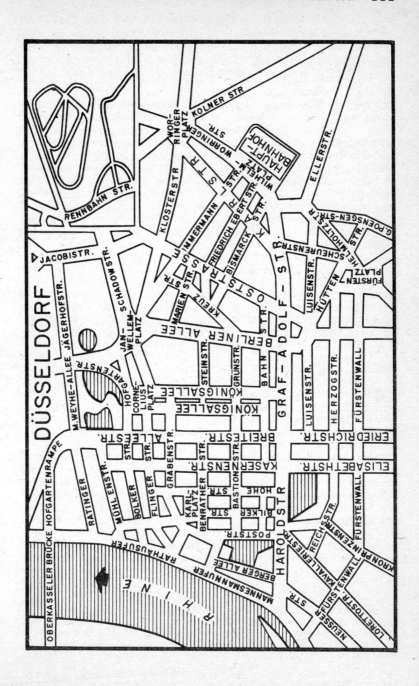

5. Düsseldorf

After 85% of this large city on the right bank of the Rhine was destroyed in World War II, it could easily have grown into just another ugly manufacturing town. Instead, Düsseldorf followed a modern trend in reconstruction, and today it is the most elegant and modern metropolis in the Rhine Valley.

THE SIGHTS: As in all German cities, there is the Old Town, with its marketplace, a Gothic town hall, and a few old buildings and churches such as the twisted-towered St. Lambert's. But in Düsseldorf, it's the present that is important. A walk up the **Königsalle**, affectionately called the "Kö" by Düsseldorfers, will give the outsider a quick look at what the city and its residents are really like. This famous street flanks an ornamental canal, shaded by trees and crossed by bridges. While one bank is lined with modern office buildings and important financial centers, the other is filled with elegant shops, smart cafes, and exclusive restaurants. Here you'll see attractive women dressed in the latest styles, as Düsseldorf is also the fashion center of Germany. It is especially famous for its Fashion Weeks, attracting the best designers and buyers from all over Europe.

As the capital of North Rhine–Westphalia, Düsseldorf is a wealthy city—the richest in Germany—with a population of more than 700,000. It's a big, commercial city full of banks and industrial offices, yet it is surprisingly clean. It has managed to incorporate parks and gardens throughout the city, some of them wedged comfortably between towering skyscrapers. The most impressive of these modern buildings is the **Thyssen House,** in the bustling center of town. Residents call the office tower the Dreischeibenhaus (three slice house), because it actually looks like three huge monoliths sandwiched together.

If you walk up the Kö toward the Triton fountain at the northern end of the canal, you'll find yourself in the **Hofgarten,** a huge rambling park. You could wander along the walks or just sit and relax for hours amid shade trees, gardens, fountains, and statues, almost forgetting you're in the very center of the city. Among the monuments is one to Düsseldorf's favorite son, the poet Heinrich Heine. The Hofgarten is a good central point for seeing the major attractions of Düsseldorf as well as nearly all the museums and other cultural attractions on the perimeter of the park.

The **Jägerhof Castle,** at the east end of the park, was an 18th-century hunting lodge. Today it houses an outstanding collection of modern art, including works by Picasso, Georges Braque, Juan Gris, Fernand Léger, Max Ernst, Salvador Dali, René Magritte, Joan Miró, Kirchner, Kandinsky, Chagall, Jackson Pollock, Mark Tobey, Robert Rauschenberg, Roy Lichtenstein, Andy Warhol, Frank Stella, and others. The museum also has a number of works by Paul Klee—so many, in fact, that the Klee exhibition is rotated at regular intervals since all cannot be shown at the same time. The top floor of the baroque castle is devoted to porcelain, with an exceptional collection of Meissen ware, some going back as far as 1710. Some fine gold and silver work as well as a few antiques add to the variety of this collection. The Jägerhof is open daily, except Monday, from 10 a.m. until 5 p.m. Admission: 1 DM (57¢).

The **Goethe Museum,** housed in the court gardener's cottage in the Hofgarten, is sponsored by the Anton and Katharina Kippenberg Foundation. Mr. Kippenberg was the owner of the famous Insel-Verlag publishing house in Leipzig, and as a young bookseller, began collecting Goethe memorabilia. Düsseldorf joins Frankfurt and Weimar in having Goethe museums. Opened in 1956, this museum contains about 75,000 items relating to the famous German poet—so many that not all can be exhibited because of lack of space.

Among such important documents as the first draft of Goethe's poem, "Noble be man, helpful and good . . ." and the first edition of *Werther,* are such esoteric items as a collection of glasses from spas frequented by Goethe. There's even a special room on the second floor devoted to *Faust.* The museum is open Tuesday through Sunday from 10 a.m. to 5 p.m. (closed Mondays). Admission is .50 DM (29¢).

The **Kunstmuseum,** at the Ehrenhof in one of Düsseldorf's most delightful locations between the Hofgarten and the Rhine, is one of the largest and most comprehensive museums in the Rhineland. The museum is famous for its collection of paintings (Rubens, C. D. Friedrich, Brücke, Blaue-Reiter) and sculptures from the late Middle Ages to the 20th century and for its print room with a collection of Italian drawings. It is also a focal point for glass, and, naturally, a collecting area and research center for Düsseldorf art from the time of Schadow to the present day. The Kunstmuseum is open daily (except Monday) from 10 a.m. to 5 p.m. Enter through the main gate at 5 Ehrenhof. Admission is free.

THE TOP HOTELS: Inter-Continental, 5 Karl-Arnold-Platz (tel. 43-48-48), is the star hotel in Düsseldorf, a pace-setting modern establishment. Other German hotel designers could learn from this deluxe hostelry. Placed at the edge of the city, across from the Hilton, it's an attractive, high-rise building, with its own entrance plaza and open swimming pool terrace. The service is efficient. Its rooftop restaurant, the Belle Époque, offers set dinner-dances at from 33 DM ($18.93) to 66 DM ($37.86). It opens at 6 p.m., and closes at 2 a.m. The entertainment in the turn-of-the-century setting is lively, the decor art nouveau. The Brasserie is in the old Germanic tavern style, offering moderately priced lunches and dinners. The Herold Bar and lounge is one of the main social centers of the city, set against a background of heraldic shields, old lanterns, and antiques. In addition to the three restaurants, there is a sauna with a massage service. The bedrooms, created by an internationally known designer, have coordinated colors with traditional furnishings. Most singles range in price from 108 DM ($61.95) to 160 DM ($91.78); doubles, 143 DM ($82.02) to 205 DM ($117.59).

Düsseldorf Hilton, 20 Georg-Glock-Strasse (tel. 43-49-63), and its adjoining congress centers are between the Kennedy Damm and the Rhine, close to the city, airport, and fair grounds. It is exactly what you would expect from a Hilton. Provided are well-designed and streamlined bedrooms, each with a handsomely equipped tile bath. Single rooms cost from 109 DM ($62.52) to 139 DM ($79.73), although they may go as high as 159 DM ($91.20). Doubles start at 149 DM ($85.47), going up to 180 DM ($103.25) and 198 DM ($113.57). The most expensive rooms are on the upper floors. But no matter what you pay, the view is good and the rooms attractively styled. Those added conveniences are there, too: the color TV outlets, radios, direct-dial phones, mini-bars, whatever. The public lounges reflect a progressively ultramodern decor, utilizing free-form sculpture and contemporary paintings. Most popular is Neptune's Club, with its swimming pool, sauna, and massage facilities, as well as a fitness center and solarium. The San Francisco Restaurant is famous for its creative cuisine, and at the Club 1001, it's disco time every night from 10 until 4 a.m. Most agreeable is the Hofgarten-Restaurant, a glassed-in garden room for informal dining, where you can order a set meal for only 19.50 DM ($11.19). Late in the afternoon, there's a Happy Hour, with recorded music.

Breidenbacher Hof, 36 Heinrich-Heine-Allee (tel. 86-01), seems to have been designed to coddle the well-heeled German and his meticulous frau.

Dating back to 1806 (although rebuilt when it was partially destroyed in World War II), it is Düsseldorf's leading traditional hotel, bordering on the luxurious. It was the leader long before the "upstarts" such as the Hilton and the Inter-Continental came along. Everything for plush living is to be found here, including a nightclub, the beautiful Regine's Club and a grill room with orchestral background music during the cocktail hour. The Breidenbacher Eck, with its intimate atmosphere, is also a magnet. The main drawing rooms and lounges have traditional furnishings—somewhat glamorized by a sprinkling of antiques, gilt mirrors, paintings, and bronze chandeliers. Unquestionably, the service is excellent. All bedrooms have private baths, telephone, radio, TV, and traditional furnishings. You pay from 160 DM ($91.78) to 175 DM ($100.38) in a single, from 210 DM ($120.46) to 240 DM ($137.66) in a double.

Steigenberger Park-Hotel, 1 Corneliusplatz (tel. 86-51), is a sedate, old-fashioned Germànic hotel which survived World War II. In fact, it has survived the decades and now must look with envy upon its more contemporary competitors. Nevertheless, it's still a prestige hotel, maintaining a good service level in the true old-world style. The lounges have been mildly modernized, as have the bedrooms, which are very comfortable. All the accommodations come with private bath; singles rent for 121 DM ($64.41); doubles, 160 DM ($91.78). Both prices include breakfast, service charge, and tax. The distinguished Rôtisserie attracts a well-dressed clientele, many from the fashion industry. Before dinner, drinks are served in the cozy Étoile Bar. During fair weather, breakfast is offered on the terrace overlooking the garden.

MEDIUM-PRICED HOTELS: Eden, 29–31 Aderstrasse (tel. 38-10-60), is a first-class hotel, catering to a business clientele. In spite of its name, it is more solid than lush. A lot of care has gone into making the bedrooms comfortable. But the baths, in most of the doubles, are more luxurious—tiled and spacious, with two basins and large fluffy towels. Singles are 70 DM ($40.15) with shower and 85 DM ($48.76) with complete bath. Double rooms with bath are from 130 DM ($75.57), all these rates including breakfast as well. A high level of cleanliness is maintained throughout. The position of the Eden is fairly central, with private parking in a rear courtyard. The reception area is small, but adequate, leading to a combination grill-restaurant-bar.

Esplanade, 17–18 Fürstenplatz (tel. 32-05-61), is a Germanic modern building, opening onto a quiet plaza, with fountains and trees. The Esplanade boasts an informal country-style dining room, a good cuisine, a slightly plush restaurant with bar, a heated swimming pool (plus a gymnastic room for your push ups), and a Scandinavian sauna. Not surprisingly, it seems to attract health faddists. The bedrooms are equipped with radios, phones, and private baths with tub or shower. Singles, depending on the plumbing, go for from 92 DM ($52.77) to 120 DM ($68.83). Doubles are 138 DM ($79.16) to 168 DM ($96.36). These prices include breakfast. You'll find the rooms comfortably modern and agreeable.

Atlantik, 3 Fürstenplatz (tel. 32-60-56), opening onto an attractive tree-filled square, is modern, but not glaringly so. For example, its small lobby is quite traditional. Although breakfast only is provided, the facilities of its neighboring sister hotel, the Esplanade, are available to Atlantik guests. Singles range from 49 DM ($28.11) to 75 DM ($43.02), depending on the plumbing. A double with running water costs from 79 DM ($45.31) to 85 DM ($48.76): with bath, from 105 DM ($60.23) to 130 DM ($75.57). Prices include breakfast.

BUDGET HOTELS: Graf Adolf Hospiz, 1 Stresemannplatz (tel. 36-05-91), is one of the better links in the Deutsche Verband Hospiz chain. The Düsseldorf link offers you a super-clean, reasonably priced accommodation well situated about three blocks from the railway station. You can relax in the nice reception lounge, then take an elevator to one of the 100 good-sized rooms, furnished in a trim contemporary manner. Because of the odd shape of the building, baths are present, but usually as an afterthought in design. Depending on the plumbing, singles run from 53 DM ($30.40) to 85 DM ($48.76). The most expensive doubles, those with bath and toilet, cost from 115 DM ($65.96) to 130 DM ($75.57). The atmosphere is fine, the rooms facing the street equipped with soundproof windows. The breakfast room on the first floor offers you a fair view of the morning crowd rushing to work. The morning meal is included in the rate.

Wurms, 23 Scheurenstrasse (tel. 37-50-01), offers 30 bedrooms that are most recommendable. It's in a five-story stucco building, close to the Graf-Adolf-Strasse, leading to the Rhine and about four blocks from the railway station. The accommodations are honestly furnished in dark wood which has been personalized with brightly colored bedspreads and curtains. Bathless singles are 35 DM ($20.08), increasing to 90 DM ($51.62) with bath. Bathless doubles go for 75 DM ($43.02); with bath, 90 DM ($51.62).

Hotel an der Oper, 15 Heinrich-Heine-Allee (tel. 80-621), next to American Express, is standard modern and utterly basic, with an absolute minimum of a reception area. The bedrooms are extremely simple, but adequate for only an overnight's stay. Bathless singles cost 40 DM ($22.94), 50 DM ($28.68) with bath. Bathless doubles are 80 DM ($45.89), increasing to 90 DM ($51.62) to 100 DM ($57.36) with bath. Taxes, service, and breakfast are included.

Pension Lindenau, 176a Karl-Rudolf-Strasse (tel. 38-18-79), is a tiny corner pension, suitable for low-cost overnighting. More small town in character than big city, it is somewhat cluttered, but ever so clean. With its flowers and pictures, the combination breakfast and TV room provides a homey touch. The friendly owner speaks a bit of English—enough to make you feel at home. Bedrooms are basic, containing only hot and cold running water. Singles go for 45 DM ($25.81); doubles, 70 DM ($40.15). These rates include breakfast.

Haus Runkel, 23 Kurfürsterstrasse (tel. 36-06-61), is in a renovated building off Karlstrasse, about four blocks from the railway station. The rooms are hit and miss—equipped with varying styles of furniture. Singles without bath are 40 DM ($22.94) to 45 DM ($25.81), increasing to 48 DM ($27.53) to 60 DM ($34.42) with shower. Bathless doubles go for 59 DM ($33.84) to 80 DM ($45.89); with shower, from 85 DM ($48.76) to 100 DM ($57.36). Breakfast is served free in a lounge that looks more characteristically like a former beer tavern. The management also runs the **Hotel Grosser Kurfürst,** 18 Kufürsterstrasse (tel. 35-76-47), which is housed in a more modern building. The rooms are better organized, but there's no furniture to spare. Bathless singles cost 42 DM ($24.09) to 45 DM ($25.81); with shower, 52 DM ($29.83) to 65 DM ($37.28). Bathless doubles range from 59 DM ($33.84) to 65 DM ($37.28), peaking at 72 DM ($41.30) to 90 DM ($51.62) with bath. Frankly, both hotels are somewhat overpriced for what they offer, but in Düsseldorf a budgeteer often doesn't have a choice.

Rheinpark, 13 Bankstrasse (tel. 49-07-86), is a 30-room, antiseptically modern little hotel, about three blocks from the Rhine. You are quite far away from the center, but a streetcar stopping nearby will quickly bring you to the Königsallee. The hotel's in a colorless concrete building, with no proper reception area, but rooms are clean, the furnishings banal oakwood modern, the walls nicely decorated with old pictures. All rooms have running water, and there's a shower on each floor. Singles cost from 35 DM ($20.08) to 56 DM ($32.12); doubles, from 70 DM ($40.15) to 100 DM ($57.36).

The **Jugendherberge,** Düsseldorf-Oberkassel, is the least expensive place to stay in the city (take bus no. 34 from the rail station). A youth hostel catering to people from all continents, it charges only 8 DM ($4.59) for a dormitory bed, plus 4 DM ($2.29) for sheets.

THE TOP RESTAURANTS: M&F, 14 Königsallee (tel. 32-60-01), is a deluxe haute-cuisine establishment where you dine in a stately, dignified atmosphere in keeping with the standards of the restaurant. It's in the most fashionable part of Düsseldorf, on the second floor, with some outside tables providing an ideal view of the promenade and canal. M&F stands for Müllers und Fest, famous for their outstanding wines. (Bottles of their fabulous wines are sold in the winery around the corner.) The cuisine is international, with Italian and French dishes providing added spice to the repertoire. Here are but a few suggestions, and you'll note that the prices are not exactly low. Cream of mushroom soup costs 7.75 DM ($4.45); breast of chicken with mushrooms and asparagus in a sauce suprême, 21 DM ($12.05). The average meat, fowl, or fish is around 32 DM ($18.36). Closed Sundays. Note: do not confuse M&F with the less expensive **KD** restaurant on the lower floor, with its sidewalk tables. Each is quite different.

Walliser Stuben, 46 Aderstrasse (tel. 37-47-57), offers rustic-style dining in a Swiss-style chalet. It's a cozy world of rough plaster walls, crude beams, bare wooden tables, a grandfather clock, a gleaming collection of brass ladles, pewter mugs, gilt-framed oil paintings, and field flowers in copper urns. Various dining areas provide semiprivacy. Waiters in colorful hand-embroidered smocks place overscale pepper and salt mills on each table. The Stuben is Swiss-owned with a Swiss chef—so you can't lose! It's not cheap, but the extra you pay is worth it. On the impressive à la carte menu, take note of the following: Specialties of the chef include noisette of lamb with fresh basil at 40 DM ($22.94); filet of turbot with tomato flan, 36 DM ($20.65); a fricasee of snails at 20 DM ($11.47); and a salad of the thigh of the duck with honey and thyme, 26 DM ($14.91). The chef also prepares a selection of sorbets at 15 DM ($8.60) per serving.

Schneider-Wibbel-Stuben, 5 Schneider-Wibbel-Gasse (tel. 156-05), is in Düsseldorf's famous Altstadt alleyway—with boutiques, a theater, and a museum—just off the Rhine. You get the finest fish dinners in Düsseldorf, and this attractive restaurant, which avoids any gimmicky decor, is dedicated to the expert preparation of fish. One of its three dining rooms honors the lobster, priced according to weight, of course, and prepared in practically any style. You can also dine at a counter, as in a New England oyster bar, or at one of the cozy booths. Appetizers include a cocktail of Greenland crayfish at 12 DM ($6.88) or a cream soup at 4 DM ($2.29). House specialties include blue carp at 8 DM ($4.59) and Nordland salmon at 25 DM ($14.34). Most desserts average around 6 DM ($3.44). The restaurant is closed Sundays.

A MEDIUM-PRICED RESTAURANT: Zum Schiffchen, 5 Hafenstrasse (tel. 32-71-76), has plenty of atmosphere. A golden model ship on top of the step-gabled building reminds you of its location, only a block from the Rhine. The interior of the 1628 structure relies heavily on the Germanic tavern tradition of scrubbed wooden tables and rustic artifacts. Good, hefty portions are the rule of the kitchen, open from noon to 3 p.m. and from 5 p.m. till midnight.

Specialties start at 8.50 DM ($4.88), going up to 25.90 DM ($14.86). The Schiffchen roast plate for two costs 43 DM ($24.66). The menu's large, the service rather hectic, the clientele friendly. Zum Schiffchen is the perfect place to sample Düsseldorf's own beer.

LOW-BUDGET DINING WITH ATMOSPHERE: Irish Pub Bei Fatty, 13 Hunsrückstrasse, is a sentimental favorite. Housed in a building dating from 1648, it has been the traditional dining and drinking spot for Düsseldorf artists. Nowadays, the alleyway out front is bombarded with discos at every door, but the pub tenaciously holds onto its atmosphere of Bohemia. Artist-guests have contributed the paintings on the walls; the atmosphere remains cluttered and charming, with red gingham cloths, lots of copper kettles and pots, ornate pumpkin-shaped glass lanterns, and frosted lights shining softly on the pewter plates. At a horseshoe-shaped bar, you may want to order a quick or "long" predinner drink. The Irish salmon plate goes for 12.50 DM ($7.17), or else you may prefer Dublin crab on toast, 4.90 DM ($2.81). A cheddar cheese sandwich costs 4.50 DM ($2.58). Of course, there is Irish coffee at 6.50 DM ($3.73). Scotch or Irish whiskey costs in the 4-DM ($2.29) to 5-DM ($2.87) range.

   Zum Schlüssel, Gatzweilers house-brewery, 43–47 Bolkerstrasse, is the original site of the famous Gatzweilers Alt brewery. The style is that of a classic German gasthaus, with an abundance of wood, ceramics, and pictures, capturing the aura of a country inn. The service, proffered by courteous, shirt-sleeved waiters, is lightning swift. You may not meet any fellow countrymen; this establishment is as Germanic as the Rhine. Featured are set lunches, running from 2.90 DM ($1.66) to 12.90 DM ($7.40). Actually, there are more than 30 meals to choose from for less than 8 DM ($4.59). The aroma and taste are good, and there's plenty to eat. Try the eisbein (pig knuckles) for 11.60 DM ($6.65), both filling and delicious. A huge bowl of soup costs from 1.65 DM (95¢) to 3 DM ($1.72). If you want only to drink, there's a side bar—but it's for men only. A quarter of a liter of the house beer, Gatzweillers Alt, costs just .90 DM (52¢).

6. Koblenz

   Just 55 miles southeast of Cologne, the city of Koblenz has stood at the confluence of the Rhine and Mosel Rivers for more than 2000 years. Its strategic point in the mid-Rhine region has made Koblenz a vital link in the international river trade routes of Europe. Tourists often find themselves here at either the start or finish of a steamer excursion of the Rhine Valley. Right in the heart of the wine country, Koblenz is surrounded by vine-covered hills dotted with old castles and fortresses.

THE SIGHTS: The town itself was heavily bombed during World War II, but many of the important historical buildings have been restored. For the best overall view of the town, go to the point where the two rivers meet. This is called **Deutsches Eck** (corner of Germany). From the top of the base, where a huge statue of Wilhelm I once stood, you can see the Old Town and across the Rhine to the Ehrenbreitstein Fortress.

   The focal point of the Old Town is the **Liebfrauenkirche** (Church of Our Lady), a 13th-century Gothic basilica built on a Romanesque foundation. Of particular interest are the unusual onion-shaped spires on the top of the church's twin towers. The early 18th-century **Town Hall** was formerly a Jesuit college. In the courtyard behind the hall is an unusual fountain dedicated to the youth of Koblenz and called *The Spitting Boy*—and that's just what he does! At the edge of the Old Town, near the Deutsches Eck, is Koblenz's oldest and most attractive church, **St. Castor's,** dating from 836. This twin-towered Romanesque basilica was the site of the Treaty of Verdun in the 9th century, dividing Charlemagne's empire.

The **Ehrenbreitstein Fortress,** across the Rhine from Koblenz, can be reached by chair lift, but if you have a fear of heights, you can drive via the Pfaffendorfer Bridge just south of the Old Town. The fortress was built on a rock, towering 400 feet above the Rhine. The present walls were built in the 19th century by the Prussians, on the site of the tenth-century fortress of the archbishops of Trier. It was the headquarters of the American Occupation Army following World War I. From the stone terrace, you can see for miles up and down the Rhine, a view that includes not only the town of Koblenz, but also several old castles along the Rhine and the terraced vineyards of the region.

THE TOP HOTEL: Diehl's, am Rhein, Ehrenbreitstein (tel. 7-20-10), is the most important hotel in Koblenz, built right on the banks of the Rhine, across the river from the town. All of its public rooms, lounges, and dining rooms, plus three-quarters of its bedrooms, face the river directly. You can watch the sun set on the water from your bedroom. It's an old-style hotel, which often accommodates groups. The furnishings are standard, but there is unquestioned comfort for your marks. Another advantage, besides the magnificent views, is the sliding scale of room prices. A single with shower goes for 44 DM ($25.24), increasing to 60 DM ($34.42) with private bath. Doubles with showers or private baths range in price from 70 DM ($40.15) to 90 DM ($51.62). Breakfast is included. Lunch is 14 DM ($8.03); a dinner, 20 DM ($11.47).

A MEDIUM-PRICED HOTEL: Kleiner Riesen, 18 Rheinanlagen (tel. 3-20-77), is one of the few city hotels lodged right on the banks of the Rhine. In fact, its dining room terrace and most of its bedrooms are close enough to wave at the boats as they go by. The hotel itself is a large, overgrown chalet, informal, with several living rooms and comfortable, clean bedrooms. A double with bath costs 110 DM ($63.10); a single with bath, 60 DM ($34.42). Bathless singles are 35 DM ($20.08). Nicely situated away from the town traffic, it has a peaceful small-town quietness.

BEST BUDGET HOTELS: Sophienhöhe, 3 Lehrohl (tel. 0261/7-20-96), is a gracious hillside home which has been converted to accommodate paying guests. It's across the river from Koblenz, but so are several of the better hotels. Lodged off a steep, winding road, it sits on a ledge, providing a romantic view of the Rhine (be there at sundown!). All its family-size bedrooms seem to have a share in this spectacular panorama, as does the dining room, with its projected tower room—a place where breakfast becomes a memorable meal. Two hard-working women keep everything immaculate. The furnishings throughout are adequate, with generous helpings of comfort. Bathless doubles cost 55 DM ($31.55), increasing to 80 DM ($45.89) with bath. Singles without bath are only 35 DM ($20.08). Breakfast's included.

Trierer Hof, 1 Deinhardplatz (tel. 3-10-60), a private hotel built back in 1786 and converted into a gasthof as early as 1789, was considered "revolutionary" at the time of its conversion. It is situated behind the schloss in the midst of gardens and only a quarter of a mile from the Deutsches Eck where the

Rhine meets the Mosel. Most of the bedrooms and lounges are overscale, although the furnishings are unimaginative. Per-person rates are as follows: 25 DM ($14.34) in a single without bath, 48 DM ($27.53) with bath, including breakfast. In a bathless double, two persons pay 54 DM ($30.97), this price rising to 80 DM ($45.89) with private bath. The hotel is easy to spot, next to the Koblenz Theatre.

Im Dortmunder, 92 Löhrstrasse (tel. 3-42-05), is a regular with traveling business people who know they can always get a clean and inexpensive overnight accommodation—without frills but with comfortable beds. The hotel's on a busy street near the main railway station. The reception desk is on the second floor. Including breakfast, rates are 24 DM ($13.77) in a bathless room, 26 DM ($14.91) with shower, 32 DM ($18.36) with bath.

Gasthaus Christ, 32 Schützenstrasse (tel. 3-77-02), is a modest little inn on a quiet street where life is informal and friendly. Rooms are simple, but clean and fairly comfortable. A distinct bargain is a bathless double renting for only 36 DM ($20.65), including breakfast. The use of the shower is an extra 4 DM ($2.29) for two persons. No singles are available.

READERS' HOTEL SELECTIONS: "Five minutes from the pier at the Rhine and five minutes from the train station, is the **Hotel Kornpforte,** 11 Kornpfortestrasse (tel. 3-11-74). Its accommodating management offers a pleasant double room without bath but with breakfast for 50 DM ($28.68) to 60 DM ($34.42)" (Jim and Linda Masini, Chicago, Ill.). . . . "We stayed at **Hotel Treffpunkt,** la Casinostrasse (tel. 3-19-97). It costs 26 DM ($14.91) each for a room with private shower. The room was large and superclean, and breakfast was included. The owner's husband is from Milwaukee, so, of course, she speaks English" (Beth Daniell, Atlanta, Ga.). . . . **"Kramer,** 12 Kardinal-Krementz-Strasse (tel. 4-13-40), is a small, 20-room, family-run hotel, with an elevator, in a quiet section within easy walking distance from the railroad station and main shopping areas. The hotel is pleasingly decorated and spotlessly clean, charging 30 DM ($17.21) without bath and 36 DM ($20.65) with bath, including a large breakfast. Mr. Kramer, the owner, speaks good English and is most helpful" (Robert J. Dickson, Charleston, W. Va.). . . . "We found a pleasant room within walking distance of the railroad station, in **Hotel Reinhard** (Garni), 60 Bahnhofstrasse (tel. 3-48-35). We were greeted by an attractive host, R. Mallabré, who spoke English. The cost of bed and breakfast for two was 56 DM ($32.12), service included" (Mrs. Berdena Koehler, Elmwood, Neb.). . . . "We stayed at the **Haus Morjan,** 14 Rheinzollstrasse (tel. 341-87). Right near where the Rhine steamers stop, it is delightful, though small. In a nice bedroom with a balcony, we were charged 64 DM ($36.71), including breakfast for two. We could walk out and see the traffic on the river" (Graham and Rhonda Kelly, Sydney, Australia). . . . "We stayed at the **Hotel National,** 47 Roonstrasse (tel. 1-41-94), run by Rita Blasius. This was within walking distance of the rail and boat connections. A double room costs 55 DM ($31.55), complete with hot and cold running water and breakfast. The hotel has an elevator, but no dining room, though there is an excellent restaurant nearby. The owner will gladly give directions. The hotel lies in a quiet neighborhood away from the busy section of town" (Mr. and Mrs. Henry Meyers, Augusta, Mich.). . . . **"Park-Hotel,** 1 Arenberg (tel 0261/6-88-80), is in the suburbs but can be reached easily by bus or car. It is modernized and exceptionally clean. Our double room with breakfast cost 45 DM ($25.81), including parking. The hotel is fine except for its location if you are not driving. It is near the large museum of Ehrenbreitstein Citadel, a fortress)" Stanley and Dorothy Sandelius, Stockton, Calif.).

WHERE TO DINE: Bit Stuben, 36 Rizza Strasse, is a traditional restaurant with wooden tables and chairs. Red-and-white napkins and tinted windows make for a cozy ambience. The food is good, and the service polite. Soups range from 3.75 DM ($2.15) to 6.50 DM ($3.73). Typically Germanic main dishes go from 6 DM ($3.44) to 19 DM ($10.90). More elaborate meals include sole meunière at 24 DM ($13.77) or rumpsteak in the American style, with a tomato salad and french fries, at 18 DM ($10.32). A wide choice of desserts is available at prices ranging from 3.75 DM ($2.15) to 7 DM ($4.02).

Weinhaus Hubertus, 54 Florinsmarkt (tel. 3-11-77), across from the Old Rathaus Museum, offers both rooms and meals in the Old Town. It looks like an old timbered country inn, with boxes of red geraniums at the windows. The furnishings and the decor of the rooms are family style, offering a homey atmosphere. Family antiques are placed throughout. The owner, Richard Caldeway, welcomes guests to his large, warm, and friendly dining room. Wooden chairs and wooden tables covered with white napkins provide an intimate setting, enhanced by candlelight. Soups begin at 2.50 DM ($1.43). Main dishes start as low as 6 DM ($3.44), going up to 17.50 DM ($10.04). Game specialties in season go from 12.50 DM ($7.17). You may rent a room as well, costing from 36 DM ($20.65) to 45 DM ($25.81) for two persons with hot and cold running water only.

WINE-TASTING: Weindorf, at the foot of the Pfaffendorfer Bridge, right on the Rhine, is the center for tasting the wines of the vineyards of the Mosel and Rhine regions. It's actually a timbered wine village where everyone gathers on festive evenings. In fair weather, you'll prefer to do your sampling in the open courtyard—or on the river-view terrace. Let someone else do the driving afterward.

READERS' SELECTION AT BACHARACH: From Koblenz we got off at a small town called Bacharach. At first it didn't look interesting, but once we passed through one of the gates of the wall surrounding the front of the town, we were transported back to the Middle Ages. It is untouched by time—small, narrow, cobblestoned streets, picture-book hotels, and friendly people. The town is 31 miles from Koblenz, the same distance from Mainz.

"We stayed at a hotel, the **Altkölnischer Hof,** 2 Blücherstrasse (tel. 13-39), which is open only from April to October. The town is small enough, so simply ask someone who will direct you to it. Here we had a double room for 46 DM ($26.39) without shower. The hotel's restaurant has a never-ending list of culinary delights at very reasonable prices, main dishes beginning at 14 DM ($8.03). The owners also speak English well. The hotel also looks as if it were from the Middle Ages, with a white exterior and black crisscrossing beams.

"We left Koblenz at 2 p.m. and arrived at Bacharach at 5:30 p.m. The most enjoyable part of the trip was to arrive at Bacharach in peak European holiday season and not have to fight crowds to find a hotel. The Rhine trip from Koblenz to Bacharach is through one of the most colorful sections of the Rhine Valley, with its castles and Lorelei Rock. The next day it's possible for readers to take the train from Bacharach station (about a quarter of a mile down the road from the hotel) to Bingen and then on to Mainz" (Peter and Barbara Jones, Oshawa, Ontario, Canada).

7. Mainz

In spite of its size—Mainz has a population of nearly 200,000—this 2000-year-old city at the confluence of the Rhine and Main Rivers is still a provincial wine town. Since the Romans brought the first vine stalks to Mainz in 38 B.C., it has been the center of the wine-producing regions of the Rheingau and Rheinhessen. It's a festive city, with its annual Wine Fair taking place each August and September. The most celebrated merrymaking is at the All Fools capers at Carnival each spring, broadcast throughout Germany like an annual Macy's parade. In June each year, the Gutenberg Festival sponsors an excellent cultural season, a living memorial to the city's favorite son, the inventor of the movable-type printing press.

THE SIGHTS: Above the roofs of the half-timbered houses in the old section of town rise the six imposing towers of **St. Martin's Cathedral.** The Romanesque basilica, dating from 975 A.D., has been constantly rebuilt and restored, until its present form, dating mainly from the 13th and 14th centuries, is a combination of nearly every period of European architecture. Below the largest dome, a curious combination of Romanesque and baroque, is the transept, separating the west chancel from the nave and smaller east chancel. Many of the supporting pillars along the aisles of the nave are decorated with carved and painted statues of French and German saints. One of Germany's best collections of religious art is housed in the cathedral's **Diocesan Museum.** Within it are exhibitions of reliquaries and medieval sculpture, including works by the Master of Naumburg. In the 1000-year-old cathedral crypt is a modern gold reliquary of the saints of Mainz. Among the most impressive furnishings in the sanctuary itself are the rococo choir stalls and a pewter baptismal font from the early 14th century.

The **Gutenberg Museum,** opposite the east towers of the cathedral, is a unique memorial to the city's favorite son. In the modern display rooms, visitors can trace the history of printing from Gutenberg's hand press on which he printed the 42-lined Bible from 1452 to 1455, to the most advanced typesetting processes. The collections cover the entire spectrum of the graphic arts as well as phases of books and printing, illustration, and binding in all countries, past and present. The most popular—and valuable—exhibit is the famous Gutenberg Bible. The museum is open from Tuesday through Saturday from 10 a.m. to 1 p.m. and from 3 p.m. to 6 p.m.; Sunday, from 10 a.m. to 1 p.m. Closed on Monday. Admission free.

The **Mittelrheinische Landesmuseum** (Provincial Museum of the Central Rhineland), 49–51 Grosse Bleiche, is worth a visit to get a pictorial history of Mainz and the middle Rhine, from prehistoric times to the present. The most impressive exhibits are the famous Roman marble head of the Emperor Augustus, 14 A.D., and the towering Column of Jupiter, erected in Mainz by the Romans in 67 A.D. Although the original is in the museum, you may, if you are pressed for time, see the true-to-life replica in front of the Parliament building. Also of great interest is the gallery of the museum with important paintings from the 15th through the 20th centuries. The museum is open Tuesday through Sunday from 10 a.m. to 5 p.m. Closed Monday. Admission is free.

ACCOMMODATIONS: Many tourists visit Mainz on a day trip from Frankfurt, just 25 miles away. The Rhine-Main International Airport is just a 20-minute taxi ride from the center of the city. If you do plan to stay over, however, be advised that reservations are needed during the spring and autumn festival seasons. Below are our hotel recommendations in three price categories.

A Deluxe Hotel

Mainz Hilton, 68 Rheinstrasse (tel. 1-07-81). Yes, there is a Hilton on the Rhine! True, its exterior is cold—all glass and marble—but the public rooms are attractive, especially the Beer Stube and the Roman Weinstube. The Rheinbar is more elegant and the Rheingrill simulates dining aboard a luxurious Rhine River yacht. The 251 bedrooms are tastefully appointed and color coordinated, with a unified theme. The higher up you go for your overnighting, the higher the price. A single room with bath begins at a basic low of 120 DM ($68.83), ranging upward to 135 DM ($77.44). Doubles start at 135 DM

($77.44), peaking at 170 DM ($97.51). A top-floor panoramic dining room and open terrace provide a view of the river boats. The Hilton is connected to the Rheingoldhalle, one of the largest assembly halls in Europe.

The Middle Bracket

Mainzer Hof, 98 Kaiserstrasse (tel. 2-84-71), is six floors of modernity, directly on the river, almost at the point where some of the Rhine boats dock. It's a clean-cut, convenient stopover hotel on your journey down the Rhine. The furnishings in some of the bedrooms achieve a modified lushness, straight out of the boudoir tradition. The rate in a single with bath or shower is 90 DM ($51.62), rising to 134 DM ($77.86) in a double, breakfast included. The dining room, with its sweeping view of the Rhine, is attractive.

Schottenhof, 6 Schottstrasse (tel. 2-18-43), is nice and modern. Off a busy avenue, it manages to have a warm atmosphere. The actual position is on a dead-end street, leading to the railroad and transit pedestrian plaza. The furnishings and carpeting are sometimes a little dark, but the comfort inside the rooms is real. Singles with shower or bath cost from 45 DM ($25.81) to 48 DM ($27.53), and doubles with the same plumbing go from 70 DM ($40.15) to 85 DM ($48.76).

The Budget Range

Hotel am Römerwall, 53 Römerwall (tel. 2-57-80), near the university grounds, is two villas, pleasantly positioned in a garden. It attracts not only bargain seekers, but guests wanting to avoid the sterile atmosphere of the typical hotel. Here the accent is on homelike comfort, as reflected in the public living room and breakfast salon (the only meal served, incidentally). Each of the bedrooms is comfortably appointed, with heavy use made of all-white furnishings and bright, contrasting fabrics. A double with private bath and shower costs from 70 DM ($40.15) to 88 DM ($50.48), although a few singles with shower or bath go from 42 DM ($24.09) to 60 DM ($34.42). A few cheaper bathless doubles rent for anywhere from 56 DM ($32.12) to 66 DM ($37.86); bathless singles, 30 DM ($17.21) to 37 DM ($21.22). Breakfast is included in all tariffs. The owner, Frau R. Flaschl, has a good staff, who keep the bedrooms immaculate.

Hammer, 6 Bahnhofplatz (tel. 6-28-47), has been completely renewed. The furnishings are modern; there's new carpeting, and the reception is bright. The rooms are comfortable and of good size. All rooms come with private shower, bath, and toilet, radio, and a mini-bar. The rates are 49 DM ($28.11) to 55 DM ($31.55) for a single, 75 DM ($43.02) to 85 DM ($48.76) for a double, and 95 DM ($54.49) for a triple. Breakfast is included, as well as taxes and service.

Richter Eisenbahn, 6 Alicentstrasse (tel. 2-76-30), close to the station, looks more like a pension. The decoration may not always be dazzling, although the furniture often achieves an unexpected style. However, the accommodation is fair and comfortable, the prices a good bargain. Bathless singles are in the 21-DM ($12.05) to 26-DM ($14.91) range, rising to 28 DM ($16.06) with shower. Bathless doubles are priced from 46 DM ($26.39), increasing to 48 DM ($27.53) with shower, breakfast included.

READERS' HOTEL SELECTIONS: The **Weinhaus Rebstock,** 5 Leichhofstrasse (tel. 2-57-55), is a family-run operation over the top of a 'weinhaus' where delightful and enormous meals may be had at a very reasonable price. Our room was clean and spacious with a toilet on the same floor. The charge is 48 DM ($27.53) for a double, which includes a fine breakfast of homemade bread, ham, cheese, juice, and coffee. The woman and her son who seem to be in charge of the hotel are very friendly (the son speaks English fluently). The hotel is within walking distance of the Adenauer Ufer, where one boards the boat for the Rhine River tours" (Eileen S. Lane, Chicago, Ill.). . . . **"Hotel Pfeil and Continental,** 15 Bahnhofstrasse, is a three-minute walk from the railroad station and two minutes from the bus stop for the Rhine boat departures. It is over a shop, but there is an elevator. A bathless single with hot and cold running water costs 30 DM ($17.21), including breakfast, your own choice from the side table which holds cereal, cheese, jam, honey, and sausage, as well as rolls and butter" (D. Hannay, Sanderstead, Surrey, England).

WHERE TO DINE: Haus des Deutschen Weines, 3 Gutenbergplatz, is a good wine restaurant. The shields outside represent the German wine districts, and the cellar inside stocks the finest bottles from the Rheingau. An easy walk from the Dom and the Gutenberg Museum, the House of German Wines makes a fine luncheon choice, offering set meals for 17 DM ($9.75) and 30 DM ($17.21). On the à la carte menu, game is featured in season. Main dishes average 16 DM ($9.18) to 24 DM ($13.77). A recent repast began with a tasty onion soup with croutons at 4.25 DM ($2.44) and was topped by a smooth peach Melba at 7.50 DM ($4.30). The restaurant is on the second floor.

READER'S PENSION SELECTION AT BINGEN: "In the town of Bingen, about 20 miles from Mainz, I strongly recommend **Pension Harling-Schneider,** 14 Kapuzinerstrasse-Mainerstrasse (the street changes names) at the corner of Laurentzigasse, within walking distance—that is, if you have a small suitcase—of the railroad station or dock where Rhine excursion craft dock. The street out front is quiet. A bathless double costs 36 DM ($20.65). It was much nicer than some in other towns costing far more" (Allen Shields, Ann Arbor, Mich.).

8. Worms

This ancient city traces its beginnings back to the earliest civilizations—even before the Romans settled here, Germanic tribes had made Worms their capital. Siegfried began his legendary adventures, recorded in the Nibelungenlied, when he visited here. The town's most famous visitor, Martin Luther, arrived under less desirable circumstances. He was "invited" to appear before the Imperial Diet at Worms, and after refusing to retract his grievance against the Church of Rome, he was excommunicated. Now that the majority of Worms is Protestant, it has erected a huge monument to Luther and other giants of the Reformation.

Worms also has one of the oldest Jewish communities in Germany, with a synagogue dating back to the 11th century. The Hebrew cemetery is much more interesting, however, with hundreds of tombstones, some going back more than 800 years.

Towering physically and historically above all the other ancient buildings of the city is the majestic **St. Peter's Cathedral,** considered the purest Romanesque basilica in the Rhine Valley. The east choir, with a flat facade and semicircular interior, is the oldest section, dating from 1110. This was designed as the sanctuary, where the clergy performed the rites of the divine service. Lavishly decorated in baroque style during the 18th century by the famous architect Balthasar Neumann, the chancel glows with the gold and marble of the pillared enclosure for the high altar. This opulent workmanship was so large that there was no place for a proper transept. In Gothic times, the choir stalls stood in the apse, but now they had to build them into the transept. The west choir, dedicated in 1181, is more traditionally Romanesque, with a polygon-shaped exterior protruding between two round old towers. The interior has a quiet elegance, with little decoration other than the rosette window and several memorial slabs and monuments to the dead buried beneath the cathedral. Between these two extremes, which symbolize the coordination of ecclesiastical and secular power, is the nave, rather bare by comparison, where the people gather to worship. Well worth seeing is the highly decorated 14th- or 15th-century side Chapel of St. Nicolas, with its Gothic baptismal font and new stained-glass windows. The cathedral is open for visitors daily but closes during the winter for two hours each afternoon. Admission is .50 DM. (27¢).

BUDGET HOTELS: Dom-Hotel, 10 Obermarkt (tel. 62-77), is an all-purpose modern hotel, about a block from the cathedral. It's a postwar structure, built in a complex of shops and boutiques. The glass-walled bedrooms have an assortment of modern contemporary furnishings, and they offer adequate comfort. Depending on the plumbing, singles range in price from 39 DM ($22.37) to 52 DM ($29.83). Bathless doubles are tagged at 62 DM ($35.56), rising to 70 DM ($40.15) to 88 DM ($50.48) with bath. In the wood-paneled dining room, set meals are served for only 14 DM ($8.03). The guest lounge is a good place for relaxation. Altogether, it's an ideal little hotel for the in-and-out traveler.

Central, 5 Kammererstrasse (tel. 47-18). Although the rooms are not too big, they are furnished with a certain degree of comfort and warmth. Depending on the plumbing, singles range from 24 DM ($13.77) to 30 DM ($17.21); doubles, 44 DM ($25.24) to 50 DM ($28.68)—breakfast included. The reception staff speaks English fluently.

READER'S HOTEL SELECTION: "I stayed at the **Hotel Garni Hüttl,** 5–7 Peterstrasse (tel. 8-78-74), and was extremely impressed. This hotel is new, spacious, charming, very clean, and reasonably priced. A single room with shower and toilet costs 26 DM ($14.91), while a room with two beds, with like facilities, costs 48 DM ($27.52). Eighteen of the hotel's rooms have showers and toilets; the remaining nine share the plumbing. The Hotel Garni Hüttl is in the center of town and easily accessible to historic Worms. A nearby lot turns into a marketplace on Saturdays, an event that added surprise to my stay at Worms" (Naura Diehl, Stamford, Conn.).

9. The Rheingau

When God was looking for a place to set up His Paradise, so goes the story, He once considered the sunny slopes between the Taunus Mountains and the Rhine. Even though He obviously changed His mind, the Rheingau today is the kingdom of another god, Bacchus, who reigns supreme here. Nearly every town and village from Wiesbaden to Assmanshausen, no matter how small, is a major wine-producer. The names suddenly seem familiar—Bingen, Johannisberg, Rüdesheim, Oestrich—because we have seen them on the labels of many favorite wines.

The Rheingau is also rich in old churches and castles, as well as landmarks. The **Niederwald Monument,** on a hill halfway between Rüdesheim and Assmanshausen—it can be reached by cablecar from either town—is a huge statue of Germania, the *Watch on the Rhine,* erected by Bismarck in 1883 to commemorate the reunification of Germany. Below it, on a small island at the bend of the Rhine, is the infamous Mäuseturm (Mouse Tower), where, according to legend, the harsh bishop of Mainz was devoured by a swarm of hungry mice. But the real attraction of the Rheingau is the cheerful character of the wine villages and their friendly people.

In the heart of the Rheingau is the epitome of the Rhine wine towns:

RÜDESHEIM: With its old courtyards and winding alleyways lined with timbered houses, Rüdesheim is everything that a wine town should be: festive and terribly serious about its wines. The vineyards around the village date back to the Roman Emperor Probus. Besides the full-bodied Riesling, brandy and champagne are also produced here. Rüdesheim is the scene of the annual September wine festival, when the old taverns on the narrow Drosselgasse are filled with jovial tasters from all over the world. To prove how seriously Rüdesheimers take their wines, they have opened a wine museum in the old Bromserburg Castle, which traces the history of the grape with an exhibition of wine presses, glasses, goblets, and drinking utensils dating from Roman times to the present.

Top Hotel Choice

Rüdesheimer Hof, 1 Geisenheimer Strasse (tel. 20-11), is a village inn, set back from the Rhine, with a side garden and terrace where wine tasters gather at rustic tables. The atmosphere is informal; you can dine here and most certainly spend the night. A bathless double costs 63 DM ($36.14). There are a few doubles with showers or baths which go for 86 DM ($49.33) to 105 DM ($60.23). Singles without bath cost 42 DM ($24.09); with shower, 52 DM ($29.83) to 56 DM ($32.12). Most of the accommodations are roomy and comfortably furnished. Antiques are used generously throughout.

Staying here is like sampling the pulse of a Rhine village—seeing the townspeople mingling with visitors, eating the regional food, and drinking the Rheingau wines. The inn opens in February, closes at the end of October. If you're stopping by just to eat, you'll find set meals from 10.50 DM ($6.02) to 30 DM ($17.21). Fish dishes are usually in the 15-DM ($8.60) to 18-DM ($10.32) range. Guests dine at cafe tables placed under a willow tree.

The Budget Range

Zum Baren, 31 Schmidtstrasse (tel. 2667), is a well-run hotel presided over by Karl-Heinz Willig, a gracious host who has shown kindness to readers of this book. He offers both singles and doubles with hot and cold running water as well as a shower and private toilet. There's also a sauna on the premises. The rate is 44 DM ($25.24) to 52 DM ($29.83) in a double, dropping to anywhere from 22 DM ($12.62) to 24 DM ($13.77) in a single, including a continental breakfast, service, and tax. The restaurant offers good plain cooking. Guests enjoy sitting out on the cozy terrace and like the central, in-town location.

READERS' HOTEL SELECTIONS: "The find of the trip was a new inn, **Gasthof Krancher,** 4 Oberstrasse (tel. 27-62), right up the hill next to the owner's own vineyard. The rooms contain hot and cold running water and are right across the court from the hotel's dining room and office. The owner speaks English and is also the chef. He served steak that tasted as good as any I've had in America. He also makes his own wine and will gladly show you his grape press, vineyard tractor, and wine cellar. It was delightful to look out our window and see the grapes growing. A twin-bedded room costs 22 DM ($12.62) per person with a continental breakfast, although a single costs 25 DM ($14.34). A room with shower or toilet costs an additional 6 DM ($3.44) per person, and half pension is 36 DM ($20.65). We were able to walk from his guest house to the main street—of course, it was uphill going back, but you got a good view of the town along the way" (Mr. and Mrs. Henry Meyers, Augusta, Mich.). . . . "**Hotel Gastatte Hohn,** 1 Niedsewaldstrasse (tel. 23-66), is a two-minute walk from the bustling center of town. Our very modern and well-furnished room was equipped with a shower and was quite clean. The charge is 26 DM ($14.91) per person per day, including breakfast" (Susan L. Davison, Herford, West Germany).

A Hunting Lodge at Niederwald

Waldhotel Jagdschloss Niederwald (tel. 0-67-22) is perched high in the hills, three miles from the center of Rüdesheim itself. It's a world apart, attracting visitors for romantic weekends along with families on holiday. Part of the compound was the former hunting lodge of the dukes of Hesse. That tone is reflected in the entrance hall, with its hunting museum decor.

A wide-view terrace has been enclosed, allowing for a panoramic sweep over the Rhine Valley. Vines have been trailed under a glass arbor roof. The rates are from 31 DM ($17.78) to 35 DM ($20.08) in a bathless single, from 68 DM ($39) in a bathless double. In a double with bath, the rate ranges from 88 DM ($50.48) to 104 DM ($59.65), dropping to 52 DM ($29.83) to 68 DM ($39) in a single with bath. Half board costs an extra 18 DM ($10.32) per person.

Although off the main travel route, the schloss is restful and rewarding. From Rüdesheim, drive toward Presberg (the Jagdschloss signs will appear).

READERS' SELECTION AT MITTELHEIM: "Although at first reluctant to tell the masses of 'our' find, we promised Mrs. Berg back in Mittelheim that we would: Have a terrace with a view of the Rhine, Wilhelm Berg's own wine, a beautiful, spotlessly clean room and a delicious breakfast at the **Pension W. Berg**, 10 Weinheimer Strasse (tel. 33-90), in the quaint town of Mittelheim (Orstrich-Winkel), ten minutes from busy Rüdesheim, all for 32 DM ($18.36). We first learned of the hospitable Bergs and their lovely pension five years ago. After being so pleased with what we found then, we went back. Many things have changed in that area on the Rhine, but the Pension Berg is still a remarkable bargain. Within easy reach: the wine museum (in an old castle) in Rüdesheim, the peaceful Niederwald, Marienthal Kloster, Schloss Vollrads, and a swimmenbad. There's an unlimited supply of Mr. Berg's wines, proudly brought up from the cellar as Mrs. Berg rushes out with beautiful wine glasses—at the unbelievably low price of $2" (Mr. and Mrs. Murray Apelbaum, Brooklyn, N.Y.).

ASSMANSHAUSEN: At the northern edge of the Rheingau, this old village is built on the slopes on the east bank of the Rhine. The half-timbered houses and vineyards seem precariously perched on the steep hillsides, and the view of the Rhine Valley from here is awe-inspiring. Assmanshausen is famous for its fine red Burgundy-style wine, and . . .

A Notable Inn

Krone, 10 Rheinstrasse (tel. 22-36), is one of a few inns in Germany with so distinguished a pedigree. Built right on the banks of the Rhine, surrounded by its own lawns, gardens, and swimming pool, it traces its origins back 400 years. The inn is overscaled—a great big gingerbread fantasy. Not to be missed is a small second-floor lounge, virtually a museum, with framed letters and manuscripts of some of the more celebrated personages who have stayed here— Goethe, for one. There's a stack of 37 autograph books, signed by writers, painters, diplomats, and composers.

Your actual bedroom may either be in a building from the Middle Ages, a Renaissance structure, or a postwar house. The bedrooms have a decided old-inn character, spacious with traditional furnishings. A single room, bathless, ranges in price from 35 DM ($20.08) to 40 DM ($22.94); singles with bath, 60 DM ($34.42) to 70 DM ($40.15). Bathless doubles are priced at 60 DM ($34.42) to 70 DM ($40.15); doubles with bath, 90 DM ($51.62) to 140 DM ($80.30). Breakfast is 8 DM ($4.59) extra.

The public rooms are time-seasoned, with a preponderance of antiques, old oak paneling, antlers, framed photographs, antique clocks, and oil paintings, all heavy Teutonic.

Even if you're not overnighting, you may want to stop over to sample one of the finest meals you're likely to be served on the Rhine. For example, you might begin with real turtle soup at 7 DM ($4.02) or a half-dozen snails at 9.50 DM ($5.45), and follow with fresh salmon at 34 DM ($19.50) or broiled Rhine eel with dill at 26 DM ($14.91). In season, the house specialty is a saddle of venison for two persons at 74 DM ($42.45). For dessert, try the eisbecher Krone at 7.50 DM ($4.30). Stocked in the rock-hewn cellars is one of the finest assortments of Rhine wines in the world.

The Moderate Range

Alte Bauernschänke (tel. 23-13) is owned by Konrad Berg and his family, who are known as wine-growers. They have completely renovated two of the oldest mansions of the town, turning them into a hotel and restaurant. The interior decor is luxurious, with tapestries, carpeting, and ornate furniture. The comfort is great, and the welcome hearty. Near the church inside the village, the hotel is not far from the Rhine, about a quarter of a mile. A bathless double costs 40 DM ($22.94), increasing to anywhere from 78 DM ($44.74) to 88 DM ($50.48) with bath. These prices include breakfast. The restaurant of the hotel provides a folkloric experience, with musicians playing every night. A goulash soup, a peppersteak with fresh green beans and french fries, plus a half bottle of Mr. Berg's red wine, will cost a maximum of 30 DM ($17.21) per person. If you order and select from the menu less lavishly, you can get away for 18 DM ($10.32).

Low-Cost Rooms and Meals at Inns

Unter den Linden, 1 Rheinstrasse (tel. 22-88), is a converted Rhine-fronting villa, which places heavy emphasis on its cuisine and terrace wine drinking. A new building has been added at the rear, offering units for overnight. If there is a choice of rooms, avoid the rear location because of heavy railroad traffic. The line runs 30 yards from your window, and a train passes by every three minutes. Up front, the dining room now overflows onto part of an open terrace. There's a minimum of public lounges, the space being eaten up primarily by tables. In front is a wide terrace shaded by a grape arbor and linden trees. In summer, revelers fill up every table. English is spoken, the food is good, and the wine is superb. The accommodations are a bargain. All are pleasantly decorated and comfortable. Bathless doubles cost 50 DM ($28.68), increasing to 64 DM ($36.71) with complete bath. A bathless single begins at 30 DM ($17.21). A dish of the day is featured in the dining room. On one recent occasion we enjoyed filet of smoked Black Forest trout at 9.50 DM ($5.45). Meals in the 14-DM ($8.03) to 23-DM range are offered. The soup of the day costs 3 DM ($1.72). Desserts, such as an apple tart with cream, add another 5 DM ($2.87) to your bill.

Hotel-Café Post (tel. 23-26). Coming from Rüdesheim, you'll discover this inn alongside the Rhine. The owner, Joseph Hötger, is the concierge of the Krone. He offers a good bargain in immaculately kept rooms, furnished in a modern, practical style. A single without bath costs 25 DM ($14.34); a double without bath, 32 DM ($18.36) to 40 DM ($22.94). A double with bath and toilet ranges in price from 60 DM ($34.42) to 75 DM ($43.02). Half-pension per person per day goes from 35 DM ($20.08) to 60 DM ($34.42), depending on the plumbing in the room you occupy. The food is simple and fine, and you can dine in a room overlooking the Rhine traffic. A continental breakfast costs 6 DM ($3.44). A lunch is 16 DM ($9.18); dinner, 18 DM ($10.32).

SAMPLING THE HOSPITALITY OF THE RHEINGAU: Everywhere you turn in this vine-laden region, you come upon little village inns, or massive castles converted into hotels. We have selected a few of the most unusual and enjoyable.

Burg Schwarzenstein (tel. 88-50), in the old monastery town of Johannisberg, is a restaurant installed in a fort, surrounded by vineyards. The establishment nestles in the ruins of a turreted tower, with dining tables on a 100-foot terrace overlooking the valley. The patio is covered with bearing grapes. For colder weather, there is an indoor dining room also affording a panoramic view. Some people come here just to sample the wine, especially the 1976 Johannisberger Kochsberg Hölle Riesling No. 22 for 60 DM ($34.42) a bottle. The food is good, too, with main dishes beginning at 14 DM ($8.03), soups at 3 DM ($1.72) to 6.90 DM ($3.96), and desserts at 6 DM ($3.44). Johannisberg is reached from Rüdesheim by taking the road to Winkel (from there proceed on a northwestern route for approximately 1½ miles).

Hotel Schwan, in Oestrich, 5 Rheinallee (tel. 30-01), is one of the most celebrated inns in Germany. You might spend the night in the favored tower room with its seven windows overlooking the Rhine, descend the cantilevered wooden staircase built in 1628, or taste the Rheingau wine, Oestricher Lenchen, while sitting on a Rhine-fronting terrace. The innkeeping family, the Winkel-Wenckstern, keep their Swan preening proud, hospitable and friendly. This is an inn of Renaissance gables and a half-timbered facade. It opens onto the little front garden facing a boat landing dock.

The bedrooms have been brought up to date with modern plumbing and comfortable furnishings. Doubles with private bath, including tax and service, go for 110 DM ($63.10) to 160 DM ($91.78). Dining here is genuinely excellent, with main dishes in the 15-DM ($8.60) to 30-DM ($17.21) range. You'll also find a historical wine cellar here, with racks of rare vintages and huge wooden casks of "open wines."

A Castle Hotel on the Rhine

Hotel Schloss Reinhartshausen (tel. 40-81) is in Erbach, the site of one of the finest Rheingau wines, the "Marcobrunner." On the banks of the Rhine, this 18th-century palace was the property of Prince Frederick of Prussia, the heir to the Hohenzollern throne. It is both a famous and a fashionable oasis and follows faithfully the prince's decision to restore it skillfully and convert it to receiving paying guests in style and comfort. The hotel enjoys a reputation for its cellar and vineyard. Across the Rhine is the hotel's large farm, from which much of the produce for the kitchen originates. The cuisine is of an exceptional international standard. A typical menu might include cream of lobster soup with cognac at 9 DM ($5.16); chateaubriand with béarnaise sauce for three, 52 DM ($29.83); and an apple pancake, 8 DM ($4.59).

The castle hotel is elegantly appointed, the salons intricate, with gold and white paneling, family portraits (some of them the greats of Germany), carefully tended antiques, rare Oriental rugs, and Empire bronze urns. The bedrooms are regal, yet retain a country house character—each with its own style and personality. Nearly all have private baths or showers, with doubles going from 90 DM ($51.62) to 150 DM ($86.04); singles without bath, 50 DM ($28.68);

with bath, 60 DM ($34.42) to 90 DM ($51.62). Lunch, breakfast, or afternoon tea is best in the wide garden terrace, where you can leisurely enjoy the prince's wine while looking at the river traffic in the distance.

10. Speyer

As one of the oldest Rhine cities of the Holy Roman Empire, Speyer early became an important religious center, culminating in the Diet of Speyer, which in 1529 united the followers of Luther in a protest against the Church of Rome. Nothing recalls this medieval German empire as much as the **Imperial Cathedral** in Speyer, perhaps the greatest building of its time.

The cathedral, begun in the early 11th century, is the largest Romanesque edifice in Germany. After several restorations in former times—the cathedral has weathered the damage of fires and wars—the silhouette of the cathedral (roofs and gables) was restored to its original shape from 1957 to 1969. Only the huge dome over the transept has kept its curved sweep. Entering the church through the single west door set in a stepped arch, you are immediately caught up in the vastness of the proportions, as the whole length of the nave and east chancel opens up before you. Lit by the muted daylight from above, it contains the royal tombs of eight emperors of the Holy Roman Empire, as well as a row of bishops' tombs. The cathedral is open from April 1 to September 30 on weekdays from 9 a.m. to 6 p.m.; on Saturdays, till 4 p.m.; and on Sundays, from 1:30 to 4:30 p.m. Off-season weekday hours are from 9 to 11:30 a.m., 1:30 to 4:30 p.m.; till 4 p.m. on Saturdays; and from 1:30 to 4:30 p.m. on Sundays. Entrance to the crypt is .50 DM (29¢). A guided tour costs 1 DM (57¢) per person.

THE LEADING INN: Wittelsbacher Hof, 2 Ludwigstrasse (tel. 7-68-28), is a stately, two-story building that has housed such famous guests as Ludwig II and Lola Montez. With its Corinthian columns and a mask of porous stone, it is a creation of the late baroque period. The present building was erected in 1709 by the Austrian baroque architect and builder, Johann Jakob Rischer (1662–1755). It was built on the medieval ruins of the main cloister of the Zisterzienser monks and known as the Eusserthaler Hof.

The Eusserthaler Hof in Speyer was (since 1277) the marketplace of the Zisterzienser monks, who brought in their products from various farms in the Palatinate (Until its total destruction in 1689, Speyer was an important mercantile center). The storage and cellar foundations of the present building are still partially extant. As early as 1525, it was known that the Eusserthaler Hof was a hostelry. After its reconstruction in 1709, the house served as the commerce registry office. In 1825, as a post office of the Kingdom of Bavaria, the house was first called the Wittelsbacher Hof.

In addition to the main restaurant, the hotel has a garden dining spot as well as an English-type pub. Rooms are well furnished and attractively maintained. Bathless singles cost from 34 DM ($19.50) to 44 DM ($25.24); with shower, from 49 DM ($28.11). Bathless doubles cost from 66 DM ($37.86), going up to 76 DM ($43.59) with shower. With complete bath, the cost is 96 DM ($55.07).

A MEDIUM-PRICED HOTEL ON THE OUTSKIRTS: Rhein-Hotel Lux-hof, at the Rhine Bridge, just outside the town (tel. 06205/3-23-33), is a hotel of unusual character. It's rather new, with many private bathrooms, but somehow the spirit of a rambling country inn has been retained. The dining rooms especially are charming and colorful, using ladderback chairs, long pine benches, a tall porcelain stove, deer antlers, and hanging copper lamps. There is an outdoor swimming pool. The bedrooms are clean, well designed, and compact, often including a small sitting area opening onto a tiny balcony. Price for a single bathless room ranges from 30 DM ($17.21) to 35 DM ($20.08); with bath, 36 DM ($20.65) to 52 DM ($29.83). Bathless doubles are in the 62-DM ($35.56) to 70-DM ($40.15) range, increasing to 80 DM ($45.89) to 90 DM ($51.62) with bath. A breakfast buffet is included.

11. Idar-Oberstein

Idar-Oberstein, medieval twin cities, has long been considered the lapidary center of Europe, with many workshops, stores, and museums of rough and cut stones from all over the world. The **Deutsche Gemmologische Gesellschaft,** which is the principal German school for training gemologists, is there, and the city has a diamond and precious stones exchange, one of fewer than 20 diamond exchanges in the world, and the only precious stones exchange.

READER'S HOTEL SELECTIONS: "We arrived late the first night and stayed at **Hotel Schutzenhof,** 175 Hauptstrasse (tel. 4-24-10). Our double room with breakfast, no bath, cost 58 DM ($33.27). We got the last room in the hotel—a small room, under the eaves, and the hotel service was obviously busy. The following day, we moved to **Hotel Zum Schwan,** 25 Hauptstrasse (tel. 4-30-81). Our double room with a big breakfast, no bath, cost 60 DM ($34.42). The room, food, and service were excellent, but it strained our budget. We stayed at a 'fremdenzimmer' our last two days, **Haus Edelstein,** 20 Hauptstrasse (tel. 4-31-49). Our double room with big breakfast cost 45 DM ($27.81). We will go back to Idar-Oberstein as we are rockhounds" (Kenneth M. Castro, Murphys, Calif.).

READER'S HOTEL SELECTION IN RHEN: "On the opposite side of the Rhine in the town of Rhen is a beautiful hotel. It is named **Konigstuhl** (tel. 244). When you get to Rhen, you'll see signs for this hotel. Follow them down winding streets to the water's edge. Here you will find the 400-year-old hotel. Our room overlooked the river, and on the opposite bank up on the hill stood Marksburg Castle. On the side of the hotel stands the ruins of another tower. The open-air veranda has tables where you can get a drink or a complete dinner for about 30 DM ($17.21). The hotel also has an indoor dining room. The menu is international and excellent. The kitchen has earned many awards for excellence. A double room with shower goes for 75 DM ($43.02), peaking at 82 DM ($47.04) with bath. It was very clean and had beautiful embroidered bed linens. The only drawback was the close proximity of the train tracks. The trains are noisy but do not run late into the night" (Karin Janik, Park Forest South, Ill.).

Germany's castle-studded river, the Neckar, is traveled in the upcoming chapter.

HEIDELBERG, STUTTGART, AND THE NECKAR VALLEY

ANCIENT CASTLE RUINS in the midst of thick woodlands, quiet university towns, busy manufacturing centers—all this truly belongs to the countryside of southwestern Germany, extending along the Neckar River from Heidelberg past medieval towns and modern cities as far as Tübingen. Although the river is now open to commercial shipping vessels as far as Stuttgart, much of the valley has remained unspoiled, its medieval privacy uninvaded.

Flowing between the Black Forest and the Swabian Alb, the Neckar has been the cradle of German royal families for centuries. The castles which lie around every bend in the river were once homes of the imperial families of Hohenstaufen and Hohenzollern. Many of the ruins were once summer palaces of kings and emperors. In the midst of all this baronial splendor, many castles and country palaces offer bed and board to travelers weary from their treks through the hills and woodlands along the river.

But before we embark on a tour of the countryside, we should visit the most fascinating city on the Neckar . . .

1. Heidelberg

Summertime in Heidelberg, according to the song from the popular operetta *The Student Prince,* is a time for music and romance. Today it's also a time when droves of tourists invade this city on the Neckar—and with just cause. Heidelberg is one of the few large German cities not leveled by the air raids of World War II, and many of its important buildings date from the latter part of the Middle Ages and the early Renaissance.

Heidelberg is, above all, a university town—and has been since 1386. Nearly 10% of the current population is made up of the huge student body. The colorful atmosphere that university life imparts to the town is felt nowhere more than in the old student quarter, with its narrow streets and lively inns.

There is a modern Heidelberg as well, centered around the green of Bismarck Square at the foot of the Theodore Heuss Bridge. The towering skyscrapers and shopping plazas contrast dramatically with the Old Town. In the new city you will find many of the best hotels and restaurants. Across the Neckar are sports grounds, a zoo, and a large botanical garden. But before exploring the sights of Heidelberg, however, let's survey the range of accommodations and restaurants.

THE TOP HOTEL: Der Europäische Hof-Hotel Europa, 1 Friedrich-Ebert-Anlage (tel. 2-71-01), is Heidelberg's glamor hotel. Fronting the city park, with a quiet inside garden, it's in the heart of the town, within walking distance of the castle, the university, and the old part of town with its student inns. Its interior is like a gracious home, with a liberal sprinkling of antiques, crystal chandeliers, bas-relief walls in the salons, and Oriental rugs. The bedrooms— 127 in all—are pleasantly traditional, done with rich taste. Each chamber is individually decorated and has a bath or shower, self-dial telephone, radio, television, and refrigerator. The rates depend on the season, the size of the room, and the location. Singles range from 89 DM ($51.05) to 99 DM ($56.79) with shower, from 115 DM ($65.96) to 125 DM ($71.70) with private bath. Double or twin-bedded rooms rent from 156 DM ($89.48) to 172 DM ($98.66). Alcove rooms with sitting room arrangement between rent for 210 DM ($120.46) and 230 DM ($131.93), and an apartment with separate sitting room goes for 300 DM ($172.08). Continental breakfast, service, and taxes are included in the rates. Meals are served in the Louis XVI restaurant, on the garden terrace where windows can be lowered to floor level, or in the finely paneled Kurfürstenstube. Before dinner, guests congregate around the curved bar in the wood-paneled drinking lounge. An elegant shopping arcade and an underground garage are on the premises.

THE MIDDLE BRACKET: Stiftsmühle, 129 In der Neckarhalle (tel. 8-05-55), a riverside hotel, a mile and a half from the old bridge (Alte Brücke), offers good food and comfortable bedrooms. Lawns and flowerbeds sweep down to the banks of the Neckar. Although the indoor dining rooms are spacious, use the wide terrace for al fresco meals in fair weather. The bedrooms are of adequate sized and well appointed. You get a bathless double for 60 DM ($34.42) to 64 DM ($36.71), 114 DM ($65.39) with complete bath. Singles with bath cost 55 DM ($31.55) to 75 DM ($43.02), only 35 DM ($20.08) without.

Zum Ritter, 178 Hauptstrasse (tel. 2-42-72), is a well-preserved rarity, a glorious old inn right out of the German Renaissance. Built in 1592 by the Frenchman Charles Bélier, it is now listed among the major sightseeing attractions of this university town, having survived the destruction of 1693. Deep in the heart of the student area of drinking houses and nightclubs, Zum Ritter holds its own. There are no public lounges; the bedrooms play second fiddle to the fine restaurant downstairs. Bathless doubles cost 70 DM ($40.15) to 75 DM ($43.02), increasing to from 90 DM ($51.62) to 150 DM ($86.04) with bath. The bedrooms are completely functional in style.

Hotel Hirschgasse, 3 Hirschgasse (tel. 4-99-22), is a historic guest house, dating from 1472. Its spacious "Saal" is still used by students for fencing and dueling. Today it is a handsome restored inn, providing meals and comfortably modern rooms for its guests. The accommodations have been remodeled, but an attempt has been made to preserve the feeling of the old character. The most expensive doubles with private baths rent for 115 DM ($65.96), although some cheaper ones go for only 95 DM ($54.49). All units have private baths and toilets.

The hotel lies on the side of the Neckar opposite the Altstadt (the antique central sector of the city). Furnishings are traditional. On a tree-shaded terrace, guests can order a leisurely breakfast or else a predinner glass of wine. The English-speaking Kraft family also welcome you to their restaurant, serving fine meals and giving good service.

Hotel Monpti, 57 Friedrich-Ebert-Anlage (tel. 2-34-83), is just what Heidelberg has always needed: a small hotel with sophisticated charm, run on a personal basis and moderately priced. The owner, Peter Mack, was born in this stately little town house in 1939. After traveling extensively, especially in Spain, he returned to his native town, intending to convert his home into a super guest house. That he has done, utilizing both his inherent and acquired taste. Built in the neoclassic style, the Monpti is a charmer, painted an olive green with a distinctive architectural trim in gleaming white. Each bedroom has color and freshness. All of the practical items are behind doors, and your chamber is furnished like a little salon. All of the 14 double rooms have private showers and toilets, as well as phones and bar refrigerators. Two persons pay from 80 DM ($45.89) to 90 DM ($51.62), and a single is charged 65 DM ($37.28), including breakfast and taxes. There's a petite breakfast room where guests gather over morning coffee. The owner has transformed the lower level (it's built on a hillside) into the bodega Vinothek, where he, his wife, and friends gather in the evening to enjoy paella. It's practically become a youth center. Hopefully, a Spanish guitarist will provide background music when you are there. The restaurant is open until 1 a.m. Free parking is on the open terrace.

Schrieder, an der Kurfürstenanlage (tel 2-50-23), is a target center of activity in Heidelberg, three blocks from the Neckar, opening onto a wide boulevard. The Schrieder, with its small garden of trees and flowers, is one of the leading second-class choices. The interior may lack élan, but there's plenty of comfort. The 85 rooms are in the modern idiom and come in varying sizes. A bathless double costs 68 DM ($39), increasing to anywhere from 97 DM ($55.64) to 130 DM ($75.57) with private bath. Depending on the plumbing and the season, singles go for anywhere from 48 DM ($27.53) to 75 DM ($43.02). The English-speaking Patriarca family are most hospitable. Public rooms include a lounge, dining room, plus an attractive breakfast salon opening onto a small rear garden.

Acor, 55 Friedrich-Ebert-Anlage (tel. 2-41-30), is a recommendable 18-bedroom hotel that was converted from an old patrician house. An elevator has been installed and the furnishings updated. Most of the rooms are compact although a few are large) and quite comfortable. Doubles with bath are 70 DM ($40.15) to 88 DM ($50.48). Singles with bath cost 52 DM ($29.83) to 65 DM ($37.28). These tabs include a continental breakfast, served in a charming little room overlooking a small rear garden. The street is busy with traffic, but soundproof windows have been installed.

Neckar-Hotel Heidelberg, 19 Bismarckstrasse (tel. 2-32-60), enjoys an enviable position, right on the Neckar River, near the center of the university town. There is no garden, but a superb view. The facilities are substantial and comfortable. The bedrooms, 35 in all, are fitted with Nordic-modern pieces. A double or twin-bedded room with bath or shower runs from 76 DM ($43.59) to 96 DM ($55.07); without bath, from 60 DM ($34.42) to 70 DM ($40.15). Depending on the plumbing, singles range from 40 DM ($22.94) to 58 DM ($33.27). These rates include breakfast, tax, and service. Breakfast is the only meal served; parking is available in the tiny lot.

Hotel Tannhäuser, Bismarckplatz (tel. 2-18-05), an inn in central Heidelberg, offers moderately priced bedrooms. The entrance lobby is absolutely minimum, the emphasis here on the comfortable and well-equipped bedrooms. A bathless double is 55 DM ($31.55), increasing to 75 DM ($43.02) with bath. Innkeeper Fritz Leipert offers an 8% reduction if stays are extended to five days. Rates include breakfast. A good restaurant is attached, serving typical Germanic meals at reasonable prices.

A BUDGET HOTEL: **Hotel zum Pfalzgrafen,** 21 Kettengasse (tel. 2-04-89), is a simple town inn, with good clean rooms. The best rooms contain private showers, and these are priced accordingly: 32 DM ($18.36) in a single, 57 DM ($32.70) in a double, and 69 DM ($39.58) in a three-bedded room. The best bargains, however, are the rooms with hot and cold running water only. Public showers are on the same floor. In these, a double or twin ranges from 43 DM ($24.66) to 46 DM ($26.39), and a single goes from 24 DM ($13.77) to 26 DM ($14.91), all tariffs including breakfast, service, and taxes.

READERS' HOTEL SELECTIONS: "The **Goldener Falke,** 204 Hauptstrasse (tel. 2-64-74), is in the old city, near the university. A room with bathtub and sink (no toilet) is 42 DM ($24.09) for two. Floors tilt slightly, but the room was very clean" (Nat and Inge Frankel, Oakland, Calif.). . . . "We've paid two visits to the **Hotel Vier-Jahreszeiten,** 2 Haspelgasse (tel. 2-41-64), which is quite elegant in comparison with its condition on our first visit in 1963. Depending on the plumbing, singles range from 32.50 DM ($18.64) to 50 DM ($28.68); doubles, 60 DM ($34.42) to 90 DM ($51.62). The price includes a continental breakfast. Our room was large and comfortable. The location was excellent; we walked to the student inns, the tram, and castle. The manager stood outside to help reserve parking areas until we moved our car" (Mrs. Willard G. Prater, Bellefontaine, Ohio). . . . "The **Hotel Roter Hahn,** 44 Hauptstrasse (tel. 2-41-57), is in the middle of the Old Town, within easy reach of everything. The price for a double room (bathless) with breakfast is in the 40-DM ($22.94) to 50-DM ($28.68) range. It is quiet and clean, with an added feature we haven't seen anywhere else: an extra padded door to the room for additional quietness. The owners, Mr. and Mrs. H. Martin Engmann, speak fluent English and are helpful and friendly" (C. H. Punnett, Richmond, B.C., Canada). . . . "**Hotel Weisser Bok,** 24 Grossmantelastrasse (tel. 2-22-31), is an antique, impressive, and homey hotel right in the center of the old city. The charge is from 38 DM ($21.80) to 45 DM ($25.81) for a double with breakfast complete with an egg. The shower, bath, and toilet are down the hall at no extra charge. To get to the hotel, take the trolley from the station and get off at the old university. Go up Mantelastrasse one-half block and you are there" (Gene McKay, Miami, Fla.).

"We stayed at **Hotel Jeske,** 2 Mittelbadgasse (tel. 2-37-33). This was the best deal we encountered all summer, Ms. Erika Jeske charges 24 DM ($13.77) to 28 DM ($16.06) for a bathless double per night. The rooms were very clean, she had the best shower we encountered on our trip, and she was very helpful in directing us to restaurants and points of interest. The best thing about staying at 2 Mittelbadgasse was the location, within 15 minutes' walking distance of everything you would want to see in Heidelberg. Ms. Jeske speaks very good English, and Americans seem to be her favorite guests" (Kenneth and Susan Johnson, New York, N.Y.). . . . "At the **Hotel Horneck,** 4 Blumenstrasse (tel. 242-47) we rented a double with shower for 50 DM ($28.68). Doubles with complete bath go for 70 DM ($40.15), breakfast included. Our morning meal was served in a charming room. The house itself is lovely and is furnished in exquisite taste and run by a pleasant woman owner" (Mrs. Ron Friend, Cremorne, Australia). . . . "**Hotel Garni Ballmann,** 28 Rohrbacherstrasse (tel. 2-42-87), is efficiently operated by the delightful owner, Maria-Theresia Jarmer. The 130-bed hotel is a favorite with groups such as a symphony company and two hostel organizations which were there during my visit. It is a few blocks from the Neckar River but not in the old section. Our double room had a shower and a wash basin. The cost is 18 DM ($10.32) per person. Mrs. Jarmer went out of her way to help me find a church service and mark a map to show me the way. You can have hot chocolate in the morning if you wish" (Pat Diehnelt, Menomonee Falls, Wisc.).

THE TOP RESTAURANT: "The **Kurfürstenstube**, Der Europaische Hof-Hotel Europa, 1 Friedrich-Ebert-Anlage (tel. 2-71-01), is the best restaurant in Heidelberg. Occupying a ground-floor wing of this outstanding hotel, the wine stuben is attractively decorated with provincial furnishings, pewter plates, and a stein collection. The menu is in English. A large collection of cold appetizers is offered, including home-pickled salmon at 19 DM ($10.90) and homemade pastry of truffled goose liver at 19.50 DM ($11.19). A good and regularly featured soup is French onion at 7 DM ($4.02), or you may enjoy lobster cream soup at 8.50 DM ($4.88) or half a dozen snails prepared according to an old French recipe, 9.50 DM ($5.45). Recommended hot dishes include roast wild boar at 24 DM ($13.77); duckling with port and green pepper in melon, 25 DM ($14.34); and filet sliced "Nowgorod," with mushrooms, sour cream, and buckwheat cakes, 26 DM ($14.91). Ask the maître d' for the specialties of the season, if you prefer. Rounding out the meal is a selection of desserts, including ice cream soufflé Grand Marnier at 7 DM ($4.02) or a choice of French cheeses from the trolley.

MEDIUM-PRICED DINING: **Kurpfälzische Wein Restaurant**, 97 Hauptstrasse, is a quiet culinary oasis in the precints of the Kurpfälzisches Museum. Housed in a baroque palace, the museum itself makes an interesting stopover before lunch. The restaurant's prices are moderate, the food good. Soups range from 3 DM ($1.72) to 5 DM ($2.87), and set meals cost from 10 DM ($5.74) to 24 DM ($13.77). From the à la carte menu, you can order such dishes as rumpsteak Madagascar (with green pepper) at 19 DM ($10.90). Desserts range in price from 3.20 DM ($1.84) to 8 DM ($4.59). From your table, you can enjoy the little garden and splashing fountain. Closed Mondays.

Zum Ritter, 178 Hauptstrasse (tel 2-42-72), is popular with both students and professors, for they know they can get not only good German cooking here, but delectable Dortmunder Actien-Brauerei beer as well. You dine either in the first-class Great Hall (the Ritter Saal), with an armored knight, or in the smaller Councillors' Chamber. Preferred is the larger room, most elegant with sepia ceilings, wainscoting, woodcarvings, and Oriental rugs. Set meals range in price from a low of 12.80 DM ($7.34) to a high of 29 DM ($16.63). The house specialty in season is saddle of venison for two, costing 65 DM ($37.28). The large international menu includes such selections as veal steak with cream sauce, 19 DM ($10.90). A good beginning might be game soup St. Hubertus with brandy foam, 6 DM ($3.44), followed by crêpes Suzette at 19.50 DM ($11.19) for two persons.

BUDGET DINING: **Heidelberg Castle Weinstube**, Schloss Heidelberg (tel. 2-00-81), is a recreation of a wine tavern, tastefully and attractively done. You'll find antique ceramic stones, natural wood trestle tables, and many framed engravings under a ceiling of ornate paneling. Tables are shared freely, and many are arranged to provide the best view of Heidelberg Castle. The weinstube is entered through the inner courtyard, reached by steep stone steps. Three-course lunches range in price from 15.20 DM ($8.72) to 25 DM ($43.02). The average main dishes in the evening are priced from 13.50 DM ($7.74) to 28 DM ($16.06). The weinstube is open for dinner from 6 to 9:30 p.m.

Solo d'oro, 172 Hauptstrasse (tel. 2-14-80), is a change-of-pace dining experience in Heidelberg. Male students bring girls here for an inexpensive meal in a colorful and moderately sophisticated atmosphere. Hopefully, you'll find a table of your own in one of the four connecting dining rooms. Often you must share—but that's part of the fun. The walls are covered with paintings by local artists. Candles burn in chianti bottles. All in all, it passes for what used to be called bohemian. Although many German dishes are available, clients come here for the Italian specialties, including pizzas in the 6.50-DM ($3.73) to 10-DM ($5.74) range, spaghetti Bolognese at 5.50 DM ($3.15), and veal piccata at 15.75 DM ($9.03). You might begin your meal with a hearty bowl of minestrone, 3.80 DM ($2.18).

STUDENT DRINKING CLUBS: **Zum Roten Ochsen** (Red Ox Inn), 217 Hauptstrasse (tel. 2-09-77), created in 1703, is Heidelberg's most famous and revered student tavern. For six generations, it's been in the Spengel family who have welcomed everybody from Bismarck to Mark Twain. It seems that every student who has attended the university has left his mark on the walls—or at least his initials. Revelers sit at long oak tables under smoke-blackened ceilings. Distinguished patrons of yore have left mementos, often framed photographs of themselves. The series of rooms is arranged in horseshoe fashion. The "U" part has a pianist who sets the musical pace. As the evening progresses, the songs become more festive and vigorous. By midnight the sounds are heard from blocks away. Motherly looking waitresses bring in huge steins of the traditional beer and plates of heavy, basic food. A mug of beer costs around 2.50 DM ($1.43). Goulasch soup is 3.80 DM ($2.18), and main dishes include such specialties as sauerbraten, Rhineland style, 15 DM ($8.60), and veal steak Cordon Bleu at 17 DM ($9.75). Desserts begin at 4 DM ($2.29).

Goldener Hecht, 2 Steingasse (tel. 2-69-84), is an old drinking tavern and restaurant combined, sitting at the corner of the Alte Brüke. Around for more than 250 years, it's been frequented by many a beer-drinking student. Still a favorite, it offers meals as well as beer and wine. Soups range in price from 2.80 DM ($1.61) to 3.80 DM ($2.18); meat dishes, from 5 DM ($2.87) to 7.50 DM ($4.30); and the dessert of the day costs from 2.50 DM ($1.43) to 4 DM ($2.29). The chef's specialty is sauerkraut garni at 7.50 DM ($4.30).

Schnookeloch, 8 Haspelgasse, is another ancient building, dating back to 1407. Right at the old bridge, the tavern attracts students who come nightly to drink and raise the rafters. During the days of the "new wine," the tempo picks up considerably. In case you want a meal, soups range in price between 2.50 DM ($1.43) and 4 DM ($2.29). Main dishes such as roast meat with vegetables average between 8.80 DM ($5.05) and 16.80 DM ($9.67). Desserts begin at 3 DM ($1.72).

THE SIGHTS: Although all the important sights of Heidelberg lie on or near the south bank of the Neckar, you must cross the river (via the 18th-century Karl Theodore Bridge) for the best overall view of the Old Town. The famous **Philosophen Weg** (Philosopher's Way), halfway up the mountain on the north bank, is best for viewing. And towering above the brown roofs of the town on the opposite bank is the rose-pink major attraction of Heidelberg, the castle.

Heidelberg Castle

In its magnificent setting of woodland and terraced gardens, the huge red sandstone castle is reached from the town below by several routes. The quickest way is the two-minute cable-car ride from the platform near the Kornmarkt (Corn Market) in the Old Town. The round trip costs 2.50 DM ($1.15). You may also drive to the winding Neue Schlosstrasse, past the old houses perched on the hillside. (Parking at the castle is 2 DM or ($1.15.) This is also a rewarding walking route because of the constantly changing view of the town and surrounding countryside. For a shorter walk, you may climb the steep Burgweg from the Corn Market, or take the more gradual walk from the Klingentor.

The castle is only a dignified ruin today; it was plundered and burned by the French in the latter part of the 17th century. Parts of the huge tower still lie in the moat where they fell after being blown up in 1693 at the command of Louis XIV. Lightning added to the destruction by striking the castle twice in the mid-18th century. But at least the magnificent structure was spared the ultimate destruction of World War II bombs, and even in its deteriorated state, it's considered one of the finest Gothic-Renaissance castles in Germany.

Entering the castle walls at the main gate, you first come upon the huge Gun Park to your left from which you can gaze down upon Heidelberg and the Neckar Valley. Straight ahead is the Thick Tower, or what remains of it after its ten-foot walls were blown up by the French. Leaving the Gun Park via Elizabeth's Gate, erected by Friedrich V in 1615 for his English wife, Elizabeth Stuart, daughter of James I, you come to the Bridge House and the bridge crossing the site of the former moat.

Through the entrance tower lies the **castle courtyard,** the heart of the complex of structures. Surrounding it are buildings dating from the 13th to the 17th centuries. You'll notice that nature has done its best to repair the ravages of war, by covering the gaping holes and roofless sections with ivy and shrubbery. Walking around the courtyard in a clockwise fashion, you come first to the Gothic **Ruprecht Building,** built about 1400. Adjacent is the **Library,** with a Gothic oriel window dating from the early 16th century. It once housed the library of Ludwig V.

The **Frauenzimmer** (Women's Rooms) was originally a three-story Gothic-Renaissance building housing the ladies of the court, but today only the ground level, the King's Hall, remains.

Along the north side of the courtyard stretches the stern palace of Friedrich IV, erected from 1601 to 1607. Less damaged than other parts of the castle, it has been almost completely restored, including the gallery of princes and kings of the German Empire from the time of Charlemagne. The palace has its own terrace, the Altan, which offers a splendid view of the plain of the Neckar as well as the Old Town. The ancient Bell Tower, at the northeast end of the Altan, dates from the early 1400s.

At the west end of the terrace, in the cellars of the castle, is the Wine Vat Building, built in the late 16th century and worth a visit for a look at the **Great Cask,** symbol of the abundant and exuberant life of the Rhineland-Palatinate. This huge barrel-like monstrosity, built in 1751, is capable of holding more than 55,000 gallons of wine.

On the east, connecting the palace of Friedrich IV to the **Ottheinrich Building,** itself an outstanding example of German Renaissance architecture, is the **Hall of Mirrors Building,** constructed in 1549—a Renaissance masterpiece of its time. Although only the shell of the original building remains, it is enough to give you an idea of its former glory, with its arcades and steep gables decorated with cherubs and sirens.

Next to Ottheinrich's palace is the Chemist's Tower, now housing the **Pharmaceutical Museum.** Entrance fee: .70 DM (40¢). The museum, on the tower's ground floor, shows a chemist's shop with utensils and laboratory equipment from the 18th and 19th centuries. It is open during the usual castle visiting hours.

Returning to the Castle Gate, you will pass the old barracks for the soldiers of the garrison. Next to the barracks is the former well house, its roof supported by ancient Roman columns. Some of the household buildings, such as the bakery, kitchen, smithshop, and butchery nearby have been restored.

In summer, you can enjoy serenades and concerts in the large castle courtyard. But the biggest spectacle is the **castle illumination,** commemorating the battles of the 17th century. Several times throughout the summer, at dates rescheduled yearly, the castle is floodlit and fireworks are set off above it.

You can visit the castle grounds at any time during the day, free. If you wish to visit the interior of the castle, you must take one of the one-hour guided tours. The fee is 2 DM ($1.15) for adults, 1.20 DM (69¢) for children. A visit to the Great Cask without the tour costs adults .70 DM (40¢); children, .30 DM (17¢).

Other Sights

Back in the town itself, a tour of the main attractions begins with the **Marketplace** in front of the attractive Rathaus. The square, on market days, is filled with stalls of fresh flowers, fish, and vegetables. At the opposite end of the square is the late-Gothic **Church of the Holy Ghost,** built about 1400. For nearly 300 years the church was the burial place of the electors, but most of the graves were destroyed in the French invasion late in the 17th century. In 1706 a wall was erected dividing the church, giving both Catholics and Protestants a portion in which to worship. The wall has since been removed and the church restored to its original plan.

Around the corner from the church is the famous old mansion, **Zum Ritter,** recommended in the hotel listings above. If you follow the Haupstrasse past the Hotel zum Ritter, you'll arrive at the **Kurpfälzisches Museum,** 97 Hauptstrasse, the Museum of the Palatinate, housed in a baroque palace. The museum presents a large collection of paintings and sculptures from six centuries, among them the Riemenschneider-Altar from Windsheim (1509) with Christ and the Twelve Apostles. There is also a cast of the jawbone of the Heidelberg Man, 500,000 years old; an Archeological collection; examples of history and culture of the Palatinate; and paintings from the Romantic period. The museum is open daily except Monday from 10 a.m. to 1 p.m. and from 2 p.m. to 5 p.m. Admission: 1 DM (57¢); students and children, .50 DM (29¢).

The Hauptstrasse also runs through the old student quarter of Heidelberg, with its student inns. Of special interest is the **Student Jail,** at 2 Augustinerstrasse. The walls and even the ceilings of the prison are covered with graffiti and drawings—including portraits and silhouettes. The last prisoners were housed here in 1914. Visiting hours are from 9 a.m. to 5 p.m. Ring the bell of the caretaker (same address) for admission, which is .50 DM (29¢).

READER'S SUGGESTION OUTSIDE HEIDELBERG: "Since Frankfurt was filled with an international book fair, we drove on and stayed in **Heppenheim** on the Bergstrasse, halfway between Frankfurt and Heidelberg. It is a lovely old town right off the autobahn. We stayed at the **Hotel Starkenburger Hof,** 7 Kaltererstrasse (tel. 06252/2416), which has an ultramodern annex. Each room had a bath, shower, and toilet, and the price for a double ranges from 48 DM ($27.53) to 52 DM ($29.83) each. Also, the dinners are very good and inexpensive. The hotel also has an indoor pool which is heated. From Heppenheim, it is only a 25-minute drive to Heidelberg" (Charles P. Holzer, Emerson, N.J.).

READERS' SIGHTSEEING SUGGESTION (LUDENBURG): "On a recent visit to Heidelberg we spent a delightful day at Ludenburg, reaching it from Bismarckplatz by trolley and bus in about a half hour. Ludenburg is a typical medieval town, considered to be the oldest German town on the right bank of the Rhine. The Romans occupied this area in the first century A.D. In the Middle Ages, it became a seat of the bishops of Worms. The present day Bishop's Palace and Chapel of St. Sebastian are the remains of the once grand episcopal residence. Also nearby are the remains of the Roman fortifications and a museum containing interesting archeological finds and rooms decorated in the traditional local fashion. In addition there are delightful inns with excellent food and local wines" (Mr. and Mrs. G. Robert Schneider, Fairfield, Conn.).

2. The Neckar Valley

Heidelberg is a good point from which to begin an exploration of the Neckar Valley. During the summer, you can take one of the boat tours along the river as far as Neckargemünd for as little as 20 DM ($11.47). But the best way to see the many attractions along the banks of the Neckar is by car. Leaving Heidelberg, drive eastward along the right bank of the river (the same as Heidelberg's Old Town) and you'll soon arrive at the medieval town of:

HIRSCHHORN: Called the gem of the Neckar Valley, this old town looks much as it did when it obtained its municipal rights in 1396. Overlooking the town and the Neckar from its fortified promontory is the 18th-century **Hirschhorn Castle.** The castle was erected on the site of an earlier Renaissance palace built by Ludwig von Hirschhorn in the late 16th century. The castle defenses date from the 14th century, and wall paintings from that period can be seen in the chapel today. Although the castle is now a hotel and restaurant, you can also visit it as a sightseeing attraction. For a view of the sharp bend of the Neckar below the town, climb to the top of the tower. Admission: .75 DM (43¢).

Hotel Burg Hirschhorn (tel. 13-73), on Highway B37 (Heidelberg-Eberbach), provides an opportunity to stay on a hilltop castle. After a stormy career, the castle settled down to serving as a hotel or dining room for wayfarers. The accommodations are divided between a palace and a guest house annex. The bedrooms are furnished in modern, with a bathroom provided on each floor. Central heating and an elevator have been installed as well. Rates are cheaper in the guest house. A single with breakfast, service, and tax included, ranges in price from 23 DM ($13.19) to 34 DM ($19.50) without bath, increasing to 42 DM ($24.09) with bath. Bathless doubles are in the 46-DM ($26.39) to 52-DM ($29.83) range, rising to 70 DM ($40.15) with bath. Half board costs 23 DM ($13.19) per person per day extra. The food is very good, particularly the veal dishes, the service is excellent, and the terrace dining views of the Neckar are superb.

EBERBACH: Just 20 miles along the Neckar from Heidelberg is the ancient Imperial City of Eberbach, which traces its municipal rights back to 1227. Its castle is even older, dating from 1012. Although the fortress was destroyed in the 15th century, its ivy-covered ruins attract many visitors today, as does the old Deutscher Hof, the medieval center of the town within the city walls.

BAD FRIEDRICHSHALL: This small town, just north of Heilbronn, is noted for its old salt mines and brine spa. At the town, two rivers, the Jagst and the Kocher, flow into the Neckar. The surrounding countryside is excellent for hiking and camping. A few miles up the Jagst River from the town is the hunting castle of Götzenburg, now a hotel.

Burghotel Götzenberg Hornberg, Neckarzimmern (tel. 27-58). In this hilltop castle, overlooking the romantic Neckar, you can climb into a great, wooden antique bed and drop all your cares. Dating from the 11th century, the castle was once owned by Götz von Berlichingen, "The Knight with the Iron Hand," who died there in 1562. His grandson sold Hornberg in 1612 to Freiherr von Gemmingen, whose descendants own it today.

Hundreds of tourists pass through the hotel portion of the castle, but, fortunately, the quarters for guests are private. The interior is handsome and colorful—somewhat like an inn, more informal than grandiose. The public rooms have beamed ceilings, thick walls, decorative paintings, an antique tin collection, engravings and forge works, and wrought-iron objects. Within a recess is a framed portrait of the castle's illustrious former owner.

Surprisingly, the castle is inexpensive for an overnight stay. Bathless singles rent for 35 DM ($20.08), increasing to 45 DM ($25.81) and 50 DM ($28.68) with shower. Bathless doubles range between 65 DM ($37.28) and 70 DM ($40.15). For a room with private bath, two persons pay 80 DM ($45.89) to 90 DM ($51.62). Breakfast is included in all the rates. If you want full board, add 30 DM ($17.21) per person. In the old horse stable of Knight Götz, a restaurant, Im Alten Marstall, was built. Charcoal meats are a specialty of the Götzen Grill.

Arrangements can be made for horseback riding, tennis, and swimming within an area of three miles. You'll enjoy walks through the hillside vineyards belonging to the castle. Best of all are the quiet, relaxing periods spent at the end of the day in front of the open fireplace.

HEINSHEIM—A BAROQUE MANOR: Hotel Schloss Heinsheim, in Heinsheim, two miles from Bad Wimpfen (tel. 10-45), is a baroque house, the family manor of Baroness von Rachnitz. It has been converted to accommodate guests and is one of the most ingratiating places in Germany. If you have only a weekend between planes in Frankfurt, try to stop here. The house is a world unto itself, with gardens, lawns, flowerbeds, woods, and a circular swimming pool at the bottom of the lawn. You can dine either under the covered loggia with its thick stone arches, or on the flagstone terrace. The house, steeped in antiquity, was built in 1730 and later rebuilt in the baroque style. Guests congregate for coffee and chatting in the classic drawing room, where an ornate ceiling, stone fireplace, and hefty antiques provide authenticity. A former carriage house has been completely restored and now offers 40 more rooms, superbly finished with wood and tapestry. There is deer hunting in the park in season. Perfectly preserved is a little baroque chapel in the garden.

Most of the produce used in the excellent menu is from the palace park farm. Meals are important here—and under the direct supervision of the baroness; she doesn't permit mediocrity. Bedrooms are available in the older or newer wings, and most have private baths. Forty rooms range from 70 DM ($40.15) to 120 DM ($68.83) with shower or bath, including breakfast. The castle can be reached by car from either the Neckar Bridge in Gundelsheim or Bad Wimpfen. It is closed from January 15 to February 15.

HEILBRONN: This city on the Neckar, 33 miles north of Stuttgart, owes its name to the holy spring (Heiligbronn) which bubbled up from beneath the high altar of **St. Kilian's Church.** The church, begun in 1020 and completed in 1529, is a combination of Gothic and Renaissance styles. The tower is nearly 210 feet high and is considered the earliest example of Renaissance architecture in Germany. Inside are some excellent woodcarvings, including the elaborate choir and altar.

Heilbronn today is mainly a thriving industrial community, noted for its manufacture of everything from machinery and automobiles to paper and soap. But its most popular product is its wine, harvested from the vineyards in the surrounding hills of Baden-Württemberg. In fact, Heilbronn is the largest producer of wine in the Neckar.

Where to Stay

Insel, Friedrich-Ebert-Brücke (tel. 8-89-31), is a completely modern hotel, built on an oasis island in the middle of the river, right in the heart of Heilbronn. Enlarged in 1972 and rebuilt in 1978, it now contains up to 120 rooms with 180 beds. Most of the bedrooms have balconies opening onto weeping willows and the park belonging to the hotel. The rooms are well designed and comfortable. All have private bath or shower, toilet, radio, and color TV. A twin-bedded room costs 108 DM ($61.95), rising to 148 DM ($84.89). A single costs 54 DM ($30.97), rising to 98 DM ($56.21). All the tariffs include breakfast from a buffet which offers cheese, sausages, juices, cereals, and fruits. The front terrace is the beer and gossip center of town, a beehive of a place. Within, there's a cozy Swabian Restaurant where you can have homemade spätzle and other well-known specialties. If you prefer French cooking, however, you may visit the hotel's restaurant in the Gallic style.

Where To Dine

Ratskeller, im Rathaus (tel. 8-46-28), is your best for dining in Heilbronn. It's a true ratskeller, unlike so many others. However, it's been given the modern treatment, with upholstered banquettes and wrought-iron grillwork. Tables are set on two levels. The prices are modest and the cuisine is regional, under the supervision of the Götz family. Soups begin at 3.50 DM ($2.01), going up to 5.50 DM ($3.15) for the good-tasting crab soup. Typical main dishes include a goulash at 20.50 DM ($11.76); peppersteak with french fries and a salad, 24 DM ($13.77); and grilled sole, 18 DM ($10.32). Desserts range from 3.75 DM ($2.15) to 6.50 DM ($3.73). There's an impressive wine list, but don't ignore the wine of the cellar, costing 3.75 DM ($2.15) to 5.50 DM ($3.15) for a quarter liter.

3. Stuttgart

Unlike many large, prosperous industrial centers, Stuttgart is not a concrete city. On the contrary, within the city limits two-thirds of the land is devoted to parks, gardens, and woodlands. Yet Stuttgart is one of Germany's largest manufacturing cities, the home of Mercedes and Porsche automobiles, Zeiss optical equipment, and many other world-famous industrial concerns. As a city interested in export and trade, it is also the home of many international trade fairs and congresses.

As a cultural center, Stuttgart is without peer in southwestern Germany. The Stuttgart Ballet performs throughout the world, highly acclaimed wherever it appears. Its State Opera and Philharmonic Orchestra are also well received—at home or abroad. In addition, Stuttgart has an abundance of theater groups, cultural festivals, and excellent museums.

Stuttgart is the capital of the southwest German Federal State of Baden-Württemberg. The city produced the philosopher Hegel, who in turn inspired Marx and Engels. It also is the third-largest wine-growing community in Germany.

ACCOMMODATIONS: No matter when you come to Stuttgart, you will probably find an international trade fair in progress, from the January glass and ceramics exposition to the December book exhibition (Stuttgart is also southern Germany's most important publishing center). Because of this, suitable accommodations may be difficult to find unless you book in advance.

The Top Hotels

Hotel am Schlossgarten, 1 Schillerstrasse (tel. 29-99-11), is the tasteful bargain of the top contenders, where you get much more comfort for your mark. It's not splashy, but offers conveniences in a dignified manner. It stands ten floors high on the railway station plaza. Most of its 125 bedrooms and apartments have their own bath, with shower or tub. The rooms have successfully skirted the line between modern and traditional. Singles with running water and toilet (corridor bath) are 85 DM ($48.76); with shower, between 100 DM ($57.36) and 105 DM ($60.23); with full bath, 90 DM ($51.62) to 120 DM ($68.83). Doubles with full bath go anywhere from 140 DM ($80.30) to 160 DM ($91.78). Included in these rates is breakfast. The public rooms are consistently decorative and sedate. The main dining room has three walls of rich walnut paneling, an Oriental carpet, a tall brass lamp, 19th-century paintings, brown armchairs, and a wall of filmy white curtains. The lounge has the same fine theme, and the hotel bar is warm and cozy. Most intimate is the Zirbelstube, all woodsy with knotty pine on the walls and ceiling and birch armchairs. You dine by candlelight in this tavern atmosphere. Note: There's a 400-car garage, costing 8 DM ($4.59) per night.

Steigenberger Hotel Graf Zeppelin, 7 Arnulf-Klett-Platz (tel. 29-98-81), is the best hotel for those who want to wheel and deal with Stuttgart business people. Although right at the railway station, it is not only attractive, but possesses dignity and style, setting a splashy modern pace. It even has a sauna and an indoor swimming pool with a wood-paneled waterside lounge. The soundproofed bedrooms are warmly and colorfully decorated, and most come complete with bath or shower, plus dial telephones, color TV, and mini-bars. Bathless singles rent for 71 DM ($40.73); with shower, 95 DM ($54.49); with complete bath, from 95 DM ($54.49) to 149 DM ($85.47). Doubles with complete bath cost 150 DM ($86.04) to 180 DM ($103.25). Continental breakfast is included. An American breakfast is available for 7.80 DM ($4.47). Guests congregate before dinner in the Apéritif-Bar before making their way to the Grill-Restaurant or the Zeppelin-Stüble. Later in the evening, there is dancing in the Scotch-Club.

Park Hotel Stuttgart, 21 Villastrasse (tel. 28-01-61), is the choice for those who seek a first-class accommodation in a secluded and quiet area. It's out of dead center, in the midst of the gardens of the Villa Berg, within walking distance of the mineral-water swimming pool surrounded by a park. Here the service is personalized. The decor is handsome and rather rich. For example, the dining room is created with wood paneling and fabric screens to provide semiprivacy. Roses adorn the white tables; molded white plastic armchairs and copper bowl droplights make for a colorful setting. The clubroom is just that, with dignified modern furnishings and a grand piano for background music.

The bedrooms are also well designed, with a decidedly personal aura. A bathless single goes for 55 DM ($31.55); with shower or full bath, 80 DM ($45.89) to 95 DM ($54.49). Doubles with shower range in price from 110 DM ($63.10) to 120 DM ($68.83); with complete bath, from 120 DM ($68.83) to 140 DM ($80.30). These rates include breakfast. If you arrive in time for dinner, there are two set meals, costing 22.50 DM ($12.91) and 27 DM ($15.41).

Hotel Unger, 17 Kronenstrasse (tel. 29-40-41), is clean-cut, survival modern. Right at the City Air Terminal, you are assured of practical, nicely designed, and most contemporary bedrooms. Since rebuilding, all rooms now contain bath or shower and toilet. In a single with shower, the cost is 65 DM ($37.28) to 70 DM ($40.15). Singles with bath go for 75 DM ($43.02). Doubles with bath are priced from 100 DM ($57.36) to 130 DM ($75.57). These rates include a continental breakfast. To garage your car costs an extra 6 DM ($3.44) nightly.

The Budget Hotels

Hotel Mack, 7 Kriegerstrasse (tel. 29-19-27), is a fairly modern little hotel on a hillside ledge, an eight-minute walk from the railway station. Homelike and cozy, it offers up-to-date bedrooms that are small and basic, but quite adequate. Bathless singles go for 39 DM ($22.37), 60 DM ($34.42) with shower. A double with shower costs 79 DM ($45.31), dropping to 70 DM ($40.15) without bath. An elevator has been installed and there's a telephone in each room. Breakfast is the only meal served.

Hotel Pflieger, 9–11 Kriegerstrasse (tel. 22-18-78), is a tiny economy hotel, just eight minutes from the railway station. Its lobby is miniature, but the bedrooms are well equipped and comfortable. There is a place to park your car, plus an elevator to take you to your room. In a double with bath, the charge is 89 DM ($51.05). A bathless single costs 39 DM ($22.37), going up to 60 DM ($34.42) with bath. The Pflieger is in a good area, central to sights you can set out for after having breakfast (included in the room price) in the pleasant modern salon.

READERS' HOTEL SELECTIONS: "An excellent, very friendly hotel is the **Koehler,** 209 Neckarstrasse, charging 26 DM ($14.91) per person for bed and breakfast. The rooms were the most modern we had in Europe, and the baths were free" (Fred R. Blanks, Greenwich, New South Wales). . . . "Within walking distance of the Stuttgart railroad station is the newly remodeled and attractive **Krönen-Hotel** (Garni), 48 Krönenstrasse (tel. 22-12-91). You're charged 68 DM ($39) for bed and breakfast for two in a room on the ground floor (partially in the basement), but with full-size windows" (Mrs. Berdena Koehler, Elmwood, Neb.). . . . **"Hotel Am Friedensplatz,** opposite the Frieden church, is a small hotel on the first floor, quiet, pleasant, clean. One of its advantages is its closeness to the railway station, some 10 or 15 minutes' walk only. Rooms without bath but with hot and cold running water cost 26 DM ($14.91) for a single, 44 DM ($25.24) in a double, breakfast, service, and taxes included. English is spoken. . . . In nearby Echterdingen, only 25 minutes on foot from the Stuttgart airport (or by frequent bus), containing an excellent restaurant is the **Gasthof Sonne.** Single rooms cost 23 DM ($13.19), and doubles are 40 DM ($22.94). The rooms are comfortable and pleasant, with hot and cold running water. Very fine meals are served for 10 DM ($5.74)" (J. Calvin Keene, Lewisburg, Penna.).

WHERE TO DINE: Alte Post, 43 Friedrichstrasse (tel. 29-30-79), is most recommendable, both for its cuisine and high standards of service. Featuring an old tavern ambience, it provides some of the finest cuisine in Stuttgart. The hors d'oeuvres are superb, including coquilles Saint-Jacques à la Nantaise, 23.80 DM ($13.65). A clear oxtail soup goes for 7.80 DM ($4.47). Among fish dishes, we'd suggest the marvelous sole soufflé Alte Post at 37.50 DM ($21.51). A special dish is rehschnitzel (venison) Waidmannsheil with spätzle, 34 DM ($19.50). Desserts include an apple cake with vanilla sauce, 8.80 DM ($5.05). Although Stuttgart is modern, this mellow inn, with its antique interior, provides a comfortable link with the Germany of old. Closed Sundays.

Fernsehturm Restaurant, in the Degerloch suburb of Stuttgart (tel. 23-46-84), is for dining high in the sky. A tourist novelty, it simultaneously gives you good food and a panoramic orientation to Stuttgart. For 4 DM ($2.29), you'll be whisked to the top and can choose between two restaurants (the lower one is more expensive). The menu is à la carte, with most main dishes costing anywhere from 12 DM ($6.88) to 25 DM ($14.34). At lunch, served till 3 p.m., a daily menu is featured for 20 DM ($11.47). On a higher level is a coffeeshop which many visitors patronize just for drinks, although hot meals are served. At the bottom of the tower there are two restaurants, one in a Black Forest motif, with a lovely garden terrace in the midst of an old forest. The tower is ten minutes by car from the city center and the airport, up a steep, winding road. (For a more detailed description, refer to our sightseeing section, coming up.)

Ratskeller, 1 Markplatz (tel. 24-49-51), beneath the new City Hall, is in the heart of Stuttgart. Totally modern, it pays homage to the past only in its 1904 wine vat that used to hold 9820 liters. Built in the tavern style, the Ratskeller is the best of the reasonably priced restaurants in expensive Stuttgart. Soups begin at 2 DM ($1.15), with grilled rumpsteak and vegetables costing 18.50 DM ($10.61). Bargain diners order set meals featured on the Tagesmenu (daily menu), which range in price from 8.50 DM ($4.88) to 17 DM ($9.75), including both soup and dessert.

READER'S RESTAURANT SELECTION: "Gute Stuben restaurant, 11 Kernerstrasse, near the railway station and the Friedensplatz Hotel, has an imaginative and pleasant interior and very good food. Prices are reasonable for Germany. Pork cutlet or schnitzel and bread costs 6.50 DM ($3.73). Roast pork and a full meal of large quantities of potatoes and salad goes for 9.50 DM ($5.45)" (J. Calvin Keene, Lewisburg, Penna.).

THE SIGHTS: Many of the most remarkable structures in today's Stuttgart are of advanced technological design, created by such architects as Mies van der Rohe, Gropius, Scharoun, and Le Corbusier. There is another side to the city, however. Clustered around the Schillerplatz and the 19th-century statue of that German poet and dramatist is the Old Town. But it is to the modern buildings that visitors are attracted; the **Liederhalle,** constructed in 1956 of concrete, glass, and glazed brick, is fascinating inside and out. The hall contains three auditoriums so acoustically perfect that all can stage concerts at the same time and not disturb the others. The ultramodern **City Hall** faces the old Marketplace where flowers, fruits, and vegetables are still sold in open stalls.

For the best view of the city, you can climb to the top of the 1680-foot **Birkenkopf** to the west of the city. The hill is composed of the debris of Stuttgart gathered after the air raids of World War II. The 20-minute walk to the top will be rewarded by a view of Stuttgart and the surrounding Swabian Hills, covered with vineyards and woods.

The **Television Tower** (Fernsehturm), south of the city (just off Rte. 3), offers an outstanding view of Stuttgart from a unique location. The 712-foot tower was considered an innovative design when it was constructed in 1956. You can take the elevator up 492 feet to the restaurant and observation platforms for 4 DM ($2.29).

The **castle,** in the Old Town facing the Schillerplatz, is one of Stuttgart's oldest standing structures. The huge ducal palace was originally built in the 13th century as a moated castle, but was renovated in the 16th century to a more comfortable Renaissance style and now houses the **Württembergisches Landesmuseum** (State of Württemberg Museum), which traces the art and culture of Swabia from the Stone Age to the present day. The richest pieces are displayed in the Dürnitzbau, including a survey of handicrafts in Europe, the ducal art chamber, and the Württemberg Crown Treasure, the latter containing the biggest collection of Swabian sculpture. Look also for an exhibition of costumes and musical instruments. A Roman Lapidarium is on view in the Stiftsfruchtkasten. Newly on display is one of the biggest collections of the Early Middle Ages in Germany, comprising the third to the eighth centuries A.D., the Merovingian period. The museum is open daily except Monday from 10 a.m. to 4 p.m. (Wednesdays, till 8 p.m.), charging no admission.

The **State Gallery of Stuttgart,** 32 Konrad-Adenauer-Strasse, is the city's finest art museum, exhibiting works spanning some 700 years. However, the best collection is from the 19th and 20th centuries, especially the works of the modern German Expressionists—Kirchner, Barlach, and Beckmann—as well as representatives of the Bauhaus movement—Klee and Feininger. The largest collection of non-German painters is the group of works by French artists of the 19th and 20th centuries, including Manet, Cézanne, Gauguin, Renoir, Picasso, Bracque, and Léger. The museum is open daily, except Mondays, from 10 a.m. to 5 p.m. (Tuesdays and Thursdays, until 8 p.m.). Admission is free.

Stuttgart has several unusual museums, including an umbrella museum (Schirmmuseum Hugendubel) and a Bible museum (Bibelmuseum), but the one which attracts the most visitors is the **Daimler-Benz Museum** at the Mercedes factory in the suburb of Untertürkheim (follow the Mercedesstrasse from the bridge). The museum traces the history of the automobile from the experimental vehicles of Daimler and Benz in the late 19th century. When these two companies joined forces to produce the Mercedes-Benz in the 1920s, a new era in the auto age began. Upstairs you'll find a collection of racing cars manufactured by Daimler, Benz, and Mercedes-Benz from 1899 to 1955. The museum is open Monday through Friday from 8 a.m. to 4 p.m.; Saturday, 8 a.m. to 1 p.m. Admission is free.

READER'S SIGHTSEEING SUGGESTION: "We went to Stuttgart because my husband owns a Porsche and wanted to see the factory. We were fortunate enough to have a tour through the factory, and I was asked to test-drive a Porsche just completed. It was like being on a roller coaster and marvelous sport. Both Porsche and Mercedes-Benz have tours during the day" (Mrs. George R. Hunt, Mahtomedi, Minn.).

4. Tübingen

Although often compared to Heidelberg, this quiet old university town on the upper Neckar has a look and personality all its own. The gabled medieval houses are crowded up against the ancient town wall at the bank of the river. In the summer the only movement to break this peaceful picture is the gondola-like boats poled up and down the river by students. This far upstream—25 miles south of Stuttgart—the Neckar is too shallow for commercial vessels, and Tübingen has been spared the industrial look of a trading community.

Progress has not passed the city by, however, In spite of its medieval look, it has a new residential and science suburb in the shadow of the Schoenbuch Forest north of the city, with modern medical facilities, research institutes, and lecture halls affiliated with the university. North of the botanical gardens stand the buildings of the old university, founded in 1477. Most of the buildings are in a functional neoclassical design, but they fit right in with the old city around them.

One of the unique features of Tübingen is the man-made island in the Neckar, with its promenade lined with plane trees. This street, known as the **Platanenallee,** is always alive with summer strollers who cross from the main town via the wide Eberhardt Bridge. The island also offers the best view of the town, with its willows and houses reflected in the river. Towering above the roofs of the town is the old Renaissance castle, now used by departments of the university. Visitors to Tübingen should go to the castle, at least for the dramatic view from the terraces.

The narrow streets of the Old Town wind up and down the hillside, but they all seem to lead to the old **Marketplace,** where festive markets are still held today. You'll feel like you're really stepping into the past when you come upon the scene of old country women selling their fruits and vegetables in the open square. In the center of all this activity stands the softly murmuring Renaissance fountain of the god Neptune. Facing the square is the old Rathaus, dating from the 15th century, but with more recent additions, including the 19th-century painted designs on the facade overlooking the Marketplace.

On the hillside above the Marketplace stands **St. George's Church,** the former monastery church of the Stift, an Augustinian monastery. The monastery became a Protestant seminary in 1548 and its church the Collegiate Church. Worth seeing inside are the tombs of the dukes of Württemberg in the chancel and the French Gothic pulpit and rood screen, dating from the 15th century.

BED AND BOARD: Krone Hotel, 1 Uhlandstrasse (tel. 31-036). The university town's most tasteful and prestigious hotel is right off the river, in the heart of Tübingen. The hotel is both traditional and conservative. The interior has a homelike atmosphere with a liberal use of antiques or good reproductions. The dining salon has white Louis XVI chairs, red velvet draperies, and a niche with an antique statue. The Uhlandstube, on the other hand, is more informal, with an old tavern atmosphere of beamed ceilings, leaded-glass windows, ladderback chairs, and paneled wainscoting. There is yet another provincial dining room with paneled booths, country chairs, and Oriental rugs.

The bedrooms are consistent with the public rooms, all personalized with a well-planned arrangement of furniture. Many of the baths are decoratively tiled, with stall showers. The per-person cost of the rooms (including tax, service, and breakfast) is 36 DM ($20.65) in a bathless room, and 70 DM ($40.15) with private bath (almost all of the rooms have private baths). The owners, Karl and Erika Schlagenhauff, provide some of the best meals in town (recommendable even if you're not an overnighter). The menu is international. Typical dishes include filet of sole fried in butter at 28 DM ($16.06), wienerschnitzel at 20 DM ($11.47), and tournedos Rossini, 28 DM ($16.06).

Hotel am Schloss, 18 Burgstrasse (tel. 210-77). This comfortable, chalet-style hotel is only a two-minute walk from the old Marktplatz, on a narrow street opposite the entrance to the baroque castle. It couldn't be more central, yet at the same time away from the hustle and bustle. The bedrooms are somewhat basic, but spacious. The furnishings are contemporary, and each room has a telephone, central heating, and either hot and cold water or a private bath. For the latter, two persons are charged 60 DM ($34.42), only 45 DM ($25.81) without bath. Singles pay anywhere from 27 DM ($15.49) without bath to 40 DM ($22.94) with shower.

5. Schwäbisch Hall

Technically, this medieval town is not in the Neckar Valley, but if you miss it in your travels through this region, you will have missed one of the treasures of southwestern Germany. Lying in the heart of the forests of the Swabian Alb, just 40 miles east of Heilbronn, the town clings to the steep banks of the Kocher River, a tributary of the Neckar. The houses of the Old Town are set on terraces built into the hillside, and from the opposite bank they appear to be arranged in steps, overlooking the old wooden bridges on the river.

The **Marketplace** is possibly the most attractive in all of Germany. Flanking the square are fine old-timbered patrician houses and at the lower end of the sloping square, the baroque Rathaus (Town Hall). In the center of the square is a 16th-century Gothic fountain, decorated with statues of St. George and St. Michael. Behind the fountain is a decorative wall holding the pillory, where offenders in days gone by were left to be jeered at by the townspeople. Today the square is the scene of festive occasions, such as the annual Kuchenfest (Salt Maker's Festival), celebrating the ancient industry which grew up around the springs in Schwäbisch Hall.

On the northern side of the Market Square, facing the Town Hall, are the imposing 54 large stone steps, delicately curved, leading up to **St. Michael's Cathedral.** The cathedral is a 15th-century Gothic Hallenkirche with a Renaissance tower. Many of the pews date from the 15th century, plus St. Michael's altarpiece in the side chapel. The church is open daily from 8 a.m. to 5 p.m. Admission is .50 DM (29¢).

BED AND BOARD: Ratskeller, 12 am Markt (tel. 61-81), right on the Market Square, is an attractive stone building, much of it dating from 1400. The hotel has been completely renewed, installing new furnishings in its high-standard modern rooms. The major installation was a heated swimming pool. Singles with toilets and showers begin at 53 DM ($30.40), and doubles go for 95 DM ($54.49), breakfast included. A sauna bath is an extra 8.50 DM ($4.88). Downstairs, the restaurant serves the best food in town, with set meals ranging in price from 17.50 DM ($10.04) to 31 DM ($17.78).

Hotel Goldener Adler, 11 am Markt (tel. 63-64) is an old-world coaching inn, as authentic as you are likely to find. It stands on one side of the little stage-set Market Square, a beguiling place at which to spend the night and have a meal. You can drive through the central arcade, where carriage wheels of old rolled by. The bedrooms upstairs are casual, but spacious and tidy. A double room with private bath rents for 70 DM ($40.15) to 90 DM ($51.62), dropping to 50 DM ($28.68) to 60 DM ($34.42) without bath. Singles, depending on the plumbing, cost from 32 DM ($18.36) to 48 DM ($27.53). The main dining room is oak paneled, with crude country chairs, red tablecloths, a beamed ceiling, and framed costume prints. Your three-course meal starts as low as 11.50 DM ($6.60), ranging upward to 26 DM ($14.91). Many international specialties are offered in the evening, including nasi-goreng at 25 DM ($14.34) and fondue bourguignonne for two at 44 DM ($25.24).

Hotel Hohenlohe, 14 Weilertor (tel. 61-16), is a modern hotel, built right on the Kocher River, in the historic Freie Reichsstadt district. From its bedroom floors, a dramatic view unfolds. The accommodations are comfortable, compact, with bright color accents. Most of them contain private baths as well. A bathless single rents for 31 DM ($17.78) to 33 DM ($18.93), increasing to 37 DM ($21.22) with shower, 43 DM ($24.66) with bath. Bathless doubles cost 56 DM ($32.12) to 60 DM ($34.42), 64 DM ($36.71) to 72 DM ($41.30) with bath. These rates include breakfast on an open-view roofdeck. The hotel's restaurant offers set meals for 11 DM ($6.31) to 82 DM ($41.30), the latter including, on one recent occasion, crab cocktail and roast pheasant. The family of Theo Dürr are most hospitable.

From the Neckar, we travel to another major river of tourist interest, the Mosel.

THE MOSEL VALLEY

THOSE RETURNING from Germany singing the praises of the Rhine as the most scenic of German rivers have definitely not taken the short trip up the Mosel River. Weaving its snakelike path through the mountains west of the Rhineland, the Mosel (Moselle) encounters town after town whose sole purpose seems to be to beautify the banks of the river. Nearly every village and every hill has its own castle or fortress, surrounded by vineyards where young, green grapes are grown for the popular wines.

Many of the Mosel wines are superior to those of the Rhine Valley, and in spite of their lightness, they are rich and full-bodied wines. Mosel wines have the lowest alcoholic content—only about 9%—of any white wine in the world. Because of this, they are best enjoyed in their youth. Their freshness deteriorates with age.

Although the Mosel actually begins in the hills of France, its most colorful portion is the last 120 miles before it flows into the Rhine at Koblenz. Along these banks, the visitor enjoys the loveliest landscapes, the most legend-rich countryside, and, of course, the best wines. In recent years, locks have been built at strategic points along the river to enable modern vessels to sail the waters which once transported Roman ships. The locks have been incorporated into the landscape, and thus far have not hurt the appearance of the river.

If you enter Germany via France or Luxembourg, the Mosel is a good route by which to begin your tour of the German countryside. By following its path through the mountains, you'll first arrive at the major city of . . .

1. Trier (Trèves)

As the Romans spread out over Europe, they established satellite capitals and imperial residences for ruling their distant colonies. Of all the subcapitals, only August Trevorum (Trier) became known as Roma secunda (the second Rome). For nearly five centuries, well into the Christian era, it remained one of Europe's most powerful cities—politically, culturally, and religiously.

Although officially founded by the Romans under Augustus in 15 B.C., the history of Germany's oldest city actually dates back much farther. In 2000 B.C., according to legend, the Assyrians established a colony here, and archeological findings indicate an even earlier civilization. Most of the buildings and monuments still standing today, however, date from Roman and later periods.

Trier is an important gateway, lying on the western frontier of Germany. Just six miles from the Luxembourg border, it is the first major city on the Mosel, a very German city, rich in art, festivities, and tradition. It became a major market city in 958, a fact commemorated by the Market Cross placed in the old Hauptmarkt by the archbishop. Because of its location, it is one of Germany's largest exporters of wine, as a visit to the huge wine vaults beneath the city will confirm. Tours of the vaults and special wine tastings can be arranged through the city tourist office in the Porta Nigra.

THE SIGHTS: When the last Roman prefect left Trier in about 400, he left behind a vast collection of monuments to the centuries of Roman domination. The **Porta Nigra** (Black Gate), is the best preserved Roman relic in Germany, the only survivor of the great wall which once surrounded Trier. The huge sandstone blocks, assembled without mortar, were held together with iron clamps, the marks of which can still be seen in the blackened stones. From the outside of the gate, the structure appeared to be simply two arched entrances between rounded towers leading directly into the town, but intruders soon discovered that the arches only opened into an inner courtyard where they were at the mercy of the protectors of the town.

During the Middle Ages, the Greek hermit Simeon, later canonized, chose the east tower as his retreat. After his death, the archbishop turned the gate into a huge double church. When Napoleon invaded the Mosel, however, he ordered all the architectural changes to be removed and the original Roman core restored. The Porta Nigra is open daily from 9 a.m. to 6 p.m. Admission: .50 DM (29¢).

The **Imperial Palace** district, stretching along the site of the former eastern wall of the city, begins with the huge Roman palace known today as the **Basilica.** Although much of the original structure, built in 310 A.D., has been demolished, the huge hall which remains gives some idea of the grandeur of the original palace. Believed to be the throne room, its hall is 220 feet long, 90 feet wide, and 98 feet high. The windows are arranged in two tiers within high-rising arches in which fragments of some of the original wall paintings can be seen. The unique method of Roman central heating through ducts beneath the floor was used to warm this huge hall from five large heating chambers outside the walls. Today the parish church of the Protestant community is housed within the northern end of the hall.

Adjacent to the Basilica is the **Electoral Palace,** built in the 17th century as the residence for the archbishops and electors. Originally designed in the style of the German Renaissance, the rebuilding in the 18th century created a more baroque appearance with the addition of a rococo wing facing the **Palace Gardens.** The formal gardens, full of ponds and flowers, are decorated with rococo statues.

The **Imperial Baths,** at the south end of the Palace Gardens, were erected in the early fourth century by Constantine I. Of the huge complex—more than 284 yards wide—only the ruins of the hot baths remain. These baths were among the largest in the entire Roman empire, and although never completed, were used in connection with the Imperial Palace, and built about the same time.

The **Amphitheatre,** just outside the site of the old Roman walls, is the oldest Roman construction in Trier, dating from 100 A.D. The stone seats, arranged in three circles separated by broad promenades, held a capacity of nearly 20,000 people.

St. Peter's Cathedral, north of the Palace Gardens and Basilica, incorporated part of the former palace (fourth century) of the Empress Helena, mother of Constantine, into its precincts. This structure influenced the style adopted by the archibishop when he added the Romanesque facade in the 11th century. The Gothic and baroque additions in later centuries only helped to pull the ecclesiastical architecture into a timeless unity. The interior is also unique, combining elaborate baroque furnishings with the spacious Gothic vaulting and archways. The treasury contains many important works of art, including the tenth-century St. Andrew's altar, an unusual portable altar—if you could lift it—made of gold. But the most valuable treasure is the Holy Robe, alleged to be the seamless garment of Christ, brought to Trier by the Empress Helena. The relic is so fragile that it is only displayed every 30 years (last shown in 1959).

The **Liebfrauenkirche** (Church of Our Lady), separated from the cathedral by a narrow passageway, is the parish church of Trier and is more pleasing esthetically than its older sister. The first example of French Gothic in Germany, it was begun in 1235. The ground plan is in the shape of a Greek cross, creating a circular effect with all points equidistant from the central high altar. The structure is supported by 12 circular columns, rather than the typical open buttresses. The interior is bathed in sunlight, which streams through the high transoms. Although the restoration after the war changed some of the effect of the central construction, the edifice is still unique among German churches. Most of the important works of art have been placed in the city's museum; the sepulchre of Bishop Karl von Metternich is among the most interesting of those remaining. The black marble sarcophagus is a sculptured likeness of the canon, who represented the archbishopric during the Thirty Years' War.

The **Landesmuseum,** between the Imperial Roman Baths and the audience hall (Basilica), at the edge of the Palace Gardens behind the medieval city wall, is one of the outstanding museums of Roman antiquities north of the Alps. Numerous reliefs from funerary monuments show daily life in Roman times. The museum's most famous and popular exhibit is the *Mosel Ship,* a sculpture of a wine-bearing vessel crowning a big funerary monument of the third century A.D. Besides numerous ornamental and figurative mosaics and frescoes, ceramics, and an outstanding numismatic collection, prehistoric and medieval art and sculpture are also exhibited. The museum is open daily from 10 a.m. to 4 p.m.; Sunday, from 10 a.m. to 1 p.m. Admission is free.

The **Episcopal Museum,** also near the Palace Gardens, contains valuable pieces of religious art from the Trier diocese. Among the most important is the ceiling painting from Constantine's imperial palace, recently discovered under the cathedral. Also included are medieval sculptures and other works of art from the treasures of the churches of Trier. The museum is open weekdays from 10 a.m. to noon; Sundays and holidays, 10 a.m. to 1 p.m.

A FIRST-CLASS ACCOMMODATION: Dorint Porta Nigra, Porta-Nigra-Platz (tel. 7-81-61), is Trier's most important hotel, offering a desirable accommodation that combines style, comfort, and position. Across from the Roman ruins, it is a six-story modern building whose interior is decorated with primitive colors and contemporary furnishings. However, the grill room is in the old style, with ladderback chairs and wood paneling. The bedrooms are refreshing, particularly those with bright-red sofas, panels of blue draperies, and bone-white walls. Usually, a sitting area is provided. The baths are ornately tiled. Rates depend on the view and size, with singles priced at 72 DM ($41.30); doubles, from 102 DM ($58.51). Guests enjoy drinks in the intimate bar before dining in the traditional restaurant, ablaze with red. A cafe with an entire wall of glass provides a semipanoramic view of the Roman ruins. The hotel has taken over the Europäischer Hof next door to make a larger hotel (see below).

A MEDIUM-PRICED HOTEL: Europäischer Hof, 1–3 Paulinstrasse (tel. 7-81-61), across from the Porta Nigra, is another excellent accommodation choice. It's under the same ownership as the more prestigious Dorint Porta Nigra, but charges less. In a bathless single, the price is 30 DM ($17.21) to 32 DM ($18.36). Bathless doubles rent for 48 DM ($27.53) to 68 DM ($39). Most of the bedrooms have views opening onto the Roman ruins. Although without baths, the rooms themselves are functional and comfortable. There is no lounge to speak of, except for the sunny breakfast room. The reception area is on the second floor.

BUDGET CHOICES: Hotel Monopol, 7 Bahnhofsplatz (tel. 7-47-55), is one of your best lodging possibilities if you're seeking a low-budget accommodation directly across from the railroad station. The rooms are immaculately kept and of good size. Singles range in price from 29 DM ($16.63) for a bathless room, going up to 44 DM ($25.24) for a unit with more elaborate plumbing. In a double without bath the tariff is 46 DM ($26.39), increasing to 60 DM ($34.42) with shower, and peaking at 74 DM ($42.45) with full bath. The management has employed a friendly, helpful staff.

    Dom Hotel, 18–20 Hauptmarkt (tel. 7-47-10), is a homogenous, 80-year-old combination of gingerbread Germanic and modern comfort. The rates are low, the positioning, at the Hauptmarkt, colorful. Most of the bedrooms overlook the flower and vegetable market as well as Trier's leading restaurant, the Zum Domstein. Halfway along the Roman Trail, the exterior greets you in its bulbous, gargoyle fashion, with its ornate gable and an onion tower crowning a corner circular, bay-windowed bedroom. Inside, it is homey and immaculate, presided over by a courtly manager who speaks English quite well. The rooms, while small, are comfortable, with modern furnishings. The per-person rate, including breakfast, ranges from 26 DM ($14.91) to 38 DM ($21.80) nightly; the different prices are based on the size of the room, the view, and plumbing. Breakfast is the only meal served.

READERS' HOTEL SELECTIONS: "Walking from the train station, I found the **Hotel Kurfürst Balduin,** about one or two blocks down, at 22 Theodor-Heuss-Allee (tel. 4-86-10). It turned out to be a real find. For 29 DM ($16.63), you can have a comfortable, quiet, clean room and a generous breakfast (judged by the usual continental standards). The charge is 60 DM ($34.42) to 65 DM ($37.28) for a large, beautiful, double room with lounge, private bath, and toilet. The hotel is a bit old-fashioned (no elevator), but charmingly appointed, with good-sized rooms, a lounge-coffee room with TV for the guests, and a very amiable proprietor who speaks excellent English" (Lore J. Wagner, Geneva, N.Y.). . . . "**Hotel Wiener Hof,** 25 Bahnhofstrasse (tel. 4-85-47), offers a bathless single room with hot and cold running water for 27 DM ($15.49). A shower is available three yards from the bedroom door. For breakfast, included in the price, you have egg as well as cheese, jam, and honey" (D. Hannay, Sanderstead, Surrey, England). . . . "Our bicycle tour group had reservations at **Warsberger Hof, Hotel im Kolpinghaus,** 42 Dietrichstrasse (tel. 7-51-31). This is a quiet, clean, small hotel one block from Hauptmarkt Square. The hotel courtyard was ideal for parking our bicycles. Breakfast brought generous servings of sausage with hard rolls and jam. The German-speaking husband and wife who run the place are friendly and showed an interest in us. The cost was 18 DM ($10.32) per person per night, double occupancy" (Pat Diehnelt, Menomonee Falls, Wisc.).

THE TOP RESTAURANTS: Zum Domstein, 5 Hauptmarkt und Dom (tel. 7-44-90), overlooking the flowerstands and the fountain on the Hauptmarkt, is the preferred choice for dining. Opening onto an inner courtyard, it features authentic local cuisine and sets a high culinary standard. The three dining rooms have a true gemütlich atmosphere, in the best of the Germanic tavern tradition. English is spoken. No matter what you order, it's traditional to test the Mosel, Saar, and Ruwer wines. For 12 DM ($6.88), you're given six different wines of the local region, lined up so that you can drink them in proper order. In addition, 14 open wines and about 200 bottled ones are in the cellar awaiting your selection. No matter what you decide to eat, the dish at the next table will appear more tempting. Soups are priced from 3.50 DM ($2.01) to 7.50 DM ($4.30). A typical Germanic offering is Rheinischer sauerbraten, kartoffelklosse, and apfelkompott at 15.50 ($8.89). Main dishes are in the 9-DM ($5.16) to 25-DM ($14.34) range. Desserts are from 3.50 DM ($2.01) to 7.50 DM ($4.30). In winter you'll want to find a spot near a huge tile stove. You can also have a look at the Römischer Weinkeller. The room is in the area of the double cathedral (from 326 A.D.), excavated in 1970. Original Roman artifacts, many of them connected with food and cooking, decorate the cellar room. In the Römischer Weinkeller you are served dishes prepared according to recipes attributed to Marcus Gavius Apicius, said to have been the foremost chef at the court of the Roman Emperor Tiberius.

Ratskeller zur Steipe, Hauptmarkt, is one of the most tasteful ratskellers along the Mosel, created out of an ancient crypt Romanesque friezes decorate the walls. Guests sit at tables on different levels, enjoying the exquisite Mosel wines. Set lunches range in price from 7.50 DM ($4.30) to 21 DM ($12.05). On the à la carte menu, try the peppersteak for two at 45 DM ($25.81). Beer begins at only 1.25 DM (72¢).

Im Simeonstift Brunnenhof, at the Porta Nigra (tel. 4-85-84), is nestled in historic ruins, occupying a portion of an old cloister and providing an excellent place at which to dine. You select a table in what was once a great hall, although in fair weather you may prefer the courtyard, where you can enjoy the splashing fountain and the purity of line of the Roman arches. The food is somewhat standardized, but good. Set meals in the 9-DM ($5.16) to 21-DM ($12.05) range are offered from 11:30 a.m. to 2:30 p.m. Desserts are only 2 DM ($1.15).

READER'S RESTAURANT SELECTION: "Braun's Fisch-Gastatätten, 28 Fleischstrasse, is a fast-service fish restaurant with waitress service. Fleischstrasse comes into Hauptmarkt place. For lunch I had delicious halibut with mixed salad and french fries for 7.70 DM ($4.42). Braun's is a 50-year-old restaurant and has branches in Aachen, Bremerhaven, Dortmund, Essen, Frankfurt, Mildescheim, Koblenz, Cologne, Mainz, München-Gladbach, and Wiesbaden. The food is good and economical, the service fast" (Pat Diehnelt, Menomonee Falls, Wisc.).

READER'S HOTEL SELECTION OUTSIDE TRIER: "Our find of the season is an inn on the road between Trier and Bernkastel called St. Michael (tel. 233), in the village of Wintrich-Mosel. It is not only a hotel, but wine cellars as well. Herr Quint, the proprietor (the inn has been in his family since 1602), speaks good basic English and is warm and friendly as is his wife. He is also a vintner, and has his own stock of wines, eaux de vie, and other products for sale per bottle at a cost ranging from 3.50 DM ($2.01) to 18 DM ($10.32). The charge for a room with bath and toilet is 11 DM ($6.31) to 16 DM ($9.18) per person. For 5 DM ($2.87) per person, you can enjoy breakfast, which is most adequate, with good coffee, two kinds of homemade bread (one a delicious raisin), with butter and preserves, a soft-boiled egg, and two varieties of sliced wurst" (Susan H. Briggs, APO New York).

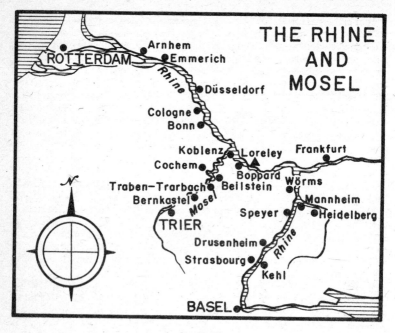

2. Zell

This old village, stretching along the east bank of the mosel, is best known for its excellent wine, Schwarze Katz (Black Cat). The grape is king here, as you will realize if you come to Zell during the annual wine festival.

Nowhere does the wine and the festivity of Zell rule more than at the **Hotel Schloss Zell,** 8 Schlossstrasse (tel. 40-84), one of the very special places in all of Germany. Installed in a 14th-century castle-like bastion, it is ruled by the Jakob Bonn family. Right in the heart of Zell, its twin domed towers are a village landmark. Because of high taxes and the ever-constant need for maintenance, the Bonn family now receives paying guests in 15 bedrooms (try for the ornate one used by Kaiser Maximilian, the last cavalier, in 1512, or the honeymooners' special in the tower).

The salons and the drawing room are filled with antiques—a flamboyant use of gilt, ornate inlaid woods, stained glass, bronze, and crystal. Be sure to see the settee given to Josephine by Napoleon. Favored guests who stay more than one night are invited into the private drawing rooms, in themselves museums of antiquity. For an accommodation here, you pay 45 DM ($25.81) per person in a bathless room, 50 DM ($28.68) with shower, and 55 DM ($31.55) to 75 DM ($43.02) with your own bath. Taxes are included. Closed December 15 through January 15.

Dining at Schloss Zell is a gastronomic event worth crossing the Mosel for—or even the Rhine! One woman makes a weekly pilgrimage here just to sample the vineyard snails in garlic and tarragon at 12 DM ($6.88) for a half dozen. Specialties include freshwater trout—caught in the nearby streams—

prepared in Mosel wine for 25 DM ($14.34). The Mosel eel, also cooked in Mosel wine, is famous, costing 25 DM also. Set lunches range from 20 DM ($11.47) to 35 DM ($20.08). A special treat: The Bonn family is the owner of the original Schwarze Katz (Black Cat) Mosel wine and sells a bottle for 15 DM ($8.60); occasionally, guests buy as many as ten bottles to take with them. Try it and you'll understand why.

On the left bank of the Mosel, five miles from Zell and 20 from Cochem, stands the little wine village of **Alf.** The surroundings are idyllic, especially if you climb up to the Marienburg. From there, you get a fine view overlooking the Mosel and the vineyards of Zell.

3. Traben-Trarbach

Thanks to their central location on the Mosel, halfway between Koblenz and Trier, the twin cities of Traben and Trarbach have become the wine capitals of the Mosel Valley. The garden-like promenades on both banks of the river are perfect viewpoints for the annual international speedboat and waterskiing competitions held on the Mosel. The July wine festival attracts visitors from all over Europe to the romantic old wine cellars and taverns of the towns. But behind all the bustle and activity, Traben-Trarbach is proud of its sightseeing attractions, and especially of its thermal springs and health resort, **Bad Wildstein,** just south of town.

Above Trarbach, on the east bank of the river, stands the 14th-century **Grevenburg Castle,** which, with five other now-in-ruins castles in the vicinity, was the scene of hard-fought battles to gain control of this strategic spot on the Mosel. On the opposite bank, above Traben, are the ruins of Mont Royal, an important fortress built in the late 17th century by the invading Louis XIV.

If you plan to stay over, you might try **Clauss-Feist,** am Moselufer (tel. 64-31), in Traben, a heavily Germanic structure right on the banks of the Mosel. It was created in an ornamental style around 1900 by the architect Moehring, and utilizes such adornments as elaborate timberwork, a domed tower, a highly pitched roof, gables, and dormers. A special feature is the ivy-covered terrace, where you can dine. Inside, stained-glass windows are set in ecclesiastical frames, and overstuffed chairs are drawn up around Victorian fringed "parlor tables," resting under vaulted ceilings. The accommodations are warmly decorated and cost 40 DM ($22.94) to 52 DM ($29.83), increasing to 58 DM ($33.27) to 68 DM ($39) with bath—quite a bargain. It's an architectural hodgepodge, but fun if you're in the mood.

Zur Post, 17 Gestade (tel. 30-01), is a genuine humble village inn, with a colorful exterior—shutters, window boxes for summer flowers, tiny windows inserted in the small bedrooms under the eaves, and tubs of flowers on the sidewalk. Some 30 beds are offered in 17 bedrooms, some of them in a nearby guest house. A bathless double rents for 54 DM ($30.97), with breakfast included. The cuisine is hearty, and the wines are excellent with more than 100 selections. In season, eel is recommended. Zur Post is open from February through November only. It's within walking distance of the town, right below the castle.

READER'S WINE CELLAR SELECTION: "**Bacchus Keller,** Gestadestrasse, is a lovely wine cellar at which to spend your evening singing, dancing, and tasting wine with the local people. The band plays favorite German songs. You must buy wine by the bottle, the cost starting at 14 DM ($8.03). We had a terrific evening" (Nancy Gilbert, Alexandria, Va.).

4. Bernkastel-Kues
Like Traben-Trarbach, this town is split into twin villages on opposite banks of the Mosel. In a valley of wine towns, Bernkastel stands out as the most colorful, with its old Markplatz surrounded by half-timbered buildings in perfect condition, dating from as early as 1608. In the center of the square stands **St. Michael's fountain** (17th century), which flows with wine during the annual September wine festival. Above the town stand the ruins of the 11th-century **Landshut Castle,** worth a visit for the dramatic view of the Mosel from the promontory on which it stands. During the wine festival, the castle is lit by floodlights and fireworks.

In accommodations and food, the following are recommended:

Drei Könige (Three Kings), 1 Bahnhofstrasse (tel. 23-27), is like a sleeping palace. It's an ornate gingerbread relic, standing on the banks of the Mosel, its architecture characterized by gables, bay windows, and a timbered tower. In all, there are 40 bedrooms, many of which have private baths. The rooms are comfortable. Try for a river view. Bathless singles peak at 30 DM ($17.21), at 45 DM ($25.81) with shower. The most expensive accommodations—the doubles with private bath—cost anywhere from 76 DM ($43.59) to 85 DM ($48.76), although you can get bathless doubles in the 56 DM ($32.12) to 60 DM ($34.42) range. If you do have a bathless room, however, you'll have to pay 4.50 DM ($2.58) to take a bath. Continental breakfast is included. In the wine cellar, you can sample Mosel wine.

Ratskeller, Markt (tel. 4-23), traces its origins back to 1608 and occupies the most colorful real estate in Bernkastel-Kues, opening onto a square of half-timbered houses and a 17th-century fountain dedicated to an angel. The Town Hall itself is in a Renaissance style, and sports a bay window adorned with pots of red geraniums. Although it has experienced a rocky history, the cellar today is a tavern of charm and good food (every dish here is washed down with superb wines of Bernkastel). A pianist in the evening encourages dancers to join in the Mosel polka. Main dishes, with salad, range in price from 9.55 DM ($4.48) to 24.50 DM ($14.05), and include such hearty fare as rumpsteak, wienerschnitzel, game (in season), and Mosel fish. Desserts cost from 2.75 DM ($1.58) to 6 DM ($3.44), and soups go from 2.75 DM ($1.58) to 5.50 DM ($3.15).

5. Beilstein
On the east bank of the Mosel, this ancient wine town has an unusual marketplace hewn right into the rocky hillside. Above the town stands the former cloister church and the ruins of the 12th-century Metternich Castle.

You can sample the wines that made Beilstein famous at its favorite inn, **Haus Lipmann** (tel. 3-73). The centuries pass by, and time has been more than kind to this 1795 timbered inn, in one of the oldest and most unspoiled villages along the Mosel. It's owned by one of Germany's most unforgettable characters, Herr W. Lipmann, a down-to-earth, most democratic gentleman who represents the sixth generation which has tended the vast riverside vineyards that have won fame for his family. Try either his Ellenzer Goldbäumchen or Beilsteiner Schlossberg.

The spots for drinking and dining are so tempting that it's difficult making a decision. Most popular in summer, however, is the vine-covered terrace, with a statue of Bacchus, overlooking the Mosel. Of course, there's the antique-filled tavern itself, or the wood-paneled Rittersaal, with its impressive collection of old firearms and pewter. Candles are lit at night; in the cooler months, fires burn in either the tall walk-in-fireplace or the tiny peasant open hearth, with its copper kettle on a crane. Main dishes are in the 9.80-DM ($5.61) to 18.50-DM range ($10.61). The Mosel eel in dill sauce is classic, but especially delectable is the fresh trout.

Lucky is the person who can spend the night. Bathless doubles cost only 40 DM ($22.94); singles, 24 DM ($13.77). A few doubles with shower go for 50 DM ($28.68). These rates include breakfast. The bedrooms are furnished in a homey manner—some old pieces, some new, much of undetermined origin. Preferred are the rooms with their own balconies. Activities are so hectic at grape harvest time that the hotel closes down.

6. Cochem

In one of the best wine regions of the Mosel Valley, this medieval town is crowded against the left bank of the river by a huge vineyard-covered hill. The town itself is a typical wine village, with its wine tastings and festivals. But the biggest attraction is **Reichsburg Cochem,** a huge castle at the top of the mound behind the town. Originally built in 1027, it was almost completely destroyed by the army of Louis XIV in 1689. It has since been completely restored after the original ground plans, and its medieval ramparts and turrets created a dramatic backdrop for the town. To reach the castle, follow the steep footpath from the center of town. The 15-minute walk is well worth it for the views of the town below and the Mosel. Although you can visit any time, the interior of the castle is open from 9 a.m. to 6 p.m. daily. Guided tours are conducted at regular intervals. Admission is 3 DM ($1.72) for adults, 2.50 DM ($1.43) for students, and 1.50 DM (86¢) for children.

THE TOP INNS: Alte Thorschenke, 3 Brückenstrasse (tel. 70-59), is both a hotel and a wine restaurant, one of the oldest, best known, and most colorful, along either side of the Mosel. Innkeeping has been refined to its ultimate here, in a romantically conceived building with timbers, towers, and many antiques, including some bedrooms with four-posters. Built originally in 1332, it was remade into a hotel in 1960, when a modern wing was added, offering rooms with private baths. Most of the accommodations have old wooden beds, chests, and armories. You reach them via a cantilevered wooden staircase that has creaked for centuries—and probably will for a few more! Of course, there is an elevator in the rear if you want to make it easy on yourself. Prices for rooms are as follows: 28 DM ($16.06) to 46 DM ($26.39) for a bathless single, 45 DM ($25.81) to 65 DM ($37.28) with bath. Bathless doubles (these are the antique-filled rooms) are 59 DM ($33.84) to 83 DM ($47.61), rising to 82 DM ($47.04) to 110 DM ($63.10) in the new wing with private baths. If you want a room with one of the old-fashioned beds, ask for the *himmelbetten* (heaven beds). Not to be ignored are meals in the tavern, accompanied by Mosel wines. In the summer, guests often take their lunch at one of the sidewalk tables. Set midday meals range in price from 15 DM ($8.60) to 25 DM ($14.34) with à la carte main courses costing from 12 DM ($6.88) to 35 DM ($20.08).

The 500-year-old wine castle of Baron von Landenberg in Eller is seven kilometers from Cochem. Guests of the hotel can visit the old wine cellars and enjoy tasting the wines.

Germania, 1 Moselpromenade (tel. 2-61), is a big, old resort-style hotel, complete with dormers and balconies, as well as dining terraces surrounded by red geraniums. Best of all, it's right on the Mosel, with a view of Cochem Castle. The interior oozes with charm, leaning heavily on traditional wood paneling, provincial antiques, and lots of Teutonic artifacts. Part of the hotel dates back to 1749, although modernization has erased much antiquity. A bathless single ranges in price from 36 DM ($20.65) to 38 DM ($20.80); singles with bath, 42 DM ($24.09) to 48 DM ($27.53). Bathless doubles go from 56 DM ($32.12) to 62 DM (35.56), from 74 DM ($42.45) to 85 DM ($48.76) with complete bath.

Burg Hotel, 23 Moselpromenade (tel. 71-17), is the happy domain of the Müller family, who offer guests a warm and friendly welcome. The family has renovated the inn, providing more private baths, showers, and toilets for the bedrooms. The furnishings are traditional, with a few antiques lending added style, and some rooms have balconies, opening onto views of the Mosel. Bathless singles range in price from 30 DM ($17.21) to 34 DM ($19.50), increasing to anywhere from 32 DM ($18.36) to 45 DM ($25.81) with bath. Bathless doubles go for 50 DM ($28.68) to 62 DM ($35.56), rising to 90 DM ($51.62) for the most expensive rooms with private baths. However, the bargain of the house is a double with bath, sans river view, costing only 65 DM ($37.28).

The food is still the best you may expect in town. Main dishes are in the 12-DM ($6.88) to 25-DM ($14.34) range. Specialties include game fricassee with bits of asparagus and rice; trout meunière; and rumpsteak with mushrooms, french fried potatoes, and a salad. A tremendous selection of the best Mosel wines are in the 15-DM ($8.60) to 30-DM ($17.21) bracket. The hotel offers an indoor swimming pool, sauna, solarium, and TV room.

READER'S RESTAURANT SELECTION: "I especially enjoyed **Hans Felden's** clean, quiet, comfortable restaurant just south of the bridge on the west side of the Mosel River. Mr. Felden personally took our orders, and when I ordered milk, he asked if I wanted it cold or warm. I ordered it cold, and it came in a cup, a surprising custom to me. My fine evening meal of pork schnitzel, french fries, marinated green beans, and marinated shredded carrots was about $4. I wanted to share this peaceful place with your readers so I asked for a piece of paper with the name of his restaurant on it. Mr. Felden gave 11 of his different wine labels from his own brands. He specializes in Riesling wines such as Volwiger Herrenberg. His address is on the labels, 'Hans Felden of Cochem/Mosel Weinhaus, Weinbau, Windellerei.' Apparently in Cochem, Hans Felden doesn't need an address. Just ask for his weinhaus and prepare to enjoy well lit, friendly surroundings and excellent food" (Pat Diehnelt, Menomonee Falls, Wisc.).

7. Eltz Castle

This magnificent castle, completely surrounded by woodlands, can be reached in an hour's walk from **Karden,** in about 40 minutes from **Moselkern,** or, more conveniently, in about 15 minutes if you arrive via **Münstermaifeld** (with a remarkably beautiful Gothic abbey church) and **Wierschem.** The original structure, built from the 12th to 17th centuries, has been preserved in all its medieval glory. The romance of the Middle Ages really comes alive here, with no modern conveniences nearby to distract you from your dalliance in history. Completely surrounding a large inner court, the castle houses four separate residences, furnished with pieces from the Gothic period, including some fine old paintings. From April to October 31, the castle is open daily from 9 a.m. to 5:30 p.m. (from 10 a.m. on Sundays). Admission is 4.50 DM ($2.58) (less for groups). If you want to fortify yourself before the trek back to town, two small restaurants lie within the castle walls.

READER'S DINING SELECTION AT BRAUNEBERG: "Between Trier and Bernkastel-Kues, we ate at a place we truly enjoyed. It has expanded greatly since we first discovered it, and this has been charmingly and attractively accomplished. The food—abundant and deliciously prepared—and the efficient, friendly service have not suffered. We were as delighted with our meal—eaten by the window with a view of the Mosel—as we had been in the past, and would highly recommend it to anyone stopping there. We had a complete wienerschnitzel dinner with french fries and a delightful German vegetable salad for 8.80 DM ($5.05) each. The place is **Lindenhof,** 5551 Brauneberg-Mosel (tel. 06534/448). It also has rooms for rent if you'd like to stay over" (Mrs. H. L. Briggs, APO New York).

After the Mosel, the Black Forest is explored in the next chapter.

Chapter VIII

THE BLACK FOREST

1. **Baden-Baden**
2. **Badenweiler**
3. **Freiburg**
4. **Wildbad**
5. **Freudenstadt**
6. **Titisee**

WHEN YOU VISIT this region in southwestern Germany, don't expect to come upon a little elf working on a cuckoo clock in his tiny gingerbread shop. What you will find, however, is nearly as exciting and altogether more enjoyable. The Black Forest is full of charming people and hospitable little villages which have retained their traditional flavor.

This region of Germany (called Schwarzwald) covers a triangular section of the large province of Baden-Württemberg roughly 90 miles long and 25 miles wide. The pine- and birch-studded mountains are alive with fairytale villages, sophisticated spas, and modern ski resorts. The peaks in the southern part of the forest reach as high as 5000 feet, excellent for skiing in winter and hiking or mountain climbing in summer. The little lakes of Titisee and Schluchsee are popular for boating, swimming—and, of course, winter skating. Fish abound in the streams and lakes, and deer romp through the groves of pine.

Besides the cuckoo clock and the many toys manufactured in the Black Forest, this region is noted for another product—kirschwasser, a delicious, unsweetened cherry brandy, derived from the fruit of its black, twisted cherry trees. This, along with Black Forest bacon and peasant-style rye bread, constitutes a memorable meal.

Although the ideal way to explore the Schwarzwald is on foot, your time and energy would probably run out before the many scenic attractions did. So motoring is the best alternative. The roads through the forest are excellent—especially the **Schwarzwald Hochstrasse** (Black Forest High Road), running from Baden-Baden to Freudenstadt. This scenic route offers many opportunities to park your car and explore the countryside. Many of the side roads leading off the High Road are in good condition as well and take you to little villages, ancient castles, and rolling farmlands.

The adventure of the Black Forest begins at its gateway city:

1. Baden-Baden

In the 19th century, the nobility of Europe discovered Baden-Baden, where the bath-conscious Roman Emperor Caracalla had taken the waters more than 1500 years before. Most of the titles and crowns are merely dust collectors today, but the legacy left by these Romans and Romanovs has made the resort on the edge of the Black Forest the most elegant and sophisticated playground in Germany. The clientele may have changed, but Baden-Baden still evokes an aura of 19th-century aristocracy, combined with the most modern facilities.

THE SIGHTS: The center of activity is the **Lichtentaler Alee**, the park-promenade lining the bank of the Oosbach River (affectionately called the Oos—pronounced ohs), which rùns through the center of town. As you stroll along this promenade, you'll be amazed at the variety of exotic shrubs and trees, the colorful patches of rhododendrons, azaleas, roses, and zinnias. At the north end of the park, on the banks of the babbling stream, are the buildings of the Kurgarten, including the classical Kurhaus. Behind its sparkling white columns and facade is the oldest casino **(Spielbank)** in Germany where for more than 200 years everyone from Dostoevsky's Alexei Ivanovitch to the Prince of Wales have tested their luck at the roulette wheel or the baccarat tables. The various rooms of the casino were designed more than 125 years ago in the style of an elegant French chateau, not unlike Versailles. In all this splendor, you can gamble year round, using real gold and silver chips. The minimum stake is 5 DM ($2.87), but visitors are not obliged to play. The historic gaming rooms may be viewed daily from 10 a.m. to noon on a conducted tour costing 1.50 DM (86¢). If visitors want to gamble later, a full day's ticket is available for 5 DM ($2.87). A jacket and necktie are mandatory for male visitors.

Although most of the bathing establishments, including the old Friedrichsbad and the ultramodern Neues Augustabad, are on the opposite side of the Oos, in the heart of the Old Town, the spa gardens contain the **Pump Room** (Trinkhalle), where visitors can sip the radioactive, chloride water. Built in the 19th century, the loggia of the hall is decorated with frescoes of Black Forest legends. The springs of Baden-Baden have been recognized for more than 2000 years, and yet their composition is almost the same today as when the Romans built their baths here in the third century. The remains can still be seen today beneath the Römerplatz in the old section of the city.

Above the Römerplatz stands the Renaissance castle **Neues Schloss** (New Castle), built in the 16th century by the margraves of Baden to replace their 12th-century castle. The terraces offer an excellent view of the entire city. The castle today houses the **Zähringer Museum,** containing many fine works of German art, including paintings by Lucas Cranach. Especially interesting is the collection of fine china and Meissen porcelain. For a visit to the museum, telephone 2-55-93 or make an appointment with the Information Center, 1 Augusta-Platz, 757 Baden-Baden (tel. 27-52-02).

Baden-Baden is the ideal choice for sports and outdoor enthusiasts who would like to settle in for a few days of golf, tennis, or horseback riding. Horse-lovers will also enjoy the international racing season each August at Iffezheim Track. The surrounding countryside is good for hiking and mountain climbing. During the winter months, Baden-Baden is still very active. As the gateway to the Black Forest, it is a convenient center for numerous ski resorts—and after a day on the slopes, you can return to a soothing swim in the thermal pools of the baths before a night out at the casino.

THE TOP HOTELS: **Brenner's Park,** an der Lichtentaler Allee (tel. 2-30-01), is the Rolls-Royce resort hotel of Baden-Baden. It's a short walk from the heart of town, on the little River Oos, in the midst of beautiful gardens. Some of its international habitués wouldn't dare let a year go by without making an appearance here for the cure. It's a glamorous place at which to stay, with orchestra music nightly for dancing and gourmet dining in the Schwarzwald Grill. One almost overlooks the fact that interwoven in the hotel life are extensive health facilities. There's a new indoor swimming pool on the premises, including a sauna with open-air space solarium, massage, and exercise room. The public rooms are fashionably conceived—each providing a rich background for the chic attire of its guests.

Rates are complicated, depending on the season as well as the size and placement of your room. The winter low is from November through April; the high season is from May until November 1. The accommodations themselves are richly furnished and spacious. Bathless singles in high season range in price from 45 DM ($25.81) to 80 DM ($45.89); with shower, 100 DM ($57.36) to 128 DM ($73.42); with private bath, 110 DM ($63.10) to 180 DM ($103.25). Twin-bedded rooms with bath are 180 DM ($103.25) to 290 DM ($166.34). A complete luncheon costs 33 DM ($18.93); a complete dinner, 36 DM ($20.65).

Steigenberger Hotel Europäischer Hof, 2 Kaiserallee (tel. 2-35-61), which stands opposite the Kurgarten and the famous casino, has just completed an extensive renovation. It stands adjacent to the Oos River which runs at the edge of the Kurpark. Actually, it's a pair of hotels joined together which were built when it was considered important to provide dramatic living facilities. Its colonnaded, classic central hallway is stunning, and many of its suites and bedrooms open off its balconies. Offered are 140 well-furnished rooms, equipped with radio, phone, and, for the most part, color television. The atmosphere is one of elegance in this distinguished hotel. Single rooms range in price from 55 DM ($31.55) to 129 DM ($73.99), with twins going for 120 DM ($68.83) to 192 DM ($110.13), these tariffs including a large buffet breakfast. The restaurant facilities reflect a traditional atmosphere, and the food is of high standard, with both regional and international dishes appearing on the bill of fare.

Bellevue, Lichtentaler Allee and 22–24 Maria-Viktoria-Strasse (tel. 2-37-21), is "not a palace—but a big, styled manor house with antique furnishings," according to the realistic appraisal of the owners, the Saur family. It is grandiose, set in its own park, near the Rosengarten, about a ten-minute walk from the center of town. It essentially attracts a mature clientele. It has well-kept gardens, an informal and attractive drinking lounge, a wood-paneled study graced with a six-foot fireplace and old paintings, a music room splendidly furnished in Biedermeier, and a dining room surrounded by walls of glass for the garden view. The rooms are spacious and traditionally furnished, the rates complicated, depending on the size, season, and type of bath in your room. Bathless singles range in price from 55 DM ($31.55) to 70 DM ($40.15); with shower and/or bath, 88 DM ($50.48) to 120 DM ($68.83). Bathless twins go for anywhere from 100 DM ($57.36) to 130 DM ($75.57); with bath or shower, 110 DM ($63.10) to 220 DM ($126.19).

Steigenberger Badhotel Badischer Hof, 47 Lange Strasse (tel. 2-28-27), with its colonnaded facade, is on a busy street in the center of town, but its rear opens onto an expansive garden with a wide balustraded terrace, flower beds, and a lawn around a stone fountain. Once a Capuchin monastery stood on this site, but gave way to a spa hotel in 1807. Then the Badhotel began its career as a social center for famous personalities who spent "the season" there, taking the cure. One of its most distinguished guests, composer Carl Maria von Weber, wrote: "The beautiful dining room with its high ceiling, the tastefully decorated casino, and the fine stone-encased bathing facilities will make this guest house more and more popular with the years." And so they have. You'll look in amazement at the colonnaded, four-story-high hallway, with its great staircase and encircling balustraded balconies. Giant bronze torchiers stand at the base of the staircase, and antiques are tastefully used. Other public rooms are attractive and old-world. The well-furnished bedrooms are priced according to size and view, as well as season. All the accommodations have private baths. Singles range from 83 DM ($47.61) to 109 DM ($65.52); doubles, from 110 DM ($63.10) to 150 DM ($86.04). A buffet breakfast is included. Many rooms have private balconies, and all have thermal water piped into the private baths.

THE MIDDLE BRACKET: Bad-Hotel zum Hirsch, 1 Hirschstrasse (tel. 2-38-96), has been operated as a hotel by the same family since 1689. A plaque in the dining room traces the family tree. It's a tranquil compound of several buildings, and throughout the centuries constant modernization has taken place. In spite of the physical improvements, the antique furnishings have been retained, making the hotel a living museum of the fine period pieces. The more formal dining room is dominated by crystal chandeliers and paneled walls. The Kleines restaurant is equally attractive, with blue velvet provincial armchairs, classic draperies, and much crystal. There are several sitting and drawing rooms each tastefully furnished. A breakfast terrace rests under a glycinia arbor, and an inner courtyard garden is a tranquil oasis. Consistently interesting are the old-style bedrooms, each individually furnished as in a country home. Bathless singles are 36 DM ($20.65) to 44 DM ($25.24); with bath, 70 DM ($40.15) to 86 DM ($49.33). Twin-bedded rooms with bath or shower are 125 DM ($71.70) to 140 DM ($80.30). Breakfast is included. All the rooms have thermal water piped in. One of the special advantages of staying here is the abundant spa facilities at reasonable fees. Frau Peters, who was born in 1899, when Germany was quite a different country, still operates the hotel, keeping her knowing eye on everything—including your comfort.

Waldhotel Der Selighof, 125 Fremesbergstrasse (tel. 2-33-85), on the outskirts of Baden-Baden, stands in a wooded park adjoining a golf course. It seems more a country club than a hotel. The house is presided over by a gracious owner, Doris Oberst, who collects original paintings and antiques. There is a quietness and purity of air here—either at the open-air swimming pool in the garden, or at a table on the terrace where you can have a slow-paced breakfast. The dining room, with all-glass walls, allows uninterrupted views of the woods and park. The living room provides a proper background for a well-spent evening, and the study is decorated in a country-house theme, with an open fireplace and antiques. There is, in addition, a country-style drinking lounge, with a collection of plaques, prints, plates, and tiles, plus a heated indoor pool. To stay here in a comfortable, well-furnished room is not prohibitively expensive. A single with shower ranges from 50 DM ($28.68) to 70 DM ($40.15), going up to 63 DM ($36.14) to 82 DM ($47.04) with a complete bath. A double with shower costs from 80 DM ($45.89) to 100 DM ($57.36), rising to 90 DM ($51.62) to 140 DM ($80.30) with a full bath. Breakfast is included.

THE BUDGET CHOICE: Hotel am Markt, 18 Marktplatz (tel. 2-27-47), sits like a pleasant country inn on the old marketplace, far removed from the grandeur of the upper-bracket social life of Baden-Baden. It's a gem of a situation, with a tiny terrace cafe in front with window boxes of petunias. Best of all is the quietness, interrupted only by the chimes from the church across the square. There is no lounge to speak of, rather a tavern-style dining room with deep-toned wooden dado, deeply set small-paned windows, and straight-back country armchairs—in all, a relaxed and informal atmosphere. Innkeeper Herr Bogner has set the following prices for the upper-level bedrooms, each comfortably but simply furnished. Bathless singles are 26 DM ($14.91) to 28 DM ($16.06); bathless doubles, 54 DM ($30.97) to 56 DM ($32.12). A single with a private bath (shower) costs 35 DM ($20.08) to 38 DM ($21.80); a double with shower or bath, 62 DM ($35.56) to 66 DM ($37.86). Breakfast is included.

READERS' HOTEL SELECTIONS: "An agreeable and reasonable hotel, within a mile of downtown Baden-Baden, is the **Familienhotel Friedrichsruh,** 20 Seelachstrasse (tel. 7-22-48). We had a lovely room overlooking the mountains with a beautiful, clean, and elegant bathroom. The dining room was really lovely, and the food excellent. Our best breakfast in Germany was served there. A bathless double rents for 52 DM ($29.82) and up, breakfast included" (Mrs. George Gussman, Silver Spring, Md.). . . . "About three or four kilometers outside of Baden-Baden on the way to the village of Varnholt, we stayed at **Haus Roderswald** (tel. 56-28), a lovely pension on top of a hill in the midst of vineyards. The view of the valley and vines from our balcony off the room was outstanding. The room was clean, and we had a tiled bath with shower which was private. The Wecker family operates the pension, and both speak English and are quite cordial. Breakfast (with egg) was excellent, served in a glass-enclosed dining room overlooking the villages of Varnholt, Steinbach, and Neuweier. The price is 45 DM ($25.81) for a double" (Robert A. Klocke, Williamsville, N.Y.).

THE TOP RESTAURANTS: Mirabelle, 1 Kaiserallee (tel. 2-96-11), is a fine place to dine in Baden-Baden. It's especially dramatic when the musicians play in the shell bandstand at the edge of the park. The cuisine is French. Your meal might begin with green pepper soup at 9 DM ($5.16) or salade nouvelle at 18 DM ($10.32), then follow with one of these tempting main dishes: scallops at 28 DM ($16.06); duckling with oranges, 28 DM also; or filet of veal with spinach, 30 DM ($17.21). The restaurant is open from 6 p.m., but closed Mondays. In addition to the formal dining room, the Boulevard, on a covered portico with floor-to-ceiling windows opening onto the esplanade, is open all day from 11 a.m. The cuisine is international, and a meal will cost between 10 DM ($5.74) and 18 DM ($10.32).

Stahlbad, 2 Augustaplatz (tel. 2-45-69), provides dining in the French manner. And what a production it is! Mrs. Elisabeth Schwank does the cooking, as she has for almost 30 years, and her daughter, Mrs. Ursula Monch, welcomes you in the dining room. The atmosphere evokes a glorified tavern, chock-full of gourmet memorabilia. Every square inch is covered with a colorful collection of framed prints, copper cooking and serving equipment, antique pewter plates, mugs and engravings. An open kitchen whets your appetite for the good food being prepared here. Soups begin at 6.50 DM ($3.73). Some of the specialties are peppersteak at 35 DM ($20.08) or venison steak at 45 DM ($25.81). Two other dishes which have won esteem are fresh sole in a curry sauce, 35 DM ($20.08), and lobster thermidor, priced according to weight and lethally expensive.

A BUDGET RESTAURANT: Wienerwald Krokodil, 2 Muhlengasse (tel. 2-31-71), is hidden away in a shopping area, just two minutes from the park. This spacious, tavern-style restaurant, with a rustic interior, contains several dining rooms offering good and inexpensive food. The specialty is Wienerwald-grillhendlt, half a grilled chicken, costing 6.30 DM ($3.61). Another good main dish is the Wienerwald-schnitzel at 9.90 DM ($5.68), served with a mixed salad, and the Texas steak, with french fries and a salad, 13.95 DM ($8). To begin with, liver dumpling soup at 2.60 DM ($1.49) is favored by many German diners. You might like it, too. Apfelstrudel costs 2.30 DM ($1.32) and is the most classic dessert. Service is good, and the place is friendly.

2. Badenweiler

Halfway between Freiburg and Basle, near the Swiss border, is the tiny spa of Badenweiler. The town authorities are so intent on keeping their community spotless that you will be required to park your car at the entrance. The designers of the Kurpark used the natural hillside setting to its best advantage by planting the cypress and cedar trees in groves around the walks and buildings. The springs of the spa have been known since Roman times. In fact, the well-preserved Roman baths still stand today within the spa gardens.

In spite of its appearance of a sleepy little German village, Badenweiler offers its visitors a wide range of entertainment and activity, from summer concerts in open-air pavilions to winter skiing. For another attraction of this area, you'll have to leave the city and drive about 12 miles south to the **Bürgeln Castle**. Built in 1764 by order of the abbott of St. Blasien, the castle sits on an extension of the Blauen, the southernmost reaches of the Black Forest. The castle offers a view of the surrounding countryside as far as the Swiss Alps. On a clear day, you can see Basle and the bend in the Rhine as it flows into Switzerland. The gardens around the castle are a delight in summer. Guided tours are conducted through the baroque palace daily, except Tuesday, at regular intervals between 10:15 a.m. and 5 p.m. Admission for adults is 2 DM ($1.15); children, 1 DM (57¢).

THE TOP HOTELS: Römerbad, 1 Schlossplatz (tel. 701), is a palatial hotel, where discerning guests find a proper setting for resort living in addition to taking the cure. It's a bone-white structure, with domes, balconies, a mansard roof, plus a huge open-air swimming pool set in a woodland, amid lawns and flower beds. The interior has opera-house grandeur with rooms opening off its elegant reception hall ringed with a white balustraded balcony. Furnishings are discreetly high fashion, employing excellent antiques and tones of gold balanced with white or Wedgwood blue in the small dining room. Provincial furniture, a medallion collection, and bird prints make for an interesting decor. A wood-paneled drinking lounge is popular in the evenings, and there's a stately dining room as well, which contrasts sharply with an informal outdoor barbecue. The most recent addition is an enclosed swimming pool, with walls of glass to allow views of the neighboring park. In addition, there are numerous spa facilities and massage rooms.

Rates, including continental breakfast, are 80 DM ($45.89) to 120 DM ($68.83) for a single with bath, 130 DM ($75.57) to 180 DM ($103.25) for a double with similar plumbing. The half-pension charge is 30 DM ($17.21) extra per person; full board, 40 DM ($22.94) per person extra. Two tennis courts with pro are reserved for guests.

Park, 6 Ernst-Eisenlohr-Strasse (tel. 50-91), is like a pair of Italian palaces on the side of the hill with a pastoral view. Within, traditional furnishings give a country estate look to the main living room. An enclosed thermal swimming pool makes the Park even more tempting. Bedrooms vary greatly in size and style, but each is nicely appointed and comfortable. Most have good views. The full-board price for a bathless single goes from 90 DM ($51.62) to 98 DM ($56.21); with bath, 126 DM ($72.27) to 136 DM ($78). Bathless doubles with three meals range in price from 160 DM ($91.78) to 168 DM ($96.36); with bath, 225 DM ($129.06) to 245 DM ($140.53). The management is reluctant to rent rooms without pension.

THE MIDDLE BRACKET: Ritter, 2 Friedrichstrasse (tel. 50-74), is an informal chalet building, with its own gardens and an annex with modern apartments. Its main building contains many traditional, but attractive, bedrooms, most with private baths. Bathless singles range from 35 DM ($20.08) to 45 DM ($25.81); doubles, 54 DM ($30.97) to 64 DM ($36.71). With private bath, singles rent for 60 DM ($34.43); doubles, 90 DM ($51.62) to 100 DM ($57.36). Rates include breakfast. The public rooms have a pleasant informality. The grillroom restaurant, for example, has a rustic theme, with a beamed ceiling and many trailing vines and plants. The swimming pool is modern, with one glass wall opening onto the lawn and woods. The Ritter lies just a short walk to the Kurpark and town social center.

WHERE TO DINE: Grill Restaurant, Parkstüble, Park Hotel, 6 Ernst-Eisenlohr-Strasse (tel. 50-91), is the gathering spot for those who want to dine out in Badenweiler. Although separate, it is within the Park Hotel. The interior is rustic. One room, for example, has wood-paneled walls adorned with primitive paintings, provincial furniture, and a coved ceiling. Best of all, the atmosphere is friendly and the food is good. On the à la carte menu, you can order lobster soup at 8 DM ($4.59); sole Nantua, 24 DM ($13.77); or ox tongue in Madeira, 15 DM ($8.60). Desserts start at 4.75 DM ($2.72), rising to 18 DM ($10.32), the latter for crêpes Suzette for two.

3. Freiburg

This, the largest city in the Black Forest region, is often overlooked by tourists because it is off the beaten track. But visitors to Freiburg will be rewarded with one of the most scenic and interesting cities in southwestern Germany. Its strategic location at the southern edge of the Black Forest brought the town under the rule of the Austrian Habsburgs in 1368, and it remained theirs for more than 400 years. This same location is an awe-inspiring sight when you first arrive in Freiburg today. If you enter from the Rhine plain on the west, you are faced with the town silhouetted against huge mountain peaks towering more than 3000 feet. Within an hour you can reach most of these peaks by car, or in less time by funicular.

One of the most interesting facts about Freiburg's situation is its remarkable climate. In early spring, the town is usually bursting into bloom while the mountain peaks are still covered with snow. In the fall, the smell of new wine fills the narrow streets while reports of snowfalls on the nearby peaks are already reaching the ears of the townfolk. The reason for this unusual weather is that Freiburg lies in the path of warm air currents which come up from the Mediterranean through the Burgundy Gap, balanced by the winds from the Black Forest hillsides. The two forces join together to make Freiburg a year-round attraction.

The winter "call of the slopes" makes Freiburg a sports center. No matter what the weather, it is easy to get to this city via the efficient German Federal Railway, whose fastest trains stop at this junction en route to the Swiss Alps. It is also the home of a 400-year-old university, which has claimed among its faculty and alumni great scholars, scientists, and humanists such as Erasmus, Zasius, and Waldseemüller (the first geographer to put America on the map).

THE SIGHTS: A town of historical interest and significance—Marie Antoinette "slept here" on her way to marry Louis XVI—Freiburg offers a number of well-preserved monuments, beginning with . . .

Freiburg Cathedral

Towering over the Münsterplatz (Minster Square), where the busy weekly market is still carried on today, the cathedral forms a grand sight with its unique spire of filigree-like stonework. This steeple sits on an octagonal belfry, whose historic bells include a five-ton wonder dating from 1250. Although construction of the church was begun in 1200 in Romanesque style, the builders had incorporated the styles of every Gothic period, as well as a bit of Renaissance, by the time it was completed in 1629. The overall look, however, is mainly Gothic, with heavy buttresses above the north and south walls, which are decorated with statues of biblical characters.

Entering the cathedral through the south door, you find yourself in the transept facing an early 16th-century sculpture of the Adoration of the Christ Child by the Magi. Turning left into the nave, you'll see at the far end of the aisle, at the entrance to the tower, a 13th-century statue of the Virgin flanked by two adoring angels, a fine example of French Gothic art. Resting against one of the Renaissance pillars along the aisle is a carved 16th-century pulpit, with stairs winding around the curve of the column. The figures below the stairs are likenesses of the townspeople of the period, including the sculptor himself.

Of particular interest throughout the cathedral are the stained-glass windows, many of which are hundreds of years old. The oldest are the small round windows in the south transept, which date from the 13th century. Some of these, however, have been removed to the Augustinian Museum and replaced by more recent panels.

The vaulted chancel is the real treasure house of art within the cathedral. Most impressive is the painted altarpiece by Hans Baldung Grien, dating from 1516, above the high altar. If you follow the aisle around behind the choir, you can also see the reverse side of the work, depicting the Crucifixion. Each of the 12 chapels around the choir has its own important works of art, including the elaborate rococo font in the Stürzel Chapel and a 16th-century altarpiece by von Staufen in the Locher Chapel.

The cathedral can be visited at any time between 9 a.m. and 6 p.m., but entrance to the choir is limited to weekdays from 10 a.m. to noon and from 2 p.m. to 5 p.m. Closed Mondays. The tower is open from 9:30 a.m. to 5 p.m. (Sundays, from 2 p.m.) Admission is 1 DM (57¢). Winter hours (October through May) for both the choir and tower are usually reduced to 10 a.m. to 4 p.m.

Around the Old Town

Across the Münsterplatz from the cathedral is the **Kaufhaus,** the most colorful building in Freiburg. The Gothic structure, with magnificent oriel windows at each end, was originally an ancient emporium to which a balcony was added in 1550. Above the massive supporting arches, the facade is decorated with the statues of four emperors of the Hapsburg dynasty—all but one of whom visited Freiburg during their reigns. The red-painted building is still used today as the town's official reception hall.

The **City Hall,** on the attractively planted Rathausplatz just west of the Münsterplatz, became a happy marriage of two 16th-century merchants' houses when an arcade was built between them in 1900. The Renaissance houses are in excellent condition, and among the decorations on the oriel windows and facades, the one which is most commented upon is the relief of "The Maiden and the Unicorn."

The **Augustiner Museum** is housed in the former church and monastery of the Order of St. Augustine and contains the town's finest collection of art, including religious art spanning more than 1000 years. Among the treasures are some of the original stained-glass windows from the cathedral and the most important part of its medieval gold and silver treasure, brought here for safe-keeping. The best works—in the collection of medieval art—include the painting by Grünewald of the *Snow Miracle,* as well as works of Hans Baldung Grien (the best pupil of Albrecht Dürer). Besides, there is a rich collection of fine "oberrheinische" late-Gothic wooden sculpture. Well presented is the folk art from the Black Forest in the upper story. The museum is open daily, except Monday, from 10 a.m. to 5 p.m. (Sunday, until 1 p.m.). Admission: 1.50 DM (86¢) for adults, .75 DM (43¢) for children. On Wednesdays and Sundays entrance is free; guided tours on Thursdays at 3 p.m.

INNS AND WEINSTUBEN: Weinstuben zum Falken, 30 Rathausgasse (tel. 3-69-84), near the cathedral, is a sedate old wine tavern which avoids gimmicky trappings. Its own character is all it needs. Innkeeper Herr Haas-Ihringer not only provides the best of the local cuisine, but has enough beds to accommodate 30 guests. He charges 30 DM ($17.21) to 34 DM ($19.50) for a bathless single, 48 DM ($27.53) for a single with bath. Bathless doubles cost 42 DM ($24.09) to 56 DM ($32.12), increasing to 60 DM ($34.42) and 84 DM ($48.18) with bath. These prices include a good breakfast. His three floors of inn-like rooms are pleasant, nicely furnished, and immaculately kept. Some have an oblique view of the cathedral tower.

The restaurant is quickly recognized by its row of six-foot-high potted bay trees. The tavern is colorful, with paneled oak walls, cut-out Bavarian stools, and an unusual white porcelain stove standing in the center. Set lunches range in price from 14 DM ($8.03) to 24 DM ($13.77). From the à la carte menu, you may want to consider veal liver à la Meyer, 24 DM ($13.77), or other main dishes priced from 12 DM ($6.88) to 31 DM ($17.78). Desserts average around 7.50 DM ($4.30). The inn is on a traffic-free pedestrian mall.

Weinstube zur Traube, 17 Schusterstrasse (tel. 3-21-90), is another old wine tavern near the cathedral. Its reputation for good food challenges that of the Zum Falken. Most attractive, it has boxes of abundantly growing red geraniums, wrought-iron torchiers, and a handsome decor. It's expensive—but worth it. Many main dishes are prepared for two persons, at prices ranging from 56 DM ($32.12). Peppersteak, served with french fries and house salad, is 25 DM ($14.34); veal liver in the Berlin style, 25 DM also; and tournedos, 28 DM ($16.06). Closed Mondays.

Rappen, 13 Münsterplatz (tel. 3-13-53), may be newly built, but the Schanz family has done it in the Black Forest manner, with a wrought-iron hanging sign, little dormer windows in its steep roof, and window boxes and shutters. Hopefully, you'll get a room overlooking the Gothic cathedral. There are three dining rooms on the street, all with beamed ceilings, leaded-glass windows, coach lanterns, and a collection of decorative plates and prints. The women who make your beds and wait on you at mealtimes wear Black Forest costumes. Doubles with shower are 64 DM ($36.71); with complete bath, 74 DM ($42.45). Breakfast is additional. Whether you dine on the sidewalk terrace or inside, the cuisine is commendable for local dishes.

Oberkirchs Weinstuben, 22 Münsterplatz (tel. 3-10-11), is where you'll be saturated with old Freiburg—and love it. Innkeeper Herr Johner-Oberkirch provides excellent regional cooking and comfortable rooms for overnight guests. In the cellar are dozens of six-foot-high wooden kegs of wines. The setting is pure picture postcard—on a little square, with step-gabled roofs. An old wrought-iron sign hangs over the entrance, and red and white tables are set out front for wine sampling or meals.

The main weinstube is old, with dark paneled walls holding framed engravings and prints, plus a monumental ceiling-high ceramic stove made with ornate decorative tiles. Crude country chairs are set around the tables. Main dishes range between 14 DM ($8.03) and 24 DM ($13.77) on the à la carte menu, the latter for young pheasant. However, set lunches in the 15-DM ($8.60) to 25-DM ($14.34) range are the best buys, and include the soup of the day. In the rear is a modern complex, fronting an open patio with a fish pond. Bathless singles are 35 DM ($20.08) to 45 DM ($25.81), rising to 65 DM ($37.28) and 80 DM ($45.89) with shower. Doubles cost 65 DM ($37.28) if bathless. A few doubles contain private baths, costing between 100 DM ($57.36) and 130 DM ($75.57), depending on the size and the view. Breakfast is included.

READER'S HOTEL SELECTION: "A good place to stay is the **Hotel Atlanta,** within easy walking distance of the town center. A double room costs 63 DM ($36.14), including breakfast" (Mrs. William Blakely, Los Angeles, Calif.).

READER'S RESTAURANT SELECTIONS: "There are two very fine places to eat at Freiburg im Breisgau. One is the **Hotel Engel Horben,** 7801 Harben-Langackern. It is up in the mountains above the city. A local family took us there, where we enjoyed the wild game. It is not fancy to look at, but the service is outstanding. A wild boar dinner costs 18 DM ($10.32); reindeer dinner, 19.50 DM ($11.19); and veal, 15.50 DM ($8.89). It is worth driving up the mountain. . . . The other restaurant is in Glottertal, which is near Freiburg. It is at the **Hotel Hirschen** (tel. 07684/215), which has a charming atmosphere, excellent service, and also serves wild game. Waitresses dress in Bavarian costumes at this first-class place. Dinners are in the 15-DM ($8.60) to 20-DM ($11.47) range. Some meals will go higher, but the whole experience will be elegant" (Mrs. William Blakely, Los Angeles, Calif.).

4. Wildbad

This tiny town in the valley of the Enz River is one of the best known spas in the Black Forest. Although not as elegant as nearby Baden-Baden, Wildbad lacks none of its important facilities and attracts visitors from all over Germany —and Europe—to its own promenades and thermal springs. The river which flows through the town divides the smart, colonnaded shopping streets and the spa center.

The thermal springs in the spa gardens are popular for both drinking and bathing. Among the many unusual baths is the **Graf-Eberhard Bath,** dating from the 19th century and decorated in an exotic Moorish style, with sunken baths and colorful tiles. In contrast, the newer **Kurhaus** is terraced with glass walls opening onto lush greenery and thermal pools where you can bathe year round.

One of the biggest attractions of Wildbad is its scenery. The paths and roads in the surrounding woodlands are always alive with strollers; the streams teeming with fish and fishermen. A cable railway runs from the town to the top of the **Sommerberg,** a 1000-foot peak overlooking the town and popular with skiers and sightseers alike.

MIDDLE-BRACKET ACCOMMODATIONS: Kurhotel Post, 2 Kurplatz (tel. 676), is a beguiling inn, right in the heart of everything. In fact, its open dining terrace, with abundant flower boxes and plants, is suspended bridge-like across a river wending its way through the spa.

Once the Post was a humble guest house, but as the years passed by, it was enlarged. In 1827, it became known as a gastronomic center, and in 1921, it came under the wings of the Fritzsches, who provided modern plumbing for most of the bedrooms (more than a third have a bath with either shower or tub).

Bathless singles cost around 30 DM ($17.21) to 42 DM ($24.09), although the most expensive doubles with private bath add up to 87 DM ($49.90) to 100 DM ($57.36). Even if you can't dine on the terrace, there is a garden room with an informal atmosphere of Windsor chairs and mile-long vines. In addition, there is an attractive tavern-like Weinstube grill.

A BUDGET GUEST HOUSE: Gästehaus Rothfuss, 47 Olgastrasse (tel. 33-68), is a chalet-like, family-run hotel, built on the side of the hill—a virtual sun magnet. It's a steep walk from the center of town, although benches for resting are placed all along the way. Wide balconies surround the house, allowing private areas for sunbathing and breakfasts. The garden has abundant roses and geraniums, tended by Frau Richter. She and her husband, Heinz, keep a family staff busy seeing that everything is highly polished. Even the grandmother gets into the act! The little sitting room is personalized, cluttered, and intimate. The dining room seems to be all tables and glass windows, providing one with a woodland view. Prices are quite low. Bathless singles are 21 DM ($12.05) to 26 DM ($14.91), and a few have toilets. Bathless doubles are 43 DM ($24.66). Doubles with shower and toilet peak at 56 DM ($32.12). Breakfast is included.

5. Freudenstadt

Although this sunny resort has no castle overshadowing it as many German villages do, it certainly has an enormous castle square. This plot of land, now the largest marketplace in Germany, was laid out in the 16th century for a castle that was never built. But history's loss is today's gain, because the market square which greets the visitor to Freudenstadt is a maze of lawns and concrete, broken by patches of flowers and kiosks. The buildings surrounding the square are mainly modern, since the air raids of World War II almost completely destroyed the city. A few of the old Renaissance structures on the square have been reconstructed, up to their neat little archways and gabled roofs.

Originally founded by Protestants, the town takes pride in its **Stadtkirche,** dating from the 17th century. The unusual L-shaped architecture of the church brings the two main aisles together at right angles. Over the entrances stand identical towers, topped with rounded domes and narrow spires. The church's most important treasure is the reading desk dating from the 12th century. The desk itself is supported by carved and painted likenesses of the writers of the four Gospels.

Freudenstadt's popularity springs not from the town itself, but from its ideal location in the midst of the best hiking and camping country in the Black Forest. Trails wind for hundreds of miles in the nearby hills, and in winter the snow-covered paths become excellent ski trails.

THE TOP HOTEL: Golf Hotel Waldlust, 92 Lauterbadstrasse (tel. 20-51), is the most luxurious hotel in the area—an old-style building on the side of a hill, at the edge of town. Quite conveniently, it's next to the Kurhaus itself. This chalet provides tasteful, interesting, and comfortable accommodations. Its interior draws upon the past; where there are no antiques, you'll find serviceable and attractive reproductions. Rooms exist for every event and mood, ranging from an intimate piano bar to a rustic Zwitscherstube for wine and snacks. You can have your coffee under a red-and-white canopy overlooking a woodsy view, or lounge in the drawing room, with its mahogany furnishings and gilt paintings. The main dining room is warmly decorated in pinks and browns, with a classical 19th-century atmosphere. All rooms contain private baths. Singles range from 65 DM ($37.28); doubles, from 125 DM ($71.70). For meals, you pay an extra 35 DM ($20.08) per person. Otherwise, a set luncheon goes for 20.50 DM ($11.76), a table d'hôte dinner for 43 DM ($24.66).

INNS—DINING AND LODGING: Post Hotel, 5 Stuttgarterstrasse (tel. 24-21), is a recommendable country-style, vine-covered inn. It's just off the marketplace, with a wrought-iron sign prominently displayed over its doorway. Inside, the Post has been given the 1950s-modern treatment. Excellent meals are provided in the spacious dining room and at cafe tables on the terrace. The Luz family has taken over this historic inn, providing good value for your marks. All rooms now have private baths, with singles ranging from 48 DM ($27.53) and doubles from 80 DM ($45.89) to 93 DM ($53.34). Set lunches cost from 14 DM ($8.03) to 33 DM ($18.93).

Ratskeller, 8 Marktplatz (tel. 26-93), is a small inn directly on the marketplace. It's charmingly old-world in style: the lower rooms are set back with three Romanesque colonnades, and the other levels have windows with shutters and windowboxes of red geraniums. The Ratskeller is managed by M. E. Nickol, who disarmingly says, "We are a little house, but a fine house." The main dining room is traditional, with its dark paneled walls and ceiling. Tables are arranged around a tiled stove. Down below is the antique wine cellar, all bricked—even its steep coved ceiling. The Ratskeller has a distinguished cuisine, with many international specialties. Try, for example, the sole meunière at 24 DM ($13.77); medallion of veal, 21 DM ($12.05); or tournedos sauté Tour d'Argent, 24 DM ($13.77). Desserts start as low as 3 DM ($1.72), going up to 6 DM ($3.44). A winding, open staircase leads to the well-kept, homey bedrooms. A bathless single is 30 DM ($17.21); with bath, 33 DM ($18.93). Bathless doubles are 50 DM ($28.68); with bath, 54 DM ($30.97), including breakfast.

6. Titisee

After a brisk session of ice skating on the lake or horseback riding through the hills, you can return to your homey inn in this tiny resort. The hospitality of Titisee knows no hour nor season. This year-round resort on the banks of Lake Titisee, just 20 miles southeast of Freiburg, is as popular for winter sleigh rides and skiing as it is for summer swimming, boating, and fishing. The surrounding mountains, including the **Feldberg,** the highest point in the Black Forest (5000 feet), are ideal for hiking and mountain climbing.

The town of Titisee is a well-staffed spa, with important therapeutic thermal baths, and various treatments for cardiac and vascular disorders, as well as for rheumatism and intestinal diseases. It has all the other facilities of a resort town, too, including concerts in the open-air pavilion, tennis courts, and various social events.

Shoppers gravitate to the waterfront stores where they find good buys in Bavarian enamelware and Hummel figurines.

Later, at night, a Bavarian marching band plays, its members going from one hotel to another.

THE TOP HOTELS: Schwartzwaldhotel am See, 12 Seestrasse (tel. 81-11), reigns supreme in Titisee as the most fashionable hotel. It gets "A" for position, in the heart of the village, right on the lakeside, with an unimpared view. Most of its life centers around its waterside courtyard. Plants and garden furniture make for an easy life on the wide sun terrace. The dining room is provincial in style, the sun room a multitude of vines and plants (the latter is an ideal spot for breakfast). Inviting also is a rustic weinstube for drinks before or after your meal. Its decor has a barn theme, with horseshoes, brasses, alpine chairs, and wrought-iron lamps. A large, enclosed swimming pool has an all-glass wall on the lakeside. It's fun to swim here. Accommodations are wide ranging, going from spacious to closet-sized. A bathless single in high season costs 55 DM ($31.55), rising to 70 DM ($40.15) with complete bath. A double without bath is 84 DM ($48.18), increasing to 165 DM ($94.64) with complete bath in high season. If you're not on the full-pension plan, you can order a three-course dinner for anywhere from 20 DM ($11.47) to 44 DM ($25.24).

Seehotel Wiesler, Strandbadstrasse (tel. 83-30), may well be the most attractive place to stay around the lake. It's built in a modernized chalet style, long and low, with three floors of bedrooms, each with its own balcony. Bedrooms are country style, with traditional furnishings. A bathless single costs from 38 DM ($21.80) to 54 DM ($30.97); with shower or bath, 56 DM ($32.12) to 62 DM ($35.56). Doubles with showers or baths go from 58 DM ($33.27) to 66 DM ($37.86). Full-pension terms in a single range from a low of 59 DM ($33.84) to a high of 72 DM ($41.30). In a double, the full-pension charge is from 56 DM ($32.12) to 62 DM ($35.56) per person, these rooms with showers or baths.

Kurhotel Brugger am See, Strandbadstrasse (tel. 82-38), is one of the leading hotels around the waterfront. It's a modified chalet, with balconies and an all-window dining room. Its cafe and konditorei have an open-beamed ceiling and country-style chairs. The interior is contemporary, done in harmonious colors. On the premises are several cure baths and an indoor pool. Bedrooms are fair-sized. A single without bath goes from 38 DM ($21.80) to 40 DM ($22.94). With a complete bath, the tariff ranges from 42 DM ($24.09) to 48 DM ($27.53). In a double with bath, the charge goes from 72 DM ($41.30) to 92 DM ($52.77), depending on the quality of the room. Half pension is an extra 30 DM ($17.21) per person.

READER'S SELECTION AT TRIBERG: "Twice **Parkhotel Wehrle,** Marktplatz (tel. 4081), was our 'big splurge.' Rooms are furnished with antiques. Bathless singles cost from 35 DM ($20.08); bathless doubles, 60 DM ($34.42). With bath, singles are 52 DM ($29.83) to 72 DM ($41.30); doubles, 80 DM ($45.89) to 112 DM ($64.24). Smoked Black Forest trout is a specialty, and it's most delicious. Parking is free, and the hotel is within walking distance of the famous waterfalls as well as a most interesting museum of native crafts and costumes" (Mrs. Willard G. Prater, Bellefontaine, Ohio). [*Authors' Note:* Triberg makes for a charming stopover in the Black Forest. The waterfalls referred to are called Gutach, and they're the highest in Germany, spilling down in seven stages. The town is one of the best places in the Black Forest to make purchases of woodcarving. The provincial museum carries an intriguing collection of cuckoo clocks.]

READER'S SELECTION AT BIRKENDORF: "Birkendorf is near Stühlingen, Germany, and near Schaffhausen, Switzerland. It is a picture-book village, a gold medal winner in the 1973 national competition to find the best-kept villages in the Federal Republic of Germany. It lies in the Hochschwarzwald where there are more open fields and fewer dense forests. We stayed and ate at the **Hotel Pension Sonnenhof,** 3 Hauptstrasse (tel. 360). The annex of the hotel has a swimming pool which we could use. A bathless single costs from 20 DM ($11.47) to 24 DM ($13.77); bathless doubles, 37 DM ($21.22) to 48 DM ($27.53). Doubles with bath go from 52 DM ($29.83) to 60 DM ($34.42)" (Pat Dichnelt, Menomonee Falls, Wisc.).

Coming up, more romantic scenery.

Chapter IX

LAKE CONSTANCE

1. Constance (Konstanz)
2. Meersburg
3. Lindau

EVEN THOUGH THREE nations—Austria, Germany, and Switzerland—share the 162-mile shoreline of this large inland sea, the area around Lake Constance is united in a common cultural and historical heritage. The hillsides sloping down to the water's edge are covered with vineyards and orchards and dotted with colorful hamlets and busy tourist centers. The mild climate and plentiful sunshine make Lake Constance a popular vacation spot for lovers of sun and sand, as well as for sightseers and spa-hoppers. A well-organized network of cruise ships and ferries links every major center around the lake.

Lake Constance is actually divided into three lakes, although the name is frequently applied only to the largest of these, the **Bodensee.** The western end of the Bodensee divides into two distinct branches. The **Überlingersee,** a long fjord. On the other hand, the **Untersee** is more irregular, jutting in and out of the marshlands and low-lying woodlands. It is connected to the larger lake by only a narrow channel of water—actually, the young Rhine, whose current flows right through the Bodensee. Tip: The blue felchen, a pike-like fish found only in Lake Constance, furnishes the district with a tasty and renowned specialty.

Our exploration of Lake Constance begins with the city on the Rhine which bears the same name.

1. Constance (Konstanz)

Crowded against the shores of Lake Constance by the borders of Switzerland, this medieval town had nowhere to grow but northward across the river. Today, the modern resort city lies on both banks of the infant Rhine as it begins its long journey from the Bodensee to the North Sea. This strategic position has made Constance the most important city on the lake since a Roman fortification was established here under Claudius in 41 A.D.

The city's claim to historical fame is due to the fact that it was the chosen site of the great Christian Reform Council, held here from 1414 to 1418, when the delegates from the entire Christian world temporarily increased the population by 600%! During this period, the Catholic church resolved its quarrel over the claims of three rivals for the papacy by electing a fourth individual, Martin V, as pope.

THE SIGHTS: The best way to see Constance is from the water. Several pleasure ships offer tours across the lake to Meersburg, or just along the shoreline of the city itself. (Ferries to Meersburg leave every ten minutes, day or night, the price depending on the size of your car. For the average compact car and two passengers, expect to pay 10 DM or $5.74). The water's edge is the most fascinating part of Constance, as the little inlets weave in and out of the land, around ancient buildings and the city gardens where concerts are held outdoors during the summer.

Below the gardens is the city's most significant structure, the **Council Building,** originally constructed as a storehouse in 1388, but used for many important meetings during its early years. None was so important, however, as the meeting here in November 1417 of the Roman Conclave which elected Cardinal Otto of Colonna as Pope Martin V. The hall was restored in 1911 and decorated with murals depicting the history of the town. On the harbor in front of the building is a huge obelisk erected in memory of Count Ferdinand Zeppelin, a citizen of Constance who invented the first dirigible airship in the late 19th century.

From the water you can also see the towers of the massive Romanesque **basilica** rising behind the city garden. Begun in 1052 on the foundation of an even older cathedral, the church took centuries to complete—the neo-Gothic spire was added only in 1856. During the Council of Constance, the members of the synod met here. Most interesting is the view from the top of the tower, looking out onto the lake and the sections of the city.

An Excursion to Mainau Island

Just four miles north of Constance, in the arm of the Bodensee known as the Überlingersee, is the unusual island of Mainau, a tropical paradise. Here palms and orange trees grow in profusion and fragrant flowers bloom all year, practically in the shadow of the snow-covered Alps. In the center of this botanical oasis is an ancient castle, once a residence of the Knights of the Teutonic Order. Today both the castle and the island are owned by a Swedish count, but can be visited by the public. You can get to the island either by tour boat from Constance, or by walking across the small footbridge connecting Mainau to the mainland just north of the city.

STAYING AT A CONVERTED MONASTERY: Steigenberger Hotel Insel, 1 auf der Insel (tel. 2-50-11), is a successful example of the transformation of a lakeside 13th-century Dominican monastery into a first-class, comfortable hotel. Its situation is prime for the area—on an island, with its own lakeside gardens and dock (the hotel has a private yacht for use of guests). The step-gabled building is gray, with an inner Romanesque cloister. The informal dining room has Windsor chairs, wood-paneled walls, and planters of flowers, not to mention ecclesiastical arches and pillars. The bedrooms are well coordinated, with homey patterned fabrics. The furnishings are fine, and most doubles have a living room look with sofas, armchairs, and coffee tables. All rooms have their own bath. The cost ranges from 69 DM ($39.58) to 99 DM ($56.79) in a single and from 98 DM ($56.21) to 148 DM ($84.89) in a double.

At twilight, guests gather at the intimate Zeppelin Bar. Very clublike, its walls are cluttered with framed letters and documents. (The man who pioneered the airship also turned this abbey into a hotel.) A gemütlich spirit prevails in the Weinstube, with its knotty pine bar, pine chairs and tables, parquet floors, ceramic collection, and decorative green and white eight-foot-high tiled stove in the corner. Here guests order wine, beer, and light snacks.

WHERE TO DINE: St. **Stefanskeller,** 41 Stefansplatz (tel. 2-35-66), seems like a setting for an operetta—an old Germanic inn, with lots of local flavor. Beside the Romanesque church of St. Stephen's down a narrow street, it sits next to an antique shop. You descend a flight of steps, screened by stained glass. On carved alpine chairs, you dine at bare wood tables by candlelight. The wainscoting of the dining room depicts local folklore, including a scene of St. George slaying the dragon. Waitresses in regional dress place wicker baskets of small, crisp warm rolls on the tables. An ornate serving bar has open shelves of wine, colored glassware, and copper urns of seasonal flowers. Almost anything you select for your meal will be interesting and well cooked. The cuisine is French, so you might begin with a pâté maison at 11 DM ($6.31), then follow with a main course such as gratin fruits de mer at 18.50 DM ($10.61) or peppersteak at 26 DM ($14.91). More than 145 different wines are offered.

2. Meersburg

Like the towns of the lake district of Italy, this village on the northern shores of Lake Constance cascades in terraces down the hillside until it touches the water. Although you can drive into town as far as the New Castle, it's best to leave your car at the northern edge and explore on foot. In the center, the streets become nothing but narrow promenades and steps wandering up and down the hillside.

THE SIGHTS: Entering the town through the ancient **Obertor** (upper gate), you're in the Marketplace and facing the 16th-century Rathaus (Town Hall), containing a typical German Ratskeller. Leading off from this is the **Steigstrasse,** the most interesting street passing between rows of half-timbered houses whose arcades serve as covered walkways above the street. Nearby is the **Old Castle,** with its ancient Dagobert's Tower dating from 628, the oldest German castle still standing. The interior contains exhibits of medieval weapons and armor, as well as a group of furnished rooms where the German poetess Annette von Droste-Hülshoff lived and died. Adjoining is the **Castle Mill** (1620), with a 28-foot wooden water wheel, the oldest of its kind in Germany. Guided tours are conducted daily through the castle from 9 a.m. to 6 p.m.

Even more interesting is the **New Castle,** a masterpiece by the leading German baroque architect, Balthasar Neumann. Erected in 1750, the castle was the residence of the prince-bishops of Constance. The attractive chapel in the left wing is especially worthy. Note also the huge double staircase, with rococo grillwork alternated with graceful baroque statuary. Perched on the crest of the steep hill which plunges to the lake below, the castle affords an excellent view.

On the promenade below stands the **Great House,** dating from 1505 and now housing ticket offices for the railway and for steamer lines on Lake Constance. Regular ferry service to Constance leaves from the dock on the outskirts of town.

INNS WITH ATMOSPHERE: Brandners 3 **Stuben,** 1–3 Winzergasse (tel. 60-19), is a Hansel and Gretel timbered weinhaus-restaurant-hotel. Potted trees stand at the doorway, along with window boxes of red geraniums. It's in the heart of the village—known not only for its old-world dining rooms, but for its modernized bedrooms. Innkeeper Peter Nicolaus knows his job well. He offers his guests immaculate rooms that are colorful and attractive, well appointed and not overpriced. All rooms contain showers or complete baths. Doubles range in price from a low of 70 DM ($40.15) to a high of 80 DM ($45.89), with singles going for from 45 DM ($25.81). If you come here to eat, the average set meal is 15 DM ($8.60). From the à la carte menu, try trout amandine at 16 DM ($9.18) or trout Konstanz at 16 DM also. Rumpsteak Mexican is 19 DM ($10.90) and pork steak with cherries, 16 DM ($9.18).

Weinstube Löwen, 2 Marktplatz (tel. 60-13), is an old inn, right on the market square, colorful for such a village. Its facade is a raspberry pink with green shutters, window boxes filled with red geraniums, and vines reaching the upper windows under the steep roof. For more than 50 years it's been run by the Stadelhofer-Langeder family, who have updated its interior—especially the bedrooms, which are almost all modernized by now. All rooms have baths of some sort. Singles with showers rent for 27.50 DM ($15.77) to 35 DM ($20.08). Doubles with shower cost from 49 DM ($28.11), peaking at 65 DM ($37.28) with bath. The family has made everything homelike. For example, in the entry, with its provincial furnishings, are subtropical plants, a cage of canaries, a spinning wheel, and a mandolin on the wall. The Weinstube is wood paneled with a white ceramic stove in the corner. On the shelves are hunting and farming artifacts.

Gasthof zum Bären, 11 Marktplatz (tel. 60-44), is a picture-book inn, right in the heart of the village—a delightful place to stay. A five-story corner building with step gables, it has window boxes overflowing with red geraniums, an ornately decorated corner tower with steeple, plus a tangle of purple wisteria crawling over most of the facade. Innkeepers are the Gilowsky-Karrer family, who speak a little English and open their guest house from March to November. They treasure Zum Bären, which was built in the year 1510 and has been owned by their family since 1851. It is furnished with tavern pieces and alpine stools, all resting under beamed ceilings. The two dining rooms are colorfully primitive, and the bedrooms are most attractive. The cost for a single room is 26 DM ($14.91), rising to 48 DM ($27.53) in a bathless unit, although these contain only hot and cold running water. In a single with shower and toilet, the charge is 35 DM ($20.08), going up to 66 DM ($37.86) in a double, all these quotations including a continental breakfast.

WHERE TO DINE: Weinstube zum Becher, Hollgasse (tel. 90-09), is a wine restaurant, where guests congregate as in a "gentlemen's club." You'll find a wealth of old oak, copper, and antiques. In the background is an unusually fine collection of wines of the region. Michael Benz directs the establishment and offers such dishes as veal in a piquante sauce, 12 DM ($6.88); wienerschnitzel, 16 DM ($9.18); and beef Stroganoff, 18 DM ($10.32). In season the chef specializes in game at prices that go from 19 DM ($10.90) to 27 DM ($15.49). Soups cost from 4 DM ($2.29), and desserts are in the 5.50-DM ($3.15) to 8-DM ($4.59) range.

3. Lindau

Its unique setting on an island at the eastern end of the Bodensee made Lindau such a popular tourist attraction that it outgrew its boundaries and spread to the shores of the mainland. The garden city, stretching for five miles along the shoreline, caters to your every whim—from bathing to baccarat. The island also offers a look into the past of the former Free Imperial City.

Connected to the mainland by a road bridge and a causeway for walkers and trains, Lindau is easy to reach. It lies just at the edge of the Austrian frontier and is an important transportation link between the western part of Lake Constance and the towns of Austria and Switzerland, which lie directly across the water.

THE SIGHTS: Whether you arrive at Lindau by boat or train, a tour of the Ferieninsel (Holiday Island) begins with the **old harbor,** seen from the lakeside promenade. The massive Mangturm, the old lighthouse, stands on the promenade as a reminder of the heavy fortifications that once surrounded the city. It also marks the point where Lindau was once divided into two islands (now filled in). The entrance to the harbor is marked by two monumental silhouettes —the 108-foot **New Lighthouse** (19th century), and the **Bavarian Lion,** standing guard as yachts and commercial ships pass by below. From the promenade, you can gaze out past these monuments over the water to the Alps on the opposite side of the lake.

In the center of the town, the **Hauptstrasse** is the main street of the Alstadt. The most easily recognized building is the **Old Rathaus,** erected in 1422 on the site of a vineyard. The stepped gables are typical of the period, but the building's facade also combines many later styles of architecture. The interior, once used by the Imperial Diet as a Council Hall, is now the town library.

Just north of the Hauptstrasse, with its half-timbered houses, is the town's most familiar landmark, the round **Diebsturm** (Thieves' Tower), with its turreted roof. Next to it is the oldest building in Lindau, **St. Peter's Church** (11th century), which houses a war memorial chapel. In the church is a group of frescoes painted by Hans Holbein the Elder.

Returning to the Hauptstrasse, which cuts through the exact center of the island, follow the street eastward to the **Haus zum Cavazzen,** considered the handsomest patrician's house on Lake Constance. Rebuilt in 1730 in the style of a baroque country mansion, it houses the municipal art collections. Included are exhibits of sculpture and painting from the Gothic, Renaissance, and baroque periods of the town's history. Some of the rooms are furnished with period pieces showing how wealthy citizens lived in the 15th and 16th centuries. The 18th-century murals on the facade have been restored.

Passing across the Marketplace and by the Collegiate Church and St. Stephen's Church—both baroque—you come to the strange pile of rocks known as **Heathen's Wall,** dating from Roman times. Beyond this is the solitude of the **Stadtgarten** (Town Gardens), which, though peaceful during the day, livens up at night when the wheels of the town's casino begin to whirl and spin.

LAKESIDE HOTELS (MEDIUM PRICED): A trio of hotels, under the same ownership and management, have taken over the best lakeside estate. They are right on the promenade facing the small harbor, with its monuments, a stone sphinx, and lighthouse. The threesome are appropriate for three budget levels. The most expensive is the Bayerischer Hof, followed by the middle-income Reutemann, and then the economical Seegarten. A framed family tree in the Bayerischer Hof traces the lineage of the owners (the Spaeth family) back to the year 1660. The Reutemann has a special dining and dancing restaurant shared by all three hotels (closed in winter)—**Zum Lieben Augustin,** a romantic tavern, where spirits fly high under a beamed ceiling. Tyrolean chairs and tables are set on two levels, and a small orchestra plays in the background.

Bayerischer Hof, Seepromenade (tel. 50-55), is first class in atmosphere and service. It rises five stories high, one side facing the railway station plaza, the other the lake. Three-quarters of its rooms have a good view. The lesser chambers overlook a narrow thoroughfare. The dining room has dignity, with wide screen windows to allow a view for everyone. The lounges are tastefully decorated in traditional fashion, with antiques and reproductions, and Oriental rugs on parquet floors. In a bathless single, the rates are 42 DM ($24.09) to 63 DM ($36.14); with private bath, 63 DM ($36.14) to 102 DM ($58.51). Doubles with private bath are 181 DM ($103.82) to 200 DM ($114.72). Breakfast is included.

Reutemann, Seepromenade (tel. 50-55), is a villa-style structure, next door to the Bayerischer Hof, containing its own waterfront garden, with red and yellow outdoor furniture amid the lemon trees and wisteria vines. Open all year, the Reutemann is unself-consciously and traditionally furnished in fine style. Most rooms are large, some have tiled baths, heated towel racks, huge tubs, and endless hot water. It, too, has its own glassed-in dining room, where adequate meals are served in a dignified manner by an East Indian staff. Bathless singles are 39 DM ($22.37) to 51 DM ($29.25); with full bath, 50 DM ($28.68) to 78 DM ($44.74). All doubles have private baths and cost from 104 DM ($59.65) to 154 DM ($88.33). Rates include breakfast, and, as in all three hotels, you can have it American style with fresh orange juice, ham, and eggs.

Seegarten, Seepromenade (tel. 50-55), has the most attractive facade of the trio. It's built like a Bavarian villa, with little flower-filled balconies and trailing vines. It, too, has an informal lakefront garden with flowerbeds and furniture for sunbathing. The public rooms are modest and traditional, but attractive. The bedrooms are really quite spacious and handsome, especially the lake-view ones (at higher prices, naturally). Bathless singles cost from 39 DM ($22.37) to 48 DM ($27.53); with bath, 57 DM ($32.70) to 64 DM ($36.71). All doubles have private baths, costing from 92 DM ($52.77) to 115 DM ($65.96). Across the street, a garage services all three hotels.

THE BUDGET CHOICES: Lindauer Hof, an der Seepromenade (tel. 40-64), is the best budget hotel in Lindau—certainly the least expensive directly on Lake Constance. It's right in the center of activity, close to the boat docks and harbor, yet only a five-minute walk from the railway station plaza. An eye-catching, shuttered and gabled building, it faces a square, with a second-floor waterview terrace. Here you can dine under a flourishing wisteria vine. The lounge has an attractive collection of Empire and Biedermeier furniture. The bedrooms are nicely decorated, each in a unique fashion. Try for one with a view of the plaza and lake. The rate for a bathless single ranges from 37 DM ($21.22) to 40 DM ($22.94), going up to a peak 52 DM ($29.83) with shower and toilet, overlooking the lake. Bathless doubles go from 70 DM ($40.15) to 75 DM ($43.02), reaching a maximum 100 DM ($57.36) for those doubles with private baths, overlooking the lake. It's open Easter to mid-October.

Insel, 42 Hauptstrasse (tel. 50-17), only a quarter of a mile from the lake, is a completely renovated accommodation, with a bit of a reception room, plus an elevator. The upstairs rooms are comfortable and furnished with modern pieces. The breakfast room opens onto the traffic-free Hauptstrasse, described under sights. Bathless singles rent for 25 DM ($14.34), increasing to 43.50 DM ($24.95) with shower and toilet. Bathless doubles cost 50 DM ($28.68) to 56

DM ($32.12), rising to 69 DM ($39.58) to 76 DM ($43.59) with private bath. Hans Grattinger and his wife provide a warm welcome.

On the same street is the **Gasthaus Zum Sünfzen,** 1 Hauptstrasse (tel. 58-65), owned by the same family as the Insel. In an old arched house/restaurant—all wooded with windows in the antique glass style—it offers pleasant groups of tables covered with red-and-white napkins. The food is great, the cost low. Soups run from 3 DM ($1.72) to 5 DM ($2.87); desserts, 3 DM ($1.72) to 7.50 DM ($4.30). Main dishes include such choices as rumpsteak at 17.20 DM ($9.87). Set menus range from 10.50 DM ($6.02) to 16.50 DM ($9.30).

WHERE TO DINE: Spielbank Restaurant, 2 Oskar-Groll-Anlage (tel. 52-00), is the most prestigious restaurant in Lindau—perfect for a celebration meal. It is, in reality, a pavilion right on the lake, with scenic views. Surprisingly, you won't have to break the bank at the casino to dine here. For example, set lunches range from 22 DM ($12.62). In the evening, main dishes on the à la carte menu average 25 DM ($14.34).

In the following chapter, we head inland to the most romantic strasse in Germany.

Chapter X

THE ROMANTIC ROAD

1. **Bad Mergentheim**
2. **Rothenburg**
3. **Dinkelsbühl**
4. **Nördlingen**
5. **Augsburg**
6. **Füssen**
7. **The Royal Castles**

NO AREA OF GERMANY is more aptly named than this. Even if the road which runs through central Bavaria isn't romantic itself, the medieval villages and 2000-year-old towns through which it passes certainly are. The Romantic Road (Romantische Strasse) stretches for 180 miles between the cities of Würzburg, on the north, and Füssen, in the foothills of the Bavarian Alps.

You may, if you wish, take the regular bus tour, accompanied by an English-speaking guide, which traverses the entire route each day. But the best way to see this stretch of Germany is by car, stopping whenever the mood suggests and then driving on through miles of vineyards and over streams until you arrive at the Alpine passes in the south.

If you begin your tour of the scenic route at the north, you'll find yourself, after leaving the Franconian city of Würzburg, in Bad Mergentheim.

1. Bad Mergentheim

From the name you can guess that this little town along the northern stretches of the Romantic Road is a spa resort community, but that is only one of the faces of Bad Mergentheim. In fact, it was only as recently as 1826 that the healing springs of the town were accidentally rediscovered (archeological evidence indicates that they had been known in the Bronze and Iron Ages). Perhaps the spa side of the town is the one that will interest you most, since, after a few weeks of German beer and sausages, you may wish to shed a few pounds. Bad Mergentheim, among its various treatments, offers a cure for obesity.

But a more pleasant cure for the overweight tourist would be a walking tour through the crooked, narrow streets to the old **Marketplace** with the **Town Hall,** the town's major sightseeing attraction, and the **Mergentheim Palace,** on the opposite bank of the Tauber from the spa facilities. The palace was the seat of the Knights of the Teutonic Order from 1527 until their dispossession by Napoleon in 1809. During its residence in this Renaissance castle, the order was a politically influential one, straying from its original purpose as a religious and military order founded during the Crusades. Especially interesting is the palace church, redesigned in the 18th century by Balthasar Neumann and François Cuvilliés in a rich baroque style with colorful frescoes and elaborate rococo altars. Tours are conducted from March to October on Sunday from 10 a.m. till noon and on Tuesday through Saturday from 2:30 p.m. till 5:30 p.m.; from November to February, on Sunday from 10 a.m. till noon and Tuesday through Saturday from 2:30 p.m. till 4 p.m. Admission is 1.50 DM (86¢). There are possibilities for excursions to Markelsheim for wine tests or to see the *Stuppacher Madonna,* a beautiful medieval painting in Stuppach.

SPA HOTELS: Kurhaus Hotel, 4–6 Dr.-Leopold-Strasse (tel. 56-2-52), is an elegant, contemporary resort hotel of advanced architectural design, set in a green park, close to the promenade. Its dining room alone makes eating an event—you dine under a high wooden ceiling, with all-glass walls overlooking the gardens. Also well conceived is the two-story-high lounge, with a mezzanine and black leather and birch armchairs clustered around glass and chrome coffee tables. In the TV room, guests sit in comfortable armchairs, as in a theater. In addition, there's an intimate drinking bar, plus a garden room where *kur* waters are imbibed. Guests gather on the rooftop sundeck, with its pergola, or beside the swimming pool overlooking the lawns. Special rooms are set aside for massages, therapy, and sauna. Bathless singles are 46 DM ($26.39); with bath, 75 DM ($43.02). Bathless doubles are 60 DM ($34.42) to 80 DM ($45.89); with bath, 108 DM ($61.95) to 165 DM ($94.64). The bedrooms, decorated in a modern fashion, are comfortable. The diet meals may surprise you—if anything, they seem pretty fattening.

Hotel Garni Villa im Kurpark (tel. 70-85) is an annex to the more expensive Kurhaus, sharing the same parklike grounds and the main spa facilities. It's a gracious villa, with many rooms opening onto little flower-edged balconies. The accommodations are homelike, many treated like master bedrooms, with a pleasing combination of antiques and severe modern. Bathless singles go from 35 DM ($20.08) to 40 DM ($22.94); with bath, from 58 DM ($33.27) to 70 DM ($40.15). Bathless doubles are 64 DM ($36.71); with bath, 110 DM ($63.10).

A BUDGET CHOICE: Hotel am Markt, 40 am Oberen Markt (tel. 61-01), is an immaculate little modern hotel. Far removed from the life of a typical spa hotel, it sits right off the marketplace. There are only 36 bedrooms, most of which have private baths with shower. The rather pleasant Scandinavian furnishings are restful to the eye and body. A bathless single costs 34 DM ($19.50); bathless doubles, 55 DM ($31.55); doubles with bath, 67 DM ($38.43).

2. Rothenburg

Admittedly, if you arrive at Rothenburg's bahnhof (railway station) at the northeast corner of town, you may find it hard to believe that this is actually the finest medieval city in Europe. Modern life and industry have made an impact here too, and the first sights which greet your eyes as you leave the station are factories and office buildings. But don't be discouraged—inside those undamaged 13th-century city walls is a completely preserved medieval town, untouched by the centuries which have passed by outside.

THE SIGHTS: The only way to see Rothenburg properly is to wander through the town on foot, beginning at the typical hub of any old German village, the **Rathaus**. Set in the center of the Old Town, Rothenburg's Rathaus consists of an older Gothic section dating from 1240 and a newer Renaissance structure facing the marketplace. From the 165-foot tower of the Gothic hall, you can get a marvelous view of the town below. The belfry itself has quite a history. When fire destroyed the Gothic hall's twin (where the Renaissance hall now stands) in 1501, a guardian and his wife escaped the blaze by hanging from a window at the top of the tower. Prior to that, the tower was used as a lookout for enemy forces, but from that time on, it became a watchtower for fire. Even today, the guards have to ring the bell every quarter hour to show that they are wide awake and on the job.

The new Rathaus, built in 1572 to replace the portion destroyed in the fire, is decorated with intricate friezes, an oriel extending the full height of the building, and a large stone portico opening onto the square. The octagonal tower at the center of the side facing the square contains the grand staircase, leading to the upper hall. On the main floor is the large Court Room, the scene of the annual Whitsuntide Festival, der Meistertrunk, commemorating the preservation of the city by the heroic Burgermeister Nusch, who accepted the challenge from the conquering Commander Tilly in 1525 to drink a goblet of wine in one draught. This sounds like a simple achievement until you see the goblet on display in the local museum—it holds three and a half quarts!

On the north side of the marketplace, across from the Rathaus, is the town council's **drinking hall** (1406), where only the patrician families were allowed to drink. The most interesting feature of the tavern is the old clock on the facade facing the square. At 11 a.m., noon, 1 p.m., and 2 p.m. daily, the clock chimes and the windows on either side open to expose Commander Tilly on the left standing in amazement while Burgermeister Nusch downs the massive goblet of wine.

Leaving the marketplace, walk north on the street that opens off the square between the Rathaus and the tavern. This will lead you to the Klingengasse, a narrow old street which passes directly under **St. Jakobskirche** (Church of St. James). This church is a completely vertical Gothic edifice with three naves; the east choir, dating from 1373, is the oldest section of the church, a gift of Burgermeister Toppler, the town leader during Rothenburg's most prosperous period. The fine painted-glass windows in the choir date from the same period. To the left is the tabernacle, from 1448, which was recognized as the "free place," where condemned criminals could not be touched. The church's most important work is the Altar of the Holy Blood, created by Tilman Riemensc- hneider in 1478. A relic claimed to be the blood of Christ is kept in a piece of crystal in the Romanesque cross above the altarpiece. The most interesting work on the altar is a carving of the Last Supper, in which all the figures, save one, were carved from one piece of lime-tree. Judas, the betrayer, was carved from a separate chunk of wood.

For a look at one of the most interesting portions of the old ramparts, follow the Klingengasse northward from the church to the **Klingentor,** its top portion adorned with four oriels and a ball lantern. You can wander along the covered ramparts on this portion of the wall, and to continue your tour of the town walk on the wall west and south to the 13th-century Dominican nunnery, now housing the **Reichsstadtmuseum,** with the historical collection of the city of Rothenburg. The cloisters are extremely well preserved, and you can visit the convent hall, kitchen, and apothecary, and view the ancient frescoes and antiques. The museum collection includes period furniture and art from Ro- thenburg's more prosperous periods, plus the famous goblet that saved the town. The museum is open daily from 10 a.m. to 11 a.m. and 2 p.m. to 3 p.m. in summer; from 11 a.m. to 2 p.m. in winter. Guided tours are given at 10 and 11 a.m. and at 2 and 3 p.m.

From the museum, it's just a short walk to the **Herrengasse,** which leads back to the marketplace. This street was once the most exclusive in the Old Town, and today many of its half-timbered houses have been converted into interesting shops. On one side of the street is the 13th-century Gothic **Franciscan Church,** with an unusual rood screen separating the east choir from the naves. The church is most notable for its numerous tombs, decorated with excellent sculptures.

At the opposite end of the Herrengasse from the marketplace is the **Burgtor,** the tower which originally led to the Castle of the Hohenstaufen (destroyed in 1425). The tower once had a drawbridge, and although the moat and castle are both gone now, you can still see the holes where the ropes once raised and lowered the bridge and the huge hole, called the peat, through which hot oil or tar was poured on the enemy.

The gardens where the castle once stood jut out from the rest of the town toward the Tauber River. Just across the river from the Burggarten is the **Toppler Castle,** actually a small tower built in 1908 to commemorate the 500th anniversary of the death of the town's greatest mayor.

Returning to the marketplace, turn down the Schmiedgasse, and you'll arrive at the **Baumeisterhaus,** home of Leonard Weidmann, who built the Renaissance Rathaus. The facade is decorated with 14 carved stone figures representing the seven vices and virtues. The interior now houses a restaurant, about which more later.

READER'S TIP: "On weekends, there are open-air concerts in the courtyard under the famous clock in the marketplace. On one of the side streets you will find a puppet show with marionettes under the direction of Rolf Trexler. There is one performance each night from 8:30 to 10. It is advisable to reserve your seats early in the day. The show is in German, but can be appreciated by tourists who do not speak the language. The director personalizes each show to the audience, often mentioning the names of persons in attendance. Cost: 10 DM ($5.74)" (Karin Janik, Forest Park South, Ill.).

THE TOP HOTEL: Eisenhut ("The Iron Helmet"), 3–5 Herrengasse (tel. 20-41), is the most celebrated inn on the Romantic Road. Attracting an international crowd, it is perhaps the finest small hotel in Germany. Four medieval patrician houses, dating from the 12th century, were joined to make this colorful and distinctive inn. It's a virtual museum of antiquity. Most impressive is the three-story galleried dining hall, with ornate classic wood paneling, balconies, and a collection of ceramic mugs on display. There are additional places to dine, as well, each richly decorated and furnished, although in sunny weather, they're all deserted in favor of the multitiered flagstone terrace on the Tauber. Meals are à la carte, with soups in the 6-DM ($3.44) range. The specialty of the house is veal steak Eisenhut at 28 DM ($16.06). Another highly recommendable dish is filet of pork Nana at 23 DM ($13.19). Desserts begin at 6.50 DM ($3.73).

The main living room has a beamed ceiling, Oriental carpets, ecclesiastical sculpture, and grandfather clock. The reception lounge continues the theme, with a wooden ceiling, wide staircase, statuary, and ancestral chairs. The bedrooms are individualized, no two are alike, and antiques of distinction are used unsparingly. Your bedroom may contain hand-carved and monumental pieces, or be given a Hollywood touch, with a tufted satin headboard. Regardless, you are assured of charm, comfort, and personality. Because of the wide range of rooms, prices tend to be complicated. The highest rates are in effect from April 12 to October 31. At that time, a single with bath goes for from 93 DM ($53.34) to 104 DM ($59.65). Doubles with bath are in the 124-DM ($71.12) to 180-DM ($103.25) bracket. These prices include breakfast. The Iron Helmet is easy to find, just across the street from the Town Hall.

MEDIUM-PRICED HOTELS: Goldener Hirsch, 16–25 Untere Schmiedgasse (tel. 20-51), is a first-class hotel, a remake of an inn that dated from 1600. In the heart of town, it's housed in a rustic building, with a Blue Terrace for dining that offers a panoramic view of the Tauber and the surrounding hills. Or you may prefer to take your dinner in the blue and white Regency salon. So popular has this hostelry become that it's annexed another patrician house across the street. The bedrooms are comfortable and homelike, showing a respect for traditional taste. Prices are based on the time of year and the type of bath you request. Bathless singles are 40 DM ($22.94) to 55 DM ($31.55); with bath, from 56 DM ($32.12) to 98 DM ($56.21). Bathless doubles rent for 75 DM ($43.02) to 105 DM ($60.23), increasing to 115 DM ($95.96) to 190 DM ($108.98) with bath. Breakfast is included.

Burg-Hotel, 1–3 Klostergasse (tel. 22-52), built right on top of the old town wall, is a large timbered house, with a high pitched roof, flower garden, window boxes of geraniums, and a picket fence. The dining terrace provides a panoramic view of the Tauber River and the surrounding fields. The interior was rebuilt by the Hinckeldey family, who have good, reliable taste. Each bedroom is different, with tiled baths.. One room, for example, may have swagged and draped beds; another may be filled with antiques; yet another could be done in sleek contemporary style. In a single without bath, the rate is 31 DM ($17.78), 49 DM ($28.11) with bath. Bathless doubles are 56 DM ($32.12), rising to 97 DM ($55.64) with bath. Breakfast is served in an attractive room, with a view. The little sitting room also has nice touches, such as ecclesiastical sculpture, crystal chandeliers, and antiques combined with good reproductions.

Bären, 9 Hofbronnengasse (tel. 30-31), is one of the leading old inns of town, and it's centrally located. Although modernized, it still has 15-inch oak beams and ornate wainscoting. The bedrooms have a provincial flair, becoming quite elaborate at times, usually with coordinated colors, often with French-style furniture. Space is at a premium here. Single rooms with running water are priced from 30 DM ($17.21) to 40 DM ($22.94), increasing to anywhere from 50 DM ($28.68) to 70 DM ($40.15) with bath or shower. Twin-bedded rooms with running water cost 55 DM ($31.55) to 70 DM ($40.15), going up to 75 DM ($43.02) to 120 DM ($68.83) with full plumbing. Again, depending on the plumbing, the rate for three persons begins at a low of 95 DM ($54.49) and travels upward to 150 DM ($86.04). These tariffs include all taxes, breakfast, and the use of an indoor swimming pool and an exercise room. For the solarium and sauna, however, another charge, a small one, is levied.

Adam, 29 Burggasse (tel. 23-64), is the ultimate in an unspoiled village inn. It's one of the most recommendable in Germany for those wanting to saturate themselves in storybook atmosphere at low cost. In the heart of Old Rothenburg, it contains a wealth of beams and trailing flowers at its windows. Inside, the entrance hallway is oak paneled, setting the proper mood. Antiques are found everywhere, but the atmosphere remains informal. The dining room is important here, and it is paneled in oak, with an encircling shelf holding pewter, copper, and ceramic objects. Guests dine at bare wooden tables and peer through leaded-glass windows. The hotel is owned and run by Hans Karl

Adam, who has been called the "Julia Child" of the Germanic kitchen. Herr Adam not only prepares the food himself, but he prefers to place no condiments on individual tables. "That way," he confides, "no one will spoil my seasoning." For a mouth-watering treat, try his Tauber pastries. Each bedroom has its own personality, containing such elements as antique carved four-posters with draped testers, Biedermeier pieces, and gilt sconces. In low season, doubles with bath rent for 70 DM ($40.15), increasing to 98 DM ($56.21) in high season. Breakfast is included.

Hotel Reich Küchen Master, 8 Kirchplatz (tel. 34-06), is one of the oldest buildings in Rothenburg. It was the seat of a chief steward for Rothenburg's nobilities. The house is on different levels. You wander down the corridors to nicely furnished bedrooms with primitively painted wooden furniture. However, the plumbing is first rate. Prices are low. A single without bath is 26 DM ($14.91), rising to 38 DM ($21.80) with bath. A bathless double rents for 42 DM ($24.09), peaking at 60 DM ($34.42) with bath. In the restaurant the food is good, the choice wide. We'd recommend the Reich Küchen "master plate," including a choice of filet of pork, beef, and veal with fresh vegetables, at a cost of 40 DM ($22.94) for two persons. In season, you may prefer a leg of roebuck with mushrooms, potatoes, and cranberries, 20 DM ($11.47). A quarter of a liter of red wine costs 6 DM ($3.44).

BUDGET INNS: **Greifen,** 5 Obere Schmiedgasse (tel. 22-81), is one of the better little inns which not only offers well-cooked meals at modest prices, but has 22 bedrooms to rent as well. Just off the marketplace, it is next door to the prestigious Baumeisterhaus, recommended below. It, too, is a patrician house, dating back to the 14th century. It contains a sun-pocket garden, and here you can order your morning coffee in the midst of roses and geraniums. The bedrooms are simple, but offer good comfort, soft eiderdowns, and hot and cold running water (a few contain private baths). Singles are only 24 DM ($13.77) and 30 DM ($17.21). The rate in a double ranges from 40 DM ($22.94) to 60 DM ($34.42). The dining room is closed Mondays.

Bayerischer Hof, 21 Ansbacherstrasse (tel. 34-57), is a good and reasonably priced hotel, standing at midpoint between the railway station and the medieval walled city. Willi and Katherine Schellhaas welcome guests, housing them in one of their clean, well-furnished rooms. Without bath, they charge two persons from 36 DM ($20.65) to 40 DM ($22.94) nightly. With a private bath, the charges go up to 55 DM ($31.55) to 60 DM ($34.42). The food is very good, with many international specialties. For that reason, you may want to take the full-board rate, costing yet another 18 DM ($10.32) per person in addition to the room tariffs.

READERS' GUEST HOUSE SELECTIONS: "Don't hesitate to knock at the door of the yellow house next to the Brauhaus Rothenburg. There is no sign to indicate the **Günter Pöschel,** 22 Wenggasse. The sparkling fresh interior, the low cost, and helpful hospitality were hard to beat. A double with breakfast costs 30 DM ($17.21); a single, 15 DM ($8.60). Herr Pöschel speaks fluent English, having worked in England for a time" (Dick and Erna Cunningham, Long Island, N.Y.). . . . "Of the many cities and places visited, none was nicer or more reasonable in price than the **Gasthof zur Schranne,** 6 Schrannenplatz (tel. 22-58). Although the owner could speak no English, she could understand some, and was more than helpful. Our large, newly furnished, bright, airy room with bath cost us 44 DM ($25.24) a day for two, including tax, service, and breakfast. Some cheaper doubles rent for 38 DM ($21.80) per day. Although the gasthof doesn't look like much from the outside, I believe the whole inside has been remodeled within the last few years and is exceptionally clean and cheery. It should be noted that it is only a five-minute taxi ride from the bahnhof although after you know the location, it is a short walk" (A. L. Rastetter, Massillon, Ohio).

"We especially liked **Gastehaus Gernert,** run by Helga Gernert who speaks good English. It is just a few blocks from the station. The rate includes a good breakfast. Twin-bedded rooms with bath cost 44 DM ($25.24); singles, 28 DM ($16.06). Without bath, twin-bedded rooms cost 38 DM ($21.80) and singles 26 DM ($14.91). The rooms are extremely well kept" (Ellen and Lee Hogie, Sleepy Eye, Minn.). . . . "A nice place to stay is **Gastehaus Raidel,** 3 Wenggasse, just across the street from the Brauhaus Rothenburg. A double with breakfast costs 32 DM ($18.63). The guest house is clean and pleasant" (Mrs. William Blakely, Los Angeles, Calif.). . . . "The hotel-pension **Villa Jessl,** 28 Hornburgweg (tel. 937), isn't the most economical place in Rothenburg, but I am sure it is one of the nicest. A room with a double bed, bath, and toilet costs 65 DM ($37.28), although the rates are cheaper if you occupy a room without a bath. The tariffs include a good breakfast. Frau Rinne and her husband are fine people who make you feel at home and welcome. The villa is only about a minute's walk from the Wierzburg gate. In fact, the front rooms overlook the walls. There is a lovely garden where you can relax in the afternoons after long morning walks" (Pam Morton).

WHERE TO DINE: Baumeisterhaus, 3 Obere Schmiedgasse (tel. 34-04), is housed in an ancient patrician residence right off the marketplace. Built in 1596, it contains what is universally considered the most beautiful courtyard in Rothenburg (which, incidentally, can be visited only by guests). You must reserve well ahead in the day if you want a good table in the courtyard in the evening. The patio has colorful murals, draped serenely by vines. Even though the cuisine is good, the prices are kept low. Try, for a starter, the soup of the day, at 2 DM ($1.15). Main dishes range around 15 DM ($8.60). Desserts are priced from 3.50 DM ($2.01) to 6.50 DM ($3.73).

Ratsstube, 6 Marktplatz, enjoys a position right on the marketplace, one of the most photographed spots in Germany. The Ratsstube is a bustling center of activity throughout the day—a day which begins, incidentally, when practically every Rothenburger stops by for a cup of morning coffee, perhaps a beer. Inside, a true tavern atmosphere prevails, with hardwood chairs and tables, vaulted ceilings, pierced copper lanterns, and decorative swords. On the à la carte menu are many regional dishes, with soups starting at 2.50 DM ($1.43) and going up to 5.50 DM ($3.15). Main dishes include blood sausages with sauerkraut, 9 DM ($5.16), or a Bavarian mixed grill at 18 DM ($10.32). The Ratsstube is closed Wednesdays.

READERS' SELECTION AT SCHÖNTAL: "While traveling through the beautiful Hohenlohe region of Germany, 15 miles west of the Romantic Road and Rothenburg, we chanced upon a good pension run by a most gracious innkeeper. **Pension Zeller** (tel. 07943/6-00) is so new it isn't listed in any of the guidebooks. However, it shouldn't be missed. We had a sparkling-clean double room, with breakfast and a shower across the hall, for 36 DM ($20.65) a night. Doubles with private bath go for 46 DM ($26.39), and singles, depending on the plumbing, range from 20 DM ($11.47) to 27 DM ($15.49), these tariffs without breakfast. The innkeeper, Woltram Zeller, is very personable and speaks quite good English. Having spent some time in the United States, he even offered us ham omelets for breakfast, which we eagerly wolfed down. We used the pension as a headquarters for two days of circular trips to Rothenburg, Dinkelsbuhl, Bad Mergentheim, the Castle Weikersheim, and the beautiful Cistercian abbey (1727) right across the street from the pension in Schöntal (Mr. and Mrs. K. F. Randall, Annandale, Va.).

READER'S SELECTION AT KIRCHBERG: "We'd hoped to complete the trip from Heidelberg to Rothenburg in one day, but much difficulty in locating secondary roads delayed us. Darkness descended and we agreed to accept the next presentable place. How delighted we were! It was Kirchberg, a most picturesque old town, 30 kilometers from Rothenburg. The **Gasthaus zum Stern** (tel. 1-39) supplied a simple, but satisfactory meal at a reasonable price, although we could have ordered a few international dishes. The charge for bed and breakfast is 40 DM ($22.94) for two adults. The stenciled furniture in our room consisted of twin beds, two night tables, a large washstand, and a cupboard dated 1838. I'd gladly have purchased the latter to ship home if we could have afforded it. Breakfast was especially fine. It consisted of a boiled egg, sausage, cheese, coffee, bread, butter, assorted jams, and hot chocolate. The trip to Rothenburg was completed quickly and easily in daylight" (Mrs. Willard G. Prater, Bellefontaine, Ohio).

READERS' SELECTION AT CREGLINGEN: "We stopped at Creglingen, about ten miles northwest of Rothenburg. We stayed at **Gasthaus zum Lamm.** You don't need an address since the town is small and it is on the main street. The tariff is 38 DM ($21.80) for a double room with breakfast and without bath. The restaurant is good there, too. It is not so much the accommodations I want to emphasize. The amazing thing is the old-world living that one experiences here. It seems everyone knows everyone else. The town is built on a few hillsides. It is crammed tight, and some of the homes right in town have their barns as part of the house. Some of the stone buildings have settled and the roofs have taken a sag and present an interesting view" (Ruth and Martin S. Merritt, Akron, Ohio).

READER'S SELECTION AT LEUTERSHAUSEN: "Almost due south of Rothenburg, perhaps a scenic one hour's drive, and some 16 kilometers west of **Ansbach,** you will come upon 8801 Leutershausen (make sure you're at the right place, as there are three cities in Germany by the name of Leutershausen). For Bach music lovers, the **Bach Festival** at Ansbach, every second year, is ideal for those who enjoy classics played in the atmosphere of palace grounds amid a city steeped in culture, shops of all sorts which one will want to buy out and transport home en masse, original ancient buildings of every imaginable type untouched by World War II, street markets, and magnificent winding cobbled alleyways providing adventure and romantic color at every turn and cranny. While visiting Ansbach, where prices are suited to every pocketbook, where food is fit for a king at workingman's prices, readers should be sure to make a visit to **Leutershausen.** They might never wish to return home.

"There are gasthofs in this ancient, walled-in, medieval city, all of which provide sleepy travelers with comfort, cleanliness, and homey atmosphere and service. One in particular is Hermann Betscher's **Gasthof Neue Heimat,** on Bahnhofstrasse, just up the hill outside the ten-foot-thick ancient wall. When stopping at Hermann's you are in for a treat. A superb breakfast is included in the price of the room. Other meals are available upon request. You will meet Hermann, his wife Franziska, son Hans, daughter Petra, and grandparents, all willing to make your every need both memorable and promptly met. Hermann and his children speak excellent English.

"The city of Leutershausen was founded in the year 1000 under Kaiser Otto III. The tower of the gate into the city contains a museum you will want to explore, along with viewing the city from various levels attractive to camera enthusiasts.

"Don't miss out on the abundant charm and friendship found at the city hall **(Rathaus)** where the burgermeisters will personally extend the most remarkable hospitality and help for your needs. The present burgermeister is Dieter Gundel, who handles English with accented color to perfection. Across from the Rathaus (the burgermeister might show you from his office window) you will see the birthplace of Henry Kissinger's mother and maternal grandparents. Former Secretary of State Kissinger has visited Leutershausen for those sentimental ties, and in December 1976 his mother and father were guests of honor at the Rathaus and City Council, visiting for the first time since they fled in the 1930s.

"You will also be introduced to the history of their once native son, Gustav Weisskopf, who remains the amazing controversial contender for having flown powered aircraft prior to the Wrights at his 1900 adopted city of Fairfield, Conn. (Gustave Whitehead, his anglicized name, is 'the Father of Connecticut Aviation.') There is a small yet impressive **Weisskopf Museum** in Leutershausen, exhibiting the impressive photos of his early work and flight experiments, which is a target for any modeler or aviation buff.

"Leutershausen was bombed by the USAAF on April 19, 1945, in the hectic closing days of the war. Fifteen retreating SS troops paused outside Leutershausen's gates and fired at the oncoming American patrol. Only days before, the city had succeeded in convincing their occupying German military to leave to prevent their ancient buildings from being destroyed. Believing the city was defending itself in compliance with Hitler's decree that all would become forts, eight P-47s struck with incendiary bombs. Because of my personal acquaintance with this city, where houses appear to be made of candy for a Hansel and Gretel playlet, where ponds burst with trout, where the population is

3500, and where I have become honored as their 'Ehrenburger' (Freeman) from interests developed while serving as a major in the U.S. Air Force Reserve, I can promise you a memorable visit and stay if you simply state, 'Bill O'Dwyer sent me to discover your people and your friendship' " (William J. O'Dwyer, Fairfield, Conn.).

READER'S SELECTION AT SCHWARZENBRONN: "After trying several small towns, we finally stumbled upon Schwarzenbronn, about 6 kilometers outside Rothenburg. The **Gasthaus zum Goldenes Ross** offered us an unbelievable bargain: 50 DM ($28.68) for two connecting rooms, with one very comfortable double bed per room and a sink in each room. The shower and toilet are across the hall. The house is very clean. Breakfast is included in the price, and consists of assorted bread with butter and strawberry jam, hot chocolate, coffee, or tea, and a soft-boiled egg. The Fritz Rahn family are very hospitable, and hosted us a second night at the same bargain rate" (Donald L. Fitzgerald, APO New York).

READER'S SELECTION AT COLMBERG CASTLE: "Near Leutershausen, by not much more than five to six kilometers and on the road to Rothenburg from Leutershausen, your readers might enjoy stopping by **Colmberg Castle.** It has a superb restaurant with a great menu selection, reasonable prices, and even a room or two that would cause nostalgia for ancient times to set in. You can even have a marriage ceremony arranged upon request. What a place for a wedding, atop the old medieval fortress! The wooded hill has been converted into a zoo. The place is enjoyable for young and old alike. Peacocks by the dozens lend added color. Young women might find a modern-day knight or two in this romantic setting" (William J. O'Dwyer, Fairfield, Conn.).

3. Dinkelsbühl

Still surrounded by medieval walls and towers, this town is straight out of a story by the Grimm Brothers—even down to the gingerbread, which is one of its main products. Behind the ancient walls, originally built in the tenth century, is a dreamy village which seems to awaken only once a year for the **Kinderzeche** (Children's Festival), commemorating the saving of the village by the children. According to the story, they pleaded with the conquering Swedish troops to leave their town without pillaging and destroying it, and got their wish. The pageant includes concerts given by the local boys' band dressed in historic military costumes.

In spite of the great hordes of tourists who come here, Dinkelsbühl retains its quiet, provincial attitude. The unpaved and cobbled streets of the town are lined with fine 16th-century houses, many with exquisite carvings and paintings depicting biblical and mythological themes. In the center of the town is the late Gothic **St. George's Church,** dating from 1450 and containing a carved "Holy Cross Altar" from the same period. The pillar sculptures are excellent, many of them done by the pupils of the Gothic master Tilman Riemenschneider.

BED AND BOARD AT OLD-WORLD INNS: Goldene Rose, 4 Marktplatz (tel. 27-76), is an important landmark in the heart of this village. Intricately timbered, it rises six stories high, with a steeply pitched roof and window boxes overflowing with geraniums and petunias. It's the leading inn of Dinkelsbühl, tracing its history back to 1450. Don't expect liveried attendants, but rather a rustic, homey atmosphere. In the style of a true country inn, the dining rooms are more important than the lounges. Adding to the ambience is a wealth of oak, antiques, and portraits of sovereigns (that's Queen Victoria at the bottom of the steps). The à la carte menu offers such tempting items as French onion soup at 3.70 DM ($2.12); hummer und kraben dim dill Rahm sauce with rice, 19.50 DM ($11.19); or rumpsteak Goldene Rose, 17.50 DM ($10.04). A good variety of tasty desserts are in the 4.80-DM ($2.75) to 7.50-DM ($4.30) range (the latter price for fresh raspberries flambé). The bedrooms are modernized and have good, soft beds. Doubles without bath cost from 40 DM ($22.94), increasing to 70 DM ($40.15) with bath. A bathless single is 23 DM ($13.19), rising to 35 DM ($20.08) with shower. Breakfast is included.

Zur Sonne, 11 Weinmarkt (tel. 23-30), is most beguiling, with its pitched roof and windows overflowing with flowers. Facing the winemarket in the center of the village, it has been modernized, although it still remains a simple inn, with cottage-style chairs and windowseats. You get not only good meals here, but comfortable bedrooms (some are many flights up). A bathless double goes for 66 DM ($37.86), increasing to 75 DM ($43.02) with bath. A bathless single is 26 DM ($14.91), rising to 40 DM ($22.94) with bath. The food is good, especially the soups in the 1.80-DM ($1.03) to 2.50-DM ($1.43) range. Main dishes include wiener sauerbraten and salad at 10.50 DM ($6.02). Desserts are priced from 3.20 DM ($1.84) to 16 DM ($9.18), the latter for crêpes Suzette for two.

Deutsches Haus, 3 Weinmarkt (tel. 23-46), hides behind a fascinating facade dating from 1440 and rich in painted designs and festive woodcarvings. In a niche on the second floor of the arched entrance is a lovely 17th-century Madonna. Casually run, it features a dining room with an elaborately decorated ceiling, inset niches with primitive scenic pictures, parquet floors, and provincial chairs. Soups range in price from 1.90 DM ($1.09) to 4 DM ($2.29), with main dishes beginning as low as 7 DM ($4.02), although going up to 42 DM ($24.09), the latter the price for the chateaubriand for two persons. Desserts cost from 2 DM ($1.15) to 6.50 DM ($3.73). The bedrooms are unique. You may find yourself in one with a ceramic stove or in another with a Biedermeier desk. A single costs 36 DM ($20.65) with bath. A double without bath is rented for 42 DM ($24.09) to 45 DM ($25.81), going up to 66 DM ($37.86) with bath, breakfast included.

4. Nördlingen

One of the most irresistible medieval towns along the Romantic Road, Nördlingen is still encircled by the well-preserved city fortifications dating from the 14th and 15th centuries. You can walk completely around the town on the covered parapet, which passes 18 towers and fortified gates set into the walls.

At the center of the circular-shaped Old Town formed by these walls is the **Rübenmarkt.** If you stand in this square on market day, you will be swept into a world of the past—still alive today! The country people have preserved many medieval customs and costumes here, which, along with the ancient houses, create a living medieval city. Around the square stand a number of attractive buildings, including the Gothic **Rathaus** (Town Hall), with a Renaissance outside staircase and a collection of antiquities in the **Reichsstadt Museum** inside.

St. George's Church, on the northern side of the square, is the town's most interesting sight, and one of its oldest buildings. The Gothic hallenkirche dates from the 15th century. The fan-vaulted interior is decorated with plaques and epitaphs commemorating the town's more illustrious residents of the 16th and 17th centuries. Although the original Gothic altarpiece by Friedrich Herlin (1470) has been placed in the Reichsstadt Museum, a portion of it, depicting the Crucifixion, remains in the church. Above the high altar today stands a more elaborate baroque altarpiece. The most interesting feature of the church, however, is the 295-foot French Gothic tower, called the "Daniel." At night, the town watchman calls out from the steeple, his voice ringing through the streets of the town.

FOOD AND LODGING: **Sonne,** 3 Markplatz (tel. 50-67), is in a bull's-eye position—next to the cathedral and the Rathaus. It's practically heady from having entertained so many illustrious personalities since it opened as an inn in 1405. It has counted emperors, kings, and princes among its guests, including Frederick III, Maximilian I, and Charles V; even Goethe came this way. Also the American astronauts from Apollo 14 and Apollo 17 have stayed here. The Sonne is owned by Mrs. Truedinger, who perpetuates the tradition of hospitality. The interior has been completely modernized, providing tasteful accommodations with comfort. In a choice of dining rooms, you can order the soup of the day at 2.50 DM ($1.43); main courses, such as rumpsteak Mirabeau at 14.50 DM ($8.32); desserts, from 2.50 DM ($1.43) to 7.50 DM ($4.30). It's quite casual; the waitresses even urge you to finish the food on your plate. The bedrooms are well planned, with two price levels, depending on the plumbing you get. Bathless doubles go for 48 DM ($27.53), increasing to 56 DM ($32.12) to 75 DM ($43.02) with private bath and toilet. Breakfast, service, and taxes are included.

READER'S GUEST HOUSE AND RESTAURANT SELECTION: "**Gasthof zum Goldenes Ochsen,** 12 Deininger Strasse (tel. 09081/32-66), charges 33 DM ($18.93) for twin beds and breakfast. It is halfway between the bus stop and the railroad station and within walking distance of both. Pictures on the walls portray interesting places in Germany and the rooms have some antique furnishings. An inexpensive restaurant serving tasty veal and gnüdel or spätzle (local treats) is the **Braunes Ross,** 12 Markplatz (tel. 09081/32-26), near the bus stop and the tourist information office. Set meals range from 9.50 DM ($5.45) to 13 DM ($7.46)" (Mrs. Berdena Koehler, Elmwood, Neb.).

5. Augsburg

The 2000 years that have gone into the creation of this, the largest city on the Romantic Road, also have made it one of the most important sightseeing attractions in southern Germany. Although little remains from its early Roman period (it was founded under Tiberius in 15 B.C.), the wealth of art and architecture from the Renaissance is staggering—in quantity and scope.

THE SIGHTS: Augsburg has been an important city throughout its history, but during the 15th and 16th centuries, it was the wealthiest city in Europe, mainly because of its textile industry, and the political and financial power of its two banking families, the Welsers and the Fuggers. The Welsers, who once owned nearly all of Venezuela—among other things—have long since faded from the minds of Augsburgers. But the founders of the powerful Fugger family have established themselves forever in the hearts of the townsfolk by an unusual legacy, the **Fuggerei,** actually a miniature town established in 1519 by the Fugger family to house the poorer of the townsfolk. The quarter consists of several streets lined with well-maintained Renaissance houses, as well as a church and administrative offices, all enclosed within its own walls. As the oldest social housing project in the world, it charges its tenants a rent of only 1.71 DM per year—a rate that has not changed in more than 450 years! But the tenants must pay the balance of their debt in an unusual form of payment— each night, when the gates of the Fuggerei are closed, they are obligated to pray for the souls of their patrons.

The **High Cathedral** of Augsburg has the distinction of containing the oldest stained-glass windows in the entire world. The Romanesque windows, dating from the 12th century, are actually younger than the cathedral itself, however, which was begun in 944 on the foundation walls of an early Christian baptismal church. Partially Gothicized in the 14th century, it stands on the edge of the park which also fronts the Episcopal Palace, where the basic creed of the Lutheran Reformation was presented at the Diet of Augsburg in 1530. The cathedral remains the episcopal see of the Catholic bishop to this day. The 11th-century bronze doors, leading into the three-aisled nave, are adorned with bas-reliefs of a strange mixture of biblical and mythological characters, including an interesting scene of Adam and Eve. The interior of the cathedral, restored in 1934, contains side altars with altarpieces by Hans Holbein and Christoph Amberger. The windows in the south transept are the oldest, depicting prophets of the Old Testament in a severe, but colorful Romanesque style.

From the cathedral, follow the Hoher Weg southward past the huge Town Hall, built by Elias Holl in 1620, but badly damaged in World War II. In front of the hall is the magnificent **Augustus fountain,** forged in bronze by the Dutch sculptor Hubert Gerhard in 1594 to commemorate the founding of the city. At this point, the main street of Augsburg's Old Town begins. Extending southward from the Town Hall is the **Maximilianstrasse,** lined with old burghers' houses and studded with fountains by the Renaissance Dutch sculptor Adrien de Vries. Near the southern end of the street is the **Hercules Fountain,** and behind it, the most attractive church in Augsburg, the **Church of St. Ulrich and St. Afra.** As a tribute to the 1555 Peace of Augsburg, which recognized two denominations—the Catholics and the Lutherans—this church contains a Catholic and a Protestant church within its walls. The church itself is 15th-century Gothic, but many of the furnishings, including the three altars representing the birth and resurrection of Christ and the baptism of the Church by the Holy Spirit, are done in the later baroque style. The large pulpit looks almost like a pagoda, with decorative angels dressed in Chinese red and gold. The crypt of the church contains the tombs of the Swabian saints Ulrich and Afra, and the lance and saddle of St. Ulrich are on display in the sacristy.

The **Schaezlerpalais,** 46 Maximilianstrasse, facing the Hercules Fountain, contains the city's art galleries—and what a collection is on display here! If only the works of artists who lived in Augsburg during the Renaissance were exhibited, it would be an imposing sight. (Regrettably, however, there is no painting by Titian in all the town, although he was there twice, in 1548 and again in 1551.) Works by local artists are displayed, including Hans Burgkmair and Hans Holbein the Elder, represented by a fine drawing (his even greater son was born in a house nearby). Non-German European masters are represented by such greats as Rembrandt, Rubens, Veronese, and Tiepolo. However, the larger number of paintings are by German artists of the Renaissance and baroque periods. One of the most famous of these is Dürer's portrait of Jakob Fugger the Rich, founder of the dynasty which once elected the heads of the Holy Roman Empire. Besides the art collections, the palace-gallery contains a rococo festival hall, with gilded and mirrored wall panels and a ceiling fresco of the *Four Continents.* The galleries are open daily, except Monday, from 10 a.m. to 5 p.m. (winter, 10 a.m. to 4 p.m.). Admission is free.

The town's major collection of sculpture is displayed at the **Maximilian-Museum,** 24 Philippine-Welser-Strasse, together with works of art, highly important silver and gold, as well as scientific instruments.

Roman figures, monuments, and sepulchral finds are found in the **Römisches Museum,** 15 Dominikanergasse.

THE TOP HOTEL: **Drei Mohren Palasthotel,** 40 Maximilianstrasse (tel. 51-00-31), was one of the most renowned hotels in Germany before its destruction in 1944 in an air raid. Before that, it had been a hotel since 1723, and was known to diplomats, composers, and artists. Former guests include such names as the Duke of Wellington, Mozart, Goethe, Mascagni, Paganini, and Franklin D. Roosevelt. In 1956, it was rebuilt in a modern style. The interior treatment of the "Three Moors" incorporates stylish contemporary pieces with traditional furnishings. For example, the drawing room contains a slatted natural-wood ceiling and wall, contrasting warmly against a room-wide mural of Old Augsburg. In the dignified, formal dining room, an international cuisine is offered. More winning is the breakfast terrace, where rainbow-hued umbrellas and white garden chairs are set in view of the flowerbeds and three free-form splashing fountains. The bedrooms are restrained and restful, handsomely proportioned. Bathless singles go for 48 DM ($27.53), increasing to 72 DM ($41.30) to 88 DM ($50.48) with bath. Doubles with bath are from 125 DM ($71.70) to 145 DM ($83.17). Breakfast from the buffet is included.

THE BUDGET RANGE: The **Hotel-Gaststätte Lenzhalde,** 2 Thelottstrasse (tel. 3-34-45), is a meticulously maintained economy hotel that is well run by the Krebs family. The dining room is attractive, the food even more so. In English, you'll be welcomed to one of their roomy, pleasantly furnished accommodations. A single without bath costs 21 DM ($12.05), rising to 27 DM ($15.49) with shower. The price of a double or twin-bedded room is 40 DM ($22.94). These rooms are fitted with hot and cold running water. The use of the bath—on the same floor—is an extra 2 DM ($1.15). Tariffs quoted include breakfast.

One of the least expensive and best budget digs in the area is at Stadtbergen, about three kilometers from the heart of Augsburg, along the Augsburger Strasse in the western sector. It's the **Cafe Weinberger,** 55 Bismarckstrasse (tel. 52-30-61). The owner rents out large, light, and airy double rooms with complete private baths for 45 DM ($25.81) nightly. Singles go for 30 DM ($17.21). The place is well patronized by Germans, who know a good bargain, and its cafe is one of the most popular in the area for dinner and snacks.

The cafe is also within walking distance of **Lamm's,** which we've never visited, although it has received praise from readers as "one of the best dining spots for good food at reasonable prices." As we've been warned, don't expect frill or atmosphere—rather, good service and friendly waitresses.

READER'S MOTEL SUGGESTION: "Staying at the **Alpenhof,** 233 Dunauwörtherstrasse (tel. 41-30-51), in Augsburg-Oberhausen, was a stroke of luck. This is a fairly new motel arrangement on the order of TraveLodges in the U.S. The motel has a staff of young, helpful bellboys, a swimming pool, a sauna, and one of the finest restaurants I've found in a hotel since I have been in Germany. The menu is quite varied and very well served (with all the pomp you would expect of 'the Old World'). The motel is also very tastefully decorated in French furniture, an excellent blend of the old and the new. The menu is rather expensive, but there is a selection of daily specials that run from 10.50 DM ($6.02) to 37 DM ($21.22), which includes dessert. Bathless singles cost 29 DM ($16.63), rising to 35 DM ($20.08) and 63 DM ($36.14) with bath. Bathless doubles go from 54 DM ($30.97), increasing to 72 DM ($41.30) to 110 DM ($63.10) with bath" (J. Fred Allen, Stuttgart, West Germany).

WHERE TO DINE: Ratskeller, 2 Rathausplatz (tel. 51-78-48), true to form in German towns, is one of the best and most reliable spots for good, trustworthy meals at moderate prices. This one is especially pleasant, offering tasty set meals starting at 12 DM ($6.88). A more elaborate meal is featured at 18 DM ($10.32). However, you may want more variety and prefer the à la carte listings, including soups from 2.70 DM ($1.55) to 4.50 DM ($2.58), the latter for French onion. Main dishes, such as sole with remoulade sauce and a salad, are 18.90 DM ($10.84). The open wine list is best if you're economizing. The Ratskeller is closed Sunday from 2 p.m. and all day Monday.

READER'S RESTAURANT SELECTION: "For a change in a place to dine, we found the **Reisinger Hof,** 17 Reisingerstrasse (tel. 57-35-34), a place that in the States we'd consider 'our friendly neighborhood tavern,' but with a large, nicely decorated dining room. The owners, Karl and Inge Kugelmann, are without doubt two of the friendliest and most helpful persons I met in Germany, and the very charming Inge speaks good English. I had the largest, most delicious complete wienerschnitzel I have ever eaten in Germany for 9 DM ($5.16), and their other food is equally fine. It's about a five-minute walk from the large Holiday Inn tower" (A. L. Rastetter, Massillon, Ohio).

6. Füssen

Depending on which direction you take, Füssen is the beginning or end of the Romantic Road. Although the town has a number of attractive buildings, including a 15th-century castle once used by the bishops of Augsburg as a summer palace, Füssen's popularity lies in its ideal location as a starting point for excursions into the surrounding countryside.

Besides being the terminus of the Romantic Road, Füssen is in the foothills of the Bavarian Alps, making it equally popular with winter and summer vacationers. An added attraction to sightseers is its proximity to the Royal Castles of Neuschwanstein and Hohenschwangau.

READERS' HOTEL SELECTIONS: "Arriving in Füssen after dark, we literally stumbled onto a sparkling pension: **Hotel-Pension Christine,** 31 Weidachstrasse (tel. 72-29). The decor was elegantly modern, and the breakfast (included with the room) was served on the finest Bavarian china with classical music in the background. Single rooms with shower, toilet, and TV cost 50 DM ($28.68); with complete bath and TV, 60 DM ($34.42). Double rates are 90 DM ($51.62) with shower, toilet and TV, 100 DM ($57.36) with bath instead of shower—substantially less than the hotels at the castle site" (Lou and Bob Brum, Minneapolis, Minn.). . . . "By luck we walked out of the train station in Füssen and turned into the second street on our left, where we discovered **Pension Elizabeth,** where we had by far the most comfortable and pleasant room we stayed in on our journey. The building is set in quaint gardens, personally attended to by the owner, Mrs. Spiez, who speaks excellent English and is most helpful and accommodating. Our rooms were decorated in a delightful fashion and had hot and cold running water. All this, a filling breakfast in a German decorated breakfast room overlooking the gardens, and the chance of breathing that healthy Bavarian mountain air costs 22 DM ($12.62) for a double room" (Margaret McElroy, Sydney, Australia).

READER'S SELECTION OUTSIDE FÜSSEN: "**Heinrich und Elisabeth Hase,** 8121 Rottenbuch/Moos (tel. 08867/500), operate a pension in Rottenbuch, a short ride from Füssen or Oberammergau. They charge 10 DM ($5.74) per person for a lovely, large double room with a full breakfast, in off-season. In season, the rate is 12 DM ($6.88) per person" (Mrs. C. Roberts, St. Thomas, Ontario, Canada).

7. The Royal Castles

The 19th century saw a great Classical revival in Germany, especially in Bavaria. This was mainly because of the enthusiasm of the Bavarian kings for ancient art forms. Beginning with King Ludwig I (1786–1868), who was responsible for many of the neo-Greek buildings in Munich, this royal house ran the gamut of ancient architecture in just three short decades. It culminated in the remarkable flights of fancy of Ludwig II (Mad Ludwig). This Ludwig (1845–1886) was especially beloved by the people of Bavaria. In spite of his rather lonely life and controversial alliances—personal and political—he was a great patron of the arts.

THE SIGHTS: Although the name "Royal Castles" is limited to the castles of **Hohenschwangau** (built by Ludwig's father, Maximilian II), and **Neuschwanstein,** the extravagant king actually was responsible for the creation of three magnificent castles. The remaining two, described in other parts of the book, are Linderhof (near Oberammergau) and Herrenchiemsee (Chiemsee). These pet projects were so close to the king's heart that, when his ministers sought to check his extravagance, he became violent.

In 1868, after a visit to the great castle of Warburg, Ludwig wrote to his good friend, Richard Wagner: "I have the intention to rebuild the ancient castle ruins of Hohenschwangau . . . in the true style of the ancient German knight's castle." The following year, construction began on the first of a series of fantastic castles—a series which stopped only with Ludwig's untimely death in 1886, only five days after he was deposed because of alleged insanity.

Neuschwanstein Castle

Neuschwanstein was the fairytale castle of Ludwig II. Until the king's death, construction had taken 17 years. After his death, all work stopped—leaving a part of the interior not completed. In the years from 1884 to 1886, Ludwig lived in the rooms on and off for a total of only about six months.

Neuschwanstein was his most ambitious project, set in its isolated location atop a rock ledge high above the Pöllat Gorge. The ledge served as the foundation of the castle, and because of its unusual configuration, supported portions of the third floor as well as the first. This is obvious in the oddly shaped vestibule on the third floor, at the top of the main staircase of Untersberg marble. This hall, with its colorfully painted Romanesque vaults, is trapezoidal in shape, the walls decorated with scenes from the primitive version of the Siegfried saga.

The doorway off the left side of the vestibule leads to the king's apartments. The study, like most of the rooms, is decorated with wall paintings showing scenes from the Nordic legends (which also inspired Wagner's operas). The theme of the study is the *Tannhäuser* saga, painted by J. Aigner. The only fabric in the room is that used in the hand-embroidered silk curtains and chair coverings, all designed with the gold and silver Bavarian coat of arms.

From the vestibule, you enter the throne room through the doorway at the opposite end. This hall, designed in a Byzantine style by J. Hofmann, was never completed. The floor of the hall is a mosaic design, depicting the animals of the world. The columns in the main hall are the deep copper red of porphyry. The circular apse where the king's throne was to have stood is reached by a stairway of white Carrara marble. The walls and ceiling are decorated with paintings of Christ in heaven looking down on the twelve Apostles and six canonized kings of the Holy Roman Empire.

The king's bedroom is the most richly carved in the entire castle. It took 4½ years to complete this room alone, which, aside from the wall painting depicting the legend of *Tristan and Isolde,* is completely covered in oakwood carvings. The walls are decorated with panels carved to look like Gothic windows. In the center is a large wooden pillar completely encircled with gilded brass sconces. The bed, on its raised platform, is the most ornate furnishing in the room. The elaborately carved canopy blends into a simple Gothic design at the foot. From the balcony of the room, you can see the 150-foot waterfall in the Pöllat Gorge, with the mountains in the distance.

Passing through the winter garden and a grotto with artificial stalactites, you come to the great parlor, whose theme is the *Lohengrin* saga, expressed in the paintings of Heckel and Hauschild. Note the heavy chandelier, holding 48 candles, and studded with pieces of colored Bohemian glass.

The fourth floor of the castle is almost entirely given over to the Singer's Hall, the pride of Ludwig II—and all of Bavaria. Modeled after the huge hall at Wartburg where incidents from the saga of *Tannhäuser* were supposed to have occurred, this huge hall is decorated with marble columns and elaborately painted designs interspersed with frescoes depicting the life of *Parsifal.*

The castle can be visited year round, and in September, visitors have the additional treat of hearing Wagnerian concerts in the Singer's Hall. The rooms are open daily from 8:30 a.m. to 5 p.m. (in winter, from 10 a.m. to 4 p.m.). Admission is 4 DM ($2.29). Before returning down the slope, more energetic visitors can follow the winding path to the **Marienbrücke,** named for the mother of Ludwig II. This bridge crosses over the Pöllat Gorge at a height of 305 feet. From that vantage point, you can, like Ludwig, stand and meditate on the glories of the castle and its surroundings.

To reach that magnificence, however, you must climb a steep hill, a 25-minute walk for the energetic, an eternity for anybody else. However, mini-buses will take you up to Marienbrücke for 4 DM ($2.29). Even so, you're not transported directly to the castle, but must add on a five-minute hike to reach it. However, the most romantic way to go is by carriage, costing 8 DM ($4.59) for the ascent, 4 DM ($2.29) for the descent. (Note: Carriages require a mini-mum of 25 DM—$14.34—so round up some extra people.) However, some readers have objected to the buggy rides, complaining that too many people are crowded in. It should be pointed out that the buggy ride doesn't bring you all the way to the top. As you get out, you're faced with a steep path leading to the castle.

Hohenschwangau Castle

Although not as glamorous or spectacular as Neuschwanstein, this neo-Gothic castle has a much richer history. The original structure dates back to the Knights of Schwangau of the 12th century. When the knights faded away, the castle began to do so too, helped along by the Napoleonic War in 1809. When Ludwig II's father, Crown Prince Maximilian (later King Maximilian II), saw the castle in 1832, he purchased it, and in four years had it completely restored. Ludwig II spent the first 17 years of his life here, and later received Richard Wagner in its chambers, although Wagner never visited Neuschwan-stein on the hill above.

The rooms of Hohenschwangau are styled and furnished in a much heavier Gothic mood than the castle built by Ludwig. Many are typical of the halls of knights' castles of the Middle Ages in both England and Germany. There is no doubt that the style greatly influenced young Ludwig and encouraged his fanciful boyhood dreams which formed his later tastes and character. Unlike Neuschwanstein, however, this castle has a comfortable look about it, as if it actually were a home at one time, not just a museum. The small chapel, once a drinking hall, is still the scene of Sunday mass. The suits of armor and Gothic arches here set the stage for the rest of the room.

Among the most attractive chambers is the Hall of the Swan Knight, named for the wall paintings depicting the saga of *Lohengrin*—pre-Wagner and pre-Ludwig II. Note the Gothic grill work on the ceiling with the open spaces studded with stars. The furniture in this room, once reserved for dining, is a mixture of period Gothic, overdecorative gifts from admiring subjects, and cherry or maple Biedermeier pieces from the 19th century.

Probably the most authentically Gothic room is the huge Hall of Heroes. The paintings lining the walls depict the old German saga of Dietrich of Berne. On the long banquet table are centerpieces of hot-gilded bronze decorated with scenes from the *Nibelungen* saga.

From Ludwig's bedroom on the third floor, the young king could keep an eye on his castle on the hillside above. As in other rooms, the ceiling of the bedroom was decorated with the typically Gothic stars—with one difference; here they lit up at night!

Nearby is the music room where Ludwig and Wagner spent long hours entertaining one another at the maple piano. The small chapel in the alcove off the music room was executed by Ludwig himself. The room also contains an exhibit of emotional letters sent by the king to Wagner, expressing his great admiration for him.

The hours for Hohenschwangau are the same as for Neuschwanstein. Several parking lots nearby enable you to leave your car here while visiting both castles.

STAYING IN THE TOWN OF HOHENSCHWANGAU: Hotel Lisl und Jägerhaus, 1–3 Neuschwansteinstrasse (tel. 91-06), is a graciously styled villa, with an annex across the street. It was seemingly made to order to provide great views, as well as comfort. Both houses sit in a narrow valley, surrounded by their own gardens. In the main house, two well-styled dining rooms serve good meals. A bowl of soup costs from 2.70 DM ($1.55) to 6 DM ($3.44); Hungarian goulash, 14 DM ($8.03). The restaurant features an international as well as local cuisine, including balmi-goreng at 20 DM ($11.47). To finish, desserts are in the 4-DM ($2.29) to 8-DM ($4.59) range. If you're staying over, you'll find comfortably furnished and attractive bedrooms, renting for widely varying prices. In a bathless single, the half-pension rate is 45 DM ($25.81), rising to 70 DM ($40.15) with bath. In a bathless double, the half-pension rate is 38 DM ($21.80) per person, increasing to 55 DM ($31.55) per person in a double with complete bath.

Hotel Müller, 14–16 Alpseestrasse (tel. 92-56), is a small-town inn with many colorful elements. In the hub of village activity, its facade is adorned with dormers, flower boxes, and balconies. The dining room is in the country style, with blue fabric and natural woods, and it forms the chief social center. The stube is also popular, decorated in a provincial vein, with leather-backed chairs, beamed ceilings, and plate rails of pewter. In case you're just passing through, you can order main dishes for 11.50 DM ($6.60) to 24 DM ($13.77). On the à la carte listings, you'll find such items as soup of the day, from 2.30 DM ($1.32); veal fricassee, with asparagus and rice, at 20 DM ($11.47); and trout meunière at 14 DM ($8.03). A single starts at 45 DM ($25.81) with shower and peaks at 80 DM ($45.89) with full bath and toilet. A double without bath goes for 50 DM ($28.68) to 64 DM ($36.71), rising to 72 DM ($41.30) to 130 DM ($75.57) with a shower or complete bath. The prices for the latter rooms depend on the views of the castles.

READER'S HOTEL SELECTION AT LANDSBERG: "We found a very nice hotel in Landsberg on the Romantic Road. It is the **Hotel-Gaststatte Zederbrau,** 155 Hauptplatz, 891 Landsberg S. Lech (tel. 08191/2241). My husband, son, and I shared a room for 55 DM ($31.55), plus 15 DM ($8.60) tax per night, breakfast included. The room and the baths (which were down the hall) were spotlessly clean. We ate dinner there every night, and the food was delicious. Our dinners cost around 36 DM ($20.65) for all three of us. The proprietor does not speak English, but we were able to make ourselves understood with the German vocabulary page in your book. I should also mention that it is across from the town square statute and an old clock that chimes every hour and half hour, adding to the charm and old-world atmosphere" (Mrs. P. W. Davis, Davis Wharf, Va.).

———————

The most popular tourist section of Germany unfolds in the upcoming chapter.

THE BAVARIAN ALPS

IF YOU WALK into a rustic alpine inn along the German-Austrian frontier and ask the innkeeper if he is German, you'll most likely get the indignant response, "Of course not! I'm Bavarian." And he is undoubtedly right, because even though Bavaria is politically a part of Germany, many of its older folk can still remember the kingdom of Bavaria which did not become part of the German Reich until 1918.

Although the huge province includes not only the Alps, but Franconia, Lake Constance, and the capital city of Munich as well, we will take this opportunity to explore separately the mountains along the Austrian frontier, a world unto itself. The hospitality of the people of this area is world famous. The picture of the plump rosy-cheeked innkeeper with a constant smile on his face is no myth.

Although many travelers think of the Alps as a winter vacationland, you'll find nearly all of the Bavarian resorts and villages boast year-round attractions.

We'll begin our exploration of the Bavarian Alps with . . .

1. Berchtesgaden

Ever since Ludwig I of Bavaria chose this resort as one of his favorite hideaways—his first choice was Lola Montez's—the tourist business in Berchtesgaden has been booming. Its setting below the many summits of the Watzmann Mountain is among the most outstanding in Bavaria. According to legend, the peaks of the mountain were once a king and his family who were so evil that God punished them by turning them into rocks. The king has evidently not been completely silenced, however, because even in recent years the Watzmann has been responsible for the deaths of several mountain climbers who have endeavored to scale the one-mile-high cliff on its eastern wall.

THE SIGHTS: Berchtesgaden grew up in the Middle Ages around the powerful Augustine monastery, whose monks introduced the art of woodcarving for which the town is noted to this day. When the town became part of Bavaria in 1809, the abbey was secularized and eventually converted to a palace for the royal family of Wittelsbach. The **castle** has now been turned into a museum, exhibiting the collections of furniture and art owned by the royal family. More interesting is the adjacent **Stiftskirche** (Abbey Church), dating from 1122. The church is mainly Romanesque, with Gothic additions. One of its ancient twin steeples was destroyed by lightning and rebuilt in 1866. The interior of the church contains many fine works of art, including the high altar with a painting by Zott dating from 1669. In the vestry is a small silver altar donated by the Empress Maria Theresa of Austria.

The **Schlossplatz** (Castle Square), partially enclosed by the castle and Stiftskirche, is the most attractive plaza in town. On the opposite side of the square from the church is a 16th-century arcade which leads to the Market-place with its typically alpine houses and a wooden fountain from 1677 (re-stored by Ludwig I in 1860). Some of the oldest inns and houses in Berchtesgaden line this square. Extending from the Marketplace is the **Nonn-tal,** lined with more old houses, some of which have been built into the rocks of the Lockstein Mountain which towers above.

Although Berchtesgaden is less a sightseeing center than it is a jumping-off place for excursions into the surrounding mountains, there is one attraction: the **Salt Mines** (Salzbergwerk), at the eastern edge of town, once owned by the monastery for many years after operations began here in 1517. The mines contain two types of salt, one of which is suitable only for "salt licks" for cattle and other animals. The deposits are more than 990 feet thick and are still processed today from four galleries or "hills." Visitors on guided tours enter the mine on a small wagonlike train after donning the protective costume of the miner. After nearly a half-mile ride, they leave the train and explore the rest of the mine on foot (even taking a "wild slide"), and enjoy a ride on the salt lake in a small boat. The highlight of the tour is the "chapel," a grotto containing unusually shaped salt formations illuminated to create an eerie effect. The best thing about the 1½-hour tour is that you can take it any time of year, in any weather. Hours are from 8 a.m. till 5 p.m., from May 1 to October 15. Off-season it is open weekdays from 1 to 4 p.m. The price of admission is 4.50 DM ($2.58) for children and 8.50 DM ($4.59) for adults.

READER'S SUGGESTION IN THE ALLGÄU ALPS: "If you're ever staying in the health and ski resort of **Oberstdorf,** you'll do yourself a great injustice by not staying at the modest but immaculate guest house of Herr and Frau Knockel, **In Den Hofen,** 386 Weststrasse (tel. 29-35). This young couple made our stay as memorable as the city and the surrounding mountains through their kindness and helpfulness. A double room (with flowered balcony) cost 60 DM ($34.42) a day, including hot shower and a delicious, hearty breakfast. The TV in the breakfast room can be used when desired. As the city is a resort, you will probably have to reserve your room for a few days during the busy tourist season (summer and winter), Herr Knockel speaks English pretty well.

"Frau Knockel recommended the restaurant **Zur Alten Sennkuche,** 2 Lorettos-trasse (close to the guest house), for reasonably priced, good food. Believe it or not, most complete meals cost between 12 DM ($6.88) and 15 DM ($8.60), and light meals between 6.75 DM ($3.87) and 9 DM ($5.16)" (Claude Lillie, Bradley Beach, N.J.).

THE TOP HOTEL: Geiger Hotel, 111 Berchtesgadenstrasse (tel. 50-55), is a genuine antique! It's an ornate chalet-style inn on the upper fringes of Ber-chtesgaden. From its terraces (one with an open-air swimming pool), bed-rooms, or breakfast room, one can enjoy fantastic views of the famous moun-taintops named the Watzmann Family—mother, father, and seven children—by the natives. The "why" of this remarkable retreat is the Geiger family, who created the hotel more than 100 years ago.

Bedrooms, dining and living rooms are furnished with antiques. Biedermeier enthusiasts will revel over the several sitting rooms completely furnished in that period. Any member of the Geiger family will give you the history of any of the furnishings—especially the famous painting in the paneled drawing room of **Silent Night** (it upset everyone by depicting Mary as awaiting the birth of Jesus on a Bavarian farm). Guests like to gather in the drawing room for after-dinner coffee and cognac in front of the fireplace. Dining rooms have the requisite deer horns and wooden dado holding pewter plates. Dining is a true event here. Be sure to try the alpine river trout. The menu of the day is either 21 DM ($12.05) or 30 DM ($17.21). Have a drink of water before you depart, from the fountain where Bach drank.

The Geiger's bedrooms are comfortable, and furnished with antiques—although the plumbing may strike you as having that same characteristic, too. Prices include breakfast, and are gauged on whatever bath facilities you request, plus your view—i.e., if you have a balcony or not. Bathless rooms range in price from 42 DM ($24.09) to 67 DM ($38.43) per person, from 52 DM ($29.83) to 85 DM ($48.76) per person with bath. Half-pension terms are 22 DM ($12.62) per person daily, in addition to the room rates. An indoor swimming pool has been added.

THE MEDIUM-PRICED RANGE: Vier Jahreszeiten, 20 Maximilianstrasse (tel. 50-26), is an old inn with modern extensions that has been in the hands of the Miller family since 1876. It's in the heart of the village and has a colorful and distinguished restaurant (see our dining recommendations). The inn has been greatly remodeled and improved over the years and now brings a sophisticated level of comfort to its guests. The newer units have been furnished with many wooden pieces, and some of them are like suites with tiny sitting rooms and balconies. In addition to the main dining room, there's a terrace for summer dining and viewing. Depending on the plumbing, singles range from 55 DM ($31.55) to 65 DM ($37.28), with doubles going for anywhere from 105 DM ($60.23) to 150 DM ($86.04).

Wittelsbach, 16 Maximilianstrasse (tel. 50-61), has been modernized stylishly, now offering well-furnished bedrooms in the heart of Berchtesgaden. Its entrance is on the main street, but its better accommodations are those on the upper floors. Furnishings are neat and attractive, and maintenance is good. A single room with shower costs 43 DM ($24.66). Doubles, depending on the plumbing, range from 96 DM ($55.07), these rates including breakfast, service, and taxes.

BUDGET INNS: Watzmann, 2 Franziskanerplatz (tel. 20-55), is a country-town inn, on the square opposite the church. It's Bavarian, with shuttered windows, window boxes of red geraniums, and a wide front terrace with dining tables. Everyone seems to stop by here day or night for a beer, coffee, or lunch. Inside, the Watzmann contains huge carved wooden pillars, oak ceilings, wrought-iron light fixtures and a circular, antler-horn chandelier in the hunt dining room. Evenings there is folk singing and yodeling, with mountain musicians performing. The Piscators do the innkeeping. Bathless singles are 27 DM ($15.49); doubles, 49 DM ($28.11). Doubles with shower are 57 DM ($32.70); doubles with your own bath, 61 DM ($34.99). Breakfast is an additional 5 DM ($2.87). Simply furnished bedrooms, with an occasional antique, are kept immaculate; the beds are downy-soft. Closed November 15 through December 20.

Grassl Hotel, 15 Maximilianstrasse (tel. 40-71), is a hillside villa, with one side opening onto the main street of town and the other upon the valley below, with a spectacular view of the Alps beyond. It's a fascinating old building with overhanging balconies. Inside it has caught up to today's taste by use of simple furnishings and lots of primitive splashes of color. There is no proper restaurant, but there is a breakfast terrace and a very pleasant cafe for snacks, with wide-view windows. Bedrooms are personalized, zinging with color, and most have plenty of space. Important: Ask for rooms with a view, which are away from the noises of the street. Prices quoted are for high season (generally in the low season, there is a drop of about 10% per person). The bathless single rate (including breakfast, taxes, and service) on the street side is 29 DM ($16.63); on the view side, 31 DM ($17.78), if bathless; with shower, 50 DM ($28.68). The per-person rate in a bathless double room on the street side is 28 DM ($16.06); on the view side, a double with private bath costs 45 DM ($25.81) per person. For one or two nights, there is an extra 3-DM ($1.72) charge per person.

WHERE TO DINE: **Hubertusstuben,** in the Hotel Vier Jahreszeiten, 20 Maximilianstrasse (tel. 26-37), has been owned and directed by the Miller family since 1876. It has the most elaborate menu in Berchtesgaden. The dining room is decorated in a traditional style, and it's warm and quite intimate. The wine list is also distinguished. Among the soups, a fresh fish soup at 5.50 DM ($3.15) is presented, and you may enjoy frogs legs as an appetizer at 12 DM ($6.88). Specialties include banana steak Bombay at 19.50 DM ($11.19) and deer steak with vegetables and homemade noodles (along with almond balls) at 24 DM ($13.77). For dessert, we'd suggest the apple fritters on walnut ice cream at 5.50 DM ($3.15).

Wienerwald, 17 Maximilianstrasse, lies under a mansard roof, offering a large terrace with a view of the steep hills in the distance. It has some of the most reasonably priced food at Berchtesgaden. Try the Texas steak with french fries and a salad at 14.50 DM ($8.32) or else half a grilled hen at 6.50 DM ($3.73). The wienerschnitzel at 10 DM ($5.74) is also good. You might begin with chicken soup with noodles at 2 DM ($1.15), finishing off with apple strudel at 2.50 DM ($1.43).

THE ENVIRONS: Although time may not permit you to take every excursion through the mountains and valleys around the town, the two most popular sights make it well worth spending an extra night here.

Königssee

This "jewel in the necklace" of Berchtesgaden is very likely one of the most scenic bodies of water in Europe. Its waters appear to be a dark green because of the steep mountains which jut upward from its shores. Although the northern edge of the lake borders enough low-lying land to contain a car park and a few charming inns and bathing facilities, the rest of the lake is enclosed by mountains, making it impossible to walk along the shoreline. The only way to explore the waters, unless you are one of the mountain goats you may see on cliffs above, is by boat. **Electric motorboats**—no noisy gas-powered launches allowed—carry passengers on tours around the lake throughout the summer and occasionally, even in winter. The favorite spot on the Königssee is the tiny peninsula on the western bank. It is the only flat area surrounding the lake, and was the site of a monastery as early as the 12th century. Today, the Catholic chapel of **St. Bartholomae** is still used for services (except in winter). The clergy must arrive by boat since there is no other way to approach the peninsula. The adjacent buildings include a fisherman's house and a restaurant, where you can sample the delicious trout and salmon caught in the crisp, clean waters. At the southern end of the lake, you come to the "Salet-Alm," where the tour boat makes a short stop near a thundering waterfall. If you follow the footpath up the hillside, you'll come upon the summer pastures used by the cattle of Berchtesgaden Land.

Just over the hill is **Lake Obersee,** part of Königssee until a huge avalanche separated them eight centuries ago. The complete tour of the Königssee lasts about two hours and costs 11 DM ($6.31). If you prefer a shorter trip, you can take the boat as far as St. Bartholomae and back for 9 DM ($5.16). To reach the lake from Berchtesgaden by car, simply follow the signs south from the town (only three miles). It's also a pleasant hour walk, or a short ride by electric train or bus from the center of town.

If you'd like to stay or dine in the area, we'd suggest the **Hotel Schiffmeister,** 34 Seestrasse (tel. 10-22), a great old village inn, positioned directly on the wharf overlooking the Königssee. It couldn't be more central or more commanding. It has local architectural style, with a huge overhanging roof, tiers of wooden balconies with murals, and trailing vines. Its window-enclosed restaurants have large windows overlooking the sea and the boat landings. Often, particularly in the off-season, the hotel is booked with many groups of European vacationers who know good value. The bedrooms in the main are old-fashioned, although there are a few modernized rooms. Nothing is chic or sophisticated; rather, the place is utilitarian. The rate is about 35 DM ($20.08) per person daily with breakfast. The dining room serves some of the best grilled trout we've ever tasted—plate size and crispy with country butter. The earthy waitresses assure you it comes directly from the lake. Main dishes begin at 5 DM ($2.87), ranging upward to 16 DM ($9.18).

Obersalzberg

The drive from Berchtesgaden to Obersalzberg is along one of the most scenic routes in Bavaria, reaching a height of 3300 feet by the time you arrive at the bus station at the Hintereck Restaurant. Here you may park your car and take the thrilling ride by bus up the 4½-mile-long mountain road, blasted out of solid rock and considered an outstanding feat of construction and engineering when it was begun in 1937. At the end of the journey, after winding around numerous curves and through five tunnels, you'll arrive at your destination, the famous **"Eagle's Nest,"** built as a retreat for Adolf Hitler. To reach the house itself, you must enter the tunnel and take the 400-foot elevator ride through a shaft in the Kehlstein Mountain to its summit. The building, with its solid granite walls and huge picture windows, today houses an inn and a restaurant. The modest house belies the fact that the entire project cost in the neighborhood of $10 million!

From this eagle's-eye view, you can observe the Obersalzberg area below, where Hitler's Berghof once stood, and nearby, the house of Martin Bormann and the SS barracks, all destroyed in 1945. To the north, you can see as far as the large city of Salzburg, in Austria, and just below the mountain, to the west, the town of Berchtesgaden, with its rivers dwindling off into threads in the distance.

The bunkers and air raid shelter were built by Hitler in 1943. Three thousand laborers completed the work in nine months, connecting all the major Nazi buildings of the Obersalzberg area to the underground rooms. Although the surface houses were destroyed in 1945, the shelter, set 120 feet under-ground, is still preserved and contains kitchens, bedrooms, dining rooms, work-rooms, and all the luxuries of the above-ground existence. Most impressive are Hitler's own apartments, with adjoining rooms for the Führer's personal physi-cians and for Eva Braun.

The tours of the mountain, the Eagle's Nest, and the Obersalzberg area are conducted daily (lasting about two hours) at half-hour intervals between 9 a.m. and 5:30 p.m. The all-inclusive fee is 18 DM ($10.32). Because the roads become treacherous in winter, no tours are conducted between November and April.

In Obersalzberg, the **Turken** (tel. 24-28) is built in the alpine style with terraces, a fine restaurant, and views for everyone. On its facade is a large painted sign, "The Turk," and the foundation is stone, the windows shuttered. A large handmade sign is written across the hillside, with a rather ominous pronouncement, pointing the way to "The Bunker." Fourteen pleasantly fur-nished bedrooms are rented out, costing from 28 DM ($16.06) per person nightly. You can also dine here enjoying your meal with an Alpine vista. Prices for a simple menu begin at 15 DM ($8.60), ranging upward to 40 DM ($22.94). The inn is closed from October 20 through December.

2. Garmisch-Partenkirchen

The charm of the village that became Germany's top Alpine resort is still there, even though Garmisch-Partenkirchen has grown into the largest city in the Bavarian Alps (population 28,500). Even today you occasionally see coun-try folk in their traditional costumes, and you may even be held up in traffic while the cattle are led from their mountain grazing grounds down through the streets of town.

THE SIGHTS: The symbol of the city's growth and modernity is the **Olympic Ice Stadium,** built for the Winter Olympics of 1936, and capable of holding nearly 12,000 people. On the slopes at the edge of town is the much larger **Ski Stadium,** with two ski runs and slalom course. In 1936, more than 100,000 people watched the events in this stadium. Today it is still an integral part of winter life in Garmisch—many of the events in the annual winter competitions are held here.

Although Garmisch-Partenkirchen is more a center for winter sports and for summer hiking and mountain climbing than for sightseeing, the town and its environs offer some of the most exciting views and colorful buildings in Bavaria. The pilgrimage chapel of **St. Anton,** on a pinewood path at the edge of Partenkirchen, is all pink and silver—inside and out. Its graceful lines are characteristic of the 18th century, when it was built. The adjoining monastery pays tribute to the local men who died in the two world wars. The strange memorial consists of a collection of hundreds of photographs of the local boys who never returned from the wars.

The Philosopher's Walk in the park surrounding the chapel is a delightful spot to wander, just to enjoy the marvelous views of the mountains around the low-lying town. See especially the tallest peak of them all, the **Zugspitze,** at the frontier of Austria and Germany, the highest mountain in Germany, its summit towering more than 9700 feet above sea level. Its thrilling slopes for skiers began at the **Hotel Schneefernerhaus** at a height of 8700 feet. For a truly spectacular view of both the Bavarian and Tyrolean (Austrian) Alps, go all the way to the peak. To get to the Zugspitze summit, you have a variety of transportation choices. We will concentrate only on those from the German side, although there are also means of access from the Austrian side.

From Garmisch, you drive to Ebisee, a small lake at the foot of the mountain, and then take the underground railway leading up to the hotel. From the hotel you take the short cable-car lift to the peak. Or you may take the one-hour train ride from Garmisch, which merges with the underground railway. An alternate route is the funicular from Ebisee directly to the summit.

From Garmisch-Partenkirchen, many other peaks of the Witterstein range are accessible as well, via the ten funiculars ascending from the borders of the town. From the top of the **Wank** (5850 feet) to the east, you get the best view of the plateau on which the twin villages of Garmisch and Partenkirchen have grown up. This summit is also popular with the patrons of Garmisch's spa facilities, because the plentiful sunshine makes it ideal for the *liegekur* (deck-chair cure).

Another interesting excursion from the town is a hike through the **Partnachklamm Gorge,** lying between the Graseck and Hausberg peaks. After taking the cable car to the first station on the Graseck route, follow the paths along the sides of the slope to the right and trail the river as it cascades over the rocks. The path circles around by crossing the gorge, and returns you to the point where you entered.

THE TOP HOTELS: Posthotel Partenkirchen, 49 Ludwigstrasse (tel. 510-67), was a posting inn, and after many different stages in its development has emerged as the most prestigious hotel in town, especially when you consider the added asset of its unusually fine restaurant (refer to our dining suggestions). The bedrooms are stylish with antiques and hand-decorated or elaborately carved furnishings. You feel apart from conventional hotel life here. It's true old-world living, and Otto and Lisa Stahl, the owners, bring a personalized service.

Its facade is studded with window boxes of red geraniums, and around the front entrance are decorative murals and designs. There are two dining rooms, the larger famous for its wooden beamed ceiling, wrought-iron chandeliers, and natural-wood chairs. Huge arches divide the room, making it more intimate. In the arched, rustic Weinlokal Barbarossa, there are nooks for quiet before- or after-dinner drinks. Musicians provide background music.

New bedrooms have been built U-shaped overlooking a garden and parking for your car. Bedroom balconies are sun traps, and from them you'll have a view of the Alps. Singles with complete baths range in price from 55 DM ($31.55) to 64 DM ($36.71), and doubles go from 100 DM ($57.36) to 120 DM ($68.83).

Alpina Hotel, 12 Alpspitzstrasse (tel. 5-50-31), is a Bavarian hostelry where guests have all sorts of luxury facilities. It's really a large chalet done in a tasteful manner. Only three minutes from the Hausberg ski lifts, it has its own covered swimming pool with recreational terrace alongside, a garden with wide lawns and trees, and a large open patio, with an open-air swimming pool and surrounding terrace for sunning.

Its facade is authentic, with wide overhanging roof and Tyrolean-style entranceway and windows. A brilliant decorating job has given the rooms a sophisticated, rustic decor—beamed ceilings, provincial chairs, Oriental rugs, gilt sconce lights, and handmade chests. The open tavern dining room has two levels, and there is an extensive brick wine cellar, offering a wide and excellent choice.

Each bedroom is highly personalized, with its own color scheme and expensive, restrained furnishings. Your room may have snow-white sofa, chairs, walls, and lamps, an olive carpet, and original colorful paintings as an accent; or you may be assigned a room with sloped pine ceilings, a Spanish bedspread, and matching armchairs. Meals are served in the beamed, rustic dining room and on the sun terrace, all warmly accented by geranium red.

Room costs vary with four price seasons, with a difference ranging from about 50 DM ($28.68) to 54 DM ($30.97) in a bathless single to 120 DM ($68.83) to 148 DM ($84.89) for a double with bath. The hotel is open from December 20 to October 31.

A HOTEL FOR SPORTS PEOPLE: Golf-Hotel Sonnenbichl, 97 Burgstrasse (tel. 5-30-04), is a great blockbuster of a traditional resort hotel, at the bottom of the valley. No matter which bedroom you get, you'll have a beguiling view. There's something for everyone—a swimming pool, and golf during the summer. In winter, there is access to skiing. Bathless singles go from 40 DM ($22.94) to 44 DM ($25.24); bathless doubles, from 68 DM ($39) to 75 DM ($43.02). A single with bath ranges from 60 DM ($34.42) to 65 DM ($37.28); a double with bath, from 95 DM ($54.49) to 110 DM ($63.10). For full pension, one person pays an extra 32 DM ($18.36). During the Christmas season, prices go up. Most meals are served in the green, wood-paneled, rather formal dining room, although lighter meals are provided in the more rustic Zirbelstube.

THE MIDDLE BRACKET: Partenkirchner Hof, 15 Bahnhofstrasse (tel. 42-76), owes its fine reputation to innkeeper Karl Reindl and his family, who have made it a special Bavarian retreat. They're also known for their much-honored restaurant, the **Reindl-Grill**, considered one of the six best restaurants in all of Bavaria. It specializes in fresh lobster and crab and entrecôte, with main dishes costing from 18 DM ($10.32) to 45 DM ($25.81). The guestbook lists a glittering array of celebrated people, ranging from the Rothschilds to princesses to American governors and senators to Peggy Guggenheim. There are new balconied additions, but the main building has wrap-around verandas, giving each room an unobstructed view of the mountains and the town itself. Most bedrooms have been recently redecorated, complete with baths and balconies. Rates vary according to the facilities. Bathless singles range in price between 35 DM ($20.03) and 40 DM ($22.94); with bath, between 45 DM ($25.81) and 70 DM ($40.15). Bathless twins are tabbed at 65 DM ($37.28) to 70 DM ($40.15); with private bath and toilet, between 75 DM ($43.02) and 100 DM ($57.36). From April 1 to June 30, from October 1 to November 1, and from January 31, add 20% to all room tariffs. For half pension, add 22.50 DM ($12.91) per person to the accommodation. The hotel's facilities include a covered swimming pool, a sauna, a flowered terrace for snacks, a garden, a solarium, and an underground garage.

Clausing's Posthotel, 12 Marienplatz (tel. 5-80-71), is all Bavarian, in a colorful way. In operation 300 years as a hotel, it offers village-center accommodations under delightful circumstances. Its elaborate pink facade is decorated with baroque statues, and a long awning shades sidewalk tables for refreshments, and dining, from which you can look out across the central square. Inside are colorful public rooms, done in stylized Bavarian, with the main room serving as a center for ethnic music—group singing and yodeling every night except Thursday. Many antiques add to the ambience, and personalized touches make you feel you are on a Bavarian holiday.

Bedrooms are fresh polished, in the local decor, and you can stay here on several budget levels, according to the plumbing in your room. Bathless singles are 32 DM ($18.36) to 50 DM ($28.68); with bath, 63 DM ($36.14) to 72 DM ($41.30). Bathless doubles cost 55 DM ($31.55) to 70 DM ($40.15); with bath, 95 DM ($54.49) to 105 DM ($60.23). Most advisable is to ask for half board at an additional 20 DM ($11.47) per person daily, as you'll want to have at least one meal in one of the pleasing dining rooms. The food is good, including such featured dishes as fried brook trout and venison specialties.

Garmischer Hof, 51 Bahnhofstrasse (tel. 5-10-91), couldn't be more dead center, right in the hotel and shopping section, but its encircling balconies and small rear garden where guests sunbathe give it country Bavarian character. Bedrooms are small and comfortable for sleeping. In high season, bathless singles are 35 DM ($20.08) to 36 DM ($20.65); with bath, 46 DM ($26.39). Bathless doubles are 62 DM ($35.56); with private bath, 84 DM ($48.18).

Vier Jahreszeiten Hotel, 23 Bahnhofstrasse (tel. 44-84), is a first-class hotel with a city touch, perfect for those who are not attracted to village quaintness. Actually, looking at its rather formal modern lounge and dining room, you would never think you were in the Garmisch area. Nevertheless, there are numerous comfort-ensuring amenities: an elevator, balconies, many private bathrooms with showers, a garage, and a cozy Bavarian beer cellar, the Bierstuben. Singles without bath are 30 DM ($17.21); with bath, 42 DM ($24.09). Doubles without bath are 60 DM ($34.42); with private bath, 74 DM ($42.45). Off-season there is a 10% reduction (January 8 to 31, April 1 to June 30, and October 1 to December 15). The hotel is closed from November 1 to December 15.

BUDGET LODGINGS: Haus Erika, 45 Wettersteinstrasse (tel. 48-09), a five-minute walk from the railway station, offers not rooms, but low-cost apartments with kitchens and shower baths. However, you must book one for at least three days. The tariff for one day is 25 DM ($14.34) in a single apartment, 50 DM ($28.68) in a double. The apartments contain balconies, opening onto beautiful mountain views. The personable owner speaks English fluently.

Gastehaus Villa Maunz, 42 Mittenwalderstrasse (tel. 504-66), is a cluster of completely furnished apartments in a Tyrolean-style building at the edge of town where Mr. and Mrs. Maunz rent apartments by the week or month. Their apartment house villa is white, with a blue overhanging roof and shutters. Decorative murals adorn the facade. In a fine residential section, the apartments come in various sizes and are especially good bargains for families. You have every home comfort, as well as private balconies and personalized furnishings with complete kitchens. The two-bedroom apartment rents for 63 DM ($36.14) daily, accommodating four persons. A lower apartment, housing from six to eight guests, costs 80 DM ($45.80) daily. This latter apartment has its own washer and dryer as well as four beds.

Gastehaus Steffi, 40 Wettersteinstrasse (tel. 22-61), is a newly built chalet, with the atmosphere of a private home. It's placed pleasantly in a large garden, and most bedrooms open onto an encircling wooden balcony, providing unmarred views of the mountains. The house is only a few minutes' walk from the railway station. Ruth Manz, the owner, has 19 well-arranged and decorated rooms for rent, and her prices are reasonable. Singles rent for 24 DM ($13.77), and doubles cost from 36 DM ($20.65) to 48 DM ($27.53). These tariffs include breakfast. Rooms are equipped with private baths as well. In addition, there's a reception lounge with TV.

Gasthof Fraundorfer, 24 Ludwigstrasse (tel. 21-76), in Partenkirchen, is a family-owned inn, directly on the main street of the town, just a five-minute walk from the old church. Its original style has not been updated, and it successfully retains the character of another day. Altogether there are three floors under a sloping roof, with a facade brightly decorated with window boxes of red geraniums and decorative murals depicting a family feast. You'll be in the midst of village center activities, near interesting shops and excellent restaurants. The bedrooms are pleasant, comfortable, and adequately furnished, yet quite simple. Owners Josef and Barbara Fraundorfer are proud of their country-style meals. Depending on the plumbing, singles range in price from 22 DM ($12.62) to 27 DM ($15.49); doubles, from 44 DM ($25.24) to 55 DM ($31.55).

Maria Plachi, 10 Griesstrasse (tel. 560-52), is a newly built little chalet in the heart of Garmisch, almost behind the church on the heartbeat Marienplatz. It's freshly painted, with rooms costing the same price all year. Long balconies overhang the street and the garden in the rear. The guest house is easy to find, as it's located behind the Clausings Posthotel. Rented out are eight rooms which are kept sparkling clean by the hostess herself, Maria Plachi. Guests in the bedrooms share the baths. Rates are 14 DM ($8.03) per person, based on either single or double occupancy.

READERS' LODGING SELECTIONS: "The **Gästehaus Sebastian Trenkler,** 20 Kreuzstrasse (tel. 34-39), is a beautiful, clean, small, happy place with a splendid view of the Zugspitze, run by a friendly German woman (Frau Trenkler) and her husband. Our bill included American-style breakfasts and baths with plenty of hot water. Doubles rent for 40 DM ($22.94) to 45 DM ($25.81). Highly recommended" (J. Fitzgerald, Captain, U.S. Navy). . . . **"Zur Schönen Aussicht,** 36 Gsteigstrasse (tel. 24-74), is good, with beautiful views, removed from the noise of downtown and handy to hiking. Doubles range from 44 DM ($25.24) to 60 DM ($34.42) with private bath; bathless singles, 26 DM ($14.91)" (Dr. John A. Fust, Erie, Penna.). . . . "We found a lovely guest house, **Weyerhof Gästehaus,** 5 Partnachauen, where we paid 44 DM ($25.24) a night for a double without bath, breakfast included. A double with bath goes for 55 DM ($31.55). The owner, Irene Weyer, is so nice she even loaned us an umbrella when it was pouring rain" (Mr. and Mrs. Peter Kurtz, Fort Lauderdale, Fla.). . . . "In town, through the tunnel at the railroad station with signs to the Zugspitzbahn, is the beautifully decorated **Haus Helga,** 31 Achenfeldstrasse, alongside the Alpine Theater on the grounds of the U.S. Army Recreation Center. A single room costs 25 DM ($14.34), including breakfast, with more new marble floors than in the castles toured. As one is next to the Recreation Center, I found it easy to utilize the International Grill for inexpensive meals and the theater for American movies. Reminder, have American currency and they will not ask for the 'necessary' military I.D." (Robert F. Fera, Orchard Lake, Mich.). . . . "At the **Hotel Alpengruss,** 10 Gehfeldstrasse (tel. 26-16), we had a superbly clean, big twin-bedded room, with completely free access to the piping-hot showers, at a cost of 45 DM ($25.81) for two persons nightly. The tariff included a continental breakfast. The manager offers one of the best values in the resort" (Charlotte Wells, Artarmon, Australia). . . . "We found an excellent pension in Garmisch-Partenkirchen, the **Haus Royal,** 10 St.-Martin-Strasse. It has large rooms with private balconies, nicely furnished and immaculate. A public toilet and shower are convenient, and towels adequate. An ample continental breakfast is included in the 45-DM ($25.81) charge for two persons in twin beds. The host and hostess, Herr and Frau Steiners, are friendly and speak a little English" (Ann and C. B. Coe, Newport News, Va.).

WHERE TO DINE: Reindl's Drei Mohren, 65 Ludwigstrasse, Partenkirchen (tel. 20-75), is one of the best places to eat, and offers an outstanding choice of Bavarian dishes. The restaurant was built in 1873 and is created in a cozy, rustic style, where you can rub shoulders with the local characters. Each day a specialty is offered, made after Bavarian recipes from the 19th century. There is a wide choice of fish and game dishes. Most fish dishes cost from 8 DM ($4.59) to 17 DM ($9.75). Desserts cost from 2.20 DM ($1.26) to 4.50 DM

($2.58). An Irish coffee at 7 DM ($4.02) rounds off the meal, or perhaps an espresso at 2.20 DM ($1.26).

Posthotel Partenkirchen, 49 Ludwigstrasse in Partenkirchen (tel. 5-10-67), is renowned for its distinguished cuisine—in fact, its reputation is known throughout Bavaria. The interior dining rooms are rustic with lots of mellow, old-fashioned atmosphere. You could imagine meeting Dürer here. Everything seems comfortably subdued, including the guests. Perhaps the best way to dine here is to order one of the set menus, costing 18.50 DM ($10.61) and 28.50 DM ($16.35). These table d'hôte selections change daily, depending on the availability of seasonal produce. The à la carte menu is long and extensive, featuring such products of the season as game in the autumn. Among the selections, you can order delicious soups such as fresh cauliflower at 3.50 DM ($2.01), followed by such main dishes as veal schnitzel Cordon Bleu at 22 DM ($12.62) or a mixed grill St. James at 24 DM ($13.77). The wienerschnitzel served here with a large salad at 17.50 DM ($10.04) is the best we'd had in the resort. Or else you may prefer the entrecôte Café de Paris at 23 DM ($13.19), another fine dish.

Reindl Grill, in the Partenkirchner Hof, 15 Bahnhofstrasse (tel. 5-80-25), pleases many vacationing diners who have memories of lingering after dinner on its terrace in the warmth of a summer evening. Knowledgeable locals eat here too, and have done so for years. The grill is a first-class restaurant in every sense of the word. The whole atmosphere is very pleasant and the service commendable.

For a good opening to a fine repast, we'd suggest the salad Niçoise at 8 DM ($4.59) or else the hors d'oeuvres Reidl Grill, a good, tasty selection, costing 12 DM ($6.88). Or perhaps you'll go for the Lady Curzon soup at 5.50 DM ($3.15). Among main dishes, we'd recommend fondue bourguignonne for two, costing 21 DM ($12.05) per person or else half a grilled chicken Diable at 15 DM ($8.60). Among the fish dishes, we'd suggest fried scampi with remoulade sauce at 17 DM ($9.75) or else sole meunière at 23 DM ($13.19). We're also fond of the filet goulasch Stroganoff at 22 DM ($12.62).

For dessert, you can select a peach Melba at 6 DM ($3.44), or something more spectacular, a Salzburger nockerl for two at a cost of 6 DM per person. The restaurant is closed from mid-November to mid-December.

Goldener Engel, am Marienplatz (tel. 5-66-77), in the heart of Garmisch, is a beer stube and wine cellar, a rustic tavern in the vicinity of the Clausings Post Hotel. Your waiter is likely to wish you *guten appetit.* The place has an old-fashioned atmosphere, but not a faded look. In the autumn, Bavarians like to journey here to enjoy the game specialties, including deer stew with bread dumplings and stuffed pear at 13.50 DM ($7.74), or perhaps roast venison at 18 DM ($10.32) and roast wild boar at 21 DM ($12.05). At any time of the year you can order a sirloin steak at 16.50 DM ($9.30) or else pork hock with potato dumplings and a salad at 9.50 DM ($5.45). Fine fish is also served, including filet of sea bass at 8.50 DM ($4.88). The facade of the building is colorfully decorated in the Bavarian style.

THE VILLAGE BAR: Bei Werner's Stehausschank, Marienplatz, behind the Clausings Posthotel, is the tiniest little bar on the narrowest little street in Garmisch. It's easily spotted as you pass over a churning little stream with a splashing water wheel. It has a front bar, with its intricate woodcarving and a miniature little room in the rear with three tables. If you go here for a beer, you get caught up in a convivial atmosphere. Nothing is fancied up for tourists. The decor is hodgepodge—woodcarvings, an artificial fireplace, a rustic split-log dado, and an antler chandelier. If you're in Garmisch for long, chances are you'll make the place your "local."

ON THE OUTSKIRTS AT MURNAU: Alpenhof Murnau, 8 Ramsach-strasse (tel. 10-45), is a deluxe hotel and restaurant lying halfway between Munich and Innsbruck, off the autobahn leading to Garmisch-Partenkirchen, 15 miles to the south. Set in hilly terrain, the hotel lies in a large, pasture-like park. It's built chalet style with a widely spread, overhanging roof. Bowers of red geraniums are placed at the windows in summer. Its bedrooms are built like a motel-style Spanish hacienda, forming a courtyard. Each unit has a generous covered balcony. The view from every room is beautiful and restful.

The Alpenhof is a member of the highly selective Relais de Campagne, which means that it pampers its guests in style. The bedrooms are highly individualized, some with modern canopy beds, Oriental rugs, and a spacious bed-sitting room combination area. Singles range from 68 DM ($39) to 85 DM ($48.76); doubles, 95DM ($54.49) to 180 DM ($103.25). Tariffs include breakfast as well.

The restaurant is the best in the area. The cuisine is inspired, and the service is attentive, informal yet courteous. The dining room is in a stylized chalet style, with white plaster walls, a decorative wooden-beamed ceiling, and highback Windsor chairs. Adjoining is a wine stube created in an idealized tavern style, reminiscent of Spanish paradors.

You can order the gourmet menu at 78 DM ($44.74) or else make selections from the à la carte menu. We'd definitely recommend the chef's specialty, the soup of mussels, costing 8 DM ($4.59). For a main course, we'd suggest the veal fricassee, 17.50 DM ($10.04), or the lammsattel "fines herbes" with gratin Dauphinois, 30 DM ($17.21). For dessert, the specialty is soufflé glacé Grand Marnier, 6.50 DM ($3.73). The talented chef is Peter Ahlgrimm, who studied in France.

The Alpenhof Murnau can be used as a break on the trip from Munich to Austria. In fact, it's possible to check in after a transatlantic flight from America. Just pick up a rental car at the airport, get on the autobahn, and before you know it you're enveloped in peace and beauty. Have a swim in the garden pool, an exquisite lunch, and a nap on your balcony with its view of the Alps.

3. Chiemsee

THE SIGHTS: Although many resorts line the shores of Bavaria's largest lake, the main attractions of Chiemsee are on its two islands, Herrenchiemsee and Frauenchiemsee. From the liveliest resort, **Prien,** on the west shore, you can reach either or both of the islands via the lake steamers which make regular trips throughout the spring and summer. The round-trip fare is 4 DM ($2.29) for Herrenchiemsee, 6 DM ($3.44) for both islands.

Frauenchiemsee

Frauenchiemsee, also called Fraueninsel, is the smaller of the two islands. Along its sandy shore stands a fishing village, whose 60 boats drag the lake for its famous pike and salmon. At the festival of Corpus Christi, these boats are covered with flowers and streamers while the fishermen are dressed in Bavarian garb. The girls of the village are dressed as brides as the boats circle the island, stopping at each corner to sing the Gospels. The island is also the home of a Benedictine nunnery, originally founded in 782. The convent is known for a product called Kloster Likör—literally translated, that's cloister liqueur. Sold by nuns in black cowls with white-winged headgarb, it is supposed to be an "agreeable stomach elixir."

Herrenchiemsee

Herrenchiemsee, also called Herreninsel, is the most popular tourist attraction on the lake because of the fantastic castle—**Neues Schloss**—begun by Ludwig II here in 1878. Although never completed because of the king's death in 1886, the castle was to have been a replica of the grand palace of Versailles, which Ludwig so greatly admired. A German journalist once wrote, "The Palace, a monument to uncreative megalomania and as superfluous as the artificial castle ruins of the 19th century, is an imposing postlude of feudal architectural grandeur nonetheless." One of the architects of Herrenchiemsee was Julius Hofmann, whom the king had also employed for the construction of his fantastic Alpine castle, Neuschwanstein. When the work was halted in 1885, only the center of the enormous palace had been completed. Surrounded by woodlands of beech and fir, the palace and its formal gardens remain one of the most fascinating of Ludwig's adventures, in spite of their unfinished state.

The entrance to the palace is lit by a huge skylight over the sumptuously decorated state staircase. Symbolic frescoes personifying the four states of man's existence are alternated with Greek and Roman statues set in niches on the staircase and in the gallery above. The vestibule is adorned with a pair of enameled peacocks, the favorite bird of Louis XIV.

The **State Bedroom** is brilliant to the point of gaudiness, with practically every inch of the room covered with gilt. On the dais, instead of a throne, stands the richly decorated state bed, its purple velvet draperies weighing more than 300 pounds. Separating the dais from the rest of the room is a carved wooden balustrade covered with gold leaf. On the ceiling is a huge fresco depicting the descent of Apollo, surrounded by the other gods of Olympus. The sun god's features bear a strong resemblance to Louis XIV.

The **Great Hall of Mirrors** is unquestionably the most splendid hall in the palace, and probably the most authentic replica of Versailles. The 17 door panels contain enormous mirrors reflecting the 33 crystal chandeliers and the 44 gilded candelabra. More than 4000 candles are used to illuminate this hall, where concerts of chamber music are given on Saturday evenings throughout the summer. The vaulted ceiling is covered with 25 paintings depicting the life of Louis XIV. At the entrance to what would have been the private apartments of the king (Ludwig spent less than three weeks in the palace), is a small hall of mirrors, with mirrored panels set into the marble walls.

The **Dining Room** is a popular attraction for visitors because of the table nicknamed "the little table that lays itself." A mechanism in the floor permitted the table to go down to the room below to be cleaned and relaid between each course of the meal. Over the table hangs the largest porcelain chandelier in the world, produced by Meissen, the most valuable single item in the whole palace.

The **Royal Bedroom** is the only room in the palace to make use of rich solid colors on the walls. Set in gilded panels, royal blue silk which matches the fabric of the draperies and canopy over the bed offsets the gilded ceiling and furnishings of the room. Separating the bed from the rest of the room is a gilded balustrade like that in the throne room.

You can visit Herrenchiemsee at any time of the year. In summer, tour hours are from 9 a.m. to 5 p.m., and in winter, from 10 a.m. to 4 p.m.

Admission (in addition to the round-trip boat fare) is 4 DM ($2.29) for adults. Students and children pay 2 DM ($1.15). If you attend the Saturday evening concerts in summer, you will see yet another side of the palace. After dark, the rooms are lit by thousands of candles, sweeping you back into the magnificent period of the French court of Louis XVI—but with a definite Bavarian touch.

A RESORT HOTEL AT PRIEN: **Reinhart mit Golf Hotel,** 117 Seestrasse (tel. 10-45), has the most favored position on the lake, with a view of the castle on the crown of the island. It's a pleasant villa—just a two-minute walk to the ferry boat—in an agreeable setting with surrounding gardens, an overhanging roof and balconies, and a dining room extension, providing a lake view. The Golf portion of the hotel is an annex with its own putting course. Its picture windows overlook the lake and Alps. The cheapest per-person rate, including breakfast, is 30 DM ($17.21) in a bathless room and 40 DM ($22.94) with bath. The full-board cost per person ranges from 54 DM ($30.97) to 64 DM ($36.71). Use of the swimming pool is free, but the sauna for two costs 8 DM ($4.59). For dinner, you can choose between a simple set meal for 17 DM ($9.75), or try some of the local dishes, such as fresh fish from the Chiemsee, for 18 DM ($10.32). Soups begin at 3 DM ($1.72). Closed from October 15 to Easter.

4. Oberammergau

If you were an actor in this Alpine village, you'd be wise to find another trade to occupy you since the only theatrical production presented here is the world-famous Passion Play—with performances ten years apart. Surely the world's longest running show (in more ways than one), it began in 1634 as the result of a vow taken by the town's citizens after they were spared from the devastating plague of 1633. Lasting about eight hours, the play is divided into episodes, each of which is introduced by an Old Testament tableau connecting the incidents of Christ's suffering to the predictions of the great Prophets.

THE SIGHTS: If you visit Oberammergau on an "off" year, you can still see the **modern theater,** at the edge of town. The roofed auditorium holds only 5200 spectators, but the open-air stage is a wonder of engineering, with a curtained center stage flanked by gates opening onto the streets of Jerusalem. Although the theater and production methods are modern, the spirit of the play is marked by the medieval tradition of involving the entire community in its production. The 124 speaking parts are taken by amateur actors from the surrounding villages. The rest of the community seems to be included in the crowd scenes. The impressive array of scenery, props, and costumes is open to the public daily. The Passion Play is scheduled for the season of May through September of 1980.

Warning: It will be impossible to secure rooms in Oberammergau until after September of 1980, unless you book early in advance through a travel agent. If you're planning to visit from May to September of that year, without prepaid arrangements, you should book hotel rooms in surrounding areas, and even these are likely to be filled as well.

Admission tickets to see the Passion Play may be obtained only in connection with arrangements for lodgings and food. Accommodation arrangements are classified into about a dozen groups, including the tickets for performances. On the two-day arrangement, costs range from 191 DM ($109.55) to 375 DM ($215.60). You start with dinner on the evening prior to the play, terminating with breakfast on the day following the performance. Rates quoted include all meals.

For plays on Sundays there will be only one-night bookings, from Saturday to Sunday. The range is between 152 DM ($87.19) and 258 DM ($147.99), including meals. An advance booking fee of 8% on the total amount is added.

Aside from the actors, Oberammergau's most respected citizens include another unusual group—the woodcarvers, many of whom have been trained in the woodcarver's, school in the village. You'll see many examples of this old art form throughout the town, on the painted cottages and inns, in the church-yard and in the **Museum on the Dorfstrasse,** which has a notable collection of Christmas crèches—all hand-carved and painted—from the 18th through the 20th centuries. Also worth seeing on a walk through the village are the houses painted with frescoes by Franz Zwink (18th century) and named after fairytale cottages, such as the "Hansel and Gretel House" and the "Little Red Riding Hood House."

THE TOP INN: Alois Lang, 15 St.-Lukas-Strasse (tel. 41-41), is a name that brings memories to seasoned travelers who have made pilgrimages to the Passion Play in Oberammergau. It was in 1929 that handsome, long-haired Alois Lang was elected by the village to play the role of Christ in the pageant. Long ago the custom originated of the players having—as paying guests in their homes—visitors who came to see the now-famous production.

Within walking distance of the village center, his rustic home, now run by Fritz Lang, was built chalet style, with long bedroom extensions. The accommodations are modern Bavarian style, the beds are soft, and all is kept immaculately. Meals are elaborate, including international specialties in addition to local dishes. Be sure to try the onion soup. Equally individual is the saddle of venison in cream sauce. And to show how sophisticated this once-simple place has become, it now offers crêpes Alois Lang. You may want to dine in the inner tavern, or on the open sun terrace, where you can enjoy a view of the mountains.

All rooms have private baths. For a single, the rate ranges from 55 DM ($31.55) to 80 DM ($45.89); for a twin-bedded room, from 80 DM ($45.89) to 150 DM ($86.04). During the height of the season, pension rates are required. Half pension pays an additional 20 DM ($11.47) per person; full pension, 35 DM ($20.08) per person. The inn has a sauna, a fitness center, and the biggest private hotel park in the whole area.

THE MIDDLE BRACKET: Wolf Hotel-Restaurant, 1 Dorfstrasse (tel. 47-31), is an overgrown Bavarian chalet, right in the heart of village life. Its facade is consistent for the area, with an encircling balcony, heavy timbering, and window boxes spilling cascades of red and pink geraniums. Inside it has some of the local flavor, although certain concessions have been made: an elevator, conservative modern bedroom furnishings, a great dining hall with zigzag paneled ceiling, and Windsor chairs. The Keller is a regional rustic place for beer drinking as well as light meals.

The per-person rate for room with breakfast is 24 DM ($13.77) to 28 DM ($16.06), and for half board, 36 DM ($20.65) to 40 DM ($22.94)—for a minimum stay of three days. For private bath, toilet, and telephone, each person pays a supplement of 10 DM ($5.74), 9 DM ($5.16) for a shower. Reductions are made for children under 12.

Dining at the Wolf is economical and gracious. There are three set meals, 11 DM ($6.31), 14 DM ($8.03), and 16 DM ($9.18), although there are also à la carte listings at low prices. The soup of the day is 2 DM ($1.15), roast pork with dumplings and cabbage is 9.50 DM ($5.45), and wienerschnitzel with baked potato and salad is 14 DM ($8.03). The helpings are generous.

Alte Post, 19 Dorfstrasse (tel. 5-17), is a provincial inn, right in the heart of the village, with lots of Bavarian character. It is chalet style, with a wide, overhanging roof, green shuttered windows painted with decorative trim, a large carved crucifix on the facade, and tables set on a sidewalk under a long awning. It's the social hub of the village. The interior has storybook charm, with a beamed ceiling, tavern-style decor, a ceiling-high green ceramic stove, alpine chairs, and shelves of pewter plates.

Bedrooms are rustic, with beamed wooden ceilings, wide beds with giant posts, and, from most rooms, a view. Bathless singles are 23 DM ($13.19). Bathless doubles are 48 DM ($27.53); 54 DM ($30.97) with full bath. Breakfast is included. A main dining room is equally rustic, with a collection of hunting memorabilia. There is an intimate drinking bar. The restaurant provides excellent Bavarian dishes. There is a set menu of 11.50 DM ($6.60) for four courses, and another more splurgy one for 17 DM ($9.75). On the à la carte menu, main dishes average 10 DM ($5.74) to 14 DM ($8.03).

Hotel Schilcherhof, 17 Bahnhofstrasse (tel. 47-40), is an enlarged chalet with surrounding gardens and a new wing which provides excellent rooms. There's even a small group of apartments. In the summertime the terrace overflows with festive living and lots of beer. Five minutes away lies the Passion Theater, and also nearby, the Ammer River flows through the village. In the high season it's not easy to get a room here unless you make reservations well in advance. The per-person cost in a double ranges from 23 DM ($13.19) to 29 DM ($16.63). The cost in a single ranges from 26 DM ($14.91) to 32 DM ($18.36). Tariffs include breakfast. Although the house is built in the old style, with wooden front balconies and tiers of flower boxes, it has a fresh, new look to it.

Gasthaus Zum Stern, 33 Dorfstrasse (tel. 867), is an old-style inn where friendliness permeates, especially in the grand tavern with its huge green tiled heating stove, overhead lantern lights, and mountain-style stools. The bedrooms are consistently Alpine style, with deeply set windows, beds with fluffy eiderdowns, and hot and cold running water basins. Baths and toilets are found along the corridors. The innkeeper, Eberhard Siegmund, successfully runs a fine place with simply, although attractively furnished rooms. The per-person rate in a bathless room is 22 DM ($12.62), including a substantial breakfast. If you require a private bath, the charge rises to 26 DM ($14.91) per person.

BUDGET ACCOMMODATIONS: There are more than 100 private homes in Oberammergau which have bedrooms set aside for tourists. They are inexpensive and provide an opportunity to meet the villagers. A full list, with details such as prices and bath facilities, is available by going to or writing to the **Tourist Office,** 8103 Oberammergau, West Germany. A reservation form can be secured in advance. Usually the accommodation is in a rustic chalet (often newly built) with flower boxes at the windows, scrubbed and polished rooms, and soft beds with fluffy eiderdowns. Prices generally include a home-style breakfast, taxes, and service.

A few of the homes charge 12 DM ($6.88) per person, although the average price is 15 DM ($8.60). There are no private baths, and occasionally you are charged 2 DM ($1.15) for a bath or shower in the corridor. All the houses have central heating; many contain balconies and offer TV in the living room, plus parking space.

READER'S HOTEL SELECTION: "If I ever go back to Oberammergau, I will hope to stay at the clean attractive place of **Herr Wilheim Weber.** For one night, a single room costs 17 DM ($9.75), dropping to 16 DM ($9.18) if you stay longer. It is a lovely, quiet place on the outskirts of town behind the little railroad station. Mrs. Weber speaks some English and serves a generous breakfast" (Emily Hickey, Baileys Harbor, Wisc.).

Schloss Linderhof

Just eight miles west of the village, until the late 19th century, stood a modest hunting lodge on a large piece of land owned by the Bavarian royal family. In 1869, "Mad Ludwig" struck again, this time creating in the Ammergau Mountains a French rococo palace. Unlike Ludwig's palace at Chiemsee, the Linderhof was not meant to be a copy of any other structure of the past. And unlike his castle at Neuschwanstein, its concentration of fanciful projects and designs was not limited to the interior of the palace itself. In fact, the gardens and smaller buildings at Linderhof are, if anything, more delightful than the two-story main structure.

As you stand on the steps in front of the castle's white stone facade, you'll note that the ground floor is rather plain, with almost a complete lack of decoration, while the upper story is adorned with relief columns alternated with niches occupied by statues of mythological figures. In the center, over the three arched portals, is a large statue of Victory. Towering above the gable with its oval windows is a huge statue of Atlas supporting a world that seems just a bit too much for even him.

The most interesting rooms inside the palace are on the second floor, where ceilings are much higher because of the unusual roof plan. Ascending the winged staircase of Carrara marble, you'll find yourself at the West Gobelin Room (Music Room), with carved and gilded paneling and richly colored tapestries. This leads directly into the **Hall of Mirrors.** The mirrors are set in white and gold panels, richly decorated with gilded woodcarvings. The ceiling of this room is decorated with frescoes depicting mythological scenes—the birth of Venus and the judgment of Paris are shown here.

The two side rooms are oval shaped, each having a smaller, horseshoe-shaped anteroom. The eastern room is the **dining room,** mirrored and decorated with marble fireplaces, mythological sculptures, and an elaborately carved and gilded sideboard. The table, like that at Chiemsee, could be raised and lowered through the floor to permit the servants in the room below to reset the various courses without intruding on the shy king's privacy.

The **king's bedchamber** is the largest room in the palace, and situated in the back, overlooking the Fountain of Neptune and the cascades in the gardens. In the tradition of Louis XIV, who often received visitors in his bedchamber, the king's bed is closed off by a magnificent carved and gilded balustrade.

Even more impressive than the palace is the park in which it stands. In the popular style of the previous century, Ludwig laid out the gardens in formal parterres with geometrical shapes, baroque sculptures, and elegant fountains. The front of the palace opens onto a large pool with a piece of gilded statuary in its center. From the statue grouping a jet of water sprays 105 feet into the air.

The steep slopes behind the palace lent themselves well to the arrangement of a long cascade, made up of 32 marble steps and adorned with vases and cherubs. At the base of the cascade is the Fountain of Neptune, surrounded by a bed of flowers. Surrounding these formal terrace and garden designs is a large

English Garden, merging almost imperceptibly into the thick forests of the Ammergau.

The park also contains several other small, but fascinating, buildings—including the **Moorish Kiosk,** where Ludwig often spent hours, smoking chibouk and dreaming of himself as an Oriental prince. Unique is the **"magic grotto,"** built of artificial rock with stalagmites and stalactites dividing the cavelike room into three chambers. One wall of the grotto is painted with a scene of the Venus Mountain from *Tannhäuser.* The main chamber is occupied by an artificial lake illuminated from below, and has an artificial current produced by 24 dynamo engines. A shell-shaped boat, completely gilded, is tied to the platform called the "Lorelei Rock."

The fantasy and grandeur of Linderhof is open to the public throughout the year and makes a day trip from Munich, as well as Oberammergau. During the summer, hours are from 9 a.m. to noon and from 1 to 5 p.m. In winter, hours are from 9 to noon and from 1 to 4 p.m. Admission is 4.50 DM ($2.58) in summer, 3 DM ($1.72) in winter. The Moorish Kiosk and magic grotto are opened only from April 1 till September 30 because of snow.

A short drive from Oberammergau leads to:

Ettal Abbey

In a valley sheltered by the steep hills of the Ammergau, the Ettal Abbey was founded by the Emperor Ludwig the Bavarian in 1330. Monks, knights, and their ladies shared the honor of guarding the statue of the Virgin, attributed to Giovanni Pisano. In the 18th century, the golden age of the abbey, there were about 70,000 pilgrims every year. The Minster of Our Lady in Ettal is one of the finest examples of Bavarian rococo architecture in existence. Around the polygonal core of the church is a two-story gallery. An impressive baroque facade was built from a plan based on designs of Enrico Zuccali. Inside, visitors stand under a vast dome, admiring the fresco painted by Joh. Jacob Zeiller in the summers of 1751 and 1752.

5. Mittenwald

Seeming straight out of *The Sound of Music,* the year-round resort of Mittenwald lies in a pass in the Karwendel Range through which heavy commercial traffic once passed. The roads to the village are kept busy today as well, but the traffic now is mainly tourists who flock here with cameras and walking shoes.

Before setting out for the 60 some miles of paths winding up and down the mountains around the village, you will want to take a look at the old market town itself. Especially noteworthy—and photogenic—are the painted Bavarian houses with their overhanging eaves. Even the tower of the baroque church is covered with frescoes. On the square stands a monument to Mathias Klotz, who introduced the town's major industry—violin making—to Mittenwald in 1684. The town's museum has exhibits devoted to violins and other stringed instruments, from their conception through the various stages of their evolution.

Mittenwald also has excellent spa facilities, in large gardens landscaped with tree-lined streams and trout pools. Concerts are given during the summer in the modern music pavilion.

The most popular activities are the daily excursions into the countryside, where you are constantly exposed to refreshing changes in the scenery of the Wetterstein and Karwendel Ranges. Besides hiking through the hills on your own, you can take part in mountain-climbing expeditions, trips by horse and carriage, or coach tours from Mittenwald to the nearby villages of Bavaria. In the evening, you are treated to typical Bavarian entertainment, often consisting of folk dancing or singing, zither playing, and yodeling, but you also have your choice of spa concerts, dance bands, and cinemas.

THE INNS: Wetterstein Hotel, 1–3 Dekan-Karl-Platz (tel. 50-08), which looks like a simple country inn, with a trompe l'oeil facade in true Bavarian style, is one of the most beautiful buildings in Mittenwald and has much to offer. Inside are attractive rooms for lounging and dining and an old-fashioned bar and restaurant, the Bartholomäusstube, for drinks. There is also a sauna and massage room, as well as a heated swimming pool. Bedrooms have the alpine touch. Rates include breakfast and use of the pool. You can spend some happy hours in the hotel bar, Zur Hölle. Bathless singles are 40 DM ($22.94) to 44 DM ($25.24); with shower or bath, 48 DM ($27.53) to 56 DM ($32.12). Bathless doubles range from 70 DM ($40.15) to 75 DM ($43.02); with bath, 75 DM ($43.02) to 105 DM ($60.23). Add to this 18 DM ($10.32) for half board or 28 DM ($16.06) for all meals (required during busy periods, in order to get space). In summer, saddle horses can be rented, and in winter sleighrides are available. Each room has a radio and a telephone. If you stop only for a meal, the set offerings are 10.50 DM ($6.02) to 23.50 DM ($13.48), including soup of the day and dessert.

Alpenrose, 1 Obermarkt (tel. 50-55), has about everything one could hope for in an Alpine village inn. It's right in the center of the village, at the foot of a rugged mountain. The facade of the hotel is covered with decorative designs, with window boxes holding flowering vines. The basic structure of the inn is 14th century, although refinements, additions, and improvements have been made over the years. The present inn is truly comfortable, with modern plumbing facilities.

Its tavern room, overlooking the street, has many ingratiating features, including coved ceilings (one decoratively painted), handmade Alpine chairs, flagstone floors, and a square tiled stove in the center where one huddles during the winter months. In the cellar is the Josefikeller, where beer is served in giant steins and in the evenings musicians gather to entertain guests. The dining room provides many excellent meals, including Bavarian specialties.

Just as winning as the public rooms are the attractive bedrooms, with wood ceilings and a few antique reproductions, which are decoratively painted. In a single room, the rate ranges from 28.50 DM ($16.35) to 45 DM ($25.81) nightly, depending on the plumbing. The per-person rate in a double runs from 25 DM ($14.34) to 39 DM ($22.37), these tariffs including breakfast. The half-pension rate begins at 35 DM ($20.08) per person, going up to 50 DM ($28.68).

Rieger Hotel, 28 Dekan-Karl-Platz (tel. 17-40), is an attractive Bavarian hotel, whether snow is piled up outside or the window boxes are cascading with petunias. It's authentic, with overhanging roof, balconies, shuttered windows, and primitive murals on its facade. There are two reasons for its popularity: one is the family-style living room with beamed ceiling, wide arches, and table and armchair groupings around a three-sided open fireplace. The other attractive feature is the indoor swimming pool with a picture-window wall. Add to this room for sauna and massages (segregated except on Monday—family time—when both sexes join the crowd).

While prices are modest for room and breakfast only, you would be better advised to stay here on the full-board rate. Depending on the plumbing, the rate

with three meals a day goes from 53 DM ($30.40) to 79 DM ($45.31). Fashionably decorated, the bedrooms are pleasant and comfortable. The dining room
has a view of the Alps.

Post Hotel, 9 Obermarkt (tel. 10-94), is one of the more seasoned, established chalet hotels, housing guests all year. Owned by the Rademacher family,
it captures much of the charm required for a successful inn (the competition
is high). It's delightful to have breakfast here on the sun terrace (or on a
balcony), with a view of the Alps. Although the lobby is basic and simple
Bavarian, the tavern and dining room go all out with mountain-chalet decor—
black-and-white beams, a collection of deer antlers, and wood paneling. The
bedrooms are furnished in modern. While there are economical bed-and-break-
fast rates, you get a better buy at the full-board price. Winter rates are higher,
with full board costing 52 DM ($29.83) to 75 DM ($43.02) in a bathless double,
as against 48 DM ($27.53) to 55 DM ($31.55) in summer. With bath, the cost
is 62 DM ($35.56) to 80 DM ($45.89) in winter, 54 DM ($30.97) to 72 DM
($41.30) in summer. An indoor swimming pool, massage, and sauna are avail-
able.

WHERE TO DINE: Arnspitze, 68 Innsbruckerstrasse (tel. 10-57), is the finest
dining room in Mittenwald, housed in a chalet-style modern hotel on the
outskirts of the town. The restaurant is decorated in the old style with Alpine
features. The feeling that you can rely on the food turns out to be entirely
justified. The cookery is honesty and good—solid, satisfying, and wholesome.
You might order sole with homemade noodles or else veal steak in a creamy
smooth sauce, topped off by the dessert specialty, guglhupf-parfait Wipfelder.
For a meal composed of soup or hors d'oeuvres, a main dish with vegetables,
plus a dessert, you are likely to pay anywhere from 25 DM ($14.34) to 55 DM
($31.55). The restaurant shuts down from October 20 to December 20.

6. Starnberger See

Less than 20 miles southwest of the capital of Bavaria, this large lake is
one of the mot popular with Münchners on holiday. From the water—steamer
cruises are frequent on the lake in summer—you can observe the change in
terrain from the low-lying marshlands on the north to the Alpine ranges
towering above the lake in the south. Around the 40-mile shoreline you can
observe no fewer than six castles, including the Schloss Berg, where Ludwig
II was sent after he was certified insane in 1886. It was in the Starnberger See
that Ludwig drowned himself, along with his doctor, just a few days after he
was deposed. A cross on the water marks the spot where his body was found.

MODERATE LAKESIDE VILLAS: Hotel Seehof, 4–6 Bahnhofplatz (tel.
12-220), is the lead resort on Starnberger See. The bedrooms are mainly modern
and comfortable, and most of them contain private baths or showers. Units
open onto views of the lake. Tariffs vary according to the season. The average
double rate is 90 DM ($51.62), with shower or bath, although these rooms go
up to 105 DM ($60.23). Bathless singles are priced at 50 DM ($28.68), going
up to 72 DM ($41.30) with complete bath. Rates include breakfast and taxes.
The rustic, intimate restaurant, Tessiner Stuben, with an open fireplace,
beamed ceilings, and efficient, friendly service, offers a full scale of local and
international specialties as well as drinks.

Strandhotel Schloss Berg, 17 Seestrasse (tel. 56-21), is a villa-cum-castle,
near the lake and right over the railroad, where everything is keyed to the

holiday mood. At times, especially on weekends, it seems as if half of Munich is sunning itself on summer days on the lakeside terrace (weekdays are more tranquil). It's so popular that a modern wing has been added, providing indoor and terrace dining rooms (one with open fireplace). Bedrooms are colorful, nicely furnished, and the more expensive rooms have lake views. Bathless singles are 46 DM ($26.39); with bath, 54 DM ($30.97). Bathless doubles are 80 DM ($45.89); with private bath, 100 DM ($57.36).

7. Tegernsee

Lying 30 miles southeast of Munich, this Alpine lake and the resort town on its eastern shore have the same name. Although small, this is one of the loveliest of the Bavarian lakes, with huge peaks seemingly rising right out of the water. The lake and its string of resort towns (the finest, we think, is Rottach-Egern) are popular year round. Because the lake is quite small, it freezes over early in winter, making it an attraction for skaters.

In the town of Tegernsee, the two major sights span some 12 centuries. The oldest of these is the Benedictine monastery, now turned into a castle and village church. The other attraction is a contemporary church, one of the finest examples of modern German architecture, designed by Olaf Gulbransson of Munich.

HOTELS IN ROTTACH-EGERN: Bachmair Hotel am See, 47 Seestrasse (tel. 64-44), is perhaps the most attractive, all-around resort establishment in the entire area. A world unto itself, with every conceivable recreational facility at your disposal, it is rich in the true Bavarian spirit. The complex of nine buildings is right on the lake, surrounded by lawns and park, with wide terraces under linden trees, red and white umbrellaed tables, a covered garden room with wall-to-wall windows, white wrought-iron furniture, and garlands of vines trailing over the ceiling. Outdoors is a large, free-form swimming pool, edged by lawns for sunbathing, and there's also a beautiful, covered pool where you can swim in any weather, enjoying the view of snow-capped mountains. Extensive buildings house facilities for the cure—saunas, special baths, and massage rooms. Additional attractions are a nightclub, mini-golf, skiing, boating, and aquatic sports, bowling, ice skating, and shuffleboard on ice during winter months.

The Bachmair's interior is stylized rustic, but done with sophistication. Baroque gilt carvings, religious paintings, and country-style furniture are mixed with elegant antiques and reproductions, including Louis XV, Directoire, and Biedermeier. Each of the many sitting rooms, lounges, cafes, and restaurants has its own particular style. In the evening, the Bavarian beer hall has ethnic dances, yodeling, and zither playing, as well as conventional dance music.

Bedrooms are dramatically conceived, again combining antiques, smart decorating tricks, and an eclectic combination of furnishings. Recommended are the full-board rates. Quoted are the high-season tariffs. All rooms now have private baths. Depending on the location, singles cost from 85 DM ($48.76) to 175 DM ($100.38), and doubles rent anywhere from 140 DM ($80.30) to 220 DM ($126.19). High season is December 20 to January 7, February 10 to March 25, and June 1 to October 31, plus three days at Easter.

Seehotel Überfahrt, 27 Überfahrt (tel. 2-60-01), is a medium-size chalet resort, facing the lake and surrounded by a spectacular view of the Alps. It is, in fact, more than a resort, also having fine spa facilities. Owned by the Hurler family, and recently built, it is a happy joining together of Bavarian rusticity and modern facilities. It has the typical Bavarian architecture, with balconies (big enough for sunbathing and breakfast) and window boxes with a profusion of flowers. The interior is attractive, upper level rustic, with stylish comfort. The living room has clusters of comfortable armchairs and sofas placed to allow an unspoiled view of the lake through room-wide windows. For dining, you can use the room with booths set against view windows, or choose the more formal red and brown room, with a stage and a dance floor for weekend entertainment. The tavern, with pine stools, red-covered tables, a slat-wood ceiling, and farm artifacts, is popular in the evening.

Bedrooms show the touch of a decorator's flair. Some rooms have terraces, some balconies, some sitting-room areas. TV is available. Recommended are full-pension rates, which are almost vital for admittance from July 1 through September 30, although half board is also acceptable during that period. According to the size and exposure of your room, you pay the following: singles with a shower bath rent for 60 DM ($34.42), peaking at 120 DM ($68.83) with complete bath and a view of the lake. Again, depending on the view and the plumbing, doubles range in price from 110 DM ($63.10) to 190 DM ($108.98). Full board costs from 101 DM ($57.93) to 165 DM ($94.64) per person daily. Use of the indoor swimming pool and parking space is free to guests.

Jaedicke Hotel, 19 Aribostrasse (tel. 64-90), is a secluded, attractive Bavarian retreat, originated by Carl Jaedicke, now deceased, who won national fame for his Berlin coffeehouse and its multitiered cake. Broad lawns, shady trees with garden furniture for leisurely and restful moments, wide, encircling balconies where you can catch the morning sun while having coffee—all combine to make this an idyllic spot. The main living room, with chocolate-brown walls and filmy white draperies, is rather formal and traditional (in the gracious sense), with light-blue upholstered chairs and sofas. The inner dining room has white and olive Louis XV chairs, set on ruby-red carpets, but most guests prefer lunch served on the large paved terrace, edged with shade trees. Bedrooms are consistently tasteful, with strong and smart color usage played against chalk-white walls. All are homelike and personalized.

Owner Anita Barkholder keeps the Jaedicke open from February 1 to November 1. A bathless single ranges from 34 DM ($19.50) to 44 DM ($25.24), increasing to between 40 DM ($22.94) and 42 DM ($24.09) with shower, and peaking at 72 DM ($41.30) to 78 DM ($44.74) with private bath. Bathless doubles cost from 69 DM ($39.58) to 75 DM ($43.02), going up to 85 DM ($48.76) with shower, and peaking at 189 DM ($108.41) for the best ones with complete baths. Depending on the room, half pension ranges from 55 DM ($31.55) to 98 DM ($56.21) per person.

Coming up next: a relatively unexplored section of Germany.

FRANCONIA AND THE GERMAN DANUBE

WHEN THE GOLDEN AGE of the Renaissance swept across Germany, it seemed to concentrate its full forces on the part of northern Bavaria which had once been a Frankish kingdom. In spite of history's tendency to destroy the past through progress and war, Franconia still holds some of Germany's greatest medieval and Renaissance treasures. From its feudal cities sprang some of the greatest artists the world has seen—Albert Dürer, Lucas Cranach, Veit Stoss, Adam Krafft, and many others. As a world center for important cultural events, Franconia draws music lovers from all over the world to its annual Mozart Festival in Würzburg and Wagner Festival in Bayreuth.

The hillsides of Franconia are dotted with well-preserved medieval castles, monasteries, and interesting churches. Part of the remarkable architecture of the region owes its beauty to the limestone range along the southern edge of the province. And between these hills and the edge of the Bavarian Forest is Germany's "other" river, the young Danube. It gradually builds up its force from the many smaller streams flowing out of the Alps and Swabian Jura until by the time it reaches the Austrian border at Passau, it is powerful enough to carry commercial ships and barges. Although not as important to the German economy as the Rhine, the Danube was responsible for the growth of several influential centers in centuries past, including . . .

1. Ulm

Ulm, lying at the strategic point on the Danube where the young stream beings to take on the form of a navigable river, has been a prosperous city since the Middle Ages.

THE SIGHTS: If you approach the town from the Stuttgart-Munich Autobahn, you'll miss the best view. So sometime during your visit, cross the Danube into Neu Ulm for a look at the gables and turrets of the Old Town lining the north bank of the river. Here is the **Fishermen's Quarter,** with its little medieval houses and tree-shaded squares. Nearby are the more elaborate Renaissance patrician houses and the Gothic-Renaissance Town Hall. But the skyline and the spirit of the whole town are dominated by its major attraction:

Ulm Cathedral (Münster)

Before you even reach the city, you'll recognize the skyline of Ulm by its towering cathedral, the landmark of the medieval town. Its steeple, at 528 feet, is the tallest in the world, and the Münster itself second only to the Cologne Cathedral among the huge Gothic structures of Christendom. Without the pews, the nave of the church could hold nearly 20,000 people—more than twice the population of Ulm at the time when the cathedral was begun in 1377! When Ulm joined the Protestant movement in the early 16th century, work was suspended after 151 years of continuous building. It was not resumed until 1844, and lasted until 1880. Miraculously, the cathedral escaped serious damage during the air raids of World War II.

The exterior is almost pure German Gothic, even though bricks were often used in the walls along with the more typical stone blocks. The unique feature of Ulm's Münster, however, is that the architects placed as much emphasis on the horizontal lines as the usual Gothic vertical look. Before entering, stop to admire the main porch, whose three massive arches lead to two renaissance doors. This section dates from the 14th and 15th centuries and contains a wealth of statues and reliefs. At the pillar between the two doors is the finest sculpture on the outside of the church, *Our Lord of Dolours,* by Hans Multscher (1429).

On the inside, you can climb the tower as far as the third gallery—all 768 steps—where you can look out on the town and surrounding countryside over the Danube plain as far as the Alps.

The five aisles of the cathedral lead directly from the hall below the tower through the nave to the east chancel. The conspicuous absence of a transept heightens the emphasis on the chancel and also increases the length of the nave. Each of the five aisles is enclosed by huge pillars towering into steep arches. Above them, the ceiling is swept into net-vaults so high that many of Germany's church steeples could sit comfortably beneath them. The nave is so large that, even with the pews, it can accommodate more than 11,000 people at one service.

Up the central aisle toward the chancel, you come to the 15th-century pulpit, carved with prophets, apostles and martyrs. Above the canopy is a second pulpit, symbolizing the Holy Spirit. Just to the left is a handsomely decorated tabernacle, containing the elements of the Eucharist. The wood panels, carved with figures, date from 1470.

The chancel is entered through baroque iron gates set in the "triumph arch." Above the arch is a fresco depicting the *Day of Judgment* (1471). The other treasures are diminished by the grand choir stalls carved by Jörg Syrlin the Elder between 1469 and 1474. The 89 seats of dark oak are divided into sections, marked by busts of biblical and heathen characters. The stalls on the north side of the chancel are adorned with figures of men; those on the south, of women. The panels behind the stalls are decorated with elaborate tracery, containing figures from the Old and New Testaments, as well as several saints.

The most attractive stained-glass windows of the chancel are in the little Besserer Chapel, on the south side behind the women's choir. The five windows in this room date from the 15th century and depict scenes from the Old and New Testaments. The main south window, from the same period, represents the Day of Judgment in striking colors and figures. Although most of the windows in the side aisles of the nave were destroyed in the war, the tall Gothic windows behind the chancel were preserved.

The Ulm Cathedral is open daily, except during services on Sunday mornings. From October through February, the hours are 8 a.m. to 4:45 p.m.; in March, from 5:45 p.m.; in April, until 6:45 p.m. Beginning in May, hours begin at 7 a.m., and in the busy months of July and August, the cathedral remains open until 7:45 p.m. Admission is .50 DM (29¢); to visit both the cathedral and the tower, you pay an admission price of 1 DM (57¢).

LOW-COST INNS: Ulmer Spatz, 27 Münsterplatz (tel. 6-80-81). This corner stucco hotel-and-restaurant combination has an "impudent" position, right at the side of the cathedral, with most of its bedrooms overlooking the tower. The decor here may be slightly overdone, but one exception is the little Weinstube, where tasty meals are served in a mellowed setting of wood paneling and an interesting collection of "things." The bedrooms are fairly priced. Bathless singles are 29 DM ($16.63) to 38 DM ($21.80); singles with bath, 50 DM ($28.68); bathless doubles, 50 DM ($28.68) to 57 DM ($32.70); doubles with bath, 70 DM ($40.15) to 100 DM ($57.36). Breakfast is included. Set meals cost 7.80 DM ($4.47) to 19 DM ($10.90), although the à la carte menu has interesting main dishes, such as roast pork Schwabisch art at 16.80 DM ($9.64) or rumpsteak, 18 DM ($10.32).

Schlossbräustüble, 2 Hintere Rebengasse (tel. 6-38-39), is a quiet oasis in a busy cathedral town. It's really a country inn, where meals and rooms share equal billing. In a house set back from a narrow lane, it lies a five-minute walk from the Dom. In the front courtyard are cafe tables and strings of electric lights for evening diners. Upstairs are 20 bedrooms, furnished with care. Singles without bath cost from 22 DM ($12.62) to 26 DM ($14.91); doubles without bath, 36 DM ($20.65) to 45 DM ($25.81)—breakfast included. Set meals range from 7.80 DM ($4.47) to 10.50 DM ($6.02).

WHERE TO DINE: Ratskeller, 1 Marktplatz, offers dining on almost any budget level. It's central, close to the cathedral, and features varied menus in a pleasing and restful atmosphere. It's fairly recently renovated, with comfortable leather chairs, among other things. There is no mad rush here—just dignified dining and attentive service. Set meals range from 7.50 DM ($4.30) to 9.75 DM ($5.59). On the à la carte menu you can order a wienerschnitzel at 13 DM ($7.46). Wines begin at 4.50 DM ($2.58). Desserts range from 3 DM ($1.72) to 5.50 DM ($3.15).

READERS' HOTEL SELECTIONS: "We found a charming hostess to greet us at **Hotel zum Jungen Hasen,** 19 Hirschstrasse (tel. 6-30-28), halfway between the cathedral and railroad station. The cost is 46 DM ($26.39) for a bathless double, 60 DM ($34.42) in a double with bath, service included" (Mrs. Berdena Koehler, Elmwood, Neb.). . . . "We recommend a small, lovely, family-run hotel, **Hotel Schwarzer Adler,** 20 Frauenstrasse (tel. 2-10-93). It's just a two-minute walk from the Münster. It costs 55 DM ($31.55) for a double room with a shower. Without a shower, the charge is 50 DM ($28.68). Singles are 28 DM ($16.06) without shower, 30 DM ($17.21) with. These prices include breakfast. The rooms were nicely furnished, spotlessly clean, and the shower was spacious with lots of hot water. The restaurant seemed to be popular with the local people, and the food

was inexpensive and good. Set meals range from 7 DM ($4.02) to 15.50 DM ($8.89)"
(Mrs. D. M. Olson, Edina, Minn.).

2. Aschaffenburg

Industry in recent years has not destroyed the pastoral illusion created by
the parks and shady lanes in and around this city on the Main. Just 26 miles
southeast of Frankfurt, it is the gateway to the streams and woodlands of the
Spessart Hills. With 250 garment manufacturers in the city, it has become the
production center for men's clothing in West Germany. Yet it has remained
a peaceful, provincial town, where weekly fairs are held on the square and
seafood sold directly from the buckets of the fishermen along the banks of the
river.

THE SIGHTS: The favorite park in Aschaffenburg is the **Schönbusch Park,**
where you can ramble along shaded paths through groves of old trees. It is
across the Main (two miles on foot or by car), a marvel of planning, using the
natural surroundings as a setting for formal 18th-century gardens, wandering
lanes, temples, and gazebos. At the edge of the mirror-smooth lake is a small
neoclassic castle—really a country house—once used by the electors of Mainz.
The house is open from April 1 to September 30 from 8 a.m. to 1 p.m. and from
2 to 6 p.m., charging 1 DM (57¢) for admission. In summer, it's possible to
rent small boats to go on the lake, and the cafe-restaurant is open each day from
8 a.m. to 8 p.m.

The most impressive castle in Aschaffenburg is the huge Renaissance **St.
Johannisburg castle,** reflected in the waters of the Main. Erected in 1605–1614
by Archbishop Johann Schweickard von Kronberg to replace an earlier structure, the red sandstone castle is almost perfectly symmetrical, with four massive
lantern towers surrounding an inner courtyard. The interior is open from April
1 to September 30 from 9 a.m. to noon and from 1 to 5 p.m. Admission is 2.50
DM ($1.43). Off-season, its hours are from 10 a.m. to noon and from 1 to 4
p.m. A few treasures remain, although most of the works of art have been
removed to the Town Museum. From the gardens of the castle, you reach the
Pompeianum, built by the Bavarian King Ludwig I as a replica of the Castor
and Pollux palace discovered among the ruins of Pompeii.

The abbey **Church of St. Peter and Alexander** (Stiftskirche) has stood on
its hill overlooking the town for 1000 years. Its architecture has changed over
the centuries, however, as it was remodeled and reconstructed, until today it
stands as a combination of Romanesque, Gothic, and baroque. Its most precious treasure is the painted retable, *The Lamentation of Christ,* by the court
painter Grünewald. The interior is decorated with several paintings of the
school of Lucas Cranach, as well as a marble-alabaster pulpit by Hans Juncker.
One of the oldest pieces is a Roman-style crucifix dating from 1150. Adjacent
to the north side of the church is a Romanesque cloister from the 13th century.
The church is open to the public throughout the day, but to view the treasury
and the cloisters, you must request admission through the sacristan at 1 Stifts-
gasse. The charge is 1 DM (57¢).

BED AND BOARD AT INNS: **Romantik Hotel Post,** 19 Goldbacherstrasse
(tel. 2-13-33), is an all-around hotel, and it certainly serves the best food in
Aschaffenburg. Close to the heart of the town, its exterior may be conventional,
but there is drama inside. The focus of attention is the dining room, a stylized
version of an old posting inn, including an original mail coach, timbering on

the walls and ceiling, leaded-glass windows, and tavern chairs. Even the breakfast room has charm, with its corner fireplace of decorative tile and its raffia-seated chairs. A miniature sitting room is equally rustic, almost New England in character, with natural pine chairs, cafe curtains, and hanging oil lamps, plus lots of decorative copper.

All rooms have baths or showers. Singles with showers start at 42 DM ($24.09), peaking at 82 DM ($47.04) with private bath. Depending on the plumbing, doubles rent from 88 DM ($50.48) to 125 DM ($71.70). Each accommodation is uniquely furnished and comfortable. Dining is a special event—both to the townspeople and the Americans stationed nearby. Only problem: The menu is so long it takes all night to read it. Even diet and vegetarian menus are offered. In season, quail, venison, and stag are featured.

Wilder Mann, 1 Fischergasse (tel. 2-15-55), on a busy highway at the edge of town, is a stylized, overgrown inn, with an eclectic modern interior. The breakfast room is decorated with blue and white bentwood chairs and bronze chandeliers. The inviting entry lounge is in tones of orange and yellow, with sleek black chairs. Most treasured is a fine baroque carved wood statue of a Madonna and Child. The namesake of the inn (wild man) is the wrought-iron sculpture sign on the facade that pictures a man who will probably bring to mind the Wizard of Oz. Depending on the plumbing, singles range in price from 28 DM ($16.06) to 38 DM ($21.80). Likewise, doubles go from 55 DM ($31.55) to a high of 80 DM ($45.89). Set meals cost from 10.50 DM ($6.02) to 18.50 ($10.61), with à la carte dishes averaging around 12 DM ($6.88).

3. Bamberg

Bamberg and beer go together like barley and hops. It's been called "a beer drinker's Eden," outranking Munich in the number of breweries concentrated within its city limits. The average Bamberger drinks 50 gallons of beer a year—making the rest of the German people look like teetotalers by comparison. Many brew fanciers journey all the way to Bamberg just to sample Rauchbier, a smoked beer dating from 1536.

THE SIGHTS: Handsomely positioned on seven hills, Bamberg is a cathedral city, just 39 miles north of Nürnberg. It is considered the greatest medieval city of Germany, a powerful ecclesiastical center whose roots go back 1000 years. The **Domplatz** (Cathedral Square), the most harmonious in Germany, is dominated by **Alte Hofhaltung,** the Renaissance imperial and episcopal palace, with a courtyard surrounded by late Gothic framework buildings. Within the palace itself are the remains of the original Diet hall, built in the 11th century. Opposite is the **New Residence,** the much larger palace of the prince-bishops, dating from the 17th century. Its buildings show the influence of both Renaissance and baroque. It is open between April 1 and September 30 from 9 a.m. to noon and from 1:30 p.m. to 5 p.m. (closes at 4 p.m. the rest of the year). Admission is 1.50 DM (86¢).

On the Domplatz sits the **Imperial Cathedral,** erected in the 11th century, but rebuilt in 1237 in a Romanesque and early Gothic style. Resting on a hillside, the cathedral is a basilica with a double chancel, the eastern one raised on a terrace to compensate for the slope. The massive towers at the four corners of the church dominate the skyline of the city. The interior of the cathedral contains some of the most noted religious art in Christendom. The best known is the *Bamberg Rider,* an equestrian statue from the 13th century representing the idealized Christian king of the Middle Ages. Among the many impressive tombs is that of Emperor Heinrich II, who erected the original cathedral. Tilman Riemenschneider labored more than a decade over this masterpiece and that of the king's wife, Kunigunda, who was suspected of adultery—a fact actually commemorated in one of the scenes on the tomb! The only papal tomb in Germany—in fact, the only one north of the Alps—contains the remains of Pope Clement II, who died in 1047. He is buried in the western chancel. The cathedral may be visited at any time during daylight hours, except between noon and 2 p.m. (and during services, of course). The Cathedral Treasury, a rich collection, may be seen in the newly built **Diozesanmuseum,** 5 Kapitelshaus Domplatz. It can be visited Monday through Friday from 10 a.m. to noon and 2 to 4 p.m., Saturdays from 10 a.m. to 1 p.m., and Sundays from 10 a.m. to noon. Admission is 1 DM (57¢).

Among the other places of interest is the **Altes Rathaus,** considered the strangest town hall in Germany. Determined not to play favorites between the ecclesiastical and secular sections of the city, the town authorities built this Gothic structure (with more recent rococo overtones) on its own little island in the middle of the Regnitz River—halfway between the two factions—a true middle-of-the-road (or river) political stand! From the island you get the best view of the old fishermen's houses along the river in the section fancifully called "Little Venice."

The **E.T.A. Hoffman House,** 26 Schillerplatz, was the home of the writer, poet, and critic from 1809 to 1813. The little narrow-fronted house is filled with mementos and memorabilia of the storyteller whose strange tales formed the basis of Offenbach's famous opera, *Tales of Hoffman.* Open from April through October; admission is 1 DM (57¢).

READER'S SIGHTSEEING TIP: "We made side trips to Schloss Weissenstein (at Pommersfelden) and the churches of Vierzehnheiligen and Banz. **Schloss Weissenstein,** a superb baroque palace built 1711–1718, has a gorgeous staircase, overwhelming baroque ceilings, a splendid art gallery, and a grotto-like room decorated with shells. Weissenstein ranks with Schloss Brühl (near Cologne) and the Residence Palace at Würzburg as a gem of secular baroque. **Vierzehnheiligen,** near Bamberg, is a rococo church (1743) by Balthasar Neumann that makes one fall in love with rococo. The interior is so dazzling that one walks around as if in a trance. A short distance from Vierzehnheiligen stands **Banz,** a baroque church of astonishing beauty. Anyone who visits Bamberg should see Weissenstein, Vierzehnheiligen, and Banz" (Dr. Alfred Dorn, Long Island City, N.Y.).

A TRADITIONAL HOTEL: **Bamberger Hof Bellevue,** 4 Schönleinsplatz (tel. 2-22-16), is the principal hotel in town, a great old palace of stone, crowned by a tower and facing a little park; you'll think you're living in another era. Try to get one of the bedrooms that are large enough to contain several sitting areas. Prices for accommodations depend on the placement and size, as well as the plumbing. A bathless single is 38 DM ($21.80) to 48 DM ($27.53); with shower or tub, 55 DM ($31.55) to 75 DM ($43.02). Doubles also come in a wide range: from 54 DM ($30.97) to 76 DM ($43.59) without bath, from 74 DM ($42.45) to 110 DM ($63.10) with bath or shower. Prices include breakfast. Of the two dining rooms, the preferable one is the intimate, rustic one with Windsor armchairs and red tablecloths. The service is by especially helpful and attentive people, who give tips on the best dishes of the day. You can have set meals for 26 DM ($14.91). This is the best food in town.

WHERE TO DINE: **Würzburger Weinstube,** 6 Zinkenwörth (tel. 2-26-67), is an old, attractive, half-timbered inn on a secluded street near the river, with a courtyard in front for warm-weather dining. The bottled wines available will keep you smiling, but don't hesitate to drink the open wine of the house. Set meals are offered for as little as 14.80 DM ($8.49), going up to 23 DM ($13.19). On the à la carte listing, you'll find toast Nizza at 7.80 DM ($4.47); rainbow trout from nearby streams at 14 DM ($8.03); and tenderloin of pork, cooked in a cream sauce, at 15 DM ($8.60). The weinstube is closed from August 15 to September 5.

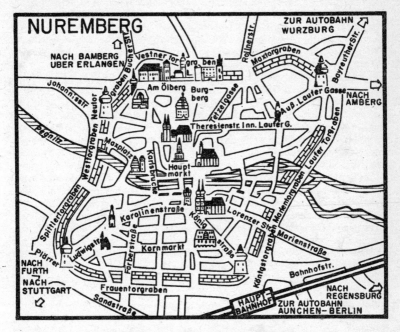

4. Nürnberg (Nuremberg)

When this, the largest city in Franconia, celebrated its 900th birthday in 1950, the scars of World War II were still fresh in its memory. Once considered the ideal of medieval splendor, Nürmberg was badly damaged by the air raids of the early '40s. Since the war, many of the most important buildings have been restored.

Tourists in Nürnberg today can see not only the ruins of the ramparts which once surrounded the city, but also the **Justice Palace** where the War Crimes Tribunal sat in 1946. You can visit some of the most impressive churches in Germany—and also the huge amphitheater where Der Führer staged his dramatic rallies.

Centuries of art and architecture went to make Nürnberg a little treasure chest of Germany.

THE SIGHTS: Nearly all the attractions of the city are within the medieval fortifications which enclose the Old Town on both banks of the little Pegnitz River. Between the main wall with rampart walks and the secondary wall once ran the waters of a protective moat. Set at the "corners" of the town are the massive stone towers of the city gates, but the remains of dozens of towers still exist along the ramparts as well.

Within these walls, the Renaissance was given its greatest impetus in Germany. The flourishing artists' workshops of Nürnberg boasted such talent as Albrecht Dürer, Veit Stoss, Peter Vischer, and Michael Wolgemut. The unparalleled Meistersingers of Nürnberg made great strides in the 14th and 15th centuries in the evolution of German music. You can still visit the Martha Church, which served as their singing school. Advanced humanistically as well as artistically, Nürnberg established its **Holy Ghost Hospital** as early as 1331. The building is supported on arches spanning one branch of the Pegnitz River. Possibly the best example of Nürnberg's passion for beauty is the **"Beautiful Fountain"** on the Marketplace. The stone pyramid, 60 feet high, dates from 1396 and is adorned with 30 figures arranged in four tiers. Within it is enclosed the symbol of Nürnberg, the journeyman's ring.

The town's most popular shrine is the **Albrecht Dürer House,** just up the cobblestone Burgstrasse from the Dürer Monument and St. Sebald's Church. It was the home of the greatest German Renaissance artist during the last 19 years of his life. Aside from the historical and artistic contents inside, the house itself is well worth the short walk up the hill. Typical of the half-timbered burghers' houses of the 15th century, the structure is the only completely preserved Gothic house in Nürnberg. The first floors are sandstone, surmounted by two half-timbered stories and a gabled roof with a view of the town below. Dürer bought this house near the medieval city walls in 1509 and painted many of his masterpieces here before his death in 1528. The building today houses a museum devoted to the life and works of the multifaceted individual who established Nürnberg as a flourishing cultural center. Many of the rooms are furnished with important historical pieces as well as copies of many of Dürer's paintings mixed with original etchings and woodcuts. The house is open daily from 10 a.m. to 5 p.m. (to 9 p.m. on Saturdays). Closed Mondays. Admission for adults is 1.50 DM (86¢); for children and students, .60 DM (34¢).

St. Lorenz Church, across the Pegnitz River from most of the sights of the Old Town, is the largest and stateliest church in Nürnberg. Begun in 1260, it took more than 200 years to complete, but the final result is one of true Gothic purity, inside and out. The twin towers flank the west portal, with its profusion of sculptures depicting the whole theme of Redemption, from Adam and Eve through the Last Judgment. Upon entering the church, you can appreciate the color and detail in the famous stained-glass Rosette above the portal. The interior of the church is defined by huge pillars which soar upward to become lost in the vaulting shafts above the nave. Each pillar is adorned with sculptures carrying on the theme introduced at the entrance. The oldest of these works is *Mary with Child,* created about 1285. The continuing theme of the sculptures urges you forward toward the single east choir, the last portion of the church to be completed (1477). Separating the choir from the nave is the **Angelic Salutation** (1519), carved in linden wood by Veit Stoss and suspended from the roof of the church just behind the Madonna Chandelier. To the left of the altar is the Gothic Tabernacle, hewn from stone by Adam Krafft (1496), its upthrusting turret repeating the vertical emphasis of the church. Above the high altar is another masterpiece by Veit Stoss, a huge carved crucifix. The church is filled with woodcarvings, paintings, and reliefs, seemingly utilizing every artists' workshop which flourished in Nürnberg during the Renaissance. Among these are the painted panels at the beginning of the choir by Michael Wolgemut, Dürer's teacher. In the first chapel on the left off the nave is a sandstone relief of the three saints, Barbara, Catharine, and Agnes (1420). Halfway up the right side is another sandstone relief by Adam Krafft, the strangulation of St. Beatrice. The beauty of the church is heightened by the well-preserved stained and painted glass, much of it dating from pre-Dürer

Nürnberg. The church can be viewed from 9 a.m. to 5 p.m. (Sunday, 2 to 4 p.m.)

St. Sebald's Church, consecrated in 1273, is a fine example of the transition in the 13th century from Romanesque to German Gothic. The nave and west choir are late Romanesque, with a narrow chancel containing a simple altar and an ancient bronze baptismal font. The larger east choir, consecrated in 1379, is pure Gothic, and contains the most important treasures of the church. Between the two east pillars is a huge 16th-century Crucifixion group dominated by a lifesize crucifix by Veit Stoss. Just behind the altar is the elaborate shrine of St. Sebald, whose remains are encased within a monument cast in brass by Peter Vischer in 1519. The nave of the church also holds several important works of art, including 14th-century statues of St. Catharine and St. Sebald and a Madonna with a Halo (1440). On the outside wall of the east choir is the tomb of the Schreyer-Landauer family, decorated with scenes of the Passion and Resurrection of Christ. The church is open daily in April and May from 9 a.m. till noon and from 2 to 5 p.m.; June through September, 9 a.m. to 6 p.m.; October, 10 a.m. to noon and 2 to 5 p.m.; November through March, 10 a.m. to noon and 2 to 4 p.m. On Sundays, November through March, noon to 4 p.m.; April through October, noon to 5 p.m. Admission to the shrine of St. Sebald costs adults .50 DM (29¢); children, .30 DM (17¢).

The **Castle of Nürnberg** looms above the city from its hilltop at the northern edge of the Old Town. For more than 500 years, from 1050 to 1571, it was the official residence of the German kings and emperors, including the zealous Crusader, Frederick Barbarossa, who entertained such exotic guests as the emperor of Byzantium and the sultan of Tyre within its walls. The castle is divided into three complexes of buildings, indicating its main periods of architecture and history: the **Imperial Castle,** the **Burgraves' Castle,** and the **Municipal Buildings of the Free City.**

The oldest portion of the complex is the Pentagonal Tower (1050). It probably dates from the previous palace of the Salian Kings, over which the Burgraves' Castle was constructed. Although the Burgraves' Castle has been in ruins since it was destroyed by fire in 1420, it offers the visitor an interesting look into the layout of a feudal castle. The heavy ramparts with the parapet walks and secret passages were used by the watchmen and guards who protected not only the burgraves, but the emperors as well, who lived in the inner core of the castle complex.

The Imperial Castle, grouped around the Inner Court within the ramparts of the Burgraves' Castle, was the residence of the kings and emperors of Germany. Most of the buildings were constructed during the 12th century, centering around the once-magnificent "Palas" built by Konrad III in 1138. The great Knights' Hall on the ground floor, and the Imperial Hall on the floor above look much as they did when King Frederick III rebuilt them in the 15th century, with heavy oak beams and painted ceilings. The rooms are decorated with period Gothic furnishings. Adjoining the Palas is the **Imperial Chapel,** the most important building in the castle complex. It consists of two chapels, one above the other in cross section, but united at the center by an open bay. Thus, the emperor could worship with his court in the upper chapel to the same liturgy as the lesser members of his retinue in the lower chapel.

The third set of buildings on the Castle Hill, built outside the Burgraves' Castle, was erected by the council of Nürnberg in the 14th and 15th centuries when it took over the responsibility of protecting the emperor. This section includes the Imperial Stables, now housing a youth hostel, the massive bastions of the fortress, and the Castle Gardens.

From April to September, the castle is open daily from 9 a.m. to 5 p.m.; from October to March, 10 a.m. to noon and 1 to 4 p.m. Admission for all parts of the castle is 2 DM ($1.15) for adults, 1 DM (57¢) for children; for the Palas only, 1.50 DM (86¢) for adults, .80 DM (46¢) for children. Even more impressive than the fortress, however, is the view of the rooms and towers of Nürnberg from its terraces.

The **Germanic National Museum,** one of the most comprehensive collections of German art and culture, is just inside the south section of the medieval city walls (near the main railway station). Its setting, incorporating the buildings of the former Carthusian monastery into its complex, covers the entire spectrum of German craftsmanship and fine arts, from its beginnings to the 20th century. The pre- and early historical section contains finds from the Stone Age to the burial sites of the Merovingians. The extensive painting and sculpture sections include works by two of the city's most important artists, Albrecht Dürer and Veit Stoss. The demonstrations of the boundless variety and richness of German handicraft play a major role in the museum's orientation toward cultural history. In this area, medieval bronze casting and tapestries, works of goldsmithery, scientific instruments, costumes, arms, armor, and toys are particularly well represented. During the last few years, the folk art section and the section devoted to historical musical instruments have been greatly expanded. The Print Room and the Numismatic Collection are among the most comprehensive of the German-speaking world. Many original parchment documents from important families are housed in the Archive. The active and broad-based scholarly programs of the museum would not be possible without its library of more than 380,000 volumes, including manuscripts, incunabula, engraved and illustrated works. Hours: Tuesday through Sunday, 9 a.m. to 4 p.m.; Thursday also 8 p.m. to 9:30 p.m. Closed Mondays year round. Admission: 2 DM ($1.15) for adults; free for students. No one pays admission on Sundays or public holidays.

The **Tucher Castle** was the summer residence of the most famous and still existing patrician family, Tucher, known for beer. The structure was built in 1534 by Peter Flötner, and it contains a small but precious collection of artworks which have been commissioned by the Tuchers since the days of the Renaissance. Called Tucher-Schlösschen, it is at 11 Hirschelgasse. Tours Monday through Friday are at 2, 3, and 4 p.m.; at 10 a.m. and 11 a.m. on Sunday. Closed Saturday. The entrance fee is 1 DM (57¢).

READERS' SIGHTSEEING TIPS: "A **Toy Museum** on Karlstrasse (two doors up from Weintraubengasse) offers the visitor three floors of handmade and industrial toys from all over the world. Toys dating back to the Middle Ages are displayed, along with a mechanical ferris wheel. Of special interest to me were dollhouse kitchens, with every utensil imaginable to minute detail. The museum is open from 10 a.m. to 5 p.m., Tuesday through Sunday; 10 a.m. to 9 p.m. on Wednesday; closed Monday. Admission is 1.50 DM (86¢) for adults and .60 DM (34¢) for children and students" (Celeste McLean, APO New York). . . . The **Handwerkerhof** is in the Waffenhof, by the Königstor, and is open daily from April 1 to December 23 (and on Sundays, too, in summer). It consists of a little world of half-timbered houses where visitors can watch craftsmen at their work, buy charming, locally made souvenirs, and indulge in eating the delicacies prepared in the restaurants. . . . **Lochgefangnisse,** the medieval prison cells and torture chambers under the old Town Hall, can be visited Monday through Friday from 10 a.m. to 4 p.m., and Saturdays and Sundays from 10 a.m. to 1 p.m. from May 2 through September 30. Admission is 1 DM (57¢)" (Carol Sanborn, Los Alamitos, Calif.).

THE TOP HOTELS: Grand Hotel, 1 Bahnhofstrasse (tel. 20-36-21), is Nürnberg's grand old hotel—it has simply no serious competition. It's a solid six-floor blockbuster, built when "hotels were really hotels"—that is, before the First World War. Across from the railway station, its convenience of location may be an asset or a curse, depending on whether you get one of the quieter rooms. The Fürstenhof Restaurant provides dignified dining, and the cuisine is international-Germanic. A wood-paneled drinking lounge is restful and conducive to winding down with a drink. The Walliser Kanne, a woodsy tavern with a Swiss-chalet ambience and walls of roughly cut pine slabs, features light meals.

Most of the Grand Hotel's 170 bedrooms are well furnished and spacious, containing private baths and showers as well. All of the double rooms are twin bedded (remember to ask for one overlooking the quiet inside court or the back street). Singles with toilet cost 61 DM ($34.99); with shower, 80 DM ($45.89) to 92 DM ($52.77); with bath, 92 DM ($52.77) to 116 DM ($66.54); with bath, from 138 DM ($79.16) to 170 DM ($97.51).

Carlton, 13–15 Eilgustrasse (tel. 20-35-35), is a first-class hotel, considered by some the best in Nürnberg. It's on a quiet street, a block from the railway station. The most formal restaurant is done in red and white, although many prefer luncheons on an outdoor stone terrace, with umbrella-shaded tables and flower garden. All of the bedrooms have private baths or showers. The accommodations are well conceived, with many modern built-in pieces. Some doubles have a pair of L-shaped sofas with coffee tables, making them combined living-sleeping rooms. Rates are based on size. All rooms have private baths. A single with shower bath costs 68 DM ($39), peaking at 95 DM ($54.49) with a full bath or toilet. Doubles with shower go from 110 DM ($63.10), increasing to 160 DM ($91.78) with full bath.

THE MIDDLE BRACKET: Hotel am Sterntor, 8–14 Tafelhofstrasse (tel. 20-31-01), is one of the railway station hotels that has been reconstructed and freshly decorated. Most important, it's not too noisy. The front lobby, with its contemporary elegance, sets the example for the nicely furnished bedrooms. Considering everything, am Sterntor is a good bet for your marks. Bathless singles cost 48 DM ($27.53), ranging upward to anywhere from 68 DM ($39) with shower to a peak 75 DM ($43.02) with bath. Bathless doubles rent for 78 DM ($44.74), climbing up to 110 DM ($63.10) with bath. Breakfast is included.

Kaiserhof, 39 Königstrasse (tel. 20-36-86), an old-fashioned hotel near the railway station, nestles behind an interesting facade of orante wrought-iron balconies. The reception area is as narrow as a bowling lane, but the bedrooms are spacious and pleasingly decorated with matching blond furniture, allowing for a petite sitting area for breakfast. Bathless singles are 25 DM ($14.34) to 33 DM ($18.93), 40 DM ($22.94) with shower, and from 46 DM ($26.39) to 50 DM ($28.68) with bath. Bathless doubles are 52 DM ($29.83) to 60 DM ($34.42); with shower or tub bath, between 75 DM ($43.02) and 95 DM ($54.49)—breakfast included. There are several rooms in which to dine. The Löwenbräu provides typical Bavarian dishes, and set meals cost from 8 DM ($4.59) to 16 DM ($9.18). On two levels, the main dining room offers a more international cuisine. The Frankenklause, for light snacks and drinks, is as cozy as a mountain chalet, with a green ceramic stove and pine walls. Most impressive is the bier and weinkeller Zum Fass, with arched pillars and decoratively painted ceilings.

Victoria, 80 Königstrasse (tel. 20-38-01), is a big, old-fashioned remake of a hotel, lodged against the main gate of the old city—within two minutes from the railway station. A handy and comfortable place to stay, it caters to the traveler who likes quiet, a traditional background, and good service. There are several lounges, a dining room, and a lower level Victorian Keller, where you can get snacks and light meals, as well as wines and beer. Breakfast is included in the room price. Bathless singles are 40 DM ($22.94) to 46 DM ($26.39), rising to 55 DM ($31.55) and 65 DM ($37.28) with bath or shower. All doubles have either a private bath or shower, with prices ranging from 78 DM ($44.74) to 90 DM ($51.62). The bedrooms are faithful to the style of the hotel—pleasantly dated, although some newer furnishings have been added recently.

THE BUDGET RANGE: Reichshof, 16–20 Johannesgasse 16 (tel. 20-37-17), is a tuck-away hotel, opening onto a little courtyard, shut off from the milling crowds. However, the interior has been modernized, although in a heavy Teutonic manner. Spacious and rather grand is the central lobby, with an open, winding staircase. Moderately priced meals are served in the dining room, and a high-speed elevator takes guests to the comfortably furnished bedrooms. The Reichshof has been owned and managed for 62 years by the Bindl family, who have set the following rates for accommodations: bathless singles, 40 DM ($22.94); singles with bath, 58 DM ($33.27) to 70 DM ($40.15); doubles without bath, 66 DM ($37.86); doubles with private shower or bath, 95 DM ($54.49) to 110 DM ($63.10). Breakfast is included, and a three-course luncheon or dinner costs 11.50 DM ($6.60) to 25 DM ($14.34).

Deutscher Kaiser, 55 Königstrasse (tel. 20-33-41), has one of the most attractive old-world exteriors of any of the Nürnberg hostelries. At the top of a vehicle-free pedestrian mall, it is built of gray stone, with step gables and a highly pitched roof studded with dormers. Three Romanesque-style arches lead into the main lobby. For 60 years, the Deutscher Kaiser has been managed and owned by the same family. Its lounges are at a minimum; the dining room rather simple, but fresh and clean; the bedrooms decorated with matching modern. The general effect is one of comfort in immaculate surroundings. Bathless doubles are 50 DM ($28.68) to 60 DM ($34.42); with shower or bath, 72 DM ($41.30) to 78 DM ($44.74). Singles with hot and cold running water cost 25 DM ($14.34) to 35 DM ($20.08); singles with bath, 50 DM ($28.68). It's difficult getting in during June, July, August, and February, as German tourists reserve then, knowing this one's a good bargain. Parking is available. In the basement is one of the Wienerwald restaurants.

Drei Raben, 63 Königstrasse (tel. 20-45-83), is a good place to consider for an overnight stopover. It offers a comfortable bed in a clean room. This modest little establishment with 41 beds is owned and run by Herr and Frau Deibel. One block from the station, it's entered from a side street. A three-passenger elevator takes you to the second-floor bedrooms. A single without bath is 25 DM ($14.34), rising to 45 DM ($25.81) with shower. A bathless double is 52 DM ($29.83), peaking at 63 DM ($36.14) with shower. Breakfast is included. Basic English is spoken. About 60 yards from the hotel is a parking lot.

The **Bavarian-American Hotel,** on the Bahnhofplatz, 3 Bahnhofstrasse, will accommodate persons with an armed services identification card. Priority is to military personnel on permanent change-of-station orders, then to personnel on temporary-duty orders. All others are accommodated on a space-available basis. Rates are $5 to $10 per person, depending on the type of room. There is a restaurant and bar. Only U.S. dollars are accepted. Space for vacationers is very limited from May through September.

READERS' PENSION SELECTION: "Pension Noris, 3 Prinzregentenufer (tel. 55-28-18), is across the street from the walled Old Town and within easy walking distance of the Hauptmarkt Platz and the Kaiserburg Castle. The streetcar stops right outside the door, with a five-minute trip to the train station. The pension is on the second floor. Our large spotless room had a balcony overlooking a lovely courtyard. Our English-speaking host was friendly and helpful. The price for two persons is 50 DM ($28.68), including breakfast of a boiled egg, cheese, cold meats, rolls, and coffee. There is limited parking" (Stanley and Dorothy Sandelius, Stockton, Calif.).

THE TOP RESTAURANTS: Goldenes Posthorn, 2 Glöckleinsgasse (tel. 22-51-53), is lodged in a building dating back to 1498. It has been acclaimed as one of the finest restaurants of Germany. The setting is fascinating, with remarkable furnishings collected through the centuries. The cozy first dining room has a grandfather clock and a full-size statue of a saint, as well as a collection of old prints, pewter, and copper urns. A second dining room is attractively rustic, with ladderback chairs. And there is yet another room—the cellar—for great wines and the best of Germanic food. The Goldenes Posthorn is as good a place as any to introduce yourself to the msot delicious sausages in Germany. Called Nürnberger rostbratwürste, they are finger-size and are usually eaten with sauerkraut and rye bread. An order of six costs 7 DM ($4.02). The restaurant is run by Nosshi A. Malak, who used to be the banquet chef for the former Egyptian president, Nasser. He and his head chef, Freddy Ernst, have received many medals and awards from different gourmet experts all over Europe. The specialty of their kitchen is an Egyptian lamb filet flamed in date liqueur, costing 19.50 DM ($11.19) for one person. A good main dish is Vienna-style roast beef with onions and a red cabbage salad at 16.50 DM ($9.46). Closed Sundays. An attractive cocktail bar has been opened on the second floor of the restaurant, where you can enjoy soft music and dancing.

Under the same management, **Langmann** stands in Fürth by Nürnberg. It's a friendly restaurant in the pre–World War I style, serving French and international specialties, as well as several rare wines.

Bimbala Vo Laff, 23 Bergstrasse, stands next to the old Nürnberg Castle. Here you will find a very charming and typical old Franconian restaurant, serving such local specialties as potato pancakes, Nürnberg sausages, home-made cheese, and many more delicacies. For our money, it has the best beer in town: Arnold Bier fresh from the barrel. Expect to spend anywhere from 15 DM ($8.60). The owner, Warner Becker, will entertain you with his guitar and by singing folk songs.

Heinzrolf Essig Bratlein, 3 Weinmarkt (tel. 22-51-31), is Heinzrolf Schmitt's new restaurant in one of the oldest houses in the city. It is a narrow, timbered structure dating back to 1550, which formerly housed a vinegar factory. The house has small windows and is decorated with antiques, giving a warm, rich ambience. You may eat at small wooden tables covered with immaculate linen, either on the first or second floor. If the weather is warm enough, you may choose to have your meal outside, protected from the street by shrubbery. Soups are in the 5.50-DM ($3.15) to 8-DM ($4.59) range. Main dishes include a turbotin with sauce crevette for 27 DM ($15.49) and a beef filet with pepper for 26 DM ($14.91). Desserts range in price from 7.50 DM ($4.30) to 12.50 DM ($7.17). The restaurant is open in the evening, Mondays through Saturdays. Herr Schmitt formerly operated the Goldenes Posthorn.

LOW-COST DINING WITH ATMOSPHERE: Nassauer Keller, 2 Karolinenstrasse (tel. 22-59-67), occupies the cellar of one of the most romantic buildings in Nürnberg, opposite the Church of St. Lorenz. It features an original cuisine, specializing in trout and game in season. Soups range from 3.50 DM ($2.01) to 4.50 DM ($2.58). Main dishes include wienerschnitzel Cordon Bleu at 17.50 DM ($10.04) or filet of venison with mushrooms and cranberries at 18.50 DM ($10.61). Desserts begin at 3.80 DM ($2.18), going up to 7.50 DM ($4.30). Closed Sundays.

Ratsstuben, 2 Rathausplatz (tel. 22-78-11), is a reconstructed tavern in the old Town Hall, with Gothic windows opening onto the square behind the Hauptmarkt. Its chef provides an authentic Nürnberger cuisine at low prices. If you prefer to order from the à la carte menu, try the soup of the day for 1.80 DM ($1.03); fish filet, 6.90 DM ($3.96); grilled steak with mushrooms, peas, and french fried potatoes, 18.50 DM ($10.61); and desserts, from 2.60 DM ($1.49) to 5.90 DM ($3.38).

Weinstuben Steichele, 2 Knorrstrasse (tel. 20-43-78), is the coziest inn in Nürnberg. Try to arrive on a Thursday when the cooks bake a delicious ham in bread dough. The entrees average around 7.50 DM ($4.30) to 10.50 DM ($6.02). A good-tasting and very filling set luncheon menu is offered for just 18.50 DM ($10.61). The restaurant is closed on Mondays. Incidentally, if you're looking for a bargain place to stay, you can find lodgings here, costing from 28 DM ($16.06) to 35 DM ($20.08) per person. Expect extremely modest, but clean, appointments.

READER'S RESTAURANT SUGGESTION: "We found a charming little place to eat in Nürnberg, with very reasonable prices and friendly management. First we were hesitant to go in (the walls were full of 'student art'), but we did not regret it a bit. The place is **Geststätte Burgschanke,** 2 Albrecht-Dürer-Strasse (tel. 22-59-22). The owner is Frau Else Kaak. The place is clean, they like children, and the food was very good. Expect to pay from 11.50 DM ($6.60) and up for a meal here" (John F. Szblya, Pullman, Wash.).

READER'S SELECTION IN PARSBERG: "We happened onto the **Zum Hirschen,** 1 Dr.-Boecale-Strasse (tel. 50-10), in Parsberg, between Regensburg and Nürnberg, just a few kilometers from the autobahn. The town itself is not much of a tourist attraction, although there is a lovely church and, of course, a castle. But the Zum Hirschen is a typical small German guest house which served food 'just out of this world.' Dishes include pears with blueberries, beef with cognac butter, liver with bacon, and many other delights at prices ranging from 11 DM ($6.31) to 18 DM ($10.32). All in all, it was the best meal we had during our entire trip. The simple and comfortable rooms range in price from 18 DM ($10.32) to 23 DM ($13.19) per person" (Mrs. Paul L. Barndt, Quakertown, Penna.).

5. Würzburg

For the German, the South begins at Würzburg, the loveliest baroque city in all the country.

THE SIGHTS: Remaining faithful to the Catholic church throughout the Reformation, this city on the Main has been called "the town of Madonnas" because of the more than 300 statues of its patron saint which adorn many of the house fronts. The most famous statue of the Virgin is the *Patrona Franconiae,* a sweeping baroque Madonna which stands with the statues of other Franconian saints along the buttresses of the **Alt Mainbrücke,** Germany's second-oldest stone bridge, dating from the 15th century.

During the last few weeks of World War II, Würzburg was shattered by a series of bombing raids. In a miraculous rebuilding program, every major building has been restored. Much of the original splendor of the city was due to the efforts of one man—the greatest master of the German baroque, Balthasar Neumann (1687–1753). As court architect to the Prince-Bishop of Würzburg, his major accomplishment is the pride of the entire baroque world, the Residence.

The Residence

Begun in 1720 to satisfy the passion for elegance and splendor of the Prince-Bishop Johann Philipp Franz von Schönborn, this palace is the last and finest of a long line of baroque castles built in Bavaria in the 17th and 18th centuries. Completed within 20 years, the great horseshoe-shaped edifice was the joint effort of the best Viennese, French, and German architects working under the leadership of Neumann. Because it was built in such a short time, the castle shows a unity of purpose and design not usually evident in buildings of such size.

Leading upward from the vestibule at the center of the castle is the **Treppenhaus** (staircase), standing detached in the lower hall and branching into twin stairways at a landing halfway to the second floor. This masterful creation by Neumann is the largest staircase in German baroque art. The high, rounded ceiling above it is decorated with a huge fresco by Tiepolo. At the center, Apollo is seen ascending to the zenith of the vault. The surrounding themes represent the four corners of the world, the seasons, and the signs of the zodiac. The illusion of the painting is so thorough it appears to be overflowing onto the walls of the upper hall.

At the top of the staircase, you enter the White Hall, whose deliberate absence of color provides the ideal transition between the elaborate staircase and the connecting **Imperial Hall,** the culmination of the splendor of the entire castle. Based on Neumann's design, Tiepolo worked on this room in conjunction with the accomplished sculptor and stucco artist, Antonio Bossi. The walls of the hall are adorned with three-quarter marble pillars with gilded capitals. In the niches between the columns are original sculptures of Poseidon, Juno, Flora, and Apollo by Bossi. The highlight of the hall, however, is in the graceful combination of the white and gold stucco work and the brilliantly colored paintings on the upper walls and ceiling. The work is so well done that it is difficult to tell where the paintings leave off and the relief work begins. On the flat part of the ceiling, Tiepolo has depicted an allegorical scene of Apollo escorting the bride of Frederick Barbarossa to the emperor. The paintings between the upper, rounded windows glamorize important incidents in the history of Würzburg.

The other important attraction in the Residence is the **Court Chapel,** in the southwest section. Since light only enters the chapel from one side, Neumann placed the window-arches at oblique angles, thus creating a muted effect. The rectangular room is divided into five oval sections, three with domed ceilings. Colored marble columns define the sections, their gilded capitals enriching the ceiling frescoes by Byss. Bossi trimmed the vaulting and arches with intricate gilded stucco work. At the side altars, Tiepolo painted two important works—*The Fall of the Angels* on the left and *The Assumption of the Virgin* on the right.

The **Court Gardens,** at the south and east sides of the Residence, are entered through the gate next to the Court Chapel. The terraces are connected by walks and stairways and end in a large orangerie on the south side. The various gardens are laid out in geometric designs and studded with little statues by Johann Peter Wagner, plus several fountains spouting from sunken parterres.

From April through September, you can visit the Residence daily from 9 a.m. to 5 p.m. During the winter, hours are reduced to 10 a.m. to 4 p.m. Closed

Mondays, throughout the year. Admission is 2 DM ($1.15). During the summer, the Mozart Festival is held in the upper halls.

The Marienberg Fortress

The Marienberg Fortress, over the stone bridge from the Old Town, was the residence of the prince-bishops from 1253 until 1720, when the transition was made to the more elegant "Residence." Although portions of the stronghold have been restored, the combination of age and wartime destruction has taken a serious toll on its thick walls and once impenetrable ramparts. But what remains is worth a visit. One of the oldest churches in Germany, the **Marienkirche,** dating from the eighth century, stands within its walls. In the former arsenal and Echter bulwark, to the right of the first courtyard, is the **Main-Franconian Museum,** housed here since 1946. A real treasure house, the museum contains a history of Würzburg in art, from marble epitaphs of the prince-bishops to a carved wood model of the town in 1525. Works by the greatest aritsts engaged by patrons of Würzberg art are included here—a famous collection of sculptures by Tilman Riemenschneider, paintings by Tiepolo, sculptures by Peter Wagner, and sandstone figures from the rococo gardens of the prince-bishops' summer palace. A further tribute to one of the few industries of the city—that of winemaking—is paid in the presshouse, the former wine vaults of the fortress. Historic wine casks and carved cask bases and a large collection of glasses and goblets make an interesting conclusion to the museum and castle tour. The fortress is open daily, except Monday, from 9 a.m. to 5 p.m. (from 10 a.m. to 4 p.m. in winter). Admission is 1 DM (57¢). The museum, entered separately, is open from 10 a.m. to 5 p.m. (from 10 a.m. to 4 p.m. in winter). The charge here is 1.50 DM (86¢). (On the first Sunday of each month, admission is free.)

THE TOP HOTEL: Rebstock, 7 Neubaustrasse (tel. 5-00-75), is unique and impressive, worth a detour for a stopover for a night or two. Housed in a palace, it is decorated with style and flair. The facade is attractive, with its neoclassic pilasters, baroque plaster window trim, and a steep roof studded with tiny dormers. Through a classic doorway, you enter a wide foyer adorned with carved wooden doors and an old Spanish sea chest. A red carpet guides the way to the reception area.

The interior is splashy in a tasteful way, using ingenuity. Some of the best of contemporary furnishings have been well coordinated with the old. The main parquet-floor restaurant has been entirely redecorated. The wooden ceiling, hand-painted, is indirectly lighted. The gourmet is served here from delicate dishes prepared by master cooks. The Fränkische Weinstube also completely redone, comes with oak beams, stark-white walls, wooden chairs matching the ceiling, wooden tables, and a gilded baroque painting along with a carved Madonna. Here, guests gather for local wine and meals.

The bedrooms are equipped with wall-to-wall draperies and matching sofas, a pair of deep armchairs, along with a bare wood coffee table. Baths are colorfully tiled. Singles range in price from 60 DM ($34.42) to 70 DM ($40.15); twin-bedded rooms, 110 DM ($63.10) to 150 DM ($86.04). Breakfast, included, is served in the courtyard under a trellis, next to a splashing fountain.

THE BUDGET RANGE: Gasthof Greifenstein, 1 Häfnergasse (tel. 5-16-65), is recommendable if you want the good simple life. It's a true tavern, abounding in village atmosphere, just off the Marienkapelle, with its colorful food market.

The dining room tavern is stage center, and the upper-floor bedrooms have a private entrance. The Greifenstein is easy to spot, with its shutters and window boxes dropping with bright geraniums. All rooms have basins with hot and cold running water, and some contain private baths. Depending on the plumbing, singles range from 27 DM ($15.49) to 34 DM ($19.50). Doubles go from 40 DM ($22.94) to 48 DM ($27.53), priced according to size and location. If you prefer more modern accommodations, you can ask to be booked into the new wing, offering some of the most comfortable rooms in Würzburg. Forty-five of these contain complete private baths, renting for 72 DM ($41.30), including breakfast. The bathless doubles, including breakfast, range between 65 DM ($37.28) and 75 DM ($43.02). A new underground parking garage provides space for the cars of hotel guests. For a hearty Germanic cuisine, the restaurant is economical. Soups begin at 1.20 DM (69¢), and main dishes range between 7 DM ($4.02) and 15 DM ($8.60). A large glass of beer is 1.80 DM ($1.04). A city parking space is nearby. The innkeeper is Adolf Schraud.

READERS' HOTEL SELECTION: "Hotel Sankt Josef, 87 Würzburg (tel. 5-31-41), is in the center of the Old Town but is a modernized hotel that is also spotlessly clean. It has a spacious breakfast room and serves an excellent morning meal. The English-speaking owner is very helpful. A double room with breakfast costs 45 DM ($25.81), plus 4 DM ($2.29) extra to park the car in the garage. The owner's hobby is raising flowers on his patio, so the hotel is graced with his lovely blossoms, which also appear on each breakfast table" (Stanley and Dorothy Sandelius, Stockton, Calif.).

WHERE TO DINE: Wein-und-Fischhaus Schiffbäuerin, 7 Katzengasse (tel. 4-24-87), is one of the best restaurants in the region. A combined wine house and fish restaurant, it is across the river in an old half-timbered building on a narrow, hard-to-find street. The situation is about one minute from the old bridge. The house specializes in pike, perch, blue carp, and eel. Most of these dishes are priced at 100 grams. For example, blue carp costs 2.20 DM ($1.26) per 100 grams; pike, 2.70 DM ($1.55) per 100 grams; and eel, 3 DM ($1.72) per 100 grams. Fish appetizers average around 4.50 DM ($2.58), and oxtail soup beings at 2.50 DM ($1.43). The restaurant is closed on Mondays and from January 15 to 31.

READER'S SUGGESTIONS FOR WÜRZBURG: "For meeting GIs and young Germans, I'd suggest the **Bundschuh** at 1 Ursulinergasse (near the base of the old Saint's Bridge, the Alte Mainbrücke), as well as the **Omnibus,** a basement cave on Theatrestrasse, near the intersection with Semmelstrasse. Other activities might include (1) visiting the Kiliani fair, with its rides and specially brewed beer, sold by the liter only (in the first two weeks of July); (2) renting a rowboat or kayak from the concession between the Ludwigsbrücke and the Alte Mainbrücke; and (3) taking one of the river cruises which leaves from near the 'old crane' close to the intersection of Roentgen Ring and the river. Prost!!" (Frank L. Rubino, U.S. Army).

6. Bayreuth

If you arrive in this city on the Main during the late summer months, you may think the whole town (some 60,000 people) has turned out to pay homage to the great operatic composer who once lived (and died) here. Indeed, for one month each year, everything else in Bayreuth stops for the **Wagner Festival.** Stores which usually display their own commercial items place recordings of Wagnerian operas in the windows. Landladies become so concerned that guests will be late for the evening's performance that they may offer to press a tuxedo or wash and iron a shirt.

THE SIGHTS: The operas of Wagner are dispensed like a musical Eucharist from the **Festspielhaus** at the northern edge of town. Pilgrims from all over the world gather here for performances in the theater, designed by the composer himself as the perfect setting for his epic operas. Although the opera house is far from perfect in appearance, it is an ideal Wagnerian theater, with a huge stage capable of swallowing up Valhalla, and beautifully balanced acoustics throughout the entire auditorium. When the festival was opened here in 1876 with the epic *Ring Cycle,* it was so well received that the annual tradition has been carried on ever since. When the composer died, his wife Cosima, daughter of Franz Liszt (who also is buried in Bayreuth), took over. Today Wagner's grandchildren produce the operas, with exciting modern staging and excellent musicians brought here from all over the world.

The **Markgräfliches Opernhaus** (Margraves' Opera House), although not as large nor as acoustically perfect as the house that Wagner built, is certainly a more glamorous structure from an architectural point of view. Considered the oldest and finest baroque theater in Germany, it was opened in 1748 by Bayreuth's patron of the arts, the Margravine Wilhelmine, sister of Frederick the Great. Behind its weathered wooden doors is a world of gilded canopies and columns, ornate sconces and chandeliers, and staircases leading to plush boxes. Today, the opera house, which seats only 500 people, is used for Bayreuth's "second" festival, the **Franconian Weeks' Festival** usually held in late May. The greatest of the baroque composers—Mozart, Rameau, and Handel—would be pleased to see their works performed in such surroundings. If you don't catch a performance, you may visit the opera house April through September, from 9 a.m. to 11:30 a.m. and 1:30 to 4:30 p.m., and October through March from 10 to 11:30 a.m. and 1:30 to 3 p.m. Guided tours, in German only, are conducted daily, except Monday, for 1 DM (57¢).

The **New Castle,** in the center of town just a few blocks from the Margraves' Opera House, also shows the influence and enlightened taste of the talented and cultured Wilhemine. Built in the mid-18th century after fire nearly destroyed the Old Palace, the castle has been well-preserved in a baroque style, with a definite French touch. The apartments of Wilhelmine and her husband, the Margrave Friedrich, are decorated in a late rococo style, with excellent period furnishings. The castle also contains the **Regional Historical Museum** and **Bavarian Art Gallery,** with excellent paintings and an interesting coin collection. A small section of the palace's east wing is devoted to the **Wagner Memorial,** with mementos and possessions of the composer, including a death mask. The various museums and apartments of the castle can be visited daily, except Monday. Hours, April through September, are 10 a.m. to noon and from 1 to 5 p.m.; October through March, from 10 a.m. to noon and 1:30 p.m. to 3:30 p.m. Admission is 1 DM (57¢). While touring the rooms, you should take the opportunity to wander through the adjacent court garden, planned in a natural, English style.

The Margraves of Bayreuth also had a pleasure palace outside the city—the **Hermitage,** just three miles northeast of Bayreuth, reached via a road lined with chestnut trees planted in honor of Frederick the Great. This summer palace was built in 1718 as a retreat by Margrave Georg Wilhelm. The fascinating structure almost looks as if it were hewn out of a huge rock, but the interior again felt the baroque touch of Margravine Wilhelmine. Especially interesting are the Japanese salon and the rococo music room. The castle is set in a park, full of formal as well as English-style gardens. The palace and gardens are open daily from 9 a.m. to 11:30 a.m. and from 1 to 4:30 p.m. (in winter, from 10 to 11:30 a.m. and 1 to 2:30 p.m.). Admission is 1.50 DM (86¢).

THE TOP HOTEL: Bayerischer Hof, 14 Bahnhofstrasse (tel. 2-30-61), is the leading Bayreuth hotel. It's near the railway station, yet on a quiet street, with a small garden of weeping willows and a swimming pool. An elevator takes you to the fifth-floor roof-garden restaurant, overlooking the Festival House and the environs of Bayreuth. All in all, "The Hof" is a substantial hotel, combining contemporary furnishings with traditional. Some bedrooms have French pieces; others are in Nordic modern. Bathless singles range in price from 28 DM ($16.06) to 32 DM ($18.36); with shower or bath, between 36 DM ($20.65) and 58 DM ($33.27). Bathless doubles go from 45 DM ($25.81) to 52 DM ($29.83); with shower or tub, between 55 DM ($31.55) and 95 DM ($54.49). Breakfast is included. Preferred for drinking is the Hans Sachs Stube, an air-conditioned replica of an old inn, with small private boxes. On the wall are pictures of the most famous singers who have performed in Bayreuth. The kitchen turns out Franconian specialties, with set meals in the 7.50-DM ($4.30) to 15-DM ($8.60) bracket. Half a pint of beer costs 3 DM ($1.72). The Bayerischer Hof has added an indoor pool, sauna, and solarium.

THE BUDGET RANGE: Am Hofgarten, 6 Lisztstrasse (tel. 6-56-05), is a private home on a residential street, with a rear garden opening onto the castle grounds. Ingeniously rebuilt, it provides personalized accommodations at low prices. The Bauernstube for drinks has a country theme, with alpine chairs and a wooden ceiling; the dining room is pine paneled, with a trio of picture windows. But best of all is the garden in the back, with its little terrace, lawn, and flowerbeds. Although small, the bedrooms are decorated attractively. For example, one may be all white and pink, with Louis XV–style furniture, including a crystal chandelier; or else an accommodation might be provincial, with a postered bed and a painted armoire. Bathless singles start as low as 30 DM ($17.21). With bath or shower, a single rents for 42 DM ($24.09). Bathless doubles are from 43 DM ($24.66) to 55 DM ($31.55), rising to 70 DM ($40.15) with bath, breakfast included. The manager, Franz Bettermann, will help you find your way around the town. Interest note: Look at a plaque on the house opposite am Hofgarten. It says that Franz Liszt lived there; the street is named after him.

Goldener Anker, 6 Opernstrasse (tel. 6-55-00), is the unquestioned choice for opera enthusiasts, especially Wagner buffs. Next door to the Opera House, it has been "the hotel" for distinguished composers, singers, operatic stars, even maestros for more than 200 years. Framed photographs on the time-seasoned, oak-paneled walls are museum treasures. The guestbook includes such signatures as Richard Strauss, Elisabeth Schwarzkopf, Toscanini, Thomas Mann, Fritz Kreisler, Bruno Walter, and Lauritz Melchior. The inn is furnished with unusually fine antiques and Oriental rugs. Your bed may be a towering wooden structure, or an elaborate brass. Depending on the plumbing, singles range in price from 35 DM ($20.08) to 48 DM ($27.53); doubles, 65 DM ($37.28) to 85 DM ($48.76)—these tariffs including breakfast, taxes, and the service charge. There are 28 bedrooms in all, each one different. The dining room is like a fine old club room, with rich paneling and paintings. The food is good and agreeable. Main dishes are priced from 7.50 DM ($4.30) to 22.50 DM ($12.91).

READER'S GUEST HOUSE SELECTION: "If you love the music of Wagner (as I do), but want to be economical, I suggest a stay at the **Gasthof Herzog,** 2 Herzog (off Kulmbacherstrasse, tel. 4-13-34). This is a simple, charming inn accommodating 30 guests, run by Herr Hans Behmer and his family. There is a friendly atmosphere in the facility that I find unmatched anywhere I have been. Herr Behmer thrives on happy guests. A single is 21 DM ($12.05) to 25 DM ($14.34) without bath. A double is from 35 DM ($20.08) to 46 DM ($26.39). Breakfast is included—served on a sunny porch with geraniums when the weather is good. Other meals may be had at reasonable prices, 9 DM ($5.16) to 14 DM ($8.03)" (W. H. Lockey Jr., Richmond, Va.).

DINING ON THE OUTSKIRTS: Jagdschloss Thiergarten, in Thiergarten (tel. 2-11), was an 18th-century hunting lodge, belonging to the margraves of Bayreuth. Just four miles outside of Bayreuth, it opens onto a wide and sweeping view of surrounding farmland. (By car, take the Bayreuth-Sud exit, drive about 1.2 miles on highway B-2 to Wolfsbach, turn right to the lodge). It is mainly a restaurant, and its former drawing rooms now serve as dining rooms. The principal salon is circular and classic, with crystal chandeliers, oil paintings, huge paneled doors, and antiques. Background music is played, perhaps Beethoven or Bach. Some palatable suggestions include Parisian onion soup at 4.50 DM ($2.58); saddle of Venison, 24 DM ($13.77); veal filet, 24 DM also. A specialty of the chef is sole Monte Carlo at 26 DM ($14.91). Desserts begin at 7 DM ($4.02). Bathless singles range from 30 DM ($17.21) to 35 DM ($20.08), going up to 45 DM ($25.81) to 55 DM ($31.55) with bath. Bathless doubles are 52 DM ($29.83), rising to anywhere from 75 DM ($43.02) to 85 DM ($48.76) with private baths. Breakfast, pleasant to take on the sunny terrace, is an extra 7 DM ($4.02).

GERMANY'S OLDEST CASTLE: Burghotel Lauenstein, Lauenstein, near Ludwigsstadt (tel. 09263/256), is a fairytale stone castle, the oldest in Germany, dating back to 915 when it was built as a sprawling fortress. Approached by a narrow and winding road, it stands like a crown on the mountain, often veiled by clouds. The location near the East German border is private, although it lies only 47 miles north of Bayreuth and 18½ miles from Kronach.

Acquired by the State of Bavaria, the castle has a central core with stone towers, turrets, and a narrow moat. This is unused. The hotel is in the manor house which partially encircles the castle. The part in active use has recently been modernized, turning it into a simple yet comfortable hotel.

Its 22 bedrooms vary in size and character. Some have reproductions of peasant furniture and other hand-decorated pieces of the region. All rooms have spectacular views. Several of the accommodations have private baths; others share tower bathrooms with monumental tubs. Bathless singles cost 25 DM ($14.34), rising to 31 DM ($17.78) with shower. Bathless doubles are tabbed at 30 DM ($17.21) per person, rising to 33 DM ($18.93) per person with shower. Meals are regional and well prepared, with half pension ranging in price from 40 DM ($22.94) to 43 DM ($24.66) per person. The hotel is operated by the Wagner family, who attract a sophisticated clientele.

There is no grand hall or lounge with coats of armor. But there is a dining room, with mountain-style furnishings. Weather permitting, meals are served on the newly built covered veranda with a panoramic view of the neighboring Franconian woods. The castle shuts down in February.

7. Regensburg

The architecture which remains from its 2000 years of history testifies to the past grandeur of the city on the Danube which, by the beginning of the Gothic era, had already reached its peak. Fortunately, the wars of this century did not touch Regensburg, and its remarkable buildings and towers offer an unspoiled look into history. Of its ancient structures many are not just museum pieces, but are actually in use today. The best example of this is the **Stone**

Bridge, built in 1146 on 16 huge arches—in continuous service for more than 800 years.

THE SIGHTS: Regensburg is a city of churches—and for good reason. When Christianity was introduced into Germany, this city became the focal point from which the religion spread throughout the country and even into Central Europe via the Danube. The most majestic of these churches is the towering **St. Peter's Cathedral,** on the Domplatz. Begun in the 13th century on the site of an earlier Carolingian church, it was inspired by the French Gothic style. Because of its construction of easily corroded limestone and green sandstone, the edifice is constantly being renewed and renovated. The massive spires of the two western towers, only added in the mid-19th century, were almost completely replaced in 1955 with a more durable material. Most impressive are the well-preserved stained-glass windows in the high choir (14th century) and south transept (13th century). Most of the pillar sculptures on the aisles of the nave were made in the cathedral workshop in the mid-14th century. The two little sculptures in the niches on opposite sides of the main entrance (inside the cathedral) are called "The Devil" and "The Devil's Grandmother" by the townsfolk.

You can also visit the treasures of the cathedral (**Domschatzmuseum**), which shows goldsmith works and splendid textiles from the 11th to the 19th centuries. Entrance is through a portal at the northern nave in the cathedral. Open April to October on Tuesday through Saturday, 10 a.m. to 5 p.m.; Sundays, noon to 5 p.m.; closed Mondays. During the winter months, it is generally open only on weekends. The charge is 2 DM ($1.15).

Crossing the cathedral garden, you enter the **Cloister,** with its Romanesque All Saints' Chapel and St. Stephen's Church. The ancient frescoes on the walls of the chapel depict liturgical scenes from All Saints' Day. The 11th-century Ottonian church of St. Stephen contains an altar made of a hollowed limestone rock with openings connecting to a martyr's tomb. Although the cathedral is open during the day, you may visit the cloisters and St. Stephen's Church only with the regular guides: April to October, daily at 10 and 11 a.m., 2 and 3 p.m.; during the winter months, daily at 10 a.m. and 2 p.m. The charge is 3 DM ($1.72).

Among the remnants of the Roman occupation of Regensburg, the ancient **Porta Praetoria,** behind the cathedral, is the most impressive, with its huge stones piled in the form of an arched gateway. Through the grille beside the eastern tower you can see the original level of the Roman street nearly ten feet below (which is why you often step down into the ancient churches of Regensburg). The city's **Municipal Museum** at Dachauplatz contains other relics of the Roman period, including the stone tablet marking the establishment of the garrison here in the second century, several Christian tombstones from that period, and a stone altar to the Roman god Mercury.

No town hall in Germany has been preserved better than Regensburg's **Altes Rathaus.** The Gothic structure, begun in the 13th century, contains a **Reichssaal** (Imperial Diet Hall), where the Perpetual Diet sat from 1663 to 1806. In the basement of the Town Hall are the dungeons, with the only torture chamber in Germany preserved in its original setting. The rooms and dungeons of the Rathaus are open daily for tours only at regular intervals throughout the morning and afternoon. Admission is 2 DM ($1.15).

WHERE TO STAY: Karmeliten, 1 Dachauplatz (tel. 5-43-08), is a traditional hotel with a young modern look. It's the best hotel in town, set on a square, about three blocks from the river and a four-minute walk to the Dom, reached via an open-air fruit and vegetable market. In the bedrooms, the public lounges, and the dining room, the sleek furnishings are Nordic inspired, relieved by balloon lamps, bentwood chairs, and modern paintings. The overall effect is unpretentious, but comfortable. The doubles are generally spacious, with over-scale armchairs drawn up at long coffee tables. Bathless singles range in price from 40 DM ($22.94); with bath, from 50 DM ($28.68) to 54 DM ($30.97). Bathless doubles go from 56 DM ($32.12) to 62 DM ($35.56); with bath, 82 DM ($47.04). Rates include breakfast, service, and taxes. Set meals are available, ranging in price from 14 DM ($8.03) to 21 DM ($12.05), although extensive à la carte listings are offered as well.

WHERE TO DINE: Ratskeller, 1 Rathausplatz (tel. 5-17-77), is traditional and unspoiled. Here, you get the best meals for your money in Regensburg. Just five minutes from the Dom, this comfortable, middle-class establishment consists of two dining rooms, with vaulted ceilings, paneled walls, and painted crests. The cooking is good, in the true Germanic tradition, although internationally inspired offerings are introduced to give added variety and flair. At your adjoining table, you'll likely find a Regensburg matron taking time out between shopping sprees. The best buy is the set luncheon, ranging in price from 12.50 DM ($7.17) to 17 DM ($9.75). On the à la carte menu, soups begin at 2.40 DM ($1.38), followed by such offerings as veal schnitzel Cordon Bleu at 16.50 DM ($9.46) and the Indonesian nasi-goreng at 12.50 DM ($7.17). An always reliable dish is the entrecôte with french fries, at 17 DM ($9.75).

8. Passau

One of the most popular reasons for visiting this "Dreiflüssetadt" (town of three rivers) on the Austrian frontier is to take one of the numerous boat tours along the Danube and its tributaries, the Inn and Ilz Rivers, which join the Danube at Passau. The sightseeing trips range from a one-hour, three-river tour to a steamer cruise downriver to Vienna. But before you wander off from this medieval city, you'll find it worthwhile to stop to see—

THE SIGHTS: The Old Town is built on a rocky spur of land, formed by the confluence of the Inn and Danube, just 75 miles downstream from Regensburg. To best appreciate its setting, cross the Danube to the **Veste Oberhaus,** a medieval episcopal fortress towering over the town and the river. Note how many of the houses are joined together by arches, giving them a unity of appearance. As you view the town, you can sense in its architecture that it is more closely allied to northern Italy and the Tyrolean Alps than to its sister cities to the north.

Dominating the scene are the twin towers of **St. Stephen's Cathedral.** The original Gothic plan of the church is still obvious in spite of its reconstruction in the 17th century in the style of grand baroque. Its most unusual feature is the huge octagonal dome over the intersection of the nave and transept. The interior of the cathedral is mainly Italian baroque—almost gaudy, with its many decorations and paintings. Of particular interest is the east wing, which remains from the Gothic period. The cathedral's newest addition is a huge organ—possibly the largest in the world—built in 1928 and placed in an 18th-century casing. Concerts are given every day at noon during the summer.

Below the cathedral, on the bank of the Danube, is the attractive Marketplace with its **Rathaus**. Dating from the 13th century, Passau's Town Hall is a colorful structure, its facade decorated with painted murals depicting the history of the town. Inside, the huge Knights' Hall contains two large 19th-century frescoes depicting incidents from the German epic, the legend of the Niebelungen.

LOW-COST INNS: Zur Laube, am Dreiflusseck (tel. 21-11), is an old inn, right on a tiny plaza overlooking the Danube, near the point where it joins the Inn. Brewery owned, it is managed by the energetic and enlightened Bruno Graswald, who has style and joie de vivre. True to simple innkeeping fashion, there is no guest lounge. The bedrooms have a special flair, with natural slatted pine ceilings, strong colors on the walls, decorator lamps and mirrors, and blond contemporary furnishings. Bathless singles cost 28 DM ($16.06), increasing to 32 DM ($18.36) to 38 DM ($21.80) with bath. Bathless doubles go for 60 DM ($34.42) or 90 DM ($51.62) with bath.

Tables for dining open directly on the little plaza, with plates set under a colonnade of arches. Every guest has a view of the barge traffic on the Danube. The major dining room inside has coved ceilings and a sophisticated provincial decor. An inner salon has tables with a view of a fountain pond where fresh fish are stocked. Meals are good and attentively served. A specialty is trout with morsels steamed in foil (opened and served at your tableside) at a cost of 19.50 DM ($11.19). Most main dishes are cooked to order to guarantee their freshness. A cheese fondue costs 18.50 DM ($10.61) for two persons. For dessert, you might want to pay homage to across-the-border Austria by ordering a Salzburger nockerl in caramel sauce at 14 DM ($8.03) for two persons. A special feature is Irish coffee at 8.50 DM ($4.88).

Weisser Hase, 23 Ludwigstrasse (tel. 3-40-66), has been completely rebuilt. One would never know that it traces its history back to 1512. The only clue would be a pair of antique family portraits hanging over a tufted Victorian sofa in a little salon. The Weisser Hase is in the heart of Passau, off Ludwigsplatz, halfway between the Dom and the railway station. It straddles the peninsula, between the Danube and the Inn Rivers. The Weinstube has a Bavarian-Austrian decor, with much woodcarving, red table coverings, and provincial chairs. The accommodations are clean and comfortable, with modern furnishings. Bathless singles range in price from 31 DM ($17.78); bathless doubles go for 48 DM ($27.53). Singles with bath or shower are from 45 DM ($25.81), while doubles with private bath or shower are 75 DM ($43.02) to 90 DM ($51.62), breakfast included.

Schloss Ort, am Dreiflusseck (tel. 340-72), is a remake of a 1250 castle, standing right on the banks of the Inn River, rising five stories directly from the water's edge. The most dramatic feature of the bedrooms is that they provide views of where the rivers converge. All is modern inside; chrome and plastic set the tone. But the situation is decidedly glamorous, the rooms fresh. Bathless singles rent for 32 DM ($18.36); with shower, 39 DM ($22.37). Bathless doubles cost 57 DM ($32.70), increasing to 80 DM ($45.89) with private bath. Your morning meal is best when taken on the open terrace overlooking the Inn River. Riverboat excursions begin at the dock right at the foot of the schloss.

Schwarzer Ochse ("Black Ox"), 22 Ludwigstrasse (tel. 21-19), is a rustic and basic inn in the heart of town, just a few minutes' walk from the cathedral. Two rather attractive dining rooms are all you'll get in the way of public rooms. However, both feature a surprising array of international dishes, including filet

244 DOLLARWISE GUIDE TO GERMANY

goulasch Stroganoff at 16 DM ($9.18) and peppersteak, 18 DM ($10.32). Lunches are a bargain at 11 DM ($6.31) and 18 DM ($10.32). The bedrooms are comfortable, the bedding fresh, the eiderdown fluffy—and the cost low. In a bathless single, one person pays 26 DM ($14.91), and in a double with bath, the charge is a peak 37 DM ($21.22) per person.

WHERE TO DINE: Heilig-Geist-Stift-Schenke, 4 Heiliggeistgasse (tel. 26-07), is a little inn born in 1358! It's easily found, across from the Hotel Weisser Hase, previously recommended. Many good and low-cost regional dishes emerge from its ancient kitchen, including Serbian bean soup at 3 DM ($1.72) a bowl. Typical main dishes include sirloin steak with french fries at 12.50 DM ($7.17) or a grilled pork cutlet at 8 DM ($4.59). Definitely worth sampling for dessert is the Salzburger nockerl at 7.50 DM ($4.02). Closed Wednesdays.

LOWER SAXONY AND NORTH HESSE

THE WIDE EXPANSE between Frankfurt and Hamburg is probably Germany's most neglected tourist area, and yet it holds some of the most pleasant surprises for sightseeing. Some of the best preserved medieval timbered towns stand in the flatlands and rolling hills of Lower Saxony and North Hesse, as well as many of the most important spas.

Extending from the Netherlands to the East German border, this area includes a wide variety in its landscape, from the busy port of Bremen to the isolation of the Lüneburg Heath. It even contains one of Germany's best winter resort areas, the **Harz Mountains.** These mountains and the flatlands around the Weser River nearby gave rise to some of the most familiar legends and fairy tales in Western literature.

We'll begin our tour of Lower Saxony and North Hesse with its most famous city, the Free and Hanseatic City of Bremen.

1. Bremen

Whether you arrive at "this ancient town by the gray river" by land, sea, or air, you are instantly aware that Bremen is closely tied to the sea. The sights and smells of coffee, cocoa, tropical fruit, lumber, and tobacco give this port city an international flavor. In the days of the transatlantic ocean crossing, most travelers disembarked at Bremerhaven, Bremen's sister port 40 miles up the Weser River. Many visitors rushed immediately off in all directions from the port, ignoring the treasure right under their noses—Bremen, second only to Hamburg among German ports.

Germany's oldest coastal city was already an important port when it was made an episcopal see in 787. In the 11th century, under the progressive influence of Archbishop Adalbert, Bremen became known as the "Rome of the North." During the Middle Ages, it was one of the strongest members of the Hanseatic League and remains one of Europe's most important port cities.

GETTING AROUND BREMEN: Tram tickets cost 1.20 DM (69¢), although preferable is a booklet of ten tickets available at reduced prices when purchased in advance. A two-day "runabout" ticket costs only 3.50 DM ($2.01). **Taxi** charges start at 2.80 DM ($1.61), thereafter being .75 DM (43¢) per 1.20 kilometers. **Sightseeing tours** of the city by bus depart from the main railway station. From the beginning of May until the end of October, tours start daily at 3 p.m. From November to April, the tour leaves on Sundays at 10:30 a.m. The cost is 10 DM ($5.74) for adults, 5 DM ($2.87) for children under 10. Tickets must be purchased beforehand at the **Tourist Information** booth, opposite the main railway station. It is open weekdays from 8 a.m. to 9 p.m. (tel. 31-46-19).

ACCOMMODATIONS: Before we explore the impressive array of sights, let's see what Bremen holds in the way of accommodations.

A Deluxe Choice

Park Hotel Bremen, in Bürgerpark (tel. 34-00-31), is a peaceful world only five minutes by taxi from the heart of the city. Its situation is in a park setting where the life is restrained. The bedrooms vary from impressive suites to cozy singles, but all offer comfort, and many have a lake view. Single rooms with shower and toilet go from 85 DM ($48.76) to 115 DM ($65.96); doubles with bath and toilet range from 150 DM ($86.04). You can enjoy well-prepared meals in any of several dining rooms, including a New England–style grill. Many French dishes are included in the menu. The Halali Bar, with its open terrace in summer, is a good spot for drinks and relaxation. The English-speaking staff is noted for hospitable service.

First-Class Hotels

Columbus, 5–7 Bahnhofsplatz (tel. 31-41-61), is a skillfully updated modern building across from the railway station. In the reading and cocktail lounge, a room-wide mural honors the hotel's namesake. The bedrooms, as well as the public rooms, combine reproductions of traditional furniture with good modern. A liberal decorative use of paintings, tapestries, and Oriental rugs gives a warm colorful touch. Soundproofing in the rooms cuts down the busy traffic noise on the street outside. A bathless single with a toilet costs from 55 DM ($31.55) to 58 DM ($33.27); with bath or shower, from 78 DM ($44.74) to 105 DM ($60.23). Doubles with bath and toilet go from 115 DM ($65.96) to 170 DM ($97.51). Breakfast is included.

Hotel zur Post, 11 Bahnhofsplatz (tel. 31-45-05), may well be a close contender for Bremen's leading modern hotel. The present structure has had four ancestors, the first built in 1889. The latest renovation has created up-to-date accommodations. Bathless singles cost from 37 DM ($21.22) to 46 DM ($26.39), increasing to 70 DM ($40.15) with bath. All doubles have shower baths or else complete baths, ranging in price from 85 DM ($48.76) to 136 DM ($78.01). It's an ideal choice for train passengers, who can refresh themselves after their journey in the hotel's free swimming pool.

The Medium-Priced Range

Übersee, 27 Wachtstrasse (tel. 32-01-97), doesn't look like a hotel—but it is, and a practical and efficient one at that. It occupies the top four floors of a modern business building a short block from the canal. Adjoining the Böttcherstrasse, it is a satisfactory combination of the new and the old. The bedrooms are modern, efficient, and immaculate, many with double sinks, and sofas as well as desks. Not much color, but the essentials are there. The cost of rooms is widely varied, according to the plumbing you choose. Bathless singles rent for 29 DM ($16.63) to 41 DM ($23.52); bathless doubles are 61 DM ($34.99) to 70 DM ($40.15). With bath or shower, the price in a single goes up to 62 DM ($35.56); in a double, 72 DM ($41.30) to 89 DM ($51.05). A big continental breakfast, consisting of crusty raisin bread, cold ham, and cheese, is included in the room rate. Groups often gravitate here.

The Budget Range

Schaper-Siedenburg, 8 Bahnhofstrasse (tel. 31-01-06), is a conservative business-type hotel, just a block from the railway station. Breakfast, included in the rates, is taken in a charming room with tinted windows. The rooms (100 beds in all), are modest, but each is adequate and comfortable. The front rooms are somewhat noisy, so be sure to ask for a room in the back. Bathless singles rent for an inclusive 30 DM ($17.21); bathless doubles cost 55 DM ($31.55) to 59 DM ($33.84). With bath, singles cost 45 DM ($25.81); doubles, 75 DM ($43.02) to 78 DM ($44.74).

Pension Tietjen, 22 Slevogtstrasse (tel. 34-15-59), is a small house with a few bedrooms on a tiny residential street about half a mile from the railway station and close to Bürgerpark. If your requirements are minimal, you'll find it comfortable. The furniture is modern, although not exceptional. The prices are fairly high compared to a hotel, but many guests like it. Singles without bath cost 30 DM ($17.21), rising to 50 DM ($28.68) in a bathless double, breakfast included. A shower or bath is in the corridor.

DINING IN BREMEN: As a seaport, Breman has developed its own style of cooking, concentrating much of its effort, naturally, on seafood from Scandinavia and the North Sea.

The Top Restaurants

Deutsches Haus-Ratsstuben, 1 am Markt, combines pure local color on a comfortable level with the best food in town. The six-story, high-gabled patrician building sits on the Marketplace, opposite the famous Ratskeller, directly facing the square. You dine on either of two levels, including the second-floor Ratsstuben. If the time is right, you may catch festive group singing, especially on Saturday nights. The food is excellent from the mock turtle soup, at 6 DM ($3.44), to the creamy desserts, priced at 4 DM ($2.29) to 7.50 DM ($4.30). Meat dishes are usually in the 8.50-DM ($4.88) to 18-DM ($10.32) range. For seafood, try the sole meunière, priced according to weight.

Set meals range from 22 DM ($12.62) to 28 DM ($16.06). This restaurant is highly recommended for cuisine, atmosphere, and location.

The **Ratskeller,** in the 500-year-old Rathaus, is one of Germany's most celebrated dining halls—and certainly one of the best. It's filled, especially on Saturday nights, with the townspeople, who have adopted it as a social club. The wine list is outstanding, probably the longest list of German wines in the world. Some of the decorative wine kegs have actually contained wine for nearly 200 years. Glasses of wine begin as low as 2.75 DM ($1.58). It's traditional for friends to gather in the evening over a good bottle of Mosel or Rhine wine. Beer is not served in the Ratskeller. Set lunches are served daily in the 12-DM ($6.88) to 20-DM ($11.47) range. The starred items of the menu are available at night only. You may prefer the Hubertus topf for 20 DM ($11.47) or the game ragoût with orange and vegetables for 22 DM ($12.62). Rumpsteak costs 14.80 DM ($8.49), and the soup of the day goes for 5.50 DM ($3.15).

Robinson, 3 Böttcherstrasse, is a series of dining rooms in a variety of styles, reflecting Bremen's international nature as a port city. One room is inspired by Copenhagen, another perhaps by an Italian trattoria, Montmartre, or Granada. The Fischerstube—for seafood lovers—in a chateau style, has especially good sole and hors d'oeuvres platters. You may choose the old Bremen herring filet in cream sauce for 23.50 DM ($13.48), or else lamb filet cutlet with tarragon for 24.50 DM ($14.05). Two six-course menus are available at 39.50 DM ($22.66) and 52 DM ($29.83). In the same building is the intimate Flett. Both the restaurant and grill are popular, not only for the wide assortment of international dishes, but also for the good wines and excellent, strong, coffee. Service is rather hectic; closed Sundays.

The Medium-Priced Range

Martini Grill-Restaurant, 2 Böttcherstrasse, in keeping with the mood of the famous street where every building is an original, is as contemporary at the avant-garde theater next door (it lies just off the theater's lobby). The imaginative decor consists of a ceiling of crisscrossed sticks and a wall of pressed natural pebbles. Balloon lights hang above the tables. Halfway between the Marketplace and the Weser River, the restaurant is convenient to all the major sights, shopping, and, of course, the theater. Fresh fish, much of it from Norway, is the specialty. The sole is priced according to weight; the heilbuttschnitte (halibut steak) is 18.40 DM ($10.55). The mock turtle soup, at 3.60 DM ($2.04), is a delicious introduction to Bremenese cooking. Lighter eaters may prefer the bauern omelet with french fries, at 7.80 DM ($4.47). Closed Sundays.

Alte Gilde, 24 Ansgaritorstrasse, is housed in one of the most ornately decorated houses in Bremen. In spite of the modern buildings surrounding it, the structure, with its gilt gargoyles and sea serpents, clings tenaciously to the past. The restaurant itself (entrance on Hutfilterstrasse) is in the vaulted cellar of the 17th-century structure. The house specialty is "Alte-Hanse Platte," reminiscent of Old Bremen, 42 DM ($24.09) for two persons. Set lunches with soup and dessert range from 9.50 DM ($5.45) to 19.75 DM ($11.33). For a safe, but typically German, choice, try the pork steak à la Kempinski with poached eggs and a béarnaise sauce at 17.75 DM ($10.18). Soups begin at 4.75 DM ($2.72), and desserts start at 6.75 DM ($3.87).

The Budget Range.

Alt Bremer Brauhaus, off Sogestrasse, is like dining in an 18th-century village. Each "house" in this restaurant faces on the "square," where there is dancing every night of the week from 7:30 p.m. till 1:45 a.m. to live music, and even on Sunday morning from 11 a.m. till 2 p.m. Each house, as you've guessed, is a dining room, whose windows give clients a view of the dance floor. The beer garden atmosphere becomes very lively if you arrive on the right night. Main dishes range from 7.95 DM ($4.56) to 24.05 DM ($11.50). The Bremer chicken soup, at 4.25 ($2.44), is a good appetizer. Desserts cost from 2.90 DM ($1.66) to 5.10 DM ($2.93).

THE TOP SIGHTS: The most practical way to see Bremen is on foot. If you don't like to explore on your own, guides are available for walking tours, as well as inexpensive motorcoach tours of the entire city.

The main sights center around the **Marktplatz,** the "parlor" of Bremen life for more than 1000 years. The 30-foot statue of the city's protector, **Roland,** erected in 1404, still stands today, his sword raised toward the cathedral, symbolizing Bremen's declaration of freedom against the Church. Shortly after the statue was put up, Bremen became Germany's first Protestant state.

The **Rathaus** (Town Hall) has stood for 560 years on the Marketplace, although it has seen several periods of transformation. The original Gothic foundations remain basically unchanged, but the upper section reflects the 17th-century Weser Renaissance style in the facade, with the tall windows alternated with relief statues of Charlemagne and the electors of the Holy Roman Empire. The Upper Hall, part of the original structure, contains a beautifully carved oak staircase dating from the early 17th century and a huge mural (1537) depicting *The Judgement of Solomon* and typifying the hall's original character as a council chamber and courtroom. In the Lower Hall are ancient oak pillars and beams supporting the building, and below, the historic wine cellar, the previously recommended "good Ratskeller of Bremen." At the west end of the Rathaus is one of the most recent additions, a modern sculpture of Bremen's famous visitors from the land of Grimm—the Bremen Town Musicians. The donkey, dog, cat, and cock are stacked, pyramid style, in a constant pose for the ever-present cameras. For sightseeing tours of the Town Hall, inquire at the information booth at the **New Town Hall** (entrance opposite the cathedral).

St. Peter's Cathedral is set back from the square, but towers majestically over all the other buildings in the Altstadt (Old Town). Originally designed in 1043 as the archbishop's church, it has since been rebuilt twice—in the 16th and 19th centuries. Dating from the early church, however, is the Romanesque **East Crypt,** containing the tomb of St. Adalbert and an organ on which Bach once played. The West Crypt, from the same period, houses a bronze baptismal font, a fine example of 12th-century workmanship. There is even an interesting collection of mummies in the ancient chapel in the cathedral cellar. Guided tours are conducted hourly throughout most of the day, except Sundays and holidays.

Across the square from the Rathaus stands another example of a happy merger of Gothic and Renaissance architecture, the **Schütting,** a 16th-century guildhall now used by the Chamber of Commerce. In direct contrast to these ancient masterpieces is the modern (1966) **"Haus der Bürgerschaft,"** home of Bremen's Parliament. The new structure was scaled down to fit in with its surroundings. Even though the architecture is a maze of glass, concrete, and steel, it does not look entirely out of place.

Other Sights

The **Böttcherstrasse,** running from the Marketplace to the Weser River, is a brick-paved reproduction of a medieval alley, complete with shops, restaurants (see recommendations above), museum, and galleries. The street was the brainchild of a wealthy Bremen merchant, Ludwig Roselius, and designed to present a picture of Bremen life, past and present. Dedicated in 1926 and rebuilt after World War II, the street is one of Bremen's biggest attractions. Try to visit around noon, 3 p.m., or 6 p.m., when the Meissen bells strung between two gables set up a chorus of chimes for a full 15 minutes. Besides the fine handicraft and pottery shops, the street also contains buildings of historical significance. The **Paula Modersohn-Becker House,** at no. 8, is dedicated to Bremen's most important contemporary painter and contains many of her best works, including several self-portraits and some still lifes. The **Roselius House,** next door, is a 16th-century-style merchant's manor housing Roselius's collection of medieval objets d'art and furniture.

The **Schnoor,** the old quarter of Bremen, has undergone restoration by the "Custodian of Ancient Monuments." The cottages of this east end district, once the homes of simple fishermen, have been rented to artists and craftsmen in an effort to revive many old arts and crafts. Tourists visit not only for the atmosphere but for the unusual restaurants, shops, and art galleries.

The **Rampart Walk** is a green park where the ramparts protecting the Hanseatic city used to stand. The gardens divide the Old Town from the newer extensions of the city. Extending along the canal (once Bremen's crown-shaped moat), the park is a peaceful promenade just a few short blocks from the Marktplatz. Its major attraction is an ancient windmill, still functioning.

ORGANIZED TOURS OF THE PORT OF BREMEN: To see Bremen, you have to visit the busy harbor and docks, as these are the lifeblood of the city. Circular tours of the harbor, lasting 1¼ hours, depart daily (subject to change) at 10 a.m., 11:30 a.m., 1:30 p.m., 3:15 p.m., and 4:30 p.m. from the dock just below **St. Martin's Church** (just follow the Böttcherstrasse from the Marketplace). The 7-DM ($4.02) tickets can be purchased on the pier. Children up to 14 years old are charged half fare.

2. Hannover

Every student of English history is aware of the important role which the House of Hannover played in the political history of Great Britain. For more than 100 years, until a woman named Victoria split the alliance, Britain and Hannover were ruled simultaneously by German monarchs, some of whom preferred to live in their native state (much to the annoyance of the British!).

The city of Hannover today has lost much of its political influence, although it is the capital of the province of Lower Saxony. It has, instead, become one of Germany's most important hubs of industry, transportation, and commerce. The annual industry trade fair is world-famous. Held the last ten days in April, the Hannover Fair has grown to be the largest trade fair in the world. Producers and buyers from around the globe meet en masse. Thanks to its central location in West Germany, the city has become a major railway terminus. Its international airport is a convenient shuttle point for flights to Berlin.

The Green Metropolis is a masterpiece of modern planning, combining parks and tree-lined streets with bold and imaginative solutions to a large city's traffic problems. Before we explore the treasures these streets hold, however, let's check into a hotel.

ACCOMMODATIONS: Hannover is a business person's city, and the hotel accommodations reflect this in the super-abundance of deluxe and first-class hotels which are big on comfort but rather short on romance.

A Deluxe Hotel

Hotel Inter-Continental, 11 Friedrichswall (tel. 1-69-11), opposite the Rathaus, is the finest hotel in northern Germany. It's a splendid contemporary palace of comfort, with built-in style, where you get the most for your money. Heavily patronized by American, German, and Japanese business people, the hotel has many fine public facilities, including a garage, shopping center, beauty salon, currency exchange, barbershop, drugstore, and a large international newsstand. Each of the 300 ultramodern rooms has its own tiled bath and shower, a radio, color TV, direct-dial telephone, and a mini-bar. In the widest possible price range, single rooms begin at 100 DM ($57.36) and spiral upward to 162 DM ($92.92). Double rooms begin at 140 DM ($80.30) and range upward to 205 DM ($117.59). Prices include tax and service. A third person in a room pays an additional 46 DM ($26.39).

The Inter-Continental's spacious but intimate Prinz Taverne is one of Hannover's most popular restaurants. The food and service are both outstanding. Two à la carte specials on the dinner menu: filet of sole "belle vue" for 36 DM ($20.65) and filet de veau au citron (marinated sirloin of veal with lemon-pepper) for 34 DM ($19.50). For cocktails before dinner, or for an evening of live entertainment and dancing afterward, stop in at the Grenadier Lounge, a disco. There's usually a combo for dancing, or you may prefer just to relax and sip your drink in the raspberry-hued chairs. And you only pay for what you drink here—no admission or cover charge. Besides the Prinz Taverne, the Inter-Continental has two other restaurants, for lighter and less expensive meals: the Bierstube, for beer and snacks, and the Brasserie, opening onto a view of the Rathaus, for snacks, breakfast, and full-course meals.

First-Class Hotels

Kastens Hotel, 2 Luisenstrasse (tel. 1-61-51), just 300 yards from the main railway station and a few minutes by car from the airport, was Hannover's leading hotel until the Inter-Continental came along. For many, however, it remains the traditional favorite, having been in the same family since it was established by Heinrich Kasten in 1856. The 220 extensively modernized rooms are agreeable and well maintained. Bathless singles rent for 49 DM ($28.11) to 69 DM ($39.58); singles with bath, 89 DM ($51.05) to 109 DM ($62.52). All doubles have private baths, renting from 148 DM ($84.89) to 168 DM ($93.36). The hotel has several dining facilities, including a restaurant, grill-room, and a cozy bar. There is a parking garage for 100 cars. The English-speaking staff is helpful and efficient.

Hannover EuroCrest Hotel, 117 Tiergartenstrasse (tel. 52-30-92), in the suburb of Kirchrode, is an excellent choice, although a long haul from the center of town. The ultramodern rooms, often decorated in sunflower gold and chocolate brown, all contain private baths, showers, bidets, radios, and direct-dial telephones. The filmy white curtains at the windows are drawn back to look out on a Deer Park and woodland. A double room with French bed and shower rents for 92 DM ($52.77) if occupied by one person, 118 DM ($67.68) if occupied by two. A studio or twin-bedded room rents for 148 DM ($84.89) for two persons. Extra beds cost an additional 24 DM ($13.77). Breakfast is included. Hearty fare and good wines and beer are served in the semirustic Royal Stable. The attractive bar, Old Smithy, has a warm and inviting atmosphere. The hotel can easily be reached from the Hannover-Anderten exit (just a mile away) of the Hamburg-Frankfurt-Basle autobahn.

The Medium-Priced Range

Hotel am Leineschloss, 12 am Markt (tel. 32-71-45), across from the City Hall, is a surprise discovery, the best for value in Hannover. It's the preferred hotel for those who want to be in the heart of the old section, yet it's quiet despite its central location. It's like being snuggled warmly in contemporary comfort in old-world surroundings. The generously sized rooms, with their bright colors, are housed in an avant-garde modern structure. Most units have sitting areas big enough for a leisurely breakfast. Every room has either a bath or shower as well as toilet. Singles with shower rent for 92 DM ($52.77); doubles with bath, 120 DM ($68.83) to 143 DM ($82.02). The individual service and ultramodern comfort may make you want to prolong your stay. There is a garage, or you can park in the space in front of the hotel. The only meal served is breakfast, included in the rates.

The Budget Range

Rummels Europäischer Hof, 4 Luisenstrasse (tel. 1-76-44), is just the right place for one-night stopovers. It's a modest railway station hotel next door to Kastens. The excellent restaurant, Le Coq d'Or, recommended below, is on the same premises. The hotel's rooms are furnished in basic modern. The double windows and double doors keep out most of the noise. Bathless singles rent for 32 DM ($18.36) to 48 DM ($27.53); bathless doubles, for 65 DM ($37.28) to 88 DM ($50.48). With private shower or bath and toilet, the price in a single is 42 DM ($24.09) to 63 DM ($36.14), rising to 75 DM ($43.02) to 110 DM ($63.10) in a similarly equipped double. Breakfast, service, and taxes are included.

Hotel Loccumer Hospiz, 16 Kurt-Schumacher-Strasse (tel. 1-46-57), a short walk from the station, is one of the best economy finds in the city. The rates are reasonable, considering the general comfort and amenities offered. The utilitarian rooms are small, the service and frills minimal, but it's a good stopover. Bathless singles cost 40 DM ($22.94) to 50 DM ($28.68); bathless doubles, 66 DM ($37.86) to 72 DM ($41.30). With private bath, the price in a single increases to 55 DM ($31.55) to 78 DM ($44.74); a double, to 76 DM ($43.59) to 96 DM ($55.07). Prices include service and tax, plus breakfast. The standard Germanic fare in the hotel's dining room is quite good.

Am Rathaus, 21 Friedrichswall (tel. 32-62-68), is a modern hotel directly facing the Town Hall. It offers a good choice of small, although comfortable, rooms—well furnished with oak pieces. The hotel is immaculately kept as well. The reception is small, but the welcome is big. An elevator takes you to one of the guest bedrooms. All rooms now have private baths or showers, the price in a single going from 64 DM ($36.71) to 72 DM ($41.30), increasing to 88 DM ($50.48) to 96 DM ($55.07) in a double.

A Country Retreat Near the Herrenhausen Gardens

Georgenhof, 20 Herrenhäuser Kirchweg (tel. 71-22-44), is really a country inn incongruously positioned within the city. Sitting in its own private park near the famous Herrenhausen Gardens, the hotel is the quietest, most secluded retreat in Hannover. Single rooms range from 35 DM ($20.08) to 85 DM ($48.76), depending on plumbing and location. Doubles range from 65 DM ($37.28) to 140 DM ($80.30). There is an additional charge of 8 DM ($4.59) for use of the public bath. The rooms are clean and pleasant, furnished with a mixture of antiques and traditional furniture, often hand-painted pieces. The Georgenhof's restaurant is the finest in Hannover. All selections are à la carte and rather expensive, but well worth the price. For an appetizer, try the turtle soup at 7.50 DM ($4.30). The difficulty then is in choosing the main course—they're all tempting. The specialties include deep-fried prawns at 26 DM ($14.91) and breast of chicken suprême at 18.50 DM ($10.61). A selection of international dishes is also featured, including Valencian paella at 52 DM ($29.83) for two persons. Desserts range from 5.50 DM ($3.15) to 12.50 DM ($7.17). Seafood and fresh fish, prepared in the nouvelle cuisine style, cost from 25 DM ($14.34) to 42 DM ($24.09), and game dishes go from 27.50 DM ($15.77) to 45 DM ($25.81). In summer, tables are set out on the terrace, overlooking a restful garden, and pond. The Georgenhof is highly recommended for both food and lodging.

READERS' HOTEL SELECTIONS: "The owners of the **Hotel Rena,** Fred and Rosi Kurkofka, will welcome guests at any hour, even late at night. They speak English, and children and pets are welcome. The address is 86 Alte Peiner Heer Strasse, just five minutes from the **Berlin-Köln** autobahn exit of **Buchholz** (tel. 61-16-93). Without bath, doubles range from 38 DM ($21.80) to 46 DM ($26.39); with bath, from 48 DM ($27.53) to 58 DM ($33.27). On weekdays authentic German meals are available for reasonable prices. The set menu changes daily" (Steve Willing, Granada Hills, Calif.). . . . **"Hotel an der Marktkirche,** 10 Gruppenstrasse (tel. 1-24-13), is virtually opposite the Ratskeller and Old Town and yet is only a brief walk to the shopping center. In small but comfortable rooms, the charge is 25 DM ($14.34) per person per day, including breakfast" (Susan L. Davison, Herford, West Germany).

DINING IN HANNOVER: Besides the fine food served in many of the hotels' dining rooms and restaurants, including the Hotel Inter-Continental, Kastens, and the Georgenhof, Hannover enjoys a wide variety of cuisine in its numerous restaurants. You can find anything from a hamburger to chop suey if you wish, but we have concentrated our recommendations on the more continental choices.

Le Coq d'Or, 4 Luisenstrasse, right near the railway station, serves the best food in the center of town. The typical tavern decor is the setting for a real adventure in French cuisine. The specialties of the day feature full-course dinners ranging from as low as 16.50 DM ($9.46) to 27 DM ($15.49), the latter including, for example, a mixed salad, mussels, game (in season) with vegetables, plus cheese and zabaglione.

The **Ratskeller,** in the historic old Town Hall, 60 Köbelingerstrasse (tel. 1-53-63), as in most German cities, is one of the most popular dining spots for townspeople and visitors alike. Patrons dine in two rooms at tables set under vaulted brick arches. The lunches are among the best bargains in town. From noon to 3 p.m., a complete luncheon, including soup, main course, and dessert, ranges from 16 DM ($9.18) to 34 DM ($19.50). The à la carte appetizers in the evening include soups costing from 6 DM ($3.44) to 9.50 DM ($5.45). Main-dish specialties include Oriental steak, 21.75 DM ($12.48); filet steak Café de Paris, 29 DM ($16.63); and wienerschnitzel, 19.50 DM ($11.19).

THE SIGHTS: No matter where you go in Hannover, you will not be far from a park or garden. But if you have time to explore only one of these, it might be the **Herrenhausen Gardens,** the only surviving example of Dutch/Low German early baroque-style gardening. Designers from France, the Netherlands, England, and Italy, as well as Germany, worked together to create this masterpiece of living art. The **Grosser Garten,** dating from 1666, is the largest, consisting of a huge rectangle surrounded by a moat. Within the maze of walks and trees are examples of French baroque, rococo, and Low German rose and flower gardens. The Grosser Garten also contains the highest fountain in Europe, shooting jets of water 270 feet into the air, and the world's only existing baroque hedge-theater (1692), where Shakespeare, Molière, and Brecht are still performed today, along with ballets and jazz concerts. The smaller 17th-century **Berggarten,** across the Herrenhauserstrasse from the Grosser Garten, is an impressive botanical garden with several houses containing rare orchids and other tropical flowers. The gardens are open daily, in season, from 8 a.m. to dusk. The Grosser Garten is illuminated on Wednesday, Saturday, and Sunday from May 1 to October 1.

The **Market Church,** on the Market Square, is one of Hannover's oldest structures, built in the mid-14th century. Its Gothic brick basilica houses several important religious works, including a 15th-century carved altarpiece and a bronze baptismal font. The **Rathaus** (Old Town Hall), facing the square, dates from 1425. Although badly damaged during the war, it has been magnificently restored and now houses a museum and the civic archives.

The "new" **City Hall** is a huge structure, dating from 1901. It is a good place to visit for a panoramic view of Hannover from its 100-meter tower. The building itself is made more attractive because it sits in the **Machpark,** reflected in a small lake, just a short distance from the extensive **Machsee,** a man-made lake frequented by Hannoverians for its beach, boating, and restaurants.

The **Kestner Museum,** next to the City Hall, contains treasures representing 6000 years of history. Its Egyptian collection is one of the finest in Germany. Other exhibitions include medieval arts, prints, sculpture, porcelain, glass, and coins. The museum is open from 10 a.m. to 4 p.m. Tuesdays, Thursdays, and Fridays; from 10 a.m. to 8 p.m. on Wednesdays; and from 10 a.m. to 6 p.m. on Saturdays and Sundays. Admission is free.

3. Celle

The well-preserved town of Celle stands at the edge of a silent expanse of moorland, looking like something out of a picture book. Its ancient half-timbered houses were spared in the air raids of the war, and the legends carved on their beams seem to live on today. Most of the houses date from the 16th and 17th-centuries—the oldest was built in 1526—but they are in such good condition that they could have been built in this century. One of the landmarks of the town is the **Palace of the Dukes of Brunswick and Lüneburg,** a square Renaissance castle with huge towers at each corner. The palace's bizarre 16th-century Renaissance chapel was designed by Martin de Vos, with galleries and elaborate ornamentation. But the pride of the castle—and of the town—is its baroque theater, the oldest in Germany (1674) and still in regular use today. The Ducal Palace is open daily for guided tours only, from 9 a.m. to noon, and from 2 p.m. to 4 p.m. Admission is 1 DM (57¢) for adults and .50 DM (29¢) for children.

For a picture of life as lived in 16th- and 17th-century Celle, visit the **Bomann Museum,** one of Germany's finest regional museums, with extensive exhibits illustrating the life on the moors and in the town. Included is a complete 16th-century farmhouse, as well as rooms from old cottages, period costumes, and Hannoverian uniforms from 1803 to 1866. In the portrait gallery of Brunswick-Lüneburg dukes, you can see pictures of the electors, later kings of England and Hannover.

ACCOMMODATIONS: If you're stopping over—either for lodgings or meals—you might consider one of the following.

The Upper Bracket

Parkhotel Fürstenhof, 55–56 Hannoverschestrasse (tel. 2-70-51), far superior to any other accommodation, is surprisingly sophisticated for such a provincial town. Standing at the edge of Celle, it is a small-scale manor house flanked with timbered wings which house antique shops, boutiques, and a beer stube. The brick courtyard in front of the salmon-colored mansion is shaded by a towering ash tree. The hotel's interior has formal neoclassic paneling and a collection of antiques, many of them removed from castles—almost high-fashion furnishings. A modern annex beyond the rear courtyard contrasts with the main building in its use of daring and refreshing colors in the rooms and apartments. On the lower level is a tiled swimming pool. All rooms have toilet facilities, and depending on whether you prefer bath or shower, the price of a single room ranges from 65 DM ($37.28) to 115 DM ($65.96). Doubles range from 100 DM ($57.36) to 160 DM ($91.78), which includes breakfast, use of the hotel's indoor swimming pool, service, and taxes. Besides the heated swimming pool, the hotel also has a sauna and massage rooms for guests.

Fürstenhof's restaurant, **Endtenfang,** is warmly formal, done in autumnal colors. The elegant dining room is decorated with painted tapestries. It is known for its Ducal duck, after an old recipe from the court of Celle. The bar room is in the ancient vaults of the mansion. Fine food and wines are the order of the day here. The beer tavern built into the old coach house is more informal, with its old wooden tables and farm artifacts.

The Medium Range

Hotel Celler Hof, 11 Stechbahn (tel. 2-80-61), is on the street where tournaments of knights were once held. Considering the old-world architecture of the hotel and its neighboring timbered houses, the interior furnishings are incongruously modern, but quite pleasing. The Celler Hof's advertisement of "internationaler komfort" holds true for all the guest rooms. Bathless singles rent for from 34 DM ($19.50) to 58 DM ($33.27); bathless doubles, for 68 DM ($39) to 88 DM ($50.48). With bath or shower, the price in a single goes from 64 DM ($36.71) to 118 DM ($67.68); in a double, from 89 DM ($51.05) to 138 DM ($79.16). Prices include breakfast, service, and taxes.

The next-door restaurant, **Heid'Rose,** offers set lunches beginning at 15 DM ($8.60).

WHERE TO DINE: Historischer Ratskeller, 14 am Markt (tel. 2-23-97), is a plusher version of the typical German town hall dining room. The food, as well, is superior to the usual ratskeller fare. The attentive waiters are constantly passing by, carrying silver platters heaped with spicy, flavorful dishes. Complete lunches, including soup and dessert, range in price from 10.50 DM ($6.02) to 30 DM ($17.21). At night, the à la carte menu is varied, with main courses averaging 18 DM ($10.32) to 25 DM ($14.34).

Bürgerkeller Löwenbräu, 34 Bergstrasse, is a small restaurant with two rooms. One is dedicated to serious beer drinkers. The other is for those who want a good and copious meal at a bargain price. You can fill up for as little as 10 DM ($5.74) to 12 DM ($6.88). But for 25 DM ($14.34) to 30 DM ($17.21), you can enjoy a gargantuan repast. Most recently we had wild game in a brown cream sauce with peaches, green beans, potato croquettes, and cranberries. To help this feast along, a quarter of a liter of the local beer is recommended.

4. Lüneburg and the Heath

Motorists driving south from Scandinavia through the Baltic port of Lübeck often find themselves on the Old Salt Road leading to the Hanseatic city of Lüneburg. The road was so named because it was the route by which the heavy salt deposits of Lüneburg were delivered to the countries of Scandinavia during the Middle Ages. Most of the buildings of the Salt City are from its most prosperous period—the 15th and 16th centuries. Although the medieval brick buildings are the most prevalent, seven centuries of architecture are represented in this 1000-year-old city. The rising gables of the once-patrician houses range from Gothic to Renaissance to baroque.

THE SIGHTS: The **Rathaus** (Town Hall) is a perfect example of several trends in architecture and design. You'll enter through a Gothic doorway into a magnificent Renaissance hall, then suddenly find yourself in a baroque chamber. The Great Council Room is its most outstanding feature, with sculptures and bas-reliefs by Albert von Soest (1578). From the painted beamed ceiling in the Fürstensaal, chandeliers made of antlers hang down, adding a festive touch.

Because of its heavy salt deposits, Lüneburg remains an important spa, even today. In the Kurpark is a bathing house where visitors take brine mud baths. In the spa gardens there are also indoor swimming pools, sauna baths, and tennis courts.

Lüneburg is the ideal starting point for excursions into the **Lüneburg Heath.** The soil of the heath is sandy and is mainly covered with brush and heather, although there are a few oak and beech forests in the northern valleys. The heath covers nearly 3000 square miles and includes many beauty spots for the outdoorsman. The **Wilsede National Park** is a 100-square mile sanctuary for plants and wildlife, and for people as well. Strict laws enforce the maintaining of the thatched houses and rural atmosphere. The heath is especially beautiful in late summer and early autumn, when the heather turns shades of deep purple. The pastoral scene of shepherds, sheep, and undulating hills is peaceful.

You may wish to return to Lüneburg to spend the night, or at least for a meal before continuing on to Hamburg, Hannover, or some other destination.

WHERE TO STAY: **Romantik Hotel Zum Heidkrug,** 5 am Berge (tel. 3-12-49), is a brick inn, once a salt warehouse, dating from 1485. The friendly oasis, filled with antiques, is worth a special trip from as far away as Hamburg (35 miles). The innkeeper, Brich Topper, has retained the old beamed ceilings and mellow wood in the rooms and the lounges. The quarters are immaculate, with lots of old-fashioned comfort. There are only eight rooms, so it's best to reserve. Singles with bath rent for 38 DM ($21.80); doubles with bath, 68 DM ($39). Prices include service and breakfast. A closed garage is available for patrons and guests. The dining room serves excellent meals and is popular with many of the local townsfolk as well as visitors from nearby cities and villages. Main-course dishes include veal steak with green beans at 22.50 DM ($12.95) and sole King George at 18 DM ($10.32). Desserts range from 3 DM ($1.72) to 7 DM ($4.02).

WHERE TO DINE: The **Ratskeller,** 1 Markplatz, is a good alternative dining choice. Right on the town Marketplace, the town's dining hall offers a varied menu, including game (in season) with fresh mushrooms, French-style green beans, and cranberries at 22 DM ($12.62). Other main dishes are in the 16-DM ($9.18) to 30-DM ($17.21) range. Soups begin at 3 DM ($1.72).

5. Braunschweig (Brunswick)

Between the Harz Mountains and Lüneburg Heath, Braunschweig (Brunswick, in English) is the second-largest town in Lower Saxony. Henry the Lion fortified and improved the town, making it his residence. Brunswick was one of the chief cities of the Hanseatic League.

Brunswick is a main stopover on the Hannover-Berlin route. Motorists nearing the East German border in the late afternoon or early evening might want to stop at Brunswick to spend the night.

Up until 1918 the city was a German duchy. Brunswick was virtually destroyed in World War II, but it has been rebuilt. The "isles of tradition"—that is, the castle square and the old town market—were restored authentically.

The castle square of **Burgplatz** is in the Romanesque style. In the center is a lion monument, **Löwendenkmal,** the emblem of Brunswick. The sculpture was erected by Henry the Lion in 1166.

Dominating the square is the cathedral of Brunswick, **St. Blasius,** dating from 1173. The chancel contains the tombs of the Dom's founder, Henry the Lion, and his consort, Mathilda of England. Emperor Otto IV is also entombed here. The remains of the Guelphs of the Brunswick line from 1681 are in the vaulting beneath. The most outstanding artwork is a triumphal cross carved by Master Imerwald in the mid-12th century.

The **Burg Dankwarderode,** also at Burgplatz, was built after 1865. It contains the celebrated Treasure of the Guelphs, consisting of silver and gold religious objects and dozens of reliquaries, some from as far back as the 11th century. It is open from 10 a.m. to 4 p.m. Tuesday to Sunday.

The **Herzog Anton Ulrich-Museum,** 1 Museumstrasse (tel. 15-51), was founded in 1754 by Carl I, Duke of Braunscheig. It is now housed in a neoclassical building designed in 1886, and includes on the first floor the art library and print room with drawings by Cranach, Dürer, Holbein, Rembrandt, Rubens, and prints from the 15th century to the 20th century. On the second floor, the picture gallery has paintings by Cranach, Van Dyck, Tintoretto, Rubens, Rembrandt, Vermeer, Holbein, and Giorgione, among others. An antique collection containing the Mantuan Onyx Vase together with a large collection of Renaissance and baroque minor artworks are on the third floor. Hours are from 10 a.m. to 4 p.m. Tuesdays through Sundays; 10 a.m. to 8 p.m. Wednesdays; closed Mondays. Admission is free.

At the **Alstadmarkt** is the old **Town Hall,** a gem of Gothic architecture from the 13th century. From there you can walk to the **Gewandhaus,** the cloth merchant's hall, characterized by its richly ornamented Renaissance facade. Nearby is **St. Martin's Church,** from 1180. Originally a Romanesque basilica, it was enlarged in the 13th century in the Gothic style. Its Annenkapelle is from 1434 and is the first chapel in the south aisle.

WHERE TO STAY (BUDGET): Frühlings Hotel, 7 Bankplatz (tel. 2-67-18), may not win style awards, but it does excel at comfort. It's a substantial, 72-bedroom corner hotel, with a modern Germanic look. There is a respectable dining room, plus a cozy bar and lounge. Most of the adequately furnished bedrooms have tiled private baths. Bathless doubles go for 50 DM ($28.68), increasing to 80 DM ($45.89) with a private bath. Taxes, service, and breakfast are included in these tariffs. Nearby is a community parking garage.

WHERE TO DINE (MODERATE): Gewandhaus, 1 Altstadtmarkt (tel. 4-44-41), is a stone building dating from 1352 and located on the most beautiful square of Brunswick. Once it was a guildhouse for sailmakers, and later it acquired an elegant Renaissance facade. Its fine wines are kept in a 1000-year-old cellar. Rhine and Mosel wines are a specialty. In the midst of this antiquity, well-prepared international dishes are served. Specialties include tournedos Monte Carlo at 23 DM ($13.19) and sole Ceylon at 19 DM ($10.90). Closed Sundays.

    Haus zur Hanse, 7 Güldenstrasse (tel. 4-61-54), is another historic restaurant. Built in 1567, it lies behind a half-timbered structure with the most interesting facade in Brunswick. Plan to make an evening of it. For openers, we'd recommend onion soup at 3.50 DM ($2.01), followed by snails French style at 9 DM ($5.16), and veal steak Hortense in a cream sauce at 24 DM ($13.77). Another specialty is grilled king-size prawns in tarragon butter at 23.50 DM ($13.48). The ice soufflé Grand Marnier at 6 DM ($3.44) makes a good finish.

6. Hildesheim

    Just 15 miles southeast of Hannover, the town of Hildesheim basks in the glory of its 1150 years. The history of the community is closely tied to a romantic tale about the rose tree, still flourishing today, which supposedly marked the spot for the founding of the seat of the bishopric. As with most episcopal sees, Hildesheim became a free city and prospered as a center, not only for the church, but for art and industry as well.

THE SIGHTS: Some of the original ramparts, built by the bishop about 1000 A.D., are standing around the Old Town. The streets are lined with many old houses with overhanging upper stories and elaborately adorned wooden facades. The **Rathaus** (Town Hall), dating from the 15th century, contains frescoes illustrating the history of the city. The chief attraction, however, remains the **cathedral,** which, although badly damaged during World War II air raids, has been magnificently restored. The present structure, built in the 11th century, occupies the site of the original building of the early 9th century. Although the basilica is Romanesque in design, the side chapels are Gothic and the dome is classical. The 11th-century bronze bas-relief doors were turned out by local artisans under St. Bernward, bishop of Hildesheim. The cathedral also contains a treasury full of valuable works, including the intricately designed bishop's staff. Within the church are also many important works of art, and last but not least, the Romanesque cloister at the end of the cathedral houses the town's most valuable possession, the **rose tree.**

The **Roemer-Pelizaeus Museum** is unique in Germany, containing one of the world's most impressive collections of Egyptian antiquities, including sarcophagi, statues, and even the chapel of a 4500-year-old coffin-tomb of one Egyptian official. The museum is open daily (except Monday) from 10 a.m. to 4:30 p.m.; Saturdays, 10 a.m. to 1 p.m. Admission is 1 DM (57¢).

THE TOP HOTEL: Hotel Rose, 7 Markt (tel. 19-55), across the Marketplace from the historic Town Hall, is completely modern with most attractive accommodations. Many people stay here during the Hannover Fair (just a six-minute drive from the autobahn) when the hotels of Hannover are fully booked. All rooms contain private baths and showers. Many have terraces overlooking the Marketplace. Single rooms rent for 70 DM ($40.15), doubles for 110 DM ($63.10) to 140 DM ($80.30). The **Restaurant Arnold** on the premises offers the most sophisticated dining in town, with selections from a wide-ranging international menu, which offers entrees costing from 15.50 DM ($8.89) to 49 DM ($28.11). Set meals go from 14.50 DM ($8.32) to 21.50 DM ($12.33). A good selection of wines rounds out the menu. Patrons and guests of the hotel and restaurant may park in either the parking lot or the hotel's subterranean garages.

THE BUDGET CHOICE: Hotel Weisser Schwan (White Swan), 29 Schuhstrasse (tel. 3-41-43), is like an inn in an English market town, and it's the best economy choice. However, expect no frills and no special hotel facilities. The owner keeps the rooms clean and comfortable. The modest brick facade faces a busy boulevard in the center of town, halfway between the cathedral and the Marketplace. Bathless singles rent for 26 DM ($14.91), going up to 33.50 DM ($19.22) with shower. Bathless doubles go for 44 DM ($25.24) to 52 DM ($29.83), rising to 48 DM ($27.53) to 54 DM ($30.97) with shower. Rates include breakfast, and set lunches are available in the attractive dining room for 8.50 DM ($4.88) to 15.50 DM ($8.89). Soups range in price from 1.50 DM (86¢) to 3.75 DM ($2.15), and desserts are priced from 2 DM ($1.15) to 4.50 DM ($2.58). Parking is often possible around the nearby St. Andrew's Church.

BUDGET DINING: The **Ratskeller,** 1 Markt, is an attractive dining room under a vaulted ceiling in the cellar of the old Rathaus. Every attempt has been made to create a cozy atmosphere. Main courses are priced from 8.50 DM ($4.88) to 23 DM ($13.19), the latter price for a kalbashaxl. Soups go from 2.80 DM ($1.61) to 5.80 DM ($3.33), and desserts are priced at 7 DM ($4.02).

7. Minden

Also in the "Land" of North Rhine–Westphalia, Minden is just 44 miles from Hannover—so it's included in this chapter for convenient touring purposes. On the left bank of the Weser, the old Hanseatic city is famous in history as the site of the Battle of Minden, fought in 1759 at which time the British infantry defeated the French cavalry in the Seven Years' War.

Minden's most interesting building is its cathedral, in the center of town. Characterized by a Romanesque facade, the Dom has somewhat the look of a fortress. Inside, its most valued art treasure is a Romanesque crucifix from the 11th century.

The **Mittellandkanal** merits a visit, too. It crosses the Weser by means of a 1200-foot-long bridge, allowing the canal to go from the Münster to Hannover without benefit of locks.

In the environs, **Porta Westfalica,** or the Westphalian Gap, is a natural geological attraction. From either the Bismarck Tower or the monument to Kaiser Wilhelm across the river, there is a panoramic view of the Weser as it enters the plains of North Germany.

WHERE TO STAY: Victoria, 11 Markt (tel. 2-22-40), is a good, sturdy hotel, heavy in style and furnishings. Everything's a little dull, but comfortable. Bathless singles range in price from 26 DM ($14.91) to 30 DM ($17.21), increasing to 35 DM ($20.08) to 45 DM ($25.81) with bath. Bathless doubles cost 54 DM ($30.97), rising to 80 DM ($45.89) with bath and breakfast included.

WHERE TO DINE: Ratskeller, 1 Markt (tel. 2-58-00), is known for its bierkeller Tonne. A nicely vaulted cellar from the Middle Ages, its original stones intact, the Ratskeller features set lunches and dinners from 8 DM ($4.59) to 21 DM ($12.05). A specialty is leg of veal Ratskeller, with potatoes Lyonnaise and a hollandaise sauce, 19 DM ($10.90). Other dishes include steak tartare at 12.50 DM ($7.17) and a medallion of veal with mushrooms at 14 DM ($8.03).

8. Detmold

Detmold was the capital of Lippe, a former Land of the German Reich After World War II, it was incorporated into North Rhine–Westphalia and is included in this chapter for convenient touring purposes, not geographical designations.

Until 1918, Detmold was the center of the family of Prince Bernard of Holland when Lippe was a principality.

About ten miles from Bad Pyrmont, Detmold is a center for many tours. Following are several examples: **Teutoburger Forest,** where visitors travel a distance of four miles to the **Hermannsdenkmal** (Arminius Monument), to commemorate the victory of native tribes against the Roman legions in 9 A.D. With the dawn of German nationalism, the monument was completed in 1875. Armed with a sword, the copper statue of hero Arminius stands more than 50 feet high. In summer you can visit from 8 a.m. to 6 p.m., providing you don't mind climbing 75 steps for a panoramic view (admission: .50 DM or 29¢).

Another three miles and you're at **Externsteine,** the famous collection of limestone rocks (known in English as the Extern Stones). Beside a lake, this was a place of pagan workshop, although it was turned into a pilgrimage site for Christians in the Middle Ages. A remarkable bas-relief, the *Descent from the Cross,* was carved into the rock in the 12th century.

Back in Detmold, you can visit the **Palace of Detmold,** a Renaissance building from the 16th century, although the interior decoration is from the 18th and 19th. The front wing of the inner courtyard is exceptional, in the Weser Renaissance style. Tapestries of the 17th century—most of them woven in Belgium—were based on cartoons by Rubens and La Brun. Hours are from 9 a.m. to noon and from 2 to 5 p.m. daily, from April 1 till October 31, except Tuesdays and Saturdays, when hours are 10 to 11 a.m. and 3 to 4 p.m. Admission is 3 DM ($1.72).

WHERE TO STAY: Detmolder Hof, 19 Langestrasse (tel. 2-82-44), was a 16th-century hostelry, with a handsome landmark gable. Tradition still prevails, as reflected by the sumptuous hall, with its marble and luxurious carpeting not to mention the deluxe dining room, with bright silver settings and valuable antiques. The large bedrooms are also tastefully furnished. With all of this, the cost is still not exorbitant: bathless singles from 34 DM ($19.50) to 40 DM ($22.94); with bath, 44 DM ($25.24) to 50 DM ($28.68); bathless doubles, 60 DM ($34.42) to 68 DM ($39); with bath, 70 DM ($40.15) to 78 DM ($44.74)—breakfast included. The culinary reputation is high, and the wine cellar is excellent.

9. Hameln

Halfway from Hannover to Bad Pyrmont or Detmold lies Hameln (Hamelin in English), most notorious for its folklore history. It was the town of the world's most famous ratcatcher, the Pied Piper, immortalized by both Goethe and Robert Browning.

The legend is that in 1284 the town was infested by rats. There appeared a piper who, for a fee, offered to lure the vermin into the Weser River. The ratcatcher kept his bargain; the stingy denizens of Hameln did not, claiming he was a sorcerer. He reappeared the next Sunday and played a tune that lured all the children, except one lame boy, into a mysterious door in a hill. The children and the Pied Piper were never heard from again. The story is retold every summer Sunday at noon in a special performance at Town Hall. In the shops of the town, you can buy rats made of every conceivable material, even candy ones.

In Lower Saxony, Hameln traces its history back to the 11th century. The most interesting buildings include **Minster,** dedicated to St. Boniface and built in the Gothic style; the **Rattenfängerhaus** (ratcatcher's house), with frescoes illustrating the Pied Piper legend; and the **Hochzeitshaus** (wedding house), with its trio of attractive gables. The finest houses in the town are built in what is known as the "Weser Renaissance" style, dating from the late 16th century. You can admire these nicely sculpted houses, as you stroll along pedestrian streets.

WHERE TO STAY: Zur Krone, 30 Osterstrasse (tel. 74-11), is an old house with real antique furniture, comfortable and very clean, in the center of the historic town. A lot of copper utensils are placed all around, giving it a rustic aura. The dining rooms and breakfast salons are small, although numerous. Bathless singles go for 35 DM ($20.08), rising to 55 DM ($31.55) with shower. A bathless double is priced at 60 DM ($34.42), going up to 95 DM ($54.49) with shower, those tariffs including a continental breakfast.

READERS' HOTEL SELECTION: "Hotel Garni Birkenhof, 1a Hugenottenstrasse (tel. 2-87-52), is within easy walking distance of the Old Town and the marvelous bronze sculpture of the Pied Piper leading the children out of Hameln. The hotel reeks with old-world charm. Our spacious third-floor room for two was 50 DM ($28.68), including breakfast and parking" (Stanley and Dorothy Sandelius, Stockton, Calif.).

WHERE TO DINE: Rattenfängerhaus, 28 Osterstrasse (tel. 38-88), is the Renaissance building from 1603 referred to earlier as the "ratcatcher's house." The outside is well preserved and most inviting. The inside is also historical looking, with small wood windows, antiques, and pictures. It's practically like eating in a museum. Soups range from 3.50 DM ($2.01) to 6.50 DM ($3.73).

The house specialty is rumpsteak Madagascar with green pepper, potato croquettes, and green beans, costing 21.50 DM ($12.33). Another specialty is
rattenschwanze Bali-reis with salad, costing 40 DM ($22.94) for two persons,
and a "mouse-catcher" plate, a pork filet, at 21 DM ($12.05). Desserts go from
2.40 DM ($1.38) to 6 DM ($3.44).

10. Upper Weser Valley

Running for 273 miles, the Weser River winds along Germany's "fairytale
country." Sleeping Beauty, the characters in the Grimm Brothers' fairy tales,
and the tall tales of Baron Münchausen were created here.

This most interesting day tour traditionally begins at Hann. Münden. At
this point the Fulda and Werra Rivers meet. Many end their tour in the Pied
Piper town of Hameln in the north. The most romantic way to see the river
is on a paddle-steamer in summer.

HANN. MÜNDEN: In the center of town are hundreds of half-timbered
houses built in many styles. At the confluence of the Werra and Fulda Rivers,
the Weserstein (stone) commemorates the joining. In the medieval town, you
can park your car and begin your exploration of "Hannoversch Münden" by
going inside **St. Blaise's Church.** In the nave is the tomb of William of Brunswick, who died in 1503. With its trio of gables, the **Town Hall** is also interesting. The facade is a good example of the style known as "Weser Renaissance."
From here, you can branch out and tour the already-mentioned medieval
houses. The tombstone of the much maligned Doctor Eisenbart is also in Hann.
Münden. He is honored every year at a colorful folk festival.

If you're anchoring in for a day or so, the following recommendation is
suitable.

Hotel Pension Haus Weserland, 55 Kattenbühl (tel. 88-63), is an old-
fashioned resort-style hotel, seemingly like a spa accommodation, with abundant public rooms and spacious bedrooms. The physical plant is spread out and
somewhat impersonal, but the hotel's position is stellar, with a view of the town
and rivers. In adequately furnished doubles, the rate in a bathless room is 53
DM ($30.40), rising to 70 DM ($40.15) with bath, these tariffs including
service, taxes, and breakfast. Dining is in a glassed-in room or on a weather-
sheltered rear garden terrace. The hotel is closed from December 10 to February 8.

After leaving Hann. Münden, you have to detour west of the river at a
marked turnoff to reach—

SABABURG: Across forest roads you arrive at **Sababurg Castle** where Sleeping Beauty supposedly slumbered. In summer you generally have to park down
below and walk up, as the limited space at the top is almost always filled. This
castle is in Hesse, and it's partially in ruins, but it is believed to have inspired
the Grimm Brothers. For .60 DM (34¢), you can explore it.

The **Burghotel Sababurg** (tel. 05678/1052) lies in Hofgeismar-Sababurg,
13 kilometers north from Kassel. The hotel, run by Mr. Koseck, is beautifully
furnished with antique reproductions, renting out 16 bedrooms, a dozen of
which contain private baths. Nearly all of the well-furnished rooms open onto
views. Depending on the plumbing, singles range in price from 30 DM ($17.21)
to 40 DM ($22.94), and doubles are priced from 60 DM ($34.42) to 75 DM
($43.02). Demi-pension (breakfast and dinner) costs an extra 20 DM ($11.47)
per person daily. The inn shuts down from January 5 to February 25. If you're

stopping by to dine, expect to pay from 20 DM ($11.47) to 35 DM ($20.08) for a meal. There is no restaurant service from November to March. However, summer feasts—announced by blowing horns—are staged in the fortress ruins, with wild pig or spitted bullock, a glass of wine at fireside, or a romantic dance by torchlight. Game and fish dishes, along with spit-grilled items, are also offered.

Again, you have to traverse the Reinhardswald, an oak forest, to reach the main route along the Weser.

The next recommended stopover is at—

KARLSHAFEN: This is a baroque town founded in 1699 by the Huguenots. It lies at the confluence of the Diemel and the Weser. In the town is one of the most interesting stopovers for both food and lodgings along the Weser River. It is previewed below.

Hotel zum Schwan, 3–4 Conradistrasse (tel. 10-44), is an elegant although miniature spa, situated beside the main bathhouse and opposite the town pond on which swans float. Built in 1765, it has the baroque facade of a small palace, with an entrance terrace overlooking the river. Life is informal here, although the rococo dining salon is rather grand, with its paneled walls and monumental ceramic stove. The living room is modern, and in the rear is an attractive courtyard garden. Breakfast is served in a period-piece room, with beaded hanging lampshades and lace curtains. Singles cost 30 DM ($17.21) if bathless, and range from 40 DM ($22.94) to 47.50 DM ($27.25) with shower and toilet. Bathless doubles go for from 55 DM ($31.55), and range from 75 DM ($43.02) to 95 DM ($54.49) with a bath or shower and a toilet. All prices include breakfast. Add 25 DM ($14.34) per person for full pension. If you stop only for a meal, expect to pay from 14 DM ($8.03) to 20 DM ($11.47). English is spoken. The hotel is closed from December 15 to February 15.

Continuing north along the river, you reach—

FÜRSTENBURG: On a hill overlooking the right bank, a castle-factory has been making a famous porcelain since 1747.

From there, the approach is easy to—

HÖXTER: This town is filled with Renaissance and baroque buildings. The most interesting is called **Dechanei,** or the deanery, and it stands to the right of St. Nicholas's Church. The house is twin gabled and dates from 1561. A walk down the **Westerbachstrasse** reveals many half-timbered medieval buildings. Dating from the 11th century, **St. Kilian's Church** contains an outstanding Renaissance pulpit. It's decorated with motifs in alabaster.

Take the Bahnhofstrasse from Höxter for about two miles to **Corvey,** where the remains of a Carolingian abbey stand. The oldest part of the abbey, and the only part still left from the original structure, is the west facade. The lower parts are examples of Romanesque art from the ninth century. Guided tours are conducted through the abbey from April 1 to October 31 from 9 a.m. to noon and from 1 to 5 p.m. for an admission of 1 DM (57¢).

You can also dine within the castle precincts at **Schloss-Restaurant,** Schloss Corvey (tel. 83-23). In summer ask for a table on the garden terrace. This restaurant is installed in the former living quarters of the castle. It's surrounded on two sides by well-trimmed linden trees. The great hall is used mainly for special events, and the tavern-style dining room offers luncheons and dinners with a fairly large international repertoire of dishes. The waiters are cordial, and the food is well prepared. Main dishes range from 12 DM ($6.88) to 36 DM ($20.65).

Continuing on, we reach our final goal at—

BODENWERDER: Thirteen miles south of Pied Piper's Hameln lived Baron Münchausen and his son. The Münchausen name has gone down in literary history. A hunting lodge owned by the baron is now a pilgrimage site for dreamy souls. Münchausen's narrative about his "travels and campaigns" in Russia increased in popularity and was translated into many languages. The original author was Rudolf Erich Raspe, who apparently became acquainted with Freiherr von Münchausen upon his retirement in 1760 in the Russian service against the Turks. He was widely known for his tall tales about his prowess as a sportsman and a soldier. Many of the stories for which Münchausen is known were actually inspired by other tellers of tall tales and were included in subsequent editions.

11. Goslar

Time seems to have stood still in this ancient Hanseatic town at the foot of the Harz Mountains. In spite of the progress and growth of Goslar, the old portion of the town looks just as it did hundreds of years ago. The 600-year-old streets are still in use today and the carved, half-timbered houses are more than just monuments to the past. Many of them are actually used as homes today, or as offices of various organizations.

Goslar owes its early prosperity to the mines in the Harz Mountains, from which silver was drawn as early as 968. Even today, the town works the lead and zinc mines in nearby Rammelsberg.

THE SIGHTS: To best explore this 1000-year-old town, park your car, put on a pair of comfortable shoes, and set out on foot. That way you won't miss any of the numerous attractions that await you, beginning with the **Rathaus** (Town Hall), one of the oldest and perhaps the most impressive of town halls in Germany. Begun in the 12th century, the main section was not constructed until 1450. This part of the structure consists of an open portico with huge Gothic crossvaulting, topped by the burghers' hall. The open arcade on the ground level was used for centuries as a market by the townspeople. The open gallery on the second floor was closed up with stained-glass windows in the 17th century. In the early 1500s, the original assembly hall in the Rathaus was turned into a **Hall of Homage,** and lavishly decorated with a cycle of 55 paintings called *The Incarnation of God in Jesus Christ.* The paintings, which cover the walls and ceilings of the room, include not only works depicting the life of Christ, but other biblical characters as well. Many of the faces are actually the portraits of townspeople of the period.

The **Marketplace,** in front of the Rathaus, was for a long time the town's hub of activity. In the center of the large square is a 13th-century fountain with two bronze basins and the traditional German Imperial Eagle at the top. Even today, townspeople and visitors alike gather in the square at 6 o'clock each evening to hear the clock concert and to watch the parade of people, including the zinc miners, returning home from the Rammelsberg mines.

The churches of Goslar provide an interesting look into the architectural history of the area. Many of the oldest churches—five had already been built by 1200—have been expanded and altered from their original Romanesque style to their current Gothic appearance. The Romanesque **Market Church,** opposite the Rathaus, still has its 700-year-old stained-glass windows and a 16th-century bronze baptismal font. The **Neuwerk Church** has retained its purely Romanesque basilica, and its well-preserved sanctuary contains a richly decorated choir and stucco reliefs. The **Jakobikirche,** dating from the 11th century, has been transformed into a Gothic masterpiece, complete with baroque altars. The church contains the famous *Pietà* by Hans Witten (1520). The **Frankenberg Church** dates from the 12th century, but was completely remodeled in the 1700s. Over the elaborate baroque pulpit and altars hangs the intricately carved "Nun's Choir Gallery," bedecked with little gilded saints and symbols.

One of the reminders that Goslar was once a free Imperial and Hanseatic city is the **Breites Tor** (Wide Gate), a fortress with 23-foot-thick walls and ramparts stretching to the **Kaiserpfalz** (Imperial Palace). The palace, rebuilt in the 19th century along the lines of its 11th-century original, is a huge Romanesque hall. Within its walls is the 12th-century twin-storied chapel of St. Ulrich, containing the sarcophagus of Emperor Henry III.

For a quick and less exhausting look at the history of Goslar, visit the **Civic Museum,** which has interesting displays of the early town, models of the architecture, and several important relics of the past. The museum also contains an important exhibition of 1000 years of mining, including a large geological collection from the Harz Mountains.

Incidentally, for hikers and other outdoor enthusiasts, Goslar is the ideal starting point for day trips and excursions into the Harz Mountains. Not only are these hills famous for their minerals and Harz canaries, but they also contain some of Germany's best skiing resorts and several important spas.

For the demonology expert, the Harz is rich in tales of witchcraft and other folklore. Walpurgis Eve (Witches' Sabbath) is still celebrated in the hills each year.

Meanwhile, back in the town itself, you'll find suitable accommodations.

THE TOP HOTEL: Der Achtermann, 20 Rosentorstrasse (tel. 2-10-01), was completely gutted and has been restored. The historic structure is the leading hotel in Goslar, and its reputation is known throughout the Harz region as well. The 92 rooms—enough for 140 guests—are completely modernized, each with private bath, TV, and radio. All rooms now have private baths, singles costing from 45 DM ($25.81) to 52 DM ($29.83), doubles going for 85 DM ($48.76) to 95 DM ($54.49). In addition to the major dining room, the hotel also has an intimate bar and a bierstube. The latter is housed in a circular medieval tower for which the hotel is named. Incorporating the tower into the structure, the hotel has created an old-world atmosphere in the bierstube, with time-blackened oak and snug nooks for drinking.

THE MEDIUM-PRICED CHOICE: Kaiserworth, 3 Markt (tel. 2-11-11), right in the heart of town, is a great big old-fashioned Germanic hotel. The building dates from 1494 and is considered a sightseeing attraction. Below the eaves are carved baroque statues of the German emperors. The hotel's exterior is Gothic, with an arched arcade across the front of the structure, topped by a turreted oriel window facing the Marketplace. The rooms are large; in fact, the corner rooms are big enough to be suites. Room 21 (a corner room) offers the best view of the Marketplace and the six o'clock concert by the clock on the square. Bathless singles rent from 30 DM ($17.21) to 55 DM ($31.55); bathless doubles, from 65 DM ($37.28) to 80 DM ($45.89). With bath, the price goes up to 65 DM ($37.28) to 85 DM ($48.76) in a single and 90 DM ($51.62) to 150 DM ($86.04) in a double. The rooms are designed with an accent in comfort. On the ground floor, the hotel has a sedate, wood-paneled breakfast room and a vaulted-ceilinged dining room, Die Worth. Step through a 1000-year-old cistern and you are in the cellar restaurant, the Dukatenkeller, with its vaulted ceilings, stone pillars, and ecclesiastical chairs.

THE BUDGET CHOICE: Goldene Krone, 46 Breite Strasse (tel. 2-27-92), near the Breites Tor (Wide Gate), is a village inn, complete with a friendly, stocky innkeeper and his plump wife who attend to the rooms and the meals. The intricately timbered building sits on a busy street along with other old structures. If you enjoy local color, this hotel is a real find. Singles without bath rent for 25 DM ($14.34), going up to 28 DM ($16.06). Doubles without bath cost 50 DM ($28.68) with shower. Included are breakfast and taxes. The rooms are simple, but homelike and clean. The food and drink available are good and inexpensive. Set lunches cost from 10 DM ($5.74) to 30 DM ($17.21), including soup and dessert.

READERS' HOTEL SELECTION: "At the **Hotel zum Breiten Tor,** 53 Breiten, the prices are very reasonable: 24 DM ($13.77) for a single, 40 DM ($22.94) for a double. Breakfast is 7 DM ($4.02). The beds are comfortable featherbeds, and the rooms are clean and simply furnished. They serve the best breakfast we had in our travels. It was the usual rolls, bread, egg, juice, coffee, tea, meat, cheese, and jam, but it was as much as you could eat. The hotel restaurant serves delicious meals, with main meals of meat, potatoes, a vegetable, soup, and dessert costing from 7.50 DM ($4.30) to 12.50 DM ($7.17). The portions are generous. Full pension costs 44 DM ($25.24). The people who run the hotel are friendly and helpful. The hotel is right across from the Breiten Tor" (Sue and Geoff Stanton, Racine, Wisc.).

BUDGET DINING: Ratsweinkeller, Ratsplatz, is the most rustic and also the most attractive dining room in Goslar. Right in the heart of town, in the cellar of the Town Hall, the restaurant is a stone crypt with vaulted ceilings and arches, stained-glass windows, wrought-iron lanterns, and trestle tables. The food is good, if uninspired, and the portions are hearty. The menu consists of heavy Germanic cooking. In season, roast game is featured with wild mushrooms, mashed apples, and berries, at prices that begin at 14.50 DM ($8.32). Soups cost from 3.50 DM ($2.01) to 5 DM ($2.87), and desserts are in the 5.50-DM ($3.15) to 8-DM ($4.59) range. A set lunch costs 13.80 DM ($7.92).

12. Göttingen

A city in Lower Saxony, Göttingen was pronounced "famous for its sausages and university" by Heinrich Heine. The university in this Gothic town is one of the most respected and oldest in Germany, and it suffered little damage during World War II.

Medieval romanticism and the vivacity of student life, particularly as lived in the numerous taverns, make Göttingen worth a day's visit. By making a slight detour, you can visit the university town before exploring the fairytale country of the Upper Weser Valley. Göttingen is halfway between Bonn and Berlin.

In 1737 George II, king of Great Britain and Ireland and elector of Hannover, opened the "Georgia Augusta University," and in time Göttingen became the most popular university town in Europe. The university granted absolute freedom in doctrine and research. For the first time, female as well as Jewish students were admitted.

The **Town Hall** dates from 1369, although it wasn't completed until 1443. Before the Town Hall is a modern fountain of a goosegirl, around which students congregate. Around the Town Hall, the **Markplatz** is the most interesting section of Göttingen. A visit here is traditionally capped by going to one of the student taverns (see below for recommendations).

In the center of Göttingen are some old churches. **St. Alban's** is the church of the "old village," and is said to have been founded by St. Boniface. The present structure dates from 1423. **St. John's** is characterized by two octagonal towers, and **St. James's** is graced by a tower rising 243 feet, the tallest in town.

In the center of Göttingen you can wander down narrow streets, looking at wide-eaved, half-timbered houses. Some of the facades are carved and painted.

WHERE TO STAY (MEDIUM PRICED): Zur Sonne, 10 Paulinerstrasse (tel. 5-67-38), is in the core of Göttingen, at the rear of the Gothic Town Hall. The hotel sleeps 120 guests, mostly in rooms with private baths or showers. Good comfort and convenience are bought at moderate prices: singles are in the 38-DM ($21.80) to 48-DM ($27.53) range; doubles, from 65 DM ($37.28) to 85 DM ($48.75)—breakfast included. A guarded car park is opposite the hotel, or you can park in the hotel's underground garage.

WHERE TO DINE (MODERATE): Alte Krone, 13 Weenderstrasse (tel. 5-66-40), is the finest restaurant in the university town. It continues to win high and justified praise. Once a part of a famous, but now defunct, hotel, Alte Krone provides meals for discriminating diners. You enter through a coved drinking room, with book covers attached to the ceiling. Dining is in one of four intimate rooms. The central chamber is sedately paneled in wood; another contains hunting mementos, including rifles and small antlers. The service by the young student waiters is gracious. Very elaborate set luncheons range in price from 36.50 DM ($20.94) to 48.50 DM ($27.82). On the à la carte menu, specialties include hummerkrabbenspiess (lobster and crab) at 27 DM ($15.49) and crêpes Suzette for two persons at 18 DM ($10.32).

Junkernhaus, 5 Barfüsserstrasse, is a traditional restaurant steeped in ancient traditions. Dating from 1503, it is a black and white timbered corner building with ornate carvings. Inside this atmospheric hostelry are three dining rooms with beamed ceilings and woodcarvings. Main dishes cost from 13.75 DM ($7.89) to 24.85 DM ($14.25), and complete dinners range from 16.50 DM ($9.46) to 22.75 DM ($13.05).

Zum Schwarzen Bär, 12 Kurzestrasse (tel. 5-82-84), is a fine restaurant, also housed in a black and white timbered circa-1500 building. It still has the original stained-glass leaded windows. The facade has name plates of well-known guests. Inside, the ambience is tavern style, with a ceramic stove in the corner and dining rooms with intimate booths. Service is courteous and friendly. Innkeeper Viktor Kainrath suggests Puzsta schinken at 16 DM ($9.18) or nasi-goreng at 12.50 DM ($7.17). Wienerschnitzel is also offered at 16 DM ($9.18). Desserts are from 6 DM ($3.44).

READERS' SUGGESTION: "The presence of a large university makes the city a haven for student nightlife and good fellowship. The pub **Norgelbuff,** 23 Gronerstrasse (tel. 5-51-54), is the central gathering spot for young people interested in good folk music and low-priced beer. Herr Klaus Richter, the host, has guest artists from all over Europe performing twice a week to jam-packed audiences. On other nights, local musicians sometimes grace the pub with impromptu numbers that are equally enjoyable. Herr Richter speaks English and welcomes all visitors to his establishment, which is a gathering place for young people from all areas of the world. The entrance fee is usually 3 DM ($1.72), going up to 4 DM ($2.29) on Saturdays. In the pub, a soft drink goes for 1.20 DM (69¢), a beer for 2.20 DM ($1.26)" (Stuart and Ann Bunnell, Oakland, Calif.).

13. Kassel

Much of Kassel's 1000-year history went down in ruins in World War II, but the modern city which rose from the rubble holds its own culturally and industrially. Known as a city of gardens, the Kassel of today has been designed with traffic-free promenades and pedestrian tunnels. Public parks and sports grounds offer residents and visitors relaxation and entertainment.

THE SIGHTS: Culturally, Kassel has earned fame as the home of the **Documenta,** possibly the world's most important international art exhibition. Its modern State Theatre sets the stage for impressive operatic and dramatic productions. Long a center for drama and the arts, Kassel also boasts the **Ottoneum,** the oldest permanent theater building in Germany (1604), now housing the **Natural Science Museum.**

Visitors to Kassel are drawn here for a variety of reasons—for the art exhibitions, for individual and trade conferences, or for the theatrical productions. But no matter why they come, everyone eventually visits Kassel's biggest attraction:

Schloss Wilhelmshöhe

Built on a small wooded slope where a monastery once stood, this 18th-century baroque castle was the residence of Napoleon's brother, the king of Westphalia, during the Napoleonic era and later became the summer palace of Kaiser Wilhelm II. The apartments are richly and lavishly furnished with good period pieces, and art lovers go to Kassel just to see the fine collection of Dutch, Flemish, Italian, and German Old Masters in the castle. There is one of the most important Rembrandt collections in the world, including three self-portraits of the artist. The collection also includes works by Dürer, Lucas Cranach, Rubens, Van Dyck, and Frans Hals, as well as Titian, Piazzetta, Jan Liss, and others. In addition to the picture gallery of Old Masters, the castle also houses a collection of Greek and Roman sculpture, gold, and pottery.

Also interesting in the huge **castle park,** unique in Europe because of its layout across the slopes of Habichtwald. The crowning feature of the park is the massive **Hercules Monument,** constructed in the early 18th century to a height of 250 feet. From the foot of the monument, a series of waterfalls cascades down the slope of the 800-foot hill. The park also contains the **Löwenburg Castle,** a romantic imitation of a ruined English castle, built at the same time as the Wilhelmshöhe. The park and castles are open daily from 10 a.m. to 5 p.m. (slightly shorter hours in winter). Admission to Schloss Wilhelmshöhe is 1 DM (57¢); to Löwenburg Castle, 1 DM also; and to the Hercules Monument, 1.50 DM (86¢). The castle grounds are open free to the public during the same hours indicated above.

Other Sights

The Waldeck Region, the Reinhards Forest, and Kassel were responsible for the birth of many legends and tales about witches, sleeping princesses, strange beasts, and magic spells. These tales had a profound influence on the Brothers Grimm, who lived in Kassel from 1798 to 1830. The Brüder-Grimm-Museum, 4 Brüder-Grimm-Platz (tel. 1-98-16), contains letters, portraits, and mementos of the famous brothers and their relatives. The most interesting exhibit is a collection of editions of their fairy tales from the first copy to the present day. Admission to the museum is free. Nearby is Kassel's second-largest park, the **Karlsaue,** extending along the bank of the Fulda River. The park contains the ruins of the orangerie, flanked by the **Marble Pavilion,** worth a visit for a look at the 12 statues of mythological characters.

The **Hessisches Landesmuseum** and **Neue Galerie** in the city contain exhibits of interest. In the former, there are four departments: prehistory; Hessian folk art; European arts and crafts, including French and Germanic art nouveau, armoires, glassware, and medieval triptychs and sculpture; and for the science buff, there is the astronomy and physics collection, containing priceless scientific instruments dating as far back as Copernicus.

The New Gallery, on the green terrace high above the river Fulda, houses German and international paintings, sculpture, and objects from 1750 to today. There are many works of the Tischbein family and the elder Kassel school. Modern artists such as Lovis Corinth, Max Ernst, Paul Klee, Ernst Ludwig Kirchner, Joseph Beuys, Richard Hamilton, and Claes Oldenburg are also represented.

Admission to the Landesmuseum and the gallery is free. They are open from 10 a.m. to 5 p.m. daily except Mondays.

ACCOMMODATIONS: In Kassel, you have a choice of living in a fine hotel within the city proper, or in motel-like comfort on the outskirts.

An Upper-Bracket Hotel Near the Castle

Schloss Hotel Wilhelmshöhe, 2 Schlosspark (tel. 3-00-61), is misnamed. It's not an old castle at all, but completely modern in the tradition of an American motel. Built directly across the street from the palace, and next to what were once the imperial stables, the hotel has many private terraces with views of the rolling castle park and its buildings. The bedrooms are comfortable and decorated in a bright, airy style. Single rooms range in price from 40 DM ($22.94) to 110 DM ($63.10), depending on the plumbing. Doubles go for 100 DM ($57.36) to 135 DM ($77.44). Adjoining the hotel is an excellent restaurant-cafe where complete lunches range from 17.25 DM ($9.89) to 42 DM ($24.09). A selection is made from the dessert wagon for 3 DM ($1.72). In fair weather, you can dine at a cafe table on the terrace, listening to band music and enjoying the panorama of Kassel.

The Medium-Priced Range

Park Hotel Hessenland, 2 Obere Königstrasse (tel. 1-49-74), near the Town Hall, couldn't be more convenient for viewing the Flemish masterpieces in the museum across the street. It's the leading hotel within the city proper, and its success has brought about a new addition, with most of the rooms having balconies overlooking the museum gardens. The bedrooms are standard modern, fairly large, with built-in conveniences. One person in a room with hot and cold running water pays 30 DM ($17.21); with shower, the price goes up to 40 DM ($22.94); with full bath, the cost is 70 DM ($40.15). The hotel is also convenient to the town's best restaurants, or, if you prefer, it has its own dining facilities as well as a grillroom.

WHERE TO DINE: Däche, 4 Obere Königstrasse (tel. 1-37-61), next door to the Park Hotel, serves some of the best food in town in its dignified atmosphere. The modern rustic decor belies the fact that the menu is one of the most sophisticated in the city. The luncheon menu, including soup, main course, and dessert, ranges in price from 13 DM ($7.46) to 18 DM ($10.32). For the less expensive price, we recently enjoyed cauliflower soup, schweinschnitzel Montmarte, and cassata regal. The evening menu is à la carte, beginning with soups at 4.50 DM ($2.58). Specialties include filet steak à la Beaujolais at 23.50 DM ($13.48) and sole for 21 DM ($12.05). The dessert feature is a parfait Grand Marnier at 9 DM ($5.16).

The **Ratskeller,** 8 Obere Königstrasse, a few doors from the Däche, is seemingly everyone's favorite place for dining. The attractive, semirustic atmosphere makes people forget their troubles and helps them relax and enjoy their meals. You can find the tables shared by a diverse clientele, from white-haired matrons to young people, from business people to Kassel's students and their professors. The Ratskeller serves both international specialties and regional dishes such as the famous schmeckewöhlerchen, 9.50 DM ($5.45); ratsherrentopf, 13.80 DM ($7.92); and altdeutsches schnitzel, 11 DM ($6.31). Among the international dishes you will find green noodles Florentine style, 13.80 DM ($7.92); medallions of pork Alsatian style, 16.80 DM ($9.64); and grilled filet of pork on a spit, herdsman style, 13 DM ($7.46). At lunchtime there is a special menu prepared for clients in a hurry. Dishes at lunch run from 9 DM ($5.16) to 18 DM ($10.32). A set luncheon is offered daily for around 12.50 DM ($7.17). The extraordinary ice cream menu is well known.

Chapter XIV

HAMBURG

1. Hotels
2. Restaurants
3. Sights
4. Hamburg After Dark

HAMBURG IS A CITY with many faces. A trip through the canals makes you realize why it has been called "the Venice of the North." A walk down the neon-lit Reeperbahn at night assures you that it is the "wickedest city in Europe." A ride around the Alster Lake in the center of the city reveals the elegance of its finest parks and buildings. A view from the old tower of the baroque church of St. Michael opens on the steel-and-glass buildings of modern Hamburg. A Sunday morning visit to the Altona fish market gives you a good look at the stout, Wagnerian housewives mingling with the late-nighters from Reeperbahn.

Above all, Hamburg has a unique and versatile personality. It's a flexible city—it has had to be to recover from the many disasters during its 1100-year history. Not the least of these was the almost total destruction of this North Sea port during World War II. But the industrious Hamburgers seized this as an opportunity to rebuild a larger and more beautiful city, with huge parks, impressive buildings, and cultural institutions.

GETTING AROUND HAMBURG: A word to the wise—park your car and use the public transportation in this busy and, at times, frantic city. Hamburg's **U-Bahn** is one of the best subway systems in Germany, serving the entire downtown area, and connecting with the **S-Bahn's** surface trains in the suburbs. This train network is the fastest means of getting around, but if you refuse to go underground, the slower **streetcars** and **buses** offer a good alternative. The advantage of surface travel, of course, is that you get to see more of the city. Fares range between 1 DM (57¢) and 2 DM ($1.15), depending on the distance you go. The S-Bahn fare ranges from a low of 1.50 DM (86¢) to 2.50 DM ($1.43).

A **Day Ticket** is recommended, as it allows you to use, within the central zone, several methods of transportation (buses, trams, U- and S-Bahn underground services). It is valid between 9 a.m. and 4:30 a.m. the following morning and costs 4 DM ($2.29) as of this writing. You can travel by express (Schnell) or S-Bahn first class for an additional 1.50 DM (86¢). Children, 4 to 12, accompanied by adults, pay only .75 DM (43¢). Day tickets are obtainable at the U- and S-Bahn ticket offices, on buses, trams, boats, and at automatic machines.

Taxis are available at all hours by telephoning 4-10-11 or 44-11-81. Bare fare is 2.80 DM ($1.61), and from .75 (43¢) to 1 DM (57¢) is charged for each additional kilometer (five-eighths of a mile).

HELPFUL INFORMATION CENTERS: Tourist Information, Bieberhaus, near the railway station (tel. 24-12-34), is open Monday through Friday from 7:30 a.m. to 6 p.m.; Saturdays, until 1 p.m. At the airport arrival hall is another tourist information counter, open Monday to Friday from 8 to 11 p.m. Both of these centers will assist with maps, accommodation reservations, and inquiries by telephone, plus give tips and advise of local tours by bus and boat.

1. Hotels

With more than 14,000 hotel beds in Hamburg, the visitor has a wide selection of accommodations to choose from, ranging from luxurious living overlooking the Alster, to friendly, clean boarding houses in the suburbs. But Hamburg is an expensive city, and you'll find an abundance of first-class hotels, but a limited number of budget accommodations, especially in the city proper. During a busy convention period, you may have trouble finding a room on your own. In such a case, go to the hotel information desk at the airport or the main railway station. But if you reserve in advance, there are excellent choices available to you.

THE DELUXE HOTELS: Vier Jahreszeiten (Four Seasons), 9 Neuer Jung-fernstieg (tel. 3-49-41), is a warm, mellowed hotel. Its position is great, right on the Binnenalster. Built in the baronial style, with rich wood paneling, it evokes a memory of the grand hotels of 1910. Ancestral paintings, ecclesiastical woodcarvings, tapestries, and antiques are everywhere mixed with comfortable upholstered pieces. The large rooms are handsomely furnished and immaculately kept, and despite the large size of the hotel (200 rooms), personal service is a hallmark. Single rooms with bath range from 135 DM ($77.44) to 198 DM ($113.57). Double rooms with bath go from 185 DM ($106.12) to 295 DM ($169.21). The inclusive prices vary with the view and size of accommodations. A continental breakfast is an additional 11 DM ($6.31). All rooms contain color TV and direct-dial telephones.

The hotel's dining room, bedecked with garlands and four large porcelain cherubs, is an attractive setting for the excellent international cuisine. There's also an informal country-style luncheon room, furnished in Biedermeier style. The tea room, Condi, is a favorite afternoon rendezvous point. International bands play in the hotel's own nightclub. Garage and parking facilities are available for guests. The Simbari Cocktail Bar is new, and there is also a wine shop as well as a confectioner's shop, selling the chef's own pastry.

Atlantic Hotel, 72 an der Alster (tel. 24-80-01), is Hamburg's other prestige hotel, its glistening neoclassic facade opening onto the lake. The interior is conservative and traditional, with a definite formal aura. Emphasis is on service and comfort, and the entire staff contributes to the smooth-running operation. The lounges are spacious and comfortable, as are most of the rooms. Many decorator touches, such as flowery fabrics and subtle prints, add to the warmth of the rooms. Try to get one of the rooms overlooking the Alster, where you can breakfast while watching the boats sailing on the smooth water. A single with shower costs 143 DM ($82.02), rising to 163 DM ($93.50) with bath. Doubles with bath costs 216 DM ($123.90) to 276 DM ($158.31). Prices include service, taxes, and breakfast.

The hotel's facilities include the Atlantic Rendezvous, a drinking lounge with clusters of deep armchairs where you can meet for long drinks. Lobster is a specialty in the Atlantic-Grill, the hotel's restaurant, but a wide variety of excellent international cuisine is also served.

C.P. Hamburg Plaza, 2 Marseillerstrasse (tel. 35-10-35), stands tall in the Planten un Blomen Park. It's recently built, with all this decade's luxurious accoutrements, including a penthouse bar and disco, sun terrace, swimming pool, sauna, shopping arcade, and three restaurants serving a cuisine ranging from gourmet to rustic. All 570 rooms come with bath, individually controlled air conditioning, color TV, radio, and direct-dial telephone. Incidentally, it's Germany's tallest hotel. Singles range from 122 DM ($69.98) to 152 DM ($87.19); doubles, from 160 DM ($91.78) to 200 DM ($114.72).

FIRST-CLASS HOTELS: **Hotel Berlin,** 1 Börgfelderstrasse (tel. 2-50-43-51), about one-half mile from the central railway station, at the intersection of main thoroughfares, is a convenient hotel, particularly for motorists. But the main reason for staying here—it has the best food of any hotel in Hamburg. Its conservative and restful Kroepels Restaurant serves an excellent French cuisine. It's a modern hotel with a wide range of amenities; the rooms, in contemporary style, emphasize comfort. Prices vary according to size and placement. Bathless singles range from 65 DM ($37.28). Singles with bath go from 95 DM ($54.49). Doubles with bath cost from 135 DM ($77.44), plus 9.50 DM ($5.45) for breakfast. The Y-shaped structure also houses a barbershop and hairdresser. There's an intimate bar in the lobby, convenient for the thirsty traveler. You can park in the 100-car garage. The English-speaking staff is cooperative.

Hamburg Euro Crest Hotel, 1 Mexicoring (tel. 6-30-50-51), overlooks the Stadtpark, just 15 minutes from the heart of Hamburg, ten minutes from the airport. Each of the 125 attractively furnished guest rooms has its own bath or shower, as well as bedside radio and direct-dial phone. A single with shower goes for 98 DM ($56.21) to 102 DM ($58.51). Doubles with shower or bath cost from 130 DM ($75.57). No charge is made for children sharing rooms with adults.

Hanseatic dishes and international fare are offered in both the Windsor Restaurant and the Friesenstube. The motel also houses a cocktail lounge and intimate bierstube. To reach the motor hotel, follow the signs to Geschäftsstadt Nord (City North) from the autobahn exit. It is just 11 kilometers from the Elbe Bridges exit of the Hannover-Bremen-Hamburg autobahn and six kilometers from the Hamburg-Horn exit of the Lübeck-Hamburg autobahn.

MEDIUM-PRICED HOTELS: The **Prem Hotel,** 9 an der Alster (tel. 24-22-11), is a favorite rendezvous in Hamburg. An attractive and sophisticated clientele makes this "white house on the Alster" its home in Hamburg during frequent trips to the city. Originally a mansion, the hotel has been in the possession of the Prem family since it was first established in 1912. The glistening white facade overlooks the Alster, and the rear faces a quiet garden with umbrella-covered tables. The splendid interior shows off a highly personalized collection of French-style antiques and reproductions, many of them Louis XV. The reception salons are dignified but not at all austere. Everywhere there are interesting accessories, such as the tall inlaid clock in the lobby and 18th-century porcelain figurines in some of the rooms. Most of the bedrooms are furnished with white and gold Louis XV–style pieces. The hotel is the best value in town in the middle-bracket category. Bathless doubles rent for 93 DM

($53.34); doubles with private bath are 109 DM ($62.52) and 135 DM ($77.44). All the rooms are sunlit and cheery, but the garden-facing accommodations are much quieter than the front rooms on the Alster. You can enjoy a pleasant breakfast at 8 DM ($4.59) in the white and gold dining room jutting out into the garden. The restaurant also serves delicious lunches and dinners.

Hotel Bellevue, 14 an der Alster (tel. 24-80-11), near the Prem and just a short ride from the central station, enjoys the same sensational view of the Alster. Although the building itself is like a glistening town house with some ornate Venetian touches on its facade, it has been considerably modernized. Some of the larger rooms contain traditional furnishings, but the newer singles are ultramodern, often in the Scandinavian style. Many theatrical celebrities make this their Hamburg choice. The front windows open onto the lake, but the back rooms, away from the busy boulevard, are quieter. Bathless singles rent for 39 DM ($22.37) to 44 DM ($25.24). Singles with private bath cost 71 DM ($40.73) to 76 DM ($43.59); doubles with bath or shower, from 109 DM ($62.52) to 139 DM ($79.73). Prices include service and taxes, plus a breakfast buffet. All rooms contain self-dial telephones. The Alster Restaurant on the premises serves a fine international cuisine. In the Pilsener-Urquell Stuben and Ina Bar, soloists provide nightly music on the Hammond organ. Parking is available in the hotel's garage.

Hotel Park-Hochhaus, 15 Drehbahn (tel. 34-16-56), in the center of Hamburg, is fast rising in popularity; the spacious lobby is often filled with tour groups. The rooms are furnished in an ultramodern style, with sudden splashes of dramatic color. Singles with shower and toilet rent for 72 DM ($41.30); doubles with shower and toilet, for 88 DM ($50.48). A single room with full bath ranges from 83 DM ($47.61) to 93 DM ($53.34); doubles with full bath, from 99 DM ($56.79) to 115 DM ($65.96), inclusive. The restaurant and grill-bar on the premises are popular with the townspeople who have been enticed there by the good German and international fare. The large dining room is decorated in a modified tavern style. Ample garage space is provided for hotel patrons.

Alster-Hof, 12 Esplanade (tel. 34-17-81), is a serviceable, efficient hotel on a quiet street near the Binnenalster. Most of the decor, especially in the public rooms and lounges, is in modern, but heavy German taste, although some of the bedrooms have lighter pieces. Bathless singles rent for 48 DM ($27.53); with shower and toilet, the price goes up to 64 DM ($36.71); with private bath, the tab increases to 85 DM ($48.76). Doubles range from 80 DM ($45.89) to a high of 150 DM ($86.04), depending on bath and location. All rates include breakfast. There's also a good restaurant on the hotel premises. One of the better known middle-bracket hotels of Hamburg, the Alster-Hof is well recommended.

BUDGET CHOICES: **Wedina Hotel,** 23 Gurlittstrasse (tel. 24-30-11), is a friendly little family-style hotel just a minute from the lake and a five-minute walk from the railway station. Most of the bedrooms open onto a small, informal rear garden. It's a pleasant, quiet retreat, owned and run by an English-speaking family. Bathless singles rent for 40 DM ($22.94) to 47 DM ($26.96); bathless doubles, for 60 DM ($34.42) to 70 DM ($40.15). With bath, the price in a single is 55 DM ($31.55) to 60 DM ($34.42); in a double, 74 DM ($42.45) to 90 DM ($51.62). Breakfast is included, and these tariffs also cover the use of a swimming pool. No parking facilities are available other than metered parking in front of the hotel.

Rüdesheimer Hof, 19 Lange Reihe (tel. 24-28-64), near the main station, belongs to the Wienerwald hotel group. The rooms are large and clean, with ample furnishings in a functional style. A single costs 30 DM ($17.21); a double, 50 DM ($28.68), rising to 62 DM ($35.56) in a double with bath. The establishment is small, only six rooms, but a good bargain. Breakfast, included in the price of the room, is served in a nicely decorated salon. In addition, you may order a cold snack to take with you for the day for 7 DM ($4.02) and up. Naturally, you're invited to eat in the nearby Wienerwald, with meals in the 6.75-DM ($3.87) to 17-DM ($9.75) bracket.

Dammtorpalais Schmelzer, 34 Moorweidenstrasse (tel. 44-35-33), is in a building on the outskirts of Hamburg not far from "Fernsehsturm" and Congress Center. A wide selection of pensions is offered on every floor, although the Dammtorpalais Schmelzer is preferred for its position on the ground floor. The owner, Peter Schmelzer, welcomes you in your own language and pays personal attention to each of his guests. Twelve large and comfortably furnished rooms are offered. The rooms—mainly with showers—are often big enough to accommodate three or four. A bathroom is on the floor. The prices for single rooms depend on the size and situation, ranging from 38 DM ($21.80) to 45 DM ($25.81), the latter with shower. For doubles, the rate is 38 DM ($21.80) to 45 DM ($25.81), increasing to 70 DM ($40.15) with shower. Included are a continental breakfast, service, and taxes.

Savoy, 54 Steindamm (tel. 24-66-48), quite close to the station, is recommended in an emergency only. It's basically a traveling salesperson's hotel, with adequately furnished rooms. Singles without bath rent for 40 DM ($22.94), rising to 50 DM ($28.68) with shower. Bathless doubles cost 55 DM ($31.55), jumping to 75 DM ($43.02) with bath, breakfast included.

READERS' PENSION SELECTIONS: "We were directed to a small but clean pension called **Any Nix,** 7a Hartungstrasse. The rate is 40 DM ($22.94) for a double, and it is very comfortable. The woman who runs it (Any Nix) speaks no English but is very friendly. When she wants to tell you something, she just keeps repeating it in German until you understand. Her place is highly recommended and very cheap for Hamburg" (Jerry Pelletier, Banff, Alberta, Canada). . . . "I found a place on my own within two blocks of the bahnhof, **Hotel Alt Nürnberg,** 15 Steintriveg, costing 80 DM ($45.89) in a double with bath. The rooms are clean, roomy, and airy, with a bath and shower on each floor. The only disadvantage is that there is no elevator, a considerable drawback to those living on the fifth floor" (Kevin Cullinane, Somerville, Mass.). . . . "I found a very friendly and clean place with the family **Hugo Reimann,** 39 Lornsenstrasse, Hamburg-Schenefeld (tel. 8-30-77-71). For bed and breakfast (egg) the cost is 24 DM ($13.77) per night. There is good S-Bahn and bus service to the inner city of Hamburg" (I. Tregent, Toorak, Australia).

2. Restaurants

Hamburg life is eternally tied to the sea, and nothing reflects this more than the cuisine. Lobster from Helgoland, shrimp from Büsum, turbot, plaice, sole from the North Sea, and fresh oysters in huge quantities, make up the Hamburger's diet. Of course there's also the traditional meat dish, Hamburger steak, called stubenkücken, and the favorite sailor's dish, labskaus, made with cured meat, potatoes, herring, and gherkins. The eel soup is probably the best known of all Hamburg's typical dishes. The sweet-and-sour eel soup is said to contain more than 75 different ingredients.

THE TOP RESTAURANTS: W. Schümanns Austernkeller, 34 Jungfernstieg (tel. 34-62-65), is admittedly one of the most expensive restaurants in town, but this one is really worth it. You'll pay dearly for a dozen oysters in this "oyster cellar," but what a treat for those who can afford it! Available from September through April, the chef makes his selections as if he were buying pearls. When you enter this belle époque restaurant, founded in 1884, you are instantly transported into the grand, elegant world of the Kaisers. You can dine "in state" here, with your own waiter in formal attire in one of the tiny private dining salons on the long passageway. Each salon is decorated differently, ranging from intimate country style to Empire, with silk damask wall coverings, paneled dado, doors with large brass handles, and gilt mirrors. There are even a few Biedermeier-style salons. The restaurant, incongruously housed in a commercial building, has been in the same family for more than 90 years. The service is the most superb in all of Hamburg.

The Hamburger crab soup at 10 DM ($5.74) makes a good beginning, followed by the house specialty, a Schümanns seeungenplatte at 46 DM ($26.39), a delicious fish plate with a lobster sauce. Desserts are tempting—especially the crêpes Alaska at 17.50 DM ($10.04).

Peter Lembcke, 49 Holzdamm (tel. 24-32-90), is not only one of Hamburg's leading restaurants with truly good food, but also one of the friendliest places in town. In its unprepossessing location on the second floor of an old town house, it attracts a widely diverse clientele, from sculptors to bankers. The good-hearted, helter-skelter service adds to the charm of the restaurant—but the food is the real attraction here. Lembcke specializes in the cuisine of northern Germany, including the most local dish of all, labskaus, at 17 DM ($9.75). A house specialty that may not please everybody, but attracts a loyal following of gourmets, is the eel soup at 19 DM ($10.90), with dill and fruit swimming in the broth along with the eel. Possibly a more appealing dish to the tourist palate is the house-style bouillabaisse at 32 DM ($18.36). Besides the best rau kalbs filet for 33 DM ($18.93), the restaurant also serves excellent steaks. There seems to be no end to the menu. For dessert we recommend the strawberry gelatin dish with whipped cream at 6.50 DM ($3.73). It's so fantastic that the waiters sometimes congratulate you on your good judgment in ordering it! Lembcke's is invariably crowded, and late arrivals without reservations must wait it out in the foyer—so phone ahead.

Alsterpavillon, 54 am Jungfernstieg, is a modern pavilion built right on the Binnenalster. Cafe tables are placed outside in summer when the lake takes on a festive air. The food isn't ignored, however, just because of the dramatic location. Both service and cuisine make this one of the finest dining choices in Hamburg. The sole meunière in chive butter is a delicious selection at 33 DM ($18.93). Other specialties include Strasbourg sauerkraut with pork, 14.50 DM ($8.32). A good beginning for any meal is Matjes herring at 10.50 DM ($6.02). Set lunches are also served daily from 16.50 DM ($9.30) to 24 DM ($13.77). A concert is given daily from 3 to 10 p.m.

Restaurant im Finnlandhaus, 41 Esplanade, is a panoramic restaurant, close to the heart of the city. While the setting is Finnish, with warm autumnal colors and stylish molded armchairs, the cuisine is mainly Germanic, with a few Finnish specialties offered. It's a chic place to dine, in the modern glass Finland House near the Binnenalster. Take the elevator to the top, where the restaurant opens on three sides to spectacular views of the city. On the à la carte menu, a good beginning is the Brazil avocado with crabmeat at 15 DM ($8.60). In season, the wild duck is an excellent choice for two at 48 DM ($27.53). Finnish specialties include smoked reindeer with scrambled egg, 15 DM ($8.60); Finnish reindeer soup, 8 DM ($4.59); grilled moose steak, 40 DM ($22.94); cranberries with whipped cream, 9.50 DM ($5.45). Desserts begin at 7 DM ($4.02) and range upward to 12 DM ($6.88). The restaurant is open daily, except Saturdays and Sundays, and serves meals from noon to 10 p.m.

A MEDIUM-PRICED RESTAURANT: Ratsweinkeller, 2 Grosse Johannis-strasse (tel. 36-41-53), is one of the most impressive and distinguished ratskell-ers in northern Germany. The theme is suggested at the entrance, where you'll find a stone statue of Bacchus. The main dining hall has high vaulted ceilings; wood-paneled columns and antique ship models add to the decor. Medieval scenes are depicted on the three large stained-glass windows. The city takes pride—and deservingly so—in the culinary offerings of its Ratskeller. One excellent dish is the halibut steak in a curry sauce, 16.50 DM ($9.46). The fresh sole bonne femme, at 25 DM ($14.34), is heavenly and served in large portions. Try the Hamburg crab soup at 6.50 DM ($3.73). Desserts are in the 4.50-DM ($2.58) to 8-DM ($4.59) range. Luncheon specials are offered daily from 11:30 a.m. to 3 p.m., including soup and dessert, and range from 12 DM ($6.88) to 25 DM ($14.34). The service is smooth. Listen for the great-grandfather clock to chime the quarter hour, resounding throughout the chambers. Closed Sun-days and holidays.

On the Outskirts

Fernsehturm Restaurant, 2 Lagerstrasse, is perched halfway up Ham-burg's 900-foot television tower in the suburb of Rotherbaum. As the fully air-conditioned restaurant revolves (one complete turn each hour), a panoramic view of Hamburg unfolds. The food doesn't try to compete with the view, but it is good. Angus beef is the specialty here; Angus steak with a Bordelaise sauce goes for 30 DM ($17.21). Soups are in the 4-DM ($2.29) to 8-DM ($4.59) range. Lunch is served daily from noon to 2:30 p.m. and dinner from 6:30 to 10:30 p.m. Families often go up for coffee and kuchen satt, 7.50 DM ($4.30), between 3:30 and 5:30 p.m. Visitors must have a 2.50-DM ($1.43) ticket to go up in the tower.

Alte Mühle, 34 Alte Mühle, a Bergstedt (tel. 6-04-91-71), is a restaurant in a residential quarter, near a waterfall with an old mill. Home-style Germanic fare is featured, including pig's trotters with sauerkraut and potatoes at 13.50 DM ($7.74). Many Hamburgers make the journey out here just to enjoy the fresh carp with melted butter, horseradish, and potatoes, 14.50 DM ($8.32). Blue trout is another feature at 14.50 DM, also. However, the chef delivers his peak performance when he served venison with red cabbage, 19 DM ($10.90). After an opulent meal, you can take a walk through the pond-filled woods and watch the horses nearby.

BUDGET RESTAURANT: Vegetarische Gaststätte, 11a Alsterarkaden, a refreshing change of pace, is the oldest vegetarian restaurant in the world—and certainly the best known. Entered via an arcade in the center of the city, the restaurant is on the second floor. There are two folding chairs halfway up the two flights for the older vegetarians who have trouble navigating the steps all at once. The restaurant, which has been around since 1892, consists of three generous rooms, one of them terrace-style surrounded by windows. Care is taken in the preparation of the vegetables, which are usually overcooked in Germany. Soups cost 3.50 DM ($2.01); most vegetable plates go for around 8 DM ($4.59); salads, for around 2.90 DM ($1.66) to 3.20 DM) ($1.84). Yogurt fans will find the product here, at 1.60 DM (92¢) to 1.75 DM ($1), among the best. Desserts go for around 3 DM ($1.72) to 3.50 DM ($2.01). The restaurant is open daily from 11:15 a.m. to 7 p.m.; until 3:30 p.m. on Saturday. Get your check as you enter.

3. Sights

Hamburg was subject to several severe bombings in the summer of 1943, and more than half the city—including 295,000 houses—was completely destroyed. Thousands more structures were badly damaged. Instead of restoring many of the completely demolished buildings, therefore, the city fathers decided on a creative plan of action, and today Hamburg is Germany's showplace of ultramodern architecture. Many historic structures stand today, side by side with towering steel-and-glass buildings. The 4½ square miles of parks and gardens are a vital part of the city. Hamburgers are extremely proud of their 22 square miles of rivers and lakes as well.

The **Alster** is the perfect starting point for a pleasurable exploration of Hamburg. This huge lake, rimmed by the city's most important and attractive buildings, sparkles with the white sails of small boats and ripples with the movement of motor launches. The lake is divided by the Lombard and John F. Kennedy Bridges into the **Binnenalster** (Inner Alster) and the larger **Aussenalster** (Outer Alster). The Binnenalster is flanked on the south and west by the **Jungfernstieg,** one of Europe's most famous streets, and Hamburg's most vital artery—and also its best shopping district. For landlubbers, the best view of the Alster is from this "maiden's path," but for the best overall look at the city and its waterways, take a one-hour **boat tour** around the Alster. During the long summer season, boats run hourly every day from 10 a.m. to 4 p.m. Expert English-speaking guides point out the landmarks of the city while bright-colored spinnakers and steamers pass by. The price for the tour is 6 DM ($3.44) for adults, 3 DM ($1.72) for children 4 to 6 years of age.

The **Port of Hamburg** is the world's fifth-largest harbor, stretching for nearly 25 miles along the Elbe River. More than 1500 ships call at this important port each month, connecting it with 1000 other cities throughout the world. Since 1189 the stretch of water has been one of the busiest centers for trade on the continent, making Hamburg one of Germany's wealthiest cities.

Before you tour the harbor, however, get a good overall view from the tower of the nearby **St. Michael's Church,** Hamburg's favorite landmark. It is considered the finest baroque church in the north of Germany. And the view from the top of the hammered copper tower (1762) is magnificent. Church and tower are open weekdays from 9 a.m. to 5:30 p.m., Sundays from 11:30 a.m. to 5:30 p.m. (in winter, 10 a.m. to 4 p.m. weekdays, 11:30 a.m. to 4 p.m. Sundays). Take the elevator or climb the 400 steps. Then, for a closer look at the river's activity, take one of the tours conducted every half hour in summer by the **HADAG Line,** from 10 a.m. to 4 p.m. Running commentaries are given by the guides in English as well as German. Departure is from St. Pauli landing stage at Entrance 3. The price of the tour is 7 DM ($4.02) for adults, 4 DM ($2.29) for children, 4 to 14.

The **Altstadt** actually has little left of the old architecture, but there are a few sights among the canals (fleets) which run through this section from the Alster to the Elbe. The largest of the older buildings is the **Rathaus,** which is actually modern compared with many of Germany's town halls. Hamburg's City Hall is a Renaissance-style structure, built in the late 19th century on a foundation of 4000 oak piles. Its 160-foot clock tower overlooks the **Rathausmarkt** and the **Alster Fleet,** the city's largest canal. A few blocks away is **St. Petri Cathedral,** built in the 12th century and renovated in 1842. The lionhead knocker on the main door is the oldest piece of art in Hamburg, dating from 1342. Although the nearby 14th-century church of **St. Jacobi** was destroyed in the last war, its tower and the famous Arp-Schnittger organ were rebuilt.

The **Hamburger Kunsthalle,** Glockengiesserwall, containing the works of the world's greatest painters and sculptors, is the leading art museum in northern Germany. One of the most outstanding works is the Grabow Altarpiece, painted for the St. Petri-Kirche in 1379 by Master Bertram, Hamburg's first painter known by name, and the leading master of 14th-century Germany. The 24 scenes on the wing-panels are a free adaptation of the medieval text, "The Mirror of Human Salvation," and depict the story of mankind from the Creation to the Flight into Egypt. Particularly interesting is the creation of the animals, in which a primitive Christlike figure is surrounded by the animals of his creation, from the fish of the sea to the fowl of the air. As a sardonic note—or possibly prophetic—one little fox is already chewing the neck of the lamb next to it. In the center panel of the Crucifixion, Master Bertram has depicted prophets, apostles, and saints; in a band above, more prophets appear in medallions. The wise and foolish virgins are lined up above the center shrine.

The museum also contains works by Master Francke, a Dominican monk, including the altar of St. Thomas of Canterbury (1424) with the first representation of the murder in the cathedral. There is a remarkable collection of Dutch and local paintings of the 17th century. Van Dyck, Rubens, Rembrandt, Claude Lorrain, de Champaigne, Tiepolo, Goya, Boucher, and Fragonard are well represented, and the German school particularly by Mengs, Denner, and Tischbein. Emphasis is laid on 19th-century art, beginning with Wilson, Reynolds, and Fuseli. Friedrich's landscapes and Runge's visions are hardly to be seen better anywhere else where work of the Romantic movement is seen. The Nazarenes (Overbeck, Cornelius) are followed by the British Pre-Raphaelites (Rossetti, Burne-Jones, Dyce). Later trends are marked by Leibl, Menzel, Meissonier, Corot, Daubigny, Courbet, Millet, Böcklin, Feuerbach, and von Marées. Notable works by French Impressionists are the *Nana* by Manet and paintings by Cézanne, Degas, Monet, Renoir, and Sisley. Twentieth-century artists are represented by Kirchner, Picasso, Chagall, Kandinsky, Klee *(Golden Fish* and *Revolution of the Viaduct),* Ernst, Magritte, Léger. Examples of Constructivism and recent Western art trends are displayed. Sculpture of the 19th and 20th centuries—by Rodin, Maillol, Renoir, Matisse, Marini, Moore, Calder, Segal, Fraesel, Luginbuehl, Nachi, and Caro—is shown. Hours are 10 a.m. to 5 p.m., Tuesday to Sunday (Wednesday, to 7 p.m.). In addition, seven or eight exhibitions are staged every year, some of international importance.

The **Hagenbeck Zoo,** at Stellingen, in the northwest suburbs, was the first of its kind. In 1908 it opened with a new idea in zoo planning—large herds of animals kept in open-air pens without cages. It worked, and many zoos in Europe and America have since adopted this type of design. In addition, the Hagenbeck Zoo has been responsible for capturing, selling, and training many wild animals in zoos and circuses throughout the world. Although completely destroyed during the war, the zoo is again functioning as well as before, with the most modern animal houses found anywhere. Open daily from 8 a.m. to one hour before dusk, admission is 8 DM ($4.59).

SOME NOTES ON SHOPPING: A stroll through the city center is like taking a look at one large international shop window. Hamburg is a city of merchants. In general, stores are open from Monday to Friday from 9 a.m. to 6:30 p.m. (on Saturday, 9 a.m. to 2 p.m.). Unfortunately, the interesting shops are not concentrated in just one location. Two of the oldest and most important shopping streets, **Grosse Bleichen** and **Neuer Wall,** run parallel to the canals, connected transversely by Jungfernstieg and Ufer Strasse on the Binnenalster.

Seek out, in particular, **Harry Rosenthal's** bazaar cellar on Bernhard-Nocht-Strasse, where you can purchase curios from all over the world. Most of the merchandise was brought here by sailors seeking a little extra cash after the clip joints of St. Pauli had taken their money.

4. Hamburg After Dark

Hamburg is the cultural center of northern Germany. Its State Opera is known throughout the world; its three symphony orchestras and several chamber groups have produced some of the finest recordings of classical works, and give frequent and varied concerts all year long. The city's 15 theaters offer the visitor everything from operetta to Shakespearean tragedies.

For a more active and lively evening, you can visit the streets of **St. Pauli,** where the famous Reeperbahn has become a synonym throughout the world for the most exciting and wicked entertainment. But before we take on the wild life, let's look at some more "civilized" entertainment around.

The **Hansa Theatre,** 17 Steindamm, is a North German variety show which claims that it's intelligible to all foreigners. The humor is so broad that that's surely true. The acts include Spanish flamenco dancers, magicians pulling rabbits out of hats, and aerialists balancing on wires above the stage. Each show usually has about 40 performers. There are special tables for smoking and drinking. Two shows are performed daily, one at 4 p.m. and another at 8 p.m. If you go to the 8 o'clock show, you're out by 11 p.m. Prices range from 10 DM ($5.74) to 15 DM ($8.60) for the 4 p.m. show, increasing to 15 DM ($8.60) to 20 DM ($11.47) on weekends. For the 8 p.m. show, tickets range from 18 DM ($10.32) to 25 DM ($14.34), increasing to 20 DM ($11.47) to 26 DM ($14.91) on Saturday night.

THE "INFAMOUS" REEPERBAHN: For the true nightlife of Hamburg, you have to go where the action is, on the Reeperbahn in the St. Pauli quarter of the city. The hottest spots are on a tawdry little side street called Grosse Freiheit, meaning Great Freedom. St. Pauli is the sailors' quarter. Sailors, in fact, have more experience in taking care of themselves than the innocent abroad, so be on guard.

The streets are lined with pornography shops, interspersed with clubs with names such as Las Vegas and San Francisco. A word of warning: German law requires restaurants and nightclubs to display their price list. Know the cost of your drinks before ordering. If the management refuses to give you a price list, get up and leave, unless you've already fallen in love with someone and are prepared to risk anything. And a final bit of advice: This section is *not* for women traveling alone.

The **Colibri,** 34 Grosse Freheit (tel. 31-31-25), is the safest haven among the sex clubs. *Warning:* Not for prudes. Its shows are among the most erotic you'll see in Germany, but this is the main attraction of Reeperbahn nightlife. For the sake of delicacy, we won't go into any detailed description of the acts, but by now, you probably get the gist. You'll pay 20 DM ($11.47) for beer and schnapps (a combination that is automatic, even if you don't care for schnapps). The shows are long, seemingly endless, and 80 attractions are advertised each night. This is the only club on this street that we can recommend. The other are definitely "off limits."

JAZZ: Hamburg has become firmly established as the number one jazz city in Germany. Famous stars in the music field also make appearances here.

Personally, we've found the best jazz at **Markthalle,** 9–21 Klosterwall, near the Central Station (tel. 33-78-09). This is not like your typical jazz club at all. Rather, it's a series of boutiques and dining areas set in a market place. For an admission fee of about 7 DM ($4.02), you are admitted to the performing area, which is an indoor amphitheater with a stage and a large central section. You can listen to the artists in concert fashion or else view them in the theater-in-the-round style. Seats are really backless benches. You're allowed to bring beer or other drinks into the hall as you listen to the music.

Another good spot we're fond of is **Dennis' Swing Club,** 25 Papenhuderstrasse (tel. 2-29-91-92), which lies in a residential part of Hamburg. Here you are usually charged no minimum and no admission. It's a completely informal atmosphere for jazz, and it's operated by Dennis Busby, who is not only the owner and manager, but the piano player and bartender as well. He's been an accompanist to some of the finest Stateside jazz talents, and old friends who remember him from those days are always passing through Hamburg. About 80 people can show up here on a good night. When a name artist shows up (often unannounced), Dennis may suddenly decide to impose a door charge of about $10 per person. But he assures you that you'll hear something good for that.

READER'S SELECTION AT WEDEL: "We spent a relaxing Sunday afternoon in Widel, 23 kilometers west of Hamburg, reached via B431. As the ships of various nations go past, they are welcomed in their native language as well as German, and their national anthem is played in salute. We had lunch at **Willkomm-Höft-Schulauer Fährhaus,** 29 Parnasstrasse (tel. 04103/23-03), with its dining terrace. The food was very good and fairly reasonable, sauerbraten costing 16 DM ($9.18)" (Dora R. Parker, Denver, Colo.).

From Hamburg, we strike out for Germany's northernmost province, Schleswig-Holstein.

Chapter XV

SCHLESWIG-HOLSTEIN

1. Lübeck
2. Kiel
3. Schleswig
4. Westerland (Sylt)

YOU WALK ALONG THE DUNES and hear the roaring waves breaking fiercely on the rocks. Or perhaps you lie on a tranquil beach while tiny waves lap at your feet. Sounds inconsistent, doesn't it? But not in Schleswig-Holstein. This northernmost province of Germany borders both the turbulent and chilly North Sea and the smooth, gentle Baltic. And between these two bodies of water are rolling groves and meadows, lakes and ponds, and little fishing villages with thatched cottages. But there's more to life in this part of Germany than peaceful country living. Fashionable seaside resorts line the North and Baltic Seas. Even in the coldest weather you can swim in heated seawater at the resorts of Westerland and Heligoland. In Kiel, you can wander around the harbor and explore Schleswig with its Viking ghosts.

But let's begin our tour of Germany's north country with a visit to the Queen of the Hanseatic Cities, Lübeck.

1. Lübeck

It is said that nothing testifies to the wealth of an old European city as much as the size and number of its church spires. If this is so, Lübeck is rich indeed, for no less than seven towering steeples make up the skyline of this Hanseatic city. It has prospered since it was made a Free Imperial City in 1226 by the Emperor Frederick II. Lübeck held this position for 711 years, until 1937. In addition, it was the capital and Queen City of the Hanseatic League for hundreds of years, and retains the title even though the economic and political importance of the League dissolved with its last meeting in 1630.

Lübeck is a city of high-gabled houses, massive gates, and strong towers. The rich Hanseatic merchants decorated their churches with art treasures and gilded their spires to show off their wealth. Many of these survivors of nearly 900 years of history stand side by side today with modern housing developments, and the neon lights of the business district shine out on the streets and narrow passageways of bygone days. West Germany's top custodian of national monuments has called Lübeck "richer in antiquities than any other German city."

Lübeck has two famous sons: Thomas Mann and Willy Brandt. As a young man, Brandt, who was later the West German chancellor and Nobel Peace Prize winner, opposed the Nazis so stubbornly he fled his hometown on a boat to Norway. Mann, too, won a Nobel Prize. However, his was for literature. His novel, *Buddenbrooks,* was set in his hometown and catapulted the 27-year-old author to international fame in 1902.

The city is the world's marzipan capital. According to legend, Lübeckers, riding out a long siege, ran out of flour and started grinding up almonds to make bread. So delighted were they with the results, they've been doing it ever since. To sample a marzipan on home turf, go to the Niederegger shop across from the Rathaus.

THE SIGHTS: The Old Town of Lübeck is surrounded by the Trave River and its connecting canals, giving it an island-like appearance. Although it suffered heavily during World War II (it is estimated that one-third of the city was leveled), most of the damaged buildings have been repaired or reconstructed. Today, Lübeck stands, as always, with a wealth of historic attractions.

The **Holstentor** (Holsten Gate), just across the south bridge from the Altstadt (Old Town), is the first greeting for visitors entering from the railway station. At one time it was the main entrance, built in the 15th century as much to awe visitors with the power and prestige of Lübeck as to defend it against intruders. To the outside world, the towers look simple and defiant, rather like part of a great palace. But on the city side they contain a wealth of decoration, with windows, arcades, and rich terracotta friezes. Within the gate is a municipal museum, housing a model of Lübeck as it appeared in the mid-17th century.

The **Salt Lofts,** if viewed from the river side near the Holstentor, are among the most attractive buildings in Lübeck. These buildings, dating from as early as the 16th century, were once used to store the salt brought here from Lüneburg before it was exported to Scandinavia. Each of the five buildings is slightly different, reflecting several trends in Renaissance gabled architecture.

The **Rathaus** (Town Hall) traces its origins back to 1230. Although it has been rebuilt several times, there are remains of the original structure in the vaulting and Romanesque pillars in the cellar and the Gothic south wall. The towering walls have been made with open-air medallions to relieve the pressure on the Gothic-arcaded ground floor and foundations. It is estimated that within an area of two square miles around the city hall stand 600 medieval houses. Nearby is **Petersgrube,** the finest street in Lübeck, lined with some of the best preserved structures in Europe, one dating from 1363.

St. Mary's Church (Marienkirche), across the Marketplace from the Town Hall, is the most outstanding church in Lübeck, possibly in northern Germany. Built on the highest point in the Old Town, its flying buttresses and towering windows leave the rest of the city's rooftops at its feet. St. Mary's is undoubtedly one of the finest examples of Gothic brick churches, and the largest of its kind in the world. Originally planned as a Romanesque basilica, it was somehow switched to Gothic style and designed as a Westphalian hall-church instead. Some of its greatest art treasures were destroyed in a fire in 1942. After the fire, the original painted decoration on the walls and clerestory was discovered. The bells from the original tower were struck in a World War II air raid, fell, and embedded themselves in the floor of the church, where they remain to this day. Organ concerts have been revived during the summer months, carrying on the tradition of St. Mary's most famous organist, Dietrich Buxtehude (1668–1707).

Other Sights

Many of the art treasures of old Lübeck have been preserved in **St. Anne's Museum,** a former convent built in 1502. The museum is devoted mainly to religious works and statues, many of which had been removed from the bombed churches of the city.

Among the other important churches of Lübeck, the **cathedral,** built in the early 13th century, is the oldest church in the town. Badly damaged in 1942, it has not yet been completely repaired, but the slender twin spires again tower over the quiet south end of the Altstadt. The 14th-century **St. Catherine's** is the only monastic church within the city, built by the Franciscan order with a light spaciousness and severe, clean lines.

The **Seamen's Guild House** (Haus der Schiffergesellschaft) is one of the last of the elaborate guild houses of Hanseatic Lübeck, built in 1535 in Renaissance style, with stepped gables and high Gothic blind windows. It is worth seeing just for the medieval furnishings and beamed ceilings in the main hall, now a restaurant (see recommendation below). A walk through the old streets of Lübeck reveals a constant use of brick as the local building material. The city insisted on this after fires in the 13th century. The effect is one of unity among all the houses, churches, shops, and guildhalls.

THE TOP HOTEL: Lysia, auf der Wallhalbinsel (tel. 7-10-77), enjoys a garden setting opening onto a canal. The accommodations in back are more desirable, as the front bedrooms open onto railway tracks. The Lysia is right at the entrance to Old Lübeck. The excellently designed chambers are colorful and compact, almost motel-like. A single room with shower and toilet ranges in price from 75 DM ($43.02) to 98 DM ($56.21). A twin-bedded room with shower or tub and toilet is in the 105-DM ($60.23) to 140-DM ($80.30) bracket. Rates include a breakfast from the Scandinavian buffet. The Safari bar in the cellar is popular with young people. Also on the premises is a cafe-konditorei, as well as Duell-Stuben for beer drinkers. Tables outside are hedged in by boxes of geraniums.

THE MIDDLE BRACKET: Jensen, 4–5 Obertrave (tel. 7-16-46), is one of the best in the medium-priced field. Right on a canal, near Holstentor, it offers the finest views from its bedroom windows of any hotel in the city. The view is of the Hanseatic brick architecture across the canal. The rooms are furnished in modern style—modest, but comfortable, as befits a town inn. For a double with bath, two persons pay 90 DM ($51.62) to 95 DM ($54.49). The bathless doubles, however, are a greater bargain at 66 DM ($37.86) to 71 DM ($40.73). Singles cost 55 DM ($31.55) to 57 DM ($32.70) in a room with bath, only 37 DM ($21.22) to 38 DM ($21.80) without bath. Breakfast is served in a room with picture windows overlooking the old canal—a delightful way to begin your day. Either lunch or dinner is good in the warmly decorated tavern-style restaurant.

Kaiserhof, 13 Kronsforder Allee (tel. 7-91-011), is a successful remodeling of a patrician town house as a hotel. Outside the center, it sits on a tree-lined boulevard. Since she fled from East Germany with her family, the gracious owner, Ruth Klemm, has created a fashionable homelike environment here for her guests. Every room is uniquely furnished, combining period pieces with modern. Most of her bedrooms have private showers and baths; an elevator takes guests to all floors. The most expensive doubles—that is, the largest ones with the best views—rent for 109 DM ($62.52), although the average rate for two persons is 88 DM ($50.48). Mrs. Klemm rents a few singles with bath—each with a sofa and desk—for 59 DM ($33.84) to 75 DM ($43.02). An elaborate and authentic Scandinavian sauna has been installed opening off the rear garden. On weekdays the sauna is segregated between men and women, on weekends it's mixed!

DINING WITH ATMOSPHERE: Schabbelhaus, 48 Mengstrasse (tel. 7-20-11), is like the informal wing of a palace. On a medieval street, you make your way to this classic example of Hanseatic architecture. (The old Schabbelhaus was destroyed by a 1942 air raid. The new Schabbelhaus was installed in two patrician buildings dating from the 16th and 17th centuries.) Inside, in an atmosphere of German baroque (note the painted ceilings), you get the most attentive service and the best food in Lübeck. In the restaurant, ceiling-high studio windows overlook the small gardens; a pair of 15-foot-high armoires hold linen and glassware which are eventually placed on scrubbed wooden tables with pewter candlesticks. Set lunches are 23 DM ($13.19). À la carte fare includes such tempting items as Lübecker crab soup at 7 DM ($4.02); chicken curry, 18 DM ($10.32); and peppersteak, 24 DM ($13.77). A wooden staircase and balcony lead to two rooms devoted to memorabilia of Thomas Mann.

Haus der Schiffergesellschaft, 2 Breitestrasse (tel. 7-67-76), opposite the Church of St. Jakobi, basks in the Hanseatic tradition. Memorabilia such as ships' models hang from the ceiling and decorate the walls. Dining in this mellowed Baltic atmosphere is like entering a museum of Hanseatic architecture. The restaurant was once patronized exclusively by sailors and other men of the sea. Today, good food (and large portions!) is served on scrubbed-oak plank tables as you sit in a carved high-backed wooden booth, showing coats of arms from Baltic merchants. Often, you must share a table here. Meals, including soup and dessert, are in the 26-DM ($14.91) to 40-DM ($22.94) range. The more expensive price includes such elaborate dishes as sole meunière (one pound) with a salad.

The **Ratskeller,** 13 Markt (tel. 7-20-44), is one of the finest town hall dining cellars in Germany. You make your way through the flower vendors on the square outside to enjoy the offerings of an ambitious chef. High standards and excellent food are the order of the day. The huge menu is backed up by a good wine list. As befits a seaport, fish is the house specialty. Wide-ranging delicacies are offered, including some high-priced lobster and caviar. Soups are in the 3.75-DM ($2.15) to 7-DM ($4.02) range, and main dishes include fish grilled müllerin art at 17.50 DM ($10.04) or filet Stroganoff at 23 DM ($13.19). Desserts go from 2.75 DM ($1.58) to 18 DM ($10.32), for Crêpes Suzette for two.

2. Kiel

Even the name of this port and fishing city—it means haven for ships in old Anglo-Saxon—shows the importance of the sea to the growth and prosperity of Kiel. The perfect natural harbor at the end of the seven-mile-long extension of the Baltic Sea made Kiel a center for commerce with other northern European countries. The opening of the Kiel Canal in 1895 connected the Baltic Sea with the North Sea and western trade.

Keil Week, held each June, is a further example of the port's close ties with the sea. This week of special events, held each summer for the past 80 years, includes the famous and spectacular regattas, in which hundreds of yachts race on the waters of the Roadstead. In 1972, the Olympic yacht races were held on the waters at Schilksee. Stretches of sandy beaches in the nearby resorts make the port an important Baltic vacation spot as well.

Although Kiel is nearly 1000 years old, there is little in the way of streets or buildings to make the casual visitor believe that the town ever was anything other than a completely modern city. Almost all of its buildings were destroyed in World War II, and in their place is an admirable example of modern town planning. Kielers are proud of their broad streets, spacious squares, and green parks in the heart of town.

THE SIGHTS: Most of the attractions of Kiel center in and around the harbor. For the best overall look at the city and the Roadstead, go to the top of the Town Hall's 350-foot tower. For a closer view, wander the **Hindenburg Embankment** stretching for two miles along the west side of the fjord, opposite the shipyards. It's also one of the best spots from which to watch the exciting regatta.

The **Sea Fish Market,** on the east bank of the fjord, is one of the largest in the world, and a fascinating spot to visit, if the smell doesn't turn you off. You'll see a wide variety of sea life here.

If you have the time, take a short steamer trip to one of the nearby Baltic towns, such as Laboe with its sandy beach. Steamers and ferries also connect Kiel with Baltic ports in Denmark, Norway, and Sweden.

THE TOP HOTEL: Conti-Hansa Hotel, 7 am Schlossgarten (tel. 5-12-44), is an attractive three-story modern structure built at the edge of a park with a pond, across from the ferry dock for the Scandinavian countries. Half of the bedrooms overlook the harbor, the other half the park. You can snuggle into your modern bedroom after an excellent meal in the restaurant. Guests tend to gravitate to the parkside dining terrace overlooking the streets and lawns. There are 60 bedrooms, each one having a telephone, toilet, shower or tub, and some of the doubles have a spacious living room area—costing an additional fee, of course. Singles range in price from 55 DM ($31.55) to 79 DM ($45.31); doubles, from 90 DM ($51.62) to 124 DM ($71.13). There's a cocktail bar and a parking lot.

THE MIDDLE BRACKET: Kieler Yacht Club, 70 Hindenburgufer (tel. 8-50-55), is exactly what its name implies—a yacht club with unusually fine guest facilities. It's an old classic building, standing back from the harbor, with an adjoining motel-style annex of contemporary design. It's the most spirited and ideal accommodation in Kiel. Prices are lower in the older portion. For example, in the old building, doubles with bath are 80 DM ($45.89), increasing to 120 DM ($68.83) in the annex. Singles with bath are 52 DM ($29.83) in the old part, 65 DM ($37.28) in the new. Breakfast is an additional 8.50 DM ($4.88) per person. The newer rooms are designed yacht-cabin style; the older rooms have more space and are pleasantly furnished and decorated. There is a multitiered restaurant where the tables are staggered to provide the best views. The Mastenkeller in the basement is for beer drinking. Note: the front rooms with water views are preferred, although the accommodations in the back open onto greenery. On the waterside, chairs and sidewalk tables are placed on terraces surrounded by planters of roses.

THE TOP RESTAURANTS: Restaurant im Schloss, 80 Wall (tel. 9-11-58), is the finest and most elegant restaurant in Kiel—as well as the most expensive and formal. The service is superb, as are the food and choice of wine. It's a modern restaurant, across from the embarkation point for boats to Scandinavian countries. In a stone building overlooking the harbor, the Schloss looks like a contemporary museum set in a park. If you reserve, you can get one of the window tables opening onto the water. Set menus are offered for 17 DM ($9.75), 19 DM ($10.90), and 24 DM ($13.77).

Ratskeller Kiel, 9 Fleethörn (tel. 9-54-94), provides an ambitious menu and excellent food, plus a huge choice of dishes. Its three dining rooms have been modernized, the Windsor chairs making for a tea-roomy atmosphere. The cellar opens through arches onto a view of the platz. Favored dishes include rumpsteak with beans and french fries at 19.50 DM ($11.19), and filet steak with béarnaise sauce at 26 DM ($14.91). There are many fish specialties as well, including some of the best and freshest Baltic herring at 17.50 DM ($10.04) you are likely to sample in any port. Set lunches are offered from 17.50 DM ($10.04) to 27.50 DM ($15.77).

BUDGET DINING: König-Haus, 4 Willestrasse, is newly constructed by the Könige Brewery. From the outside it has brick walls, dark windows, and green shades. The interior is decorated in the old Prussian style, with high-backed chairs and benches covered with leather. Guests dine at wood tables over which hang heavy bell-like green lamps. Dinners cost from 8.50 DM ($4.88) to 18 DM ($10.32), with soups priced at 3.50 DM ($2.01). Naturally, you can order Könige pilsener at 2.10 DM ($1.20).

3. Schleswig

This one-time Viking stronghold on the Schlei (an arm of the Baltic Sea) is Schleswig-Holstein's oldest town, and it is steeped in all the myths and legends that go with such a long history. Even the seagulls—whose eggs are a delicacy here—have a legend of their own. According to tradition, the birds nesting on Seagull Island in the middle of the Schlei are actually the fellow conspirators of Duke Abel, who, in 1250, murdered the duke's brother, King Eric. The crime was discovered when the king's body, weighted with chains, washed ashore from the Schlei. The duke went mad and eventually died and was impaled and buried in the Tiergarten. But his followers, according to the story, were doomed to nest forever on Seagull Island.

Fortunately, legends are not the only survivors in this ancient city. The bombing raids of World War II did not touch Schleswig, and it stands today an impressive witness to 1200 years of history.

THE SIGHTS: A tour of the important attractions usually begins in the Altstadt (Old Town), with a visit to the jewel of Schleswig—

St. Peter's Cathedral is a magnificent brick Romanesque-Gothic hall-church begun in the 11th century. The towering spire makes the rest of the Old Town seem like so many doll houses by comparison. Inside is the outstanding Bordesholm Altarpiece, a powerful work, carved in oak by Hans Brüggemann (1514–1521) for the convent at Bordesholm. It was brought to the cathedral in 1666. Its elaborately carved Gothic panels contain a total of nearly 400 figures. The cathedral and cloisters also contain art treasures, including the *Blue Madonna* by J. Ovens, and 13th-century frescoes on the walls and ceilings. The cathedral is open daily from 9 a.m. to 5 p.m., except Sundays, when visiting hours begin at the close of the morning service. Winter hours are slightly shorter. There is no charge for admission.

Schloss Gottorf lies on a small island in the Burgsee, a bay at the west end of the Schlei. A bridge connects the island with the town. As you walk around the harbor, the panorama of the Old Town and the widening bay open up behind you. The castle itself is the largest in Schleswig-Holstein. Although the foundations date from the original 12th-century ducal palace, the present structure was built mainly in the 16th and 17th centuries, and reconditioned since 1948 for use as a museum.

The **Provincial Museum for Prehistoric and Early Times** is one of the two museums housed in Schloss Gottorf. Exhibitions include displays of reindeer hunters and Vikings, models, artifacts, and even some rune stones in the Haithabu Room (Haithabu was the Viking name for Schleswig). Housed in a separate building next door is the most remarkable exhibit, the **Nydam Boat,** a fourth-century Viking ship found in the Nydam marshes in 1863. In glass cases in the same room are moor-corpses, artifacts, and weapons found with the ship, all adding up to one of the major archeological finds in northern Germany.

The **Schleswig-Holstein State Museum,** also housed in the castle, contains an exceptional collection of fine and applied arts from medieval times to the 20th century (paintings, sculpture, furniture, textiles, weapons, and arms, plus folk art). Outstanding are the famous Gothic "King's Hall," the 17th-century ducal living rooms with rich stucco ceilings, and the Renaissance chapel with a private chamber for the ducal family decorated with intricate and elaborate carving and inlays. Two separate buildings east of the castle contain the collections of contemporary art in Schleswig-Holstein and the ethnological collections, plus extensive displays of implements and tools representing the rural life of farmers, artisans, and fishermen in Schleswig-Holstein. The same 1 DM (57¢) ticket admits you to both museums. From April through October, the museums are open from 9 a.m. to 5 p.m. daily, except Mondays. Hours are slightly shorter during the winter months.

BUDGET HOTELS: Strandhalle, 2 Strandweg (tel. 2-20-21), is the best hotel in Schleswig. Actually, it's more of a holiday resort—right on the water with rowboats, its own swimming pool in a beautiful garden, a natatorium with steam bath, and alpine sun. It's owned and run by Gerda and Kurt Kries, who set the informal atmosphere in the homey and comfortable rooms. You should ask for a room opening onto the water, with a view of the yacht harbor. Bathless singles range in price from 32 DM ($18.36); with shower, from 40 DM ($22.94). Doubles with shower or complete bath and toilet cost from 90 DM ($51.62). Breakfast is included. Half pension is priced at 20 DM ($11.47) per person additional, full pension at 26 DM ($14.91), which is a good buy considering the tasty fish dishes available. The wine list contains more than 250 different kinds of wine. You can bake out in the sauna, or take a cool dip in the pool.

On the Outskirts

Waldhotel am Schloss Gottorf, an der Stampmühle (tel. 2-32-88), is a brick mansion lodged on a grassy plateau surrounded by a park and pine trees. It's on the outskirts of Schleswig, en route to the castle and approached by a winding driveway. A secluded holiday retreat, it's a fine bargain. There are no lounges to speak of, but the emphasis is placed on the sunny dining room and the bedrooms (large enough to have breakfast in, unless you prefer your morning coffee on the front terrace). To stay one night costs between 25 DM ($14.34) and 30 DM ($17.21) per person. Some accommodations have toilets and baths. Full board is available for from 46 DM ($26.39) to 52 DM ($29.83) per person per day. All prices include breakfast, and you can also get moderately priced luncheons and dinners.

Gasthaus Haddeby, Rte. 76 (tel. 3-22-30), is a historic roadside inn less than a mile from Schleswig. It's good for an overnight stopover. There's a Viking inn signpost outside, and the general character inside is like a Danish *kro* (inn). The food is good for such a simple inn. It's certainly economical: doubles, with hot and cold running water, rent for 45 DM ($25.81). Try for a room with a view opening onto the garden, as those accommodations fronting the road tend to be noisy. The restaurant is in the cozy provincial style, with interesting local dishes offered, especially fish. Bouillabaisse goes for 3.75 DM ($2.15) as an appetizer. Other dishes include filet of herring at 8.75 DM ($5.02) and veal kidneys at 17.50 DM ($10.04). A light soufflé costs 6 DM ($3.44).

WHERE TO DINE: Schloss Keller, Schloss Gottorf (tel. 3-29-90), on the lower level of the already-recommended castle, is a fine choice for dining. There's also a cafe for light snacks and refreshments. The main courses in the restaurant (which include soup of the day) are in the 11.50-DM ($6.60) to 19.50-DM ($11.19) range. The cuisine is typically and reliably Germanic, with dishes such as wienerschnitzel, rumpsteak, and sole. The dining room is pleasant, the cooking good.

4. Westerland (Sylt)

Although the mineral spas are a favorite summer spot for vacationing Germans, many prefer to "take the waters" at the seacoast or in the crisp freshness of the Frisian Islands in the North Sea. The long, narrow island of Sylt and its capital, Westerland, are popular with northern Europeans drawn here by the invigorating sea air. Sylt is Germany's northernmost point, lying just west of the Germany-Denmark border.

Salty air and pounding surf are not the only attractions of Westerland. It is a fashionable, chic resort with huge hotels, fine restaurants, a promenade overlooking the sea, and a gambling casino. In addition, it has some of the best therapeutic facilities of any seaside spa. The basic therapy here is sunshine, pure air, and seawater, but in recent years mud baths have also become a popular method of treatment. The spa has facilities for the treatment of everything from heart disease to skin irritations.

Some of the more remote sections of the dunes have been turned into nudist beaches for purists in the art of sunshine therapy. In addition to bathing, there are facilities in and around Westerland for horseback riding along with surf, golf, tennis, as well as more sedentary entertainment such as the theater and concerts.

When the sunlight begins to fade at the end of each day, the **Casino** (Spielbank) becomes the center of activity. In the center of town, it is housed in the same building as the town hall. All major games are played here: baccarat, roulette, and blackjack. The Casino bar serves the best drinks in town. It is open daily from 5 p.m.

The only link between the mainland and Sylt—other than car ferry—is the causeway running from the town of Neibüll. However, this causeway is only a railroad track, so if you wish to bring your car to the island, you'll have to load it on the train at Niebüll for the long slow ride. The fare ranges from 50

DM ($28.68) to 100 DM ($57.36), depending on the size of the car. Passengers pay 10 DM ($5.74) per person for a one-way trip. Trips are frequent during the busy summer season, although sporadic from mid-September through April.

THE TOP HOTELS: Stadt Hamburg, 2 Strandstrasse (tel. 70-58), is the superior hotel on the island. It's more like a well-appointed country home than a hotel, with its gleaming white entrance reached through a white picket fence with street lanterns. It's built close to the street, next to the Casino, and its rear windows overlook a well-kept lawn. The interior is bright and cheerful, with sophisticated country-estate furnishings (antiques intermixed with good reproductions), including wing-backed chairs and floral-covered armchairs. Each of the 85 bedrooms is individually furnished, with homelike touches. In high season, bathless singles go from 45 DM ($25.81) to 59 DM ($33.84); with shower or tub baths, from 59 DM ($33.84) to 102 DM ($58.51) with TV. The per-person rate in a double without bath ranges from 30 DM ($17.21) to 45 DM ($25.81); with shower or tub baths, from 55 DM ($31.55) to 105 DM ($60.23). Half pension (most recommendable) costs 70 DM ($40.15) to 145 DM ($83.17) per person. You'll want to take your morning meal in the breakfast room, with its blue-and-white ceramic stove. Guests gather on cooler evenings around the open fireplace. For what it offers, the Stadt Hamburg is a bargain. It has all this and style, too.

The hotel's restaurant serves some of the best cookery at the resort, offering set meals from 22 DM ($12.62) to 28 DM ($16.06). Among the à la carte dishes, we'd recommend the lobster soup at 11.50 DM ($6.60) and the filet of plaice at 20.50 DM ($11.76). By request only, the chef will make you his special apple pancake for dessert, costing 7.50 DM ($4.30).

Wünschmann Hotel, 4 Andreas-Dirks-Strasse (tel. 50-25), is the second choice for accommodations. This hotel may be in the core of a modern building plaza (with more than two dozen boutiques), but its inner aura is one of comfortable old-world tranquility. Breakfast is the only meal served, and it is offered in a woodsy and informal room, a pleasant place to begin the day. The bedrooms are one of a kind—all with strong colors, all cheerful, each with its own bath or shower. The high-season rates are as follows: singles range from 52 DM ($29.83) to 75 DM ($43.02); doubles, from 78 DM ($44.74) to 162 DM ($92.92). All rooms have private showers or baths. Breakfast is an extra 8 DM ($4.59). The tariffs include taxes and service. The hotel is in the heart of the tourist belt of Westerland, yet only minutes from the sand dunes.

Dünenburg, 9 Elisabethstrasse (tel. 60-06), is standard modern, set a block from the town center and beach. All its front bedrooms face the water and contain balconies (the higher up you go, the better the accommodation). Every bedroom is immaculate, comfortable, nicely furnished, and each has its own shower and toilet, color TV, and mini-bar. High-season rates are charged from June 1 to September 30. Singles with shower and toilet range in price from 73 DM ($41.87); doubles with bath and balcony, from 130 DM ($75.57).

Viking Hotel, 8 Dr.-Nicolas-Strasse (tel. 70-31), is a five-story, mansion-style hotel, which opens onto streets half a block from the water. It provides fine accommodations at fair prices. The public rooms, as well as the bedrooms, are spacious and informal. The interior is comfortable and adequate, especially because of its convenience to the sea, swimming pool, and beach. The high-season rates are as follows: bathless singles, from 38 DM ($21.80) to 54 DM ($30.97); singles with shower or tub bath, from 48 DM ($27.53) to 60 DM

($34.42). Bathless doubles rent from 64 DM ($36.71) to 90 DM ($51.62); with private bath, from 90 DM ($51.62) to 110 DM ($63.10). Breakfast is included.

THE BUDGET CHOICE: Vier Jahreszeiten, 40 Johann-Möller-Strasse (tel. 2-25-28), is the best economy choice. It's like an informal country inn, practically in the sand dunes, although right in the heart of the resort activity—about a five-minute walk to the Casino and swimming pool. Most of its bedrooms embrace the sea, and the lifestyle here is simple and informal. It's easy to spot—bone white with red tiled roof. In high season, one person pays anywhere from 35 DM ($20.08) to 55 DM $31.55), depending on the plumbing. Breakfast is an additional 8 DM ($4.59).

WHERE TO DINE: Altfriesische Weinstuben, 5 Elisabethstrasse (tel. 70-11), is highly recommended. At this brick tavern, the food and service are excellent. But be warned—it's expensive! The specialty is lobster, priced according to weight. Helgoländer lobster soups range from 5.50 DM ($3.15) to 10 DM ($5.74). Chicken suprême is a delight at 16 DM ($9.18); eel in dill sauce, also excellent, is 24 DM ($13.77). Another house favorite is bouillabaisse Marseillaise at 46 DM ($26.39).

Stadt Hamburg Stuben, 2 Strandstrasse, offers top-rate cuisine in an attractive setting. The menu is so wide ranging it makes selection difficult. Even if you aren't a guest at the hotel, you're welcome to drop in, either for lunch or dinner. Set meals range in price from 21 DM ($12.05) to 25 DM ($14.34), although you'll pay 48 DM ($27.53) for the menu gastronomique. On the à la carte listings, the smoothest beginning is cream of lobster soup with cognac, 12.50 DM ($7.17). There are many seafood specialties, such as filet of fresh North Sea plaice baked in egg, with béarnaise sauce, parsley potatoes, and lettuce salad, at 20 DM ($11.47), or an elegant sole Colbert, the price varying daily beginning at 22 DM ($12.62). Desserts range from 4 DM ($2.29) to 9.50 DM ($5.45), although an order of apple pancake costs 11 DM ($6.31).

The Kurhaus Westerland houses both the Restaurant Strandvogt and the Cafe Frisia, standing at the Strandpromenade with views of the open sea. Reasonably priced seafood is featured, with most fish (and it's fresh) dishes ranging in price from 14 DM ($8.03) to 25 DM ($14.34). The flounder is especially good. There's also a big choice of meat dishes. Hours are from 11 a.m. to 3 p.m. and from 6 to 10:30 p.m.

The tour of West Germany is over. And now we head east to Berlin.

Chapter XVI

BERLIN

1. Hotels
2. Restaurants
3. Sights
4. West Berlin After Dark
5. A Tour of East Berlin
6. Side Trip to Potsdam

IF YOU WERE ONE of the pilots engaged in bringing supplies to the people of Berlin in the great airlift of 1948 and 1949, you wouldn't recognize the city today. The same optimistic spirit and strength of will which caused the remarkable Berliners to survive the destruction of the war and the postwar Soviet blockade of the city have caused the creation of a new West Berlin, a metropolis unequaled in Germany—or in the world. Huge structures of steel and glass now tower over streets where less than 30 years ago only a pile of rubble lay. Parks which were once reduced to muddy swamplands and battlefields are again bringing forth lush forests and gardens. Children play in a quiet side street right within the shadow of the one thorn in the flesh of the city—the Berlin Wall.

The tragedy of the city is that it is no longer one Berlin, but two. Families and friends are divided by the concrete and barbed wire through the center of the metropolis. But most of them have adjusted to the fact, and life goes on from day to day in this, the most sophisticated, lively, friendly city in Germany.

With the Cold War waning, and nothing is more symbolic of that than the admission of both Germanys to the United Nations, Berlin is, in the words of two observers, "losing its status as 'the island of freedom in a red sea.' " In fact, as both Germanys normalize relations, it is now relatively easy for West Berliners to travel to East Berlin. East Germans, reportedly, are still having difficulty crossing the border.

The center of West Berlin activity is the 2½-mile-long street named the **Kurfürstendamm,** but called the Ku-damm by Berliners, who seem to have a habit of irreverently renaming every street and building in the city. Along this wide boulevard you'll find the best hotels, restaurants, theaters, cafes, nightclubs, shops, and department stores. As the showcase of West Berlin, it is the most elegant and fashionable spot in the city.

Before getting into the sights, sounds, and tastes of this exciting city, we'll survey the hotel situation. But even before this, a look at transportation: getting to and around Berlin.

GETTING TO BERLIN: At present, travel is no problem between West Berlin and West Germany. Several airlines make regular flights from Hannover, Hamburg, Frankfurt, Munich, and other cities, to the Tegel Airport right in West Berlin. It is also accessible by car, bus, and train. The days of East German roadside inspections and endless delays seem at an end, since the signing of a treaty between the two countries in 1972.

There are three major points of entry for motorists traveling from West Germany to West Berlin. The shorter (approximately two hours) route is at the border town of Helmstedt, east of Hannover. You can also go east from Frankfurt in the direction of Bad Herzfeld toward the East German border. Finally, another autobahn is north of Nürnberg, with a crossing at Rudolphstein.

You can pass through customs 24 hours a day. Although there are gasoline stations en route to Berlin, it is wise to begin the trip with a full tank. You must carry the proper traveling papers for your car and your passport, of course; you'll have to cross the West German and East German checkpoints at the border.

You'll also have to declare your intention of visiting West Berlin to the East German border guards. You surrender your passport and pay a 5-DM ($2.87) visa fee. Rarely does any guard speak English, although cryptic words are sometimes understood. Under favorable circumstances, all the border formalities need take no more than 20 minutes. The trip itself from any point in West Germany is about 2½ hours.

Along the route, you'll notice speed limits posted. Obey them religiously. Fleets of police cars patrol the autobahn. Many hide out in concealed places waiting for speeders. Occasionally cars are stopped indiscriminately, and all of a driver's luggage is tediously inspected.

Warning: Stop only at wayside parking zones clearly designated with a large "P" or at gasoline stations. Along the way you'll pass villages and towns. Do not be fooled into thinking you can leave the autobahn without police detection. If you venture into any of these towns without the proper documents, you are invariably subject to arrest.

In case of a breakdown along the badly paved autobahns, boxes are placed at strategic points. However, if you seem to be a long way from a box, police cars will often find you and send a hauling truck if required.

Eventually you'll reach the Berlin Ring Road which encircles both Berlins. Take the sign to West Berlin. Don't be misled. The East Germans call their Berlin simply "Berlin," not East Berlin. Proceed to the border check, passing through East German customs once again and across West German lines.

READER'S WARNING TO EURAILPASS HOLDERS: "I took a train from Lucerne, Switzerland, to Berlin Germany. Through misinformation, I was under the impression that I would be going through East Germany on a strip of land owned by West Germany, and that my Eurailpass would be valid. This was false, and I got stuck buying a first-class ticket and paying a fine to the tune of $30 to the East Germans. The important thing to know is to obtain a ticket from the last West German city to Berlin. On my trip from Berlin, I got a ticket from Berlin Zoological Garden to Helmstedt (the first West German city I passed through). Also, visas are made out on the train by the East Germans" (Mark Ballard, Burbank, Calif.).

TRANSPORTATION IN THE CITY: Because West Berlin is completely surrounded by East Germany, even its airport, which in most large cities is normally quite a drive from the center, lies within the city limits. Economically, this is a great boon to the visitor, since public transportation is convenient to

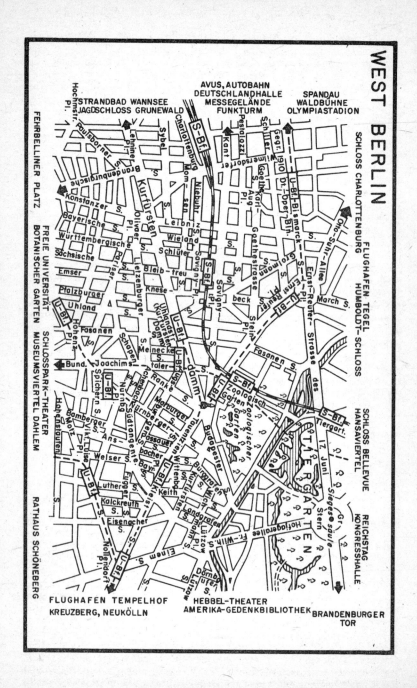

all points. For example, the 30-minute ride from Tegel Airport to the center of the city via bus A9 costs only 1.50 DM (86¢).

The Berlin transportation system consists of **buses,** the underground (U-Bahn), and the S-Bahn (surface trains). Fares for the U-Bahn and buses, which run only from about 4:30 a.m. to 1 a.m. (except for a few additional night buses), run 1.50 DM (86¢) for a single fare. The less expensive S-Bahn goes for 1 DM (57¢), and is operated under the administration of East Berlin. Both the U-Bahn and S-Bahn run in both West and East Berlin. One U-Bahn and one S-Bahn line have been established for frontier-crossing traffic. Another U-Bahn line goes through East Berlin without a stop.

A special service to tourists is the **Touristenkarte,** a ticket good for unlimited travel on the U-Bahn and buses (but not on the S-Bahn). These tickets can be purchased at the **BVG information booth** across from the bahnhof (railway station), in front of the zoo. A ticket valid for two days costs 20 DM ($11.47).

Taxis are readily available throughout Berlin as well, either by hailing them on the street, or by calling 69-02.

1. Hotels

The day of *Grand Hotel,* when the lives of gamblers, ballerinas, noblemen, and stenographers became intertwined behind those revolving doors, is no more. The prewar ideal of luxury has been replaced by ultramodern comfort and conveniences. In many of Berlin's newest hotels, electric eyes and pushbuttons have made doormen and elevator operators obsolete. If you're still looking for that personal touch, Berlin has that too, in the many small hotels and pensions in the vicinity of the "Ku-damm."

Since Berlin is the scene of frequent trade fairs and conferences, it's wise to make reservations in advance, especially at the deluxe and first-class hotels. With more than 12,500 beds throughout the city, however, you should have no problem finding accommodations to suit both your taste and your pocketbook. We'll survey some of the best choices in all price categories below.

ON OR OFF THE KURFÜRSTENDAMM: Here are the most central hotels in Berlin—in all price ranges.

A Deluxe Choice

Bristol Hotel Kempinski Berlin, 27 Kurfürstendamm (tel. 88-10-91), is a legend in Berlin. A century ago, Kempinski was the name of one of the most renowned restaurants in Germany. In 1952, it rose out of the debris of World War II to become a landmark hotel, enjoying a position in the "island city" similar to the Waldorf-Astoria in New York. Business people who want to conclude international deals select the Kempinski as their base of operation, knowing they will be assured of a dignified ambience, attentive service, and a dramatic setting in the center of the city.

The decor is conservatively traditional, although everything—from tapestries to antiques to Persian carpets—seems special. The lobby sets the relaxed mood, with its fine and comfortable groupings of furniture. A high-level cuisine is served in the Restaurant Kempinski, although many discriminating diners prefer the grillroom, with its open hearth. For quick snacks, try the Café Carrousel coffeeshop, which opens into a Kurfürstendamm terrace. The Bristol Bar is low key, with patent-leather chairs and a pianist playing soft background music. An outstanding feature is the Kempinski pool, a recreation center with an inside swimming pool (24 by 48 feet), sauna, massage, solarium, fitness center, and pool bar.

The bedrooms—335 in all, with full air conditioning, color TVs, direct-dial telephones, and fully stocked mini-bars—match the taste level of the public rooms. The accommodations are richly carpeted; the furnishings, a selection of antique reproductions combined with modern. A single room with complete bath ranges in price from 130 DM ($75.57) to 160 DM ($91.78). Doubles with complete bath range from 160 DM ($91.78) to 210 DM ($120.46). Dining tip: Try the Friday evening buffet which costs 35 DM ($20.08) for adults, half that for children.

If you would like to experience an added touch of class, try the Kempinski Luxury Limousine Service. You can use it for transportation from and to the airport, or for a sightseeing tour, in an old-fashioned, chauffeur-driven Daimler limousine.

First-Class Hotels

Parkhotel Zellermayer, 15 Meinekestrasse (tel. 88-20-51), is a modern well-recommended hotel which has both interest and character. Near the Kurfürstendamm, it offers an interior of style and flair, escaping the doldrums of most Berlin hostelries with its innovative concepts in decoration. For example, the bedrooms have wide-ranging themes, going from the Caribbean, with a natural wicker bed, to contemporary, with built-in sofas and tartan bedspreads. All rooms have telephone, TV, radio, are soundproofed, and contain private baths. Singles are between 75 DM ($43.02) and 125 DM ($71.70); twin-bedded rooms, between 118 DM ($67.68) and 150 Dll ($86.04). A continental breakfast is included. The main lounge is conservatively appointed, with leather couches —quite tasteful and not commercial looking. Meals are provided in the Pavillon du Parc restaurant, styled in a garden theme, or in the Grill-Restaurant. Drinks are offered in the Jockey-Bar, with its pinto-skin-covered stools. More recently opened is the only dietary restaurant in Berlin.

Arosa, 79–81 Lietzenburgerstrasse (tel. 88-20-11), has a deceivingly austere facade, giving no clue as to the charm, style, and flair of its interior. It's strongly recommended for many reasons, but most especially because it opens onto a rear courtyard and garden with a good-sized, open-air swimming pool and terrace for relaxation and refreshments. On the premises is a specialty restaurant, the Relais Suisse, a successful recreation of a country inn, with a rough wooden ceiling, heavy beams, alpine chairs, pine tables, not to mention excellent provincial cuisine.

The main living room of the Arosa has a country flavor, with a rounded open fireplace, pine ceiling, and groups of good armchairs arranged in clusters. The drinking lounge evokes the turn of the century, with its fringed hanging lamps, ornate cash register, and wood paneling. The bedrooms are skillfully styled as well, with bone-white walls, built-in sofa beds (often with bright-red covers), and white Windsor chairs with red cushions. Altogether, a sophisticated, youthful look. All of the accommodations have private baths or showers; singles rent for 65 DM ($37.28) to 85 DM ($48.76); doubles, for 110 DM ($63.10) to 140 DM ($80.30). Rates include breakfast.

Hotel am Zoo, 25 Kurfürstendamm (tel. 88-30-91), sits snugly on the main street of Berlin. Substantial and well maintained, it was built when bedrooms were expansive, so you'll have plenty of space to tuck away your overweight luggage. The rooms are well furnished, clean and comfortable. All rooms now have private baths, and singles range in price from 75 DM ($43.02) to 95 DM ($54.49), with doubles going for 130 DM ($75.57) to 155 DM

($88.91), depending on the type of plumbing. Breakfast is included. Dining is recommended at the old Germanic restaurant, where the atmosphere is authentic and interesting.

The Budget Hotels

Aviv, 82–84 Lietzenburgerstrasse (tel. 883-34-13), is one of the best budget establishments in Berlin. First, its location is good—just five minutes from the Kurfürstendamm, in a modern building near a fascinating group of boutiques, restaurants, and nightclubs. Two elevators lead to an airy, spacious lounge, with semitropical plants and attractive contemporary furnishings, that makes you feel you're going to pay more than you do. The Aviv is run by a kindly woman who speaks English. The rooms are modern in a nice way—quite attractive, with a picture window and glass door opening onto a balcony. Some contain large sitting areas, with a sofa, armchairs, and coffee table. Best of all is a hide-away kitchen where you can prepare your own breakfasts (sink, refrigerator, hotplate, and equipment). The larger doubles with balcony cost 100 DM ($57.36); the smaller ones, 76 DM ($43.59). No charge is made for converting the sofa into a third bed. A superb buy!

Frühling am Zoo, 17 Kurfürstendamm (tel. 881-80-83). There is no elevator, but this hotel offers one of the best budget accommodations right in the heart of West Berlin. Just two minutes from the Memorial Church, it occupies the upper floors of a corner building, directly on the Kurfürstendamm. The reception area is tiny, but the old-fashioned, chandeliered bedrooms are spacious, comfortable, and well maintained. Singles with shower cost from 46 DM ($26.39), peaking at 65 DM ($37.28) with complete bath. Doubles with shower go for 73 DM ($41.87), rising to 98 DM ($56.21) with complete bath. Included is breakfast, served in a handsome, formal salon overlooking the busy boulevard.

Astoria, 2 Fasanenstrasse (tel. 312-40-67). This rebuilt and modernized hotel is just off the Kurfürstendamm, near the Bahnhof Zoo. Its exterior looks somewhat like a town house. You can stay here for a modest amount of money in a rather expensive section of Berlin—especially if you ask for a room without a private bath. A double-bedded accommodation without bath ranges in price from 65 DM ($37.28) to 90 DM ($51.62) with bath. Bathless singles go for 40 DM ($22.94), rising to 55 DM ($31.55) with bath. Breakfast is included in the rates. The bedrooms contain all the necessary comforts. The miniature dining room is restrained, with wood paneling, yellow walls, and orange chairs.

Bogotá, 45 Schlüterstrasse (tel. 881-05-01). Although you're just off the Kurfürstendamm, when you walk into the Bogotá you'll think you're in a small town on the northern coast of Spain. When you hear Spanish spoken, your impression will be confirmed. The lobby is Iberian in character, with a high beamed ceiling, an open wooden staircase leading through an arch to the bedrooms, a wooden balcony, and a heavy bronze chandelier. There are 118 bedrooms, some of which have private showers; otherwise, each room contains hot and cold running water. Singles go from 38 DM ($21.80) to 58 DM ($33.27), the latter price for one with shower. Bathless doubles are 58 DM ($33.27), increasing to 78 DM ($44.74) with shower. Rates include breakfast. The rooms are elbow-action clean. To economize, ask about staying here on a half- or full-board arrangement and taking your meals in the downstairs restaurant.

Borse, 34 Kurfürstendamm (tel. 881-03-21), is ideally situated for those who want to be right in the swing of things. The hotel is run like an inn, with its lower floor and overlook sidewalk devoted to its restaurant. To check in, you wend your way through the diners. An elevator takes you to the upstairs rooms, which are small, but clean and comfortable, sometimes brightly decorated. Doubles with private bath rent for 100 DM ($57.36), including breakfast, service, and taxes. Singles with full bath range between 60 DM ($34.42) and 70 DM ($40.15).

Cortina, 140 Kantstrasse (tel. 313-90-59), is a modest, well-maintained little pension, just off the Kurfürstendamm. Its prices won't break the bank. Bathless singles cost 35 DM ($20.08); doubles, 56 DM ($32.12). Rates include use of the corridor bath, as well as a continental breakfast. It's not fancy, yet there's a pleasant feeling of roominess and cleanliness. A friendly, English-speaking management helps out, too. Hot and cold running water, as well as a telephone, are in every room. Many doubles have a little sitting area where you can have your morning meal.

NEAR THE MEMORIAL CHURCH AND ZOO: The bomb-flattened area between the Memorial Church and Zoo has become the new hotel belt of Berlin. Here was enough space to build and accommodate the superluxurious hotels. Kurfürstendamm changes character at the church and becomes less a promenade shopping street and more an avenue of first-class hotels. It is the most prestigious place in Berlin to stay.

Deluxe Hotels

Intercontinental Berlin, 2 Budapesterstrasse (tel. 26-10-81), rising 14 stories with its stark checkerboard facade, is now a Berlin landmark. Among the top trio of deluxe hostelries, it is a world apart—prestigious, tasteful, ingenious, dramatic. It not only adjoins but is almost a part of Berlin's famous Tiergarten, or Zoo. The Intercontinental is set in its own garden, with a horseshoe arcade, onto which most of its restaurants, cafes, and boutiques open.

A few singles with shower bath go for 115 DM ($65.96), although most singles contain complete baths, ranging in price from 130 DM ($75.57) to 160 DM ($91.78). Doubles begin at 180 DM ($103.25), going up to 540 DM ($309.74) for the ultimate suite. Each accommodation has an overhead shower, radio, telephone, color TV with English-speaking programs, and mini-bar. The hotel also maintains 24-hour room service.

The theatrically designed dining rooms recapture some of the spirit of the 17th century, with waitresses in the appropriate apparel. The main dining is in Zum Hugenotten. The Garten Laube is formed around a small house with a garden; it takes its theme from a famous society magazine published in Berlin between 1851 and 1930. The Pavilion Bar, with its white piano and intimate dance floor, features a happy hour between 6 and 8 p.m.

Palace, Europa-Center (tel. 26-20-11), may well be the most convenient, popular, and substantial home base for business people in Berlin who are always seen milling about its luxurious lobby. It's within the all-purpose complex, the Europa-Center, with its mini-Rockefeller Center facilities—even a skating rink at the side of the Memorial Church. Facilities within the Palace are impressive as well: parking, a florist, a swimming pool with sauna, a bank, a multitude of boutiques, hairdressers, two important restaurants, an intimate Empire cocktail lounge, a movie theater, and a travel agency. Although the Palace building is modern, the tasteful decor is more conservative, using soft autumnal colors. The bedrooms are decorated with well-upholstered pieces, good reproductions of antiques intermixed with clean-cut, comfortable modern. Each of the soundproofed rooms has a private, richly tiled bath, TV, telephone, and radio. Singles range between 68 DM ($39) and 132 DM ($75.72); double-bedded rooms are 140 DM ($80.30); twin-bedded rooms are between 160 DM ($91.78) and 184 DM ($105.54). Breakfast is included.

First-Class Hotels

Berlin Ambassador, 42–43 Bayreutherstrasse (tel. 24-01-01), is an upper-grade contemporary hotel, whose dining rooms and lounges are among the most well conceived and designed of any Berlin hotel in this price range. The main lounge sets the pace, with its sophisticated steel-and-leather modern chairs gathered around a spherical copper and glass open fireplace that looks something like a space capsule. The favored dining spot is the French restaurant, paneled in wood, with one glass wall opening onto a winter garden of canopied greenery. The grillroom and bar are also alluring, and a snackbar settles instant hunger pangs. A lively crowd is drawn to the heated rooftop swimming pool, with its sun lounge. In addition, bodies from many nations are baked in a genuine log-cabin sauna before being massaged.

Bedrooms are excellent and well planned, with expensive, tasteful furnishings. Each has a shower in its private bath, a radio, and direct-dial telephone. A single with shower starts at 118 DM ($67.68), going up to 123.50 DM ($70.84) with private bath. A twin-bedded room with bath is between 167 DM ($95.79) and 177 DM ($101.53).

Schweizerhof, 21–31 Budapesterstrasse (tel. 2-69-61), has brought honors and success to its Swiss owners. Built in a fashionable and convenient section, close to the Memorial Church and opposite the Zoo, it is clearly a winner in every department. The service, the amenities, and the comfort are first class. However, the overall effect is not one of lavishness—rather, dignified restraint. Increased patronage has led to a whole new wing of streamlined bedrooms, both substantial and comfortable. An Olympic-size swimming pool, even a nightclub, suggests that the Schweizerhof is one of the leading first-class hotels of Berlin. The bedrooms are more traditional than daring, each containing a private bath (most with shower attachments). Singles range all the way from 99 DM ($56.79) to 140 DM ($80.30); doubles, from 140 ($80.30) to 170 DM ($97.51). Most recommendable is the Schweizerhof Grill, offering a fine Helvetian cuisine, backed by Swiss wines. You can also dine in the Zunft-Stube and the Schützen-Stubli, after having had a predinner drink in the Wappen-Bar. Every Thursday evening at 7:30, a 16th-century program featuring a torchlight dinner with a ballad singer is staged at the hotel's Old Market restaurant.

Hotel Berlin, 62 Kurfürstenstrasse (tel. 26-92-91), is a true international hotel, built honeycomb modern, with its own grounds and gardens. Each room has an inset balcony, just large enough for breakfast. This chain hotel is noted primarily for its Berlin-Grill, considered the finest dining room in the city. But it has a claim to fame as a hotel as well. It is used primarily by travelers who want everything at their fingertips—not only a top restaurant, but consistently good service and up-to-date accommodations. The latter are especially good—rather ultramodern in style, each with a private telephone, bath, or shower and toilet. Singles go for 84 DM ($48.18); doubles, 126 DM ($72.27).

The Savoy, 9–10 Fasanenstrasse (tel. 31-06-54), was the only Berlin hotel to survive World War II. Erected in the 1920s, it was once filled with Russian aristocrats, who stopped off here before going on to Cannes. Nowadays, it attracts conservative travelers who appreciate a traditional ambience and setting, just minutes from the Kurfürstendamm. Persian carpets, crystal chandeliers, and contemporary upholstered pieces add a warm note. "Germanic modern" accommodations have private baths or showers—most rooms have sitting areas with TV, couch, and desk. Rates, including tax, service, and continental breakfast, are as follows: singles with shower or tub bath range from 85 DM ($48.76) to 95 DM ($54.49). Twins with shower or bath go from 135 DM ($77.44) to 150 DM ($86.04). The American Bar, dining room, and garden are most popular.

Sylter Hof, 116 Kurfürstenstrasse (tel. 213-20-01), is recently built, offering rich trappings at moderate prices. The main lounges are warmly decorated in an old-world style, with glittering chandeliers, Louis XV and provincial chairs, and such antiques as a glistening armoire and a grandfather clock. The bar-lounge is seductive, serving drinks to guests seated in velvet armchairs nestling on Persian rugs. The dining room is more conservative, done in green. Although small, the bedrooms are warmly appointed, with compact, traditional furnishings, plus private tiled baths. Singles rent for 82 DM ($47.04); doubles, for 120 DM ($68.83). Garage parking is available.

Medium-Priced Hotels

Hamburg, 4 Landgrafenstrasse (tel. 26-91-61), is one of the newer streamlined hotels, offering modern accommodations at reasonable prices. The Hamburg, with its checkerboard facade of glass and two-toned marble, is a five-minute walk from the Kurfürstendamm. Each bedroom contains its own tiled bath and shower, telephone, radio, and TV, if requested. Singles are 79 DM ($45.31) to 83 DM ($47.61); a twin-bedded room is 107 DM ($61.38) to 120 DM ($68.83). An extra bed in your room costs an additional 24 DM ($13.77). A buffet breakfast is included.

The decor of the rooms is most satisfactory, a combination of Nordic modern with wall-wide draperies and comfortably upholstered armchairs. Other facilities include a cocktail lounge behind open white grillwork, where the bartender prides himself on international brews. Best of all is the outstanding living room, with its clusters of deep, well-styled, velvet-upholstered armchairs arranged around tables or the stone fireplace with copper slats.

President Hotel, 16–18 an der Urania (tel. 213-80-61), is the latest of a cluster of ultramodern hotels, whose white marble facade and streamlined decor seem right in step. About a ten-minute walk from the Kurfürstendamm, this hotel rises seven floors, with glistening bands of picture windows. An expansive roof garden, with a panoramic view, is its most winning feature; a Nordic sauna, its most restful. Bedrooms are geared more for efficiency than high style, with lots of swivel armchairs, and trim sofas which convert into extra beds. In addition, each room has its own bath, radio, TV, mini-bar, and direct-dial phone. Singles with shower are 90 DM ($51.62). Doubles with a full bath are 130 DM ($75.57). A supplementary bed costs 30 DM ($17.21).

SOUTH OF THE KURFÜRSTENDAMM: This area is better known as

no-man's land—with no special geographical boundaries except for its northern border. Only a few hotels are in this area, as it is mostly a residential and shopping section.

The Medium-Priced Choice

Alsterhof, 1–3 Würzburger Strasse (tel. 213-70-01), is a relatively unknown modern hotel which is an excellent buy. Set back from the street, it rises seven stories. The lounges and reception area have walls of glass. Recent and welcome additions: Grill-Room with bar and a TV room. Each of the 77 bedchambers has its own private bath, radio, TV, mini-bar, and telephone, and is furnished with fine-grained contemporary wooden pieces. Many contain sitting areas as well. Singles with shower are 60 DM ($34.42) to 65 DM ($37.28); with complete bath, 71 DM ($40.73) to 81 DM ($46.46). A double-bedded room rents for 110 DM ($63.10) to 120 DM ($68.83). Breakfast is included.

The Budget Choice

Dom Hotel, 33 Hohenzollerndamm (tel. 87-97-80), is quite economical. This modern building, with its absolute minimum lobby, provides good sleeping rooms. Bathless singles range between 20 DM ($11.47) and 30 DM ($17.21), increasing to 45 DM ($25.81) with bath. Bathless doubles rent for 55 DM ($31.55); with private bath, from 58 DM ($33.27) to 60 DM ($34.42). A continental breakfast is 5.50 DM ($3.15) extra. Meals are served in the friendly restaurant, the Domklause. Young visitors enjoy the Dom's proximity to the Riverboat disco.

IN CHARLOTTENBURG: This is an area combining private residences, apartment houses, and hotels, about a five- to ten-minute taxi drive from the Memorial Church and Kurfürstendamm. Its main artery, Bismarckstrasse, is where you'll find the Deutsche Oper and the Schiller Theatre.

A First-Class Choice

Seehof, 11 Lietzensee-Ufer (tel. 32-10-51), is perhaps the most attractive and enjoyable hotel in Berlin. It's comparatively unknown, as it lies in the residential section of Charlottenburg. Yet it's only five minutes from the center by taxi. The hotel borders Lake Lietzen. You start your day here with a swim in the rooftop, glassed-in pool, then order breakfast at one of the garden tables. The blue-and-white checkerboard facade opens onto a tree-shaded street. On the waterside stone terrace in the rear you can have refreshments, sunbathe, or take your lunch.

The living room is styled like a country house, with a natural stone wall, a planter, a window wall, and low couches for relaxed conversation. The main dining room is seductively designed; a pianist plays soft background music. Drinks are available in the rustic tavern bar. The bedrooms, while small, are well conceived, with splashes of color against stark-white walls. Most of the accommodations have slim-line sofas, armchairs, and cocktail tables. A single with toilet ranges in price from 66.50 DM ($38.14); with bath, from 114 DM ($65.39). Doubles with bath go from 132 DM ($75.72) to 182 DM ($104.40).

Medium-Priced Hotels

Europäischer Hof, 10 Messedamm (tel. 30-20-11), built in 1966, stands halfway between the Olympia Stadium and the Europa-Center, and adjacent to the Berlin Exhibition Grounds and the new Congress Center, at the end of the Federal and Berlin City Highways. Its modern features are attractive and winning. Crowning its top floor is a garden-style terrace restaurant, the Bellvue, one of the most panoramic spots for luncheons in the city. Its bedrooms have full baths, with wall-wide glass windows. Radios, telephones, desks, and armchairs add to the modern comforts. Single rooms cost from 86 DM ($49.33); doubles, 128 DM ($73.42)—breakfast included. For predinner drinks, there's an intimate wood-paneled bar and cocktail lounge. It's a leader in the moderately priced field if you don't mind the long haul.

Hotel am Studio, 80–81 Kaiserdamm (tel. 30-20-81), is recommended to those seeking a bright and cheery accommodation at lower than usual prices for what you get. This 80-bedroom structure of bands of marble and glass windows is built in the Charlottenburg district, near the Olympic Stadium and next to the Radio and Television Center. Two subway stops are nearby. The bedrooms are pleasantly decorated and comfortable. Each of the rooms has its own private bath. Singles go for 56 DM ($32.12); doubles, anywhere from 80 DM ($45.89) to 90 DM ($51.62)—including breakfast, service, and taxes. Your morning meal will be served in a sun-filled salon.

IN GRUNEWALD: The Green Forest of Berlin is the pleasantest residential section of the city, with tree-shaded streets and many town houses which were spared the destruction of war. It's ideal for a peaceful night's sleep.

Schlosshotel Gehrhus, 4–10 Brahmsstrasse (tel. 826-03-55), offers a rare opportunity to live in an Italian Renaissance-style palace in the Grunewald residential section of Berlin. It was created in 1912 by Dr. Pannwitz, personal attorney to Kaiser Wilhelm II. The palace was built as a showcase to house the attorney's outstanding art and china collection. Gehrhus miraculously escaped destruction in World War II. On a shady street—it is reached via a formal driveway—it is a 15-minute taxi ride from the center. Surrounding the estate are tranquil, parklike gardens.

Inside, the architectural grandeur remains the same. Gilt is used flamboyantly. The two-story grand hall contains an elaborate staircase and minstrel gallery. Glittering chandeliers glow in the French-style salons, with their brocaded walls.

The bedrooms vary greatly, ranging from grand to average. A bathless single costs 48 DM ($27.53) to 68 DM ($39), rising to 100 DM ($57.36) with bath. Bathless doubles begin at 90 DM ($51.62), going up to 130 DM ($75.57) to 155 DM ($88.91) with bath. Even though they're not guests of the hotel, many tradition-minded Berliners come here just to have coffee or tea—perhaps a nostalgic reminder of the past. Others use the Gehrhus for fashionable weddings, receptions, and cocktail parties.

READERS' PENSION SELECTIONS: "In Berlin, we stayed at the **Pension Konstanz,** 1 Konstanzerstrasse (tel. 881-4246). A two-bedded room costs from 56 DM ($32.12) to 70 DM ($40.15), those figures including a nice breakfast. The higher price is for the one room with bath. It was recommended at the airport information office, and turned out to be a pleasant place, left over from Old Berlin" (Guy H. Raner Jr., Chatsworth, Calif.). ... "**Pension Savignyplatz,** 52 Grolmannstrasse, second floor, rents for 25 DM ($14.34) per night without breakfast in a single, the price going up to 38 DM ($21.80) in a double. It's not far from Kurfürstendamm and Zoo-Station, and the rooms are better than the price would suggest (Rolf Hepke, Achim, West Germany).

2. Restaurants

If it's true that optimism and appetite go hand in hand, the West Berliners must be among the most optimistic people in Europe! In breads alone, the visitor is likely to be tempted by a dozen varieties, including brötchen, mohnbrötchen, milchbrötchen (all types of rolls), graubrot (rye), pumpernickel, and several others. If you're interested in local food, these breads go equally well with the "Berliner schlachteplatte" (cold plate), or pig's trotters cooked with sauerkraut and pea puree.

But Berlin does not limit itself to German cuisine—nearly every major nation on the globe is represented here by a restaurant. Only the thickness (or thinness) of your wallet and the flexibility of your tastebuds need determine your choices. And don't think that an excellent dinner in Berlin has to be expensive. On the contrary, as you'll see in our recommendations below, you can have a memorable dinner in a completely unheralded wine restaurant or sidewalk cafe.

THE TOP RESTAURANTS: Berlin-Grill, Berlin Hotel, 62 Kurfürstenstrasse (tel. 26-92-91), is Berlin's leading candidate for in-depth preparation of haute cuisine. You feel absolutely coddled dining here as a train of serving carts with your choices is brought to your chair. Salads are made on the spot—and pretested. Many of the dishes are prepared right at your table, for your closest scrutiny. After any finger food is served, you get hot, scented towels. Everything is top-grade—no substitutes, in the food, service, or atmosphere. Fresh flowers placed on the tables add yet another warming note.

The cuisine is Germanic-international. Many of the soups are prepared and served right at your table, including Burgundian snail soup at 7.50 DM ($4.30). Specialties of the house feature a brochette of fish with a herb sauce and creole rice at 21.50 DM ($12.33); a skewered loin of veal with vegetables and saffron rice, 34 DM ($19.50); and fresh chicken with fines herbes, 71 DM ($40.73) for two persons. Cherries jubilee at 8.50 DM ($4.88) makes for a flaming dessert.

Maître, 10 Meinekestrasse (tel. 883-84-85). This French restaurant, along with the Berlin-Grill, serves the best food in the city. It's run by Henri Levi and Mme. Marguerite Rahn. Monsieur Levi not only helps seat guests, but often advises them on what to order and helps with the wine selection if asked. He makes one feel immediately relaxed and comfortable; a meal here is like being a guest in his home. The restaurant is open from noon to 3 p.m. and from 6 to midnight. It's closed Sundays and serves dinner only on Mondays. For an appetizer, we'd suggest escargots en petits pots at 11 DM ($6.31). Among the most recommendable classic French dishes are pot-au-feu at 29 DM ($16.63); rognons de veau (veal kidneys), 28 DM ($16.06); and the peppersteak, 31 DM ($17.78). A good dessert is délice antillais with rum chocolate at 8.50 DM ($4.88). The restaurant avoids a gimmicky decor. Its series of dining rooms are sedately decorated. All attention—and rightly so—goes to the cuisine.

Ritz, 26 Rankestrasse (tel. 24-72-50), is one of the most celebrated restaurants of Germany. It's unique, and exotic; the chef feels equally at home roaming through Chinese, Arabic, Russian, Indian, Japanese, or even Korean cuisines—not to mention those of Germany, Italy, Switzerland, and France. To be completely international, the menu is printed in Japanese. English is spoken, however. The key to the success of the Ritz is the choice ingredients imported from all over the world.

The background for this exotic cuisine is a Germanic version of an Oriental and Far East decor. You dine in semiprivate booths. The woodwork is rich Venetian red. The walls with a background of raffia are covered with displays of savory condiments, spices, earthenware cookware, wine bottles, and in a niche an aquamarine ceramic Buddha.

In season, lobster and oysters are the specialties, and these dishes are prepared in infinite ways. For a curious opener, you might try Siamese peacock soup at 6.25 DM ($3.59). Also good is the Indonesian boula-boula soup at 6.25 DM. Among the host of specialties are such dishes as filets of roebuck with hazelnut cream, 20.50 DM ($11.76); chamois-bucksteak with sour cherries, Albanian style, 28 DM ($16.06); and Russian chicken Koljanka, 18.50 DM ($10.61). A dessert specialty is Burgunder wein crêpes at 9 DM ($5.16). Closed Sundays.

MEDIUM-PRICED DINING: In this category, West Berlin has dozens of dining spots. Here are the best choices.

A Place with Atmosphere

Mampes Gute Stube, 14 Kurfürstendamm (tel. 881-71-01), is a genuine Old Berlin restaurant. You expect the cast from *Grand Hotel* to walk in at any minute. Housed in a building that survived World War II, the "stube" couldn't be more traditional, although you'd never know it, judging by the modern glassed-in sidewalk tables outside on the Kurfürstendamm. Inside, the dining nooks are more atmospheric, with dark woods and leather, as well as tiled tables. Set menus are available at 15.75 DM ($9.03) and 18.50 DM ($10.61). Recommended are the chicken fricassee at 11.50 DM ($6.60) or the veal steak at 15.50 DM ($8.89). The sole meunière is also good at 12.50 DM ($7.17). For dessert, try the sour cherries with fresh cream at 6.50 DM ($3.73).

For Danish Smørrebrød

Kopenhagen, 203 Kurfürstendamm (tel. 881-61-19). The Danes are among the finest cooks in Europe. Just ask them! Their most famous specialty is smørrebrød (literally, bread and butter), on which they are likely to pile everything from a slice of Danish cheese to steak tartare crowned by a raw egg. These open-face sandwiches, when prepared correctly, are a delight. Copenhagen more than a quarter of a century ago invaded Berlin (not the other way around!). The selection of smørrebrød is so huge that you may spend half your lunchtime deciding what to order. Favored are marinated herring at 6 DM ($3.44) and roast beef with remoulade sauce at 12.50 DM ($7.17). However, the liver Pâté at 9 DM ($5.16) is heartily recommended as well. A special smørrebrød is the aquavit cream cheese at 6.75 DM ($3.87). Naturally, you'll want to accompany your meal with a Danish Carlsberg beer at 3.75 DM ($2.15) a bottle. Hot main dishes, Danish style, are featured as well, including lobster soup at 4.75 DM ($2.72). A good main course is game pie, with Cumberland sauce and a Waldorf Salad, at 24 DM ($13.77) for two. Desserts range from 3.50 DM ($2.01) to 7 DM ($4.02), and many are elaborate concoctions.

For Czech Cuisine

Zlata Praha, 4 Meinekestrasse (tel. 881-97-50), serves the best Eastern European cuisine of any restaurant in Berlin. Featured are Hungarian, Bulgarian, and Austrian wines in the 18-DM ($10.32) to 25-DM ($14.34) range. However, the pièce de résistance is the special tap-drawn beer, Pilsner Urquell das Echte, costing 4 DM ($2.29). Actually, if your palate isn't Slavic, you may want to steer clear of this brew. Otherwise, it makes the perfect drink for toasting your Czech friends at the next table. Most of the food seems inspired by the Prague kitchen. Although many of the dishes may be esoteric to you, you'll recognize the Balkan salad at 7 DM ($4.02) and the bean soup at 3.50 DM ($2.01). Among the main-dish specialties are the paprika schnitzel at 15.50 DM ($8.89) and the sauerbraten at 16 DM ($9.18). Few can resist the topfer strudel at 7.50 DM ($4.30). Owner Roschi Biro is a most gracious host, and seemingly never tires of being asked, "How did you happen to come to Berlin?" Go after 5 p.m. only, and never on Sunday.

Dining with a View

Funkturm, Messegelände (tel. 303-83-75). Dining in towers enjoys a vogue in Germany bordering on madness. West Berlin is not without its high-rise cuisine, and the Funkturm in the Charlottenburg district of West Berlin scores by serving good food. At this panoramic restaurant, the local Berlin dishes are notable. Try, for example, boiled brisket of beef, with a red beet salad and creamed horseradish, 14 DM ($8.03). A more international offering is the sole meunière at 21 DM ($12.05). Onion soup, at 5.50 DM ($3.15), makes a good beginning; the peach Melba, at 6.50 DM ($3.73), a worthy finale.

A Terrace on the Kurfürstendamm

Drei Bären (Three Bears), 22 Kurfürstendamm (tel. 882-10-76). Sitting at a table on the canopied sidewalk terrace of this most central of Berlin restaurants, you're likely to be closely inspected by the passersby. They'll either look at you or your food, depending on which is more interesting! At the Three Bears, your personal charms are in for some competition, because the cuisine is quite good—and rather elaborately served at times. Should you want to remove yourself from the scene of action, you can ask to be seated on the second floor. A typical dinner might include oxtail soup at 3.50 DM ($2.01), followed by brook trout at 16 DM ($9.18) or chicken fricassee at 14.50 DM ($8.32). The chef's specialty is peppersteak at 24 DM ($13.77). A fresh fruit salad at 5.50 DM ($3.15) is a good dessert choice.

BUDGET DINING: Of the many budget dining spots in West Berlin, here are our top choices:

A Beer Hall

Schultheiss Bräuhaus, 220 Kurfürstendamm (tel. 881-70-50), sits diagonally across from the deluxe Bristol-Kempinski Hotel. Ever since its appearance on the scene, it has fast gained admirers, making it one of the leading beer hall restaurants in West Berlin. You can dine on the terrace, in the midst of planters filled with greenery, or go inside to the dark and more mellowed tavern, selecting one of several rooms. Beer barrels have been converted to cozy dining nooks. Under the beams and against a background of rustic trimmings, large, hearty portions are served. The prices are low. For example, a fresh soup is made daily, costing 3 DM ($1.72). Typical dishes include a thick pork cutlet in brown gravy, with salad and freshly done french fries, at 12.50 DM ($7.17). A Sülze cotelet with potato salad costs only 7.75 DM ($4.46), and a country breakfast (that is, an omelet with bacon) goes for 9.50 DM ($5.45).

Tradition on a Budget

Hardtke's, 26 Meinekestrasse, right off the Kurfürstendamm, is the best all-around budget restaurant in Berlin. A traditional favorite, it was well known before the war. Restored after a bombing, it is in the old style, with dark beams and wood paneling—heavily Teutonic in flavor—along with Heidelberg steins, pewter, scrubbed wooden tables, and wrought-iron chandeliers. A copper-topped serving bar is always kept shiny clean. There are many cozy booths for pleasant, leisurely dining. The prices are low, as exemplified by a bowl of soup at 2.50 DM ($1.43) or a hearty portion of french fries at 2.50 DM also. If you want a most filling snack, order bockwurst with potato salad at 5 DM ($2.87). A large schinkenhaxe costs 15 DM ($8.60); grosses eisbein (pig's trotters),

12.50 DM ($7.17). The restaurant is noted for its sausages. Set meals—served until 4 p.m.—range in price from 9.75 DM ($5.59) to 12 DM ($6.88).

DINING IN A RATSKELLER: **Ratskeller Schöneberg,** Schöneberg Rathaus, John F. Kennedy·Platz (tel. 71-01-41). This ratskeller is on the square which became famous when former President Kennedy made his now legendary "Ich bin ein Berliner" speech. Many Americans, when visiting the square and the Freedom Bell inside, like to stop off here for food. The wines are really good, and they can be ordered to accompany one of the set luncheons, priced reasonably at 10.50 DM ($6.02) and 21 DM ($12.05). Among the à la carte items, the main dishes are fairly ambitious, including such offerings as steak Diane at 20.50 DM ($11.76) or veal schnitzel Cordon Bleu, with a fresh salad and french fries, 19.50 DM ($11.19). The day's soup is invariably good, priced at 2.75 DM ($1.58) per bowl. Desserts begin as low as 2.75 DM also, although you'll pay 5 DM ($2.87) for a peach Melba.

DINING AT EUROPA-CENTER: This 22-story skyscraper—crowned by a revolving Mercedes star—is a virtual culinary United Nations. Many visitors take all their meals in Berlin here and enjoy a widely varied cuisine.

Good for the budget is **Edelweiss,** decorated in the old beer tavern style. It makes an especially attractive place at which to dine. Soups begin at 3.50 DM ($2.01), and you can order a pork chop plate for 12.50 DM ($7.17). Six of those delectable Nürnberg sausages, with potatoes, go for 9 DM ($5.16). Desserts begin at 3.50 DM ($2.01). On weekend nights, a Bavarian band plays.

Also recommendable is the **Alt Berlin** (Old Berlin), whose decor lives up to its name. Especially festive in the evening, it contains rooms in the old-fashioned Berlin tavern style.

Actually, the independent eateries in the Europa-Center attract more business than the House of Nations. For example, **Alt Nürnberg,** on the ground level, is more successful in its antique theme than the Alt Berlin. It handsomely and dramatically captures the old style of a German tavern, complete with copper lanterns and dark woods. It is not expensive either, with soups beginning at 3 DM ($1.72) and main dishes such as pork plates going for 10.50 DM ($6.02). The house specialty is a plate of Nürnberger rostbratwurstl. You can have 12 of these delectable finger-size sausages for 12 DM ($6.88). They're usually served with sauerkraut and brown bread.

The **Tokyo,** on the second floor, is one of the best Japanese restaurants in Berlin. Festively decorated, it is a bright, glassed-in structure, with paper lanterns. A set sukiyaki dinner costs 28 DM ($16.06), including an appetizer, soup, main dish, salad, rice, dessert, and Japanese tea. Sukiyaki by itself is 21.50 DM ($12.33); an order of teriyaki steak, 22 DM ($12.62).

During the day you may want to visit the **i-Punkt Café** after going up to the viewing platform (1.50 DM or 86¢, incidentally). Coffee begins at 3.75 DM ($2.15); beer, 4 DM ($2.29). A slice of cake is 3 DM ($1.72). Picture windows provide a panoramic view.

READER'S RESTAURANT SELECTIONS: "In Berlin two of the best budget restaurants serving noninstitutional-tasting food are in museums. The first is the **Dahlem Museum,** which offers hot food from 11:30 a.m. to 2:30 p.m., with meat, potato, and salad plates starting at 8 DM ($4.59). Cold food is available throughout the day. The second is the Weissbierstube in the **Berlin Museum** on Lindenstrasse. Here there is a smörgasbord where you can combine meat, vegetables, and salad for 8 DM ($4.59). Also, the staff serves the city's most characteristic drink, the Berlinerweisse, white beer with a shot of raspberry flavoring. Open from 11 a.m. to 6 p.m." (Gail Walker, Needham, Mass.).

. . . "Eating well and relatively inexpensively in downtown West Berlin is not easy, but try the **Schwejk Prager Gasthaus,** 4 Ansbacherstrasse (tel. 213-7892). It's open daily from 6 p.m., two blocks east from the Memorial Church at the very center of the city, then two doors south. Bohemian specialties are served in a neighborhood-tavern atmosphere, with some scrubbed tables and a small drinking/eating bar with individual placemats. We had superb boneless pork cutlets and crackling broiled pork shanks (schweinhaxen) with salad and excellent sauerkraut, generous servings costing 12.50 DM ($7.17) each. Good-size bowls of thick borscht or libber-ball soup go for 3.50 DM ($2.01) each. Other persons near us ordered huge 'toasts' with meats and vegetables piled on top. Excellent Pilsner Urquell is available for 3 DM ($1.72) per .41 liter. The waiters speak English" (Cameron N. Lusty, St. Petersburg, Fla.).

3. Sights

In the midst of the daily whirl of working, shopping, dining, and entertainment, Berliners along the Kurfürstendamm often glance at the sobering reminder of less happy days. At the end of the street stands the **Kaiser Wilhelm Memorial Church,** destroyed in World War II. Only the shell of the old neo-Romanesque tower (1895) remains, as a symbol of West Berlin after the war. In striking contrast to the ruins, a new church has been constructed west of the old tower seating 1200 people in its octagonal hall, and lit solely by the hundreds of colored-glass windows set into the honeycomb framework. Dedicated in 1961, the church has an overall look best described by the nickname given it by Berliners, "the lipstick and powder box." You can wander through the ruins any day from 9 a.m. to 9 p.m. Ten-minute services are held in the modern church daily at 5:30 p.m. and 6 p.m. for those going home from work.

This remarkable combination of old and new is what Berlin is all about. Although there is much more new than old in this city, which suffered more than any other European metropolis during World War II (except perhaps Warsaw), Berlin offers a multitude of sights for the visitor.

MODERN BERLIN: In World War II, one out of every three Berliners lost his home. After the rubble was cleared away—a major problem in itself for this isolated city—the great task of rebuilding began. It took the united effort of many of the world's greatest architects to create the splendid example of modern Berlin which lies just north of the Tiergarten. The **Hansa Quarter** (U-Bahn to Hansaplatz) was a direct result of the great Interbau (international builders' exhibition) of 1957, when architectural designers from 22 nations constructed homes and apartments in this district, along with shops, schools, churches, even a cinema, library, and museum. The excitement here is in the variety: each of the nearly 50 architects, including Gropius, Niemeyer, and Düttman, was able to express himself in his own way. Even Le Corbusier submitted a design for an apartment house, but the structure would have been too gigantic for the quarter. You can see it today where it was built in the less congested western section of the city, near the Olympic Stadium. The **Corbusier House,** called Strahlende Stadt (radiant city) is Berlin's largest housing complex—and one of the biggest in Europe. Its 530 apartments (more than 1000 rooms) can house up to 1400 people. Typical of the architect's style, even this tremendous building rests on stilts.

Berlin's highest building sits in the heart of the city's activity. The 22-story **Europa-Center,** just across the plaza from the Kaiser Wilhelm Memorial Church, is the largest self-contained shopping center and entertainment complex in Europe. This town-within-a-town opened in 1965 and has been fascinating Berliners and outsiders alike ever since. Besides its three levels of shops, restaurants, nightclubs, bars, and movie houses, it contains hundreds of offices, a car park, and an observation roof from which you can view every part of the city.

THE ZOO AND AQUARIUM: You wouldn't expect to find anything more than a handful of tiny animal cages in the center of a city where space is at such a premium. Yet, in West Berlin, where the proportion of green parkland is surprisingly large in comparison to many of the large cities of Europe, you can see the oldest, largest, and finest zoo in all of Germany. Just a short walk north from the main street of town, the Ku-damm, it occupies almost the entire southwestern corner of the huge Tiergarten.

Until World War II, the zoo boasted thousands of animals of every imaginable species and description, many of them familiar to Berliners by nicknames. The tragedy of the war struck here as well as in the human sections of Berlin, and by the end of 1945, only 90 animals had survived. For the past 35 years, however, the city has been rebuilding its large and unique collection until today there are more than 13,000 animals and birds, some of them housed here to prevent their becoming extinct. The zoo has the most modern birdhouse in Europe, with more than 700 different species of birds. Furthermore, great and small cats from all over the world can be seen in a Carnivore House, and in the Nocturnal House the visitors can watch the way of life of nocturnal animals. The monkey center is a popular spot, and in the Berlin Zoo you can see breeding groups of apes (no fewer than six gorillas, ten orangutans, and four chimpanzees). There are also large open ranges where wild animals can roam in a simulated natural habitat.

In the center of the zoological gardens is a large and excellent restaurant where you can dine indoors or out. On the patio in summer you may have the added treat of dinner music furnished by the old organ grinders.

The Aquarium, on the edge of Budapesterstrasse, is as impressive as the adjacent zoo. Its collection of more than 3,000 fish and reptiles holds a strange fascination for every visitor. The second floor is devoted entirely to creatures that live entirely under water, with one section for saltwater fish and one for those that live in lakes and streams. Benches are along the viewing promenade so you can sit and watch your favorite turtle or octopus for as long as you wish. But even more intriguing is the terrarium on the third floor, with a huge crocodile collection. You can even walk into the terrarium on a bridge over the reptile pit—but don't lose your balance! Around the outside are several glass cases containing nearly every known species of snake and lizard, and a small terrarium at the corner with giant tortoises, and on the third floor, you can watch the world of insects.

The zoo is open daily from 9 a.m. to 6:30 p.m. (it closes at dusk in winter), and charges 4 DM ($2.29) admission. The aquarium, with its separate entrance, is open from 9 a.m. to 6 p.m. (until 7 p.m. on Sundays and holidays). Admission is 3.50 DM ($2.01), but you can purchase a combined ticket for 6 DM ($3.44) which will admit you to both the aquarium and the zoo.

THE DAHLEM MUSEUM: War is no respecter of persons or objects, and the art collections of Berlin suffered tragically in 1945. Although many smaller paintings of the national museums of Berlin were stored in inoperative salt mines during the war, many larger works, including eight paintings by Rubens and three by van Dyck, were destroyed by fire. Some works which survived are now in East Berlin, where many of Berlin's finest galleries were located before the war. Of the paintings which were relegated to the West and passed from nation to nation in the late 1940s like so many decks of cards, most have now been returned to Berlin and are permanently ensconced in the Dahlem, making it one of Germany's finest galleries. Of the nearly 1500 paintings in its possession, more than 600 are on display.

The first floor has several rooms devoted to early German Masters, with panels from altarpieces dating from the 13th, 14th, and 15th centuries. Note the panel of *The Virgin Enthroned with Child* (1350), surrounded by angels which resemble the demons so popular in the later works of Hieronymus Bosch. Eight paintings make up the Dürer collection in the adjacent rooms, including several portraits and a Madonna, with a crown held above her head by two cherubs whose bodies fade into puffs of smoke.

Two contemporaries of Dürer, Albrecht Altdorfer and Lucas Cranach the Elder, are both represented by paintings of *The Rest on the Flight into Egypt*. Note the contrasts between the two works, the former in the Renaissance style, with a town as the background setting and tiny angels playing in an elegant fountain in the foreground. Cranach, on the other hand, chose a quiet pastoral setting and confined the colors and action to the characters themselves, seemingly ready to pose for a family portrait.

Another gallery on the first floor is given over entirely to Italian painting. Here you'll find five Raphael Madonnas, works by Titian *(The Girl with a Bowl of Fruit),* Fra Filippo Lippi, Botticelli, and Coreggio *(Leda with the Swan).*

Furthermore, on the first floor, are early Netherlands paintings from the 15th and 16th centuries (van Eyck, van der Weyden, van der Goes, Bosch, and Bruegel).

The second floor is devoted mainly to Flemish and Dutch Masters of the 17th century, with no less than 24 works by Rembrandt alone! Among the most famous of the great painter's works in the Dahlem are *The Man with the Golden Helmet,* and the warmly human *Head of Christ.* Several portraits and biblical scenes make up most of the balance of this excellent collection. In spite of the several works by Rubens which were burned after the war, you can still see 19 on display here, including the charming *Child with a Bird,* and one of his landscapes, showing milkmaids tending cattle.

In the not-too-distant future, the Dahlem will be moving to newer and larger quarters in the southeastern part of the Tiergarten. But until then, we will remain deprived of the more than 800 works packed in the vaults of the museum. The rest of the building is occupied by several other museum exhibitions, including the **Department of Sculpture,** with its bas-relief on Carrara marble by Donatello of a serene Madonna and Child (1422). The **Department of Prints and Engravings** contains several pen and ink drawings by Dürer, including his signed (1511) sketch of the *Holy Family at Rest.* There's even a landscape sketch by Rembrandt.

The **Ethnographical Museum** houses arts and artifacts from Africa, the Far East, the South Seas, and North and South America. Many of the figures and ritualistic masks are grotesquely beautiful, presenting a striking contrast in art, especially after a visit to the gallery of paintings. In addition to all the above museums, the Dahlem also houses the Museums of Far Eastern Art, Islamic Art, and Indian Art, all only recently opened in striking new exhibition areas.

You can visit any of the collections at the Dahlem Tuesday through Sunday from 9 a.m. to 5 p.m. Closed Monday. Admission to all departments is free. To get there, take bus 1, 10, or 68 or the U-Bahn to the Dahlem-Dorf stop.

CHARLOTTENBURG PALACE: Perhaps Napoleon exaggerated a bit in comparing this palace to the great Versailles when he invaded Berlin in 1806, but Charlottenburg was, in its heyday, the most elegant residence for the Prussian rulers outside the castle in Potsdam. Begun in 1695 as a summer palace for the friend of the arts, Electress Sophie Charlotte, wife of King Frederick I (Elector Frederick III), the little residence got out of hand until it grew into the massive structure you see today, branching out in long narrow wings from the main building. When you visit the palace, you should plan on spending the day, since it contains not only the apartments of Prussian royalty, but several museums as well.

When you pass the heavy iron gates and enter the courtyard, you'll immediately encounter a baroque equestrian statue of the pompous Great Elector himself, by Andreas Schlüter. The main entrance to the palace is directly behind, marked by the 157-foot-high cupola capped by a gilded statue of Fortune. Inside you'll find a columned rotunda with stucco reliefs depicting the virtues of the Prussian princes in mythological terms.

From this vestibule, you can take guided tours of the **Historical Rooms** between Tuesday and Sunday, from 9 a.m. to 5 p.m. (tours leave every hour and cost 1 DM). Since they are in German only, you'll have to be content to appreciate the works of art without the running commentary. If you wish to prepare for what you'll be seeing, you can buy the English translation of the guide's lecture in book form at the ticket counter.

Although parts of the palace were badly damaged during the war—most of it has now been completely restored—many of the furnishings were saved, especially the works of art, and are again on display. The main wing contains the apartments of Frederick I and his "philosopher queen." Of special interest in this section is the **Reception Chamber,** in the left projection of the wing. This large room is decorated with frieze panels, vaulted ceilings, and mirror-paneled niches. The tapestries on the walls (1730) depict famous men in the style of Plutarch's *Lives.* Included are scenes of Pericles in battle and the sacrifice of Theseus on Delos.

At the far end of the west wing is the **Porcelain Chamber,** whose walls are decorated solely by various pieces of Oriental porcelain, hung on the walls, standing on pedestals, some even partly inserted into the walls or suspended by metal rings. The unusual effect is heightened by the profusion of mirrors.

The **New Wing** (Knobelsdorff Wing), built in 1740–46, contains the apartments of Frederick the Great, which have in essence been converted into an outstanding museum of excellent paintings, many of which were either collected or commissioned by the king. Most of the ground-floor apartments are galleries of portraits mixed with fine examples of period furniture, but the real treasures are on the upper floor. Here you can see several works by Watteau, including *The Tradesign of the Artdealer Gersaint,* purchased by Frederick the Great in 1745 for the concert hall of the palace. Another room is devoted to Boucher tapestries depicting love affairs among the gods, including Bacchus and Ariadne on Naxos, and Venus seducing Vulcan at his forge. In addition to the fine works of art in this wing, it is interesting to notice the decoration on the walls and ceilings of the rooms. Of course, many rooms have been virtually reproduced since the war, but the variety of wall coverings and ceiling paintings is, nevertheless, fascinating.

The Charlottenburg Museums

The **Egyptian Museum** is in the east guardhouse at the entrance to the palace. It's worth a trip just to see the bust of **Nefertiti,** dating from the

Amarna period of Egypt (about 1400 B.C.). In addition, you can see seals and plaques that go back to the invention of writing, about 3000 B.C., and prehistoric implements which date back even further. Room 7 contains several objects relating to the Egyptian belief in the afterlife, including a traveling boat, complete with all the necessities for the long journey. The rooms trace the history of Egypt right down to the Greco-Roman period, and you can even see writings of the Coptic Church in the early years after the crucifixion of Christ. The museum is open daily, except Tuesday, from 9 a.m. to 5 p.m. (Sundays, from 10 a.m.) There is no admission charge for this or any of the other museums.

The **Museum of Greek and Roman Antiquities** is housed in the west guardhouse, just opposite the Egyptian Museum. The collection here includes some of the finest Greek vases of black- and red-figured style dating from the sixth to the fourth century, B.C. Of the several excellent bronze statuettes, one, the *Zeus of Dodone* (470 B.C.), shows the god about to cast a bolt of lightning, which looks remarkably like a hero sandwich! The most unusual exhibits are a large collection of ancient jewelry and of funerary portraits from Egypt. Those from the first and second centuries A.D. are especially well preserved and surprisingly realistic. Museum hours are from 9 a.m. to 5 p.m. on Monday, Thursday, and Friday; Saturday and Sunday, from 10 a.m. to 5 p.m.; Wednesday, 2 p.m. to 9 p.m. Closed Tuesdays.

The **Museum of Applied Arts,** housed in the New Wing of the palace (first floor), consists of 11 rooms of domestic and ecclesiastical art from the Middle Ages through the 18th century. Among the tapestries, porcelain figurines, and jewelry (including an interesting watch collection), is the outstanding **Guelph Treasure,** a collection of medieval church treasures in gold and silver. More impressive than the precious metal is the reliquary made in Cologne in 1175. It is formed like a Byzantine church, in the shape of a cross, with an umbrella-like cupola supported by carved biblical figures. In niches on either side of the Crucifixion scene at the base are carvings of the Apostles. You can visit the museum any day except Tuesday from 9 a.m. to 5 p.m. (from 10 a.m. on Sunday).

The **Prehistoric and Early History Museum,** in the western extension of the palace facing the Klausener Platz, contains several rooms devoted to art and artifacts discovered mainly on German soil, with a few interesting pieces from the Near East and Orient thrown in. The first five rooms are the most interesting, grouping the exhibits into ages of man, from 1,000,000 B.C. up to the millennium before Christ. You can visit any day, except Tuesday, at the same hours as the Applied Arts Museum above.

In addition to the exhaustive—and exhausting—collections in the interior of the palace buildings, you can enjoy a relaxing ramble through the palace gardens, where, just a few years ago, lay a field of mud and swampland created by the ravages of war. The gardens have been restored, however, and landscaped much as they were in the days of Friedrich-Wilhelm II. Boxing in the formal gardens are two rows of cypresses leading to a lake complete with swans and other waterfowl. To the west of the cypress grove, between the English Gardens and the Prehistory Museum, stands the **Mausoleum,** practically unharmed during the war. Beneath its small temple are the tombs of King Friedrich-Wilhelm II and Queen Louise, sculptured by Rauch, as well as several other interesting funerary monuments of the royal Prussian family.

Charlottenburg lies in the quarter of Berlin of the same name, just west of the Tiergarten. You can get there by a number of routes, including the U-Bahn to either Sophie-Charlotte-Platz or Richard-Wagner-Platz, or by buses 21, 74, or 86.

A TOUR ALONG THE BERLIN WALL: The ideological rift between East and West Berlin, which grew out of the dissolution of the Kommandantura of the Big Four powers in 1948, suddenly became a stark reality in August 1961. Most West Berliners have adjusted to the fact that the wall marks the eastern end of their world, but for the visitor, the concrete and barbed wire barrier still holds an awe-inspiring, sobering fascination.

After a bracing cocktail or cup of coffee at the Hilton Hotel we'll begin a tour of the area of West Berlin along the Wall. If you follow Budapesterstrasse eastward from the hotel, you'll soon reach the entrance to the **Tiergarten,** Berlin's largest park. The road which enters the park at this point is called the Hofjäger (hunter's ground) Allee, reminding us of its 16th-century use by the electors of Brandenburg. When seen by those who trudged into Berlin in 1945, the park was a dreary battlefield laid waste. Children play safely here today amid the young trees planted since the war to replace the ancient forest cut down to supply fuel in the cold winters of 1945–46. If you wander from the main roads, you'll come upon rustic bridges, fishponds, and peaceful, isolated paths and streams.

At the center of the park, where the Hofjäger Allee meets the wide avenue now called the Strasse des 17 Juni (named in memory of those East Berliners who were killed in the unsuccessful uprising against the Soviets on June 17, 1953), is the highest point in the park, the **Victory Column.** This beloved landmark of West Berlin now sits on a traffic circle called the Grosser Stern (Big Star). Erected in 1873, the yellow sandstone column is hollow and you can climb the 290 steps to the observation platform at the top, 210 feet above the street. Towering above the platform is the gilded bronze statue of Victory, 27 feet high, commemorating the German military accomplishments in the Franco-Prussian Wars. The observation platform is open daily (except Monday) from 10 a.m. to 5 p.m. (till 4 p.m. in winter), and admission is .50 DM (29¢).

If you follow the Strasse des 17 Juni eastward from the Grosser Stern, it will take you directly to the Wall. As you proceed, however, you'll pass several attractions worth at least a quick visit. About halfway between the Victory Column and the Wall, set at the northern edge of the Tiergarten near the Spree River, is the **Kongresshalle,** built as the American contribution to the 1957 Interbau, when the world's greatest architects constructed several important buildings in West Berlin. Given to the people of Berlin in the following year, this huge convention hall is irreverently, but affectionately—and perhaps appropriately—called the "pregnant oyster," because of the spans of concrete which curve across the roof and end in open arches on each side. The auditorium alone seats 1250, and is equipped with modern translation equipment and other facilities. In addition the building houses a 400-seat theater, conference rooms, a garden cafe, and a restaurant. So huge is the hall that it has its own waterworks, which supply not only the building, but the large pool and fountain just below the wide outer staircases as well. Guided tours are conducted daily between 10 a.m. and 5 p.m. for 1 DM (57¢), except when conventions are in progress.

Back on the Strasse des 17 Juni, you'll next come to the **Soviet War Memorial,** lying on the left side of the street, on the wrong side (West Berlin side) of the Wall. Built in 1946 from the marble of Hitler's former Berlin headquarters, the semicircular colonnade is guarded night and day by Soviet soldiers. On top of the memorial is a large bronze statue of a solider in battle uniform, holding a bayonet. Above the inscription are the dates 1941–45, and a wreath enclosing a hammer and sickle. Once a popular spot for demonstrations against the Soviets, the memorial and its guards are now also guarded by British soldiers and West German police.

At this point you can see the Wall and past it to the famous landmark of old Berlin, the **Brandenburg Gate,** and beyond it the former main street and promenade of Berlin, the **Unter den Linden.** The gate itself represents a unique combination of cooperation between the sectors of the divided city. When the Quadriga (a chariot drawn by four horses) atop the gate was destroyed during the war, and the gate itself badly damaged, the people of East and West Berlin were anxious to have it restored. The Senate of West Berlin had a new Quadriga hammered in copper and presented it to the administration of East Berlin to place on the newly repaired colonnade. Thus, even though West Berliners don't get to their beloved landmark often, they can still admire it through the barbed wire barrier. On special occasions it is illuminated at night.

Just north of this point, along the West Berlin side of the Wall, lies the large square called the **Platz der Republik,** only a sand dune until it was developed as the home of the German Parliament in the 18th century. At the eastern side of the square, right next to the Wall, sits the 19th-century **Reichstag,** the neo-Renaissance Parliament building.

Turning now to the west side of the square, make for the street called Umgehungs-Strasse, which cuts south through the Tiergarten. As you leave the park on the south side, you'll see the wavy roof of the modern **Philharmonie** (Philharmonic Hall), an outstanding example of modern functional design (1963). Its unusual layout allows the audience to sit on all sides of the orchestra, yet the technical and acoustical aspects of the hall permit you to hear and see well from any point. The Philharmonie is the home of the renowned Berlin Philharmonic Orchestra, under the baton of world-famous conductor Herbert von Karajan. You can purchase tickets for performances at the office in the main lobby of the hall Monday through Friday from 3:30 to 6 p.m., and on Saturday and Sunday from 11 a.m. to 2 p.m. If you wish to get to the hall directly from the center of Berlin's activity on the Ku-damm, take bus 29.

From Kemper Platz in front of the Philharmonie, follow Bellevuestrasse southeast to **Potsdamer Platz,** a rather dreary square which was once the most active spot in all of Berlin. Along the street leading to the square, you can still see some of the streetlamps which added their nighttime charm to the old city. The square is now referred to as the three sector corner because it is the meeting place of the British, American, and Soviet sectors of the city. Cutting right through the middle of the square is the hated Wall. Because most of the buildings around the square have been destroyed, you can glimpse the Reichstag, the Brandenburg Gate, and other important buildings along the Wall from this vantage point. On the East Berlin side, buildings have been cleared away for about 100 yards, creating a sort of no-man's land where a number of daring escapes from East Germany have been attempted—many of which have failed tragically. Raised high on the West Berlin side is an illuminated newspaper, emphasizing the contrast between western freedom and eastern suppression.

If you don't intend to visit East Berlin, but would still like at least a glimpse of it, you can get your best look from the observation platform, near the Potsdamer Platz. A photo-mural here shows the square in its heyday in 1929 and as it looks today. Another mural shows the near-massacre of the East Germans on June 17, 1953, when they began their unsuccessful revolt against the Soviet oppression of East Germany. A light note is added to the sobering scenes by the souvenir shops and ice cream stands nearby.

NEW NATIONAL GALLERY: In its ultramodern glass-and-steel home designed by Mies van der Rohe, this gallery is a sort of sequel to the art housed at the Dahlem. Here you'll find works of 19th- and 20th-century artists with a heavy concentration on the French Impressionists—Manet, Renoir, Monet, and Pissarro. An adjoining room offers a comparison in style in the works of the German Impressionists of the same period—Liebermann, Slevogt, and Corinth. Earlier 19th-century German artists are represented as well, including Leibl and Caspar David Friedrich *(A Man and Woman Contemplating the Moon).*

The 20th-century collection includes a number of works by Max Beckmann, Edvard Munch, and Kirchner—*Brandenburger Tor* (1929) is among the most popular—as well as a few paintings by Francis Bacon, Dufy, Picasso, Max Ernst, and, of course, Paul Klee.

Small exhibitions on the second floor are free, although you'll have to pay changing fees for the larger shows. Admission to the downstairs gallery is free. The gallery is open from noon to 8 p.m. Mondays; from 9 a.m. to 5 p.m. Tuesdays, Wednesdays, Thursdays, Saturdays, and Sundays; closed Fridays. The museum is on the Potsdamerstrasse just south of the Tiergarten and near the Wall. You can get there by taking bus 24, 29, 48, 75, or 83.

SCHÖNEBERG TOWN HALL: Of special interest to Americans, this seat of the West German administration since 1948 was the scene of John F. Kennedy's memorable "Ich bin ein Berliner" speech on June 26, 1963, just a few months before he was assassinated. Berliners, taking the speech literally as well as symbolically, have renamed the square around the building the John F. Kennedy Platz. Built in 1911, the facade of the hall is not as outstanding as the interior. Here you'll find many paintings—especially portraits of political leaders of the past—and an exhibition of the history of the Schöneberg quarter of Berlin. Note the eight tinted-glass panels in the vestibule with scenes of various sections of Berlin, each with its own coat of arms.

From the 237-foot-high tower of the hall, a replica of the Liberty Bell is rung every day at noon. A gift from the American people in 1950, the Freedom Bell, as it is called, symbolizes U.S. support in the determination of West Berliners to preserve their freedom. The document chamber contains a testimonial presented with the bell bearing the signatures of 17 million Americans who gave their moral support in the struggle. You can visit the Liberty shrine on Wednesdays and Sundays between 10 a.m. and 3:30 p.m.

BOTANICAL GARDEN: In the Dahlem quarter of West Berlin, 6–8 Koenigin-Luise-Strasse (tel. 831-40-41), near the Dahlem Museum, the huge Botanical Garden contains vast collections of European and exotic plants in the open and in 15 greenhouses, among which the most popular ones are: the big palm house, one of the largest in the world, with its palms, bamboos, and tropical flowers; and the Victoria house, where *Victoria amazonica* and *Victoria cruziana* are in bloom in late summer. The flowers of those South American water lilies reach up to 15 inches in diameter and last only two nights, turning from pure white to blood red in their short lifetime, then dropping off to be replaced by new blossoms. During the summer, the garden is open from 8 a.m. to 8 p.m. (Sundays and public holidays, 9 a.m. to 8 p.m.). In winter the garden is closed at dusk. Admission is 1.50 DM (86¢).

A unique approach to botany is represented in the **Botanical Museum** near the entrance to the gardens. Here you can see dioramas and exhibit cases portraying the history and significant facts of plant life around the world. The museum is open Tuesdays to Sundays from 10 a.m. to 5 p.m.; Wednesdays, 10 a.m. to 7 p.m. Admission is free.

OLYMPIC STADIUM: Built in 1936 by Werner March for the 11th Olympic Games, this stadium seating 100,000 people was the first in Europe to supply all the facilities necessary for modern sports. Hitler expected to see the "master race" run off with all the awards in the 1936 Olympics, and you can imagine his disappointment when a black American named Jesse Owens took four gold medals for the U.S. team!

The stadium area covers a total of 330 acres, including a swimming stadium, a hockey arena, tennis courts, and riders' exhibition grounds. But the main attraction is the arena itself, so large that, if the seats were laid end to end, they would stretch for more than 25 miles! The playing field in its center lies 47 feet below ground level. You can take the elevator to the top of the 260-foot platform where the huge Olympic bell hangs. From this point you have a panoramic view of Berlin to the east. Since the Olympic Stadium lies just northwest of the Radio Tower, you can reach it in a few minutes by a brisk walk. If you come directly via U-Bahn, take the train one stop past the Radio Tower stop to the Theodore-Heuss-Platz.

RADIO TOWER (FUNKTURM): Nearly every sizable town in Germany seems to have a television tower, but this steel frame construction predates them all—in fact, it predates television! Erected in 1924–26, it sits on a base of porcelain pedestals. Popularly called the tall dwarf, the tower has been converted to a television transmitter, but if you visit here it will likely be either for the restaurant (at 170 feet) or for the excellent view of Berlin and its environs (as far as Potsdam) from the observation platform at 457 feet. The speedy elevator reaches the top in hardly more than half a minute. The elevator is in operation from 10 a.m. to 11 p.m., but if you wish you can climb the seemingly endless stairs to the restaurant. Admission to the platform is 2 DM ($1.15). The tower sits in the large fairgrounds in the western section of West Berlin. To get there, take the U-Bahn to the Kaiserdamm stop, or the S-Bahn to the closer Witzleben stop.

ORGANIZED TOURS: West Berlin and East Berlin can be difficult to navigate on your own. Many of the attractions of West Berlin are spread out, and the border formalities of East Berlin may intimidate the less adventurous. Therefore, you may need the security of an organized tour. The best ones are operated by **Severin & Kühn,** 215–216 Kurfürstendamm (second floor; tel. 883-10-15). Across from the Bristol-Kempinski Hotel, this agency offers a host of tours, including some interesting excursions into East Germany.

Their big tour combines East and West Berlin, costs 30 DM ($17.21) and lasts 4½ hours (there's an extra 15-DM or $8.60 guidance fee in East Berlin). The tour leaves at 10 a.m. Or, if you prefer, you can take—for 20 DM ($11.47) each, plus guidance fee—two separate tours of East and West Berlin, spending three hours in the west, 3½ hours in the east. If you want to stay just in West Berlin, you can take another three-hour tour, including a visit to the New National Gallery if you go on the 10 a.m. tour (the 2:30 p.m. tour visits the Egyptian Museum, with its celebrated bust of Nefertiti). The cost is 20 DM ($11.47).

A separate tour (passports required) of East Berlin leaves at 10 a.m. and 2 p.m. The fare is 20 DM ($11.47), plus an extra guidance fee in East Berlin. The 2 p.m. jaunt is preferred, as it takes in the important Pergamon Museum.

An even more exotic tour is the one to Potsdam and Sans Souci, leaving on Tuesday, Thursday, and Saturday from May 1 to October 31, beginning at

9:30 a.m. and lasting eight hours. The cost is 70 DM ($40.15), with lunch included. You go on a guided visit to the world-famous Sans Souci Palace, explore the Orangerie and the Chinese Tea House. On the full-day tour, you visit not only the New Palace, but also the ancient Palace of the Crown Prince, Cecilienhof, where the "Four Power Agreements" of 1945 were concluded. A lunch or coffee break is taken at the Interhotel Potsdam. An abbreviated five-hour tour is offered at 1 p.m., at a cost of 56 DM ($32.12) (instead of lunch, you get coffee and cake). This afternoon tour is available Wednesday, Friday, and Sunday from May 1 to October 31; Tuesday, Thursday, and Saturday from November 1 to April 30.

SOME NOTES ON SHOPPING: The central shopping destination for all Berliners are Kurfürstendamm (its Fifth Avenue), Tauentzienstrasse, and am Zoo. Each quarter of Berlin has shopping centers as well. The show windows of the Ku-damm are in sparkling contrast to the drab stores of East Berlin.

The **Royal Porcelain Factory**, known as KPM, is at 1 Wegelystrasse, and it's been in existence since 1763. King Frederick the Great once purchased the factory, and today it's known as the State Porcelain Factory. Its products carry a distinctive official signature, an imperial orb and the letters "KPM." Guided tours let you look at the work of the employees, and you can buy beautiful pieces of porcelain here. Because of small defects—many visible only to experts—the prices of these "seconds" are quite reasonable.

THE BUMMELPASS: This pocket-sized booklet is your welcome package from the Berlin Tourist Office. Each of its pages contains a voucher—perforated for easy use—for some little present during your visit to Berlin: a free glass of Berlin beer, a Berliner schnaps called "Saurer with Persiko," or even a free pickled egg at a bohemian watering spot! In addition, some of the coupons offer reductions when purchasing souvenirs, e.g., KPM porcelain or pleasure-boat trips on the Havel River in summer. The Bummelpass is valid year round, and can be obtained through your travel agent or at the offices of the **Berlin Tourist Information Service,** either at Tempelhof Airport or 20 Hardenbergstrasse.

4. West Berlin After Dark

"A Teutonic determination to achieve offbeat gaiety." That's how one writer described Berlin nightlife. Berliners certainly do try their best to keep their city going well after dark. The seductive, intriguing cabaret life of prewar Berlin may have faded, but the spirit and determination are still there. So get yourself together, and get ready for a night on the town, Berlin style.

MAKING THE SCENE: There is such a variety of nightspots to choose from in Berlin—cabarets, saloons, cafes, discos, beer halls. Let's start with:

The Top Nightclub

The **Red Rose** (tel. 261-47-90), although on the lower level of the Europa-Center, is, as of this writing, the top nightclub in Berlin. It's one of the dressiest spots in town—except for the topless bardamen—but you needn't pay a fortune for a good time here. With a 6-DM ($3.44) door charge, and a minimum of 20 DM ($11.47) for a double whiskey, you can enjoy a pleasant evening. The nonstop shows, which begin at 10:30 p.m., feature a variety of international acts, from Caribbean bongo players to Italian acrobats. You'll usually find a well-known singer or musical group as well—and, of course, several exotic striptease acts.

The Old Cafe Life

There is no better way to begin or end your evening than taking a table at the **Café Kranzler**, 18–19 Kurfürstendamm. At the turn of the century, Berlin was famous for its cafes. Many survived until World War II. But after the war, the momentum of cafe life was never revived—some scattered to such points as Frankfurt, some never rose from the debris. However, the Kranzler continues in the old tradition and does so exceedingly well. Its bright, breezy orange and white decor lifts the fog from many a gray day in Berlin. You can anchor at a sidewalk table on the Kurfürstendamm in fair weather, or take a table inside when the cold winds blow, peering outside through the glass-fronted entrance. Many begin their day over breakfast (as little as 5 DM, or $2.87), served till noon. Throughout the day and evening, coffee costs 2.50 DM ($1.43), and those delicious cakes begin at 3 DM ($1.72). The more prosaic beer is 3 DM also.

Phone a Friend

Resi, 32 Hasenheide (tel. 691-10-03), is legendary for its table phone service and pneumatic table mail system. The ballroom itself is spectacularly large, looking straight out of a 1935 movie set. You go in, select a table, and wait for the action to happen, perhaps start it yourself if your phone doesn't ring at once or the pneumatic tube doesn't bring you a love letter right away. The Resi has been on the scene since it reopened in 1951, but it never seems to wane, gaining new converts every night among the post-30 set. When you reach your seat, you will find a map showing all the table numbers. Since the ballroom is so vast, you may want to stroll around, jotting down a few numbers before placing that important call. However, don't assume that all the calls are romantic; many guests are just having fun—at your expense! Language barriers only add to the confusion. All in all, there are 250 telephones, and hundreds of letters circulate nightly on the pneumatic tube. In addition to the technical entertainment, the Resi is known for its water shows. Within one minute 9000 jets discharge 8000 liters of water. And if you're not impressed with that statistic, know that 100,000 colored lights are needed for the colossal effects. A Kloster-Keller, also with a table phone system, has been installed as well, capturing the atmosphere of an Old Berlin beer cellar. The entrance fee is 5 DM ($2.87); the least expensive bottle of wine at one of the tables is 29 DM ($16.63). Closed Mondays.

Ladies' Choice

Café Keese, 108 Bismarckstrasse, offers what the Germans call a ball paradox. This is a fancy way of saying that the women have a chance to ask the men to dance, instead of the other way around. It's really an old-fashioned Teutonic atmosphere. People go here who actually like to dance—the familiar way, holding each other in their arms! While this custom may seem quaint to readers of more advanced modern tastes, it still continues to pack them in at the Keese. Of course, the management also encourages more "unconventional" dancing as well. The orchestra plays music—quite slowly, at times—and the place is often jammed, especially on Saturday nights. If you're a lone male, and fear the women will mob you if you make an appearance on the floor, you can remain perched at the bar. Incidentally, the management reserves the right to kick out any male patron who turns down a female request to dance! Actually, the Keese is something of a matrimonial bureau, always announcing new statistics about the number of people who have met and fallen in love on its premises and later gotten married. Men are requested to wear jackets and ties; women, anything seductive. No entrance fee is charged. Inside, you can order a beer at 6 DM ($3.44)—the cheapest way to spend an evening here, incidentally—or most whiskeys at 9.50 DM ($5.45) a shot. The least expensive bottle of wine begins at 30 DM ($17.21).

For Jazz

Quartier Latin, in a refurbished movie theater not far from the Berlin Philarmonie on Matthäikirschstrasse, is a hotbed of avant-garde music. Most of the original seats from the theater are in place, although the stage itself is not used. Rather, its present operators have covered the orchestra pit with plywood, making for a temporary platform on which the musicians can play. In the balcony is a restaurant operated independently of the jazz club. To enter, you'll pay an admission of 2.50 DM ($1.43). Beer begins at 1.50 DM (86¢), although hard liquor costs from 3.50 DM ($2.01).

The "Gardens" of Eden

The **New Eden Saloon,** 71 Kurfürstendamm, is an outgrowth of the now-defunct Old Eden, but it's an entirely different "paradise." One newspaper writer termed this garden "too elegant and expensive for vagabond types." Essentially what you get here is dancing to a smooth orchestra and striptease. One lone male, sitting close to the scene of action, appraised the strippers as "advanced in their craft." Rolf Eden, who was the MC that night, corrected him. "It's an art," he said. Certainly the carefully selected girls strip with flair and style, each having a unique act. Shows, three nightly, begin at 10:30, midnight, and 2 a.m. The last acts are usually the liveliest. The entrance is 5 DM ($2.87); the cloakroom charge, 1 DM (57¢). A Pilsner costs 9.90 DM ($5.68); a double whiskey, 26 DM ($14.91).

Big Eden, 202 Kurfürstendamm, bills itself as a dance paradise for 2000 people. It certainly is that and more! Boys dance with boys, by themselves, or occasionally even with a girl! The latest electronic gimmicks—all zany—decorate the place, the creation of the fertile mind of Rolf Eden himself. The strobe system alone may send you into a trance. Here, you'll find a wonderful melange of Berlin youth, in every conceivable form of dress (or lack of it!), dancing to recorded music. As befits the means of most of the clientele, prices are kept low. For example, you pay a regular 4-DM ($2.29) entrance fee; 5.50 DM ($3.15) on Saturdays. This is applied to your first drink (beer, whiskey, vodka, etc.).

Nostalgia

Berlin Palast, 26 Kurfürstendamm (tel. 882-29-22), keeps alive the nostalgia of prewar Berlin when ladies wore silk and beaded gowns and their escorts were attired in pomp-and-circumstance uniforms, with glistening gold braids and medals. It's like a miniature "show biz" Austrian palace, with an abundance of gilt and crystal. In the rear is a paneled, domed rotunda, surrounded by boxes with tables for refreshments and light meals. A telephone is placed on each table. At one side, international dance and show bands are presented, as are top disc jockeys. The bands play for dancing nonstop. Cocktails and long drinks are in the 6-DM ($3.44) to 12-DM ($6.88) range, with beer starting at 4 DM ($2.29). You pay a 3-DM ($1.72) entrance fee. The club is open from 3 p.m. to 5 a.m.

Next door is the **Zigeuner Keller,** 26 Kurfürstendamm, which draws devotees of string orchestra and zither music. You can even waltz here. Beer begins at 4 DM ($2.29); whiskey, at 9 DM ($5.16).

The Discos

Riverboat, 174 Hohenzollerndamm (tel. 87-84-76). The building itself is unprepossessing; you think you're taking an elevator to a floor in a warehouse. But once inside you feel you've boarded a real Mississippi riverboat. The ambitious decor gives one the impression that he or she is on the largest boat ever known on the U.S. mother river. It's like wandering in a labyrinth, with galleyways, portholes, as well as photostat blow-ups of the actual craft that sailed the river. Although some nights can be slow, the Riverboat at its most active has been known to have a band and four disc jockeys. There are offshoot galleys, where a person can enjoy a quiet beer. If you're alone, you can "cruise" because you'll find many young Berliners in your same predicament. Should you bring someone, you stand a chance of losing him or her in the crowd, as the Riverboat really packs them in. The boat doesn't navigate on Mondays, but does so admirably on other nights of the week. There's space for 2000 people. The entrance fee is usually 2 DM ($1.15), increasing to 3 DM ($1.72) on Fridays, 4 DM ($2.29) on Saturdays. Once inside, you'll pay 3.50 DM ($2.01) for beer, 5 DM ($2.87) for a shot of whiskey. Take the U-Bahn to Fehrbelliner Platz.

Cheetah, 13 Hasenheide, is a totally plastic world! Taking the name of the famed New York disco of the '60s, it is a projection of the world of tomorrow, an architectural melange of lily-padded wonder. It's multitiered—you can perch high or low depending on your mood. An orange glow flatters everybody. Live groups are booked. The entrance fee is 2 DM ($1.15). Once inside, you can order a beer at 3 DM ($1.72), a whiskey (a small shot) at 3 DM also.

Big Apple, 13 Bundesallee. If you're in your late teens, you'll find lots of friendly souls at the Big Apple, one of Berlin's leading discos. Boys dance with girls, boys dance with boys—it really doesn't matter here. Everybody is liberated. If you're a young boy who likes girls, you'll find plenty of them in attendance—sometimes shockingly attractive (Berlin girls are said to be the most beautiful in Germany). The music from live rock bands is loud, the words usually in English. The entrance fee is 3 DM ($1.72) on regular nights, increasing to 6 DM ($3.44) on weekends. When entering, you're given a card marked "Verzehrbon," which, along with 3 DM ($1.72), will get you a beer.

Where the "Girls" Are

Troika, 5 Wittenbergplatz. At this exotic cabaret, the herren become damen. The transvestite acts featured nightly are among the best in the city. For example, you might be entertained by a sultry, boa-draped striptease star from Rio de Janeiro. Or you might see an entertainer looking like a gun moll from the 1940s. Of course, latter-day derivatives of Marlene Dietrich are always in vogue. You don't pay an entrance fee, although you're charged 7 DM ($4.02) for Becks beer or 12 DM ($6.88) for a scotch whiskey. Go late.

Gambling

One of the biggest attractions for visitors is the **Spielbank** or gambling casino which is at the Europa-Center (entrance on Budapesterstrasse). It is open daily from 3 p.m. to 3 a.m. Inside you'll find 14 roulette tables, in addition to tables for baccarat and blackjack. The bar is the longest in Berlin, and it's a popular watering spot between rounds at the tables. There's also a restaurant serving an expensive international cuisine.

Beer Hall Revelry

Münchner Hofbräuhaus, 29 Hardenbergstrasse, across from the Kaiser Wilhelm Memorial Church. Although this Berlin namesake has little to do with the celebrated Hofbräuhaus of Munich, it does provide one of the most gemütlich evenings in Berlin. Near the center of the room, a seven-piece brass band plays Bavarian music. Dancers choose their partners to take them out to the large floor. Prussians, of course, are not Bavarians, and their dancing reflects this. But it's good fun, nevertheless. The hall itself is attractively decorated, with carved wood chairs and pine tables—sort of half modern, half rustic. Beer is served in gray and blue ceramic steins at 4.20 DM ($2.41) for a half liter, 7.50 DM ($4.30) for a full liter. You can also order food here, with soups beginning at 5 DM ($2.87) and the famous weisswürste—the white sausages of Munich—at 5.50 DM ($3.15). Main dishes are in the 5.20-DM ($2.98) to 17.50-DM ($10.04) range, the latter for the hefty schweinhaxe. Desserts begin at 4 DM ($2.29). The beer hall opens at 6 p.m., but it's best to go later. Admission is 3 DM ($1.72) on weekdays, 4 DM ($2.29) on Saturdays.

5. A Tour of East Berlin

No sightseeing trip to Berlin would be complete without at least a day trip into the eastern sector of the city. For it was here, prior to World War II, that the real center of Berlin lay: the best museums, the finest churches, the most important streets. Although the city you see today on the opposite side of the wall may not be the exciting, lively city of prewar days, it still has many attractions.

If you are of the "safety in numbers" school, perhaps one of the already-recommended tours (see "Organized Tours" in this chapter) offered by the **Severin & Kühn Line,** at 216 Kurfürstendamm (tel. 883-10-15), is the best way for you to tour East Berlin. A four-hour tour of the major sights of East Berlin leaves each afternoon and costs an inclusive 20 DM ($11.47). This tour has the added advantage of cutting through the red tape of border crossing (but carry your passport). You, however, have the disadvantage of being almost completely confined to your bus seat except for a few quick museum stops. You don't have the opportunity to explore the city as you would on your own.

For a more realistic picture of life in East Berlin, we recommend a personal tour of the city, either by car or on foot. As of this writing, citizens of Western nations should have no problems in entering East Berlin—or, more important, in returning to the West.

CROSSING THE BORDER: The control point for non-Socialist countries is **Checkpoint Charlie.** To reach it on West Berlin's U-Bahn, take the train from the Zoologischer Garten station to Hallesches Tor. At that station, board the train for Kochstrasse, which is only one stop away. This station is the exit point for the wall crossing.

All you need to take with you is your passport, a few marks and if you are driving, your "green card." If all goes well, you should be through the customs inspection within 20 minutes—that is, if the person in front of you isn't carrying 35 copies of *Time* magazine. We've seen East German customs officials tediously go through every page of a magazine before permitting access to its owner!

You must also exchange the equivalent of 6 DM ($3.44) into East German marks before entry. And you might as well spend it because you can't bring it out again! The exchange rate—again, as of this writing—is the same for both East and West German marks. Additional West German marks can be brought with you without restriction (you must declare them, however), and you can exchange them during your visit at the offices of the Bank of Industry and Commerce. You probably won't find this necessary, however, since many shops, restaurants, and hotels will accept foreign currency (including West German marks).

Before passing through Customs, you should pay a visit to the "House at Checkpoint Charlie," the **Museum of the Wall.** This small building houses exhibits depicting the tragic events leading up to and following the erection of the Wall. You can see some of the instruments of escape used by East Germans, including chair lifts, false passports, even a mini-sub! Photos document the building of the Wall, the establishment of escape tunnels, and the dramatic postwar history of both parts of Berlin from 1945 until today, including the airlift. One of the most moving exhibits is the display on the staircase of drawings by school children in 1961–62 who were asked to depict both halves of Germany in one picture. You can also see works by well-known German painters. On the floor above, you can look out toward East Berlin from the observation platform. Visit the museum any day between 9 a.m. and 8 p.m. There is a 2-DM ($1.15) admission fee (1 DM, or 57¢, for groups).

Tourists can also travel to East Berlin on the S-Bahn train which is boarded at the Zoologischer Garten station. This train is entirely above ground. You can purchase a round-trip ticket for 3 DM ($1.72). Take the train to Friedrichstrasse which is right in East Berlin.

Leave the train and go to the counter marked "Einreise." There you surrender your passport and get an entry card which you fill out; note your number. You sit in a waiting room until your number is called out on the loudspeaker. The last three numbers on your card are called out—unfortunately in German only.

When you're called up, go to a window marked "Passausgabe." Pass along to the guard under a large red, yellow, and black wooden flag to get your card stamped. Proceed to the money exchange window where you are required to make the already-mentioned obligatory 6-DM ($3.44) currency conversion into East German marks. You'll be given the East German marks in a small plastic bag.

Friedrichstrasse station is only a block from Unter den Linden. However, if you wish to begin your sightseeing on the main square, Alexanderplatz, you can take a taxi, one of which is usually found waiting outside the station exit. At the base of the tower on the square is a tourist information office, dispensing data in English.

To return to West Berlin, go back to the station on Friedrichstrasse. Proceed to the Customs offices which are in a modern annex to the station across from the taxi stand. Present your passport and card at the entrance marked "Entrance for Foreigners." At this point you'll be required to exchange any East German marks in your possession back into West German marks.

THE SIGHTS: There is no better way to begin your tour of East Berlin than by walking down its world-famous street . . .

Unter den Linden

The linden trees for which this street was named have been replanted, and many of the old buildings have been restored, but the prewar gaiety and glamor of the Unter den Linden have never returned. The palaces which once lined this street have either been destroyed or turned into lecture halls for Humboldt University, which numbers among its former students the young Karl Marx.

The contrast between the prewar and postwar thoroughfares is obvious from the beginning of Unter den Linden at the **Marx-Engels Platz.** This large "people's square," built in 1951, was once the site of the 16th-century Imperial Palace. Rather than restore the damaged structure after World War II, however, the Soviets, in their rebuilding program, chose to level it completely and create the square instead. Today, it is the scene of staged demonstrations against capitalism.

Beginning at the square, walk down the left side of Unter den Linden, past the Palais Unter den Linden (restored in 1969) to the Opera Cafe. This former 18th-century palace, complete with gardens and fountains, is now used as a nightclub, wine tavern, and concert cafe, especially popular with the crowds from the adjoining **German State Opera House.** After 200 years of almost continuous performances, the State Opera Company was made homeless in 1941 when bombs almost completely destroyed the structure. In 1955, the new opera house, built to the original (18th-century) plans of Knobelsdorff, opened with Wagner's *Meistersinger.* The neoclassic hall seats nearly 1500 in its three tiers and box stalls. In addition, it contains smaller concert halls such as the Apollo Hall, a copy of a room in the Sanssouci Castle at Potsdam.

Directly behind the opera house (on Bebelplatz) is the once-magnificent **St. Hedwig's Cathedral,** now the Cathedral of the Berlin diocese. The entrance to the building is marked by a series of columns. The huge copper dome is designed after the Pantheon in Rome. Although still under construction, the cathedral is open for inspection. You can walk in and survey the ruins, even make a contribution if you feel like it. On our last visit, only two men were working inside. At this rate, we estimate a completion date of the year 2000. Pictures outside show the Dom as it looked in 1905.

Facing the cathedral on the Bebelplatz is the Royal Library, now part of the Humboldt University. The facade of this building is worth a passing glance because of its rather unusual shape. (The curved wings of the structure have prompted irreverent Berliners to christen it the Kommode—chest of drawers.)

Continuing down the Unter den Linden, you'll pass the Old Palais, once the residence of Kaiser Wilhelm, but currently in use by Humboldt University. Next are several buildings and administrative facilities of the East German government (East Berlin is the capital of East Germany). Near the end of the street sits the Soviet Embassy, the first of the buildings on Unter den Linden to be restored after the war. The ground floor of this palace-like structure contains propaganda shops and travel agencies offering information about holidays within the Soviet Union.

The walking tour brings us now to the **Brandenburg Gate,** forming not only the end of the Unter den Linden, but the end of East Berlin as well. From this angle, you get the best view of the gate, with its two classical gate houses flanking the heavy Roman attica. From the East Berlin side you can also appreciate the Quadriga at its best since the "best" side of the horses is not displayed to West Berliners.

The right side (on your left from Brandenburg Gate) of Unter den Linden is mainly taken up by embassies and buildings of the Humboldt University, but the two sights worth crossing the street for (the Memorial and the Museum of German History) lie at the end nearest the Marx-Engels Platz.

Memorial for the Victims of Fascism and Militarism

It's much less exhausting to call this classical temple by its older name, the **Neue Wache.** Previous to its current use, the building was a memorial to the dead of other German wars, including World War I. Today, however, it contains the ashes of an unknown soldier (placed there in 1969) to commemorate the heroism of the resistance fighters who fought for the freedom of the German Democratic Republic (East Germany). The main attraction here, for Westerners at least, is not the memorial itself but the 11 a.m. changing of the guard ceremony in front of the building. Tourists cluster around for picture taking while the guards look on stoically. U.S. soldiers enjoy having their pictures taken while making faces at the unmoving guards. But when the clock strikes 11, the crowds scatter as the goose-stepping soldiers begin their ceremony. Anyone standing in the way is likely to get a great black boot on a tender spot, because nothing deters these guards from their rigid discipline.

The Museum of German History

In what must be the most beautiful arsenal of all time, this museum, at 2 Unter den Linden, offers you a chance to see a real propaganda center in action. Grouped in exhibits representing various periods of German history from 1789 to 1949, the museum draws some rather far-fetched contrasts between the horrors of capitalism and the ideal socialist state. Military uniforms, photo-murals, and models depict the German attempts at colonialism; documents and photos show the social inequality—champagne parties of capitalists versus the squalid rooms of the working classes in 1900. In the room dealing with the Second World War, you'll see photos of the Krupp armament factories, along with a profit chart for the heavy wartime production of guns and ammunition. In the same room are anti-Nazi posters and photos of Hiroshima. The section devoted to 1945–49 includes pictures of the Nürnberg trials, along with many Communist propaganda posters of the critical point in Berlin's history.

The museum building is much easier to take than its contents. Originally constructed as an arsenal and war trophy museum in 1695 in a subdued baroque style, it is a perfectly square structure, with a large center courtyard, where chamber concerts are held in the summer. Above the windows are the most outstanding features of the facade, the sculpted heads of 22 dying warriors by Andreas Schlüter (1696). The museum is open weekdays from 8 a.m. to 7 p.m. (from 9 a.m. to 4 p.m. on Saturdays and Sundays). Admission is M .50 (29¢); students, M .30 (17¢).

ART MUSEUMS: The old Berlin of prewar days was proud of its fine museums, many of which came under East German control when the boundaries were set up for the divided city. On the island in the Spree, which marks the beginning of the Unter den Linden, you'll find the greatest concentration of these. One must remember in visiting the wealth of ancient art and treasures within some of the historical museums that German archeologists of the 19th and early 20th centuries led the way in the studies of ancient civilizations.

Pergamon Museum

A museum complex, this building houses several departments. But if you have time for only one exhibit, run—don't walk—to the back hall of the U-shaped building to see the **Pergamon Altar.** This Greek altar (160 B.C.) is so large that it has a huge room all to itself. Nearly 50 steps lead from the museum floor up to the colonnade. Most fascinating is the frieze around the base, tediously pieced together over a 20-year period. Depicting the struggle of the Greek gods against the giants as told in Hesiod's *Theogony,* the relief is strikingly alive, with its figures projected as much as six feet from the background. This, however, is only part of the attraction of the **Department of Greek and Roman Antiquities,** housed in the north wing of the museum. Here you'll also find a Roman market gate discovered in Miletus, sculptures from many Greek and Roman cities, including a statue of a goddess holding a pomegranate (575 B.C.), which was found in southern Attica where it had lain beneath the ground for 2000 years wrapped in lead. So well preserved was the goddess that you can still see flecks of the original paint on her garments.

The **Near East Museum,** in the south wing, contains one of the largest collections anywhere of antiquities discovered in the lands of ancient Babylonia, Persia, and Assyria. Among the exhibits is the Processional Way of Babylon with the **Ishtar Gate,** dating from 580 B.C.; its glazed tiles are as colorful now as when they led to the throne room of Nebuchadnezzar II nearly 2600 years ago. Cuneiform clay tablets document much of the civilization of the period which created ceramics, glass, and metal objects while Europe was still overrun with primitive tribes.

The museum's upper level is devoted to the Islamic Museum, the East Asiatic Collection, and the Museum of Folklore. Although these suffered great losses during the war, the collections contain many noteworthy items. Of special interest are the miniatures, carpets, and woodcarvings in the Islamic Museum.

Opening hours may vary from day to day in the Pergamon Museum, so it's best to check in advance. Generally, hours are from 9 a.m. to 6 p.m. every day (Mondays and Tuesdays only for the Near East Museum and the three halls of ancient architecture, including the Pergamon Altar). Admission is M 1.05 (60¢); students, M .50 (29¢).

The Bode Museum

According to East Berlin authorities, the West Berliners broke up a set when they allegedly stole the bust of Nefertiti from the Egyptian Museum. You see, the head of her husband, King Ikhnaton, still remains on the east side of the Wall. Even without the world-renowned queen, the Bode Museum contains tons of the most significant Egyptian collections in the world. Exhibits vary in size from the huge sphinx of Hatshepsut (1490 B.C.) to fragments of reliefs from Egyptian temples. Of special interest is the "Burial Cult Room," where coffins, mummies, and grave objects are displayed along with life size X-ray photographs of the mummies of humans and animals.

Adjoining the Egyptian Museum is the **Papyrus Collection,** containing about 25,000 documents of papyrus, ostraca, parchment, limestone, wax, and wood in eight different languages. On the opposite side of the staircase is the **Collection of Early Christian and Byzantine Art,** with a rich display of mosaics, icons, panel paintings, and even gravestones dating from the third through the 18th centuries. Directly behind this museum is the **Sculpture Collection and Art Gallery,** devoted mainly to German and Dutch paintings of the 15th and 16th centuries on the lower level, and Italian, Flemish, Dutch, English, and

French masters of the 14th through the 18th centuries on the second floor. Among the sculptures are several pieces from the churches and monasteries, including a sandstone pulpit support by Anton Pilgram (1490) carved in the shape of a medieval craftsman. The museum is open daily, except Monday and Tuesday, from 9 a.m. to 6 p.m.; Friday, 10 a.m. to 6 p.m. Admission is M 1.05 (60¢); students, M .50 (29¢).

Altes Museum (Old Museum)

This 19th-century building would be worth a visit even if it were empty. The facade is supported by 18 Ionic columns. The central vault room was restored in similar style while the rest of the building was modernized and air-conditioned to display more than 40,000 prints and drawings. Among the most valuable works here are about 135,000 illustrations by Botticelli for Dante's *La Divina Commedia*. Sketches, woodcuts, and engravings by Dutch, German, English, and French masters are supplemented with drawings by 19th- and 20th-century artists, including a number of works by Edvard Munch, whose art Hitler considered scandalous. Propaganda is present here too, in hundreds of pieces categorized as "GDR socialist art." But don't let that keep you away—the Botticellis and the Old Masters are worth wading through the hundreds of WPA-type drawings.

The Old Museum has the same hours as the Bode Museum (above); admission is M 1.05 (60¢) for adults, M .50 (29¢) for students. As you leave, note the Neues Museum (New Museum) directly behind this museum. This attractive structure, although still in ruins, is scheduled for restoration.

The National Gallery

Next door to the New Museum, this gallery mainly contains 19th- and 20th-century paintings and sculpture. The Nazi campaign against degenerate art depleted this collection during World War II, but you can still see quite a few works by Cézanne, Rodin, Degas, Liebermann, Tischbein, and Corinth. Many of the German works of the 19th century show scenes of court life at Wilhelm I's "Königsberg." The best of these are by Adolph von Menzel (1815–1905), who also is represented in the numerous sketches and drawings included in the museum. You can also see several paintings by one of Germany's greatest portrait artists, Max Liebermann (1847–1935). On the top floor is a large collection of watercolors, many of them satirical. Hours and admission for the National Gallery are the same as those for the Old Museum (above).

OTHER ATTRACTIONS: Not to be outdone by the cities of western Germany, East Berlin has constructed a massive **Television Tower** (opened in 1969) which is the second-highest structure in Europe (1100 feet)—second only to the tower in Moscow. It's worth the M 4 ($2.29) or M 2 ($1.15)—for students—you'll pay to take the 60-second elevator ride to the observation platform, 610 feet above the city. From this isolated vantage point, you can clearly distinguish most of the landmarks of both cities. On the floor above, you can enjoy a piece of cake and cup of coffee for M 7 ($4.02)—M 4 ($2.29) for students—as the tele-cafe slowly revolves, making one complete turn every hour. By the time the revolution is completed, you'd better be on your way, however, or the guard will throw you out. The tower is open to visitors daily from 9 a.m. to 11 p.m.

At the foot of the tower stands one of Berlin's oldest churches, the brick Gothic **Marienkirche** (St. Mary's). Constructed in the 15th century, it is especially notable for the wall painting depicting the *Dance of Death* (1475), discovered beneath a layer of whitewash in the entrance hall of the church in 1860. Also worth seeing is the marble baroque pulpit carved by Andreas Schlüter (1703).

On the opposite side of the TV Tower stands the **Alexanderplatz,** today's center of East Berlin activity. Several modern buildings now line the square, including an HO Department Store and the Congress Hall. Information and tickets pertaining to events in East Berlin are available at the Berolina House on the square, open from 9 a.m. to 7 p.m., Monday through Friday (Saturday, until 4 p.m.)

The **Soviet War Memorial** in Treptow Park, along the Spree, is the final resting place of more than 5000 Soviet soldiers. Entering the park, you pass between two huge red granite pylons in the form of stylized flags, each towering over a bronze sculpture of a kneeling Soviet soldier. The cemetery itself consists of five large communal graves flanked by 16 raised stone sarcophagi. On them, bas-reliefs portray the events of World War II. At the end of the "Grove of Honor" stands the Memorial Statue, atop the Mausoleum which contains the "Book of Honor," listing the 5000 victims of the war who are buried here.

Many readers have asked the way to the **Reichschancellery,** Hitler's bunker where on April 30, 1945, the Third Reich came to an end with the suicide of the German dictator. Hitler had proclaimed it would last 1000 years. Although the Reichschancellery once stood within walking distance of Checkpoint Charlie after one crosses into East Germany, it does not exist today. The Russians bombed the area totally, and what was left was bulldozed by the Soviets. The Communists did not want to create a memorial of any kind to Hitler. The site today is an open space. Only a mound of rubble marks the spot where the Nazi nerve center once stood. At one time the building of marble and glass was vast. Art adorned its great halls. The bunker was built 50 feet below ground following the bombing of Hitler's military headquarters.

READER'S SIGHTSEEING SELECTION: "For those interested in the Nazi period, there is a **synagogue** left standing that was firebombed by the Nazis during Kristallnacht on November 10, 1938. That was the night that some of the people of Germany went around firebombing and destroying synagogues throughout the country. It has been retained untouched as a memorial. The building is at 28 Oranienbergstrasse. It is reached as follows: follow Friedrichstrasse away from Checkpoint Charlie all the way to Oranienbergstrasse and turn right for about five blocks. The synagogue is on the left-hand side of the street. It is, incidentally, quite a hike from Checkpoint Charlie, across the river and past the rail station" (Toni L. Kamins, Briarwood, N.Y.).

HOTELS: Because there is so much to see in East Berlin, you may want to spend more than a day's visit. If so, you can make arrangements with travel bureaus or the East German tourist office for a proper visa for overnight stopovers. What follows are the major hotels of East Berlin.

Interhotel Stadt Berlin, DDR 1026 Berlin, Alexanderplatz (tel. 2190), is the showcase hotel of East Berlin, a 2000-bed establishment with 37 floors standing impressively to the side of the heartbeat Alexanderplatz. Its public facilities are modern and spacious, with lobbies overflowing with large groups of Russians and touring Eastern Europeans or business people. Luggage from group travel is often piled high. The architecture is self-described as "des neuen sozialistischen Berlins." A single room costs from M 100 ($57.36) to M 110 ($63.10), the double rate going from M 120 ($68.83) to M 140 ($80.30).

In the Rotisserie, specialties are served. Facing the big plaza is a milk bar where you can order coffee and light meals from 11 a.m. to 11 p.m. If you go to the second-floor restaurant, the Zillestube, you'll find an ethnic decor and cuisine. Here the specialty is Berliner eisbein (pig's trotters) with sauerkraut, costing M 9.50 ($5.45). In addition, other catering facilities include a Nachtbar and an international restaurant, where individual entrees cost M 10 ($5.74) and a complete meal might run M 35 ($20.08). The Panoramic Restaurant on the top floor is open from 11 a.m. till midnight. Other facilities include a garage, barbershop, beauty parlor, and sauna.

Interhotel Berolina, 1026 Berlin, Karl-Marx-Allee (tel. 21-095-41), is smaller than the nearby Interhotel Stadt Berlin. There are 677 beds in rooms furnished in "DDR modern." Each accommodation contains a private bath. The per-person rate in a single or double ranges from M 60 ($34.42) to M 75 ($43.02). The hotel's dining room provides an authentic German cuisine. The restaurant is open from 6 a.m. till midnight. A game specialty we recently enjoyed was accompanied by apple sauerkraut and potatoes. It's called "Wildschweinbraten in Sahne mit Apfelrotkraut und Schwenkkartoffeln bereits," and the cost is M 14 ($8.03). A gastronomique menu, including specialties of Berlin, goes for M 38 ($21.80). On the lower level is a wine restaurant, Bodega, open from 6:30 p.m. till 2 a.m. Drinks, including not only wine but excellent beer, are offered in addition to food. Another spot for drinks is the Nachtbar which remains open till 2 a.m. In summer, you can enjoy coffee on the garden terrace, perhaps request the "Theaterplatte Berolina," a variety of mixed cold meats, at M 35 ($20.08).

Interhotel Unter den Linden, 108 Berlin, Unter den Linden (tel. 22-003-11), is our third and final recommendation. It stands on the most famous street of Berlin, within walking distance of the S-Bahn station. Handy for visiting the major museums of the capital, it is impersonally modern, containing 443 beds in generously proportioned rooms, all with private baths and soft beds. The per-person rate ranges from M 55 ($31.55) to M 65 ($37.28). In the lounge is the Hallenbar and the Hallencafé, open from 10 a.m. till 3 a.m., where you can order international drinks. The pastries are good. The main restaurant, open until midnight, features international dishes, with a complete meal costing M 28 ($16.06). À la carte prices range from M 7 ($4.02) to M 20 ($11.47).

RESTAURANTS: East Berlin is gaining a string of international restaurants, all of which reflect the cuisines of Communist countries. There's even a Nachtbar Havanna.

Gaststättenensemble Fernsehturm, 1026 Berlin, Alexanderplatz (tel. 21-040), is housed in the previously recommended Television Tower. If you're visiting just for the view and coffee, see "Other Attractions." For more serious dining, the main restaurant is open from 10 a.m. till midnight. Regional specialties, costing M 20 ($11.47), feature such dishes as herring filets in an apple cream sauce, pork cutlets with ham and cheese, and a fish platter. On the ground level, the Tagescafé is self-service. Featured is a Berliner Hackepeter for M 4.50 ($2.58). This is a generous plate of chopped meat, with mix-it-yourself condiments, topped by an egg. You can also order pea soup with bockwurst at M 2.75 ($1.58). The typical dish of pig's trotters with sauerkraut and potato salad is only M 7 ($4.02). Young Berliners come here for evening dancing to contemporary music.

Operncafé, 108 Berlin, 5 Unter den Linden (tel. 20-002-56), is the leading cafe of East Berlin, a good choice if you're visiting the State Opera House next door. The building itself is a remodeled version of a former structure built for royalty in 1733. The atmosphere is historic, but the interior is modern. You have a choice of places at which to eat, drink, or dine. In the cellar is a bar, on the street floor a cafe, and upstairs two restaurants. The cafe has a modest opera theme, with red and white chairs grouped around a small dance floor with a bandstand. An orchestra plays in the evenings until 9:30. Lots of green plants and framed theater prints add extra glamor. From 10 a.m., you can order light snacks, Berliner cakes, tea, or coffee in the M-4 ($2.29) to M-7 ($4.02) range. Ice cream begins at M 4 ($2.29). A Berlin Pilsner beer is M 2.75 ($1.58). The second-floor Weinrestaurant offers more formal dining. Here, specialties include curried pork at M 7 ($4.02) and a porterhouse steak for two persons at M 20 ($11.47). On a lower level, the Nachtbar is open from 9:30 p.m. till 4:30 a.m. At least 70 varieties of drinks are offered.

Restaurant Moskau, 1026 Berlin, 34 Karl-Marx-Allee (tel. 27-940-52), is a restaurant and cafe devoted to Russian specialties. Soviet generals in long woolen coats often dine here, attesting to the authenticity of the recipes and the decor of the room, inspired by one of the "republics" of the Soviet Union. Specialties from the Russian kitchen include a Kiever cutlet, chicken "Tabaka," and "Bauernteller" (a Russian peasant's dish). Prices are in the M-9 ($5.16) to M-30 ($17.21) range. Of course, you can order Russian vodka, even Russian champagne (listed as SU-Sekt). The restaurant is open Monday through Friday from 11 a.m. to 11 p.m. A coffee bar, Mokkabar, has an outside mural, evoking the WPA days, showing workers striving for the dignity of man. There are also a Tanzcafé, open from 3 till midnight, and a Nachtbar, serving from 9 p.m. till 4 a.m. On certain nights of the week shows are presented.

Lindencorso, 108 Berlin, 17 Unter den Linden (tel. 22-024-61), offers five areas for food, drinks, and entertainment. It is one of East Berlin's most fashionable cafes on an historic street, although its interior is plastic modern. It overlooks the previously recommended Hotel Unter den Linden. At Das Konzertcafé, open till midnight, you can dance to modern music. In summer Das Boulevard-cafe offers 180 guests a chance to sit out and absorb the unique atmosphere of the city. The major spot for dining is the Weinrestaurant, seating 116 guests. It is open from 11 a.m. till midnight. A three-course meal is featured for M 25 ($14.34). Such regional dishes as fried liver with red cabbage and potatoes are offered. The restaurant is closed on Mondays. On the Kaffeegedecke you can order pastries and espresso at M 8 ($4.59). Finally, the Nachtbar Havanna offers entertainment from 7:30 p.m. till 1 a.m. (on weekends, until 2 a.m.). International drinks and Cuban specialties are served.

Ermeler Haus, 102 Berlin, 10 Märkisches Ufer (tel. 27-940-28), is as close as you can come in the capital to dining in an old-world manner. Behind the classic facade is an elegant rococo restaurant, where you can have a light meal for only M 27 ($15.49). There are other restaurants on the premises, including a rustic cellar where you can order some of the cheapest food in East Berlin, and drink it down with Pilsner beer. The specialty is "einen Zeitungsfahrerschmaus," which is pork steak on toast with ham and mushrooms at M 9 ($5.16). It's open from 11 a.m. till midnight. On Saturday nights East Berliners congregate in the upper room to dine and dance.

Weinstube Morava, 1026 Berlin, 5 Rathausstrasse (tel. 21-232-92), offers a host of Czech specialties in a rustic restaurant opposite the Neptune fountains in front of the tall TV tower. In summer tables are set up on the terrace. The specialty here is a filling grillplatte "Morava," at a cost of M 12 ($6.88). In addition, you can order typical dishes and wine from Hungary, Rumania, and Bulgaria. The restaurant is open from noon to midnight.

The **Budapest,** 90 Karl-Marx-Allee, is another leading national restaurant. Offering both a restaurant and keller, plus a Kleine Bar, it presents the outstanding cuisine of Hungary. However, the dishes lose something in translation from Budapest. The chicken paprika is generally good, and goulash is invariably offered. Prices range from M 7 ($4.02) to M 15 ($8.60).

The **Ratskeller,** in the basement of the Rathaus on Rathausstrasse, near the TV tower, offers a more traditional German atmosphere, replete with heavy red bricks, stained glass, and dark wood beams—although the furnishings evoke an inexpensive cafeteria. Soups begin at M 2 ($1.15), and the main dishes range from M 7 ($4.02) to M 12 ($6.88). Desserts go from M 2 ($1.15) to M 4 ($2.29). The hours are from 9 a.m. to midnight.

6. Side Trip to Potsdam

Of all the tours possible from both Berlins, the three-star attraction is the baroque town of Potsdam on the Havel River.

From the beginning of the 18th century, it was the residence and garrison town of the Prussian kings. World attention focused on Potsdam from July 17 to August 2, 1945, when the Potsdam Conference took place here.

The town, 16 miles from East Berlin, can be reached by a short bus or train ride (two local rail lines service it). However, if you plan to spend the night, you must make arrangements in advance for a hotel and a proper visa. You can do this at the offices of American Express in West Berlin.

Better yet, if you're in New York or passing through, you can visit the **German American Inc. Travel Service,** 215 West 98th St., Suite 6D, New York, NY 10025. There, a former East Berliner, Max Kurz, the director, will answer your questions and make arrangements for travel in the GDR.

At Potsdam, a British air raid in April 14, 1945, destroyed much of the center of the old city, but the major attraction, **Sans Souci Park,** and its palace buildings, survived.

With its palaces and gardens, Sans Souci Park was the work of many famous architects and sculptors. The park itself covers an area of about one square mile. Arrangements for tours of the park can be made at the **Tourist Pavilion,** 15 Potsdam, Schopenhauerstrasse (tel. 238-19). The charge for admission is only 1 mark (57¢) per person. The length of the tour is about 1½ hours. Note: To visit any historic buildings within the park is an extra admission charge. Also, at the pavilion you can make arrangements to tour the town for only 1 mark.

Frederick II (called "The Great") chose Potsdam rather than Berlin as his permanent residence. The style of the buildings he ordered erected are called "Potsdam rococo," an achievement primarily of Georg Wenzeslaus von Knobelsdorff.

Knobelsdorff built **Sans Souci Palace,** with its terraces and gardens, as a summer residence for Frederick II. The palace was inaugurated in 1747 and called Sans Souci, meaning free from worry.

It is open throughout the year. From March to October, hours are from 9 a.m. to 5 p.m.; from November to February, from 10 a.m. to 4 p.m. Guided tours, costing M 1.50 (86¢), last 40 minutes and are conducted frequently throughout the day.

The palace itself is a long, one-story building crowned by a dome and flanked by two round pavilions. Of all the rooms, the music salon is the supreme point of the rococo style. The elliptically shaped Marble Hall is the largest in the palace. As a guest of the king, Voltaire is said to have lived in the last general room from 1750 to 1752. A small bust of Voltaire commemorates that event.

The **Picture Gallery** (Bildergalerie) was built between 1755 and 1763. Its facade is similar to that of Sans Souci Palace. The interior is considered one of the most flamboyant rooms in the GDR. A collection of some 125 paintings is displayed, including works from both the Italian Renaissance and baroque periods. Dutch and Flemish masters are also exhibited. Represented are such artists as Rubens, Terbrugghen, van Dyck, Vasari, and Guido Reni, as well as Caravaggio. Concerts at the Potsdam Park Festival take place here. In summer the hours are from 10 a.m. till 5:30 p.m. with guided tours conducted every hour on the hour. The tour lasts 30 minutes. Admission to the museum is M .50 (29¢), plus another M .50 for a guide.

To the west of Sans Souci is the **Orangerie,** built between 1851 and 1860. It was based on designs of Italian Renaissance palaces. Its purpose was to shelter southerly plants during the cold months. In the central core, with its twin towers, is the Raphael hall, with 47 copies of that master's paintings. In addition, you can visit five lavishly decorated salons. The Orangerie is open daily from 10 a.m. to 5:30 p.m. Guided tours are offered from M .50 (29¢). To ascend the tower, you pay a supplement of M .25 (14¢).

The largest building in the park is the **New Palace** or Neues Palais, built between 1763 and 1769, at the end of the Seven Years' War. Frederick II called it a "fanfaronade." Crowning the center is a dome. The three Graces bear the crown on the lantern. The rooms inside were used as a residence for members of the royal family. Filled with paintings and antiques, they were decorated in the rococo style. The most notable chamber is the Hall of Shells, with its fossils and semiprecious stones. At the Palace Theatre, also in the rococo style, concerts take place every year from April to November. The palace is open in summer from 9 a.m. to 5:15 p.m. and in winter from 10 a.m. to 4:15 p.m. You can either be admitted individually, or take a guided tour leaving every half hour in summer. The length of the tour is 50 minutes, and the admission is M 1.55 (89¢).

Reached by tram lines 1 and 4, **Charlottenhof Palace** stands south of Ökonomieweg. It was built between 1826 and 1829 to the designs of Karl Friedrich Schinkel, the greatest master of neoclassical architecture in Germany. He erected the palace in the style of a villa, and designed most of the furniture inside. The palace is open daily from 10 a.m. to 5:30 p.m., costing M 1.05 (60¢) for admission. The tour lasts 30 minutes.

Neighboring the palace, the **Roman Baths** are on the north of the artificial lake, known as "machine pond" or Maschinenteich. This group of buildings was constructed between 1829 and 1835, based in part on designs by Schinkel. The baths were strictly for the romantic love of antiquity, having no practical purpose. They can be visited on guided tours at regular intervals in summer from 10 a.m. to 5:30 p.m. for an admission of M .50 (29¢).

With the proper visa, as mentioned, and with arrangements made at a travel bureau before you visit, you can spend the night at Cecilienhof Palace.

On the Heiliger See or "holy lake" in the northern parts of Potsdam lies the **New Garden.** It is about a mile northwest of Sans Souci. The nephew and successor to Frederick the Great, Friedrich-Wilhelm II, ordered the gardens laid out.

To the north of the 200-acre park, **Cecilienhof Palace** was completed in the style of an English country house. It was ordered built by Kaiser Wilhelm II between 1913 and 1916. The 176-room mansion became the new residence of the then Crown Prince Wilhelm of Hohenzollern. It was occupied as a royal residence until March 1945 when the crown prince and his family fled to the West, taking many of their possessions with them.

Cecilienhof was the headquarters of the 1945 Potsdam Conference. For the conference, 36 rooms had to be quickly reconditioned. Truman represented the United States, and Stalin, of course, represented the Soviet Union. Churchill at first represented Great Britain, although at the time of the actual signing on August 2, 1945, Clement R. Attlee had replaced him. It is possible to visit the studies of the various delegations and see the large round table, made in Moscow, where the actual agreement was signed. Visiting hours are daily, from 9 a.m. to 5 p.m.

A double room costs M 110 ($63.10), dropping to M 65 ($37.28) in a single. Breakfast is an additional M 10 ($5.74). If you're visiting only for a luncheon, a set meal will run around M 18 ($10.32).

GERMAN VOCABULARY

English	German	Pronounced
Hello	**Guten Tag**	goo-ten-tahk
How are you?	**Wie geht es Ihnen?**	vee gayt ess ee-nen
Very well	**Sehr gut**	zayr goot
Thank you	**Danke Schön**	dahn-keh-shern
Goodbye	**Auf Wiedersehen**	owf vee-dayr-zayn
Please	**Bitte**	bit-tuh
Yes	**Ja**	yah
No	**Nein**	nine
Excuse me	**Entschuldigen Sie**	en-shool-di-gen zee
Give me	**Geben Sie mir**	gay-ben zee meer
Where is?	**Wo ist?**	voh eest
the station	**der Bahnhof**	dayr bahn-hohf
a hotel	**ein Hotel**	ain hotel
a restaurant	**ein Restaurant**	ain res-tow-rahng
the toilet	**die Toilette**	dee twah-let-tuh
To the right	**Nach rechts**	nakh reshts
To the left	**Nach links**	nakh leenks
Straight ahead	**Geradeaus**	geh-rah-deh-ous
I would like	**Ich möchte**	ikh mersh-ta
to eat	**essen**	ess-en
a room	**ein Zimmer**	ain tzim-mer
for one night	**für eine Nacht**	feer ai-neh nakht
How much is it?	**Wieviel kostet?**	vee-feel kaw-stet
The check, please	**Zahlen, bitte**	tzah-len bit-tuh
When?	**Wann?**	vahn
Yesterday	**Gestern**	geh-stern
Today	**Heute**	hoy-tuh
Tomorrow	**Morgen**	more-gen
Breakfast	**Frühstück**	free-shtück
Lunch	**Mittagessen**	mi-tahg-gess-en
Dinner	**Abendessen**	ah-bend-ess-en

1 eins (aintz)
2 zwei (tzvai)
3 drei (dry)
4 vier (feer)
5 fünf (fewnf)
6 sechs (zex)
7 sieben (zee-ben)
8 acht (ahkht)
9 neun (noyn)
10 zehn (tzayn)

11 elf (ellf)
12 zwölf (tzvuhlf)
13 dreizehn (dry-tzayn)
14 vierzehn (feer-tzayn)
15 fünfzehn (fewnf- tzayn)
16 sechzehn (zex-tzayn)
17 siebzehn (zeeb-tzayn)
18 achtzehn (akh-tzayn)
19 neunzehn (noyn- tzayn)
20 zwanzig (tzvahn- tzik)

30 dreissig (dry-tzik)
40 vierzig (feer-tzik)
50 fünfzig (fewnf-tzik)
60 sechzig (zex-tzik)
70 siebzig (zeeb-tzik)
80 achtzig (akht-tzik)
90 neunzig (noyn-tzik)
100 hundert (hoon-dert)

GERMAN MENU TERMS

SOUPS

Erbsensuppe	pea soup	**Linsensuppe**	lentil soup
Gemüsesuppe	vegetable soup	**Nudelsuppe**	noodle soup
Hühnerbrühe	chicken soup	**Ochsenschwanzsuppe**	oxtail soup
Kartoffelsuppe	potato soup		
Königinsuppe	cream of chicken	**Schildkrötensuppe**	turtle soup
Kraftbrühe	consommé		

MEATS

Aufschnitt	cold cuts	**Kassler Rippchen**	pork chops
Brathuhn	roast chicken	**Lamm**	lamb
Bratwurst	grilled sausage	**Leber**	liver
Deutsche Beefsteak	hamburger steak	**Nieren**	kidneys
		Ragout	stew
Eisbein	pig's knuckles	**Rinderbraten**	roast beef
Ente	duck	**Rindfleische**	beef
Gans	goose	**Sauerbraten**	sauerbraten
Gefüllte Kalbsbrust	stuffed breast of veal	**Schinken**	ham
		Schweinebraten	roast pork
Hammel	mutton	**Taube**	pigeon
Hirn	brains	**Truthahn**	turkey
Kalb	veal	**Wienerschnitzel**	veal cutlet
Kaltes Geflügel	cold poultry	**Wurst**	sausage

FISH

Aal	eel	**Lachs**	salmon
Forelle	trout	**Makrele**	mackerel
Hecht	pike	**Rheinsalm**	Rhine salmon
Karpfen	carp	**Schellfisch**	haddock
Krebs	crawfish	**Seezunge**	sole

EGGS

Eier in Schale	boiled eggs	**mit Speck**	with bacon
Rühreier	scrambled eggs	**Verlorene Eier**	poached eggs
Spiegeleier	fried eggs		

SANDWICHES

Käsebrot	cheese sandwich	**Schwarzbrot mit**	
Schinkenbrot	ham sandwich	**Butter**	rye bread and butter
		Wurstbrot	sausage sandwich

SALADS

Gemischter Salat	mixed salad	**Kopfsalat**	lettuce salad
Gurkensalat	cucumber salad	**Rohkostplatte**	vegetable salad

VEGETABLES

Artischocken	artichokes	**Reis**	rice
Blumenkohl	cauliflower	**Rote Ruben**	beets
Bohnen	beans	**Rotkraut**	red cabbage
Bratkartoffeln	fried potatoes	**Salat**	lettuce
Erbsen	peas	**Salzkartoffeln**	boiled potatoes
Grüne bohnen	string beans	**Sauerkraut**	sauerkraut
Gurken	cucumbers	**Spargel**	asparagus
Karotten	carrots	**Spinat**	spinach
Kartoffelbrei	mashed potatoes	**Steinpilze**	mushrooms
Kartoffelsalat	potato salad	**Tomaten**	tomatoes
Knödel	dumplings	**Vorspeisen**	hors d'oeuvres
Kohl	cabbage	**Weisse Rüben**	turnips

DESSERTS

Blatterteiggebäck	puff pastry	**Obstsalat**	fruit salad
Bratapfel	baked apple	**Pfannkuchen**	sugared pancakes
Käse	cheese	**Pflaumenkompott**	stewed plums
Klöss	dumpling	**Teegebäck**	tea cakes
Kompott	stewed fruit	**Torten**	pastries
Obstkuchen	fruit tart		

FRUITS

Ananas	pineapples	Kirschen	cherries
Apfel	apples	Pfirsiche	peaches
Apfelsinen	oranges	Weintrauben	grapes
Bananen	bananas	Zitronen	lemons
Birnen	pears		

BEVERAGES

Bier	beer	Eine Tasse Kaffee	a cup of coffee
Ein Dunkles	a dark beer		
Ein Helles	a light beer	Eine Tasse Tee	a cup of tea
Milch	milk	Tomatensaft	tomato juice
Rotwein	red wine	Wasser	water
Sahne	cream	Weinbrand	brandy
Schokolade	chocolate		

CONDIMENTS AND OTHERS

Brot	bread	Pfeffer	pepper
Brötchen	rolls	Salz	salt
Butter	butter	Senf	mustard
Eis	ice	Zitrone	lemon
Essig	vinegar	Zucker	sugar

COOKING TERMS

Gebackt	baked	Geröstet	broiled
Gebraten	fried	Gut durchgebraten	well done
Gefüllt	stuffed	Nicht durchgebraten	rare
Gekocht	boiled	Paniert	breaded

THE FROMMER/PASMANTIER PUBLISHING CORP.
380 MADISON AVE., NEW YORK, NY 10017   Date_____

Friends, please send me (postpaid) the books checked below:

$-A-DAY GUIDES

(In-depth guides to low-cost tourist accommodations and facilities.)

☐	Europe on $15 a Day	$6.95
☐	Australia on $20 a Day	$4.95
☐	England and Scotland on $20 a Day	$5.95
☐	Greece and Yugoslavia on $15 & $20 a Day	$4.95
☐	Hawaii on $25 a Day	$4.95
☐	Ireland on $15 a Day	$4.95
☐	Israel on $15 & $20 a Day	$4.95
☐	Mexico and Guatemala on $10 & $15 a Day	$5.95
☐	New Zealand on $15 and $20 a Day	$4.95
☐	New York on $20 a Day	$4.95
☐	Scandinavia on $20 a Day	$4.95
☐	South America on $15 a Day	$4.95
☐	Spain and Morocco (plus the Canary Is.) on $10 & $15 a Day	$4.95
☐	Turkey on $10 and $15 a Day	$4.50
☐	Washington, D.C. on $25 a Day	$4.95

DOLLARWISE GUIDES

(Guides to tourist accommodations and facilities from budget to deluxe, with emphasis on the medium-priced.)

☐	Egypt	$4.95	☐	Canada	$6.95
☐	England & Scotland	$5.95	☐	Caribbean (incl. Bermuda &	
☐	France	$5.95		the Bahamas)	$6.95
☐	Germany	$4.95	☐	California & Las Vegas	$4.95
☐	Italy	$4.95	☐	New England	$4.95
☐	Portugal (plus Madeira &		☐	Southeast & New Orleans	$4.95
	the Azores)	$4.95			

THE ARTHUR FROMMER GUIDES

(Pocket-size guides to tourist accommodations and facilities in all price ranges.)

☐	Athens	$2.50	☐	Los Angeles	$2.50
☐	Boston	$2.50	☐	Mexico City/Acapulco	$2.50
☐	Honolulu	$2.50	☐	New York	$2.50
☐	Ireland/Dublin/Shannon	$2.50	☐	Paris	$2.50
☐	Las Vegas	$2.50	☐	Rome	$2.50
☐	Lisbon/Madrid/Costa del Sol	$2.50	☐	San Francisco	$2.50
☐	London	$2.50	☐	Washington, D.C.	$2.50

Special Editions

☐ The Caribbean Bargain Book $6.95

(Guide to "off-season" Caribbean—mid-April to mid-December—and the resorts that slash rates 20% to 60%; includes the Bahamas.)

☐ Where to Stay USA $4.95

(Guide to accommodations in all 50 states, from $3 to $20 per night.)

Include 60¢ for first book, 25¢ for each additional book for postage and handling.

Enclosed is my check or money order for $ _____

NAME _____

ADDRESS _____

CITY _____ STATE _____ ZIP _____